FICTIONS OF EMPIRE

NEW RIVERSIDE EDITIONS

Series Editor for the British Volumes
Alan Richardson

For a complete listing of our American and British New Riverside Editions, visit our web site at **http://college.hmco.com.**

NEW RIVERSIDE EDITIONS
Series Editor for the British Volumes
Alan Richardson, Boston College

Fictions of Empire

*Complete Texts with Introduction
Historical Contexts • Critical Essays*

JOSEPH CONRAD
Heart of Darkness

RUDYARD KIPLING
The Man Who Would Be King

ROBERT LOUIS STEVENSON
The Beach of Falesá

Edited by John Kucich
UNIVERSITY OF MICHIGAN, ANN ARBOR

Houghton Mifflin Company
BOSTON • NEW YORK

Sponsoring Editor: Michael Gillespie
Editorial Development: Bruce Cantley
Project Editor: Carla Thompson
Associate Production/Design Coordinator: Christine Gervais
Manufacturing Manager: Florence Cadran
Marketing Manager: Cindy Graff Cohen

Cover image: © EyeWire

Credits appear on page 421, which is a continuation of the copyright page.

Printed in the U.S.A.

Library of Congress Control Number: 2001133336
ISBN: 0-618-08488-6
1   2   3   4   5   6   7   8   9-QF-06   05   04   03   02

CONTENTS

ABOUT THIS SERIES
Alan Richardson

The Riverside imprint, stamped on a book's spine or printed on its title page, carries a special aura for anyone who loves and values books. As well it might: by the middle of the nineteenth century, Houghton Mifflin had already established the Riverside Edition as an important presence in American publishing. The Riverside series of British poets brought trustworthy editions of Milton and Wordsworth, Spenser and Pope, and (then) lesser-known writers like Herbert, Vaughan, and Keats to a growing nation of readers. There was both a Riverside Shakespeare and a Riverside Chaucer by the century's end, titles that would be revived and recreated as the authoritative editions of the late twentieth century. Riverside Editions of writers like Emerson, Hawthorne, Longfellow, and Thoreau helped establish the first canon of American literature. Early in the twentieth century, the Cambridge editions published by Houghton Mifflin at the Riverside Press made the complete works of dozens of British and American poets widely available in single-volume editions that can still be found in libraries and homes throughout the United States and beyond.

The Riverside Editions of the 1950s and 1960s brought attractive, affordable, and carefully edited versions of a range of British and American titles into the thriving new market for serious paperback literature. Prepared by leading scholars and critics of the time, the Riversides rapidly became known for their lively introductions, reliable texts, and lucid annotation. Though aimed primarily at the college market, the series was also created (as one editor put it) with the "general reader's private library" in mind. These were paperbacks to hold onto and read again, and many a "private" library was seeded with the colorful spines of Riverside Editions kept long after graduation.

Houghton Mifflin's New Riverside Editions now bring the combination of high editorial values and wide popular appeal long associated with the Riverside imprint into line with the changing needs and desires of twenty-first-century students and general readers. Inaugurated in 2000 with the first set of American titles under the general editorship of Paul Lauter, the New Riversides reflect both the changing canons of literature in English and the greater emphases on historical and cultural context that have helped a new generation of critics to extend and reenliven literary studies. The series not only is concerned with keeping the classic works of British and American literature alive, but also grows out of the excitement that a broader range of literary texts and cultural reference points has brought to the classroom. Works by formerly marginalized authors, including women writers and writers of color, will find a place in the series along with titles from the traditional canons that a succession of Riverside imprints helped establish beginning a century and a half ago. New Riverside titles will reflect the recent surge of interest in the connections among literary activity, historical change, and social and political issues, including slavery, abolition, and the construction of "race"; gender relations and the history of sexuality; the rise of the British Empire and of nationalism on both sides of the Atlantic; and changing conceptions of nature and of human beings.

The New Riverside Editions respond to recent changes in literary studies not only in the range of titles but also in the design of individual volumes. Issues and debates crucial to a book's author and original audience find voice in selections from contemporary writings of many kinds as well as in early reactions and reviews. Some volumes will place contemporary writers into dialogue, as with the pairing of Irish national tales by Maria Edgeworth and Sydney Owenson or of vampire stories by Bram Stoker and Sheridan Le Fanu. Other volumes provide alternative ways of constructing literary tradition, juxtaposing Mary Shelley's *Frankenstein* with H. G. Wells's *Island of Dr. Moreau,* or Byron's *The Giaour,* an "Eastern Tale" in verse, with Frances Sheridan's *Nourjahad* and William Beckford's *Vathek,* its most important predecessors in Orientalist prose fiction. Chronologies, selections from major criticism, notes on textual history, and bibliographies will allow readers to go beyond the text and explore a given writer or issue in greater depth. Seasoned critics will find fresh new contexts and juxtapositions, and general readers will find intriguing new material to read alongside familiar titles in an attractive format.

Houghton Mifflin's New Riverside Editions maintain the values of reliability and readability that have marked the Riverside name for well over a century. Each volume also provides something new—often unexpected—and each in a distinctive way. Freed from the predictable monotony and rigidity of a set template, editors can build their volumes around the special opportunities presented by a given title or set of related works. We hope that the resulting blend of innovative scholarship, creative format, and high production values will help the Riverside imprint continue to thrive well into the new century.

INTRODUCTION
John Kucich

A s the Cambridge historian J. R. Seeley put it in 1884, the Empire was "the great fact of modern English history" (16). No one living in nineteenth-century England could have been untouched by it. Signs of its presence were everywhere—in politics, in career paths and employment opportunities, in the material fabric of everyday life. The economic fruits of empire flooded newly emergent markets of mass consumption, for example: it was in the early Victorian period that sugar, coffee, tea, tropical fruits, and cocoa became staples rather than luxury items. Increasingly, too, British technology and industrial production came to depend on resources from abroad like rubber, copper, oil, tin, and the rare metals used for steel alloys. The imperial economy grew so vast that everyone living in England would have known someone directly employed by it—either in business, manufacturing, shipping, the military, or government administration.

Politicians constantly reminded the public, too, that, without an empire, the nation's prosperity would evaporate. "Trade follows the flag" was the cry. British manufacturing had not been particularly competitive in the wake of the Industrial Revolution, and, as a result, the preservation of its overseas markets and sources of raw materials was, in Eric Hobsbawm's words, "a matter of life and death for the British economy" (74). As a result, military campaigns, conducted to protect or to expand British trade, were constantly in the headlines. Moreover, no one could have missed the innumerable international expositions, the colonial journalism (some of it supplied by Rudyard Kipling and Robert Louis Stevenson), and the books written by explorers or by globe-trotting travel writers, which never seemed to satiate a popular taste for imperial exoticism.

So it is something of a surprise that the Empire nearly disappeared from canonical British fiction in the nineteenth century. One might read through the novels of Jane Austen or Anthony Trollope and have little sense that Britons cared for anything beyond the trials of love and marriage, country balls, or the manners of upper-class life. Of course, English novelists had been fascinated by overseas adventure since *Robinson Crusoe* (1719). But the domestic fiction that predominated throughout the nineteenth century seemed to preclude even the barest mention of "the great fact" of empire. A telling instance occurs in Jane Austen's *Mansfield Park* (1814) when Fanny Price tactlessly asks her guardian, who owns a West Indies plantation, about the slave trade. To her astonishment, "there was such a dead silence! . . . my cousins were sitting by without speaking a word, or seeming at all interested in the subject" (198). Edward Said has argued that novels maintained an embarrassed silence on the subject of empire to salve the conscience of readers who might not have cared to view themselves, personally, as imperialists.

More important, Said argues, nineteenth-century fiction upholds an implicit set of hierarchies — opposing the geographic center of British life to its spatial peripheries, and the white to the nonwhite world — that posits the colonies as profoundly antithetical to England, as firmly outside the calm, order, and beauty of English domestic life. Sometimes, we can observe this process quite plainly, as in Charlotte Brontë's *Jane Eyre* (1847), in which the psychological, emotional, and moral worthiness of the fair Jane is defined in direct opposition to the subhuman savagery of her colonial counterpart, Rochester's mad Creole wife, Bertha Mason. Jean Rhys's *Wide Sargasso Sea* (1966), which reimagines Bertha sympathetically, is perhaps the most dramatic corrective to the nineteenth-century novel's marginalization of native peoples at the other end of the Empire. In Said's view, while novels can hardly be held accountable as a *cause* of imperialism, their implicit geographical and racial hierarchies helped sustain social consent to it. The nineteenth-century novel represented British imperial dominance as a benign and natural state of affairs, something to be taken for granted. This tendency is all the more important to observe, Said argues, because stories were at the heart of what Britons came to believe about regions of the world unfamiliar to them and about the British right to rule such places. As Said puts it, "the power to narrate, or to block other narratives from forming and emerging, is very important to culture and imperialism, and constitutes one of the main connections between them" (*Culture* xiii).

By the last two decades of the nineteenth century, however, the silence of British fiction on imperial subjects began to break. Rudyard Kipling, Robert Louis Stevenson, and Joseph Conrad were among the first serious writers to make empire the main subject of their work. In Stevenson's case, this meant a change in subject matter during the last five years of his life; for Kipling and Conrad, imperialism was always the principal material for their fiction. The prominence of empire in these three writers' work paralleled an unprecedented late-century rise in imperial adventure fiction for boys, by writers such as G. A. Henty, W. H. G. Kingston, and Dr. Gordon Stables, as well as a surge in colonialist fantasy writing by H. Rider Haggard, Samuel Butler, H. G. Wells, and others. As Andrew Lang noted in 1891, "There has, indeed, arisen a taste for exotic literature: people have become alive to the strangeness and fascination of the world beyond the bounds of Europe and the United States" (Green 71). A number of historians have claimed that, in the last decades of the nineteenth century, the Empire became more culturally central than it had been before and that important new narratives about imperialism—many of them critical of it—began to emerge.[1] Kipling, Stevenson, and Conrad—together with the South African–born Olive Schreiner—were the first to move imperial subjects from the periphery to the center of serious fiction, but the literary shift they represent paralleled a broad social change in British attitudes toward empire.

More than anything else, the growing cultural centrality of empire in late-century Britain sprang from the great imperial expansion during the period 1875–1914, a time when the British Empire doubled in size, increasing by 4 million square miles. Mid-Victorian British policy had generally tried to maintain rather than to expand the Empire. Trollope complacently observed, at the end of several decades of stability in 1875, "There is, I think, a general opinion that Great Britain possesses enough of the world . . . and that new territorial possessions must be regarded rather as increased burdens than increased strength" (181). An extraordinary boom in territorial acquisition was to take place during the four decades leading up to World War I, however. Intense international competition, particularly in what was called the "scramble for Africa," broke out between new colonial powers such as the United States, Russia, Italy, Germany, and Belgium and the more-established empires of Britain, France, Portugal, and the Netherlands. By 1900, 85 percent of the world's territories were directly controlled by one or another of these countries (with one-quarter of the earth controlled by England alone).

In Britain, a long economic depression (from 1873 into the early 1890s) increased international competition, and more frequent military defeats (the most alarming being General Charles Gordon's death at Khartoum in 1885 and the disastrous Boer War of 1899–1902) contributed during this period to make imperialist attitudes more aggressive and more overtly racist. The latter tendency was fueled by the popularized pseudo-Darwinian notion that the human races had separate origins and destinies, rather

---

[1] Good discussions can be found in Brantlinger (32–45) and Hobson (219–42). See also Cole, who examines the relationship between Henry Morton Stanley's popular *How I Found Livingstone* (1872) and *Heart of Darkness*.

than belonging to a single family—that they were "polygenetic" rather than "monogenetic"—which encouraged the British (and other Europeans) to regard certain races as biologically destined for subjection, or even extinction.

At the same time, however, late-nineteenth-century Britain saw the rise of new public debates about the problematics of empire—political, economic, and moral. There had been significant opposition to British imperialism in the late eighteenth century from political theorists such as Adam Smith and William Godwin and from literary figures such as William Blake, Helen Maria Williams, Walter Savage Landor, and James Montgomery. During most of the nineteenth century, however, public criticism was muted, and it only began to reemerge from the 1870s onward. Skepticism about imperial expansion marked British Liberalism under the leadership of William Gladstone throughout the 1880s, for example. Constant agitation for Home Rule in Ireland, which Gladstone supported—and which brought him down as prime minister in 1886—helped keep controversies over British colonialism at the center of political discussion. The costs of military occupation, both financial and political, were becoming unacceptable. And the emergent Labour movement was largely opposed to imperial expansion.

One symptom of these new doubts was that anxiety about the decline of empire featured prominently in the legendary decadence of fin-de-siècle culture, as comparisons between England and the late Roman Empire abounded in fiction and poetry, and in public debate more generally. For example, at the beginning of *Heart of Darkness* (1899), Marlow dwells on the striking notion that, for the Romans, London itself had been "one of the dark places of the earth" (249).[2] At the same time, however, he raises the commonplace objection to such analogies: the Roman Empire had been driven by greed, whereas the British Empire was supposedly founded on civilized principles of efficiency and hard work (an argument that was also used by pro-imperialists to distinguish between late-century imperialism and the earlier period of British conquest).

On the other hand, a nostalgia for the early, more adventurous days of imperial conquest began to surface in late-century works, as in Kipling's "The Man Who Would Be King" (1888). Stevenson, too, in his posthumously published *In the South Seas* (1896), contemplated the melancholy disappearance of native populations as a harbinger of the white race's disappearance. This pessimistic mood (which Patrick Brantlinger calls Imperial Gothic [227]) was partly the effect of demoralizing international com-

---

[2] All parenthetical references to "The Man Who Would Be King," "The Beach of Falesá," *Heart of Darkness*, and secondary readings in this volume are to this New Riverside Edition.

petition and domestic stagnation, partly a moral response to the exposure
of imperialist atrocities like those carried out by King Leopold II of Belgium in the Congo, and partly a reaction against the growing virulence
of late-century jingoism. Its sources also lay in the advances of Victorian
science. Darwin's evolutionary theory, James Clerk Maxwell's "law of en-
tropy," and Charles Lyell's discoveries of geologic change all made ideas
about cosmic or human permanence, even those embodied in empire, seem
illusory ("We live in the flicker" [250], says Marlow). In addition, fears
were raised by the new discipline of ethnography that "degeneration" could
be caused by contact between "higher" and "lower" races—a fear embedded
in Conrad's portrait of Kurtz. Poems like Alfred Lord Tennyson's "Locksley
Hall Sixty Years After" (1886) capture this widespread preoccupation with
imperial decline and fall; similarly, the narrator of Haggard's *Allan Quatermain* (1887) declares bluntly: "Civilization is only savagery silver-gilt. A
vainglory is it, and, like a northern light, comes but to fade and leave the
sky more dark" (420).

In short, while the stability of the Empire had largely been assumed during the mid-Victorian period, in the last quarter of the century imperialism
began to present itself as a set of questions. The writings of Kipling, Stevenson, and Conrad responded to a growing sense of urgency among British
readers about confronting those questions. While outright opposition to
imperialism was a minority position in England through World War I, debate about it became widespread, as well as quite complex. The attention
directed at imperial subjects by late-century writers can, of course, tell us a
great deal about the more peripheral representations of empire nested in
earlier fiction—the importance of Australia to Charles Dickens's *Great Expectations* (1861), for example, or the relationship between imperialism and
Zionism in George Eliot's *Daniel Deronda* (1876). I have thus included in
the "Chronology" references to particular works by Dickens, Eliot, Wilkie
Collins, Elizabeth Gaskell, and other mid-Victorian novelists that reward
close comparison with the stories in this volume. But, more immediately,
Kipling, Stevenson, and Conrad can reveal to us a general rethinking of
imperial attitudes and experiences in late-nineteenth-century culture, a
rethinking that prepared the way for the more forceful critiques of imperialism we find in early-twentieth-century writers such as E. M. Forster or
George Orwell.

In the twenty-first century (and, indeed, throughout much of the
twentieth), imperialism has acquired the unambiguous status of an evil,
especially as Western culture has grown increasingly self-conscious about
its racist history. The contemporary anti-imperialist consensus might make
it seem all too easy to demonstrate how the writings of Kipling, Stevenson, and Conrad remain embedded—sometimes despite themselves—in

an unenlightened political and racialist worldview. Nevertheless, it remains important to recognize the deep and often subtle involvement of late-nineteenth-century culture in imperialism, since, as Said reminds us, narratives have the power to shape their readers' sense of political reality.

In each of these three stories, for example, nineteenth-century racial stereotypes are upheld quite plainly: the superstitious gullibility of the natives in Kipling and Stevenson; the infantilizing of native peoples in all three writers; the suggestions of innate native self-destructiveness, which help to justify white rule (even Marlow's black helmsman, with whom he comes to feel a kind of sympathy, seems to cause his own death); and, above all, the pervasive irrationality of "savages." This conviction about primitive irrationality allows Kipling, for example, to allegorize the Indian Mutiny of 1857, at the end of "The Man Who Would Be King," as an act of uncontrolled, savage vengefulness. The Indian Mutiny—in which native conscripts within the British Army rose up against their white officers and, in alliance with deposed native aristocrats, seized large portions of the province of Bengal—was to some extent an organized revolutionary action. Indian historians refer to it not as a mutiny but as a rebellion. In Kipling's story, however, the homicidal rage of the Khafiristani Army, caused by the discovery that British colonizers are "only human," is seen as a fit analogy: "This business is our Fifty-Seven" (183), Carnehan laments. Moreover, the fascination of all three writers with colonial "backsliders"— that is, with those whites who have "gone native" and who seem the worse for it—further testifies to their habitual suspicion of nonwhite peoples and cultures.

Beyond the obvious racist stereotypes, these three stories also continue, in some respects, the erasure of nonwhite peoples that characterized mid-nineteenth-century canonical fiction. Readers are evidently not supposed to wonder what happens to Conrad's or Kipling's natives at the ends of these narratives. Stevenson alone among the three seems to take nonwhite characters seriously through his sympathetic portrayal of Uma in "The Beach of Falesá" (1892). But even Stevenson's story is liable to the charge Chinua Achebe lodges against *Heart of Darkness* in his now-classic essay, included in Part Five of this volume, that the significance of experience in the colonial world was always measured by British writers only through its impact on the consciousness of Europeans.

Kipling and Conrad also mystify colonial geography in ways that had traditionally been used to justify white rule. Conrad, in particular, participates in the long-standing British representation of Africa as a Dark Continent. While *Heart of Darkness* directly exposes some of the worst abuses of colonialism, it also drapes Africa in such a mysterious and monumental veil of evil that readers could not have been terribly surprised by Kurtz's impatient response: "Exterminate all the brutes!" (295). All three stories demonstrate, too, how imperial melancholy, while expressing pessimism about the colonial project, could fold subtly back into arguments in favor of imperialism. The alienation of Kipling's narrator from the bureaucratic machinery of late-nineteenth-century British rule, for example, is what fuels his nostalgic fascination with images of thrilling imperial conquest, as Carnehan and Dravot reenact in Kafiristan the eighteenth-century military and administrative conquest of India by the British. Even Stevenson, through his wistful regret over native depopulation in *In the South Seas,* seems to provide justification for the Darwinian view that "superior" races are destined to eliminate "inferior" ones.

Most important, all three stories repeat, in their own narrative trajectories, the imperial invasion of non-European territories. Each narrative's penetration of the colonial wilderness in quest of its "secret truth" makes it a reenactment of the indomitable will-to-conquest that underlies imperial exploration and domination. Of the three writers, Conrad is the most self-conscious about this resemblance between imperial and narrative aggression, as he sends his narrator up the Congo River along the exact same route taken by the brutal Kurtz and as he reminds us repeatedly of the uncanny similarities between Marlow and Kurtz—which culminate in Marlow's confusing Kurtz's face with his own reflection in the "glassy" (318) panel of the door of the apartment of Kurtz's "Intended." But all three writers were aware, in one way or another, that they raided colonial spaces for the raw materials of their trade. Stevenson once bragged to his editor, just before his arrival in Samoa:

> Nobody has had such stuff; such wild stories, such beautiful scenes, such singular intimacies, such manners and traditions, so incredible a mixture of the beautiful and horrible, the savage and civilized . . . not many people have seen more of [the South Seas] than I; perhaps no one: certainly no one capable of using the material. (*Letters* 1994–95: 6: 335)

We must remember, however, that British writers in the late nineteenth century had no alternative source of ideas and values than those offered by a deeply imperialist culture. They did not have the luxury of comfortably standing outside imperialism or of criticizing it from the perspective of antiracist or anti-imperialist discourses that have been constructed over many decades—in some cases, on the very foundations that they laid themselves. Said reminds us that the "rhetoric of blame" (*Culture* 18) will not carry us very far in understanding the relationship between imperialism and culture. Most important, easy judgments about any writer's complicity with imperialism overlook the fact that imperialism was not, itself, a unified set of values or beliefs.

The writings assembled in Part One of this volume were chosen partly to provide useful background information but also partly to demonstrate the broad range of discourses—propagandistic, scientific, sensational, political, and fictional—that flourished around imperial topics, and the complex network of ideas—often contradictory—that animated them. Outright propaganda like King Leopold's letter about the "noble" (106) work of colonization or George Trevelyan's caricatures of Indian rebels and fetishization of the British Army may seem simple enough to decode. These selections, along with those from Darwin, Kidd, and Seeley, illustrate a number of standard rationales used to justify imperial domination: the racial superiority of whites; the "natural" tendencies of the English people toward expansion; the need to relocate surplus population from Britain; the glorification of military valor; the "civilizing mission" of colonists; and, always, the health of the British economy. But many of these selections harbor complexities that make it difficult to say in what ways, exactly, their authors may have been for or against empire.

Seeley, for example, sometimes seems to regard imperialism as an evil—albeit a necessary one. William Gladstone contradicts a fundamental axiom of imperialism—that non-British peoples are unfit to rule themselves—by affirming the self-governing abilities of the Irish; but he does so only by attributing the moral norms of British imperial masculinity to the Irish, thus potentially obscuring political and cultural differences. George Washington Williams harshly criticizes the atrocities perpetrated by Leopold in the Congo, but only in the name of a humane and just colonialism. J. A. Hobson, the most systematic anti-imperialist thinker of his time, writes scathingly against colonial expansion, but only by employing an argument based on economic self-interest, rather than on moral principle. This economic argument is itself demonstrably incorrect and persuaded few even in his own time. Hobson claimed that the economic profit of the wealthy, not the nation as a whole, was the only incentive behind imperialism.[3] Nevertheless, Hobson's argument that honest Christian sentiments were used as "protective colours" (48) by more selfish imperialists remains a compelling caution against tendencies critics might have to stigmatize all British culture as hypocritical, and his account of the interrelationships between economic and political interests constitutes a powerful critique.

This mixture of progressive and regressive ideas exemplifies the tangled labyrinth of imperialist debate within which writers like Kipling, Steven-

---

[3] See Hobsbawm (60–73) for a critique of Hobson's economic theory. Hobsbawm shows that the economic benefit was very widely shared and that the expansion of markets was crucial. See also Hynes, Fieldhouse, Long, or Semmel.

son, and Conrad tried to clarify their thoughts about empire. Its complexity reveals the danger of trying to see the imperialist worldview as a fixed or a simple whole. Late-nineteenth-century discourse about imperialism was an intricate network of ideas, values, and perceptions that intersected in complex ways with basic cultural meanings. It allowed few simple or clear-cut options for opposing imperialism, just as, for example, our own time allows us few uncomplicated ways of opposing environmental destruction or rampant commodification without somehow still being implicated in them. Kipling, Stevenson, and Conrad were engaged in the dynamic but difficult process of rethinking an imperialist culture whose basic principles were often difficult to grasp, let alone to criticize or reject. Their frequent hesitations or confusions can tell us a great deal about the process by which new attitudes toward moral and political problems were forged in the late nineteenth century.

The selections in Parts One and Two are also intended to suggest that imperialism took on quite different complexions in different colonial situations, and therefore elicited a variety of different responses from writers. English intellectual life was rife with divergent responses to varying imperial situations. Gladstone may have been an anti-imperialist when it came to the Irish, for example, but that did not prevent him from being drawn into the invasion of Egypt in 1882. A prominent Liberal like John Stuart Mill may have condemned Governor Edward Eyre's massacre of Jamaican blacks in 1865, but he did not sympathize with the Indians during the 1857 mutiny. While the first few selections in Part One — those by Darwin, Kidd, Hobson, and Gladstone — document relatively general patterns of thought about imperialism, the other readings are all concerned with the particular histories of India, the South Seas, and the Congo — the three regions represented by Kipling's, Conrad's, and Stevenson's stories. In Part Two, the readings explore some of the specific circumstances shaping the perceptions of Kipling, Stevenson, and Conrad in these different colonial settings. Each writer negotiated a different colonial world, and the evaluation of imperial rule found in each writer's work is colored by the particular history and conditions he encountered.

Kipling matured as a person and as a writer in the most stable of Britain's nineteenth-century colonies, where he worked as a journalist before his literary career took off. With the one major exception of the mutiny, India had been the most durable and the most profitable of Britain's territorial possessions since its pacification in the early 1800s, and Kipling's ability to distance the violence of imperial conquest throughout "The Man Who Would Be King" — in time, in space, and in fantasy — betrays the relative complacency of Indian colonial life during the 1880s. Complicating his assumptions about colonial stability, however, was Kipling's personal relationship to India. As Ashis Nandy's biographical sketch indicates, Kipling was ambivalently poised between the colonial world, where he had been born, and England, where he had been rather traumatically educated as an outsider. Kipling's subsequent identification with colonial subjects—with his self-hatred for being a colonial himself—resulted in his ambivalent fascination with figures like the two white "loafers," Carnehan and Dravot, who are located socially somewhere between secure British rulers and downtrodden natives. To the narrator's amazement, Carnehan and Dravot can dress up as nonwhites and "pass," assuming a magical, boundary-crossing familiarity with native life to which Kipling aspired himself, as his letter to his cousin Margaret Burne-Jones reveals.

After Kipling settled more or less permanently in England in 1896, he turned militantly jingoist. Poems like "Recessional" (1897) or "The White Man's Burden" (1899), included in Part Four, represent the Kipling most Britons revered—the Bard of the Empire, as he was called. But in an early story like "The Man Who Would Be King," written when he was only twenty-one, Kipling pondered the ambiguities that link colonizers and barbarians together. The British right to rule in India is, of course, never directly questioned in the story, and whites and natives seem to inhabit two entirely separate worlds. Any moral equation of colonizers and barbarians is safely exiled into the unknown wastes of Kafiristan. Furthermore, the story demonstrates how colonial spaces give even the most degenerate white backsliders the opportunity to rediscover how powerful the core English values of discipline and loyalty can be and how colonizing work can turn even worthless slackers into true Englishmen. Nevertheless, the story raises the haunting possibility that something might be wrong with English rule in India—if only the gap between deadening bureaucratic routine and the vitality of long-lost imperial adventures, with the cross-racial intimacies (such as the bond between Carnehan, Dravot, and Billy Fish) they seem to promise. The story also makes clear that the imperial will-to-conquest is rooted largely in avarice, a thirst for personal glory, and a childish, egotistical love of the adulation of people who have been made dependent. Still, Kipling's meditations on the ambiguities and the tragedies of imperialism take place against a backdrop in which British colonial domination of India seems an irreversible historical fact.

Stevenson, seeking relief for a chronic lung condition, traveled to the South Seas at a very different stage of colonial development—at a time when imperial conquest was in full swing. The South Seas had largely been neglected by European powers until the 1880s (most writing on the South Seas before that time was done by missionaries like William Ellis). Stevenson arrived in Samoa in 1889, in time to witness Western powers acquire direct political control. While Stevenson had kept aloof from politics for most of his life, his observation of the brutalities perpetrated by Germany, Britain, and the United States in Samoa turned him into a passionate anti-imperialist. His *A Footnote to History* (1892) chronicled the injustices carried out against Samoans during the decade of the 1880s, particularly by the German government, and his nine open letters to the *Times* in the early 1890s protested indignantly the exploitation of natives by all three powers—what Stevenson called "this dance of folly and injustice and unconscious rapacity" (*Letters* 1994–95: 7: 153). In the excerpt from one of these letters included in Part Four, Stevenson actually declares himself to be a "partisan" (335) of the rebel Samoan chief—the kind of declaration that nearly provoked the British high commissioner of the western Pacific to deport Stevenson from Samoa in 1893.

The peculiarly transitional moment Stevenson observed in Samoa, in which relations between whites and nonwhites had not yet been resolved or regulated, gave him the opportunity to fraternize freely with Polynesians and to observe all the complexities of a colonial society undergoing extraordinary change. His own Scottish past, as Roslyn Jolly explains, also predisposed Stevenson to identify much more securely than Kipling could with imperial outsiders. These circumstances help make "The Beach of Falesá" the least romanticized, the most down-to-earth, and the most pro-native of the three stories in this volume. Stevenson's story proposes that the "heart of darkness" in tropical jungles is made up entirely of Western trickery. Rather than sentimentalizing a lost past of conquest and adventure, as Kipling's story does, Stevenson's narrative documents cross-cultural complexities and acutely observes social relations in the 1890s South Seas. It notes the intense conflicts between missionaries and traders; the substantial, surprising power of South Seas chiefs to control their relationship to Western trade; the high degree of mobility among Polynesian peoples (and, thus, the hybrid quality of South Seas cultures); the various accommodations often made by Western traders to native cultures; and a variety of other frankly observed features of what contemporary colonial theorists might call the "contact zone" between white and nonwhite cultures.[4]

While Stevenson never allows us to forget Wiltshire's stubborn racist attitudes, which render him a controversial figure (as Katherine Linehan argues, the first-person narration functions to expose those attitudes), the story also offers us a guardedly hopeful vision: it suggests the possibility of a biracial South Seas future through Wiltshire's half-caste children and through his homely attempts to grapple with the new problems they

---

[4]The term *contact zone,* coined by Pratt, is intended to suggest the areas of hybrid interaction between European and non-European cultures.

represent. Unlike most writers of colonial fiction, Stevenson does not mythicize the South Seas as the antithesis of Europe; rather, he seems to be asking what it might mean for whites to comprehend a non-European culture.

At the same time, however, the boyish love of mischief that pervades the life and work of the author of *Treasure Island* (1883) adds a puckish quality to Stevenson's involvement in Samoan politics, as his letter excerpted in Part Two demonstrates, and it helps graft a shoot-'em-up ending, straight out of imperial adventure fiction, onto his otherwise scrupulously realistic story. While lamenting the abuses of imperial conquest, Stevenson was nevertheless living the moment in Samoa *as* an adventure—in ways that Kipling's narrator might have envied. That love of adventure may have qualified his (and Wiltshire's) sense of the serious disparities between European and native cultures.

Of the three writers in this volume, Conrad's personal circumstances gave him the most extensive experience of imperialism, and the least reason to root himself imaginatively in any single colonial situation—or, perhaps, in any concrete response to empire. Orphaned by the imperial Russian occupiers of his native Poland, Conrad was steeped in fatalism about imperial oppression and lived in permanent exile from an early age, as W. G. Sebald's fictionalized biography movingly attests (though Sebald may also oversimplify Conrad's response to imperialism). Conrad's years of wandering the seas in the French and British merchant marines gave him both a profound and yet a detached, philosophical sympathy for imperial suffering. His voyage up the Congo in 1890 confronted him with some of the worst atrocities in the history of colonialism, which seemed only to confirm both his fatalism and his alienation. King Leopold, granted control of the Congo in exchange for permitting continued commercial access to other nations, turned the region into his own personal fiefdom from the late 1870s onward. His brutal system of forced labor killed or displaced several million native Africans (see Patrick Brantlinger's essay, 386, n. 4), in what Conrad called "the vilest scramble for loot that ever disfigured the history of human conscience and geographical exploration" (346). Leopold's excesses had been widely documented by the late 1890s, both in official reports like those of George Washington Williams and Roger Casement (mentioned by Sebald) and in exposés written by, among others, Mark Twain and Arthur Conan Doyle.

Yet faced with the most vicious imperial crimes, Conrad abstracted his experience of imperial brutality to the level of a metaphysical allegory in *Heart of Darkness*. It is difficult to say, finally, whether Kurtz's famous exclamation "The horror! The horror!" (313) stigmatizes imperial megalomania and the primitive savagery it evokes in civilized men or whether it has more to do with death, with the "darkness" of Africa and the black race, with the unsettling identity of primitive and civilized peoples, or with some other aspect of the human condition. More disturbing, it is unclear whether Marlow—or Conrad—finds something heroic in Kurtz's existential courage, his willingness to go beyond human limits and conventions to confront the worst in life ("'The horror!'," Marlow repeats to himself. "He was a remarkable man. After all, this was the expression of some sort of belief. [. . .] It was an affirmation, a moral victory" [314–315]). The very vividness of the atrocities Marlow describes, and his chastened awareness that "the conquest of the earth [. . .] is not a pretty thing when you look into it too much" (251), also compel him to generalize the meaning of suffering to a degree that contemporary critics like Achebe and Brantlinger have questioned, seeing it as a ploy sometimes to exalt European consciousness for its transcendence of mundane life.

The strikingly different receptions that these three writers' work received in England testifies in yet another way to the multidimensionality of imperial culture. Kipling's romantic ambiguities, his nostalgic delight in adventure, his contemplative but nevertheless clear endorsement of the imperial mission, and his fluid, transparent prose brought him great celebrity by the mid-1890s and a Nobel Prize in 1907. Kipling was considered a national hero, and his burial in Westminster Abbey on his death in 1936 testifies to his stature and celebrity. In particular, Kipling's sentimental ideas about India and his belief in the sanctity of "the white man's burden" were inspirational to supporters of imperialism, for whom Kipling articulated pride in empire by shrouding it in the glory of suffering and self-sacrifice.

Yet Kipling's jingosim from the late 1890s onward has blinded many readers to the multivalence of early stories like "The Man Who Would Be King," which takes a distinctly tragic view of imperial domination. At the time Kipling wrote "The Man Who Would Be King," he also wrote a number of other stories and poems that criticized the British colonial administration in India, while commiserating with the Indian victims of imperial rule.[5] It was not until a decade later that Kipling earned the criticism of Conrad (and many others) for his support of the Boer War.[6] Yet even in the late 1890s, the persistent ambiguities of Kipling's work allowed many anti-imperialists to interpret it as sympathetic to their cause. When "Recessional"

---

[5] See Ricketts (116), who describes Kipling's Liberal connections in England as a young man. See also Angus Wilson (2, 49–50, 96) for a discussion of Kipling's criticism of British brutality.

[6] Conrad wrote: "If I am to believe Kipling, this is a war undertaken for the cause of democracy. C'est à crever de rire" [It's enough to make one die laughing. ED.] (*Letters* 2: 207).

was published in 1897, for example, its allusions to British imperial missteps appealed to pro- and anti-imperialists alike. Jack Mackail, a Liberal relative of Kipling, thanked him for writing a poem that showed "all the signs of England saving up for the most tremendous smash ever recorded in history if she does not look to her goings" (Carrington 325). While Walter Besant claimed that Kipling was "the poet of the empire" and that "what Seeley taught scholars, Kipling has taught the multitude," he also admired the double-edged appeal of the poem: "I know of no poem in history so opportune, that so went home to all our hearts" (Green 256–57). It was the poignant ambivalence of Kipling's writing that helped make "Recessional" the most popular poem in the English language for several decades. Nevertheless, many contemporary critics follow Zohreh Sullivan in seeing the ambivalence and the tragic compassion in Kipling's early works as a manipulative disguise for his deeper romanticization of imperial conflicts.

In the years just before World War I, Kipling began to decline in popularity, both because his jingoism became increasingly strident and because the facility of his writing style began to be regarded as unliterary. Stevenson's judgment, in 1894, proved to be prophetic: "Even of the few best Kiplings, I am excruciatingly conscious of the journalist at the back of them" (*Letters* 1994–95: 8: 236). Only recently, as interest in the literature of imperialism has grown, has Kipling's cultural importance, as well as his stories' rich narrative complexities, begun to be reappreciated. Some of the ambiguities of "The Man Who Would Be King" may seem particularly fresh in the wake of the terrorist attacks on the World Trade Center and the Pentagon of September 11, 2001, as American and British forces try to impose a new political order on the same part of the world that stymied Carnehan and Dravot. The international war against terrorism launched in the early twenty-first century seems also to have inspired Western leaders with some of the same mixed sentiments of bellicose humanitarianism, trepidation, and sanctimoniousness expressed over a hundred years ago in "Recessional" and "The White Man's Burden." Kipling's warnings in all these works about both the magical qualities of imperial power and its impermanence may speak to us more compellingly in the coming years than they have in the recent past.

Stevenson's South Seas work, by contrast, fell on deaf ears. The early-1890s British public was much more interested in the Sudan, South Africa, and Malaysia than in the South Seas, and Stevenson's attempts to arouse their indignation were unsuccessful. He complained bitterly that he could not even interest his friends in Polynesian politics and culture. Stevenson's literary reputation had also been built on the romantic imaginativeness and the stylistic brilliance of the work that made him famous in the 1880s — enigmatic parables like "The Strange Case of Dr. Jekyll and Mr. Hyde"

(1886), Scottish romances like *Kidnapped* (1886) or *The Master of Ballantrae* (1889), and adventure fiction like *Treasure Island.* Readers were baffled by the nitty-gritty realism of his South Seas fiction, by its insistent vulgarity, and by his sudden passion for politics. As Oscar Wilde put it: "I see that romantic settings are the worst surroundings possible for a romantic writer. In Gower Street Stevenson could have written a new *Trois Mousquetaires.* In Samoa he wrote letters to the *Times* about Germans" (520).

While Stevenson's celebrity persisted into the early twentieth century, it gradually fell into decline, as modern critics came to feel that the exotic legend of his life and travels masked the conceptual thinness of much of his work. But his celebrity never at any time extended to his writings on Samoa. As is the case with Kipling, however, Stevenson's fiction is undergoing a contemporary revaluation partly as a result of his writings on imperialism. Though his South Seas fiction was less immediately influential than Kipling's writings on India, it has proven to be subtler and more sophisticated, as well as more acutely critical.

Conrad's reception has taken yet another course. *Heart of Darkness* was interpreted by reviewers, for the most part, as an attack on specifically Belgian atrocities, rather than on imperialism generally. Conrad himself had to be careful to make this interpretation possible: *Heart of Darkness* was originally published in the conservative, pro-imperialist *Blackwood's Magazine,* at a time when his reputation as an important writer was not yet secure. Conrad had to reassure William Blackwood, his publisher, of his patriotic, "justifiable" intentions: "The story is not gloomy. The criminality of inefficiency and pure selfishness when tackling the civilizing work in Africa is a justifiable idea" (*Letters* 2: 139 – 40). Reviewers failed to perceive the subtle ways *Heart of Darkness* baits the reader into seeing the story as sympathetic to British imperialism only to subvert that sympathy. Marlow may proclaim, at the beginning, that "what redeems [imperialism] is the idea only [. . .] something you can set up, and bow down before, and offer a sacrifice to" (251), and he may praise British colonial efficiency ("one knows that some real work is done in there" [254]); but the progress of the narrative undermines these pieties, clothing them both in the grotesque figure of Kurtz.

While some reviewers did praise the story as a moral tract, they tended to read its moral position in terms of the inherent limitations of whites to comprehend other races. *Heart of Darkness* was mildly celebrated in the early twentieth century for these reasons, as well as for its exotic description and narrative complexities. It was also criticized for what was seen as its obscurity, its overwrought prose, and its melodramatic qualities. But it was generally regarded as an adventure story, not as a critique of imperialism. As a reviewer for the *Manchester Guardian* wrote: "It must not be supposed that Mr. Conrad makes attack upon colonization, expansion, even upon Imperialism. In no one is the essence of the adventurous spirit more instinctive" (Sherry, *Commemoration* 135).

None of Conrad's writings brought him popular acclaim or financial reward until the 1920s, even though he was recognized as early as the 1890s by a small group of important writers—including Henry James, Stephen Crane, and Ford Madox Ford—as one of the great novelists of his time. His reputation rose, in the subsequent decades, on account of his work's modernist features: its psychological density and its self-conscious aesthetic intricacies (particularly its brilliant rhetorical flourishes, its narrative ingenuity, its use of images in abstract patterns, and its nonlinear conceptual logic). For many modernist critics, like F. R. Leavis (who enshrined Conrad as one of the three novelists making up "the great tradition," in his landmark book of that title), Conrad's political interest in imperialism seemed irrelevant to his aesthetic achievements. It has only been since the 1970s that Conrad's relationship to imperialism became the subject of great controversy, as critics have disagreed whether he reveals the horrors of imperialism or merely aestheticizes them. Conrad's having been honored for such a long time as one of the great novelists of the twentieth century is one reason why debates about the political meaning of his work have been so contentious and why writers like Achebe have found it so important to scrutinize the racial attitudes underlying *Heart of Darkness*.

The various complexities of British imperialist culture, of different colonial situations and different writers' backgrounds, of fluid reception histories, and of contemporary critical debates make it apparent that "fictions of empire" need to be situated within this complex field of meanings, rather than judged simplistically as having been either for or against empire. Nevertheless, interpretive complexity can blind us to the ways a powerful potential for anti-imperialist critique erupts quite clearly across the surface of all three narratives—if often only in fragmentary or incomplete ways or in terms the texts do not entirely control. Comparing the three stories closely can reveal some of the common critical potentials that, to one degree or another, all fictions of empire seem to unleash, whether deliberately or otherwise, and no matter what their authors' general attitudes toward imperialism might have been.

All three stories, for instance, help destabilize the conventional imperialist opposition between civilization and barbarism. Kipling's two loafers create a civilized order based on brutality, and their Masonic mumbo jumbo links developed and primitive cultures together in superstitious ritual. Stevenson reveals Case's brutality as the dark underside of "civilized" trade. Stevenson extends this collapse of differences more comically in his juxtaposition of Uma's absurd cogitations and Wiltshire's folksy reasoning.

Wiltshire himself remarks briefly on the similarities between civilized and primitive behavior (in comments that could equally well be applied to readers of adventure fiction) when he considers the natives' "fashionable boldness," their liking to be terrified by demons in the heart of darkness: "This is mighty like Kanakas; but, if you look at it another way, it's mighty like white folks too" (231). Conrad is perhaps most persistent and most self-conscious in equating civilization with the primitive: "All Europe contributed to the making of Kurtz" (294), he reminds us. Artist, scientist, businessman, writer, political agent, musician—Kurtz in his degeneration shows how both mercenary and philosophical quests (that is, the worst and best of Europe) can alike be forms of barbarism: both attempt to wrest some kind of pure value out of the contaminating, resistant wilderness. And despite their stark opposition, even Kurtz's "Intended" and his black lover are equated, strikingly, in the last pages of the narrative. In sum, these three stories may sustain some hierarchical relationships between the imperial center and the colonial periphery, but at various points they all jeopardize those relationships as well.

All three texts also defamiliarize standard imperialist attitudes by objectifying their narrator's thoughts. Each story features a narrator (and sometimes multiple narrators) who clearly cannot be identified with the author, and this distancing has the effect of estranging the narrator's more conventional assumptions. Marlow's famously naive comments about British efficiency and about the "idea" of empire are quite clearly framed ironically. Stevenson uses techniques of narratorial distancing somewhat differently, as Linehan explains, to reveal the limitations of Wiltshire's racism. Similarly, Carnehan's casual accounts of the butchery of natives, as well as his self-exculpations ("poor old Peachey that hadn't done them any harm" [184]), are presented interrogatively through Kipling's narrative framing. In general, the three stories maneuver the reader into a skeptical, questioning role in relation to the narrator, which has the potential at least to denaturalize imperialist thinking. Conrad's famous obscurity, whatever its liabilities may be, also works to defamiliarize imperialist assumptions, since the rich but murky texture of his narrative disorients moral, cultural, and philosophical values.

Finally, each story (wittingly or not) illuminates some of the fundamental motivations of imperialism—motivations that lie deeply buried beneath the standard economic or political rationales of many of the texts in Part One. All three, for example, reveal the importance of self-discovery to the imperial quest. Marlow and Kurtz both penetrate the wilderness at least partly to find themselves, and the psychological drive behind their quests appropriates colonial space as a kind of narcissistic mirror. "The most you can hope from [life]," Marlow says at the end of his journey, "is some knowledge of yourself" (314). Wiltshire's story also revolves around self-discovery, although what Stevenson's narrator learns about himself is more flattering and more consistent with conventional imperialist expectations. Wiltshire learns in the bush that, at heart, he really is an honorable Englishman—a discovery made in a more ironic key by Carnehan and Dravot.

It is difficult to distinguish these kinds of vain self-discovery from the stories' interest in imaginative self-transformation. As Ann Stoler has argued, Europeans did not simply import their own ideas into the colonies; they also *made* their identities overseas. Stoler claims that what often looks specifically European in nineteenth-century culture are "cultural and political configurations honed and worked through the politics of empire" (209). These stories, in other words, illustrate the process by which Europeans constructed their own identities (while often believing that they merely "found" them) over against the lands and peoples that they dominated.

All three stories demonstrate this process of self-discovery (or self-creation) in a variety of ways. For one thing, they show how individuals could reinvent the standard values of British culture in colonial settings, remaking them in ways that would have been prohibited at home. Kipling's journalist-narrator may be blasé about the machinery of British culture in India, but Carnehan and Dravot's rediscovery of basic English moral virtues like honor, fidelity, sobriety, and sexual restraint reinject vitality and a sense of purpose into British national identity—a reinvigoration that may account for the journalist-narrator's fascination with their experience. Kipling's story thus functioned, in part, as a reaffirmation of British national values in a time of imperial malaise. Both Kipling's and Stevenson's stories demonstrate this reaffirmation of British values as a class parable as well: in both stories, lower-class characters come to discover the moral virtues that had always traditionally been the badge of Britain's middle class. The stories thus advertised the colonies as a potential path to social respectability through moral self-rehabilitation. *Heart of Darkness* plays out this same trajectory in a subtler way, in the sense that Marlow himself discovers the "restraint" (310) that he accuses Kurtz of lacking, as well as the "fidelity" that Kurtz had betrayed—both characteristically middle-class British moral values—when he honors Kurtz's secrets at the end of the story.

Kipling's use of Masonic rituals and symbols, as the key device behind his loafers' success in Kafiristan, provides a striking mechanism for the status transformations often associated with empire. As the excerpt from Steven Knight's work suggests, Freemasonry combined a classless sense of equality—all Masons were brothers—with a rigidly hierarchical social ladder that members could climb. Freemasonry thus magically affords Carnehan and Dravot the means to escape their class position and to boost their status within social hierarchies, at the same time that it reaffirms the fundamentally hierarchical nature of British social order. Even if social mobility in the colonies was more a fantasy than a reality (optimism about imperial opportunities for self-improvement was transparently manipulated by British politicians in the late nineteenth century to defuse working-class discontent at home), the flip side of colonial social fluidity was anxiety about the social deviations such fluidity might encourage. These three stories seem generally less worried about racial difference than they are about the social deviance that results when class roles and class boundaries weaken—whether such deviance appears in the form of excessively powerful low-life figures (Carnehan and Dravot), or elite figures run amok (Kurtz), or ambivalent figures who embody the worst of both "high" and "low" social identities (Case).

Among the other volatile issues fictions of empire inevitably raise—without necessarily controlling or resolving them—are a host of questions about gender and sexual identity. As these stories indicate, colonial spaces were almost exclusively a male preserve (at least, they were commonly represented as such).[7] Carnehan and Dravot exemplify a standard theme in colonial narratives: heterosexual restraint and male "homosocial" bonding are fundamental to the maintenance of empire and transgressions against the law of celibacy can be fatal.[8] Male bonds of loyalty, which seem to replace heterosexual union as an ideal in the colonies, are affirmed in *Heart of Darkness* through the loyalty Marlow displays toward Kurtz, as he lies to the "Intended" (significantly, she is not even granted a proper name) about Kurtz's death and its meaning. Intense male bonds are also established between Wiltshire and Case but only to be betrayed—an instance of gender treason that may account for some of Wiltshire's rage at Case. All three stories indicate how colonial conditions helped consolidate certain norms for nineteenth-century British masculinity: sexual restraint, a readiness to take risks, indifference to suffering, and, above all, the sacred bond between men in the wilderness, as figured archetypically in Henry Morton Stanley's famous face-to-face encounter with David Livingstone—an encounter replayed ironically in Marlow's meeting with Kurtz. Ashis Nandy has argued that colonialism helped rigidify British masculine roles in the nineteenth century by instilling combative imperialist behavior as a national norm (see Nandy 32).

---

[7] But see the work on Victorian female travelers of Ghose, Grewal, Mills, and Morgan. See also studies of the political role of women in the colonies by Strobel and Ware.

[8] *Homosocial* is Sedgwick's term for the social (but not necessarily sexual) exclusivity between men that characterizes modern Western life and that nineteenth-century fiction, in particular, represented as central to its own psychological and political dynamics.

"The Beach of Falesá" also brings to the surface the homoeroticism sometimes embedded in colonial homosocial bonds. In the climactic fight between Wiltshire and Case, the sexual overtones are unmistakable. As Case "threw his hands up together, more like a frightened woman," Wiltshire says, "[I] drew my knife and got it in the place," eventually passing out and falling "with my head on the man's mouth" (242). This scene dramatically illuminates the erotic dimension of colonial male bonding, while also fiercely disavowing that eroticism through Wiltshire's killing of Case. In *Heart of Darkness,* the disavowal of homoeroticism is subtler and more strained. Marlow refers repeatedly to the eroticized desire both he and Kurtz's Russian disciple feel for Kurtz. "Ah, he talked to you of love" (300), Marlow says bemusedly to the Russian, unaware as yet of his own growing desire for Kurtz. "It was impossible not to—" Marlow says later, breaking off and needing the "Intended" to complete his thought: "Love him" (319). Marlow's barely repressed desire for Kurtz leads him, finally, to that classic gesture of mediated homosocial love: he desires, in some vague, sublimated way, the woman that Kurtz himself had desired.[9]

Heart of Darkness also uncovers the surprising centrality of women to the male homosocial world, despite the marginalization of women (especially white women) in colonial sites. Marlow's patronizing attitudes toward women, his notion that they live in ideal worlds, "out of touch with truth" (257), and therefore lack the strength to endure the "truth" he shares with Kurtz, point somewhat paradoxically to male homosociality's idealization of and dependence on women. The resonant epithet "Intended" suggests how deeply the motivations or intentions of the male imperial project are directed at, or devoted to, the world of women. That is, the civilized "idea" that stands behind colonial domination, from Marlow's point of view, is precisely the world of values he identifies with women: "We must help them to stay in that beautiful world of their own, lest ours gets worse" (292–293). The misogyny in this gender system, the resentment Marlow plainly feels for the centrality of (absent, idealized) women, emerges throughout his narrative, especially in his climactic suggestion that it is not death, imperialism, the primitive, or the nature of human life that inspires Kurtz's cry "The horror!" but, rather, the idealized "Intended" herself: "The last word he pronounced was—your name" (321), he tells her.

Stevenson would seem to stand apart from Kipling's and Conrad's conventional sexual values, given his frank affirmation of Wiltshire's love for Uma. Stevenson is, in fact, one of the few colonial writers to have written

[9] In her groundbreaking book, Sedgwick shows how male homosocial desire is often expressed through romantic competition between two men for the same woman, who becomes a cover and a medium for their fundamental attraction to one another.

intelligently and positively about heterosexuality, cross-racial or otherwise. Uma is clearly a counterideal to the gender system that produced the "Intended," and it is significant that Stevenson felt he had to turn to a non-European woman in order to represent women affirmatively. Uma is perhaps the only three-dimensional female character in all of Stevenson's fiction, and his willingness to endow her with both slyness and strength is pathbreaking. Nevertheless, we must remember that "The Beach of Falesá" follows in a long tradition of South Seas writing that celebrates exotic female sexuality. Herman Melville's *Typee* (1846) is a typical European representation of the South Seas as a heterosexual paradise, full of sexually unrepressed women ready to serve as helpmates or redeemers. What may appear to be a more egalitarian set of gender relations in "The Beach of Falesá" masks this tradition of sexual exoticization (a tradition whose negative side appears in Conrad's treatment of Kurtz's black lover, who, in contrast to the "Intended," is all body and emotion—a symbol for the mystery of the wilderness, and a "superb, wild-eyed and magnificent" [305] but nevertheless grotesque image of miscegenation).

Furthermore, missionary discourse in the South Seas, like the excerpt from Ellis's *Polynesian Researches* (1829) included in Part One, relentlessly imposed ideals of female domesticity on Polynesian women, in which their adoption of wifely moral responsibilities was hoped to perform something of the same function in Polynesian cultures that the "Intended" does for Marlow—to keep men from "getting worse." Wiltshire makes himself morally good for the sake of Uma, and he sees her, at least partly, as an inspirational ideal: "It came over me she was a kind of countess really, dressed to hear great singers at a concert, and no even mate for a poor trader like myself" (197). Wiltshire's upward social trajectory hinges, in part, on his ability to tie his fortunes to the kind of morally good female figure that was central to the British domestic romance. In both Ellis's and Melville's texts, the exotic sexualization and the domestic idealization of the Polynesian woman, in their complementary ways, help create sentimental narratives of reciprocity between white and nonwhite races, with all the embarrassment of conquest stripped away. It remains a question whether something similar might be said of Stevenson's use of Uma.

At the same time, in Stevenson's defense, "The Beach of Falesá" discredits exploitative attitudes toward Uma through Case, who tries to use her sexually and turns vindictive when he is rebuffed, and, to some extent, through Mr. Tarleton, who sees her primarily as an object for religious conversion. Moreover, the story does not disguise the facts of sexual exploitation in the South Seas (though Stevenson's censorious editors tried to); it does not sentimentalize the Polynesian woman as a helpmate or rescuer; it does not create unqualified illusions of cross-racial harmony achieved through heterosexuality; it does not express nostalgia for a lost sexual paradise; and, most important, it does not end with the white man abandoning his exotic fling (a standard conclusion to the Madame Butterfly plot, of which *Typee* is a classic instance). Wiltshire's love for Uma develops somewhat ambiguously—but creatively—within these traditional representations of Polynesian women. One cultural limitation that Stevenson could clearly not escape, however, was his inability to provide us with any meaningful view of Uma's interiority, or her own understanding of cross-racial romance.

Stevenson's rewriting of traditional adventure and domestic plots, as well as his willingness to incorporate two long stories told by Uma herself, suggests the potential for fictions of empire to rework and enlarge the ideological materials they inherit from imperialist culture. All these stories are, in a sense, rewritings—Kipling's, of various kinds of narratives about the conquest of India and the Indian Mutiny; Conrad's, of Homer, Virgil, Dante, Bunyan, and many others (including Stanley) who wrote narratives about transformative moral or psychological journeys; and Stevenson's, of adventure fiction, the conversion narrative, and the domestic romance. Stevenson's attempts to identify with Samoan rebels, as revealed in his letters, or to celebrate the strengths of Samoan womanhood in "The Beach of Falesá" also replay a tradition of romantic individualism found in Jean-Jacques Rousseau and other eighteenth- and early-nineteenth-century writers, who willfully tried to see the "noble savage" as a positive antithesis to civilized corruption.

That such rewritings are possible suggests that the relationship between fiction and imperialism is a dynamic one and that no preset moral judgments or interpretive formulas can tell us how that relationship should be defined or explained. The strenuous efforts of Kipling, Stevenson, and Conrad to think their way through the dilemmas of imperialism by means of these various kinds of rewritings can help us to understand the historical relationship played out between British fiction and "the great fact" of nineteenth-century imperialism. They can also help us to appreciate the crucial ways in which culture always works through the complex body of social thought to engage us in interpreting the most daunting challenges of our times.

A NOTE ON THE TEXTS

"The Man Who Would Be King" was first published in 1888, in a collection of short stories titled *The Phantom 'Rickshaw*, by the Indian publisher A. H. Wheeler. Wheeler issued six such volumes of Kipling's stories that year, in a series called the Indian Railway Library. All six volumes, then bound into a two-volume set, were republished by Macmillan in 1895, after several revisions by the author. The 1895 edition became the basis for several later editions of Kipling's work published by Macmillan through the 1930s, which came to be called the Uniform edition. Before his death, Kipling revised all his work for the Sussex edition of 1937–39, but in the interest of preserving the text read by Kipling's readers throughout the years of his greatest popularity, I have followed many editors in preferring the 1895 Macmillan edition as my copy text. I have made only a few small changes to regularize punctuation and spelling, and I have made one minor change (altering *priests* to *priest* [175]) to correct an apparent error.

The publication history of "The Beach of Falesá" is complex and controversial. Stevenson's manuscript was originally used as the basis for a serial, which ran for six issues of the *Illustrated London News* in July and August of 1892, under a different title: "Uma, or The Beach of Falesá (Being the Narrative of a South-Sea Trader)." The serial version, however, was full of "misprints abominable," as Stevenson put it (*Letters* 1994–95: 7: 363). Even more serious, Stevenson's editor had judged the story too salacious for Victorian tastes and had expurgated it. The editor entirely removed the fake marriage certificate, with its offending assertion that Uma was "illegally married to Mr. John Wiltshire for one night"—a deletion that rendered the plot incoherent. He also struck out many of the narrator's coarser expressions and cleaned up the prose to make it more palatable to middle-class tastes.

Stevenson complained bitterly, referring to his publishers at one point as "celestial idiots" (*Letters* 1994–95: 7: 413), but to little purpose. "Will it do for the young person?" he later wrote of another story. "I don't know; since 'The Beach,' I know nothing, except that men are fools and hypocrites, and I know less of them than I was fond enough to fancy" (*Letters* 1994–95: 7: 369). When the text was reset for book publication by Cassell in the volume *Island Nights Entertainments* (over Stevenson's objections that the story not be included in that volume), many of the printing errors were corrected. Stevenson then had the opportunity to go over the corrected proofs, and he made additional changes. He was able to have the marriage certificate restored, but only on the condition that the length of the fake marriage be changed from one night to one week—a compromise to which Stevenson resigned himself reluctantly. He lamented the deviation from a similar document he had once seen: "Well, well," he wrote to a friend, "if the dears prefer a week, why I'll give them ten days, but the real document, from which I have scarcely varied, ran for one night" (*Letters* 1994–95: 7: 281). Other bowdlerizations remained unchanged. The editors of the Cassell version also left out a long anecdote about Case from the first chapter, which they deleted from the serial version—a change that Stevenson called "very illogical" (*Letters* 1994–95: 7: 364) but to which he ultimately submitted.

Most subsequent editions have used the resulting text, the Cassell edition of 1893, as the standard copy text—on the grounds either that this is the final version corrected by the author or that the Cassell edition has historical precedence as the only version that was known widely to the public—until fairly recently, that is, when the text of the manuscript itself was published. While some contemporary scholars have argued for the authority of the original manuscript as the best guide to Stevenson's intentions, in light of the corruptions introduced by various editors, it seems unreasonable to assume that the editorial changes Stevenson approved in the Cassell proofs (not to mention the changes that he made to these proofs) have no legitimacy. Nevertheless, there are a number of reasons for modifying the corrected Cassell edition, in light of the manuscript. For one thing, there is the matter of the censorship, which, in the case of the revised marriage certificate, introduces an obvious absurdity and which, in other cases, alters the narrator's character or the tone of the work substantially. For another, some of the deviations from the manuscript in the Cassell version quite obviously scramble the sense of particular passages.

While purists might favor accepting the public text corrected by the author, despite these surviving errors, the unusual circumstances surrounding Stevenson's corrections make stringent notions about public texts seem a historical idealization in this case. The fact that Stevenson lived in Samoa, and that communication with his editors took weeks, deprived him of the luxury of active and constant involvement with the publication process available to writers in Europe. While Stevenson cared deeply about the details of his work, his failure to catch numerous errors of sense and consistency in the proofs suggests that he was rushed, both because of the difficulties of communication with London and because of financial pressures that forced him to work very quickly at the time. Stevenson's erratic relationships with a number of editors, trustees, and publishers, as well as the authority some of these figures assumed on account of Stevenson's remoteness, further complicated the publication process.

Neither the manuscript nor the Cassell edition, then, affords us the possibility of a definitive text of "The Beach of Falesá." Any edition of the story must inevitably reflect the critical choices of its editor. I have decided to use the 1893 Cassell version as my copy text, but I have interjected some material from the manuscript, placing it within square brackets, on occasions that seemed to warrant privileging the manuscript over the Cassell. These changes are intended to reverse apparent censorship, to restore coherence, to reflect tonal inflections sustained by similar passages elsewhere in the published text, or to achieve consistency of style.

To reverse censorship, I have restored the original marriage certificate, along with the anecdote about Case—both of which we know reflect Stevenson's intentions—and I have restored a number of incidental expressions and epithets that seem to have been removed because of their vulgarity. Restoring coherence involved reversing Cassell corrections that disrupt the sense of the manuscript version. These include such things as the dropping of *you and* (202); the changing of *recollection* to *recollections* (197); and the replacement of *early,* which makes no sense given that Wiltshire sets foot on shore at noon, by *better* (190). Restoring the sense of particular passages also meant restoring a line of dialogue (197) and converting *shy* back to *sly* (192) in order to emphasize what seems an important part of Uma's character. I have also restored the Americanisms pruned out of Wiltshire's vocabulary (*hollered* for *holla'd* [228], for example), which seem a significant part of his speech and character.

I have also restored text from the manuscript in some instances for consistency's sake—*footed* (200), for instance, to match *footed* (241); for the same reason, I have dropped an additional *and* inserted into the second sentence of Chapter 4 (223) and restored a comma (243). Also for

consistency's sake, I have changed *towards* back to *toward* [206]. I have replaced a badly garbled passage in the Cassell edition (219) with the manuscript version. I have also chosen Stevenson's manuscript in two instances
in which it supplied a stronger syntactical shading (*could* for *would* [226],
and *them* for *the* [245]) without changing the sense, and I have restored
manuscript versions when the Cassell changes created strained syntax (*were*
[234]). I have also reversed one unauthorized change made after Stevenson
corrected the proofs (*low-down* for *low* [216]). When interjecting manuscript material, I have made small alterations in spelling, capitalization, and
punctuation to create consistency with the Cassell text.

Besides these uses of manuscript material, I have made a number of
other minor changes to the Cassell text. I have regularized the spelling of a
few hyphenated words: for *to-night, to-day, to-morrow,* and *cocoa-nuts,*
I have substituted *tonight, today, tomorrow,* and *cocoanuts.* I have regularized capitalization in two cases (*Papa* and *hell*), and I have also regularized
the spelling of two names (Johnny and Galoshes). The Cassell alternates
between *O* and *Oh;* I have used the latter, more contemporary version.
Kanakaised has been changed to *Kanakaized.*

Readers who want to know more about textual variations are invited to
compare this edition with the manuscript, which has been transcribed by
Barry Mennikof (whose discussions with me, incidentally, have proved
most valuable) and published by Stanford University Press, and with editions based more narrowly on the Cassell text.

Permission to reprint from the manuscript has been generously granted
from the Huntington Library, San Marino, California.

The text of *Heart of Darkness* presents none of the editorial difficulties
of Stevenson's story. *Heart of Darkness* originally appeared in three install-
ments in *Blackwood's Magazine,* from February to April 1899. It was then
heavily revised and published in book form, together with "Youth" and
"The End of the Tether," in *Youth: A Narrative; and Two Other Stories* by
Blackwood in 1902. Like all other modern editions, mine follows the text of
the 1902 Blackwood edition. Conrad made a number of very minor corrections to this version in the Heinemann edition of 1921 — corrections that
have been adopted by most later editions. I have incorporated those changes
that regularize punctuation, spelling, or capitalization or that clearly correct errors in the sense (*those* for *these* [268], for example). I have also followed later editions in adopting *lunged* for *lounged* (290), and I have made
some small changes to regularize punctuation and spelling.

What survives of the original manuscript of *Heart of Darkness* is held at Yale University, and a typescript is held by the New York Public Library.

———

In my preparation of the notes for "The Man Who Would Be King," "The Beach of Falesá," and *Heart of Darkness*, I am indebted to previous editors of these texts, especially Roslyn Jolly, Robert Hampson, Robert Kimbrough, Hugh Haughton, and Daniel Karlin. I also received excellent research assistance from Mary-Catherine Harrison.

Part One

HISTORICAL CONTEXTS

From The Descent of Man

Charles Darwin

The virtues which must be practised, at least generally, by rude men, so that they may associate in a body, are those which are still recognized as the most important. But they are practised almost exclusively in relation to the men of the same tribe; and their opposites are not regarded as crimes in relation to the men of other tribes. No tribe could hold together if murder, robbery, treachery, etc., were common; consequently such crimes within the limits of the same tribe "are branded with everlasting infamy" (Anonymous 395);[1] but excite no such sentiment beyond these limits. A North American Indian is well pleased with himself, and is honored by others, when he scalps a man of another tribe; and a Dyak cuts off the head of an unoffending person, and dries it as a trophy. The murder of infants has prevailed on the largest scale throughout the world, and has met with no reproach; but infanticide, especially of females, has been thought to be good for the tribe, or at least not injurious. Suicide during former times was not generally considered as a crime,[2] but rather, from the courage displayed, as an honorable act; and it is still practised by some semi-civilized and savage nations without reproach, for it does not obviously concern others of the tribe. It has been recorded that an Indian Thug conscientiously regretted that he had not robbed and strangled as many travellers as did his father before him. In a rude state of civilization the robbery of strangers is, indeed, generally considered as honorable. [. . .]

The Descent of Man. Philadelphia: McKay, 1874. 133–35, 148–49, 157–58.

[1] See this able review in the *North British Review.* See also Walter Bagehot's articles on the "Importance of Obedience and Coherence to Primitive Man" (*The Fortnightly Review* 1867: 520; 1868: 457). [Darwin's note.]

[2] See the very interesting discussion on suicide in Lecky 1: 223. With respect to savages, Mr. Winwood Reade informs me that the negroes of West Africa often commit suicide. It is well known how common it was among the miserable aborigines of South America, after the Spanish conquest. [Darwin's note.]

Most savages are utterly indifferent to the sufferings of strangers, or even delight in witnessing them. It is well known that the women and children of the North American Indians aided in torturing their enemies. Some savages take a horrid pleasure in cruelty to animals,[3] and humanity is an unknown virtue. Nevertheless, besides the family affections, kindness is common, especially during sickness, between the members of the same tribe, and is sometimes extended beyond these limits. Mungo Park's[4] touching account of the kindness of the negro women of the interior to him is well known. Many instances could be given of the noble fidelity of savages toward each other, but not to strangers; common experience justifies the maxim of the Spaniard, "Never, never trust an Indian." There cannot be fidelity without truth; and this fundamental virtue is not rare between the members of the same tribe: thus Mungo Park heard the negro women teaching their young children to love the truth. This, again, is one of the virtues which becomes so deeply rooted in the mind that it is sometimes practised by savages, even at a high cost, toward strangers; but to lie to your enemy has rarely been thought a sin, as the history of modern diplomacy too plainly shows. As soon as a tribe has a recognized leader, disobedience becomes a crime, and even abject submission is looked at as a sacred virtue. [. . .]

The other so-called self-regarding virtues, which do not obviously, though they may really, affect the welfare of the tribe, have never been esteemed by savages, though now highly appreciated by civilized nations. The greatest intemperance is no reproach with savages. Utter licentiousness and unnatural crimes prevail to an astounding extent.[5] As soon, however, as marriage, whether polygamous or monogamous, becomes common, jealousy will lead to the inculcation of female virtue; and this, being honored, will tend to spread to the unmarried females. How slowly it spreads to the male sex, we see at the present day. Chastity eminently requires self-command; therefore it has been honored from a very early period in the moral history of civilized man. As a consequence of this, the senseless practice of celibacy has been ranked from a remote period as a virtue (Lecky 1: 109). The hatred of indecency, which appears to us so natural as to be thought innate, and which is so valuable an aid to chastity, is

---

[3] See, for instance, Charles Hamilton's account of the Kaffirs, Charnock xv. [Darwin's note.]

[4] Scottish explorer, one of the first Europeans to explore the Niger River, which he mapped in two expeditions. Park published *Travels in the Interior of Africa* in 1779 and was killed by African tribesmen in 1806. [ED.]

[5] McLennan (176) has given a good collection of facts on this head. [Darwin's note.]

a modern virtue, appertaining exclusively, as Sir G. Staunton remarks (2: 348), to civilized life. This is shown by the ancient religious rites of various nations, by the drawings on the walls of Pompeii, and by the practices of many savages.

We have now seen that actions are regarded by savages, and were probably so regarded by primeval man, as good or bad, solely as they obviously affect the welfare of the tribe—not that of the species, nor that of an individual member of the tribe. This conclusion agrees well with the belief that the so-called moral sense is aboriginally derived from the social instincts, for both relate at first exclusively to the community. The chief causes of the low morality of savages, as judged by our standard, are, firstly, the confinement of sympathy to the same tribe. Secondly, powers of reasoning insufficient to recognize the bearing of many virtues, especially of the self-regarding virtues, on the general welfare of the tribe. Savages, for instance, fail to trace the multiplied evils consequent on a want of temperance, chastity, etc. And, thirdly, weak power of self-command; for this power has not been strengthened through long-continued, perhaps inherited, habit, instruction, and religion.

I have entered into the above details on the immorality of savages,[6] because some authors have recently taken a high view of their moral nature, or have attributed most of their crimes to mistaken benevolence (e.g., Lecky 1: 124). These authors appear to rest their conclusion on savages possessing those virtues which are serviceable, or even necessary, for the existence of the family and of the tribe—qualities which they undoubtedly do possess, and often in a high degree. [. . .]

It must not be forgotten that although a high standard of morality gives but a slight or no advantage to each individual man and his children over the other men of the same tribe, yet that an increase in the number of well-endowed men and an advancement in the standard of morality will certainly give an immense advantage to one tribe over another. A tribe including many members who, from possessing in a high degree the spirit of patriotism, fidelity, obedience, courage, and sympathy, were always ready to aid one another, and to sacrifice themselves for the common good, would be victorious over most other tribes; and this would be natural selection. At all times throughout the world tribes have supplanted other tribes; and as morality is one important element in their success, the standard of morality and the number of well-endowed men will thus everywhere tend to rise and increase.

---

[6]See on this subject copious evidence in Lubbock, ch. 7. [Darwin's note.]

It is, however, very difficult to form any judgment why one particular tribe and not another has been successful and has risen in the scale of civilization. Many savages are in the same condition as when first discovered several centuries ago. As Mr. Bagehot has remarked, we are apt to look at progress as normal in human society; but history refutes this. The ancients did not even entertain the idea, nor do the Oriental nations at the present day. According to another high authority, Sir Henry Maine, "the greatest part of mankind has never shown a particle of desire that its civil institutions should be improved" (22).[7] Progress seems to depend on many concurrent favorable conditions, far too complex to be followed out. But it has often been remarked that a cool climate, from leading to industry and to the various arts, has been highly favorable thereto. The Esquimaux, pressed by hard necessity, have succeeded in many ingenious inventions, but their climate has been too severe for continued progress. Nomadic habits, whether over wide plains or through the dense forests of the tropics, or along the shores of the sea, have in every case been highly detrimental. While observing the barbarous inhabitants of Tierra del Fuego, it struck me that the possession of some property, a fixed abode, and the union of many families under a chief, were the indispensable requisites for civilization. [. . .]

The remarkable success of the English as colonists, compared to other European nations, has been ascribed to their "daring and persistent energy"; a result which is well illustrated by comparing the progress of the Canadians of English and French extraction; but who can say how the English gained their energy? There is apparently much truth in the belief that the wonderful progress of the United States, as well as the character of the people, are the results of natural selection; for the more energetic, restless, and courageous men from all parts of Europe have emigrated during the last ten or twelve generations to that great country, and have there succeeded best (Galton, "Heredity" 325). Looking to the distant future, I do not think that the Rev. Mr. Zincke takes an exaggerated view when he says: "All other series of events—as that which resulted in the culture of mind in Greece, and that which resulted in the empire of Rome—only appear to have purpose and value when viewed in connection with, or rather as subsidiary to . . . the great stream of Anglo-Saxon emigration to the west"(29). Obscure as is the problem of the advance of civilization, we can at least see that a nation which produced during a lengthened period the greatest number of highly intellectual, energetic, brave, patriotic, and benevolent men, would generally prevail over less favored nations.

---

[7] For Mr. Bagehot's remarks, see *The Fortnightly Review* 1868: 452. [Darwin's note.]

From Social Evolution

Benjamin Kidd

We watch the Anglo-Saxon overflowing his boundaries, going forth to take possession of new territories, and establishing himself like his ancestors in many lands. A peculiar interest attaches to the sight. He has been deeply affected, more deeply than many others, by the altruistic influences of the ethical system upon which our Western civilisation is founded. He had seen races like the ancient Peruvians, the Aztecs, and the Caribs, in large part exterminated by others, ruthlessly driven out of existence by the more vigorous invader, and he has at least the wish to do better. In the North American Continent, in the plains of Australia, in New Zealand, and South Africa, the representatives of this vigorous and virile race are at last in full possession — that same race which, with all its faults, has for the most part honestly endeavoured to carry humanitarian principles into its dealings with inferior peoples, and which not improbably deserves the tribute paid to it on this account by Mr. Lecky who counts its "unwearied, unostentatious, and inglorious crusade against slavery" amongst "the three or four perfectly virtuous acts recorded in the history of nations" (1:160).

Yet neither wish nor intention has power apparently to arrest a destiny which works itself out irresistibly. The Anglo-Saxon has exterminated the less developed peoples with which he has come into competition even more effectively than other races have done in like case; not necessarily indeed by fierce and cruel wars of extermination, but through the operation of laws not less deadly and even more certain in their result. The weaker races disappear before the stronger through the effects of mere contact. The Australian Aboriginal retires before the invader, his tribes dispersed, his hunting-grounds taken from him to be utilised for other purposes. In New Zealand a similar fate is overtaking the Maoris. This people were estimated to number in 1820, 100,000; in 1840 they were 80,000; they are now estimated at 40,000.[1] The Anglo-Saxon, driven by forces inherent in his own civilisation, comes to develop the natural resources of the land, and the consequences appear to be inevitable. The same history is repeating itself in South Africa. In the words used recently by a leading colonist of that country, "the natives must go; or they must work as laboriously to develop

---

Social Evolution. New York: Macmillan, 1894. 45–49, 55–58.

[1] *Vide* Report by Registrar-General of New Zealand on the condition of that country in 1889, quoted in *Nature,* 24th October 1889. *Vide* also Pennefather. [Kidd's note.]

the land as we are prepared to do"; the issue in such a case being already determined. In North America we have but a later stage of a similar history. Here two centuries of conflict have left the red men worsted at every point, rapidly dwindling in numbers, the surviving tribes hemmed in and surrounded by forces which they have no power to resist, standing like the isolated patches of grass which have not yet fallen before the knives of the machine-mower in the harvest field.

No motives appear to be able to stay the progress of such movements, humanise them how we may. We often in a self-accusing spirit attribute the gradual disappearance of aboriginal peoples to the effects of our vices upon them; but the truth is that what may be called the virtues of our civilisation are scarcely less fatal than its vices. Those features of Western civilisation which are most distinctive and characteristic, and of which we are most proud, are almost as disastrous in their effects as the evils of which complaint is so often made. There is a certain grim pathos in the remark of the author of a paper on the New Zealand natives, which appeared in the *Journal of the Anthropological Institute* a few years ago (Pennefather), who, amongst the causes to which the decay of the natives might be attributed, mentioned, indiscriminately, drink, disease, European clothing, peace, and wealth. In whatever part of the world we look, amongst civilised or uncivilised peoples, history seems to have taken the same course. Of the Australian natives "only a few remnents of the powerful tribes linger on. . . . All the Tasmanians are gone, and the Maoris will soon be following. The Pacific Islanders are departing childless. The Australian natives as surely are descending to the grave. Old races everywhere give place to the new" (Bonwick 210).[2] There are probably, says Mr. F. Galton, "hardly any spots on the earth that have not within the last few thousand years been tenanted by very different races" (Galton, *Inquiries* 201–02). Wherever a superior race comes into close contact and competition with an inferior race, the result seems to be much the same, whether it is arrived at by the rude method of wars of conquest, or by the silent process which we see at work in Australia, New Zealand, and the North American Continent, or by the subtle, though no less efficient, method with which science makes us acquainted, and which is in operation in many parts of our civilisation, where extinction works slowly and unnoticed through the earlier marriages, the greater vitality, and the better chance of livelihood of the members of the superior race (see Galton, *Inquiries*).

---

[2]The Bonwick quotation continues: "Are we, British people, after the *survival of the fittest* doctrine, to be some day supplanted by a more overwhelming or more cultured race?" [ED.]

Yet we have not perhaps in all this the most striking example of the pow-erlessness of man to escape from one of the fundamental conditions under which his evolution in society is proceeding. There is scarcely any more re-markable situation in the history of our Western civilisation than that which has been created in the United States of America by the emancipa-tion of the negro as the result of the War of Secession. The meaning of this extraordinary chapter in our social history has as yet scarcely been grasped. As the result primarily of an ethical movement having its roots far back in the past, the United States abolished slavery with the conclusion of the Civil War in 1865. The negro was raised to a position of equality with his late masters in the sight of the law, and admitted to full political rights. Ac-cording to the census of 1890 the negroes and persons of African descent in the United States numbered 7,470,040, principally distributed in some fifteen of the Southern States known as the "Black Belt." In some of these states the black population outnumbers the white.

Any one who thinks that the emancipation of the negro has stayed or al-tered the inexorable law which we find working itself out through human history elsewhere, has only to look to the remarkable literature which this question is producing in the United States at the present day, and judge for himself. The negro has been emancipated and admitted to full voting citi-zenship; he has grown wealthy, and has raised himself by education. But to his fellow-men of a different colour he remains the inferior still. His po-sition in the United States today is one of absolute subordination, under all the forms of freedom, to the race amongst whom he lives. To inter-marry with him the white absolutely refuses; he will not admit him to so-cial equality on any terms; he will not even allow him to exercise the polit-ical power which is his right in theory where he possesses a voting majority. Mr. Laird Clowes, whose careful and detailed investigation of this remark-able question has recently attracted attention in England, says that the im-partial observer might expect to find in some of the coloured states of the Union the government almost, if not entirely, in the hands of the negro and coloured majority; but he finds no trace of anything of the kind. "He finds, on the contrary, that the white man rules as supremely as he did in the days of slavery. [. . .]

Looking round at the nations of today and noticing the direction in which they are travelling, it seems impossible to escape the conclusion that the progressive peoples have everywhere the same distinctive features. Energetic, vigorous, virile life amongst them is maintained at the highest pitch of which nature is capable. They offer the highest motives to emula-tion; amongst them the individual is freest, the selection fullest, the rivalry fairest. But so also is the conflict sternest, the nervous friction greatest, and the stress severest. Looking back by the way these nations have come, we find an equally unmistakable absence of these qualities and conditions amongst the competitors they have left behind. From the nations who have dropped out of the race within recent times backwards through history, we follow a gradually descending series. The contrast already to be distinguished between the advancing and the unprogressive peoples of European race is more noticeable when the former are compared with non-European peoples. The difference becomes still more marked when the existence of the careless, shiftless, easily satisfied negro of the United States or West Indies is contrasted with that of the dominant race amongst whom he lives, whose restless, aggressive, high-pitched life he has neither the desire to live nor the capacity to endure.

We follow the path of Empire from the stagnant and unchanging East, westward through peoples whose pulses beat quicker, and whose energy and activity become more marked as we advance. Professor Marshall, who notices the prevailing energy and activity of the British people, and who has recently roundly asserted that men of the Anglo-Saxon races in all parts of the world not only work hard while about it, but do more work in the year than any other (1:730), only brings into prominence the one dominant feature of all successful peoples. It is the same characteristic which distinguishes the people of the great Anglo-Saxon republic of the West whose writers continually remind us that the peculiar endowment which its people have received from nature is an additional allowance of nervous energy.

A similar lesson is emphasised in the northward movement of rule and empire throughout historic times. The successful peoples have moved westwards for physical reasons; the seat of power has moved continually northwards for reasons connected with the evolution in character which the race is undergoing. Man, originally a creature of a warm climate and still multiplying most easily and rapidly there, has not attained his highest development where the conditions of existence have been easiest. Throughout history the centre of power has moved gradually but surely to the north into those stern regions where men have been trained for the rivalry of life in the strenuous conflict with nature in which they have acquired energy, courage, integrity, and those characteristic qualities which contribute to raise them to a high state of social efficiency. The shifting of the centre of power northwards has been a feature alike of modern and of ancient history. The peoples whose influence today reaches over the greater part of the world, both temperate and tropical, belong almost exclusively to races whose geographical home is north of the 40th parallel of latitude. The two groups of peoples, the English-speaking races and the Russians whose rule actually extends over some 46 per cent of the entire surface of the earth have their geographical home north of the 50th parallel.

Nor can there be any doubt that from these strenuous conditions of rivalry the race as a whole is powerless to escape. The conditions of progress may be interrupted amongst the peoples who have long held their place in the front. These peoples may fail and fall behind, but progress continues nevertheless. For although the growth of the leading shoot may be for the time arrested, farther back on the branch other shoots are always ready to take the place of that which has ceased to advance. The races who maintain their places in the van do so on the sternest conditions. We may regulate and humanise those conditions, but we have no power to alter them; the conflict is severest of all when it is carried on under the forms of the highest civilisation. The Anglo-Saxon looks forward, not without reason, to the day when wars will cease; but without war, he is involuntarily exterminating the Maori, the Australian, and the Red Indian, and he has within his borders the emancipated but ostracised Negro, the English Poor Law, and the Social Question; he may beat his swords into plough-shares but in his hands the implements of industry prove even more effective and deadly weapons than the swords.

These are the first stern facts of human life and progress which we have to take into account. They have their origin not in any accidental feature of our history, nor in any innate depravity existing in man. They result, as we have seen, from deep-seated physiological causes, the operation of which we must always remain powerless to escape. It is worse than useless to obscure them or to ignore them, as is done in a great part of the social literature of the time. The first step towards obtaining any true grasp of the social problems of our day must be to look fairly and bravely in the face these facts which lie behind them.

From The First Home Rule Bill

William E. Gladstone

Sir, the House has heard me with astonishing patience while I have endeavoured to perform what I knew must prove an almost interminable task. There is only one subject more on which I feel it still necessary to detain the House. It is commonly said in England and Scotland—and in the main it is, I think, truly said—that we have for a great number of years been struggling to pass good laws for Ireland. We have sacrificed our time; we

---

Speech given in Parliament 8 April 1886. Reprinted in *Gladstone's Speeches.* Ed. Arthur Tilney Bassett. London: Methuen, 1916. 639–43.

have neglected our own business; we have advanced our money—which I do not think at all a great favour conferred on her—and all this in the endeavour to give Ireland good laws. That is quite true in regard to the general course of legislation since 1829.[1] But many of those laws have been passed under influences which can hardly be described otherwise than as influences of fear. Some of our laws have been passed in a spirit of grudging and of jealousy. It is most painful for me to consider that, after four or five years of Parliamentary battle, when a Municipal Corporation Act was passed for Ireland, it was a very different measure to that which, in England and Scotland, created complete and absolute municipal life. Were I to come to the history of the Land Question I could tell a still sadder tale. [...]

But, Sir, I do not deny the general good intentions of Parliament on a variety of great and conspicuous occasions, and its desire to pass good laws for Ireland. But let me say that, in order to work out the purposes of Government, there is something more in this world occasionally required than even the passing of good laws. It is sometimes requisite not only that good laws should be passed, but also that they should be passed by the proper persons. The passing of many good laws is not enough in cases where the strong permanent instincts of the people, their distinctive marks of character, the situation and history of the country require not only that these laws should be good, but that they should proceed from a congenial and native source, and besides being good laws should be their own laws. In former times it might have been doubted—I have myself doubted— whether this instinct had been thus developed in Ireland. If such doubts could be entertained before the last General Election they can be entertained no longer.

The principle that I am laying down I am not laying down exceptionally for Ireland. It is the very principle upon which, within my recollection, to the immense advantage of the country, we have not only altered, but revolutionized our method of governing the Colonies. I had the honour to hold Office in the Colonial Department—perhaps I ought to be ashamed to confess it—fifty-one years ago. At that time the Colonies were governed from Downing Street.[2] It is true that some of them had Legislative Assemblies; but with these we were always in conflict. We were always fed with information by what was termed the British Party in those Colonies. A clique of gentlemen constituted themselves the British Party; and the non-British Party, which was sometimes called the "Disloyal Party," was composed of

---

[1] Under pressure from the Irish nationalist Daniel O'Connor, who had been elected to the House of Commons in 1828, the British Parliament grudgingly passed a bill granting Irish Catholics equal political rights with Protestants in 1829. [ED.]

[2] From the seat of the prime minister's government. [ED.]

the enormous majority of the population. We had continual shocks, continual debates, and continual conflicts. All that has changed. England tried to pass good laws for the Colonies at that period; but the Colonies said — "We do not want your good laws; we want our own." We admitted the reasonableness of that principle, and it is now coming home to us from across the seas. We have to consider whether it is applicable to the case of Ireland. Do not let us disguise this from ourselves. We stand face to face with what is termed Irish nationality. Irish nationality vents itself in the demand for local autonomy, or separate and complete self-government in Irish, not in Imperial, affairs. Is this an evil in itself? Is it a thing that we should view with horror or apprehension? Is it a thing which we ought to reject or accept only with a wry face, or ought we to wait until some painful and sad necessity is incumbent upon the country, like the necessity of 1780 or the necessity of 1793?[3] Sir, I hold that it is not. There is a saying of Mr. Grattan[4] — who was, indeed, a fiery and a fervid orator; but he was more than that; he was a statesman; his aphorisms are, in my opinion, weighty, and even profound, and I commend them to the careful reflection and examination of the country — when he was deprecating the surrender of the Irish Parliament, and pointing out that its existence did not prevent the perfect union of the two countries, he remarked — "The Channel forbids union; the ocean forbids separation." Is that Channel nothing? Do what you will with your steamers and your telegraphs, can you make that Channel cease to exist, or to be as if it were not? These sixty miles may appear a little thing; but I ask you what are the twenty miles between England and France? These few miles of water have exercised a vital influence upon the whole history, the whole development, and the whole national character of our people.

These, Sir, are great facts. I hold that there is such a thing as local patriotism, which, in itself, is not bad, but good. The Welshman is full of local patriotism — the Scotchman is full of local patriotism; the Scotch nationality is as strong as it ever was, and should the occasion arise — which I believe it never can — it will be as ready to assert itself as in the days of Bannockburn.[5] I do not believe that that local patriotism is an evil. I believe it

---

[3] An Irish boycott of English goods in 1780 compelled Parliament to exempt Ireland from the tariffs in force under the Navigation Acts; in 1793, agitation by Irish Catholics won them the right to vote. [ED.]

[4] Henry Grattan, Irish statesman and fierce Irish nationalist, unsuccessfully opposed the parliamentary union between England and Ireland that was imposed in 1801, when the United Kingdom was created. [ED.]

[5] The Scots and the English fought a famous battle near the village of Bannockburn, on the Scottish border, in 1314. [ED.]

is stronger in Ireland even than in Scotland. Englishmen are eminently English, Scotchmen are profoundly Scotch; and, if I read Irish history aright, misfortune and calamity have wedded her sons to her soil. The Irishman is more profoundly Irish; but it does not follow that, because his local patriotism is keen, he is incapable of Imperial patriotism. There are two modes of presenting the subject. The one is to present what we now recommend as good, and the other to recommend it as a choice of evils. Well, Sir, I have argued the matter as if it were a choice of evils; I have recognized, as facts entitled to attention, the jealousies which I do not share or feel; and I have argued it on that ground as the only ground on which it can be argued, not only in a mixed auditory, but in the public mind and to the country, which cannot give a minute investigation to the operations of that complicated question. But, in my own heart, I cherish the hope that this is not merely the choice of the lesser evil, but may prove to be rather a good in itself. What is the answer to this? It is only to be found in the view which rests upon the basis of despair and of absolute condemnation of Ireland and Irishmen as exceptions to the beneficent provisions which enable men in general, and Europeans in particular, and Americans to be capable of performing civil duties, and which considers an Irishman either as a *lusus naturae*[6] or one for whom justice, common sense, moderation, and national prosperity have no meaning; and who can only understand and appreciate perpetual strife and dissension. Well, Sir, I am not going to argue that view, which, to my mind, is founded on a monstrous misconception. I say that the Irishman is as capable of loyalty as another man — I say that if his loyalty has been checked in its development, why is it? Because the laws by which he is governed do not present themselves to him, as they do to us in England and Scotland, with a native and congenial aspect; and I think I can refer to two illustrations which go strongly to support the doctrine I have advanced. Take the case of the Irish soldier and of the Irish Constabulary. Have you a braver or a more loyal man in your Army than the Irishman, who has shared every danger with his Scotch and English comrades, and who has never been behind them, when confronted by peril for the sake of the honour and safety of his Empire? Compare this case with that of an ordinary Irishman in Ireland. The Irish soldier has voluntarily placed himself under military law, which is to him a self-chosen law, and he is exempted from that difficulty which works upon the population in Ireland — namely, that they are governed by a law which they do not feel has sprung from the soil. Consider how common it is to hear the observation, in discussing the circumstances of Ireland, that while the Constabulary are largely

---

[6] A plaything of nature. [ED.]

taken from the Roman Catholic population and from the very class most open to disaffection, where disaffection exists, they form a splendid model of obedience, discipline, and devotion such as the world can hardly match. How is this? It is because they have undertaken a voluntary service which takes them completely out of the category of the ordinary Irishman. They are placed under an authority which is to them congenial because freely accepted. Their loyalty is not checked by the causes that operate on the agricultural population of Ireland. It has grown as freely in the Constabulary and in the Army as if every man in the Constabulary and every Irish soldier had been an Englishman or a Scotchman.

From Imperialism

John Atkinson Hobson

The absorption of so large a proportion of public interest, energy, blood and money in seeking to procure colonial possessions and foreign markets would seem to indicate that Great Britain obtains her chief livelihood by external trade. Now this is not the case. Large as is our foreign and colonial trade in volume and in value, essential as is much of it to our national well-being, nevertheless it furnishes a small proportion of the real income of the nation.[1]

Although the volume and value of home industries are not directly calculable, the total income of the nation, comprising profits, wages, rents, and other gains from all sources, is approximately estimated at £1,700,000,000 per annum. This sum, of course, covers all payments, not only for productive services of land, capital and labour in the making and distributing of material wealth, but for professional and personal services as well. Real income in the shape of goods or services to this amount is consumed or saved within the year.

Imperialism: A Study. New York: Pott, 1902. 30–31, 51–52, 53–55, 76, 98–99, 207–09.

[1] This argument has been contradicted by later historians, who generally claim that imperialism was of enormous benefit to the overall national economy, that it was driven largely by the successful search for new markets, and that many factors other than economic ones (i.e., racism, fears of overpopulation, international competition, belief in "the civilizing mission," etc.) were fundamental to the expansion of empires in the late nineteenth century. See, for example, Hobsbawm 60–73, Hynes, Fieldhouse, Long, or Semmel. [ED.]

Now the total value of the import and export trade of Great Britain in 1898 (we take this year as the latest normal one for the purpose, later years being disturbed by the war factor[2]) amounted to £765,000,000. If we were to take the very liberal allowance of 5 per cent. as profit upon this turnover of trade, the annual income directly derived from our external trade would amount to a little over £38,000,000, or about one forty-fifth part of our total income.

If one is estimating the total income directly derived from taking part in processes of external trade, it would be necessary to add the salaries of commercial clerks, rents of offices, &c., paid by British mercantile firms engaged in this trade. Even then the total income derived from external trade would only play a small part in the total income of Great Britain. [...]

Seeing that the Imperialism of the last three decades is clearly condemned as a business policy, in that at enormous expense it has procured a small, bad, unsafe increase of markets, and has jeopardised the entire wealth of the nation in rousing the strong resentment of other nations, we may ask, "How is the British nation induced to embark upon such unsound business?" The only possible answer is that the business interests of the nation as a whole are subordinated to those of certain sectional interests that usurp control of the national resources and use them for their private gain. This is no strange or monstrous charge to bring; it is the commonest disease of all forms of government. The famous words of Sir Thomas More are as true now as when he wrote them: "Everywhere do I perceive a certain conspiracy of rich men seeking their own advantage under the name and pretext of the commonwealth."[3]

Although the new Imperialism has been bad business for the nation, it has been good business for certain classes and certain trades within the nation. The vast expenditure on armaments, the costly wars, the grave risks and embarrassments of foreign policy, the stoppage of political and social reforms within Great Britain, though fraught with great injury to the nation, have served well the present business interests of certain industries and professions.

It is idle to meddle with politics unless we clearly recognise this central fact and understand what these sectional interests are which are the enemies of national safety and the commonwealth. We must put aside the merely sentimental diagnosis which explains wars or other national blunders by outbursts of patriotic animosity or errors of statecraft. Doubtless at

---

[2] The Boer War (1899–1902). [ED.]

[3] The quotation, though truncated and slightly reworded, is taken from Thomas More's *Utopia*, bk. 2.

every outbreak of war not only the man in the street but the man at the helm is often duped by the cunning with which aggressive motives and greedy purposes dress themselves in defensive clothing. There is, it may be safely asserted, no war within memory, however nakedly aggressive it may seem to the dispassionate historian, which has not been presented to the people who were called upon to fight as a necessary defensive policy, in which the honour, perhaps the very existence, of the State was involved. [. . .]

What is the direct economic outcome of Imperialism? A great expenditure of public money upon ships, guns, military and naval equipment and stores, growing and productive of enormous profits when a war, or an alarm of war, occurs; new public loans and important fluctuations in the home and foreign Bourses; more posts for soldiers and sailors and in the diplomatic and consular services; improvement of foreign investments by the substitution of the British flag for a foreign flag; acquisition of markets for certain classes of exports, and some protection and assistance for trades representing British houses in these manufactures; employment for engineers, missionaries, speculative miners, ranchers and other emigrants.

Certain definite business and professional interests feeding upon imperialistic expenditure, or upon the results of that expenditure, are thus set up in opposition to the common good, and, instinctively feeling their way to one another, are found united in strong sympathy to support every new imperialist exploit.

If the £60,000,000 which may now be taken as a minimum expenditure on armaments in time of peace were subjected to a close analysis, most of it would be traced directly to the tills of certain big firms engaged in building warships and transports, equipping and coaling them, manufacturing guns, rifles, and ammunition, supplying horses, waggons, saddlery, food, clothing for the services, contracting for barracks, and for other large irregular needs. Through these main channels the millions flow to feed many subsidiary trades, most of which are quite aware that they are engaged in executing contracts for the services. Here we have an important nucleus of commercial Imperialism. Some of these trades, especially the shipbuilding, boiler-making, and gun and ammunition making trades, are conducted by large firms with immense capital, whose heads are well aware of the uses of political influence for trade purposes.

These men are Imperialists by conviction; a pushful policy is good for them.

With them stand the great manufacturers for export trade, who gain a living by supplying the real or artificial wants of the new countries we annex or open up. Manchester, Sheffield, Birmingham, to name three representative cases, are full of firms which compete in pushing textiles and hardware, engines, tools, machinery, spirits, guns, upon new markets. The public debts which ripen in our colonies, and in foreign countries that come under our protectorate or influence, are largely loaned in the shape of rails, engines, guns, and other materials of civilisation made and sent out by British firms. The making of railways, canals, and other public works, the establishment of factories, the development of mines, the improvement of agriculture in new countries, stimulate a definite interest in important manufacturing industries which feeds a very firm imperialist faith in their owners.

The proportion which such trade bears to the total industry of Great Britain is very small, but some of it is extremely influential and able to make a definite impression upon politics, through chambers of commerce, Parliamentary representatives, and semi-political, semi-commercial bodies like the Imperial South African Association or the China League. [. . .]

No mere array of facts and figures adduced to illustrate the economic nature of the new Imperialism will suffice to dispel the popular delusion that the use of national force to secure new markets by annexing fresh tracts of territory is a sound and a necessary policy for an advanced industrial country like Great Britain. It has indeed been proved that recent annexations of tropical countries, procured at great expense, have furnished poor and precarious markets, that our aggregate trade with our colonial possessions is virtually stationary, and that our most profitable and progressive trade is with rival industrial nations, whose territories we have no desire to annex, whose markets we cannot force, and whose active antagonism we are provoking by our expansive policy.

But these arguments are not conclusive. It is open to Imperialists to argue thus: "We must have markets for our growing manufactures, we must have new outlets for the investment of our surplus capital and for the energies of the adventurous surplus of our population: such expansion is a necessity of life to a nation with out great and growing powers of production. An ever larger share of our population is devoted to the manufactures and commerce of towns, and is thus dependent for life and work upon food and raw materials from foreign lands. In order to buy and pay for these things we must sell our goods abroad." [. . .]

A people limited in number and energy and in the land they occupy have the choice of improving to the utmost the political and economic management of their own land, confining themselves to such accessions of territory as are justified by the most economical disposition of a growing population; or they may proceed, like the slovenly farmer, to spread their power and energy over the whole earth, tempted by the speculative value or the quick profits of some new market, or else by mere greed of territorial acquisition, and ignoring the political and economic wastes and risks involved by this imperial career. It must be clearly understood that this is essentially a choice of alternatives; a full simultaneous application of intensive and extensive cultivation is impossible. A nation may either, following the example of Denmark or Switzerland, put brains into agriculture, develop a finely varied system of public education, general and technical, apply the ripest science to its special manufacturing industries, and so support in progressive comfort and character a considerable population upon a strictly limited area; or it may, like Great Britain, neglect its agriculture, allowing its lands to go out of cultivation and its population to grow up in towns, fall behind other nations in its methods of education and in the capacity of adapting to its uses the latest scientific knowledge, in order that it may squander its pecuniary and military resources in forcing bad markets and finding speculative fields of investment in distant corners of the earth, adding millions of square miles and of unassimilable population to the area of the Empire.

The driving forces of class interest which stimulate and support this false economy we have explained. No remedy will serve which permits the future operation of these forces. It is idle to attack Imperialism or Militarism as political expedients or policies unless the axe is laid at the economic root of the tree, and the classes for whose interest Imperialism works are shorn of the surplus revenues which seek this outlet. [. . .]

Analysis of the actual course of modern Imperialism has laid bare the combination of economic and political forces which fashions it. These forces are traced to their sources in the selfish interests of certain industrial, financial, and professional classes, seeking private advantages out of a policy of imperial expansion, and using this same policy to protect them in their economic, political, and social privileges against the pressure of democracy. It remains to answer the question, "Why does Imperialism escape general recognition for the narrow, sordid thing it is?" Each nation, as it watches from outside the Imperialism of its neighbours, is not deceived; the selfish interests of political and commercial classes are seen plainly paramount in the direction of the policy. So every other European nation recognises the true outlines of British Imperialism and charges us with hypocrisy in feigning blindness. This charge is false; no nation sees its own shortcomings; the charge of hypocrisy is seldom justly brought against an individual, against a nation never. Frenchmen and Germans believe that our zeal in promoting foreign missions, putting down slavery, and in spreading the arts of civilisation is a false disguise conveniently assumed to cover naked national self-assertion. The actual case is somewhat different.

There exists in a considerable though not a large proportion of the British nation a genuine desire to spread Christianity among the heathen, to diminish the cruelty and other sufferings which they believe exist in countries less fortunate than their own, and to do good work about the world in the cause of humanity. Most of the churches contain a small body of men and women deeply, even passionately, interested in such work, and a much larger number whose sympathy, though weaker, is quite genuine. Ill-trained for the most part in psychology and history, these people believe that religion and other arts of civilisation are portable commodities which it is our duty to convey to the backward nations, and that a certain amount of compulsion is justified in pressing their benefits upon people too ignorant at once to recognise them.

Is it surprising that the selfish forces which direct Imperialism should utilise the protective colours of these disinterested movements? Imperialist politicians, soldiers, or company directors, who push a forward policy by portraying the cruelties of the African slave raids or the infamous tyranny of a Prempeh or a Thebaw,[4] or who open out a new field for missionary enterprise in China or the Soudan, do not deliberately and consciously work up these motives in order to incite the British public. They simply and instinctively attach to themselves any strong, genuine elevated feeling which is of service, fan it and feed it until it assumes fervour, and utilise it for their ends. The politician always, the business man not seldom, believes that high motives qualify the political or financial benefits he gets: it is certain that Lord Salisbury[5] really believes that the South African war, for which his Government is responsible, has been undertaken for the benefit of the people of South Africa and will result in increased liberty and happiness; it is quite likely that Earl Grey[6] thinks that the Chartered Company which he directs is animated by a desire to improve the material and moral condition of the natives of Rhodesia and that it is attaining this object.

So Leopold, King of the Belgians, has claimed for his government of the Congo—"Our only programme is that of the moral and material regener-

[4]Primpeh (or "Prempeh") was the king of the Ashantis (who were centered in what is now Ghana); his campaign of national reunification and resistance to British control led to his arrest in 1896. He was not released until 1924. Thibaw (or "Thebaw") was the last king of Burma; his overtures to the French for protection in 1885 resulted in a British invasion and annexation of upper Burma. Thebaw and his queen, Suphayalat, were detained in Ratnagiri in India, where Thebaw died in 1916. [ED.]

[5]Robert Arthur Lord Salisbury was prime minister from 1885 to 1892 and again from 1896 to 1902. It was under his second administration that Britain prosecuted the Boer War. [ED.]

[6]Albert Henry George Grey, the fourth Earl Grey, was one of the most vigorous of late-century pro-imperialist British statesmen. In 1896 he was appointed administrator of Rhodesia, where he worked in conjunction with Cecil Rhodes to expropriate extensive amounts of territory from the Zulus. [ED.]

ation of the country."[7] It is difficult to set any limit upon the capacity of men to deceive themselves as to the relative strength and worth of the motives which affect them: politicians, in particular, acquire so strong a habit of setting their projects in the most favourable light that they soon convince themselves that the finest result which they think may conceivably accrue from any policy is the actual motive of that policy. As for the public, it is only natural that it should be deceived. All the purer and more elevated adjuncts of Imperialism are kept to the fore by religious and philanthropic agencies: patriotism appeals to the general lust of power within a people by suggestions of nobler uses, adopting the forms of self-sacrifice to cover domination and the love of adventure.

From The Expansion of England

John Robert Seeley

It is at first sight extremely perplexing to understand how we could conquer India. Here the population was dense, and its civilisation, though descending along a different stream of tradition, was as real and ancient as our own. We have learnt from many instances in European history to think it almost impossible really to conquer an intelligent people wholly alien in language and religion from its invaders. The whole power of Spain could not in eighty years conquer the Dutch provinces with their petty population. The Swiss could not be conquered in old time, nor the Greeks the other day. Nay, at the very time when we made the first steps in the conquest of India, we showed ourselves wholly unable to reduce to obedience three millions of our own race in America, who had thrown off their allegiance to the English Crown. What a singular contrast is here! Never did the English show so much languid incompetence as in the American War, so that it might have seemed evident that their age of greatness was over, and that the decline of England had begun. But precisely at this time they were appearing as irresistible conquerors in India, and showing a superiority which led them to fancy themselves a nation of heroes. How is the contradiction to be explained?

History is studied with so little seriousness, with so little desire or expectation of arriving at any solid result, that the contradiction passes almost

---

[7] See "Letter from the King of the Belgians," 107. [ED.]

The Expansion of England: Two Courses of Lectures. London: Macmillan, 1909. 228–29, 231–32, 233–41, 343–44.

unremarked, or at most gives occasion to a triumphant reflection that after all there was life in us yet. And indeed it may seem that, however difficult of explanation the fact may be, there can be no doubt of it. Over and over again in India, at Plassey, at Assaye, and on a hundred other battlefields, our troops have been victorious against great odds, so that here at least it seems that we may indulge our national self-complacency without restraint, and feel that at any rate in comparison with the Hindu races we really are terrible fellows!

But does this hypothesis really remove the difficulty? Suppose that one Englishman is really equal as a soldier to ten or twenty Hindus, can we even then conceive the whole of India conquered by the English? There were not more than twelve millions of Englishmen at the time when the conquest began, and it was made in a period when England had other wars on her hands. Clive's[1] career falls partly in the Seven Years' War of Europe, and the great annexations of Lord Wellesley[2] were made in the midst of our war with Napoleon. We are not a military state. We did not in those times profess to be able to put on foot at any moment a great expeditionary army. Accordingly in our European wars we usually confined ourselves to acting with our fleet, while for hostilities on land it was our practice to subsidise any ally we might have among the military states, at one time Austria, at another Prussia. How then in spite of all this weakness by land could we manage to conquer during this time the greater part of India, an enormous region of nearly a million square miles and inhabited by two hundred millions of people! What a drain such a work must have made upon our military force, what a drain upon our treasury! And yet somehow the drain seems never to have been perceived. Our European wars involved us in a debt that we have never been able to pay. But our Indian wars have not swelled the National Debt. The exertions we had to make there seem to have left no trace behind them.

It seems then that there must be something wrong in the conception which is current, that a number of soldiers went over from England to India, and there by sheer superiority in valour and intelligence conquered the whole country. In the last great Mahratta war of 1818[3] we had, it appears,

---

[1] General Robert Clive, victor in the Battle of Arcot in 1751 and in the Battle of Plassey in 1757. He was appointed governor of Bengal by the East India Company and was popularly considered to be the founder of the British Empire in India. [ED.]

[2] Richard Wellesley, brother of the famous Duke of Wellington (who defeated Napoleon at Waterloo), was governor-general of India from 1797 to 1805. [ED.]

[3] After the collapse of the Mogul Empire in 1707, a loose federation of semi-independent Indian states, called the Mahratta (or "Maratha") Confederacy, spread over nearly all of

more than a hundred thousand men in the field. But what! that was the time of mortal exhaustion that succeeded the great Napoleonic War. Is it possible that only three years after the battle of Waterloo we were at war again on a vast scale and had a much greater army in India than Lord Wellington had in Spain? Again at the present moment the army kept in foot in India amounts to two hundred thousand men. What! two hundred thousand English soldiers! And yet we are not a military State!

You see of course what the fact is that I point at. This Indian army, we all know, does not consist of English soldiers, but mainly of native troops. Out of 200,000 only 65,000, or less than a third, are English. And even this proportion has only been established since the mutiny,[4] after which catastrophe the English troops were increased and the native troops diminished in number. Thus I find that at the time of the mutiny there were 45,000 European troops to 235,000 native troops in India—that is, less than a fifth. In 1808 again I find only 25,000 Englishmen to 130,000 natives—that is, somewhat less than a fifth. The same proportion obtained in 1773 at the time of the Regulating Act,[5] when British India first took shape. At that date the Company's army consisted of 9,000 Europeans and 45,000 natives. Before that I find the proportion of Europeans even lower—about a seventh; and if we go back to the very beginning we find that from the first the Indian army was rather a native than a European force. Thus Colonel Chesney opens his historical view of it in these words: "The first establishment of the Company's[6] Indian Army may be considered to date from the year 1748, when a small body of sepoys[7] was raised at Madras after the example set by the French, for the defence of that settlement. . . . At the same time a small European force was raised, formed of such sailors as could be spared from the ships on the coast and of men smuggled on board the Company's vessels in England by the crimps."

In the early battles of the Company by which its power was decisively established, at the siege of Arcot, at Plassey, at Buxar, there seem almost

---

India. This alliance was the chief obstacle to British rule until the military campaign of 1818, which reduced the Marathas to a group of relatively small chieftainships. [ED.]

[4]The Indian Mutiny of 1857. [ED.]

[5]The Regulating Act established the first governor-generalship of India, based at Calcutta, and placed authority over India directly in the hands of the British government rather than the East India Company. [ED.]

[6]The East India Company, which was granted a monopoly over Indian trade by Queen Elizabeth in 1600 and which ceased operations in 1858, as a consequence of the Indian Mutiny. [ED.]

[7]Natives of India employed as soldiers by a European power. [ED.]

always to have been more sepoys than Europeans on the side of the Company. And let us observe further that we do not hear of the sepoys as fighting ill, or of the English as bearing the whole brunt of the conflict. No one who has remarked the childish eagerness with which historians indulge their national vanity, will be surprised to find that our English writers in describing these battles seem unable to discern the sepoys. Read Macaulay's[8] Essay on Clive; everywhere it is "the imperial people," "the mighty children of the sea," "none could resist Clive and his Englishmen." But if once it is admitted that the sepoys always outnumbered the English, and that they kept pace with the English in efficiency as soldiers, the whole theory which attributes our successes to an immeasurable natural superiority in valour falls to the ground. In those battles in which our troops were to the enemy as one to ten, it will appear that if we may say that one Englishman showed himself equal to ten natives, we may also say that one sepoy did the same. It follows that, though no doubt there was a difference, it was not so much a difference of race as a difference of discipline, of military science, and also no doubt in many cases a difference of leadership.

Observe that Mill's[9] summary explanation of the conquest of India says nothing of any natural superiority on the part of the English. "The two important discoveries for conquering India were: 1st, the weakness of the native armies against European discipline; 2ndly, the facility of imparting that discipline to natives in the European service." He adds: "Both discoveries were made by the French."

And even if we should admit that the English fought better than the sepoys, and took more than their share in those achievements which both performed in common, it remains entirely incorrect to speak of the English nation as having conquered the nations of India. The nations of India have been conquered by an army of which on the average about a fifth part was English. But we not only exaggerate our own share in the achievement; we at the same time entirely misconceive and misdescribe the achievement itself. For from what race were the other four-fifths of the army drawn? From the natives of India themselves! India can hardly be said to have been conquered at all by foreigners; she has rather conquered herself. If we were justified, which we are not, in personifying India as we personify France or England, we could not describe her as overwhelmed by a foreign enemy; we should rather have to say that she elected to put an end to anarchy by

---

[8] Thomas Babington Macaulay, British politician, historian, and man of letters. [ED.]
[9] James Mill, utilitarian philosopher and father of John Stuart Mill, wrote a "History of British India" in 1818. [ED.]

submitting to a single Government, even though that Government was in the hands of foreigners.

But that description would be as false and misleading as the other, or as any expression which presupposes India to have been a conscious political whole. The truth is that there was no India in the political, and scarcely in any other, sense. The word was a geographical expression, and therefore India was easily conquered, just as Italy and Germany fell an easy prey to Napoleon, because there was no Italy and no Germany, and not even any strong Italian or German national feeling. Because there was no Germany, Napoleon was able to set one German state against another, so that in fighting with Austria or Prussia he had Bavaria and Württemberg for allies. As Napoleon saw that this means of conquest lay ready to his hand in Central Europe, so the Frenchman Dupleix[10] early perceived that this road to empire in India lay open to any European state that might have factories there. He saw a condition of chronic war between one Indian state and another, and he perceived that by interfering in their quarrels the foreigner might arrive to hold the balance between them. He acted upon this view, and accordingly the whole history of European Empire in India begins with the interference of the French in the war of succession in Hyderabad that broke out on the death of the great Nizam ul Mulk (1748).

The fundamental fact then is that India had no jealousy of the foreigner, because India had no sense whatever of national unity, because there *was* no India, and therefore, properly speaking, no foreigner. So far, as I have pointed out, parallel examples may be found in Europe. But we must imagine a much greater degree of political deadness in India than in Germany eighty years ago, if we would understand the fact now under consideration, the fact namely that the English conquered India by means of a sepoy army. In Germany there was scarcely any German feeling, but there was a certain amount, though not a very great amount, of Prussian feeling, Austrian feeling, Bavarian feeling, Suabian feeling. Napoleon is able to set Bavaria against Austria or both against Prussia, but he does not attempt to set Bavaria or Austria or Prussia against itself. To speak more distinctly, he procures by

---

[10]Joseph François Dupleix, governor of the French-controlled city of Pondicherry on the southeastern coast of India, took advantage of an outbreak of civil war among native factions in southern India in 1746 and won the first decisive military victories by European forces in India. When the ruler of the province of Hyderabad, the nizam ul Mulk, died in 1748, his succession was disputed and the area plunged into chaos. Dupleix again took advantage of the situation and, after successful military and political maneuvering, won recognition as the next nizam himself. He was given the title Emperor of Southern India but was soon defeated in turn by the British. [ED.]

treaties that the Elector of Bavaria shall furnish a contingent to the army which he leads against Austria; but he does not, simply by offering pay, raise an army of Germans and then use them in the conquest of Germany. This would be the exact parallel to what has been witnessed in India. A parallel to the fact that India has been conquered by an army of which four-fifths were natives and only one-fifth English, would be found in Europe, if England had invaded France, and then by offering good pay had raised an army of Frenchmen large enough to conquer the country. The very idea seems monstrous. What! you exclaim, an army of Frenchmen quietly undertake to make war upon France! And yet, if you reflect, you will see that such a thing is abstractedly quite possible, and that it might have been witnessed if the past history of France had been different. We can imagine that a national feeling had never sprung up in France; this we can easily imagine, because we know that the twelfth century is full of wars between a king who reigned at Paris and another who reigned at Rouen. But let us imagine further that the different Governments established in different parts of France were mostly foreign Governments, that in fact the country had been conquered before and was still living under the yoke of foreign rulers. We can well understand that if in a country thus broken to the foreign yoke a disturbed state of affairs supervened, making mercenary war a lucrative profession, such a country might come to be full of professional soldiers equally ready to take service with any Government and against any Government, native or foreign.

   Now the condition of India was such as this. The English did not introduce a foreign domination into it, for the foreign domination was there already. In fact we bring to the subject a fixed misconception. The homogeneous European community, a definite territory possessed by a definite race—in one word, the Nation-State—though we assume it as if it were a matter of course, is in fact much more exceptional than we suppose, and yet it is upon the assumption of such a homogeneous community that all our ideas of patriotism and public virtue depend. The idea of nationality seems in India to be thoroughly confused. The distinction of national and foreign seems to be lost. Not only has a tide of Mussulman invasion covered the country ever since the eleventh century, but even if we go back to the earliest times we still find a mixture of races, a domination of race by race. That Aryan, Sanscrit-speaking race which, as the creators of Brahminism, have given to India whatever unity it can be said to have, appear themselves as invaders, and as invaders who have not succeeded in swallowing up and absorbing the older nationalities. The older, not Indo-Germanic race, has in Europe almost disappeared, and at any rate has left no trace in our European languages, but in India the older stratum is everywhere visible. The spoken languages there are not mere corruptions of Sanscrit, but mixtures of Sanscrit with older languages wholly different, and in the south not Sanscrit at all. Brahminism too, which at first sight seems universal, turns out on examination to be a mere vague eclecticism, which has given a show of unity to superstitions wholly unlike and unrelated to each other. It follows that in India the fundamental postulate cannot be granted, upon which the whole political ethics of the West depend. The homogeneous community does not exist there, out of which the State properly so called arises. Indeed to satisfy ourselves of this it is not necessary to travel so far back into the past. It is enough to notice that since the time of Mahmoud of Ghazni[11] a steady stream of Mussulman invasion has poured into India. The majority of the Governments of India were Mussulman long before the arrival of the Mogul in the sixteenth century. From this time therefore in most of the Indian States the tie of nationality was broken. Government ceased to rest upon right; the State lost its right to appeal to patriotism.

In such a state of affairs what is called the conquest of India by the English can be explained without supposing the natives of India to be below other races, just as it does not force us to regard the English as superior to other races. We regard it as the duty of a man to fight for his country against the foreigner. But what is a man's country? When we analyse the notion, we find it presupposes the man to have been bred up in a community which may be regarded as a great family, so that it is natural for him to think of the land itself as a mother. But if the community has not been at all of the nature of a family, but has been composed of two or three races hating each other, if not the country, but at most the village has been regarded as a home, then it is not the fault of the natives of it that they have no patriotism but village-patriotism. It is one thing to receive a foreign yoke for the first time, and quite a different thing to exchange one foreign yoke for another.

But, as I have pointed out, the surprising feature in the English conquest of India is not so much that it should have been made, as that it should have cost England no effort and no trouble. The English people have not paid taxes, the English Government has not opened loans, no conscription was ever introduced, nay, no drain of men was ever perceived, and no difficulty was ever felt in carrying on other wars at the same time, because we were engaged in conquering a population equal to that of Europe. This seems at first sight incredible, but I have already given the explanation of it. As to the finance of all these wars, it falls under the general principle which applies to all wars of conquest. Conquest pays its own

---

[11] Under the Ghaznavid dynasty beginning in the tenth century, an empire centered at the eastern Afghanistan city of Ghazni extended into northern India for three centuries. [ED.]

expenses. As Napoleon had never any financial difficulties, because he lived at the expense of those whom he vanquished in war, so the conquest of India was made, as a matter of course, at the expense of India. The only difficulty then is to understand how the army could be created. And this difficulty too disappears, when we observe that four-fifths of this army was always composed of native troops.

If we fix our attention upon this all-important fact we shall be led, if I mistake not, to perceive that the expression "conquest," as applied to the acquisition of sovereignty by the East India Company in India, is not merely loose but thoroughly misleading, and tempts us to class the event among events which it in no way resembles. I have indeed remarked more than once before that this expression, whenever it is used, requires far more definition than it commonly receives, and that it may bear several different meanings. But surely the word is only applicable at all when it refers to some action done to one state by another. There is war between two states; the army of the one state invades the other and overturns the Government of it, or at least forces the Government to such humiliating terms that it is practically deprived of its independence; this is conquest in the proper sense. Now when we say that England has conquered India, we ought to mean that something of this sort has happened between England and India. When Alexander the Great conquered the Persian Empire, there was war between the Macedonian state and the Persian, in which the latter was subjugated. When Cæsar conquered Gaul, he acted in the name of the Roman Republic, holding an office conferred on him by the senate, and commanding the army of the Roman state. But nothing of this sort happened in India. The King of England did not declare war upon the Great Mogul or upon any Nawab or Rajah in India. The English state would perhaps have had no concern from first to last in the conquest of India but for this circumstance, that it engaged five times in war with France after the French settlements in India had become considerable, and that these wars, being partly waged in India, were in a certain degree mixed up with the wars between the East India Company and the native Powers of India. If we wish clearly to understand the nature of the phenomenon, we ought to put this circumstance, which was accidental, on one side. We shall then see that nothing like what is strictly called a conquest took place, but that certain traders inhabiting certain sea-port towns in India, were induced, almost forced, in the anarchy caused by the fall of the Mogul Empire, to give themselves a military character and employ troops, that by means of these troops they acquired territory and at last almost all the territory of India, and that these traders happened to be Englishmen, and to employ a certain, though not a large, proportion of English troops in their army.

Now this is not a foreign conquest, but rather an internal revolution. In any country when government breaks down and anarchy sets in, the general law is that a struggle follows between such organised powers as remain in the country, and that the most powerful of these sets up a Government. [. . .]

Though there is little that is glorious in most of the great Empires mentioned in history, since they have usually been created by force and have remained at a low level of political life, we observed that Greater Britain is not in the ordinary sense an Empire at all. Looking at the colonial part of it alone, we see a natural growth, a mere normal extension of the English race into other lands, which for the most part were so thinly peopled that our settlers took possession of them without conquest. If there is nothing highly glorious in such an expansion, there is at the same time nothing forced or unnatural about it. It creates not properly an Empire, but only a very large state. So far as the expansion itself is concerned, no one does or can regard it but with pleasure. For a nation to have an outlet for its superfluous population is one of the greatest blessings. Population unfortunately does not adapt itself to space; on the contrary, the larger it is the larger is its yearly increment. Now that Great Britain is already full it becomes fuller with increased speed; it gains a million every three years. Probably emigration ought to proceed at a far greater rate than it does, and assuredly the greatest evils would arise if it were checked.

From Cawnpore

George Otto Trevelyan

In May 1857, a widespread insurrection among the sepoys, or Indian soldiers, of the Bengal army resulted in a violent conflict that lasted over a year. Though the exact origins of the revolt are unclear, one factor was the suspicion among the sepoys that their ammunition had been coated either with pork (unclean to Muslims) or cow (sacred to Hindus) fat. What came to be called the Indian Mutiny claimed the lives of hundreds of soldiers and civilians and threatened to destabilize the entire country. Before the rebellion was crushed in June 1858, many atrocities had been committed by both sides.

Cawnpore. London: Macmillan, 1886. 275–85.

The British public was outraged, among other things, by several massacres of British civilians, including women and children. The bloodiest of these took place at Cawnpore (now usually known as Kanpur), a city in the historical province of Bengal, 600 miles north-west of Calcutta. For the remainder of the nineteenth century, British public opinion on Indian matters was galvanized by the specter of the mutiny and its atrocities. Over fifty novels about the events of the mutiny had been published by 1900, and there were numerous sensationalized nonfictional accounts, by far the most popular of which was George Otto Trevelyan's *Cawnpore,* which details the massacre of (by Trevelyan's count) 206 British civilians, all but five of whom were women and children. More reliable historians put the number of civilians killed at Cawnpore at about 125.

Wounded as he was, Bala Rao[1] brought to Cawnpore the tidings of his own defeat. He went straight to the quarters of his brother, which were soon crowded with the leading rebels, who came to hear what had happened, and to impart their apprehensions and suggestions. The deliberations of this improvised council were at first confused and desultory. Some were for retiring to Bithoor; some for uniting their forces with the mutineers of Fut-tehgur. At length, by a slender majority of voices, it was decided to make one more stand south of Cawnpore.

When this resolution had been adopted, Teeka Singh[2] asked whether the Nana had made up his mind as to what should be done with the prisoners; and hinted that, in case things went ill, it might be awkward for some then present should the Sahibs[3] find such a mass of evidence ready to their hands; nay more, that the chances of a reverse would be considerably lessened if the captives were once put out of the way. The British were approaching solely for the purpose of releasing their compatriots, and would not risk another battle for the satisfaction of burying them. They would

---

[1] The retreating Indian troops around Cawnpore were commanded by Bala Rao, brother of the nana sahib of Bithur. The mutiny had restored to authority the nana sahib, who was the adopted son of the peshwa, or ruler, of the Bengal province defeated in the last Maratha wars of 1818. Together with the rani of Jhansi, the nana was one of the few native aristocrats associated with the mutiny. [ED.]

[2] A former trooper in the Second Cavalry, who had supposedly been a ringleader of the mutineers at Cawnpore and who had been appointed general and chief of the rebel cavalry. [ED.]

[3] A respectful term for white men in India. [ED.]

be only too glad of an excuse to avoid meeting the Peishwa[4] in the field. Dhoondoo Punth[5] was not hard to convince on such a point. Whenever bloodshed was in question, he showed himself the least impracticable of men. In the present instance he would never have required prompting, but for the importunity of the royal widows, his step-mothers by adoption, who had sent him word that they would throw themselves and their children from the upper windows of the palace if he again murdered any of their sex. As a pledge that this was no vain parade of philanthropy they had ab-stained from food and drink for many hours together. In order to anticipate their remonstrances, directions were given to set about the work forthwith. In fact, for every reason, 'twas well that it should be done quickly. The as-sembly broke up; but all who could spare the time stayed for at least the commencement of such a representation as none could hope to behold twice in a life-time.

At four o'clock in the afternoon, or between that and five, some of the Nana's people went across to the house of bondage, and bade the English-men who were there to come forth. Forth they came—the three persons from Futtehgur, and the merchant and his son; accompanied by the big-gest of the children, a youth of fourteen, who, poor boy, was glad perhaps to take this opportunity of classing himself with his elders. Some ladies pressed out to watch the course which the party took, but were pushed back by the sentries. The gentlemen inquired whither they were going, and were answered that the Peishwa had sent for them on some concern of his own. But all around was a deep throng of spectators, the foremost rows seated on the ground, so that those behind might see: while an outer circle occupied, as it were, reserved places on the wall of the enclosure. There, beneath a spreading lime-tree, lounged Dhoondoo Punth, the gold lace of his turban glittering in the sun-shine. There were Jwala Pershad; and Tantia Topee; and Azimoolah,[6] the ladies' man; and Bala Rao, the twinges of whose shoulder-blade heightened his avidity for the coming show. When this concourse was noticed by our countrymen, their lips moved as if in prayer. At the gate which led into the road they were stopped by a squad of sepoys, and shot dead. Their bodies were thrown on to the grass which bordered the highway, and became the sport of the rabble; who, doubtless, pointed to them in turn, and said: "That Sahib is the Governor of Bengal; and this is the Governor of Madras; and this is the Governor of Bombay." Such was the joke which during that twelvemonth went the round of Northern India.

---

[4]The nana sahib had claimed for himself his father's title, peishwa (or peshwa). [ED.]
[5]Given name of the nana sahib. [ED.]
[6]All former British soldiers, now high-ranking members of the rebel army. [ED.]

About half-an-hour after this the woman called "the Begum"[7] informed the captives that the Peishwa had determined to have them killed. One of the ladies went up to the native officer who commanded the guard, and told him that she learned they were all to die. To this he replied that, if such were the case, he must have heard something about it; so that she had no cause to be afraid; and a soldier said to the Begum: "Your orders will not be obeyed. Who are you that you should give orders?" Upon this the woman fired up, and hurried off to lay the affair before the Nana. During her absence the sepoys discussed the matter, and resolved that they would never lift their weapons against the prisoners. One of them afterwards confessed to a friend that his own motive for so deciding was anxiety to stand well with the Sahibs, if ever they got back to Cawnpore. The Begum presently returned with five men, each carrying a sabre. Two were Hindoo peasants; the one thirty-five years of age, fair and tall, with long mustachios, but flat-faced and wall-eyed; the other considerably his senior, short, and of a sallow complexion. Two were butchers by calling: portly strapping fellows, both well on in life. The larger of the two was disfigured by the traces of the small-pox. They were Mahommedans, of course; as no Hindoo could adopt a trade which obliged him to spill the blood of a cow.

These four were dressed in dirty white clothes. The fifth, likewise a Mussulman, wore the red uniform of the Maharaja's[8] body-guard, and is reported to have been the sweetheart of the Begum. He was called Survur Khan, and passed for a native of some distant province. A bystander remarked that he had hair on his hands.

The sepoys were bidden to fall on. Half-a-dozen among them advanced, and discharged their muskets through the windows at the ceiling of the apartments. Thereupon the five men entered. It was the short gloaming of Hindostan—the hour when ladies take their evening drive. She who had accosted the officer was standing in the doorway. With her were the native doctor, and two Hindoo menials. That much of the business might be seen from the verandah, but all else was concealed amidst the interior gloom. Shrieks and scuffling acquainted those without that the journeymen were earning their hire. Survur Khan soon emerged with his sword broken off at the hilt. He procured another from the Nana's house, and a few minutes after appeared again on the same errand. The third blade was of better temper; or perhaps the thick of the work was already over. By the time dark-

---

[7] Nickname of the native Indian woman who had superintended the quarters of the female English prisoners. [ED.]

[8] Another of the nana's titles. [ED.]

ness had closed in, the men came forth and locked up the house for the night. Then the screams ceased: but the groans lasted till morning.

The sun rose as usual. When he had been up nearly three hours the five repaired to the scene of their labours over-night. They were attended by a few sweepers, who proceeded to transfer the contents of the house to a dry well situated behind some trees which grew hard by. "The bodies," says one who was present throughout, "were dragged out, most of them by the hair of the head. Those who had clothes worth taking were stripped. Some of the women were alive. I cannot say how many; but three could speak. They prayed for the sake of God that an end might be put to their sufferings. I remarked one very stout woman, an half-caste, who was severely wounded in both arms, who entreated to be killed. She and two or three others were placed against the bank of the cut by which bullocks go down in drawing water. The dead were first thrown in. Yes: there was a great crowd looking on; they were standing along the walls of the compound. They were principally city people and villagers. Yes: there were also sepoys. Three boys were alive. They were fair children. The eldest, I think, must have been six or seven, and the youngest five years. They were running round the well (where else could they go to?) and there was none to save them. No; none said a word, or tried to save them."

At length the smallest of them made an infantile attempt to get away. The little thing had been frightened past bearing by the murder of one of the surviving ladies. He thus attracted the observation of a native, who flung him and his companions down the well. One deponent is of opinion that the man first took the trouble to kill the children. Others think not. The corpses of the gentlemen must have been committed to the same receptacle: for a townsman who looked over the brink fancied that there was "a Sahib uppermost." This is the history of what took place at Cawnpore, between four in the afternoon of one day and nine in the morning of another, almost under the shadow of the church-tower, and within call of the Theatre, the Assembly Rooms, and the Masonic Lodge. Long before noon on the sixteenth July there remained no living European within the circuit of the station.

But there were plenty at no great distance: for, about the turn of day, our force, after travelling five leagues, rested for a space in a hamlet buried amidst a forest of mango groves. A mile to northward lay the sepoy host, entrenched across the spot where the byway to Cawnpore branches from the Grand Trunk Road.[9] Seven guns commanded the approaches, and behind

---

[9]The Grand Trunk Road ran from Calcutta on the east coast northwest to Amritsar on the extreme northern frontier of India, near Lahore. [ED.]

a succession of fortified villages were gathered five thousand fighting men, prepared to strike a last blow for their necks and their booty. Havelock[10] resolved to turn the flank of the Nana: for he was aware that, if an opponent assails a native army otherwise than as it intended to be assailed when it took up its position, the general for a certainty loses his head, and the soldiers their heart. The word was given, and our column defiled at a steady pace round the left of the hostile line. The Fusileers[11] led, with two field-pieces in their rear. Then came the Highlanders, and the bulk of the artillery; followed by the Sixty-fourth, the Eighty-fourth, and the Sikh battalion. For some time the mutineers seemed to be unconscious of what was going on: deceived by clumps of fruit-trees, that screened our movement; and distracted by the sharp look-out which they were keeping straight ahead. But soon an evident sensation was created along their whole array. Their batteries began discharging shot and shell with greater liberality than accuracy; while a body of cavaliers pushed forward in the direction of our march, and made a demonstration that did not lead to much. As soon as the enemy's flank was completely exposed to the English attack, our troops halted, faced, and advanced in the order wherein they found themselves, covered by two companies of the Fusileers extended as skirmishers. Colonel Hamilton bade the pipes strike up, and led the Seventy-eighth against a cluster of houses defended by three guns. His horse was shot between his legs: but the kilts never stopped until they were masters of all inside the village. Three more pieces were captured by Major Stirling and the Sixty-fourth regiment. The rebel infantry were everywhere in full retreat; for the last half-hour nothing had been seen of the cavalry; and the battle appeared to be won.

Our fire had already ceased. The officers were congratulating each other on their easy victory: the privates were lighting their cheroots,[12] and speculating on the probability of an extra allowance of rum; when of a sudden a twenty-four pounder, planted on the Cawnpore Road, opened with fatal precision upon our exhausted ranks. Two large masses of horsemen rode forward over the plain. The foot[13] rallied, and came down with drums beating and colours flying; and the presence of a numerous staff, in gallant

---

[10] General Henry Marsham Havelock, who commanded a force of 2,000 men, set out from Allahabad and retook Cawnpore, 120 miles to the northwest, on 25 September 1857, on his way to relieving the siege at Lucknow (now spelled "Lakhnau"). For his action at Cawnpore he was awarded the Victoria Cross. [ED.]

[11] Infantry armed with rifles, the archaic term for which was *fusels*. [ED.]

[12] Cigars. [ED.]

[13] Foot soldiers, or infantrymen. [ED.]

attire, announced that the Peishwa himself was there, bent on daring something great in defence of his tottering throne. Meanwhile our artillery cattle, tired out by continual labour over vile roads and under a burning sun,
could no longer drag the cannon into action. The volunteers did whatever
might be done by a dozen and a half planters mounted on untrained
hunters.[14] The insurgents grew insolent; our soldiers were falling fast; and
the British general perceived that the crisis was not yet over. He despatched
his son to the spot where the men of the Sixty-fourth were lying down under such cover as they could get, with an order to rise and charge.

They leapt to their feet, rejoicing to fling aside their inaction: and young
Havelock placed himself at their head, and steered his horse straight for the
muzzle of the gun. [. . .]

And then the mutineers realized the change that a few weeks had wrought
in the nature of the task which they had selected and cut out for themselves.
The affair was no longer with mixed groups of invalids and civilians, without strategy or discipline, resisting desperately wherever they might chance
to be brought to bay. Now from left to right extended the unbroken line of
white faces, and red cloth, and sparkling steel. In front of all, the field
officer stepped briskly out, doing his best to keep ahead of his people.
There marched the captains, duly posted on the flank of their companies;
and the subalterns, gesticulating with their swords; and the sober, bearded
serjeants, each behind his respective section. Embattled in their national
order, and burning with more than their national lust of combat, on they
came, the unconquerable British Infantry. The grape was flying thick and
true. Files rolled over. Men stumbled, and recovered themselves, and went
on for a while, and then turned and hobbled to the rear. But the Sixty-
fourth was not to be denied. Closer and closer drew the measured tramp of
feet: and the heart of the foe died within him, and his fire grew hasty and
ill-directed. As the last volley cut the air overhead, our soldiers raised a
mighty shout, and rushed forward, each at his own pace. And then every
rebel thought only of himself. Those nearest the place were first to make
away; but throughout the host there were none who still aspired to stay
within push of the English bayonets. Such as had any stomach left for fighting were sickened by a dose of shrapnel and canister from four light guns,
which Maude[15] had driven up within point-blank range. Squadron after
squadron, battalion upon battalion, these humbled Brahmins dropped their

---

[14] Volunteers were reservists, in this case plantation owners riding horses normally used
for hunting. [ED.]

[15] Captain Francis Cornwallis Maude, commander of Havelock's artillery. Maude won
the Victoria Cross for his service the following week at Lucknow. [ED.]

weapons, stripped off their packs, and spurred, and ran, and limped, and scrambled, back to the city that was to have been the chief and central abode of sepoy domination.

From The Brotherhood

Stephen Knight

Some Freemasons claim great antiquity for Freemasonry. This is reflected in the Masonic calendar which is based on Archbishop Ussher's seventeenth-century calculation that the Creation must have taken place in the year 4004 BC. For convenience, the odd four years are ignored and Anno Lucis (in the Year of Light, when Freemasonry is deemed to have begun) is four thousand years ahead of Anno Domini—so a Masonic certificate of initiation bearing the date A.L. 5983 was issued in A.D. 1983. The implication is that Freemasonry is as old as Adam.

Throughout the eighteenth and nineteenth centuries, Masonic writers produced vast numbers of books seeking to show that their movement had a continuous history of many hundreds, even thousands, of years. Some claimed that the ancestors of the Brotherhood were the Druids or the Culdees; some claimed they were the pre-Christian Jewish monks, the Essenes. Others insisted that Freemasonry had its origins in the religion of ancient Egypt—an amalgam of the briefly held monotheism of Ikhnaton (*c.* 1375 B.C.) and the Isis-Osiris cult.

Modern Masonic historians are far more cautious. It is now accepted that Freemasonry as practised today goes back little more than three centuries. What is true, though, is that the philosophic, religious and ritualistic concoction that makes up the speculative element in Freemasonry is drawn from many sources—some of them, like the Isis-Osiris myth, dating back to the dawn of history. Rosicrucianism, Gnosticism, the Kabbala, Hinduism, Theosophy and traditional notions of the occult all play a part: but despite the exhaustive literature—one scholar estimates that some 50,000 items of Masonry had been published by the 1950s—it is impossible to determine what comes from where and when, if only because Freemasonry on its lower and more accessible levels is opposed to dogma. There is therefore no authoritative statement of what Masons believe or what the

The Brotherhood: The Secret World of the Freemasons. London: Granada, 1984. 15–16, 17–19, 20–21, 23, 33, 34–35.

Brotherhood stands for in the first, second and third degrees, to which the vast majority of members restrict themselves. Even a 33° Mason who has persevered to attain all the enlightenment that Freemasonry claims to offer could not—even if he were freed from his oath of secrecy—provide more than a purely personal view of the Masonic message and the meaning to be attached to Masonic symbolism, since this remains essentially subjective.

The comparatively short documented history of Freemasonry as an institution is nevertheless quite extraordinary. It is the story of how a Roman Catholic trade guild for a few thousand building workers in Britain came to be taken over by the aristocracy, the gentry and members of mainly nonproductive professions, and how it was turned into a non-Christian secret society enjoying association with offshoot fraternal societies with millions of adherents throughout most of the non-Communist world. [. . .]

Masonic historians seem as uncertain as non-Masons about who first saw in the obsolescent mediaeval Christian Masonic guild an organization that could be taken over and converted into a quasi-religious, quasi-secular secret society. What evidence there is indicates that this evolution began very slowly and almost by chance, and that it was only later that the potential of the Masonic guild as a clandestine power base was perceived. In other words, it appears that the original interest of the gentry in the Masonic lodges stemmed from curiosity, antiquarian interest, and a kind of fashionable search for an unconventional, exclusive social milieu— rather like a jet-set fad for frequenting working men's pubs.

There are a number of reasons why the Masonic guild should have attracted this genteel interest. First, the working (or "operative") masons' craft guild was ripe for takeover: structured in the heyday of Gothic architecture in the thirteenth century,[1] by the end of the sixteenth century the craft was dying. King's College Chapel at Cambridge, perhaps the last truly great English Gothic building, had been completed about 1512. Secondly, the highly skilled stonemasons of the Gothic age were peculiar in that many were itinerant workers, moving from church site to cathedral site as work was to be found. They had no regular headquarters like other trades, gathering in temporary lodges on site to discuss their affairs. And, as they often did not know each other as did permanent residents of mediaeval towns, they needed some method of recognition, some way of maintaining a closed shop to protect their demanding and highly esteemed profession against interlopers who had not undergone the rigorous apprenticeship necessary to acquire the mason's skills. These, as Professor Jacob Bronowski termed them, were the "industrial aristocrats."

---

[1] The term "lodge" was first used, so far as can be discovered, in 1277. [Knight's note.]

There were thus cosmopolitan romance, an exclusivity and an organized secretiveness about the masons' guild, which became increasingly moribund as baroque replaced Gothic architecture. All of this had potential fascination for men of education.

Modern Freemasonry probably originated in Scotland. The earliest known instance of a non-stonemason, a gentleman, joining a masons' lodge is John Boswell, Laird of Auchinlech, who was a member of the Lodge in Edinburgh in 1600. Apparently the first English gentleman to join an English Lodge was Elias Ashmole, founder of Oxford's Ashmolean Museum. An antiquarian deeply interested in Rosicrucianism, he joined in 1646. Masonry became so fashionable that as the seventeenth century progressed the "acceptance" (the collective term for non-stonemasons) became the majority in the Masonic Lodges. For example, in 1670 the Aberdeen Lodge had thirty-nine "accepted" members while only ten remained "operative" masons. But it was not long before the novelty in participating in the quaint and venerable doings of artisans wore thin. Men of fashion saw no reason to prolong association with working men, and they began to form their own gentlemen's Lodges. Freemasonry was launched. [...]

The "speculative" Masons inherited seven fundamental points from their "operative" predecessors:

(1) An organization with the three grades of members: Apprentice, Fellow or Journeyman, and Master Mason.

(2) A unit termed a Lodge.

(3) Legendary histories of the origins of the Masonic craft set out in the 100-odd manuscripts containing the so-called "Old Charges," the oldest being the Regius manuscript of 1390, which was in verse.

(4) A tradition of fraternal and benevolent relations between members.

(5) A rule of secrecy about Lodge doings, although the Old Charges themselves were simply lists of quite ordinary rules for the guild, which members were enjoined to keep "so help you God." As befitted a Christian grouping there were no blood-curdling oaths.

(6) A method of recognition, notably the Scottish "Mason word" traced back to 1550: unwritten but variously rendered as *Mahabyn, Mahabone* or even *Matchpin.*

(7) A thoroughly Christian foundation—the Old Charges are permeated with mediaeval Roman Catholicism.

With the demise of the original "trade union" purpose of the organization and with the eclipse not only of Roman Catholicism due to the Reformation but also the waning of Christianity with the rise of science, what was left towards the end of the seventeenth century was the framework of a secretive association, likened by one authority to a peasant's cottage ripe for extensive development as a luxury weekend home for the well-to-do.[. . .]

The transformation into a secret society meant the institution of formal oaths accompanied by penalties. But once again, before the establishment of Grand Lodge, very little is known of the development of ritual, particularly the oaths. There is evidence that rituals based on various incidents in legendary Masonic history were tried out in different Lodges—rituals perhaps based on stories of Noah's Ark and the Tower of Babel alluded to in some Old Charges. It is also probable that rituals based on the story of the building of King Solomon's temple, the principal subject of present-day rituals, were "worked" (the Masonic word meaning the acting out of the Brotherhood's ceremonies). But why this subject was chosen when the legends in the Old Charges give no special prominence to the story of Solomon's temple, no one has been able to explain satisfactorily. [. . .]

Freemasonry crossed the Atlantic to the colonies of the old empire very early on: George Washington's initiation was in 1752. Today, the dollar bill bears not only Washington's likeness but also the all-seeing-eye symbol of Freemasonry. Washington refused to become head of Masonry for the whole of the newly formed United States, and US Freemasonry came to be organized on a state-by-state basis. Today, each state has its own Grand Lodge. [. . .]

But the British—the founders of Masonry—remained throughout the nineteenth and twentieth centuries the chief propagandists for the movement. Undaunted by the loss of the first empire and with it direct control over American Masonry, the British took Masonry with the flag as they created their second empire—the one on which the sun never set. For some years membership of the Lodges set up in the empire (grouped in "Provinces" under English, Scottish or Irish jurisdiction) was confined to Europeans, apart from a handful of Indian princely exceptions. But after 1860, at first Parsees, then other Indians were brought into the Brotherhood. In British West Africa and the West Indies there were "black" Lodges as well as "white" Lodges (as in the USA), and eventually mixed Lodges were formed.

Associating the native upper and middle classes on a peculiar, profitable and clandestine basis with their white rulers, some historians believe, did much to defuse resentment of imperial domination. Despite his colour, any man rather better off than the mass of the people—who were not sought as members—could, by being a Freemason, feel that he belonged in however humble a way to the Establishment. Just how far Masonry reached is shown by the fact that on the small island of Jamaica there were no fewer than twelve Lodges, some in townships of little more than a couple of streets.

Freemasonry of itself is simply a secret environment tended by its various Grand Lodges, an exclusive society within society, there to be used by its members largely as they wish. Hence its influence, political and social, can be quite different at different times and places.

From Polynesian Researches

William Ellis

Karaimoku, the late prime minister, and present regent of the islands,[1] then arose, and said, "We have lost our king and queen,[2] they have died in a foreign land; we shall see them no more; it is right that we should weep, but let us not entertain hard thoughts of God. *God has not done wrong.* The evil is with us: let us bow under his hand: let all amusement cease; let our daily avocations be suspended; and let the nation, by prayer, and a cessation from ordinary pursuits, humble itself before God fourteen days." Before the assembly separated, Boki[3] stood up, and, in a brief outline of the voyage, narrated the most prominent events that had transpired since his departure from the islands, calling their attention in particular to the suitable and important advice he had received from his majesty the king of Great Britain, in an audience with which he was graciously favoured: viz. To return to his native country, attend to general and religious instruction himself, and endeavour to enlighten and reform the people; the peculiar circumstances of the people at this time, the increased satisfaction they had for some time felt in attending every means of instruction within their reach, and the pleasing change in favour of religion, which many had experienced, rendered this recommendation, so congenial to their feelings, from a source so distinguished, unusually acceptable. A deep and favourable impression was produced on all present, a new impulse was given to the means already employed for the instruction and improvement of the people, from

---

Polynesian Researches. Vol. 1. London: Fisher, 1831. 450–54. 4 vols.

[1] Hawaii, or as it was then known, the Sandwich Islands. [ED.]

[2] The king and queen of Hawaii, invited to visit George IV in London in 1824, both died of disease shortly after their arrival in England. [ED.]

[3] The native Hawaiian governor of the island of Oahu, who had accompanied his king and queen to England. [ED.]

which most advantageous results have already appeared. They were also made acquainted, by Boki and his companions, with the kind reception, generous treatment, and marked attentions, which the late king and queen and their suite had received while in England. This intelligence, communicated by those whose testimony would be received with the most entire credence, would at once confirm the attachment and confidence they have so long felt towards England.

No disturbance of the general tranquillity, nor change in the government of the islands, has resulted from this event. Rihoriho[4] left a younger brother, *Kauikeouli,* about ten years of age, who is acknowledged by the chiefs as his successor. A regency will govern during his minority, and the executive authority will probably continue to be exercised by *Karaimoku,* and the other chiefs with whom Rihoriho left it when he embarked for England.

The queen, who accompanied him, and who died at the same time, has left a fond mother and an affectionate people to lament her loss; she was the daughter of Tamehameha and Kalakua, and was born about the year 1797 or 1798, being two years younger than Rihoriho, and about twenty-six years of age when she left the islands. Like all the persons of distinction, she had many names, but that by which she was generally known, was *Kamehamaru* (shade of Kameha) from *kameha,* a contraction of her father's name, and *maru,* shade. She was distinguished for good-nature, and was much beloved by all her subjects. The poor people, when unable to pay their rent, or under the displeasure of the king and chiefs, or embarrassed on any other account, frequently repaired to her, and found a friend whose aid was never refused. She was also kind to those foreigners who might be distressed in the islands; and though she never harboured any, or countenanced their absconding from their ships, she has often fed them when hungry, and given them native tapa[5] for clothing.

Kamehamaru was at all times lively and agreeable in company; and though her application to her book and her pen was equal to that of the king, her improvement in learning was more gradual, and her general knowledge less extensive.

She excelled, however, in the management of his domestic affairs, which were conducted by her with great judgment and address; and though formerly accustomed to use ardent spirits, from the time she put herself under Christian instruction, she entirely discontinued that, and every other practice inconsistent with her profession of Christianity. Her attendance on the duties of religion was maintained with commendable regularity.

---

[4]The deceased king. [ED.]

[5]An unwoven fabric made from the bark of mulberry or breadfruit trees, often elaborately painted. [ED.]

Her influence contributed very materially to the pleasing change that has recently taken place, in connexion with the labours of the Missionaries in the islands. For the instruction and moral improvement of the people, she manifested no ordinary concern. Long before many of the leading chiefs were favourable to the instruction of the people, or their reception of Christianity, Kamehamaru on every suitable occasion recommended her own servants to serve Jehovah the living God, and attend to every means of improvement within their reach. It was truly pleasing to observe, so soon after she had embraced Christianity herself, an anxiety to induce her people to follow her example. At Honoruru[6] she erected a school, in which upwards of forty children and young persons, principally connected with her establishment, were daily taught to read and write, and instructed in the first principles of religion, by a native teacher whom she almost entirely supported. In this school she took a lively interest, and marked the progress of the scholars with evident satisfaction; in order to encourage the pupils, she frequently visited the school during the hours of instruction, accompanied by a number of chief women. She also attended the public examinations, and noticed those who on these occasions excelled, frequently presenting a favourite scholar with a slate, a copy-book, pencil, pen, or some other token of her approbation.

In her death, the Missionaries have lost a sincere friend, and her subjects a queen who always delighted to alleviate their distresses and promote their interests.

Her disposition was affectionate. I have seen her and the king sitting beside the couch of Keopuolani, her mother-in-law, day after day, when the latter has been ill; and on these occasions, though there might be several servants in constant attendance, she would allow no individual but her husband or herself to hand to the patient any thing she might want, or even fan the flies from her person.

The circumstances attending her departure from the islands were peculiarly affecting. The king had gone on board *L'Aigle;* but the boat was waiting to convey her to the ship. She arose from the mat on which she had been reclining, embraced her mother and other relations most affectionately, and passed through the crowd towards the boat. The people fell down on their knees as she walked along, pressing and saluting her feet, frequently bathing them with tears of unfeigned sorrow, and making loud wailings, in which they were joined by the thousands who thronged the shore.

On reaching the water side, she turned, and beckoned to the people to cease their cries. As soon as they were silent, she said, "I am going to a dis-

---

[6]Honolulu. [ED.]

tant land, and perhaps we shall not meet again. Let us pray to Jehovah, that he may preserve us on the water, and you on the shore." She then called *Auna,* a native teacher from the Society Islands, and requested him to pray. He did so; at the conclusion, she waved her hand to the people, and said, *"Arohá nui oukou"* (Attachment great to you); she then stepped into the boat, evidently much affected. The multitude followed her, not only to the beach, but into the sea, where many, wading into the water, stood waving their hands, exhibiting every attitude of sorrow, and uttering their loud *u-e! u-e!* (alas! alas!) till the boat had pulled far out to sea.

From Typee

Herman Melville

We looked about us[1] uncertain whither to direct our steps, since the path we had so far followed appeared to be lost in the open space around us. At last we resolved to enter a grove near at hand, and had advanced a few rods, when, just upon its skirts, I picked up a slender breadfruit shoot perfectly green, and with the tender bark freshly stript from it. It was slippery with moisture, and appeared as if it had been but that moment thrown aside. I said nothing, but merely held it up to Toby, who started at this undeniable evidence of the vicinity of the savages.

The plot was now thickening. A short distance further lay a little faggot of the same shoots bound together with a strip of bark. Could it have been thrown down by some solitary native, who, alarmed at seeing us, had hurried forward to carry the tidings of our approach to his countrymen?—Typee or Happar?[2]—But it was too late to recede, so we moved on slowly, my companion in advance casting eager glances under the trees on either

---

Typee: A Peep at Polynesian Life, during a Four Months' Residence in A Valley of the Marquesas. Rev. ed. New York: Wiley and Putnam, 1847. 70–74, 151–56.

[1]Unhappy with the abuse they endured on a whaling ship, the narrator and his friend Toby have run away while the ship was docked at the island of Nukuheva (sometimes spelled "Nuka-Hiva" or "Nuka Hiva") in the Marquesas Islands. Carrying only a few articles from the ship with them, they are working their way through the island forest in hopes of finding shelter among a friendly native tribe called the Happar (or "Happa"; see Stevenson, "From *In the South Seas,*" 328). [ED.]

[2]While the Happar tribe is presumed to be friendly, both toward whites and toward other natives, the Typee are universally dreaded for their warlike tendencies and for their cannibalism. [ED.]

side, until all at once I saw him recoil as if stung by an adder. Sinking on his knee, he waved me off with one hand, while with the other he held aside some intervening leaves, and gazed intently at some object.

Disregarding his injunction, I quickly approached him and caught a glimpse of two figures partly hidden by the dense foliage; they were standing close together, and were perfectly motionless. They must have previously perceived us, and withdrawn into the depths of the wood to elude our observation.

My mind was at once made up. Dropping my staff, and tearing open the package of things we had brought from the ship, I unrolled the cotton cloth, and holding it in one hand plucked with the other a twig from the bushes beside me, and telling Toby to follow my example, I broke through the covert and advanced, waving the branch in token of peace towards the shrinking forms before me.

They were a boy and a girl, slender and graceful, and completely naked, with the exception of a slight girdle of bark, from which depended at opposite points two of the russet leaves of the breadfruit tree. An arm of the boy, half screened from sight by her wild tresses, was thrown about the neck of the girl, while with the other he held one of her hands in his; and thus they stood together, their heads inclined forward, catching the faint noise we made in our progress, and with one foot in advance, as if half inclined to fly from our presence.

As we drew near, their alarm evidently increased. Apprehensive that they might fly from us altogether, I stopped short and motioned them to advance and receive the gift I extended towards them, but they would not; I then uttered a few words of their language with which I was acquainted, scarcely expecting that they would understand me, but to show that we had not dropped from the clouds upon them. This appeared to give them a little confidence, so I approached nearer, presenting the cloth with one hand, and holding the bough with the other, while they slowly retreated. At last they suffered us to approach so near to them that we were enabled to throw the cotton cloth across their shoulders, giving them to understand that it was theirs, and by a variety of gestures endeavoring to make them understand that we entertained the highest possible regard for them.

The frightened pair now stood still, whilst we endeavored to make them comprehend the nature of our wants. In doing this Toby went through with a complete series of pantomimic illustrations—opening his mouth from ear to ear, and thrusting his fingers down his throat, gnashing his teeth and rolling his eyes about, till I verily believe the poor creatures took us for a couple of white cannibals who were about to make a meal of them. When, however, they understood us, they showed no inclination to relieve our wants. At this juncture it began to rain violently, and we motioned them to lead us to some place of shelter. With this request they appeared willing to comply, but nothing could evince more strongly the apprehension with which they regarded us, than the way in which, whilst walking before us, they kept their eyes constantly turned back to watch every movement we made, and even our very looks.

"Typee or Happar, Toby?" asked I as we walked after them.

"Of course Happar," he replied, with a show of confidence which was intended to disguise his doubts.

"We shall soon know," I exclaimed; and at the same moment I stepped forward towards our guides, and pronouncing the two names interrogatively and pointing to the lowest part of the valley, endeavored to come to the point at once. They repeated the words after me again and again, but without giving any peculiar emphasis to either, so that I was completely at a loss to understand them; for a couple of wilier young things than we afterwards found them to have been on this particular occasion never probably fell in any traveller's way.

More and more curious to ascertain our fate, I now threw together in the form of a question the words "Happar" and "Mortarkee," the latter being equivalent to the word "good." The two natives interchanged glances of peculiar meaning with one another at this, and manifested no little surprise; but on the repetition of the question, after some consultation together, to the great joy of Toby, they answered in the affirmative. Toby was now in ecstasies, especially as the young savages continued to reiterate their answer with great energy, as though desirous of impressing us with the idea that being among the Happars, we ought to consider ourselves perfectly secure.

Although I had some lingering doubts, I feigned great delight with Toby at this announcement, while my companion broke out into a pantomimic abhorrence of Typee, and immeasurable love for the particular valley in which we were; our guides all the while gazing uneasily at one another as if at a loss to account for our conduct.

They hurried on, and we followed them; until suddenly they set up a strange halloo, which was answered from beyond the grove through which we were passing, and the next moment we entered upon some open ground, at the extremity of which we descried a long, low hut, and in front of it were several young girls. As soon as they perceived us they fled with wild screams into the adjoining thickets, like so many startled fawns. A few moments after the whole valley resounded with savage outcries, and the natives came running towards us from every direction.

Had an army of invaders made an irruption into their territory they could not have evinced greater excitement. We were soon completely encircled by a dense throng, and in their eager desire to behold us they almost arrested our progress; an equal number surrounding our youthful guides, who with amazing volubility appeared to be detailing the circumstances which had attended their meeting with us. Every item of intelligence appeared to redouble the astonishment of the islanders, and they gazed at us with inquiring looks.

At last we reached a large and handsome building of bamboos, and were by signs told to enter it, the natives opening a lane for us through which to pass; on entering without ceremony, we threw our exhausted frames upon the mats that covered the floor. In a moment the slight tenement was completely full of people, whilst those who were unable to obtain admittance gazed at us through its open cane-work.

It was now evening, and by the dim light we could just discern the savage countenances around us, gleaming with wild curiosity and wonder; the naked forms and tattooed limbs of brawny warriors, with here and there the slighter figures of young girls, all engaged in a perfect storm of conversation, of which we were of course the one only theme; whilst our recent guides were fully occupied in answering the innumerable questions which every one put to them. Nothing can exceed the fierce gesticulation of these people when animated in conversation, and on this occasion they gave loose to all their natural vivacity, shouting and dancing about in a manner that well-nigh intimidated us.

Close to where we lay, squatting upon their haunches, were some eight or ten noble-looking chiefs — for such they subsequently proved to be — who, more reserved than the rest, regarded us with a fixed and stern attention, which not a little discomposed our equanimity. One of them in particular, who appeared to be the highest in rank, placed himself directly facing me; looking at me with a rigidity of aspect under which I absolutely quailed. He never once opened his lips, but maintained his severe expression of countenance, without turning his face aside for a single moment. Never before had I been subjected to so strange and steady a glance; it revealed nothing of the mind of the savage, but it appeared to be reading my own. [. . .]

Returning health and peace of mind gave a new interest to everything around me. I sought to diversify my time by as many enjoyments as lay within my reach. Bathing in company with troops of girls formed one of my chief amusements. We sometimes enjoyed the recreation in the waters of a miniature lake, into which the central stream of the valley expanded. This lovely sheet of water was almost circular in figure, and about three hundred yards across. Its beauty was indescribable. All around its banks waved luxuriant masses of tropical foliage, soaring high above which were seen, here and there, the symmetrical shaft of the cocoanut tree, surmounted by its tuft of graceful branches, drooping in the air like so many waving ostrich plumes.

The ease and grace with which the maidens of the valley propelled themselves through the water, and their familiarity with the element, were truly astonishing. Sometimes they might be seen gliding along just under the surface, without apparently moving hand or foot; then throwing themselves on their sides, they darted through the water, revealing glimpses of their forms, as, in the course of their rapid progress, they shot for an instant partly into the air; at one moment they dived deep down into the water, and the next they rose bounding to the surface.

I remember upon one occasion plunging in among a parcel of these river-nymphs, and counting vainly on my superior strength, sought to drag some of them under the water; but I quickly repented my temerity. The amphibious young creatures swarmed about me like a shoal of dolphins, and seizing hold of my devoted limbs, tumbled me about and ducked me under the surface, until from the strange noises which rang in my ears, and the supernatural visions dancing before my eyes, I thought I was in the land of spirits. I stood indeed as little chance among them as a cumbrous whale attacked on all sides by a legion of sword-fish. When at length they relinquished their hold of me, they swam away in every direction, laughing at my clumsy endeavors to reach them.

There was no boat on the lake; but at my solicitation and for my special use, some of the young men attached to Marheyo's[3] household, under the direction of the indefatigable Kory-Kory,[4] brought up a light and tastefully carved canoe from the sea. It was launched upon the sheet of water, and floated there as gracefully as a swan. But, melancholy to relate, it produced an effect I had not anticipated. The sweet nymphs, who had sported with me before in the lake, now all fled its vicinity. The prohibited craft, guarded by the edicts of the "taboo," extended the prohibition to the waters in which it lay. [. . .]

Although the "taboo" was a ticklish thing to meddle with, I determined to test its capabilities of resisting an attack. I consulted the chief Mehevi, who endeavored to persuade me from my object: but I was not to be repulsed; and accordingly increased the warmth of my solicitations. At last he entered into a long, and I have no doubt a very learned and eloquent exposition of the history and nature of the "taboo" as affecting this particular case; employing a variety of most extraordinary words, which, from their amazing length and sonorousness, I have every reason to believe were of a theological nature. But all that he said failed to convince me: partly, perhaps, because I could not comprehend a word that he uttered; but chiefly, that for the life of me I could not understand why a woman should not have as

---

[3] An old warrior, who has become the narrator's principal host while among the Typee. [ED.]
[4] The son of Marheyo, Kory-Kory is the "servant" assigned to the narrator. [ED.]

much right to enter a canoe as a man. At last he became a little more ratio-
nal, and intimated that, out of the abundant love he bore me, he would
consult with the priests and see what could be done.

How it was that the priesthood of Typee satisfied the affair with their
consciences, I know not; but so it was, and Fayaway's[5] dispensation from
this portion of the taboo was at length procured. Such an event I believe
never before had occurred in the valley; but it was high time the islanders
should be taught a little gallantry, and I trust that the example I set them
may produce beneficial effects. Ridiculous, indeed, that the lovely creatures
should be obliged to paddle about in the water, like so many ducks, while
a parcel of great strapping fellows skimmed over its surface in their canoes.

The first day after Fayaway's emancipation, I had a delightful little party
on the lake — the damsel, Kory-Kory, and myself. My zealous body-servant
brought from the house a calabash of poee-poee,[6] half a dozen young cocoanuts — stripped of their husks — three pipes, as many yams, and me on his
back a part of the way. Something of a load; but Kory-Kory was a very
strong man for his size, and by no means brittle in the spine. We had a very
pleasant day; my trusty valet plied the paddle and swept us gently along the
margin of the water, beneath the shades of the overhanging thickets. Fayaway and I reclined, in the stern of the canoe, the gentle nymph occasionally placing her pipe to her lip, and exhaling the mild fumes of the tobacco,
to which her rosy breath added a fresh perfume. Strange as it may seem,
there is nothing in which a young and beautiful female appears to more
advantage than in the act of smoking. How captivating is a Peruvian lady,
swinging in her gaily-woven hammock of grass, extended between two
orange-trees, and inhaling the fragrance of a choice cigarro! But Fayaway,
holding in her delicately-formed olive hand the long yellow reed of her
pipe, with its quaintly carved bowl, and every few moments languishingly
giving forth light wreaths of vapor from her mouth and nostrils, looked
still more engaging.

We floated about thus for several hours, when I looked up to the warm,
glowing, tropical sky, and then down into the transparent depths below;
and when my eye, wandering from the bewitching scenery around, fell
upon the grotesquely-tattooed form of Kory-Kory, and finally encountered
the pensive gaze of Fayaway, I thought I had been transported to some fairy
region, so unreal did everything appear.

This lovely piece of water was the coolest spot in all the valley, and I now
made it a place of continual resort during the hottest period of the day.

---

[5] The woman living in Marheyo's household who has become the narrator's favorite. [ED.]
[6] A pasty mash made from breadfruit. [ED.]

One side of it lay near the termination of a long gradually expanding gorge, which mounted to the heights that environed the vale. The strong trade wind, met in its course by these elevations, circled and eddied about their summits, and was sometimes driven down the steep ravine and swept across the valley, ruffling in its passage the otherwise tranquil surface of the lake.

One day, after we had been paddling about for some time, I disembarked Kory-Kory, and paddled the canoe to the windward side of the lake. As I turned the canoe, Fayaway, who was with me, seemed all at once to be struck with some happy idea. With a wild exclamation of delight, she disengaged from her person the ample robe of tappa[7] which was knotted over her shoulder (for the purpose of shielding her from the sun), and spreading it out like a sail, stood erect with upraised arms in the head of the canoe. We American sailors pride ourselves upon our straight clean spars, but a prettier little mast than Fayaway made was never shipped aboard of any craft.

In a moment the tappa was distended by the breeze — the long brown tresses of Fayaway streamed in the air — and the canoe glided rapidly through the water, and shot towards the shore. Seated in the stern, I directed its course with my paddle until it dashed up the soft sloping bank, and Fayaway, with a light spring, alighted on the ground; whilst Kory-Kory, who had watched our manœuvres with admiration, now clapped his hands in transport, and shouted like a madman. Many a time afterwards was this feat repeated.

From In Darkest Africa

Henry Morton Stanley

In March 1887, the American journalist turned explorer Henry Morton Stanley, famous for his rendezvous at Lake Tanganyika in 1871 with Dr. David Livingstone (whom he greeted, famously: "Dr. Livingstone, I presume?"), began his last, three-year expedition in Africa. Stanley sailed up the Congo River along the same route taken by Conrad (and Marlow) a few years later. Stanley's chief purpose was to provide relief to the emin pasha, the title of the ruler of Equatoria, which was one of the Equatorial Provinces of Egypt, at that

In Darkest Africa, or the Quest, Rescue, and Retreat of Emin, Governor of Equatoria. Vol. 1. New York: Scribner's, 1890. 74–98. 2 vols.

[7] An unwoven fabric made from the bark of mulberry or breadfruit trees, often elaborately painted; sometimes spelled "tapa." [ED.]

time under British occupation. The emin pasha was a German Jew named Eduard Schnitzler, who had been appointed governor of Equatoria in 1885 by General Gordon (later known as the Martyr of Khartoum), the officer in command of British forces in Egypt. The emin pasha and his army of Sudanese fighters were besieged by Arab Mahdist soldiers and were badly in need of ammunition.

With funding provided by wealthy British sympathizers, the Egyptian government, and the Royal Geographic Society, Stanley led a massive expedition of nearly 800 men up the Congo River, which was felt to be the safest route to bring relief to the emin pasha. In exchange for sanction and further support, Stanley first made an agreement with Leopold II of Belgium, sole ruler of the Congo Free State. Under the terms of this agreement, Stanley was to install Tippu Tib (the nickname of an infamous Arab slave trader, Hamid Ibn Muhammad) as governor of Stanley Falls in return for Tippu Tib's help in defending the Congo Free State from Arab incursions; he was also to demand payment from the emin pasha for the ammunition Stanley provided to him in the form of the 75 tons of ivory the emin pasha was said to possess.

Stanley's party carried 2 tons of gunpowder, over 600 rifles and 100,000 rounds of ammunition, machine guns (known as Maxim automatic guns), and many other military supplies. They would have looked something like the Eldorado Exploring Expedition mentioned in *Heart of Darkness*. The progress of Stanley's expedition was reported regularly in British newspapers, and Stanley returned to a hero's reception in London on 26 April 1890, just three days before Conrad received his three-year commission from Leopold's government to serve in the Congo. This was the second convergence of Stanley's and Conrad's travels: in 1878, Conrad arrived at Marseilles one month after Stanley's celebrated arrival there, en route to England from a prior expedition in the Congo.

———

At Cape Town,[1] Tippu Tib, after remarking the prosperity and business stir of the city, and hearing its history from me, said that he formerly had thought all white men to be fools.

"Really," I said; "Why?"

———

[1] Stanley's party stopped briefly at Cape Town, South Africa, in their commissioned ship the *Madura*, as they sailed from Zanzibar, off the east coast of Africa, around the Cape of Good Hope toward the mouth of the Congo River, on Africa's west coast. [ED.]

"That was my opinion."

"Indeed! and what do you think of them now?" I asked.

"I think they have something in them, and that they are more enterprising than Arabs."

"What makes you think so, particularly now?"

"Well, myself and kinsmen have been looking at this town, these big ships and piers, and we have thought how much better all these things appear compared to Zanzibar, which was captured from the Portuguese before this town was built, and I have been wondering why we could not have done as well as you white people. I begin to think you must be very clever."

"If you have discovered so much, Tippu Tib, you are on the high road to discover more. The white men require a deal of study before you can quite make them out. It is a pity you never went to England for a visit."

"I hope to go there before I die."

"Be faithful to us on this long journey, and I will take you there, and you will see more things than you can dream of now."

"Inshallah![2] if it is the will of Allah we shall go together."

On the 18th March the *Madura* entered the mouth of the Congo River, and dropped her anchor about 200 yards abreast of the sandy point, called Banana.

In a few minutes I was in the presence of Mr. Lafontaine Ferney, the chief Agent of the Dutch Company, to whom our steamer was consigned. Through some delay he had not been informed of our intending to arrive as soon. Everybody professed surprise, as they did not expect us before the 25th, but this fortunate accident was solely due to the captain and the good steamer. However, I succeeded in making arrangements by which the Dutch Company's steamer *K. A. Nieman*—so named after a fine young man of that name, who had lately died at St. Paul de Loanda—would be placed at my disposal, for the transport to Mataddi[3] of 230 men next day.

On returning to the ship, I found my officers surrounding two English traders, connected with the British Congo Company of Banana. They were

---

[2] "If Allah wills," or "God willing." [ED.]

[3] The last port upriver from the mouth of the Congo, on a stretch of the river that was known as the Lower Congo. From this point on, because of a series of cataracts in the river, the expedition would have to proceed overland for more than 200 miles to Stanley Pool (now called Malebo Pool), where the river formed a wide bulge at the base of the Upper Congo. The Upper Congo then allowed free passage for over a thousand miles inland to Stanley Falls. [ED.]

saying some unpleasant things about the condition of the State[4] steamers. "There is a piece of the *Stanley* on shore now, which will give you an idea of that steamer. The *Stanley* is a perfect ruin, we are told. However, will you leave the Pool? The State has not one steamer in service. They are all drawn up on the banks for repairs, which will take months. We don't see how you are to get away from here under six weeks! Look at that big steamer on the sands! she has just come out from Europe; the fool of a captain ran her on shore instead of waiting for a pilot. She has got the sections of a steamer in her hold. The *Heron* and *Belgique*, both State steamers, have first, of course, to float that steamer off. You are in for it nicely, we can tell you."

Naturally, this news was very discouraging to our officers, and two of them hastened to comfort me with the disastrous news. They were not so well acquainted with the manners of the "natives" of the Lower Congo as I was. I only marvelled why they had not been politely requested to accompany their new aquaintances to the cemetery, in order that they might have the exquisite gratification of exhibiting the painted head-boards, which record the deaths of many fine young men, as promising in appearance as they.

I turned to the Agent of the British Congo, and requested permission to charter his steamer, the *Albuquerque*. The gentleman graciously acceded. This assured me transport for 140 men and 60 tons cargo. I then begged that he and his friend would negotiate for the charter of the large paddle boat the *Serpa Pinto*. Their good offices were entirely successful, and before evening I knew that we should leave Banana Point with 680 men and 160 tons cargo on the next day. The State steamer *Heron* I was told would not be able to leave before the 20th.

On the 19th the steamers *K. A. Kieman, Albuquerque,* and *Serpa Pinto* departed from Banana Point, and before night had anchored at Ponta da Lenha. The next day the two former steamers steamed straight up to Mataddi. The *Serpa Pinto* hauled into the pier at Boma,[5] to allow me to send an official intimation of the fact that the new Governor of Stanley Falls[6] was aboard, and to receive a hurried visit from two of the Executive Committee charged with the administration of the Congo State.

We had but time to exchange a few words, but in that short time they managed to inform me that there was a "famine in the country"; that "the villages along the road to the Pool were abandoned"; that "the *Stanley* was seriously damaged"; that "the Mission steamers *Peace* and *Henry Reed* were

[4] The Congo Free State, the unintentionally ironic name for Leopold's territorial preserve. [ED.]
[5] The seat of Leopold's government in the Congo Free State. [ED.]
[6] Tippu Tib. [ED.]

in some unknown parts of the Upper Congo"; that "the *En Evant* was on shore without machinery or boiler"; that "the *A. I. A.* was 500 miles above Stanley Pool"; and that "the *Royal* was perfectly rotten"; and had not been employed for a year; in fact, that the whole of the naval stock promised did not exist at all except in the imagination of the gentlemen of the Bureau at Brussels; and, said one, who seemed to be the principal of the Executive Committee, with deliberate emphasis: "The boats were only to assist you if they could be given without prejudice to the service of the State."

The gruff voice of the Portuguese captain of the *Serpa Pinto* ordered the gentlemen on shore, and we proceeded on our way up the Congo.

My thoughts were not of the pleasantest. With my flotilla of fifteen whale boats[7] I might have been independent; but there was an objection to the Congo route, and therefore that plan was abandoned. We had no sooner adopted the East Coast route than the Sovereign of the Congo State invited the Expedition to pass through his territory; the Germans had murmured, and the French Government protested at the idea of our marching through East Africa. When it was too late to order the flotilla of whale boats from Forrest and Son we then accepted the Congo route, after stipulating for transport up the Lower Congo, for porterage to Stanley Pool, and the loan of the steamers on the Upper Congo which were now said to be wrecked, rotten, or without boilers or engines, or scattered inaccessible. In my ears rang the cry in England: "Hurry up, or you may be too late!"[8] and singing through my memory were the words of Junker:[9] "Emin will be lost unless immediate aid be given him"; and Emin's appeal for help; for, if denied, "we shall perish."

"Well, the aspect of our work is ominous. It is not my fault, and what we have to do is simple enough. We have given our promise to strive our level best. It is no time for regret, but to struggle and "steer right onward." Every article of our verbal bond, having accepted this responsibility, we must perform, and it is the manner of this performance that I now propose to relate. [. . .]

On the 21st of March the Expedition debarked at the landing-place of the Portuguese trading-house of Senor Joda Ferrier d'Abren, situate at Mataddi,

---

[7] Stanley had originally considered taking his expedition up the Congo in fifteen whale boats, which would have had to be carried overland from the Lower Congo to the Upper Congo. An alternative route starting from the east coast of Africa, though considerably shorter, would have had to pass through the territories of a number of other nations, both European and African. [ED.]

[8] The cry from the wealthy backers of the expedition. [ED.]

[9] The German-born explorer Dr. Wilhelm Junker, who had been stranded together with the emin pasha since the spring of 1886. [ED.]

at a distance of 108 miles from the Atlantic. As fast as the steamers were discharged of their passengers and cargo they cast off to return to the seaport of Banana, or the river port below.

About noon the Portuguese gunboat *Kacongo* hove in sight. She brought Major Barttelot, Mr. Jephson, and a number of Soudanese and Zanzibaris;[10] and soon after the state steamer *Heron* brought up the remainder of the cargo left on board the *Madura*.

We set up the tents, stored the immense quantity of rice, biscuits, millet, salt, hay, etc., and bestirred ourselves like men with unlimited work before us. Every officer distinguished himself—the Zanzibaris showed by their celerity that they were glad to be on shore.

Our European party now consisted of Messrs. Barttelot, Stairs, Nelson, Jephson, Parke, Bonny, who had voyaged with me from Aden, Mr. Walker, an engineer, who had joined us at the Cape, Mr. Ingham, an ex-Guardsman, who was our Congo Agent for collection of native carriers, Mr. John Rose Troup, who had been despatched to superintend native porterage to the Pool from Manyanga,[11] and a European servant.

On the following day 171 porters, carrying 7 boxes biscuits = 420 lbs., 157 bags of rice = 10,205 lbs., and beads, departed from Mataddi to Lukungu[12] as a reserve store for the Expedition on arrival. There were 180 sacks of 170 lbs. each = 30,600 lbs. besides, ready to follow or precede us as carriers offered themselves, and which were to be dropped at various places *en route*, and at the Pool. Couriers were also sent to the Pool with request to the Commandant to hurry up the repairs of all steamers.

On the second day of arrival, Mr. Ingham appeared with 220 carriers, engaged at a sovereign per load for conveying goods to the Pool. Lieutenant Stairs practised with the Maxim automatic gun, which fired 330 shots per minute, to the great admiration of Tippu Tib and his followers.

On the 25th the trumpets sounded in the Soudanese camp at 5.15 A.M. By 6 o'clock tents were folded, the companies were ranged by their respective captains, and near each company's stack of goods, and by 6.15 A.M. I marched out with the vanguard, behind which streamed the Expedition, according to their company, in single file, bearing with us 466 separate

---

[10] Stanley had taken along sixty-one Sudanese fighters, mainly as a symbolic gesture to demonstrate to the emin pasha the genuineness of his mission. Through Tippu Tib, Stanley had also engaged 600 Zanzibari carriers, who were to be paid £6 apiece to carry the ammunition to the emin pasha and to carry his ivory back. In addition, he agreed to take along ninety-six of Tippu Tib's Zanzibari kin. [ED.]

[11] A village halfway between Mataddi and Stanley Pool. [ED.]

[12] A small village between Mataddi and Manyanga. [ED.]

"charges" or porter-loads of ammunition, cloth, beads, wire, canned provisions, rice, salt, oil for engines, brass rods, and iron wire. The setting out was admirable, but after the first hour of the march the mountains were so steep and stony, the sunshine was so hot, the loads so heavy, the men so new to the work after the glorious plenty on board the *Madura,* and we ourselves were in such an overfed condition, that the Expedition straggled in the most disheartening manner to those not prepared for such a sight. Arriving at the first river, the Mpozo, the *Advance* was already jointed, and we were ferried over to the other bank by fifties, and camped.

The Soudanese were a wretched sight. The Somalis[13] were tolerable, though they had grumbled greatly because there were no camels. The former showed remarkably bad temper. Covered with their hooded greatcoats, they had endured a terrible atmosphere, and the effects of heat, fatigue, and little worries were very prominent.

The next day we camped in the grounds of Palaballa, belonging to the Livingstone Inland Mission, and were most hospitably treated by Mr. Clarke, the superintendent, and ladies. As our men were so new to their work, we halted the next day. By the officers' returns I found that nine had died since leaving Zanzibar, and seventeen were so ill that we were compelled to leave them at Palaballa to recuperate.

We resumed the march on the 28th, and reached Maza Mankengi. On the road Mr. Herbert Ward was met, and volunteered as a member of the Expedition. He was engaged, and sent to Mataddi to assist Mr. Ingham with the native transport. Mr. Ward had been of late years in the service of the Congo State, and previously had wandered in New Zealand and Borneo, and was always regarded by me as a young man of great promise.

We were in camp by noon of the 29th at Congo la Lemba, on the site of a place I knew some years ago as a flourishing village. The chief of it was then in his glory, an undisputed master of the district. Prosperity, however, spoiled him, and he began to exact tolls from the State caravans. The route being blocked by his insolence, the State sent a force of Bangalas, who captured and beheaded him. The village was burnt, and the people fled elsewhere. The village site is now covered with tall grass, and its guava, palm, and lemon-trees are choked with reeds.

There was a slight improvement in the order of the march, but the beginning of an Expedition is always a trying time. The Zanzibaris carry 65 lbs. of ammunition, 9 lbs. per rifle, four days' rations of rice, and their own kit, which may be from 4 to 10 lbs. weight of cloth and bedding mats.

---

[13] A small number of Somali fighters also accompanied the expedition. [ED.]

After they have become acclimated this weight appears light to them; but during the first month we have to be very careful not to make long marches, and to exercise much forbearance.

A heavy rain detained us the early part of next day, but soon after nine we moved on and reached the Lufu River. It was a terribly fatiguing march. Until midnight the people came streaming in, tired, footsore, and sour. The officers slept in my tent, and supped on biscuits and rice.

Near the Mazamba Wood we passed Baron von Rothkirch supervising a party of Kabindas, who were hauling the *Florida's* shaft.[14] At the rate of progress they would probably reach the Pool about August next; and at the Bembezi Ford a French trader was met descending with a fine lot of ivory tusks.

We passed the Mangola River on the 31st, when I was myself disabled by a fit of sickness from indulging in the guavas of Congo la Lemba, and on the 1st April we travelled to Banza Manteka. At the L. I. Mission Mr. and Mrs. Richards most kindly entertained us. At this place a few years' mission work has produced a great change. Nearly all the native population had become professed Christians, and attended Divine service punctually with all the fervour of revivalists. Young men whom I had known as famous gin-drinkers had become sober, decent men, and most mannerly in behaviour.

I received three letters from up river, one from Troup at Manyanga, Swinburne at Kinshassa,[15] and Glave at Equator Station, all giving a distressing account of the steamers *Stanley, Peace, Henry Reed,* and *En Avant.* The first is damaged throughout according to my informants, the Mission steamers require thorough overhauling, the *En Avant* has been reduced to a barge. Mr. Troup suggests that we carry a lighter[16] or two from Manyanga to the Pool, a thing utterly impossible. We were already overloaded because of the rice we carried to feed nearly 800 people through the starving country. In order to lighten our work slightly Messrs. Jephson and Walker were despatched with our steel boat, the *Advance,* by the Congo to Manyanga.

We passed by the Lunionzo River on the 3rd, and the next day camped on the site of the abandoned village of Kilolo. During the march I passed a Soudanese trying to strangle a Zanzibari because the wearied man had

---

[14] Stanley had himself pioneered the method of transporting prefabricated steamers from Mataddi to the Upper Congo and assembling them at Stanley Pool. [ED.]

[15] Kinshassa (or "Kinshasa"), now capital of the Democratic Republic of the Congo, was at this time a small village on Stanley Pool. In the 1880s, it was nearby but separate from Leopoldville (the "Central Station," or trading post, of *Heart of Darkness*), which Stanley had established in 1881. The two settlements gradually merged, although they retained separate official identities until 1966, when both were given the name Kinshasa. [ED.]

[16] Large, flat-bottomed barge. [ED.]

slightly touched his shoulder with his box. The spleen the Soudanese show is extremely exasperating, but we must exercise patience yet awhile.

A march of three hours brought us to the Kwilu River, with the usual ups and downs of hills, which tire the caravan. At the river, which is 100 yards wide and of strong current, was a canoe without an owner. We took possession of it, and began to cross the Advance Company by tens.

The opportunity afforded by the ferriage was seized by me to write appealing letters to the Commandant at Stanley Pool to interpret the orders of the Minister of the Interior, Strauch, according to the generous spirit expressed by King Leopold when he invited us to seek Emin Pasha *viâ* the Congo. Another was directed to the Rev. Mr. Bentley, of the Baptist Mission, requesting him to remember the assistance I gave the Baptists in 1880–84, and to be prepared to lend the steamer *Peace* that I might hurry the Expedition away from the poverty-stricken region around Stanley Pool. Another was despatched to Mr. Billington, superintendent of the *Henry Reed*, in similar terms, reminding him that it was I who had given them ground at Stanley Pool. Another to the Commandant of Lukungu Station, requesting him to collect 400 carriers to lighten the labours of my men.

On reaching Mwembi the 6th April, I was particularly struck with the increase of demoralization in the caravan. So far, in order not to press the people, I had been very quiet, entrusting the labour of bringing the stragglers to the younger men, that they might become experienced in the troubles which beset Expeditions in Africa; but the necessity of enforcing discipline was particularly demonstrated on this march. The Zanzibaris had no sooner pitched the tents of their respective officers than they rushed like madmen among the neighbouring villages, and commenced to loot native property, in doing which one named Khamis bin Athman was shot dead by a plucky native. This fatal incident is one of these signal proofs that discipline is better than constant forbearance, and how soon even an army of licentious, insubordinate, and refractory men would be destroyed.

It had probably been believed by the mass of the people that I was rather too old to supervise the march, as in former times; but on the march to Vombo, on the 7th, everyone was undeceived, and the last of the lengthy caravan was in camp by 11 A.M., and each officer enjoyed his lunch at noon, with his mind at ease for duty done and a day's journey well made. There is nothing more agreeable than the feeling one possesses after a good journey briefly accomplished. We are assured of a good day's rest; the remainder of the day is our own to read, to eat, to sleep, and be luxuriously inactive, and to think calmly of the morrow; and there can scarcely be anything more disagreeable than to know that, though the journey is but a short one, yet relaxation of severity permits that cruel dawdling on the road in the suffocating high grass, or scorched by a blistering sun—the long line of carriers is crumpled up into perspiring fragments—water far when most needed; not a shady tree near the road; the loads robbed and scattered about over ten miles of road; the carriers skulking among the reeds, or cooling themselves in groves at a distance from the road; the officers in despair at the day's near close, and hungry and vexed, and a near prospect of some such troubles to recur again tomorrow and the day after. An unreflecting spectator hovering near our line of march might think we were unnecessarily cruel; but the application of a few cuts to the confirmed stragglers secure eighteen hours' rest to about 800 people and their officers, save the goods from being robbed—for frequently these dawdlers lag behind purposely for such intentions—and the day ends happily for all, and the morrow's journey has no horrors for us.

On the 8th the Expedition was welcomed at Lukungu Station by Messrs. Francqui and Dessauer. These hospitable Belgians had of their own impulse gathered four day's rations for our 800 people, of potatoes, bananas, brinjalls, Indian corn, and palm nuts.

No sooner had we all assembled than the Soudanese gathered in a body to demand more food. In fifteen days they had consumed each one 40 lbs. of biscuit and rice; and they announced their intention of returning to the Lower Congo if more rations were not served out. The four days' rations of vegetables they disdained to touch. I had resolved to be very patient; and it was too early yet to manifest even the desire to be otherwise. Extra rations of rice and biscuits were accordingly served out.

Fortunately for me personally there were good officers with me who could relieve me of the necessity of coming into conflict with wilful fellows like these sulky, obstinate Soudanese. I reserved for myself the *rôle* of mediator between exasperated whites and headstrong, undisciplined blacks. Provided one is not himself worn out by being compelled throughout the day to shout at thick-headed men, it is a most agreeable work to extenuate offences and soothe anger. Probably the angry will turn away muttering that we are partial; the other party perhaps thirsts for more sympathy on its side; but the mediator must be prepared to receive a rub or two himself.

Thinking that there would be less chance of the Soudanese storming so furiously against the Zanzibaris on the road, I requested Major Barttelot to keep his Soudanese a day's march ahead of the Zanzibaris.

It will not be surprising that we all felt more sympathy for the loaded Zanzibaris. These formed our scouting parties, and foragers, and food purveyors; they pitched our tents, they collected fuel, they carried the stores; the main strength of the Expedition consisted of them; without them the Europeans and Soudanese, if they had been ten times the number, would have been of no use at all for the succour of Emin. The Soudanese carried nothing but their rifles, their clothing, and their rations. By the time they would be of actual utility we should be a year older; they might perhaps fail us when the hour of need came, but we hoped not; in the meantime, all that was necessary was to keep them moving on with as little trouble as possible to themselves, the Zanzibaris, and us. The Major, however, without doubt was sorely tempted. If he was compelled to strike during these days, I must admit that the Soudanese were uncommonly provoking. Job would have waxed wrathful, and become profane.

The heat was terrible the day we left Lukungu—the 10th. The men dropped down on all sides; chiefs and men succumbed. We overtook the Soudanese again, and the usual scuffling and profanity occurred as an unhappy result.

On Easter Monday, the 11th, the Soudanese Company was stricken down with fever, and lamentation was general, and all but two of the Somalis were prostrated. Barttelot was in a furious rage at his unhappy Company, and expressed a wish that he had been doing Jephson's duty with the boat. I received a letter from Jephson in the evening, wherein he wrote that he wished to be with us, or anywhere rather than on the treacherous and turbulent Congo.

The following day saw a foundering caravan as we struggled most wretchedly into camp. The Soudanese were miles from each other, the Somalis were all ill; one of those in the boat with Mr. Jephson had died. Liebig,[17] and meat soups, had to be prepared in sufficient quantities to serve out cupfuls to each weakened man as he staggered in.

Lutete's was reached the next day, and the experiences of the march were similar. We suffer losses on every march—losses of men by desertion, by illness, of rifles, boxes of canned provisions, and of fixed ammunition.

At Nselo, on the Inkissi River, we encountered Jephson, who has seen some novelties of life during his voyage up the Congo rapids to Manyanga.

The sun has commenced to paint our faces a vermilion tint, for I see in each officer's face two inflamed circles glowing red and bright under each eye, and I fancy the eyes flash with greater brilliancy. Some of them have thought it would be more picturesque, more of the ideal explorer type, to have their arms painted also, and have bared their milk-white arms until they seem bathed in flame.

The 16th April we employed in ferrying the Expedition across the Inkissi River, and by 5.30 P.M. every soul was across, besides our twenty donkeys and herd of Cape goats.

---

[17] A canned preparation of meat, with the fat removed. It was named after the inventor, Baron Justus von Liebig, and marketed under the name Liebig's Extract of Beef. [ED.]

During the ferriage some hot words were exchanged between Salim, son of Massoud, a brother-in-law of Tippu Tib, and Mr. Mounteney Jephson, who is the master of the boat. Salim, since he has married a sister of Tippu Tib, aspires to be beyond censure; his conceit has made him abominably insolent. At Mataddi's he chose to impress his views most arrogantly on Lieutenant Stairs; and now it is with Mr. Jephson, who briefly told him that if he did not mind his own business he would have to toss him into the river. Salim savagely resented this, until Tippu Tib appeared to ease his choler.

At the next camp I received some more letters from Stanley Pool. Lieutenant Liebrichts, the commissaire of the Stanley Pool district, wrote that the steamer *Stanley* would be at my disposition, and also a lighter! The *En Avant* would not be ready for six weeks. Another was from Mr. Billington, who declined most positively to lend the *Henry Reed*.

One of my most serious duties after a march was to listen to all sorts of complaints—a series of them were made on this day. A native robbed by a hungry Zanzibari of a cassava loaf required restitution; Binza, the goatherd, imagined himself slighted because he was not allowed to participate in the delicacy of goat tripe, and solicited my favour to obtain for him this privilege; a Zanzibari weakling, starving amidst a well-rationed camp and rice-fed people, begged me to regard his puckered stomach, and do him the justice to see that he received his fair rations from his greedy chief. Salim, Tippu Tib's henchman, complained that my officers did not admire him excessively. He said, "They should remember he no Queen man now he Tippu Tib's brudder-in-law" (Salim was formerly an interpreter on board a British cruiser). And there were charges of thefts of a whinstone, a knife, a razor, against certain incorrigible purloiners.

At our next camp on the Nkalama River, which we reached on the 18th April, I received a letter by a courier from Rev. Mr. Bentley, who informed me that no prohibition had been received by him from England of the loan of the Baptist mission steamer *Peace,* and that provided I assured him that the Zanzibaris did nothing contrary to missionary character, which he as a missionary was desirous of maintaining, that he would be most happy to surrender the *Peace* for the service of the "Emin Pasha Relief Expedition." Though very grateful, and fully impressed with his generosity, in this unnecessary allusion to the Zanzibaris, and to this covert intimation that we are responsible for their excesses, Mr. Bentley has proved that it must have cost him a struggle to grant the loan of the *Peace.* He ought to have remembered that the privilege he obtained of building his stations at Leopoldville, Kinshassa, and Lukolela was gained by the labours of the good-natured Zanzibaris, who though sometimes tempted to take freedoms, were generally well behaved, so much so that the natives preferred them to the Houssas, Kabindas, Kruboys, or Bangalas.

On the 19th we were only able to make a short march, as each day witnessed a severe downpour of rain, and the Luila near which we camped had become dangerously turbulent.

On the 20th we reached Makoko's village. The Zanzibaris were observed to be weakening rapidly. They have been compelled to live on stinted rations lately, and their habit of indulging in raw manioc[18] is very injurious. A pound of rice per day is not a large ration for working men, but if they had contrived to be contented on this scanty but wholesome fare for a while they would not be in a robust condition, it is true, but there certainly would be less illness. During this march from the Lower Congo we had consumed up to date 27,500 lbs. of rice—about 13 tons—so that the resources of the entire region had been severely taxed to obtain this extra carriage. The natives having fled from the public paths, and our fear that the Zanzibaris, if permitted to forage far from the camp, would commit depredations, have been the main cause of their plucking up the poisonous manioc tubers, and making themselves wretchedly sick. There were about a hundred men on this date useless as soldiers or carriers.

Arriving at Leopoldville on the 21st to the great delight of all, one of my first discoveries was the fact that the *Stanley,* a small lighter, our steel boat the *Advance,* and the mission steamer *Peace* were the only boats available for the transport of the Expedition up the Congo. I introduce the following notes from my diary:

Leopoldville, April 22nd. We are now 345 miles from the sea in view of Stanley Pool, and before us free from rapids are about 1100 miles of river to Yambuya on the Aruwimi whence I propose resuming the land journey to Lake Albert.[19]

Messrs. Bentley and Whitley called on me today. We spoke concerning the *Peace.* They said the vessel required many repairs. I insisted that the case was urgent. They finally decided after long consultation that the repairs could be finished by the 30th.

In the afternoon I took Major Barttelot and Mr. Mounteney Jephson into my confidence, and related to them the difficulties that we were in,

---

[18] Also known as cassava, the starchy, tuberous roots of the manioc are a source of tapioca. [ED.]

[19] A lake in the northeast corner of the Congo Free State, on the border with the Sudan. During the reign of President Mobutu Sese Seko, when the country itself was known as Zaire, the lake was called Lake Mobutu Sese Seko. [ED.]

explained my claims on the consideration of the missionaries and the urgent necessity of an early departure from the foodless district, that provisions were so scarce that the State were able to procure only 60 full rations for 146 people, and that to supply the others the State officers had recourse to hunting the hippopotami in the Pool, and that we should have to pursue the same course to eke out the rice. And if 60 rations can only be procured for 146 people by the State authorities, how were we to supply 750 people? I then directed them to proceed to Mr. Billington and Dr. Sims, and address themselves to the former principally—inasmuch as Dr. Sims was an unsuccessful applicant for a position on this Expedition—and explain matters fairly to him.

They were absent about an hour and a half, and returned to me crestfallen—they had failed. Poor Major! Poor Jephson!

Monsieur Liebrichts, who had formerly served with me on the Congo at Bolobo, was now the Governor of the Stanley Pool district. He dined with me this evening and heard the story as related by Major Barttelot and Mr. Mounteney Jephson. Nothing was kept back from him. He knew much of it previously. He agreed heartily with our views of things and acknowledged that there was great urgency. Jephson said, "I vote we seize the *Henry Reed.*"

"No, my friend Jephson. We must not be rash. We must give Mr. Billington time to consider, who would assuredly understand how much his mission was indebted to me, and would see no difficulty in chartering his steamer at double the price the Congo State paid to him. Those who subsist on the charity of others naturally know how to be charitable. We will try again tomorrow, when I shall make a more formal requisition and offer liberal terms, and then if she is not conceded we must think what had best be done under the circumstances."

April 23rd. Various important matters were attended to this morning. The natives from all parts in this neighbourhood came to revive acquaintance, and it was ten o'clock before I was at liberty.

Ngalyema was somewhat tedious with a long story about grievances that he had borne patiently, and insults endured without plaint. He described the change that had come over the white men, that of late they had become more imperious in their manner, and he and other chiefs suspecting that the change boded no good to them had timidly absented themselves from the stations, the markets had been abandoned, and consequently food had become scarce and very dear.

Having given my sympathy to my old friends I called Barttelot and Jephson and read to them a statement of former kindnesses shown to the "Livingstone Inland Mission." "When you have spoken, request in the name of charity and humanity, and all good feeling, that Mr. Billington allow me to offer liberal terms for the charter of the *Henry Reed* for a period of sixty days."

Barttelot was inspired to believe that his eloquence would prevail, and asked permission to try in his way once more.

"Very good, Major, go, and success attend you."

"I'm sure I shall succeed like a shot," said the Major confidently.

The Major proceeded to the Mission House, and Mr. Jephson accompanied him as a witness of the proceedings. Presently I received a characteristic note from the Major, who wrote that he had argued ineffectually with the missionaries, principally with Mr. Billington, but in the presence of Dr. Sims, who sat in a chair contenting himself with uttering remarks occasionally.

Lieutenant Liebrichts was informed of the event, and presented himself, saying that this affair was the duty of the State.

Monsieur Liebrichts, who is undoubtedly one of the most distinguished officers in the Congo State, and who has well maintained the high character described in a former book of mine, devoted himself with ardour to the task of impressing Mr. Billington with the irrationality of his position, and of his obstinacy in declining to assist us out of our difficulties in which we had been placed by the fault of circumstances. To and fro throughout the day he went demanding, explaining, and expostulating, and finally after twelve hours prevailed on Mr. Billington to accept a charter upon the liberal terms offered; namely, £100 per month.

April 24th. Mustered Expedition and discovered we are short of 57 men, and 38 Remington rifles. The actual number now is 737 men and 496 rifles. Of billhooks, axes, shovels, canteens, spears, &c., we have lost over 50 per cent—all in a twenty-eight days' march.

Some of the men, perhaps, will return to their duties, but if such a large number deserts 3000 miles from their native land, what might have been expected had we taken the East Coast route. The Zanzibar head-men tell me with a cynical bitterness that the Expedition would have been dissolved. They say, "These people from the clove and cinnamon plantations of Zanzibar are no better than animals—they have no sense of feeling. They detest work, they don't know what silver is, and they have no parents or homes. The men who have homes never desert, if they did they would be so laughed at by their neighbours that they could not live." There is a great deal of truth in these remarks, but in this Expedition are scores of confirmed bounty-jumpers who are only awaiting opportunities. In inspecting the men today I was of the opinion that only about 150 were free men, and that all the remainder were either slaves or convicts.

Mr. J. S. Jameson has kindly volunteered to proceed to shoot hippopotami to obtain meat. We are giving 1 lb. of rice to each man—just half rations. For the officers and our Arab guests I have a flock of goats, about thirty in number. The food presents from the various chiefs around have amounted to 500 men's rations and have been very acceptable.

Capt. Nelson is busy with the axemen preparing fuel for the steamers. The *Stanley* must depart tomorrow with Major Barttelot and Surgeon Parke's companies, and debark them at a place above the Wampoko, when they will then march to Mswata. I must avail myself of every means of leaving Stanley Pool before we shall be so pinched by hunger that the men will become uncontrollable.

April 25th. The steamer *Stanley*, steamed up river with 153 men under Major Barttelot and Surgeon Parke.

I paid a visit to Kinshassa to see my ancient secretary, Mr. Swinburne, who is now manager of an Ivory Trading Company, called the "Sanford Exploring Company." The hull of his steamer, *Florida*, being completed, he suggested that if we assisted him to launch her he would be pleased to lend her to the Expedition, since she was of no use to anybody until her machinery and shaft came up with Baron von Rothkirch, who probably would not arrive before the end of July. I was only too glad, and a number of men were at once ordered up to begin the operations of extending the slip[20] to the river's edge.

Our engineer, Mr. John Walker, was detailed for service on the *Henry Reed*, to clean her up and prepare her for the Upper Congo.

One Soudanese and one Zanzibari died today.

April 27th. Thirteen Zanzibaris and one Soudanese, of those left behind from illness, at stations on the way have arrived. They report having sold their rifles and sapper's tools![21]

April 28th. Struck camp and marched Expedition overland to Kinshassa that I might personally super-intend launching of hull of steamer, *Florida*, which we hope to do the day after tomorrow, when the ship is finished. We are being hospitably entertained meanwhile by Mr. Antoine Greshoff, of the Dutch Company, and Mr. Swinburne of the Sanford Company.

April 29th. In camp at Kinshassa under the baobabs. The steamers *Stanley* and *Henry Reed*, towing-barge *En Avant* arrived.

April 30th. The hull of the *Florida* was launched this morning. Two hundred men pulled her steadily over the extended slip into the river. She was then taken to the landing-place of the Dutch Company and fastened to the steamer *Stanley*.

---

[20] A sloping ramp extending into the water, from which a ship could be raised or lowered. [ED.]

[21] Military implements for building field fortifications. [ED.]

Each officer was furnished with the plan of embarkation, and directed to begin work of loading the steamers according to programme.

The following orders were also issued:

The Officers commanding companies in this Expedition are—

		Company
E. M. Barttelot	Major	No. 1, Soudanese.
W. G. Stairs	Captain	" 2, Zanzibaris.
R. H. Nelson	"	" 3 "
A. J. Mounteney Jephson	"	" 4 "
J. S. Jameson	"	" 5 "
John Rose Troup	"	" 6 "
T. H. Parke	Captain and Surgeon	" 7, Somalis and Zanzibaris.

Mr. William Bonny takes charge of transport and riding animals and live stock, and assists Surgeon Parke when necessary.

"Each officer is personally responsible for the good behaviour of his company and the condition of arms and accoutrements."

"Officers will inspect frequently cartridge-pouches of their men, and keep record to prevent sale of ammunition to natives or Arabs."

"For trivial offences—a slight corporal punishment only can be inflicted, and this as seldom as possible. Officers will exercise discretion in this matter, and endeavour to avoid irritating the men, by being too exacting, or showing unnecessary fussiness."

"It has been usual for me to be greatly forbearing—let the rule be, three pardons for one punishment."

"Officers will please remember that the labour of the men is severe, their burdens are heavy, the climate hot, the marches fatiguing, and the rations poor and often scanty. Under such conditions human nature is extremely susceptible, therefore punishments should be judicious, not vexatious, to prevent straining patience too much. Nevertheless discipline must be taught, and when necessary enforced for the general well-being."

"Serious offences affecting the Expedition generally will be dealt with by me."

"While on shipboard one officer will be detailed to perform the duties of the day. He must see to the distribution of rations, ship cleaned, and that no fighting or wrangling occurs, as knifing soon follows unless checked, that the animals are fed and watered regularly. For all petty details apply to the senior officer, Major Barttelot."

An Open Letter
to His Serene Majesty Leopold II

George Washington Williams

Williams fought in the U.S. Civil War as a member of the U.S. Colored Troops, later became a Baptist minister in Massachusetts, and was subsequently elected to the House of Representatives of the Ohio General Assembly. He met King Leopold II of Belgium in the fall of 1889, while attending an antislavery conference in Brussels. In early 1890, he was informally commissioned by U.S. president Benjamin Harrison to report on conditions in the Congo, information that Harrison believed would contribute to his deliberations over whether to recommend ratification of the Berlin Act of 1885—an agreement among the European powers for carving up Africa. Williams traveled through the Congo in 1890—at the same time as Conrad—and issued a report to Harrison in October that was harshly critical of Leopold's practices. In July 1890, he was moved to write his "Open Letter" to Leopold, which was published as a pamphlet and reissued repeatedly in both Britain and the United States, where it gained considerable attention. For a full account, see Franklin's excellent study.

Good and Great Friend,

I have the honour to submit for your Majesty's consideration some reflections respecting the Independent State of Congo, based upon a careful study and inspection of the country and character of the personal Government you have established upon the African Continent.

In order that you may know the truth, the whole truth, and nothing but the truth, I implore your most gracious permission to address you without restraint, and with the frankness of a man who feels that he has a duty to perform to *History, Humanity, Civilization,* and to the *Supreme Being,* who is himself the "King of Kings."

Your Majesty will testify to my affection for your person and friendship for your African State, of which you have had ample practical proofs for

---

"An Open Letter to His Serene Majesty Leopold II, King of the Belgians and Sovereign of the Independent State of Congo, by Colonel the Honorable Geo. W. Williams, of the United States of America." Stanley Falls, Central Africa: n.p., 1890.

nearly six years. My friendship and service for the State of Congo were inspired by and based upon your publicly declared motives and aims, and your personal statement to your humble subscriber: humane sentiments and work of Christian civilization for Africa. Thus I was led to regard your enterprise as the rising of the Star of Hope for the Dark Continent, so long the habitation of cruelties; and I journeyed in its light and laboured in its hope. All the praiseful things I have spoken and written of the Congo country, State and Sovereign, was inspired by the firm belief that your Government was built upon the enduring foundation of *Truth, Liberty, Humanity,* and *Justice.*

It afforded me great pleasure to avail myself of the opportunity afforded me last year, of visiting your State in Africa; and how thoroughly I have been disenchanted, disappointed, and disheartened, it is now my painful duty to make known to your Majesty in plain but respectful language. Every charge which I am about to bring against your Majesty's personal Government in the Congo has been carefully investigated; a list of competent and veracious witnesses, documents, letters, official records, and data has been faithfully prepared, which will be deposited with Her Brittannic Majesty's Secretary of State for Foreign Affairs, until such time as an International Commission can be created with power to send for persons and papers, to administer oaths, and attest the truth or falsity of these charges.

I crave your Majesty's indulgence while I make a few preliminary remarks before entering upon the specifications and charges.

Your Majesty's title to the territory of the State of Congo is badly clouded, while many of the treaties made with the natives by the "Association Internationale du Congo,"[1] of which you were Director and Banker, were tainted by frauds of the grossest character. The world may not be surprised to learn that your flag floats over territory to which your Majesty has no legal or just claim, since other European Powers have doubtful claims to the territory which they occupy upon the African Continent; but all honest people will be shocked to know by what grovelling means this fraud was consummated.

There were instances in which Mr. Henry M. Stanley sent one white man, with four or five Zanzibar soldiers, to make treaties with native chiefs.

---

[1] The name of the governing body of the Congo, which was a thin cover for Leopold's absolute personal control. In Brussels in 1876, Leopold had convened a conference of representatives from Germany, Russia, Austria-Hungary, France, England, Italy, and Belgium and had manipulated the conference into creating *l'Association Internationale du Congo* as a fig leaf for his own personal authority in the Congo, where he later employed Henry Morton Stanley as his chief agent. The Congo Free State, or *L'Etat Indépendent du Congo,* with Leopold again as sovereign ruler, was created in 1884 as successor to the association. [ED.]

The staple argument was that the white man's heart had grown sick of the wars and rumours of war between one chief and another, between one village and another; that the white man was at peace with his black brother, and desired to "confederate all African tribes" for the general defense and public welfare. All the sleight-of-hand tricks had been carefully rehearsed, and he was now ready for his work. A number of electric batteries had been purchased in London, and when attached to the arm under the coat, communicated with a band of ribbon which passed over the palm of the white brother's hand, and when he gave the black brother a cordial grasp of the hand the black brother was greatly surprised to find his white brother so strong, that he nearly knocked him off his feet in giving him the hand of fellowship. When the native inquired about the disparity of strength between himself and his white brother, he was told that the white man could pull up trees and perform the most prodigious feats of strength. Next came the lens act. The white brother took from his pocket a cigar, carelessly bit off the end, held up his glass to the sun and complaisantly smoked his cigar to the great amazement and terror of his black brother. The white man explained his intimate relation to the sun, and declared that if he were to request him to burn up his black brother's village it would be done. The third act was the gun trick. The white man took a percussion cap gun, tore the end of the paper which held the powder to the bullet, and poured the powder and paper into the gun, at the same time slipping the bullet into the sleeve of the left arm. A cap was placed upon the nipple of the gun, and the black brother was implored to step off ten yards and shoot at his white brother to demonstrate his statement that he was a spirit, and, therefore, could not be killed. After much begging the black brother aims the gun at his white brother, pulls the trigger, the gun is discharged, the white man stoops . . . and takes the bullet from his shoe!

By such means as these, too silly and disgusting to mention, and a few boxes of gin, whole villages have been signed away to your Majesty.

In your personal letter to the President of the Republic of the United States of America, bearing date of August 1st 1885, you said that the possessions of the International Association of the Congo will hereafter form the Independent State of the Congo. "I have at the same time the honour to inform you and the Government of the Republic of the United States of America that, authorised by the Belgian Legislative Chambers to become the Chief of the new State, I have taken, in accord with the Association, the title of Sovereign of the Independent State of Congo." Thus you assumed the headship of the State of Congo, and at once organised a personal Government. You have named its officers, created its laws, furnished its finances, and every act of the Government has been clothed with the majesty of your authority.

On the 25th of February 1884, a gentleman, who has sustained an intimate relation to your Majesty for many years, and who then wrote as expressing your sentiments, addressed a letter to the United States in which the following language occurs: "It may be safely asserted that no barbarous people have ever so readily adopted the fostering care of benevolent enterprise, as have the tribes of the Congo, and never was there a more honest and practical effort made to increase their knowledge and secure their welfare." The letter, from which the above is an excerpt, was written for the purpose of securing the friendly action of the Committee on Foreign Relations, which had under consideration a Senate Resolution in which the United States recognised the flag of the "Association Internationale du Congo" as the flag of a friendly Government. The letter was influential, because it was supposed to contain the truth respecting the natives, and the programme, not only of the Association, but of the new State, its legitimate successor, and of your Majesty.

When I arrived in the Congo, I naturally sought for the results of the brilliant programme: *"fostering care," "benevolent enterprise,"* an *"honest and practical effort"* to increase the knowledge of the natives *"and secure their welfare."* I had never been able to conceive of Europeans, establishing a government in a tropical country, without building a hospital; and yet from the mouth of the Congo River to its head-waters, here at the seventh cataract,[2] a distance of 1,448 miles, there is not a solitary hospital for Europeans, and only three sheds for sick Africans in the service of the State, not fit to be occupied by a horse. Sick sailors frequently die on board their vessels at Banana Point;[3] and if it were not for the humanity of the Dutch Trading Company at that place—who have often opened their private hospital to the sick of other countries—many more might die. There is not a single chaplain in the employ of your Majesty's Government to console the sick or bury the dead. Your white men sicken and die in their quarters or on the caravan road, and seldom have christian burial. With few exceptions, the surgeons of your Majesty's Government have been gentlemen of professional ability, devoted to duty, but usually left with few medical stores and no quarters in which to treat their patients. The African soldiers and labourers of your Majesty's Government fare worse than the whites, because they have poorer quarters, quite as bad as those of the natives; and in the sheds, called hospitals, they languish upon a bed of bamboopoles without blankets, pillows, or any food different from that served to them when well, rice and fish.

---

[2] Williams wrote his letter from Stanley Falls, the furthest navigable point up the Congo River. [ED.]

[3] The harbor at the mouth of the Congo River. [ED.]

I was anxious to see to what extent the natives had *"adopted the fostering care"* of your Majesty's "benevolent enterprise" (?), and I was doomed to bitter disappointment. Instead of the natives of the Congo "adopting the fostering care" of your Majesty's Government, they everywhere complain that their land has been taken from them by force; that the Government is cruel and arbitrary, and declare that they neither love nor respect the Government and its flag. Your Majesty's Government has sequestered their land, burned their towns, stolen their property, enslaved their women and children, and committed other crimes too numerous to mention in detail. It is natural that they everywhere shrink from *"the fostering care"* your Majesty's Government so eagerly proffers them.

There has been, to my absolute knowledge, no *"honest and practical effort made to increase their knowledge and secure their welfare."* Your Majesty's Government has never spent one franc for educational purposes, nor instituted any practical system of industrialism. Indeed the most unpractical measures have been adopted *against* the natives in nearly every respect; and in the capital of your Majesty's Government at Boma there is not a native employed. The labour system is radically unpractical; the soldiers and labourers of your Majesty's Government are very largely imported from Zanzibar at a cost of £10 *per capita,* and from Sierre Leone, Liberia, Accra and Lagos at from £1 to £1/10 *per capita.* These recruits are transported under circumstances more cruel than cattle in European countries. They eat their rice twice a day by the use of their fingers; they often thirst for water when the season is dry; they are exposed to the heat and rain, and sleep upon the damp and filthy decks of the vessels often so closely crowded as to lie in human ordure. And, of course, many die.

Upon the arrival of the survivors in the Congo they are set to work as labourers at one shilling a day; as soldiers they are promised sixteen shillings per month, in English money, but are usually paid off in cheap handkerchiefs and poisonous gin. The cruel and unjust treatment to which these people are subjected breaks the spirits of many of them, makes them distrust and despise your Majesty's Government. They are enemies, not patriots.

There are from sixty to seventy officers of the Belgian army in the service of your Majesty's Government in the Congo of whom only about thirty are at their post; the other half are in Belgium on furlough. These officers draw double pay, as soldiers and as civilians. It is not my duty to criticise the unlawful and unconstitutional use of these officers coming into the service of this African State. Such criticism will come with more grace from some Belgian statesman, who may remember that there is no constitutional or organic relation subsisting between his Government and the purely personal and absolute monarchy your Majesty has established in Africa. But I take the liberty to say that many of these officers are too young and inexperienced to be entrusted with the difficult work of dealing with native races. They are ignorant of native character, lack wisdom, justice, fortitude, and patience. They have estranged the natives from your Majesty's Government, have sown the seed of discord between tribes and villages, and some of them have stained the uniform of the Belgian officer with murder, arson, and robbery. Other officers have served the State faithfully, and deserve well of their Royal Master.

Of the unwise, complicated, and stupid dual Government of the State of Congo I cannot say much in this letter, reserving space for a careful examination of it in another place. I may say that the usefulness of many a Congo official is neutralised by having to keep a useless set of books. For example, an officer is in command of a station and he wishes to buy two eggs. He makes this entry in a ruled and printed book: "For nourishment bought two eggs for two Ntaka." In another book he must make this entry: "Two Ntaka gone out of the store." And in another book he must enter this purchase *seven times!* Comment upon such supreme folly is unnecessary. We need only feel compassion for the mental condition of the man in Brussels who invented this system, and deep sympathy with its victims in the Congo.

From these general observations I wish now to pass to specific charges against your Majesty's Government.

FIRST. Your Majesty's Government is deficient in the moral, military and financial strength necessary to govern a territory of 1,508,000 square miles, 7,251 miles of navigation, and 31,694 square miles of lake surface. In the Lower Congo River there is but one post, in the cataract region one. From Leopoldville to N'Gombe,[4] a distance of more than 300 miles, there is not a single soldier or civilian. Not one out of every twenty State-officials know the language of the natives, although they are constantly issuing laws, difficult even for Europeans, and expect the natives to comprehend and obey them. Cruelties of the most astounding character are practised by the natives, such as burying slaves alive in the grave of a dead chief, cutting off the heads of captured warriors in native combats, and no effort is put forth by your Majesty's Government to prevent them. Between 800 and 1,000 slaves are sold to be eaten by the natives of the Congo State annually; and slave raids, accomplished by the most cruel and murderous agencies, are carried on within the territorial limits of your Majesty's Government which is impotent. There are only 2,300 soldiers in the Congo.

---

[4]Leopoldville is on Stanley Pool (now Malebo Pool), at the base of the Upper Congo River; N'Gombe is a village upriver from Stanley Pool. [ED.]

SECOND. Your Majesty's Government has established nearly fifty posts, consisting of from two to eight mercenary slave-soldiers from the East Coast. There is no white commissioned officer at these posts; they are in charge of the black Zanzibar soldiers,[5] and the State expects them not only to sustain themselves, but to raid enough to feed the garrisons where the white men are stationed. These piratical, buccaneering posts compel the natives to furnish them with fish, goats, fowls, and vegetables at the mouths of their muskets; and whenever the natives refuse to feed these vampires, they report to the main station and white officers come with an expeditionary force and burn away the homes of the natives. These black soldiers, many of whom are slaves, exercise the power of life and death. They are ignorant and cruel, *because* they do not comprehend the natives; they are imposed upon them by the State. They make no report as to the number of robberies they commit, or the number of lives they take; they are only required to subsist upon the natives and thus relieve your Majesty's Government of the cost of feeding them. They are the greatest curse the country suffers now.

THIRD. Your Majesty's Government is guilty of violating its contracts made with its soldiers, mechanics and workmen, many of whom are subjects of other Governments. Their letters never reach home.

FOURTH. The Courts of your Majesty's Government are abortive, unjust, partial, and delinquent. I have personally witnessed and examined their clumsy operations. The laws printed and circulated in Europe "for the protection of the blacks" in the Congo are a dead letter and a fraud. I have heard an officer of the Belgian Army pleading the cause of a white man of low degree who had been guilty of beating and stabbing a black man, and urging race distinctions and prejudices as good and sufficient reasons why his client should be adjudged innocent. I know of prisoners remaining in custody for six and ten months because they were not judged. I saw the white servant of the Governor-General, Camille Janssen, detected in stealing a bottle of wine from a hotel table. A few hours later the Procurer-General searched his room and found many more stolen bottles of wine and other things, not the property of servants. No one can be prosecuted in the State of Congo without an order of the Governor-General, and as he refused to allow his servant to be arrested, nothing could be done. The black servants in the hotel, where the wine had been stolen, had been often accused and beaten for these thefts, and now they were glad to be vindicated. But to the surprise of every honest man, the thief was sheltered by the Governor-General of your Majesty's Government.

---

[5] Zanzibaris served as mercenaries throughout Africa. [ED.]

FIFTH. Your Majesty's Government is excessively cruel to its prisoners, condemning them, for the slightest offences, to the chain gang, the like of which cannot be seen in any other Government in the civilised or uncivilised world. Often these ox-chains eat into the necks of the prisoners and produce sores about which the flies circle, aggravating the running wound; so the prisoner is constantly worried. These poor creatures are frequently beaten with a dried piece of hippopotamus skin, called a "chicote," and usually the blood flows at every stroke when well laid on. But the cruelties visited upon soldiers and workmen are not to be compared with the sufferings of the poor natives who, upon the slightest pretext, are thrust into the wretched prisons here in the Upper River. I cannot deal with the dimensions of these prisons in this letter, but will do so in my report to my Government.

SIXTH. Women are imported into your Majesty's Government for immoral purposes. They are introduced by two methods, viz, black men are dispatched to the Portuguese coast where they engage these women as mistresses of white men, who pay to the procurer a monthly sum. The other method is by capturing native women and condemning them to seven years' servitude for some imaginary crime against the State with which the villages of these women are charged. The State then hires these women out to the highest bidder, the officers having the first choice and then the men. Whenever children are born of such relations, the State maintains that the woman being its property the child belongs to it also. Not long ago a Belgian trader had a child by a slave-woman of the State, and he tried to secure possession of it that he might educate it, but the Chief of the Station where he resided refused to be moved by his entreaties. At length he appealed to the Governor-General, and he gave him the woman and thus the trader obtained the child also. This was, however, an unusual case of generosity and clemency; and there is only one post that I know of where there is not to be found children of the civil and military officers of your Majesty's Government abandoned to degradation; white men bringing their own flesh and blood under the lash of a most cruel master, the State of Congo.

SEVENTH. Your Majesty's Government is engaged in trade and commerce, competing with the organised trade companies of Belgium, England, France, Portugal and Holland. It taxes all trading companies and exempts its own goods from export-duty, and makes many of its officers ivory-traders, with the promise of a liberal commission upon all they can buy or get for the State. State soldiers patrol many villages forbidding the natives to trade with any person but a State official, and when the natives refuse to accept the price of the State, their goods are seized by the Government that promised them "protection." When natives have persisted in

trading with the trade-companies the State has punished their independence by burning the villages in the vicinity of the trading houses and driving the natives away.

EIGHTH. Your Majesty's Government has violated the General Act of
the Conference of Berlin by firing upon native canoes; by confiscating the
property of natives; by intimidating native traders, and preventing them
from trading with white trading companies; by quartering troops in native
villages when there is no war; by causing vessels bound from "Stanley-
Pool" to "Stanley-Falls" to break their journey and leave the Congo, ascend
the Aruhwimi river to Basoko,[6] to be visited and show their papers; by forbidding a mission steamer to fly its national flag without permission from
a local Government; by permitting the natives to carry on the slave-trade,
and by engaging in the wholesale and retail slave-trade itself.

NINTH. Your Majesty's Government has been, and is now, guilty of wag-
ing unjust and cruel wars against natives, with the hope of securing slaves
and women, to minister to the behests of the officers of your Government.
In such slave-hunting raids one village is armed by the State against the
other, and the force thus secured is incorporated with the regular troops. I
have no adequate terms with which to depict to your Majesty the brutal acts
of your soldiers upon such raids as these. The soldiers who open the combat are usually the bloodthirsty cannibalistic Bangalas,[7] who give no quarter to the aged grandmother or nursing child at the breast of its mother.
There are instances in which they have brought the heads of their victims
to their white officers on the expeditionary steamers, and afterwards eaten
the bodies of slain children. In one war two Belgian Army officers saw,
from the deck of their steamer, a native in a canoe some distance away. He
was not a combatant and was ignorant of the conflict in progress upon the
shore, some distance away. The officers made a wager of £5 that they could
hit the native with their rifles. Three shots were fired and the native fell
dead, pierced through the head, and the trade canoe was transformed into
a funeral barge and floated silently down the river.

In another war, waged without just cause, the Belgian Army officer in
command of your Majesty's forces placed the men in two or three lines on
the steamers and instructed them to commence firing when the whistles
blew. The steamers approached the fated town, and, as was usual with
them, the people came to the shore to look at the boats and sell different ar-

---

[6]The Aruwimi feeds the Congo River about 150 miles below Stanley Falls; Basoko is a
town just upriver on the Aruwimi. [ED.]
[7]Tribespeople from the region that is present-day Uganda. [ED.]

ticles of food. There was a large crowd of men, women and children, laughing, talking and exposing their goods for sale. At once the shrill whistles of the steamers were heard, the soldiers levelled their guns and fired, and the people fell dead, and wounded, and groaning, and pleading for mercy. Many prisoners were made, and among them four comely looking young women. And now ensued a most revolting scene: your Majesty's officers quarreling over the selection of these women. The commander of this murderous expedition, with his garments stained with innocent blood, declared that his rank entitled him to the first choice! Under the direction of this same officer the prisoners were reduced to servitude, and I saw them working upon the plantation of one of the stations of the State.

TENTH. Your Majesty's Government is engaged in the slave-trade, wholesale and retail. It buys and sells and steals slaves. Your Majesty's Government gives £3 per head for able-bodied slaves for military service. Officers at the chief stations get the men and receive the money when they are transferred to the State; but there are some middle-men who only get from twenty to twenty-five francs per head. Three hundred and sixteen slaves were sent down the river recently, and others are to follow. These poor natives are sent hundreds of miles away from their villages, to serve among other natives whose language they do not know. When these men run away a reward of 1,000 N'taka is offered. Not long ago such a re-captured slave was given one hundred "chikote" each day until he died. Three hundred N'taka-brassrod is the price the State pays for a slave, when bought from a native. The labour force at the stations of your Majesty's Government in the Upper River is composed of slaves of all ages and both sexes.

ELEVENTH. Your Majesty's Government has concluded a contract with the Arab Governor at this place for the establishment of a line of military posts from the Seventh Cataract to Lake Tanganyika,[8] territory to which your Majesty has no more legal claim than I have to be Commander-in-Chief of the Belgian army. For this work the Arab Governor is to receive five hundred stands of arms, five thousands kegs of powder, and £20,000 sterling, to be paid in several instalments. As I write, the news reaches me that these much-treasured and long-looked for materials of war are to be discharged at Basoko, and the Resident[9] here is to be given the discretion as to the distribution of them. There is a feeling of deep discontent among

---

[8] A large lake on the border of present-day Burundi and the Democratic Republic of the Congo.

[9] Ranking representative of Leopold's government. [ED.]

the Arabs here, and they seem to feel that they are being trifled with. As to the significance of this move Europe and America can judge without any comment from me, especially England.

TWELFTH. The agents of your Majesty's Government have misrepresented the Congo country and the Congo railway. Mr. H. M. Stanley, the man who was your chief agent in setting up your authority in this country, has grossly misrepresented the character of the country. Instead of it being fertile and productive it is sterile and unproductive. The natives can scarcely subsist upon the vegetable life produced in some parts of the country. Nor will this condition of affairs change until the native shall have been taught by the European the dignity, utility and blessing of labour. There is no improvement among the natives, because there is an impassable gulf between them and your Majesty's Government, a gulf which can never be bridged. Henry M. Stanley's name produces a shudder among this simple folk when mentioned; they remember his broken promises, his copious profanity, his hot temper, his heavy blows, his severe and rigorous measures, by which they were mulcted of their lands. His last appearance in the Congo produced a profound sensation among them, when he led 500 Zanzibar soldiers with 300 campfollowers on his way to relieve Emin Pasha.[10] They thought it meant complete subjugation, and they fled in confusion. But the only thing they found in the wake of his march was misery. No white man commanded his rear column, and his troops were allowed to straggle, sicken and die; and their bones were scattered over more than two hundred miles of territory.

Emigration cannot be invited to this country for many years. The trade of the Upper Congo consists only of ivory and rubber. The first is very old and the latter very poor. If the railway were completed now, it would not be able to earn a dividend for ten or twelve years; and as I have carefully inspected the line of the proposed road, I give it as my honest judgment that it cannot be completed for eight years. This is due to the stock-holders; they should be undeceived. I am writing a report on the Congo Railway, and will not present any data in this letter upon that subject.

Conclusions.

Against the deceit, fraud, robberies, arson, murder, slave-raiding, and general policy of cruelty of your Majesty's Government to the natives, stands their record of unexampled patience, long-suffering, and forgiving spirit,

---

[10] See Henry Morton Stanley, From *In Darkest Africa* n. 1 (77–78). [ED.]

which put the boasted civilisation and professed religion of your Majesty's Government to the blush. During thirteen years only one white man has lost his life by the hands of the natives, and only two white men have been killed in the Congo. Major Barttelot was shot by a Zanzibar soldier, and the captain of a Belgian trading-boat was the victim of his own rash and unjust treatment of a native chief.

All the crimes perpetrated in the Congo have been done in *your* name, and *you* must answer at the bar of Public Sentiment for the misgovernment of a people, whose lives and fortunes were entrusted to you by the august Conference of Berlin, 1884 –1885. I now appeal to the Powers which committed this infant State to your Majesty's charge, and to the great States which gave it international being; and whose majestic law you have scorned and trampled upon, to call and create an International Commission to investigate the charges herein preferred in the name of Humanity, Commerce, Constitutional Government, and Christian Civilisation.

I base this appeal upon the terms of Article 36 of Chapter VII of the General Act of the Conference of Berlin, in which that august assembly of Sovereign States reserved to themselves the right "to introduce into it later and by common accord the modifications or ameliorations, the utility of which may be demonstrated experience."

I appeal to the Belgian people and to their Constitutional Government, so proud of its traditions, replete with the song and story of its champions of human liberty, and so jealous of its present position in the sisterhood of European States, to cleanse itself from the imputation of the crimes with which your Majesty's personal State of Congo is polluted.

I appeal to Anti-Slavery Societies in all parts of Christendom, to Philanthropists, Christians, Statesmen, and to the great mass of people everywhere, to call upon the Governments of Europe to hasten the close of the tragedy your Majesty's unlimited Monarchy is enacting in the Congo.

I appeal to our Heavenly Father, whose service is perfect love, in witness of the purity of my motives and the integrity of my aims; and to history and mankind I appeal for the demonstration and vindication of the truthfulness of the charges I have herein briefly outlined.

And all this upon the word of honour of a gentleman, I subscribe myself your Majesty's humble and obedient servant,

GEO. W. WILLIAMS.
Stanley Falls, Central Africa,
July 18th, 1890.

Letter from the King of the Belgians

King Leopold II

The agents of the Congo Free State[1] have in recent times been severely tried. Their ranks have been exposed to cruel and repeated blows of fate. Identifying myself with the unanimous regret felt for such painful losses, I am anxious to pay a token of gratitude to all who have gallantly sacrificed their lives in the performance of their duty. As is the case with all great causes, the one which we serve in the Congo has had many victims. To those upholders of manly traditions and pioneers of progress who survive, I desire to address some words which my heart dictates to me.

The mission which the agents of the State have to accomplish on the Congo is a noble one. They have to continue the development of civilisation in the centre of Equatorial Africa, receiving their inspiration directly from Berlin and Brussels.

Placed face to face with primitive barbarism, grappling with sanguinary customs that date back thousands of years, they are obliged to reduce these gradually. They must accustom the population to general laws, of which the most needful and the most salutary is assuredly that of work.

In such countries, I know, strong authority must be imposed to bring the natives (who have no such inclination) to conform to the usages of civilisation. For that purpose we must be both firm and parental. In a district like the Congo the native population is at the base of the true wealth of the country, and our first object must be to secure its free expansion. Our refined society attaches to human life (and with reason) a value unknown to barbarous communities. When our directing will is implanted among them its aim is to triumph over all obstacles, and results which could not be attained by lengthy speeches may follow philanthropic influence. But if, in view of this desirable spread of civilisation, we count upon the means of action which confer upon us dominion and the sanction of right, it is not less true that our ultimate end is a work of peace. Wars do not necessarily mean the ruin of the regions in which they rage; our agents do not ignore this fact, so from the day when their effective superiority is affirmed, they feel profoundly reluctant to use force. The wretched negroes, however, who are still under the sole sway of their traditions, have that horrible

---

Appendix. *The Land of the Pygmies.* By Guy Burrows. New York: Crowell, 1898. 285–88.

[1] The Congo Free State, or *L'Etat Indépendent du Congo,* with Leopold as sovereign ruler, was created in 1884 as successor to *l'Association Internationale du Congo.* [ED.]

belief that victory is only decisive when the enemy, fallen beneath their blows, is annihilated. The soldiers of the State, who are recruited necessarily from among the natives, do not immediately forsake those sanguinary habits that have been transmitted from generation to generation. The example of the white officer and wholesome military discipline gradually inspire in them a horror of human trophies of which they previously had made their boast. It is in their leaders that they must see living evidence of these higher principles, taught that the exercise of authority is not at all to be confounded with cruelty, but is, indeed, destroyed by it. I am pleased to think that our agents, nearly all of whom are volunteers drawn from the ranks of the Belgian army, have always present in their minds a strong sense of the career of honour in which they are engaged, and are animated with a pure feeling of patriotism; not sparing their own blood, they will the more spare the blood of the natives, who will see in them the all-powerful protectors of their lives and their property, benevolent teachers of whom they have so great a need.

Our only programme, I am anxious to repeat, is the work of material and moral regeneration, and we must do this among a population whose degeneration in its inherited conditions it is difficult to measure. The many horrors and atrocities which disgrace humanity give way little by little before our intervention. Each step forward made by our people must mark an improvement in the condition of the natives. From these territories of infinite extent, nearly all of them vague and uncultivated, where the natives could only procure for themselves a meagre daily subsistence, the experience and understanding, the enterprise and initiative of the European evokes wealth and resources hitherto unsuspected. If he creates needs, he satisfies them to the full. Penetration into virgin lands is accomplished. Communication is established, roads are opened, the soil yields its produce in exchange for the articles we make and import. Legitimate trade and industry spring into vigorous life, and in proportion as economic conditions are improved, goods assume an intrinsic value. Private and public property, the basis of all social development, is defended and respected, instead of being given over to the law that "Might is Right."

This material prosperity obviously consolidates the interests of whites and negroes. Their primitive nature will not resist indefinitely the pressing appeals of Christian culture. Their education, once begun, will proceed apace. It is in its success that I see the consummation of the task undertaken by our people, and so admirably seconded by our priests and missionaries. To establish a direct immediate current of communication with the natives spread over the basin of the Congo has been the most important part of our programme, and this was done by Belgium during fifteen years, without the co-operation of any other State. The network of railways and stations has gradually put an end to the incessant warfare of tribe against tribe, village against village, and thus has brought about a rule of peace.

Geographically determined, the Congo is a state whose boundaries are occupied and guarded, a result nearly unequalled in the history of colonisation, but which is explained by the concentration of all my efforts in one field of action.

The difficulties we have encountered will be greatly reduced with the speedy completion of the railway from Bas Congo[2] to Stanley Falls.

I appeal again to the devotion of which our agents have already given so many proofs. The creation of that fresh means of communication will soon bring forth fruit. It will connect closely the Congo with the mother country, which will prompt Europe (whose eyes follow us) to take a benevolent and generous interest in all our labours, which will convey to our progress a more and more rapid and decisive impetus, and which will soon introduce into the vast region of the Congo all the blessings of Christian civilisation.

I thank our agents for all their efforts, and I reiterate the expression of my royal affection.

LEOPOLD.

---

[2] The Lower Congo. [ED.]

Part Two

―――◆―――

BIOGRAPHICAL CONTEXTS

From The Intimate Enemy

Ashis Nandy

Rudyard Kipling (1865–1936) thought he knew which side of the great divide between imperial Britain and subject India he stood. He was certain that to be ruled by Britain was India's right; to rule India was Britain's duty. He was also certain that, as one with a knowledge of both their cultures, he had the responsibility to define both the right and the duty. But is it the whole story? Or is it the last line of a story which began years ago, in Kipling's childhood in India?

Angus Wilson begins his biography of Kipling by saying that Kipling was "a man who, throughout his life, worshipped and respected . . . children and their imaginings" (1). Kipling's early life provides a clue to the childhood he worshipped and respected. He was not merely born in India; he was brought up in India by Indian servants in an Indian environment. He thought, felt, and dreamt in Hindustani, mainly communicated with Indians, and even looked like an Indian boy.[1] He went to Hindu temples, for he was "below the age of caste," and once, when he visited a farm with his parents, he walked away holding the hand of a farmer, saying to his mother in Hindustani: "Goodbye, this is my brother."

Young Kipling was deeply impressed by the romance, the colour, and the mystery of India. And the country became a permanent part of his idea of an idyllic childhood, associated with his "years of *safe* delight" and his private "garden of Eden before the fall" (Angus Wilson 3). To speak of this memory as the core of his adult self may seem overly psychological, but certainly no other non-Indian writer of English has equalled Kipling's sensitivity to Indian words, to India's flora and fauna, and to the people who inhabit India's 600,000 villages. The Indian peasantry remained for him his beloved children throughout his life.[2]

The Intimate Enemy: Loss and Recovery of Self under Colonialism. Delhi: Oxford UP, 1983. 64–70.

[1] Edmund Wilson 18. [Nandy's note.]

[2] Angus Wilson 4. [Nandy's note.]

As against this affinity to things Indian, there was his close-yet-distant relationship with his Victorian parents. He interacted with them mainly when he was formally—and somewhat ritually—presented to them by the servants. When speaking to his parents, his autobiography states, he "haltingly translated out of the vernacular idiom that one thought and dreamt in" (5). Overtly, his love, respect, and gratitude to his parents, specially his mother, were immense. Yet, at least one biographer has pointed out the gap between "the elevated, almost religious concept" of a mother's place in a son's life, as found in Kipling's stories and verses, and his own relationship with his mother.[3] Mother Alice Kipling was not apparently a woman who encouraged much emotionalism.

Also, it was through his parents that Rudyard was exposed to the most painful experience of his life. After six idyllic years in Bombay, he was sent with his sister to Southsea in England, to one Aunt Rosa for education and "upkeep." Mrs. Rosa Holloway belonged to an English family of declining fortunes, and with her husband, a retired army officer, she kept boarders. On the surface everything went smoothly. Some visitors found Mrs. Holloway a loving guardian to Rudyard and she did relate well with his sister. But it transpired after Kipling's death that his years at Southsea had been a torture. His posthumous autobiography describes Mrs. Holloway's establishment as a "House of Desolation," characterized by restrictions, bullying, persecution, and some sadism. The malefactors included both Aunt Rosa and her young son.

It must have been a lonely, hateful world for someone brought up in close proximity to nature, in a free yet capsulating world, peopled by kindly, warm, non-parental figures. To Mrs. Holloway, on the other hand, Rudyard was a stranger. Sold to the Victorian and Calvinist concept of a sinful childhood that had to be chastened, she must have found the strong-willed, defiant, uninhibited child particularly spoilt, unsaved, and reprobate. Perhaps there was an element of jealousy, too. At least one chronicler suggests that both Mrs. Holloway and her bully of a son might have sensed that the arrogant deceitful little boy had spent his time in a world quite beyond their dreary horizon.[4]

To young Rudyard, the ill-treatment at Southsea was a great betrayal by his parents. To requote a passage by his sister made famous by Edmund Wilson in the 1940s:

> Looking back, I think the real tragedy of our early days, apart from Aunty's bad temper and unkindness to my brother, sprang from our in-

---

[3] Angus Wilson 11. [Nandy's note.]
[4] Angus Wilson 32. [Nandy's note.]

ability to understand why our parents had deserted us. We had had no preparation or explanation; it was like a double death or rather, like an avalanche that had swept away everything happy and familiar . . . We felt that we had been deserted, "almost as much as on a doorstep". . . . There was no getting out of that, as we often said (Fleming 171).[5]

Some have argued that such banishment to England was normal in those times and must be considered well-motivated. Anglo-Indian parents did live with the fear of servants spoiling their children, introducing them to heathenism, and encouraging in them sexual precocity. Also, Alice Kipling's third baby had died and she was anxious about her surviving children. But the issue is not whether Rudyard was justified in feeling what he felt about his parents, but whether he actually harboured such feelings. His sister was the only person to know, and her evidence in this respect is conclusive. The other, and more serious evidence is the fact that he finally had at Southsea a "severe nervous breakdown," made more horrible by partial blindness and hallucinations (Edmund Wilson 20).

At last, Rudyard was taken away from Southsea and put in a public school which catered for children of families of a military background, mainly children planning to enter the navy. The school emphasized the military and masculine virtues. Ragging was common, the cultural compulsion to enter sports enormous. But Rudyard was a sedentary, artistically-minded child who hated sports, partly because of his dangerously weak eyesight and partly because he was already sure that he wanted to live a life of the mind. In addition, Kipling looked noticeably a non-white (at least some Indians have observed that Kipling had a tan which could not be explained away as a result of the Indian sun). The result was more misery. If his parents showed him the other side of English affection and Mrs. Holloway the other face of English authority, the bullying and ostracism he suffered as an alien-looking "effeminate" schoolboy gave him another view of the English subculture that produced the ruling élites for the colonies.

In sum, reared in the company of doting Indian servants who desanitized the Victorian though non-Calvinist and non-church-going Kipling family, young Rudyard found England a harrowing experience. It was a culture he could admire—the admiration was also a product of his socialization—but not love. He remained in England a conspicuous bicultural sahib, the English counterpart of the type he was to later despise: the bicultural Indian babu.[6] Others sensed this marginality and the resulting

---

[5] Quoted in Edmund Wilson 20. [Nandy's note.]

[6] *Sahib* is a respectful term for a white man in India; a babu is a native clerk who can write English. [ED.]

social awkwardness, and this further distanced him from English society in England and subsequently in India. His writings were to reflect this remoteness later, and he never could write about England as captivatingly as about India.[7]

Yet, his oppressive English years inevitably gave Kipling the message that England was a part of his true self, that he would have to disown his Indianness and learn not to identify with the victims, and that the victimhood he had known in England could be avoided, perhaps even glorified, through identification with the aggressors, especially through loyalty to the aggressors' values.

Kipling himself had been effeminate, weak, individualistic, rebellious, and unwilling to see the meaning of life only in work or useful activity (he was bad at figures in his school at Southsea and could not read till he was six). These were exactly the faults he later bitterly attacked in Westernized Indians. Almost self-depreciatingly, he idealized the herd and the pack and the kind of morality which would hold such a collectivity together. He never guessed that it was a short step from the Westernized Indian to the Indianized Westerner and he never realized that the marginality he scorned in the pro-Indian intellectuals and the anti-colonial liberals was actually his own.

What were the links between the two Kiplings: between the hero loyal to Western civilization and the Indianized Westerner who hated the West within him, between the hero who interfaced cultures and the anti-hero who despised cultural hybrids and bemoaned the unclear sense of self in him?

It was blind violence and a hunger for revenge. Kipling was always ready to justify violence as long as it was counter-violence. Edmund Wilson points out, with a touch of contempt, that much of Kipling's work is remarkably free of any real defiance of authority and any sympathy for the victims.[8] Actually there is more to it. Kipling distinguished between the victim who fights well and pays back the tormentor in his own coin and the victim who is passive-aggressive, effeminate, and fights back through non-cooperation, shirking, irresponsibility, malingering, and refusal to value face-to-face fights. The first was the "ideal victim" Kipling wished to be, the second was the victim's life young Kipling lived and hated living. If he did not have any compassion for the victims of the world, he did not have any compassion for a part of himself either.

But Kipling's literary sensitivities did not entirely fail him even in this sphere. He knew it was not a difference between violence and nonvio-

---

[7] On this point, see Rao 23–24. [Nandy's note.]
[8] See Edmund Wilson. [Nandy's note.]

lence, but between two kinds of violence. The first was the violence that was direct, open, and tinged with legitimacy and authority. It was the violence of self-confident cultural groups, used to facing violent situations with overwhelming advantages. The second was the violence of the weak and the dominated, used to facing violence with overwhelming disadvantages. There is in this second violence a touch of non-targeted rage as well as of desperation, fatalism, and, as the winners or masters of the world would have it, cowardliness. This violence is often a fantasy rather than an intervention in the real world, a response to the first kind of violence rather than a cause or justification for it.

In Kipling's life, the first kind of violence happened to be the prerogative of the British rulers in India; the second that of Indians subjugated in India. Kipling correctly sensed that the glorification of the victor's violence was the basis of the doctrine of social evolution and ultimately colonialism, that one could not give up the violence without giving up the concept of colonialism as an instrument of progress.

The cost of this moral blindness was enormous. The centrepiece of Kipling's life was a refusal to look within, an aggressive "anti-intraception" which forced him to avoid all deep conflicts, and prevented him from separating human problems from ethnic stereotypes. Remarkably extraversive, his work stressed all forms of collectivity, and saw the bonds of race and blood as more important than person-to-person relationships. As if their author, he hoped that the restlessness and occasional depression that had dogged him since the Southsea days could be driven off-scent by the extraversive search for cultural roots, through the service he was rendering to the imperial authority. He lived and died fighting his other self—a softer, more creative and happier self—and the uncertainty and self-hatred associated with it.

Simultaneously, the only India he was willing to respect was the one linked to her martial past and subcultures, the India which was a Dionysian counterplayer as well as an ally of the West. Probably, at another plane, like Nirad C. Chaudhuri and V. S. Naipaul after him, Kipling too lived his life searching for an India which, in its hard masculine valour, would be an equal competitor or opponent of the West that had humiliated, disowned, and despised his authentic self.

Some critics have spoken of the two voices of Kipling. One, it seems, has even named the voices the saxophone and the oboe. The saxophone was, one suspects, Kipling's martial, violent, self-righteous self which rejected pacifism and glorified soldiery, went through spells of depression, was fascinated by the grotesque and the macabre, and lived with an abiding fear of madness and death. The oboe was Kipling's Indianness and his awe for the culture and the mind of India, his bewilderment at India's heterogeneity and complexity, her incoherence and "ancient mystery," her resistance to the mechanization of work as well as man, and ultimately her androgyny. The antonyms were masculine hardness and imperial responsibility on the one hand, and feminine softness and cross-cultural empathy, on the other. The saxophone won out, but the oboe continued to play outside Kipling's earshot, trying to keep alive a subjugated strain of his civilization in the perceived weakness of another.

From A Letter to Margaret Burne-Jones

Rudyard Kipling

In the wealth of your letter I am bewildered. At which end shall I attack those six Baronial sheets and the twelve Knightly ones in a strange script? Shall I say that I agree with you about the manners of the Young Man of the present day? I will. He is a lazy, ill mannered beast *but* he is better out here than with you. Reason why. We put a higher value on our women folk 'cause they be scarcer and I fancy are a trifle more deferential to them than in England. We may speak to them or ride with them smoking *but,* the man who did not bestir himself to do everything he could for a woman travelling — yea even to giving up his seat in the mail cart to a soldier's wife, and taking her ticket etc. for her, would, an his friends knew of his conduct, be sat upon, in our particularly frank and brutal manner. 'Give you another instance. Man whom I knew and who had been out here for seven years went home the other day for three months. Average sort of a man. Holding forth in the Club on his return he said: "'Tell you what upset me. Having white women to wait at table. 'Made an ass of myself again and again by jumping up when the servant girl brought round the dinner. When I dined at hotels I always waited on myself. 'Can't stand an Englishwoman doing what's properly khitmagah's[1] work." And, would you believe it, we said with one voice: "Quite right." Your system of men being waited upon by women would strike me very queerly if I came back and so it would any man who had been out here long. No, I think we are, in many ways more courteous to our women kind than our brethren in the west; tho' the Lord he knoweth how little that is.

From *The Letters of Rudyard Kipling.* Ed. Thomas Pinney. Vol. 1. Iowa City: U Iowa P, 1990. 96–101.

[1] Waiter's (usually "khitmatgar"). [Pinney's note.]

On the second count We the young men of India stand wholly absolved. The "neat ease of mockery and disrespect" with which your young friends hide their "nobler natures" — the young imps — and the want of seriousness doesn't exist here *except* among a few army men and boys fresh from [*sic*] India. The diseased vanity which leads to this sort of moral prevarication is born in a large measure from idleness and (of course) youth. It's like distemper in pups and the best cure is making 'em work all they know. With us that particular form of cant does not exist. Everyone of us, from the youngest, has to be dealing with men and things — not sitting down and curling his downy upper lip in scorn at their ways — but actually going down into the thick of the business and working. It knocks that special sort of lunacy on the head *jut put*.[2] We don't cultivate it; priding ourselves rather on our "Earnestness" — which in English means an infinite capacity for boreing the other man with details of your own work *or* driving the government wild with appeals for more money for your district. A man who tried the "nothing new nothing true, don't matter a d——n business" would be simply laughed at for a fool. There's so much true; so much new; and the *mattering* is a question of life and death sometimes. You may tell 'em with my love that there is a God. You see him work out here which in your fenced in, railway ticket, kind of life at home you can't well do.

Better still send some of the boys out here to catch murderers; or run canals; or make railways. It would tan 'em and clean their rotten little brains a little. My faith! How angry have I grown over naught. Let me turn to the second part of your letter with its enquiries about "natives."

When you write "native" who do you mean? The Mahommedan who hates the Hindu; the Hindu who hates the Mahommedan; the Sikh who loathes both; or the semi-anglicized product of our Indian colleges who is hated and despised by Sikh, Hindu, and Mahommedan. Do you mean the Punjabi who will have nothing to do with the Bengali; the Mahrattha to whom the Punjabi's tongue is as incomprehensible as Russian to me; the Parsee who controls the whole trade of Bombay and ranges himself on all questions as an Englishman; the Sindee who is an outsider; the Bhil or the Gond who is an aborigine; The Rajput who despises everything on God's earth but himself; the Delhi traders who control trade to the value of millions; the Afghan who is only kept from looting these same merchants by dread of English interference. Which one of all the thousand conflicting tongues, races, nationalities and peoples between the Khaibar Pass and Ceylon do you mean? There is no such thing as the natives of India, any

---

[2]Immediately. [Pinney's note.]

more than there is the "People of India" as our friends the Indian delegates would have you believe. You may rest assured Wop[3] that if we didn't hold the land in six months it would be one big cock pit of conflicting princelets. Now "do the English as a rule feel the welfare of the natives much at heart." Oh Wop! If you had met some of the men I know you would cross out the sentence and weep. What else are we working in the country for. For what else do the best men of the Commission[4] die from overwork, and disease, if not to keep the people alive in the first place and healthy in the second. We spend our best men on the country like water and if ever a foreign country was made better through "the blood of the martyrs" India is that country. I couldn't now tell you what the men one knows are doing but you can read for yourself if you will how Englishmen have laboured and died for the peoples of the country. Wop dear have you ever heard of a "demoralized district"; when tens of thousands of peoples are panic stricken say, with an invasion of cholera—or dying from famine? Do you know how Englishmen, Oxford men expensively educated, are turned off to "do" that district—to make their own arrangements for the cholera camps; for the prevention of disorder; or for for [sic] famine relief, to pull the business through or die—whichever God wills. Then another man, or may be boy takes his place. Yes the English in India do do a little for the benefit of the natives and small thanks they get.

(Wednesday: Mein Gott Himmelsneeskenherrenheddof! *What* a gorgeous cold I've started, cultivated and overcome since I last wrote. 'Made me miss the mail too while Trixie[5] sent off an apoplectic envelope of twaddle. She's a bad girl is Trixie. Don't you have nothing to do with her. She makes me hand over all your letters to me and won't let me have a glimpse at your letters to her. Stay! Where was I? 'Um—yes, as Jingle[6] would say. 'Cold fever, Cataplasm. 'Sister sitting on bed, slapping hot plaster on throat askin' if it stung. Throat like superannuated organ pipe—Jus' so. Camphor, Rubinis and balsam of quinine—no balsam aniseed and Rubini's quinine—no Coleman's pectoral quinine and rubini's plaster of aniseed— I give it up. Ta-ta. 'See you again presently.)

But to return to our cousins I have endeavoured to put forward feebly the fact that the English have the welfare of the natives at heart. One year out here would show you how much truth I have *not* written. Then you de-

---

[3]Affectionate nickname for his cousin Margaret, who was the daughter of the painter Edward Burne-Jones. [ED.]

[4]The Indian Civil Service. [ED.]

[5]Kipling's younger sister, Alice. [ED.]

[6]In Charles Dickens, *The Pickwick Papers*. [Pinney's note.]

mand: Have we any interests in common? *Werry* few dear old Wop—the bulk of us—d——d few. And 'faith if you knew in what inconceivable filth of mind the peoples of India were brought up from their cradle; if you realized the views—or one tenth of the views—they hold about women and their absolute incapacity for speaking the truth as we understand it—the immeasurable gulf that lies between the two races in all things you would see how it comes to pass that the Englishman is prone to despise the natives—(I *must* use that misleading term for brevity's sake)—and how, except in the matter of trade, to have little or nothing in common with him. Now this is a wholly wrong attitude of mind but it's one that a Briton who washes, and don't take bribes, and who thinks of other things besides intrigue and seduction most naturally falls into. *When he does*—goodbye to his chances of attempting to understand the people of the land. (It's rather a Pott and Slurkian[7] thing to do but I send you herewith my "East and West"[8] an almost verbatim repro. of my confab with an Afghan gentleman (who by the way is an old friend of mine) on my way up from Rajputana the other day.[9] It may bear on what we are talking about.) Underneath our excellent administrative system; under the piles of reports and statistics; the thousands of troops; the doctors; and the civilian runs wholly untouched and unaffected the life of the peoples of the land—a life as full of impossibilities and wonders as the Arabian nights. I don't want to gush over it but I do want you to understand Wop dear that, immediately outside of our own English life, is the dark and crooked and fantastic, and wicked, and awe inspiring life of the "native." Our rule, so long as no one steals too flagrantly or murders too openly, affects it in no way whatever—only fences it around and prevents it from being disturbed. I have done my little best to penetrate into it and have put the little I have learnt into the pages of "Mother Maturin"[10]—Heaven send that she may grow into a full blown novel before I die—My experiences of course are only a queer jumble of opium-dens, night houses, night strolls with natives; evenings spent in their company in their own homes (in the men's quarter of course) and the long yarns that my native friends spin me, and one or two queer things I've come across in my own office experience. The result of it all has been to interest me immensely and keenly in the people and to show me how little an Englishman can hope to understand 'em. I would that you could see some

---

[7] The rival editors in the Eatanswill election, in *The Pickwick Papers*. [Pinney's note.]

[8] *The Civil and Military Gazette,* 14 November 1885 (uncollected). [Pinney's note.]

[9] Where Kipling had been on 7 November to report the Viceroy's opening of Mayo College. [Pinney's note.]

[10] An unfinished novel. [ED.]

of the chapters of Mother Maturin and you would follow more plainly what I mean. But this is a digression. Again you want to know whether the natives feel "affectionately" towards Europeans. No, they don't take to a European 'cos he *is* a European—but when they take to a man because they like him their attachment is rather striking. In this country every thing is done by personal influence—the personal influence of the Englishman. Only our government doesn't recognize the fact and goes centralizing and centralizing at Simla[11] until the District officers—the little kings of the counties—are reduced simply to machines for compiling statistics and lose touch with the people. A man who has the confidence of the natives can do *anything*, whether he is Civilian or Unofficial. Let me give two humble examples. The Mahommedans in the city know my Pater[12] and almost worship him in many ways, for things he's done—'specially for his kindness towards poor Mahommedans (frankly both he and I prefer Mussalmans to Hindus; they're a better lot roughly speaking). Pater is collecting exhibits for the Indo Colonial Exhibition[13] and can get through about twice as much work as other men simply because he knows the people, they know him and he handles 'em properly. Beyond a certain point however they refuse to go. They won't send valuables for exhibit across the black water *unless* they know my Pater goes with 'em. If he did they'd send *lakhs*[14] worth on his simple assurance that they would be returned uninjured. But the Pater can't go and to his assurances that everything will be safe in the hands of the other Sahibs[15] they simply reply: "Ah! but what do those Sahibs know about us or we about them. Go you yourself Sahib and you can take anything you like." Pater can't go: so much the worse therefore for the Exhibition as far as the Punjab is concerned. They (the peoples of this country) are by birth and training suspicious but if you get their confidence they'll do anything. With a few exceptions all the Englishmen who have to deal with 'em get their confidence and to do that they have to be handled like children or young horses. Another small very small instance. My own men, about 170 altogether, have rather a belief in me—primarily because I am my father's son (and in this country everyone is the son of some father—and writes his father's name down when he writes his own)

---

[11] Seat of the viceroy of India's government during the hot season. [ED.]

[12] Kipling's father, John Lockwood Kipling, who served as an instructor in craft and design and as a museum curator. [ED.]

[13] A Punjab exhibition held in 1886. [ED.]

[14] A term meaning literally 100,000 (as in rupees), often used to signify an indefinitely large sum. [ED.]

[15] A term of respect for white men in India. [ED.]

and nextly because I've laid myself out to try and understand 'em. The last
three years have just shown me how hopeless and how interesting the task
is, but also how my *wish — not* my order — can make the whole gang buckle
to and work double tides or overtime for nothing so long as they understand it was for the Chota Sahib.[16] And yet, if these men weren't paid for an
extra half hour's work, under ordinary circumstances, they'd *cry* like children. A queer people indeed. Touchy as children; obstinate as men; patient
as the High God's themselves; vicious as Devils but always loveable if you
know how to take 'em. And so far as I know, the proper way to handle 'em
is not by looking on 'em "as excitable masses of barbarism" (I speak for the
Punjab only) or the "down trodden millions of Ind groaning under the
heel of an alien and unsympathetic despotism," but as men with a language
of their own which it is your business to understand; and proverbs, which
it is your business to quote (this is a land of proverbs) and bywords and
allusions which it is your business to master; and feelings which it is your
business to enter into and sympathize with. Then they'll believe in you and
do things for you, and let you do things for them. *But* (and here you will
think me wrong perhaps) never lose sight of the fact that so long as you are
in this country you will be looked to by the natives round in [*sic*] you as
their guide and leader if anything happens. Therefore comport yourself as
such. This is a solemn fact. If anything goes wrong from a quarrel to an accident the natives *instantly* fly to a European for "orders." If a man's dying
in the road they won't touch him unless they have an Englishman to order
'em. If there's a row in the city the native policeman will take his orders
from the first wandering white man he sees and so on *ad infinitum*. This is
only the sober truth. They will go to their own District officer first and if
they can't get him to the nearest Englishman. I had almost forgotten another instance of "confidence." The financial management of the funds of
the "Durbar Sahib" — the big temple at Amritsar which is the centre of the
Sikh religion was till recently "bossed" by an Englishman on the urgent request of the Sikhs' priests. Now I believe they have a native treasurer but
that Englishman is always called in if there's any hitch. It comes to this
then — The natives aren't "affectionate" to Englishmen *qua* Englishmen but
they have a belief that they can be trusted implicitly to speak truth and
keep accounts straight — all of 'em. When they believe in any particular
Englishman affection is a mild word for their feelings. They worship him
almost. At the same time they'd perjure their immortal souls to cheat him
to the extent of d/1/2[17] English money. You can reconcile these manifold

---

[16] "Little lord," i.e., Kipling junior. [Pinney's note.]
[17] Halfpence. [ED.]

contradictions Wop as you please. But they are all pretty near the truth. Have I answered your questions at sufficient length think you? [. . .]

From A Letter to Sidney Colvin

Robert Louis Stevenson

Sidney Colvin was one of Stevenson's closest friends, and his most influential literary adviser and editor. Speaking for many of Stevenson's friends living in England, Colvin sometimes rebuked him for writing so frequently about "your beloved blacks — or chocolates — confound them; beloved no doubt to you; to us detested, as shutting out your thoughts, or so it often seems, from the main currents of human affairs . . . please let us have a letter or two with something besides native politics, prisons, *kava* feasts, and such things as our Cockney stomachs can ill assimilate" (Stevenson, *Letters* 1994–95: 8: 279n.).

---

28 September [1891]

My dear Colvin, Since I last laid down my pen I have written and re-written "The Beach of Falesá": something like sixty thousand words of sterling domestic fiction; (the story you will understand is only half that length); and now I don't want to write any more again for ever, or feel so; and I've got to overhaul it once again to my sorrow; I was all yesterday revising and found a lot of slacknesses and (what is worse in this kind of thing) some literaryisms. One of the puzzles is this: it is a first person story: a trader telling his own adventure in an island; when I began I allowed myself a few liberties, because I was afraid of the end; now the end proved quite easy and could be done in the pace; so the beginning remains about a quarter tone out (in places); but I have rather decided to let it stay so. The problem is always delicate; it is the only thing that worries me in first person tales, which otherwise (quo' Alan)[1] "set better wi' my genius."[2] There is a vast deal of

---

From *The Letters of Robert Louis Stevenson*. Ed. Bradford A. Booth and Ernest Mehew. Vol. 7. New Haven: Yale UP, 1994–95. 161–63. 8 vols.

[1] Alan Breck, one of the heroes of Stevenson's Scottish novels, featured particularly in *Kidnapped*. [ED.]

[2] See *Kidnapped*, ch. 9: "It doesn't set my genius." [Booth and Mehew's note.]

fact in the story, and some pretty good comedy. It is the first realistic South
Sea story; I mean with real South Sea character and details of life; everybody else who has tried, that I have seen, got carried away by the romance
and ended in a kind of sugar candy sham epic, and the whole effect was
lost—there was no etching, no human grin, consequently no conviction.
Now I have got the smell and look of the thing a good deal. You will know
more about the South Seas after you have read my little tale, than if you had
read a library. As to whether anyone else will read it, I have no guess. I am
in an off time; but there is just the possibility it might make a hit; for the
yarn is good and melodramatic, and there is quite a love affair—for me;
and Mr Wiltshire (the narrator) ia a huge lark, though I say it. But there is
always the exotic question;[3] and everything, the life, the place, the dialects—
traders' talk, which is a strange conglomerate of literary expressions and
English and American slang, and Beach de Mar, or native English[4]—the
very trades and hopes and fears of the characters, are all novel and may be
found unwelcome to that great, hulking, bullering whale, the public.

Since I wrote, I have been likewise drawing up a document to send in to
the President;[5] it has been dreadfully delayed, not by me, but today they
swear it will be sent in. A list of questions about the dynamite report[6] are
herein laid before him, and considerations suggested why he should answer.

5 [6] October

Ever since my last scratch I have been much chivvied about over the President business; his answer has come and is an evasion accompanied with a
schoolboy insolence, and we are going to try to answer it. I drew my answer and took it down yesterday, but one of the signatories wants another
paragraph added, which I have not yet been able to draw and as to the wisdom of which I am not yet convinced. Been off about two hours about the
clause, and a worse business. The little cutting you sent me was *not* written

---

[3] The long tradition in European writing of exoticizing South Seas subjects. [ED.]
[4] South Seas pidgin, more commonly rendered as "Beach-la-Mar." [ED.]
[5] The president of the European government in Samoa, who was appointed from among
the three consuls representing Germany, the United States, and Britain. At this time, the
president was a representative of Germany, Baron Arnold Senfft von Pilsach. Stevenson
was involved in preparing a petition to be sent to Senfft von Pilsach on behalf of many
of the white plantation owners in Samoa. [ED.]
[6] Samoan prisoners taken during a political disturbance in 1891 were jailed in the central
town, Apia, on the main island of Upolu. A rumor had been circulated—most probably
by Senfft von Pilsach's government—that the jail had been mined and that it would be
blown up if natives attempted to liberate the prisoners. [ED.]

by Fanny; it is a fabrication; what is worse we have just received it in another form, in which she is made to calumniate the captain of the German warship,[7] one of our chief friends. I have just forwarded it to him, with the proper offer to contradict. And he was trumps about it.

Next day 7 October, the right day

[. . .] We are all in rather a muddled state with our President affair. I do loathe politics; but at the same time, I cannot stand by and have the natives blown in the air treacherously with dynamite. They are still quiet; how long this may continue I do not know, though of course by mere prescription the Government is strengthened, and is probably insured till the next taxes fall due. But the unpopularity of the whites is growing. My native overseer, the great Henry Simelē, announced today that he was "weary of whites upon the beach. All too proud," said this veracious witness. One of the proud ones had threatened yesterday to cut off his head with a bush knife! There are "native outrages":[8] honour bright, and setting theft aside, in which the natives are active, this is the main stream of irritation. The natives are generally courtly, far from always civil; but really gentle and with a strong sense of honour of their own, and certainly quite as much civilised as our dynamiting President.

We shall be delighted to see Kipling.[9] [. . .]

13 October

How am I to describe my life these last few days? I have been wholly swallowed up in politics; a wretched business, with fine elements of farce in it too, which repay a man in passing, involving many dark and many moonlight rides, secret councils which are at once divulged, sealed letters which are read aloud in confidence to the neighbours, and a mass of fudge and fun, which would have driven me crazy ten years ago and now makes me smile.

---

[7]Captain Foss of the German warship *Sperber*, which arrived in Apia on 6 June and stayed on because of the political situation. [Booth and Mehew's note.]

[8]Native Samoans had committed atrocities during the recent insurrection. Stevenson was most incensed about the Samoan custom of cutting off the heads of enemies slain in combat. [ED.]

[9]Kipling, who was in Australia and New Zealand in 1891, had announced before leaving England that he intended to visit Stevenson. In his autobiography, *Something of Myself*, Kipling says that when he was in Auckland "the captain of the fruit-boat, which might or might not go to Samoa at some time or another, was so devotedly drunk" that he abandoned the idea and went to India. [Booth and Mehew's note.]

On Friday, Henry came and told us he must leave and go to "my poor
old family in Savaii":[10] why? I do not quite know—but I suspect to be tattooed—if so then probably to be married and we shall see him no more. I
told him he must do what he thought his duty. We had him to lunch, drank
his health, and he and I rode down about twelve. When I got down, I sent
my horse back to help bring down the family later. My own afternoon was
cut out for me; my last draft for the President had been objected to by some
of the signatories—not enough "hell-hound" and "atheist."— I stood out,
and one of our small number accordingly refused to sign. Him I had to go
and persuade, which went off very well after the first hottish moments; you
have no idea how stolid my temper is now. By about five the thing was
done; and we sat down to dinner at the Chinaman's[11]—the Verrey or
Doyen's[12] of Apai—Gurr[13] and I, at each end, as hosts: Gurr's wife—Fanua,
late maid of the village—her (adopted) father and mother, Seumanu and
Faitulia, Fanny, Bell, Lloyd, Joe, Austin,[14] and Henry Simelē, his last appearance. Henry was in a kilt of gray shawl, with a blue jacket, white shirt
and black neck tie, and looked like a dark genteel guest in a Highland
shooting box. Seumanu (opposite Fanny, next Gurr) is chief of Apia, a
rather big gun in this place, looking like a large, fatted military Englishman,
bar the colour. Faitulia, next me, is a bigger chief than her husband. Henry
is a chief too—his chief name, Iiga (Ee-eeng-a) he has not yet "taken" because of youth. We were in fine society, and had a pleasant meal time with
lots of fun. Then to the Opera—I beg your pardon, I mean the Circus. We
occupied the first row in the reserved seats, and there in the row behind
were all our friends—Captain Foss and his Captain-Lieutenant, three of
the American officers—very nice fellows, the doctor, etc.—so we made a
fine show of what an embittered correspondent of the local paper called
"the shoddy aristocracy of Apia"; and you should have seen how we carried
on, and how I clapped, and Captain Foss hollered "*wunderschön!*" and
threw himself forward in his seat, and how we all in fact enjoyed ourselves
like schoolchildren, Austin not a shade more than his neighbours. Then the
circus broke up and the party went home, but I stayed down, having business on the morrow.

---

[10] Hawaii. [Ed.]

[11] A small Chinese restaurant run out of a shanty in Apia. [Ed.]

[12] Verry's, a famous French restaurant in Regent Street, London. Ledoyen was in the Avenue des Champs Elysées, in Paris. [Booth and Mehew's note.]

[13] Edwin William Gurr, a fellow estate owner. [Ed.]

[14] Fanny Stevenson was Stevenson's wife; Belle Strong (Stevenson sometimes dropped
the final *e*) was Fanny's daughter and Lloyd Osbourne her son, both by a previous marriage; Joe Strong was Belle's husband, and Austin their son. [Ed.]

The next days were very largely passed trying to make up my mind how to write to *The Times*.[15] It is now done, true enough, not false I mean—but quite un*true;* not telling for instance how this mild, wild little creature[16] is as civil as a trick terrier, painfully eager to please—and came here (the poor soul) on his wedding jaunt with a pretty little wife no bigger than himself; and how there is no fault to find with him but mere folly, and the dynamite was no doubt never intended to be used, and the man is too dull to see what harm his threat could do, but thought it bold and cunning, the poor soul! Such a difference between politics and history, between a letter to *The Times* and a chapter I shall write some day if I am spared, and make this little history-in-a-teapot living. [. . .]

Robert Louis Stevenson and Samoan History: Crossing the Roman Wall

Roslyn Jolly

Robert Louis Stevenson travelled to the Pacific for health reasons in 1888 and lived there until his death in 1894. During this period he observed the expansion of European and American interests in the region as they solidified from trading and missionary links into direct forms of political control. He settled in Samoa in 1890, becoming deeply involved in local anti-imperialist politics and in the conflicts between colonising powers. In 1892 he published *A Footnote to History: Eight Years of Trouble in Samoa*, an account of the current crisis in relations between Samoa and the three powers—Germany, Britain, and the United States—which were competing to establish spheres of influence there.

Stevenson saw the European "invasion" (*Footnote to History* 19) of the Pacific as an expansion of the frontiers of Roman civilisation, which he identified with modernity and the west. As his biographer, Graham Balfour, wrote, Rome represented to Stevenson "a whole system of law and empire" (2: 122). The culture of the Pacific region fascinated him because it

---

From *Crossing Cultures: Essays on Literature and Culture of the Asia-Pacific.* Ed. Bruce Bennett, Jeff Doyle, and Satendra Nandan. London: Skoob, 1996. 113–20.

[15] One of Stevenson's indignant open letters to the editor of the *Times* about injustices in Samoa, which was published on 17 November 1891. [ED.]

[16] Senfft von Pilsach. [ED.]

had developed outside that system, and it invited the traveller to step out-side it, too. In his first travel article from the Pacific, Stevenson expressed his sense of liberation at this prospect of difference:

> I was now escaped out of the shadow of the Roman empire, under whose toppling monuments we were all cradled, whose laws and letters are on every hand of us, constraining and preventing. I was now to see what men might be whose fathers had never studied Virgil, had never been conquered by Caesar, and never been ruled by the wisdom of Gaius or Papinian. (*South Seas* 1900: 7)[1]

But as Stevenson soon learned, readers were not always prepared to follow him beyond the bounds of their own culture; musing on the poor recep-tion in England of his Tahitian poem "The Song of Rahéro,"[2] he reasoned that "the average man at home cannot understand antiquity; he is sunk over the ears in Roman civilisation; and a tale like that of *Rahero* falls on his ears inarticulate" (*Letters* 1924: 4: 56–57). This deafness of European read-ers to all that lay outside the modern, "Roman" culture of the West was the greatest problem confronting Stevenson as he set out to tell the story of Samoa, in which, he explained, "the ideas and the manners of the native ac-tors date back before the Roman Empire" (*Footnote to History* 1). Steven-son's Scottish background provided an analogy: the Samoans might be likened, he wrote, to "our tattooed ancestors who drove their chariots on the wrong side of the Roman wall" (1).

Comparisons between Scotland and Polynesia were much on Steven-son's mind when he first entered the Pacific. Both regions had experienced the repression of their indigenous culture under an imperial regime.[3] In both cases, that indigenous culture had developed outside the compass of the Roman Empire, that is, outside certain parameters of Western law and reason; so, for every "savage custom" or "superstitious belief" he encoun-tered in Polynesia, Stevenson could find "in the story of [his] fathers . . . some trait of equal barbarism" (*South Seas* 13). In 1891 Stevenson was hes-itating between writing a history of Scotland and one of Samoa;[4] when he chose the latter, he organised it around the idea that was to have provided

---

[1] Meditation on the Roman Empire and its "toppling monuments" would have been stimulated by the Stevenson party's reading on their first Pacific cruise in 1888. As Stevenson's mother recorded: "We are reading Gibbon's *Decline and Fall,* and are now in the second volume" (M. I. Stevenson 71). In the Gilbert Islands in 1889, Stevenson was still, or again, reading Gibbon; see Stevenson, *South Seas* 1900: 293. [Jolly's note.]

[2] Published in Stevenson, *Ballads.* [Jolly's note.]

[3] See Stevenson, *South Seas* 1900: 11. [Jolly's note.]

[4] Stevenson, *Letters* 1924: 4: 113–14. [Jolly's note.]

the focus for his Scottish history: the theme of "Roman civilisation face to face with our ancient barbaric life and government" (*Letters* 1924: 4: 114). Stevenson's application of the terms "barbarism" and "barbaric" to Scotland as well as Polynesia shows him taking a charged term from nineteenth-century imperialist discourse and returning it to one of its root meanings, denoting life beyond the pale of Roman civilisation. It is this radical sense of the barbaric which is suggested in the opening paragraph of *A Footnote to History*, where the unexpected image of the Samoans "on the wrong side of the Roman wall" (1) invites the reader to step back from and interrogate concepts such as barbarism which are used to differentiate and evaluate cultures. But the symbol of the Roman wall which opens *A Footnote to History* does more than this: it establishes a particular notion of the frontier in Samoa, which affects Stevenson's conception of his subject, the shape of his narrative, and the demands he makes of his readers.

First, the Roman wall signifies the finiteness of a dominant civilisation. Hadrian's Wall, dividing England from Scotland, Romans from barbarians, marked the northern boundary of the Roman Empire. It officially sanctioned the concept of a limit to an imperial culture which had previously repudiated the idea of frontiers; it was an admission that Roman civilisation was not to be co-extensive with the known world.[5] Using the analogy with Hadrian's Wall, Stevenson asks his readers to recognise the limits of Roman civilisation, and therefore the boundedness of their own cultural norms which derived from that civilisation.

Secondly, Hadrian's Wall marks a European frontier, not a New World frontier. The most influential nineteenth-century theorist of the frontier, Frederick Jackson Turner, explains the difference:

> The American frontier is sharply distinguished from the European frontier—a fortified boundary line running through dense populations. The most significant thing about the American frontier is, that it lies at the hither edge of free land (3).

Of course, very rarely was the land beyond the New World frontier "free"; Turner's formulation depended on a blindness to the presence of indigenous cultures which did not practise Western (or as Stevenson would say, "Roman") systems of property ownership. With the discursive erasure of these cultures, the New World frontier came to signify the boundary between culture and nature, energy and vacuum, signification and blankness. Even when the existence of an indigenous people could not be ignored, these oppositions could be sustained by employing two variants of the

---

[5] See Breeze and Dobson 5–29. [Jolly's note.]

"free land" myth: the doctrine of the inevitable extinction of the "lesser" races (the idea that if the land to be colonised is not empty, it soon will be) and the theory of indigenous people's "unfitness to rule," which created for purposes of colonisation the next best thing to physically empty space, a political vacuum. But these oppositions do not structure *A Footnote to History*, because Stevenson does not use the notion of the "New World" frontier on which they rest. Rather, in presenting the collision of imperial-ist and indigenous cultures in Samoa in terms of a "European" frontier— that is, a boundary between two cultures, radically different but equally present—Stevenson rejected the myth of "free land" or *"terra nullius"* which justified so much of European expansion into the non-European world during the eighteenth and nineteenth centuries.[6] This rejection had important consequences, not only for the organisation of space in his map-ping of imperialism, but also for the organisation of time in his narrative of colonial conflict. By declining to view Samoa in terms of "free land," a disappearing population or a political vacuum, he rejected one of the late nineteenth century's most powerful models for explaining the encounter between Europeans and non-Europeans, the Darwinian or Spencerian "scientific" account of imperial history. This evolutionary model was an up-dated version of the earlier "Whig" interpretation of history, which equated commercial progress with the advance of civilisation.

The terms of the imperial history Stevenson declined to write emerge very clearly from the attack on *A Footnote to History* by one of the harshest critics, the Honolulu journalist, Arthur Johnstone. Johnstone argued that given certain factors in play in the Pacific situation—the inherent fitness or unfitness of certain races to rule themselves and others, the inexorable ex-pansive force of commerce—the only possible narrative of Samoan history was an evolutionary narrative with a definite teleology; the "inevitable end" of "the extinction or absorption of the weaker race" by the stronger (89, 141, 162, 166). Because Stevenson does not follow this formula in *A Footnote to History*, Johnstone condemns his method as unscientific and his con-clusions as "historically, impossible" (162). But Stevenson's Samoan his-tory destabilises the key terms on which the Whig or Darwinian history of imperialism rested. For a start, he did not take seriously the notion that some races are inherently superior to others. As he wrote in his first South Sea letter:

> A polite Englishman comes today to the Marquesans and is amazed to
> find the men tattooed; polite Italians came not long ago to England and

---

[6] The doctrine of *"terra nullius"* or "the land belonging to no one" was the particular ver-sion of the free land myth inscribed, until recently, in Australian law. [Jolly's note.]

found our fathers stained with woad; and when I paid the return visit as
a little boy, I was highly diverted with the backwardness of Italy: so insecure, so much a matter of the day and hour, is the preeminence of race.
(*South Seas* 12)

Stevenson's scepticism about racial hierarchies shaped his history in ways
which challenged white prejudices: the "nearest thing to a hero" (*Letters*
1924: 3: 280) in the narrative is the chief Mataafa, who organised the first
successful Samoan resistance to an imperial power; throughout the work
native testimony is weighed against white testimony and sometimes preferred. But, more important than his often favourable presentation of Samoan characters is the effect that Stevenson's rejection of racial hierarchies
has on the trajectory of his narrative. If Europeans and their ways are not
seen as always and inherently superior to Polynesians and their culture, the
story of their political takeover of Samoa cannot be one of (to use Johnstone's terms) "natural evolution" and "the advance of civilisation" (141,
164). Stevenson's rejection of this plot for his history is evident in his turning back of the notion of barbarism against the Europeans. Near the end of
A Footnote to History appear two examples of European barbarity: a plot to
blow up Samoan prisoners, explicitly condemned as "barbarous" (300),
and the European attempts to incite war while the Samoans held out for
peace. In their belligerence, Stevenson writes, "our European rulers have
drawn a picture of themselves, as bearded like the pard, full of strange oaths,
and gesticulating like semaphores" (290); this image from Shakespeare's
As You Like It suggests the loose sense of barbarity as savagery—the white
officials are like violent wild animals, leopards—but also one of the root
meanings of a barbarian as one who does not speak a civilised language but
mouths meaningless sounds; "full of strange oaths, and gesticulating like
semaphores," the white officials are barbarians who cannot be understood
by those, like the Samoans, who speak the civilised language of peace.

   This image of the European rulers of Samoa regressing from civilised
speech into wild, indecipherable gestures and inarticulate sounds is one
example of the motif of regression which recurs throughout Stevenson's
history. Under the threat of war fostered by the German consul, Stevenson
writes,

> The social bond in Apia was dissolved. The consuls, like barons of old,
> dwelt each in his armed citadel. The rank and file of the white national-
> ities dared each other, and sometimes fell to on the street like rival clans-
> men. And the little town . . . had fallen back in civilisation about a thou-
> sand years. (168)

After the hurricane of 1889, which destroyed several warships in Apia harbour, the Germans and Americans saw "their formidable ships reduced to

junk; their disciplined hundreds to a horde of castaways, fed with difficulty, and the fear of whose misconduct marred the sleep of their commanders" (267). Under European government the rule of law collapsed, to be replaced by capricious personal tyrannies. The story of the Europeans' town of Apia becomes the story of its "progressive decivilisation" (172); far from embodying the law of the irresistible "advance of civilisation" which underwrote the Whig or Darwinian view of imperial history. Stevenson's account of the colonisation of Samoa is a narrative of cultural regression. In substituting this plot for the dominant late nineteenth-century plot of imperial history as evolutionary advance, Stevenson was not only reversing a historical model, but also interrogating some key terms of historical discourse in his culture. As the title of the book suggests, *A Footnote to History* disturbs its readers' sense of order and proportion in historical narrative. In offering a "footnote" as a text, Stevenson challenges his readers' sense of what an historical text is, and by what parameters of subject-matter, modes of representation, and models of explanation, it should be constituted.

Stevenson's narrative of European regression in Samoa subverts the logic and teleology of the Darwinian-Whig imperial history; and by removing the authority of the one "inevitable end," he opens up instead a range of new possibilities. If European officials can regress to the state of gibbering barbarians, why should not the tide of European commercial interests be arrested and even turned back? If European culture has shown itself at times to be barbarous, why should not Polynesian culture instead form the basis of a political solution in Samoa? Such questions are only implicit at the end of *A Footnote to History,* which tries to compromise with at least some of the conditions of European involvement in Samoa. Later, though, Stevenson went much further and advocated a solution to the Samoan problem through the full recognition of the autonomy of Samoa's distinct political culture, with the concomitant withdrawal of white political and, if necessary, commercial interests.[7] Technically "barbaric," in that it did not derive from Roman law, the traditional Samoan system of government seemed to Stevenson the only workable basis for the society's future existence.

---

[7] In a letter probably written in 1893 to the Marquess of Ripon, Stevenson advised that attempts to impose on Samoa the European model of a unified nation-state should be abandoned, and the country allowed to revert to local forms of government by multiple authorities (Stevenson, fragment of a letter dictated to Isobel Strong, HM 20533, Huntington Library, San Marino, CA). See also Johnstone 92–93, where Stevenson is quoted as having, in 1893, advocated the absolute withdrawal of the European powers from Samoa, regardless of the effect on commerce or the interests of foreign residents. [Jolly's note.]

In *A Footnote to History* Stevenson did not propose this radical political solution to his readers, but he did constantly ask them to try to conceive of cultural conditions different from their own. And so to the third implication of his opening image of the Roman wall: that, in marking the limit of one civilisation, it marked the beginning of another, the existence of which ought to be acknowledged. Throughout *A Footnote to History* Stevenson asks his readers imaginatively to cross the boundary of Roman civilisation with him, to see life on the other side of the wall. Mataafa, when he went to war with Europeans, sought to educate himself about the European code of warfare. "Let us try to be as wise as Mataafa," Stevenson writes, "and to conceive that etiquette and morals differ in one country and another" (10). When in Rome, the old saying goes, do as the Romans do; by the same token, when you have passed beyond the sphere of Roman civilisation, Stevenson suggests, do not expect the ideas and values of Roman civilisation still to apply. The difficulty of comprehending alien practices is not underestimated; the history contains a running commentary on the problems of crossing from one cultural field to another, as Stevenson tries to make various Samoan customs "thinkable by Europeans" (112). In particular, he asks his readers for "an effort of comprehension" (286) of Mataafa's behaviour in setting himself up as head of a rival "Government of Samoa" (284) to that of the official (that is, puppet) government controlled by the Europeans. To Europeans the action appeared inflammatory, rebellious, inconsistent or pointless; in Mataafa's "Samoan mind," Stevenson attempts to explain, it was "regular and constitutional" (286). It was, in fact, consistent with the "laws and customs of Samoa" which the Europeans, in their administration of Samoan affairs, had pledged to observe. The phrase "laws and customs of Samoa" comes from the Treaty of Berlin (1889) by which Germany, England and America ruled on the future form of government of a country they were simultaneously declaring independent. In *A Footnote to History*, and even more in a later letter to an English M.P., Stevenson singles out this phrase for his especial anger, because it shows the European governments paying lip-service to an idea of cultural difference into which they had no intention of inquiring or even beginning to imagine.[8] The Treaty of Berlin blandly granted the Samoan people the power to "elect" a king "according to the laws and customs of Samoa" (*Final Act*, Article 1). Stevenson argued that such an election had already taken place, although not in terms recognisable to a European. The consequent confusion was, he argued, "the result of taking a word out of one state of society,

---

[8] See Stevenson, *Footnote to History* 286–88; Stevenson, *Letters* 1924: 21: 300–01. [Jolly's note.]

and applying it to another, of which the writers know less than nothing, and no European knows much" (287). In other words, the writers of the Berlin Treaty gestured towards cultural difference while in fact making no effort to leave their own legal and political territory; at the same time they expected the Samoans to cross the frontier into Roman or Western culture, without ever admitting that there was a frontier to be crossed.

The Roman wall at the beginning of Stevenson's Samoan history signals a number of challenges which the work posed to its readers and to then current dominant models of imperial history. First, Stevenson asked his readers to recognise — as the Romans did when they built Hadrian's Wall — a limit to their own culture. Secondly, he did not present that limit as marking the beginning of nothingness, of a space from which culture was absent, of blankness awaiting European inscription (the concept which organised the "New World" frontier and the Darwinian-Whig histories which described its advance); as this essay has argued, the rejection of this notion of the frontier had important implications for the shape and teleology of Stevenson's narrative. Rather than imagining the frontier as the end of all culture, he presented the imperial frontier in Samoa as — like the Roman wall dividing Scots and Romans — a boundary between alternative cultural fields. Finally, he asked his European readers to imagine and understand the conditions of the alternative culture: to cross, imaginatively, the frontier of their own civilisation.

Letter to Marguerite Poradowska

Joseph Conrad

Dearest and best of Aunts![1]

I received your three letters together on my return from Stanley Falls, where I went as a supernumerary on board the vessel *Roi des Belges* in order to learn about the river. I learn with joy of your success at the Academy,[2] which, of course, I never doubted. I cannot find words sufficiently strong

---

From *The Collected Letters of Joseph Conrad*. Ed. Frederick R. Karl and Laurence Davies. Vol. 1. Cambridge: Cambridge UP, 1983. 58–63. 5 vols.

[1] Marguerite Poradowska, who lived in Belgium and had helped arrange Conrad's commission to the Congo as a steamship captain. [ED.]

[2] Her *Demoiselle Micia, moeurs galiciennes,* which had been published in the *Revue des Deux Mondes,* appeared under the Hachette imprint in 1889, and won one of the six French Academy prizes of 500 francs. [Karl and Davies's note.]

to make you understand the pleasure your charming (and above all kind) letters have given me. They were as a ray of sunshine piercing through the grey clouds of a dreary winter day; for my days here are dreary. No use deluding oneself! Decidedly I regret having come here. I even regret it bitterly. With all of a man's egoism, I am going to speak of myself. I cannot stop myself. Before whom can I ease my heart if not before you?! In speaking to you, I am certain of being understood down to the merest hint. Your heart will divine my thoughts more quickly than I can express them.

Everything here is repellent to me. Men and things, but men above all. And I am repellent to them, also. From the manager in Africa who has taken the trouble to tell one and all that I offend him supremely, down to the lowest mechanic, they all have the gift of irritating my nerves — so that I am not as agreeable to them perhaps as I should be. The manager is a common ivory dealer with base instincts who considers himself a merchant although he is only a kind of African shop-keeper. His name is Delcommune.[3] He detests the English, and out here I an naturally regarded as such. I cannot hope for either promotion or salary increases while he is here. Besides, he has said that promises made in Europe carry no weight here if they are not in the contract. Those made to me by M. Wauters are not. In addition, I cannot look forward to anything because I don't have a ship to command.[4] The new boat will not be completed until June of next year, perhaps. Meanwhile, my position here is unclear and I am troubled by that. So there you are! As crowning joy, my health is far from good. *Keep it a secret for me* — but the truth is that in going up the river I suffered from fever four times in two months, and then at the Falls (which is its home territory), I suffered an attack of dysentery lasting five days. I feel somewhat weak physically and not a little demoralized; and then, really, I believe that I feel homesick for the sea, the desire to look again on the level expanse of salt water which has so often lulled me, which has smiled at me so frequently under the sparkling sunshine of a lovely day, which many times too has hurled the threat of death in my face with a swirl of white foam whipped by the wind under the dark December sky. I regret all that. But what I regret even more is having tied myself down for three years. The truth is that it is scarcely probable I shall see them through. Either someone in authority will pick a groundless quarrel in order to send me back

---

[3]Camille Delcommune, first assistant manager of the Société Belge du Haut-Congo, then manager. For a further account of Conrad's relationship with him, see Sherry, *Western World*, and Jean-Aubry 58ff. [Karl and Davies's note.]

[4]The *Florida*, which Conrad had intended to command when he arrived in Kinshasa, was given to a man named Carlier at the urging of Alexandre Delcommune. [Karl and Davies's note.]

(and, really, I sometimes find myself wishing for it), or I shall be sent back to Europe by a new attack of dysentery, unless it consigns me to the other world, which would be a final solution to all my distress! And for four pages I have been speaking of myself! I have not told you with what pleasure I have read your descriptions of men and things at home. Indeed, while reading your dear letters I have forgotten Africa, the Congo, the black savages and the white slaves (of whom I am one) who inhabit it. For one hour I have been happy. Know that it is not a small thing (nor an easy thing) to make a human being happy for an *entire hour*. You can be proud of having succeeded. And so my heart goes out to you with a burst of gratitude and the most sincere and most profound affection. When will we meet again? Alas, meeting leads to parting—and the more one meets, the more painful the separations become. Such is Fate.

Seeking a practical remedy to the disagreeable situation which I have made for myself, I conceived of a little plan—still up in the air—in which you could perhaps help me. It appears that this company, or another affiliated with it, will have some ocean-going vessels (or even has one already). Probably that great (or fat?) banker who rules the roost where we are concerned will have a large interest in the other company. If someone could submit my name for the command of one of their ships (whose home port will be Antwerp) I would be able to get away for a day or two in Brussels when you are there. That would be ideal! If they wanted to call me home to take command, I would naturally pay the cost of coming back myself. This is perhaps not a very practicable idea, but if you return to Brussels in the winter, you could learn through M. Wauters what the chances are. Isn't that so, dear little Aunt?

I am going to send this care of the Princess[5] (whom I love because she loves you). Soon, probably, you will see poor, dear Aunt Gaba, and that dear and good Charles Zagórski family with their charming little daughters. I envy you! Tell them that I love them all and that I ask a little something in return. Mlle Marysieńka has probably forgotten the promise she made me about her photograph. I am ever her devoted cousin and servant. I dare not say "admirer" for fear of my Aunt Oldakowska, to whom I wish to be remembered with affection. I urge you by all the gods to keep secret from *everybody* the state of my health, or else my uncle will certainly hear of it. I must finish. I leave within an hour for Bamou,[6] by canoe, to select trees and have them felled for building operations at the station here. I shall

---

[5] The Belgian Princess Hedwige Lubomirska, with whom Conrad's aunt was on friendly terms. [Ed.]
[6] Thirty miles west of Kinshasa. [Karl and Davies's note.]

remain encamped in the forest for two or three weeks, unless ill. I like the prospect well enough. I can doubtless have a shot or two at some buffaloes or elephants. I embrace you most warmly. I shall write a long letter by the next mail.

Your affectionate nephew
J.C.K.

From The Rings of Saturn

W. G. Sebald

The Rings of Saturn is a thoroughly unconventional, postmodern novel, in which the narrator entwines both literary and nonliterary documents (which are sometimes quoted without attribution) as well as imaginative recreations of "real" scenes that may or may not have actually happened, while also weaving his own consciousness deeply into the texts and persons he describes—so much so that the narrator sometimes seems to merge with the figures about whom he is writing. The resultant dreamlike text cultivates ambiguities of many kinds. Nevertheless, this segment from Chapter 5 is probably the most evocative piece ever written on Conrad's childhood and youth, and their bearing on his voyage up the Congo River in 1890. The selection has been annotated sparsely in order to preserve the enigmatic qualities of Sebald's text, which resonate suggestively against the obscurities of *Heart of Darkness*.

On the second evening of my stay in Southwold,[1] after the late news, the BBC broadcast a documentary about Roger Casement, who was executed in a London prison in 1916 for high treason. The images in this film, many of which were taken from rare archive footage, immediately captivated me; but nonetheless, I fell asleep in the green velvet armchair I had pulled up to the television. As my waking consciousness ebbed away, I could still hear every word of the narrator's account of Casement with singular clarity, but was unable to grasp their meaning. And when I emerged hours later, from

---

The Rings of Saturn. Trans. Michael Hulse. New York: New Directions, 1998. 103–21, 127–31, 134.

[1] Small village in Suffolk, England. [ED.]

the depths of a dream, to see in the first light of dawn the test card quivering in the silent box, all I could recall was that the programme had begun with an account of Casement's meeting with the writer Joseph Conrad in the Congo. Conrad considered Casement the only man of integrity among the Europeans whom he had encountered there, and who had been corrupted partly by the tropical climate and partly by their own rapaciousness and greed. I've seen him start off into an unspeakable wilderness (thus the exact words of a quotation from Conrad, which has remained in my head) swinging a crookhandled stick, with two bulldogs: Paddy (white) and Biddy (brindle) at his heels and a Loanda boy carrying a bundle. A few months afterwards it so happened that I saw him come out again, leaner, a little browner, with his stick, dogs, and Loanda boy, and quietly serene as though he had been for a stroll in the park. Since I had lost the rest of the narrator's account of the lives of Casement and Conrad, except for these few words and some shadowy images of the two men, I have since tried to reconstruct from the sources, as far as I have been able, the story I slept through that night in Southwold.

In the late summer of 1861, Mme. Evelina Korzeniowska travelled from the small Ukrainian town of Zhitomir to Warsaw, with her boy Józef Teodor Konrad, then not quite five, to join her husband Apollo Korzeniowski, who that spring had already given up his unrewarding position as an estate manager with the intention of helping pave the way for a revolt against Russian tyranny through his writings and by means of conspiratorial politics. In mid-October the illegal Polish National Committee met for its first sessions in Korzeniowski's Warsaw flat, and over the next few weeks the young Konrad doubtless saw many mysterious persons coming and going at his parents' home. The serious expressions of the gentlemen talking in muted tones in the white and red salon will have suggested the significance of that historic hour to him and he may even, at that point, have been initiated into the clandestine proceedings, and have understood that Mama wore black, which was expressly forbidden by law, as a token of mourning for her people suffering the humiliation of foreign rule. If not, he was taken into their confidence at the end of October at the latest, when his father was arrested and imprisoned in the citadel. After a cursory hearing before a military tribunal Apollo Korzeniowski was sentenced to exile in Vologda, a god-forsaken town somewhere in the wastes beyond Nizhni Novgorod. Vologda, he wrote in summer 1863 to his Zagórski cousins, is a great three-verst marsh across which logs and tree trunks are placed parallel to each other in crooked lines; the houses, even the garishly painted wooden palaces of the provincial grandees, are erected on piles driven into the morass at intervals. Everything round about rots, decays and sinks into the ground. There are only two seasons: the white winter and the green winter. For nine

months the ice-cold air sweeps down from the Arctic sea. The thermometer plunges to unbelievable depths and one is surrounded by a limitless
darkness. During the green winter it rains week in week out. The mud
creeps over the threshold, rigor mortis is temporarily lifted and a few signs
of life, in the form of an all-pervasive marasmus, begin to manifest themselves. In the white winter everything is dead, during the green winter
everything is dying.

The tuberculosis which had ailed Evelina Korzeniowska for years advanced unimpeded in these conditions. The days that remained to her were
numbered. When the Czarist authorities granted her a compassionate stay
of sentence in order that she might spend a longer spell on her brother's estate in the Ukraine, to recover her health, it was no more than an additional torment; for after the period of reprieve expired she had to return
into exile with Konrad, despite all her petitions and applications and despite the fact that she was now more dead than alive. On the day of her
departure, Evelina Korzeniowska stood on the steps of the manor house at
Nowofastów surrounded by her relations, the servants, and friends from
the neighbouring domains. Everyone there assembled, apart from the children and those in livery, is attired in black cloth or black silk. Not a single
word is spoken. Grandmother stoically stares out past the sad scene into
the deserted countryside. On the sweeping sandy drive that curves around
the circular yew hedge a bizarre, elongated carriage is waiting. The shafts
protrude much too far forward, and the coachman's box seems a long
way from the rear of the strange conveyance, which is overloaded with
trunks and chests of every description. The carriage is slung low between
the wheels as if between two worlds drifting ever further apart. The carriage
door is open, and inside, on the cracked leather seat, young Konrad has
been settled for some time, watching from the dark the scene he will later
describe. Poor Mama, inconsolable, looked around her for the last time,
then descends the steps on the arm of Uncle Tadeusz. Those who remain
behind retain their composure. Even Konrad's favourite cousin, who is
wearing a short skirt of a tartan pattern and resembles a princess amidst the
black-clad gathering, just puts her fingertips to her lips to indicate
her horror at the departure of the two banished exiles. And ungainly Mlle.
Durand from Switzerland, the governess who has devoted herself to Konrad's education all summer with the utmost energy and who would otherwise avail herself of any opportunity to burst into tears, valiantly appeals to
her charge as she waves a farewell handkerchief: N'oublie pas ton français,
mon chéri![2] Uncle Tadeusz closes the carriage door and takes a step back.

---

[2] "Don't forget your French, my dear!" [ED.]

The coach lurches forward. The friends and relatives vanish from Konrad's view through the small window, and when he looks out at the other side he sees, in the distance, halfway down to the great gates, the district police commandant's light, open trap, harnessed to three horses in Russian fashion, drawn up on one side and the commandant himself sitting in it, the vizor of his flat cap with its red band pulled down over his eyes.

In early April 1865, eighteen months after the departure from Nowofastów, Evelina Korzeniowska died in exile aged thirty-two of the shadows that her tuberculosis had spread through her body, and of the homesickness that was corroding her soul. Apollo's will to live was also almost extinguished. He was quite unable now to devote himself to his troubled son's education, and hardly ever pursued his own work at all. The most he could do was to alter the odd line or two in his translation of Victor Hugo's *Les travailleurs de la mer.*[3] That prodigiously boring book seemed to him to mirror his own life. C'est un livre sur des destinées dépaysées, he once said to Konrad, sur des individus expulsés et perdus, sur les éliminés du sort, un livre sur ceux qui sont seuls et évités.[4] In 1867, a few days before Christmas, Apollo Korzeniowski was released from his Russian exile. The authorities had decided that he no longer constituted a threat, and gave him a passport valid for one journey to Madeira, for purposes of convalescence. But neither Apollo's financial position nor his frail state of health allowed him to travel. After a short stay in Lemberg, which he found too Austrian for his liking, he rented a few rooms in Poselska Street in Cracow. There he spent most of the time in his armchair, grieving for his lost wife, for the wasted years, and for his poor and lonely boy, who had just written a patriotic play entitled *The Eyes of Johan Sobieski.* Apollo had burnt all of his own manuscripts in the fireplace. At times, when he did so, a weightless flake of soot ash like a scrap of black silk would drift through the room, borne up on the air, before sinking to the floor somewhere or dissolving into the dark. For Apollo, as for Evelina, the end came in the spring, as it was beginning to thaw, but it was not granted to him to depart this life on the anniversary of her death. He lay in his bed till well into May, becoming steadily weaker and thinner. During those weeks when his father was dying, Konrad would sit at a little table lit by a green lamp in a windowless cabinet to do his homework in the late afternoon after school. The ink stains in his exercise book and on his hands came from the fear in his heart. Whenever the door

---

[3] One of Hugo's most famous novels, published in 1866 and translated into English as *The Toilers of the Sea* in 1867. [ED.]

[4] "It's a book about disordered destinies, about exiled, lost people, about those fated to be ostracized, a book about those who are shunned and alone." [ED.]

of the next room opened he could hear his father's shallow breathing. Two nuns with snow-white wimples were tending the patient. Without a sound they glided hither and thither, performing their duties and occasionally casting a concerned glance at the child who would soon be orphaned, bent over his writing, adding up numbers or reading, hour after hour, voluminous Polish and French adventure stories, novels and travel books.

The funeral of the patriot Apollo Korzeniowski was a great demonstration, conducted in silence. Along the streets, which were closed to traffic, bare-headed workmen, schoolchildren, university students and citizens, who had doffed their top hats, stood in solemn emotion, and at every open upper-storey window there were clusters of people dressed in black. The cortège, led by eleven-year-old Konrad as chief mourner, moved out of the narrow side street, through the centre of the town, past the Church of Mary the Virgin with its two unequal towers, towards Florian's Gate. It was a fine afternoon. The blue sky compassed the rooftops and on high the clouds scudded before the wind like a squadron of sailboats. During the funeral, as the priest in his heavy silver-embroidered vestments was intoning the ritual words for the dead man in the pit, Konrad perhaps raised his eyes and beheld the clouds drifting by, seeing them as he had never done before, and perhaps it was then that the thought occurred to him of becoming a sea captain, an altogether unheard-of notion for the son of a Polish gentleman. Three years later he expressed this wish to his guardian for the first time, and nothing on earth could put it out of his mind thereafter, not even when Uncle Tadeusz sent him to Switzerland for a summer holiday of several weeks with his private tutor, Pulman. The tutor was under instructions to remind his charge at every opportunity of the many careers that were open to him beside seafaring, but no matter what he said (at the Rhine falls near Schaffhausen, in Hospenthal, viewing the St. Gotthard tunnel under construction, or up on the Furka Pass), Konrad stuck tenaciously to his resolve. Scarcely a year later, on the 14th of October 1874, when he was not yet seventeen, he took leave of his grandmother Teofila Bobrowska and his good Uncle Tadeusz, as they stood on the platform at Cracow outside the train window. The ticket to Marseilles in his pocket had cost one hundred and thirty-seven guilders and seventy-five groschen. He took with him no more than would fit into his small case, and it would be almost sixteen years before he returned to visit his native country again.

In 1875 Konrad Korzeniowski crossed the Atlantic for the first time, on the barque *Mont Blanc*. At the end of July he was on Martinique, where the ship lay at anchor for two months. The homeward voyage took almost a quarter of a year. It was not until Christmas Day that the *Mont Blanc*, badly damaged by winter storms, made Le Havre. Undeterred by this tough initiation into life as sea, Konrad Korzeniowski signed on for further voyages to the West Indies, where he visited Cap-Haïtien, Port-au-Prince, St. Thomas and St. Pierre, which was devastated soon afterwards when Mont Pelée erupted. On the outward sailing the ship carried arms, steam-powered engines, gunpowder and ammunition. On the return the cargo was sugar and timber. He spent the time when he was not at sea in Marseilles, among fellow sailors and also with people of greater refinement. At the Café Boudol in the rue Saint-Ferréol and in the salon of Mme. Déléstang, whose husband was a banker and ship owner, he frequented gatherings that included aristocrats, bohemians, financiers, adventurers, and Spanish Legitimists. The dying throes of courtly life went side by side with the most unscrupulous machinations, complex intrigues were connived at, smuggling syndicates were founded, and shady deals agreed. Korzeniowski was involved in many things, spent more than he had, and succumbed to the advances of a mysterious lady who, though just his own age, was already a widow. This lady, whose true identity has not been established with any certainty, was known as Rita in Legitimist circles, where she played a prominent part; and it was said that she had been the mistress of Don Carlos, the Bourbon prince, whom there were plans to instate, by hook or by crook, on the Spanish throne. Subsequently it was rumoured in various quarters that Doña Rita, who resided in a villa in rue Sylvabelle, and one Paula de Somogyi were one and the same person. The story went that in November 1877, when Don Carlos returned to Vienna from inspecting the front line in the Russo-Turkish war, he asked a certain Mme. Hannover to procure for him a Pest chorus girl by the name of Paula Horváth, whose beauty had caught his eye. From Vienna, with his new companion, Don Carlos travelled first to see his brother in Graz and then onward to Venice, Modena and Milan, where he introduced her in society as the Baroness de Somogyi. The rumour that the two mistresses were in reality one person originated in the fact that Rita vanished from Marseilles at the exact moment in time when the Baroness, supposedly because Don Carlos was having a crisis of conscience prompted by the imminent first holy communion of his son Jaime, was either dropped by the Don or married off to the tenor Angel de Trabadelo, with whom she appears to have lived in London in happiness and contentment until her death in 1917. While the matter of whether Rita and Paula were identical must remain unresolved, it is beyond doubt that the young Korzeniowski sought to win the favour of either the one or the other lady, irrespective of whether she had grown up as a goatherd in the highlands of Catalonia or as a goosegirl on the shores of Lake Balaton; just as there is no question that this love story, which in some respects bordered on the fantastic, reached its climax in late February 1877, when Korzeniowski shot himself in the chest, or was shot by a rival. To this day it is unclear whether this wound, which mercifully posed no threat to Korzeniowski's life, was inflicted in a

duel, as he himself later claimed, or, as Uncle Tadeusz suspected, in a suicide attempt. Either way, the dramatic gesture, which the young man, who
saw himself as a Stendhalien, evidently meant to cut the Gordian knot,
took its inspiration from the opera, which at that time determined the social mores and in particular the expressions of love and longing, in Marseilles as in most other European cities. Korzeniowski had seen and heard
the work of Rossini and Meyerbeer at the Théatre de Marseille and, above
all, was enraptured by the operettas of Jacques Offenbach, which were as
much in vogue as ever. A libretto entitled *Konrad Korzeniowski and the
Carlist Conspiracy in Marseilles* could easily have been the making of another of them. In actual fact, however, Korzeniowski's French apprentice
years came to an end when he left Marseilles for Constantinople aboard
the SS *Mavis* on the 24th of April 1878. The Russo-Turkish war was over,
but from the ship, as he later reported, Korzeniowski was still able to see
the army camp at San Stefano, a vast city of white tents, where the peace
treaty had been signed, passing by like a mirage. From Constantinople the
steamer proceeded to Yeysk, at the far end of the Sea of Asov, where it took
on a consignment of linseed oil with which, as the Lowestoft harbour register records, it reached the east coast of England on the 18th of June 1878.

From July until early September, when he left for London, Korzeniowski made three round trips as an ordinary seaman aboard the *Skimmer of
the Seas,* a coaster that plied between Lowestoft and Newcastle. Little is
known of how he spent the second half of June in the fishing port and
bathing resort of Lowestoft, which could not have afforded a greater contrast to Marseilles. Doubtless he rented a room and made whatever enquiries were necessary for his plans. In the evenings, when the darkness
settled upon the sea, he will have strolled along the esplanade, a twenty-
one-year-old foreigner alone amongst the English. I can see him, for instance, standing out on the pier, where a brass band is playing the overture
from *Tannhäuser* as a night-time serenade. And as he walks homeward past
those who remain to listen, with a gentle breeze coming off the water, he is
intrigued by the ease with which he is absorbing a hitherto quite unfamiliar language, a language he will one day employ to write the novels that will
win him worldwide acclaim, whilst for now it fills him with an altogether
new sense of purpose and confidence. By his own account, Korzeniowski's
first English tutors were the *Lowestoft Standard* and the *Lowestoft Journal,*
in which, during the week of his arrival, the following motley assortment
of news items was brought to the public's attention: an explosion in a mine
in Wigan cost two hundred lives; in Rumelia there was a Mohammedan
uprising; in South Africa the kaffir unrest had to be suppressed; Lord
Grenville expatiated on the education of the fair sex; a despatch boat was
sent to Marseilles to take the Duke of Cambridge to Malta, where he was

to inspect the Indian troops; a housemaid in Whitby was burnt alive when her dress, onto which she had accidentally spilt paraffin, caught light at an open fire; the steamship *Largo Bay* left the Clyde with three hundred and fifty-two Scottish emigrants aboard; a Mrs. Dixon of Silsden was so overjoyed to see her son Thomas, who, after ten years' absence in America, suddenly turned up at her door, that she had a stroke; the young Queen of Spain was growing weaker by the day; work on the fortifications of Hong Kong, where two thousand coolies were slaving, was approaching completion; and in Bosnia, so the *Standard* reports, all highways are infested with bands of robbers, some of them mounted. Even the forests around Sarajevo are swarming with marauders, deserters and francs-tireurs of all kinds. Travelling, therefore, is at a standstill.

In February 1890, twelve years after his arrival in Lowestoft and fifteen years after his departure from the station at Cracow, Korzeniowski, who now had British citizenship and his captain's papers and had seen the most far-flung regions of the earth, returned for the first time to Kazimierówka and the house of his Uncle Tadeusz. In a note written much later he described his arrival at the Ukrainian station after brief stops in Berlin, Warsaw and Lublin. There his uncle's coachman and majordomo were waiting for him in a sleigh to which four duns were harnessed but which was so small that it almost looked like a toy. The ride to Kazimierówka took another eight hours. The majordomo wrapped me up solicitously, writes Korzeniowski, in a bearskin coat that reached to the tips of my toes and put an enormous fur hat with ear flaps on my head, before taking his seat beside me. When the sleigh started off, to a soft and even jingle of bells, a winter journey back into childhood began for me. The young coachman, who was perhaps only sixteen years old, found the way across the endless snow-covered fields with an unfailing instinct. When I commented on his astounding sense of direction (Korzeniowski continues), never hesitating and not once taking a wrong turn, the majordomo replied that the young fellow was the son of Joseph, who had always driven grandmother Bobrowska of blessed memory and later served Pan Tadeusz with equal loyalty, until cholera ended his days. His wife, the majordomo said, died of the cholera too, which reached us when the ice was breaking, and so did a whole houseful of children, and the only one who survived was this deaf mute sitting in front of us on the box. He was never sent to school and no one ever expected he would be much use for anything till it turned out that horses were more obedient to him than to any other stable-boy. And when he was about eleven it emerged on some occasion or other that he had the map of the entire district in his head, complete with every bend in the road, so accurately you'd think he'd been born with it. Never, writes Korzeniowski, have I travelled better than that day as we journeyed into the settling dusk. As in the old days, long ago, I saw the sun going down over the plains, a great red disc sinking into the snow as though it were setting upon the sea. Swiftly we drove on into the gathering dark, into the infinite white wastes that met the starry skies at the horizon, where villages amidst trees floated like shadowy islands.

Before he set off for Poland and the Ukraine, Korzeniowski had applied for a job with the Société Anonyme Belge pour le Commerce du Haut-Congo.[5] Immediately after his return to Brussels he called in person on the managing director, Albert Thys, at the Société's main offices in rue de Brederode. Thys, whose shapeless body was forced into a frock coat that was far too tight, was sitting in a gloomy office beneath a map of Africa that covered the entire wall, and the moment Korzeniowski had stated his business, without further ado, he offered him the command of a steamer that plied the upper reaches of the Congo, because the captain, a German or Dane by the name of Freiesleben, had, as it happened, just been killed by the natives. After two weeks of hasty preparation and a cursory medical, conducted by the Société's ghoulish doctor, Korzeniowski took the train to Bordeaux, where in mid-May he embarked on the *Ville de Maceió*, bound for Boma. At Tenerife he was already beset with dark premonitions. Life, he wrote to his beautiful and recently widowed Aunt Marguerite Poradowska in Brussels, is a tragicomedy—beaucoup de rêves, un rare éclair de bonheur, un peu de colère, puis le désillusion, des années de souffrance et la fin[6]—in which, for better or worse, one had to play one's part. In the course of the long voyage, in this dispirited frame of mind, the madness of the whole colonial enterprise was gradually borne in upon Korzeniowski. Day after day the coastline was unchanging, as if the vessel were making no progress. And yet, wrote Korzeniowski, we passed a number of landing places and trading posts with names like Gran' Bassam or Little Popo, all of them seeming to belong in some sordid farce. Once we passed a warship anchored off a dreary beach where not the smallest sign of any settlement was to be seen. As far as the eye could reach there was nothing but ocean, sky, and the hair-thin green strip of bush vegetation. The ensign hung limp from the mast, the ponderous iron vessel rose and fell on the slimy swell, and at regular intervals the long six-inch guns fired off shells into the unknown African continent, with neither purpose nor aim.

Bordeaux, Tenerife, Dakar, Conakry, Sierra Leone, Cotonou, Libreville, Loango, Banane, Boma—after four weeks at sea, Korzeniowski at last

---

[5] Anonymous Belgian Society for Commerce in the Upper Congo. [ED.]

[6] "Many dreams, an occasional flash of happiness, a little anger, then disillusion, years of suffering followed by the end." [ED.]

reached the Congo, one of those remote destinations he had dreamt of as a child. At that time the Congo had been but a white patch on the map of Africa over which he had often pored for hours, reciting the colourful names. Little was marked in the interior of this part of the world, no railway lines, no roads, no towns, and, as cartographers would often embellish such empty spaces with drawings of exotic beasts, a roaring lion or a crocodile with gaping jaws, they had rendered the Congo, of which they knew only that it was a river measuring thousands of miles from its source to the sea, as a snake coiling through the blank, uncharted land. Since then, of course, detail had been added to the map. The white patch had become a place of darkness. And the fact is that in the entire history of colonialism, most of it not yet written, there is scarcely a darker chapter than the one termed *The Opening of the Congo.* When the Association Internationale pour l'Exploration et la Civilisation en Afrique[7] was established in September 1876, it was with a declaration of the most high-minded intentions and ostensibly without any vested national or private interests. Exalted personages representing the aristocracy, the churches, the sciences, industry and finance, attended the inaugural meeting, at which King Leopold, patron of the exemplary venture, proclaimed that the friends of humanity could pursue no nobler end than that which brought them together that day: to open up the last part of our earth to have remained hitherto untouched by the blessings of civilization. The aim, said King Leopold, was to break through the darkness in which whole peoples still dwelt, and to mount a crusade in order to bring this glorious century of progress to the point of perfection. In the nature of things, the lofty spirit expressed in this declaration was later lost from sight. As early as 1885, Leopold, now styled Souverain de l'Etat Indépendent du Congo,[8] was the sole ruler of a territory on the second longest river on earth, a million square miles in area and thus a hundred times the size of the mother country, and was accountable to no one for his actions. Ruthlessly he set about exploiting its inexhaustible wealth, through trading companies such as the Société Anonyme Belge pour le Commerce du Haut-Congo, the soon legendary profits of which were built on a system of slave labour which was sanctioned by all the shareholders and all the Europeans contracted to work in the new colony. In some parts of the Congo, the indigenous people were all but eradicated by forced labour, and those who were taken there from other parts of Africa or from overseas died in droves of dysentery, malaria, smallpox, beriberi, jaundice, starvation, and physical exhaustion. Every year from

---

[7] International Association for Exploration and Civilization in Africa. [ED.]
[8] Sovereign of the Congo Free State. [ED.]

1890 to 1900, an estimated five hundred thousand of these nameless victims, nowhere mentioned in the annual reports, lost their lives. During the same period, the value of shares in the Compagnie du Chemin de Fer du Congo[9] rose from 320 Belgian francs to 2,850.

On arrival in Boma, Korzeniowski transferred from the *Ville de Maceió* to a small river steamer, by which he reached Matadi on the 13th of June. From there he went overland, since numerous waterfalls and rapids make the Congo unnavigable from Matadi to Stanley Pool. Matadi was a desolate settlement, known to its inhabitants as the town of stones. Like an ulcer it festered on the rubble thrown up over thousands of years by the infernal cauldron at the end of this three hundred-mile stretch of the river, which remains untamed even today. Buildings with rusty corrugated iron roofs were dotted randomly below the high crags through which the water forced its way, and amongst these, on the scree, and on the steep riverbank slopes, gangs of black figures were everywhere at work or moving in bearer columns that ran long lines across the rough terrain. Here and there an overseer in white suit and white pith helmet stood by. Korzeniowski had already been for a day or so in this arena reminiscent of a quarry, where the constant noise of the rapids filled the air, when (as Marlow later describes in *Heart of Darkness*) he came upon a place some way off from the settlement where those who were racked by illness, starvation and toil had withdrawn to die. As if after a massacre they lay there in the greenish gloom at the bottom of the gorge. Evidently no one cared to stop these black shadows when they crept off into the bush. I began to distinguish the gleam of the eyes under the trees, says Marlow. Then, glancing down, I saw a face near my hand. The black bones reclined at full length with one shoulder against the tree, and slowly the eyelids rose and the sunken eyes looked up at me, enormous and vacant, a kind of blind, white flicker in the depths of the orbs, which died out slowly. And as this man, scarcely more than a boy, breathed his last, those who were not yet worn out were carrying hundredweight sacks of provisions, crates of tools, explosive charges, gear and equipment of every description, engines, spare parts, and sections of ships' hulls through the swamps and forests and across the sun-scorched uplands, or were working in the mountain range of Palaballa and by the M'Pozo river, building a railway to link Matadi with the upper reaches of the Congo. Korzeniowski made that arduous journey himself, along a route where presently the settlements of Songolo, Thumba and Thysville would be established. He had with him a caravan of thirty-one men and, as his troublesome travelling companion, an overweight Frenchman named

---

[9] Congo Railway Company. [ED.]

Harou, who invariably fainted whenever they were miles from the nearest shade, so that for long distances he had to be transported in a hammock. The march took well-nigh forty days, and during this period Korzeniowski began to grasp that his own travails did not absolve him from the guilt which he had incurred by his mere presence in the Congo. Though he did in fact continue upriver from Léopoldville, aboard the steamer *Roi des Belges*, to the Stanley Falls, he now regarded his original plan of taking up a command for the Société Anonyme with revulsion. The corrosive humidity of the air, the sunlight pulsing to the heartbeat, the unchanging haze that hung over the river, and the company he had to keep aboard the *Roi des Belges*, which struck him increasingly, as the days went by, as unhinged—he knew that he would have to turn back. Tout m'est antipathique ici, he wrote to Marguerite Poradowska, les hommes et les choses, mais surtout les hommes. Tous ces boutiquiers africains et marchands d'ivoire aux instincts sordides. Je regrette d'être venu ici. Je le regrette même amèrement.[10] Back in Léopoldville, Korzeniowski was so sick in body and in soul that he longed for death. But it was to be another three months before this man, whose protracted bouts of despair were henceforth to alternate with his writing, was able to depart homeward from Boma.[. . .]

The first news of the nature and extent of the crimes committed against the native peoples in the course of opening up the Congo came to public attention in 1903 through Roger Casement, then British consul at Boma. In a memorandum to Foreign Secretary Lord Lansdowne, Casement—who, so Korzeniowski told a London acquaintance, could tell things that he, Korzeniowski, had long been trying to forget—gave an exact account of the utterly merciless exploitation of the blacks. They were compelled to work unpaid throughout the colony, given a bare minimum to eat, often in chain-gangs, and labouring to a set timetable from dawn to dusk till in the end they literally dropped dead. Anyone who travelled the upper reaches of the Congo and was not blinded by greed for money, wrote Casement, would behold the agony of an entire race in all its heart-rending details, a suffering that eclipsed even the most calamitous tales in the Bible. Casement made it perfectly clear that hundreds of thousands of slave labourers were being worked to death every year by their white overseers, and that mutilation, by severing hands and feet, and execution by revolver, were among the everyday punitive means of maintaining discipline in the Congo. King Leopold invited Casement to Brussels for a personal talk

---

[10]"Everything here is repellant to me. Men and things, but men above all. All these African shopkeepers and ivory merchants with sordid instincts. I regret having come here. I even regret it bitterly." (Compare "Letter to Marguerite Poradowska," 133). [Ed.]

aimed either at defusing the tension created by Casement's intervention or at assessing the threat his activities posed to the Belgian colonial enterprise. Leopold explained that he considered the work done by the blacks as a perfectly legitimate alternative to the payment of taxes, and if the white supervisory personnel at times went too far, as he did not deny, it was due to the fact that the climate of the Congo triggered a kind of dementia in the brains of some whites, which unfortunately it was not always possible to prevent in time, a fact which was regrettable but could hardly be changed. Since Casement's views could not be altered with arguments of this kind, Leopold availed himself of his royal privilege in London, as a result of which, with a certain duplicity, Casement was on the one hand praised for his exemplary report and awarded the CMG, while on the other hand nothing was done that might have had an adverse effect on Belgian interests. When Casement was transferred to South America some years later, probably with the ulterior motive of getting his troublesome person out of the way for a while, he exposed conditions in the jungle areas of Peru, Colombia and Brazil that resembled those in the Congo in many respects, with the difference that here the controlling agent was not Belgian trading associations but the Amazon Company, the head office of which was in the city of London. In South America too, whole tribes were being wiped out at that time and entire regions burnt to the ground. Casement's report, and his unconditional partisanship for the victims and those who had no rights, undoubtedly earned him a certain respect at the Foreign Office, but at the same time many of the top-ranking officials shook their heads at what seemed to them a quixotic zeal incompatible with the professional advancement of otherwise so promising an envoy. They tried to deal with the matter by knighting Casement, in express recognition of his services to the oppressed peoples of the earth. But Casement was not prepared to switch to the side of the powerful; quite the contrary, he was increasingly preoccupied with the nature and origins of that power and the imperialist mentality that resulted from it. It was only to be expected that in due course he should hit upon the Irish question—that is to say, his own. Casement had grown up in County Antrim, the son of a Protestant father and a Catholic mother, and by education and upbringing he was predestined to be one of those whose mission in life was the upholding English rule in Ireland. In the years leading up to the First World War, when the Irish question was becoming acute, Casement espoused the cause of "the white Indians of Ireland." The injustice which had been borne by the Irish for centuries increasingly filled his consciousness. He could not rid his thoughts of the fact that almost half the population of Ireland had been murdered by Cromwell's soldiers, that thousands of men and women were later sent as white slaves to the West Indies, that in recent times more than a million

Irish had died of starvation, and that the majority of the young generation were still forced to emigrate from their native land. The moment of decision for Casement came in 1914 when the Home Rule programme proposed by the Liberal government to solve the Irish problem was defeated by the fanatical resistance of Ulster Protestants with the support, both open and covert, of various English interest groups. We will not shrink from Ulster's resistance to Home Rule for Ireland, even if the British Commonwealth is convulsed declared Frederick Smith, one of the leading representatives of the Protestant minority whose so-called loyalism consisted in their willingness to defend their privileges against government troops by force of arms if necessary. The hundred-thousand-strong Ulster Volunteers were founded. In the south, too, an army of volunteers was raised. Casement took part in the recruiting drive and helped equip the contingents. He returned his decorations to London, and refused the pension he had been offered. In early 1915 he travelled to Berlin on a secret mission, to urge the government of the German Reich to supply arms to the Irish army of liberation and persuade Irish prisoners of war in Germany to form an Irish brigade. In both endeavours Casement was unsuccessful, and he was returned to Ireland by a German submarine. Deadly tired and chilled to the bone by the icy water, he waded ashore in the bay of Banna Strand near Tralee. He was now fifty-one; his arrest was imminent. All he could do was to send the message *No German help available* through a priest, to stop the Easter rising which was planned for all Ireland and was now condemned to failure. If the idealists, poets, trade unionists and teachers who bore the responsibility in Dublin nonetheless sacrificed themselves and those who obeyed them in seven days of street fighting, that was none of his doing. When the rising was put down, Casement was already in a cell in the Tower of London. He had no legal adviser. Counsel for the prosecution was Frederick Smith, who had risen to become Director of Public Prosecutions, which meant that the outcome of the trial was as good as decided before it began. In order to pre-empt any petitions for pardon that might have been made by persons of influence, excerpts from what was known as the Black Diary, a kind of chronicle of the accused's homosexual relations found when Casement's home was searched, were forwarded to the King of England, the President of the United States, and the Pope. The authenticity of this Black Diary, kept until recently under lock and key at the Public Records Office in Kew, was long considered highly debatable, not least because the executive and judicial organs of the state concerned with furnishing the evidence and drawing up the charge against alleged Irish terrorists have repeatedly been guilty, until very recent times, not only of pursuing doubtful suspicions and insinuations but indeed of deliberate falsification of the facts. For the veterans of the Irish freedom movement it was in any case inconceivable that one of their martyrs should have practised the English vice. But since the release to general scrutiny of the diaries in early 1994 there has no longer been any question that they are in Casement's own hand. We may draw from this the conclusion that it was precisely Casement's homosexuality that sensitized him to the continuing oppression, exploitation, enslavement and destruction, across the borders of social class and race, of those who were furthest from the centres of power. As expected, Casement was found guilty of high treason at the end of his trial at the Old Bailey. The presiding judge, Lord Reading, formerly Rufus Isaacs, pronounced sentence. You will be taken hence, he told Casement, to a lawful prison and thence to a place of execution and will be there hanged by the neck until you be dead. Not until 1965 did the British government permit the exhumation of the remains of Roger Casement, presumably scarcely identifiable any more, from the lime pit in the courtyard of Pentonville prison into which his body had been thrown.

Part Three

FICTIONS OF EMPIRE

The Man
Who Would Be King

Rudyard Kipling

Brother to a Prince and fellow
to a beggar if he be found worthy [1]

The Law, [2] as quoted, lays down a fair conduct of life, and one not easy to follow. I have been fellow to a beggar again and again under circumstances which prevented either of us finding out whether the other was worthy. I have still to be brother to a Prince, though I once came near to kinship with what might have been a veritable King and was promised the reversion of a Kingdom—army, law-courts, revenue, and policy all complete. But, to-day, I greatly fear that my King is dead, and if I want a crown I must go hunt it for myself.

The beginning of everything was in a railway train upon the road to Mhow from Ajmir. [3] There had been a Deficit in the Budget, [4] which necessitated travelling, not Second-class, which is only half as dear as First-class, but by Intermediate, which is very awful indeed. There are no cushions in the Intermediate class, and the population are either Intermediate, which is Eurasian, or native, which for a long night journey is nasty, or Loafer, [5] which is amusing though intoxicated. Intermediates do not buy from refreshment-rooms. They carry their food in bundles and pots, and buy

---

[1] An unattributed maxim alluding to the spirit of brotherhood in Freemasonry. Freemasonry was an English secret society with far-flung branches throughout the world. Although Freemasonry originated in the seventeenth century, its adherents believed it to be an ancient body of wisdom that had been revealed, at various stages of history, to God's Chosen Peoples—which included Jews, Christians, Muslims, and others. Freemasonry had been deeply rooted in British India since the eighteenth century, where, somewhat paradoxically, it served to open up social intercourse across class ranks for soldiers of the British Army, who were sometimes frustrated by the closed hierarchical stratification both of military life and of the caste system in India. At the same time, the (more open, climbable) hierarchy of the Masonic Lodges touched on a deep cultural affinity between Britons and Indians, as well as a source of profound mutual respect, given the orderly class structures of both societies. Kipling was inducted into Freemasonry in 1885 and maintained loose ties to it throughout his life. See Stephen Knight, "From *The Brotherhood*," 64–68. [ED.]

[2] The law of Freemasonry. [ED.]

[3] Ajmir (sometimes spelled "Ajmer") is an ancient city in the historic Rajputana region of northwest India, on the main railroad line running southwest from Delhi to Bombay. A branch line ran from Ajmir 270 miles south to Mhow. [ED.]

[4] The narrator is out of money. There was, incidentally, a severe deficit in the budget of the British government of India in 1887–88. [ED.]

[5] A very broad category of disreputable whites, including scamps, con artists, jacks-of-all-trades, roustabouts, etc. [ED.]

sweets from the native sweetmeat-sellers, and drink the road-side water. That is why in the hot weather Intermediates are taken out of the carriages dead, and in all weathers are most properly looked down upon.

My particular Intermediate happened to be empty till I reached Nasira-bad,[6] when a big black-browed gentleman in shirt-sleeves entered, and, following the custom of Intermediates, passed the time of day. He was a wanderer and a vagabond like myself, but with an educated taste for whisky. He told tales of things he had seen and done, of out-of-the-way corners of the Empire into which he had penetrated, and of adventures in which he risked his life for a few days' food.

"If India was filled with men like you and me, not knowing more than the crows[7] where they'd get their next day's rations, it isn't seventy millions of revenue[8] the land would be paying—it's seven hundred millions," said he; and as I looked at his mouth and chin I was disposed to agree with him.

We talked politics—the politics of Loaferdom that sees things from the underside where the lath and plaster is not smoothed off—and we talked postal arrangements because my friend wanted to send a telegram back from the next station to Ajmir, the turning-off place from the Bombay to the Mhow line as you travel westward. My friend had no money beyond eight annas[9] which he wanted for dinner, and I had no money at all, owing to the hitch in the Budget before mentioned. Further, I was going into a wilderness where, though I should resume touch with the Treasury,[10] there were no telegraph offices. I was, therefore, unable to help him in any way.

"We might threaten a Stationmaster, and make him send a wire on tick,"[11] said my friend, "but that'd mean inquiries for you and for me, and I've got my hands full these days. Did you say you are travelling back along this line within any days?"

---

[6] The first stop after leaving Ajmir, on the way to Mhow. [ED.]

[7] Possible allusion to Job 38. 41 or to Luke 12. 24. [ED.]

[8] The approximate rate of taxation imposed by the British on all of India in the mid-1880s was 75 million pounds. [ED.]

[9] 16 annas made a rupee. A rupee was worth approximately 1s6d (1 shilling, sixpence) in 1888. Half a rupee, therefore, would have been worth ninepence—a paltry sum for a dinner. [ED.]

[10] Presumably, the newspaper for which he works. Although the loafer takes the narrator to be a fellow loafer, the narrator is actually a "roving correspondent" for a newspaper. [ED.]

[11] On credit. [ED.]

"Within ten," I said.

"Can't you make it eight?" said he. "Mine is rather urgent business."

"I can send your telegram within ten days if that will serve you," I said.

"I couldn't trust the wire to fetch him now I think of it. It's this way. He leaves Delhi on the 23rd for Bombay. That means he'll be running through Ajmir about the night of the 23rd."

"But I'm going into the Indian Desert,"[12] I explained.

"Well *and* good," said he. "You'll be changing at Marwar Junction to get into Jodhpore[13] territory—you must do that—and he'll be coming through Marwar Junction in the early morning of the 24th by the Bombay Mail. Can you be at Marwar Junction on that time? 'Twon't be inconveniencing you because I know that there's precious few pickings to be got out of these Central India States—even though you pretend to be correspondent of the *Backwoodsman*."[14]

"Have you ever tried that trick?" I asked.

"Again and again, but the Residents[15] find you out, and then you get escorted to the Border before you've time to get your knife into them. But about my friend here. I *must* give him a word o' mouth to tell him what's come to me or else he won't know where to go. I would take it more than kind of you if you was to come out of Central India in time to catch him at Marwar Junction, and say to him: 'He has gone South for the week.' He'll know what that means. He's a big man with a red beard, and a great swell[16] he is. You'll find him sleeping like a gentleman with all his luggage round him in a Second-class compartment. But don't you be afraid. Slip down the window, and say: 'He has gone South for the week,' and he'll tumble.[17] It's only cutting your time of stay in those parts by two days. I ask you as a stranger—going to the West,"[18] he said with emphasis.

---

[12] A northern desert on the border between India and Pakistan, also known as the Desert of Thar. [ED.]

[13] The main railway line from Delhi to Bombay ran 200 miles southwest to Ajmir, then to Marwar Junction another 75 miles to the southwest. At Marwar Junction, another line branched north to Jodhpore (or "Jodhpur"), which was the last stop on the way to the Indian Desert. [ED.]

[14] Fictional name for an Indian newspaper. Kipling worked as a journalist for the *Civil and Military Gazette*. [ED.]

[15] British representatives at the local, native courts. [ED.]

[16] Stylishly dressed, dandified man. [ED.]

[17] Understand. [ED.]

[18] These mysterious directional references are allusions to Freemasonry, in which all points of the compass have symbolic significance. [ED.]

"Where have *you* come from?" said I.

"From the East," said he, "and I am hoping that you will give him the message on the Square[19]—for the sake of my Mother[20] as well as your own."

Englishmen are not usually softened by appeals to the memory of their mothers, but for certain reasons, which will be fully apparent, I saw fit to agree.

"It's more than a little matter," said he, "and that's why I asked you to do it—and now I know that I can depend on you doing it. A Second-class carriage at Marwar Junction, and a red-haired man asleep in it. You'll be sure to remember. I get out at the next station, and I must hold on there till he comes or sends me what I want."

"I'll give the message if I catch him," I said, "and for the sake of your Mother as well as mine I'll give you a word of advice. Don't try to run[21] the Central India States just now as the correspondent of the *Backwoodsman*. There's a real one knocking about here, and it might lead to trouble."

"Thank you," said he simply, "and when will the swine be gone? I can't starve because he's ruining my work. I wanted to get hold of the Degumber[22] Rajah down here about his father's widow, and give him a jump."[23]

"What did he do to his father's widow, then?"

"Filled her up with red pepper and slippered her[24] to death as she hung from a beam. I found that out myself and I'm the only man that would dare going into the State to get hush-money for it. They'll try to poison me, same as they did in Chortumna when I went on the loot[25] there. But you'll give the man at Marwar Junction my message?"

He got out at a little roadside station, and I reflected. I had heard, more than once, of men personating correspondents of newspapers and bleeding small Native States with threats of exposure, but I had never met any of the caste before. They led a hard life, and generally die with great suddenness. The Native States have a wholesome horror of English newspapers, which may throw light on their peculiar methods of government, and do

---

[19] *On the square* colloquially meant "honestly," but the square is also an important Masonic symbol, usually denoting fairness. [ED.]

[20] In Freemasonry, the *Mother Lodge* refers to the central organization and meeting place in a given country. [ED.]

[21] Practice confidence tricks. [ED.]

[22] Fictional native state, as is Chortumna. [ED.]

[23] Rob him. [ED.]

[24] Beat her. [ED.]

[25] *Loot* is derived from a Hindu word for plunder. To be *on the loot* meant to be engaged in acquiring ill-gotten gains. [ED.]

their best to choke correspondents with champagne, or drive them out of their mind with four-in-hand barouches.[26] They do not understand that nobody cares a straw for the internal administration of Native States so long as oppression and crime are kept within decent limits, and the ruler is not drugged, drunk, or diseased from one end of the year to the other. They are the dark places of the earth, full of unimaginable cruelty, touching the Railway and the Telegraph on one side, and, on the other, the days of Harun-al-Raschid.[27] When I left the train I did business with divers Kings, and in eight days passed through many changes of life. Sometimes I wore dress-clothes and consorted with Princes and Politicals,[28] drinking from crystal and eating from silver. Sometimes I lay out upon the ground and devoured what I could get, from a plate made of leaves,[29] and drank the running water, and slept under the same rug as my servant. It was all in the day's work.

Then I headed for the Great Indian Desert upon the proper date, as I had promised, and the night Mail set me down at Marwar Junction, where a funny little, happy-go-lucky, native-managed railway runs to Jodhpore. The Bombay Mail from Delhi makes a short halt at Marwar. She arrived as I got in, and I had just time to hurry to her platform and go down the carriages. There was only one Second-class on the train. I slipped the window and looked down upon a flaming red beard, half covered by a railway rug. That was my man, fast asleep, and I dug him gently in the ribs. He woke with a grunt and I saw his face in the light of the lamps. It was a great and shining face.

"Tickets again?" said he.

"No," said I, "I am to tell you that he is gone South for the week. He has gone South for the week!"

The train had begun to move out. The red man rubbed his eyes. "He has gone South for the week," he repeated. "Now that's just like his impidence. Did he say that I was to give you anything? 'Cause I won't."

"He didn't," I said, and dropped away, and watched the red lights die out in the dark. It was horribly cold because the wind was blowing off the sands. I climbed into my own train — not an Intermediate Carriage this time — and went to sleep.

---

[26] A barouche is a four-wheeled carriage, and if it were drawn by four horses, it would be an elegant means of transportation. *Drive them out of their mind* is a facetious way of saying they would be bribed in style. [ED.]

[27] The caliph of Baghdad in *The Arabian Nights*. [ED.]

[28] Political agents were official British advisers in native states. [ED.]

[29] The way food would be served by a roadside hawker. [ED.]

If the man with the beard had given me a rupee I should have kept it as a memento of a rather curious affair. But the consciousness of having done my duty was my only reward.

Later on I reflected that two gentlemen like my friends could not do any good if they forgathered and personated correspondents of newspapers, and might, if they black-mailed one of the little rat-trap states of Central India or Southern Rajputana, get themselves into serious difficulties. I therefore took some trouble to describe them as accurately as I could remember to people who would be interested in deporting them; and succeeded, so I was later informed, in having them headed back from the Degumber borders.

Then I became respectable, and returned to an Office where there were no Kings and no incidents outside the daily manufacture of a newspaper. A newspaper office seems to attract every conceivable sort of person, to the prejudice of discipline. Zenana-mission[30] ladies arrive, and beg that the Editor will instantly abandon all his duties to describe a Christian prize-giving in a back-slum of a perfectly inaccessible village; Colonels who have been overpassed for command sit down and sketch the outline of a series of ten, twelve, or twenty-four leading articles on Seniority *versus* Selection; missionaries wish to know why they have not been permitted to escape from their regular vehicles of abuse and swear at a brother-missionary under special patronage of the editorial We; stranded theatrical companies troop up to explain that they cannot pay for their advertisements, but on their return from New Zealand or Tahiti will do so with interest; inventors of patent punkah-pulling machines,[31] carriage couplings and unbreakable swords and axle-trees[32] call with specifications in their pockets and hours at their disposal; tea-companies enter and elaborate their prospectuses with the office pens; secretaries of ball-committees clamour to have the glories of their last dance more fully described; strange ladies rustle in and say: "I want a hundred lady's cards printed *at once*, please," which is manifestly part of an Editor's duty; and every dissolute ruffian that ever tramped the Grand Trunk Road[33] makes it his business to ask for employment as a proof-reader. And, all the time, the telephone-bell is ringing madly, and

---

[30] Missionary work done among Indian women. *Zenana* meant the women's quarters of a house. [ED.]

[31] A punkah was a large interior fan, hence, a mechanically driven fan. [ED.]

[32] A fixed lateral bar with bearings on either end, to which the wheels of a carriage or train would be attached. [ED.]

[33] The Grand Trunk Road ran from Calcutta on the east coast northwest to Amritsar on the extreme northern frontier of India, near Lahore. [ED.]

Kings are being killed on the Continent, and Empires are saying—"You're another,"[34] and Mister Gladstone[35] is calling down brimstone upon the British Dominions, and the little black copy-boys are whining, *"kaa-pi chay-ha-yeh"* (copy wanted) like tired bees, and most of the paper is as blank as Modred's shield.[36]

But that is the amusing part of the year. There are six other months when none ever comes to call, and the thermometer walks inch by inch up to the top of the glass, and the office is darkened to just above reading-light, and the press-machines are red-hot of touch, and nobody writes anything but accounts of amusements in the Hill-stations[37] or obituary notices. Then the telephone becomes a tinkling terror, because it tells you of the sudden deaths of men and women that you knew intimately, and the prickly-heat covers you with a garment, and you sit down and write: "A slight increase of sickness is reported from the Khuda Janta Khan[38] District. The outbreak is purely sporadic in its nature, and, thanks to the energetic efforts of the District authorities, is now almost at an end. It is, however, with deep regret we record the death, etc."

Then the sickness really breaks out, and the less recording and reporting the better for the peace of the subscribers. But the Empires and the Kings continue to divert themselves as selfishly as before, and the Foreman thinks that a daily paper really ought to come out once in twenty-four hours, and all the people at the Hill-stations in the middle of their amusements say: "Good gracious! Why can't the paper be sparkling? I'm sure there's plenty going on up here."

That is the dark half of the moon, and, as the advertisements say, "must be experienced to be appreciated."

It was in that season, and a remarkably evil season, that the paper began running the last issue of the week on Saturday night, which is to say Sunday morning, after the custom of a London paper. This was a great

---

[34] Threatening each other, name-calling. [ED.]

[35] William Gladstone was prime minister of England from 1868 to 1874, from 1880 to 1885, for a few months in 1886, and finally from 1892 to 1894. His Liberal, anti-imperialistic policies and his responsibility for several major military defeats (particularly the botched mission that led to the death of General Gordon in the Sudan in 1885), along with his controversial support for Irish Home Rule in 1886, earned Gladstone the indignation and contempt of conservatives like Kipling. [ED.]

[36] Mordred was King Arthur's nephew. His shield was blank because he did not perform any heroic deeds, and thus did not have the right to decorate it. Mordred eventually helped bring about the fall of King Arthur. [ED.]

[37] British settlements in interior hill towns. [ED.]

[38] Fictional name, meaning roughly "God-knows-town." [ED.]

convenience, for immediately after the paper was put to bed, the dawn would lower the thermometer from 96° to almost 84° for half an hour, and in that chill—you have no idea how cold is 84° on the grass until you begin to pray for it—a very tired man could get off to sleep ere the heat roused him.

One Saturday night it was my pleasant duty to put the paper to bed alone. A King or courtier or a courtesan or a Community was going to die or get a new Constitution, or do something that was important on the other side of the world, and the paper was to be held open till the latest possible minute in order to catch the telegram.

It was a pitchy black night, as stifling as a June night can be, and the *loo,* the red-hot wind from the westward, was booming among the tinder-dry trees and pretending that the rain was on its heels. Now and again a spot of almost boiling water would fall on the dust with the flop of a frog, but all our weary world knew that was only pretence. It was a shade cooler in the press-room than the office, so I sat there, while the type ticked and clicked, and the night-jars[39] hooted at the windows, and the all but naked compositors wiped the sweat from their foreheads, and called for water. The thing that was keeping us back, whatever it was, would not come off, though the *loo* dropped and the last type was set, and the whole round earth stood still in the choking heat, with its finger on its lip, to wait the event. I drowsed, and wondered whether the telegraph was a blessing, and whether this dying man, or struggling people, might be aware of the inconvenience the delay was causing. There was no special reason beyond the heat and worry to make tension, but, as the clock-hands crept up to three o'clock and the machines spun their fly-wheels two or three times to see that all was in order before I said the word that would set them off, I could have shrieked aloud.

Then the roar and rattle of the wheels shivered the quiet into little bits. I rose to go away, but two men in white clothes stood in front of me. The first one said: "It's him!" The second said: "So it is!" And they both laughed almost as loudly as the machinery roared, and mopped their foreheads. "We seed there was a light burning across the road, and we were sleeping in that ditch there for coolness, and I said to my friend here, The office is open. Let's come along and speak to him as turned us back from the Degumber State," said the smaller of the two. He was the man I had met in the Mhow train, and his fellow was the red-bearded man of Marwar Junction. There was no mistaking the eyebrows of the one or the beard of the other.

I was not pleased, because I wished to go to sleep, not to squabble with loafers. "What do you want?" I asked.

---

[39]Nocturnal birds in the same family as whippoorwills. [ED.]

"Half an hour's talk with you, cool and comfortable, in the office," said the red-bearded man. "We'd *like* some drink—the Contrack doesn't begin yet, Peachey, so you needn't look—but what we really want is advice. We don't want money. We ask you as a favour, because we found out you did us a bad turn about Degumber State."

I led from the press-room to the stifling office with the maps on the walls, and the red-haired man rubbed his hands. "That's something like," said he. "This was the proper shop to come to. Now, Sir, let me introduce to you Brother[40] Peachey Carnehan, that's him, and Brother Daniel Dravot, that is *me,* and the less said about our professions the better, for we have been most things in our time. Soldier, sailor, compositor, photographer, proof-reader, street-preacher, and correspondents of the *Backwoodsman* when we thought the paper wanted one. Carnehan is sober, and so am I. Look at us first, and see that's sure. It will save you cutting into my talk. We'll take one of your cigars apiece, and you shall see us light up."

I watched the test. The men were absolutely sober, so I gave them each a tepid whisky and soda.

"Well *and* good," said Carnehan of the eyebrows, wiping the froth from his moustache. "Let me talk now, Dan. We have been all over India, mostly on foot. We have been boiler-fitters, engine-drivers, petty contractors, and all that, and we have decided that India isn't big enough for such as us."

They certainly were too big for the office. Dravot's beard seemed to fill half the room and Carnehan's shoulders the other half, as they sat on the big table. Carnehan continued: "The country isn't half worked out because they that governs it won't let you touch it. They spend all their blessed time in governing it, and you can't lift a spade, nor chip a rock, nor look for oil, nor anything like that without all the Government saying—'Leave it alone, and let us govern.' Therefore, such *as* it is, we will let it alone, and go away to some other place where a man isn't crowded and can come to his own. We are not little men, and there is nothing that we are afraid of except Drink, and we have signed a Contrack on that. *Therefore,* we are going away to be Kings."

"Kings in our own right," muttered Dravot.

"Yes, of course," I said. "You've been tramping in the sun, and it's a very warm night, and hadn't you better sleep over the notion? Come tomorrow."

"Neither drunk nor sunstruck," said Dravot. "We have slept over the notion half a year, and require to see Books and Atlases, and we have decided that there is only one place now in the world that two strong men can

---

[40] A Masonic term of address. [ED.]

Sar-a-*whack*.[41] They call it Kafiristan.[42] By my reckoning it's the top right-hand corner of Afghanistan, not more than three hundred miles from Peshawar.[43] They have two-and-thirty heathen idols there,[44] and we'll be the thirty-third and fourth. It's a mountaineous country, and the women of those parts are very beautiful."

"But that is provided against in the Contrack," said Carnehan. "Neither Woman nor Liqu-or, Daniel."

"And that's all we know, except that no one has gone there, and they fight, and in any place where they fight a man who knows how to drill men[45] can always be a King. We shall go to those parts and say to any King we find—'D'you want to vanquish your foes?' and we will show him how to drill men; for that we know better than anything else. Then we will subvert that King and seize his Throne and establish a Dy-nasty."

"You'll be cut to pieces before you're fifty miles across the Border," I said. "You have to travel through Afghanistan to get to that country. It's one mass of mountains and peaks and glaciers, and no Englishman has been through it. The people are utter brutes, and even if you reached them you couldn't do anything."

"That's more like," said Carnehan. "If you could think us a little more mad we would be more pleased. We have come to you to know about this country, to read a book about it, and to be shown maps. We want you to tell us that we are fools and to show us your books." He turned to the bookcases.

"Are you at all in earnest?" I said.

"A little," said Dravot sweetly. "As big a map as you have got, even if it's all blank where Kafiristan is, and any books you've got. We can read, though we aren't very educated."

I uncased the big thirty-two-miles-to-the-inch map of India,[46] and two smaller Frontier maps,[47] hauled down volume INF-KAN of the *Encyclopædia Britannica,* and the men consulted them.

---

[41] *Sarwat* means "wealth." Of more relevance, though, in 1841, Sir James Brooke organized a ragtag army and became ruler of Sarawak in Borneo, founding a dynasty of white sovereigns that lasted until the mid–nineteenth century. [ED.]

[42] This was the contemporary name for an as yet poorly explored mountainous region north of India, stretching across parts of northeastern Afghanistan and Pakistan. Very little was known about the area in 1888. Kipling's knowledge came almost entirely from the *Encyclopedia Britannica.* [ED.]

[43] City in present-day Pakistan, at the eastern approach to the Khyber Pass (usually spelled "Khaiber" by Kipling), the famous gateway to central Asia. [ED.]

[44] This information, like much of what we are told about Kafiristan, is fictional. [ED.]

[45] Teach them military skill and discipline, especially in the handling of weapons. [ED.]

[46] Standard map produced by the India Survey Department in 1886. [ED.]

[47] Also issued by the India Survey. [ED.]

"See here!" said Dravot, his thumb on the map. "Up to Jagdallak,[48] Peachey and me know the road. We was there with Roberts' Army.[49] We'll have to turn off to the right at Jagdallak through Laghmann territory.[50] Then we get among the hills — fourteen thousand feet — fifteen thousand — it will be cold work there, but it don't look very far on the map."

I handed him Wood on the *Sources of the Oxus.*[51] Carnehan was deep in the *Encyclopædia.*

"They're a mixed lot," said Dravot reflectively; "and it won't help us to know the names of their tribes. The more tribes the more they'll fight, and the better for us. From Jagdallak to Ashang.[52] H'mm!"

"But all the information about the country is as sketchy and inaccurate as can be," I protested. "No one knows anything about it really. Here's the file of the *United Services' Institute.*[53] Read what Bellew[54] says."

"Blow Bellew!" said Carnehan. "Dan, they're a stinkin' lot of heathens, but this book here says they think they're related to us English."

I smoked while the men pored over Raverty,[55] Wood, the maps, and the *Encyclopædia.*

"There is no use your waiting," said Dravot politely. "It's about four o'clock now. We'll go before six o'clock if you want to sleep, and we won't steal any of the papers. Don't you sit up. We're two harmless lunatics, and if you come tomorrow evening down to the Serai[56] we'll say good-bye to you."

"You *are* two fools," I answered. "You'll be turned back at the Frontier or cut up the minute you set foot in Afghanistan. Do you want any money or a recommendation down-country? I can help you to the chance of work next week."

"Next week we shall be hard at work ourselves, thank you," said Dravot. "It isn't so easy being a King as it looks. When we've got our Kingdom in

---

[48] Small town east of Kabul, the capital of present-day Afghanistan. [ED.]

[49] During the Second Afghan War of 1878–80, a force commanded by Lord Roberts attacked Kabul, and then won a famous battle over Afghans in western Afghanistan that enabled the installation of a pro-British amir. [ED.]

[50] Laghmann (also spelled "Laghman") is a province in northeastern Afghanistan. [ED.]

[51] John Wood wrote *A Journey to the Source of the Oxus* in 1841 about a commercial expedition to Afghanistan. [ED.]

[52] A town in northeastern Burma, near the border with China. [ED.]

[53] A British government organization that offered lectures and issued bulletins on military matters. [ED.]

[54] Henry Bellew served the British government at Kabul as a political consultant and authored several books on Afghanistan.

[55] Major Henry Raverty, soldier and author of a book on Afghanistan. [ED.]

[56] An inn built around an open courtyard. [ED.]

going order we'll let you know, and you can come up and help us to govern it."

"Would two lunatics make a contrack like that?" said Carnehan, with subdued pride, showing me a greasy half-sheet of notepaper on which was written the following. I copied it, then and there, as a curiosity—

> This Contract between me and you persuing witnesseth in the name of God—Amen and so forth.
> (One) That me and you will settle this matter together; i.e. to be Kings of Kafiristan.
> (Two) That you and me will not, while this matter is being settled, look at any Liquor, nor any Woman black, white, or brown, so as to get mixed up with one or the other harmful.
> (Three) That we conduct ourselves with Dignity and Discretion, and if one of us gets into trouble the other will stay by him.
> Signed by you and me this day.
> Peachey Taliaferro Carnehan.
> Daniel Dravot.
> Both Gentlemen at Large.

"There was no need for the last article," said Carnehan, blushing modestly; "but it looks regular. Now you know the sort of men that loafers are—we *are* loafers, Dan, until we get out of India—and *do* you think that we would sign a Contrack like that unless we was in earnest? We have kept away from the two things that make life worth having."

"You won't enjoy your lives much longer if you are going to try this idiotic adventure. Don't set the office on fire," I said, "and go away before nine o'clock."

I left them still poring over the maps and making notes on the back of the "Contrack." "Be sure to come down to the Serai tomorrow," were their parting words.

The Kumharsen Serai[57] is the great four-square sink of humanity where the strings of camels and horses from the North load and unload. All the nationalities of Central Asia may be found there, and most of the folk of India proper. Balkh and Bokhara there meet Bengal and Bombay,[58] and try to draw eye-teeth.[59] You can buy ponies, turquoises, Persian pussy-cats, saddle-bags, fat-tailed sheep and musk in the Kumharsen Serai, and get

---

[57]*Kumharsen Serai* was an inn and courtyard frequented by paupers and transients. [ED.]

[58]Balkh is a town in northern Afghanistan; Bokhara is a town north of Afghanistan, in Uzbek; Bengal was a province of northeastern India and eastern Pakistan; and Bombay is a city on the west coast of India. [ED.]

[59]To fleece each other. [ED.]

many strange things for nothing. In the afternoon I went down to see whether my friends intended to keep their word or were lying there drunk.

A priest attired in fragments of ribbons and rags stalked up to me, gravely twisting a child's paper whirligig. Behind him was his servant bending under the load of a crate of mud toys.[60] The two were loading up two camels, and the inhabitants of the Serai watched them with shrieks of laughter.

"The priest is mad," said a horse-dealer to me. "He is going up to Kabul to sell toys to the Amir.[61] He will either be raised to honour or have his head cut off. He came in here this morning and has been behaving madly ever since."

"The witless are under the protection of God," stammered a flat-cheeked Usbeg[62] in broken Hindi. "They foretell future events."

"Would they could have foretold that my caravan would have been cut up by the Shinwaris[63] almost within shadow of the Pass!" grunted the Eusufzai[64] agent of a Rajputana trading-house whose goods had been diverted into the hands of other robbers just across the Border, and whose misfortunes were the laughing-stock of the bazar. "Ohé, priest, whence come you and whither do you go?"

"From Roum[65] have I come," shouted the priest, waving his whirligig; "from Roum, blown by the breath of a hundred devils across the sea! O thieves, robbers, liars, the blessing of Pir Khan[66] on pigs, dogs, and perjurers! Who will take the Protected of God to the North to sell charms that are never still to the Amir? The camels shall not gall, the sons shall not fall sick, and the wives shall remain faithful while they are away, of the men who give me place in their caravan. Who will assist me to slipper the King of the Roos[67] with a golden slipper with a silver heel? The protection of Pir Khan be upon his labours!" He spread out the skirts of his gaberdine and pirouetted between the lines of tethered horses.

"There starts a caravan from Peshawar to Kabul in twenty days, *Huzrut*,"[68] said the Eusufzai trader. "My camels go therewith. Do thou also go and bring us good luck."

---

[60] Dolls sculpted in mud or clay. [ED.]

[61] Variant of *emir,* or native ruler.

[62] Tribesman from a region of central Asia largely contained within present-day Uzbekistan (sometimes spelled "Uzbek"). [ED.]

[63] Tribesmen from areas south of the Khyber Pass. [ED.]

[64] Tribesmen from areas north of the Khyber Pass (sometimes spelled "Yusufzai"). [ED.]

[65] Turkey. [ED.]

[66] Fictional Muslim name, combining the words for saint and prince. [ED.]

[67] Czar of Russia. [ED.]

[68] A term of great respect, similar to *your Honor.* [ED.]

"I will go even now!" shouted the priest. "I will depart upon my winged camels, and be at Peshawar in a day! Ho! Hazar[69] Mir Khan," he yelled to his servant, "drive out the camels, but let me first mount my own."

He leaped on the back of his beast as it knelt, and, turning round to me, cried: "Come thou also, Sahib,[70] a little along the road, and I will sell thee a charm—an amulet that shall make thee King of Kafiristan."

Then the light broke upon me, and I followed the two camels out of the Serai till we reached open road and the priest halted.

"What d'you think o' that?" said he in English. "Carnehan can't talk their patter, so I've made him my servant. He makes a handsome servant. 'Tisn't for nothing that I've been knocking about the country for fourteen years. Didn't I do that talk neat? We'll hitch on to a caravan at Peshawar till we get to Jagdallak, and then we'll see if we can get donkeys for our camels, and strike into Kafiristan. Whirligigs for the Amir, O Lor! Put your hand under the camel-bags and tell me what you feel."

I felt the butt of a Martini,[71] and another and another.

"Twenty of 'em," said Dravot placidly. "Twenty of 'em and ammunition to correspond, under the whirligigs and the mud dolls."

"Heaven help you if you are caught with those things!" I said. "A Martini is worth her weight in silver among the Pathans."[72]

"Fifteen hundred rupees[73] of capital—every rupee we could beg, borrow, or steal—are invested on these two camels," said Dravot. "We won't get caught. We're going through the Khaiber with a regular caravan. Who'd touch a poor mad priest?"

"Have you got everything you want?" I asked, overcome with astonishment.

"Not yet, but we shall soon. Give us a memento of your kindness, *Brother*. You did me a service, yesterday, and that time in Marwar. Half my Kingdom shall you have,[74] as the saying is." I slipped a small charm compass[75] from my watch-chain and handed it up to the priest.

"Good-bye," said Dravot, giving me hand cautiously. "It's the last time we'll shake hands with an Englishman these many days. Shake hands with him, Carnehan," he cried, as the second camel passed me.

---

[69] Get ready. [ED.]

[70] A term of respect for white men in India. [ED.]

[71] The Martini-Henry was a standard issue military rifle, with a single-action breech bolt. [ED.]

[72] Variant term for Afghans. [ED.]

[73] Approximately 100 pounds. [ED.]

[74] A possible allusion to Mark 6. 23. [ED.]

[75] A Masonic charm, since the compass is a key Masonic symbol. [ED.]

Carnehan leaned down and shook hands. Then the camels passed away along the dusty road, and I was left alone to wonder. My eye could detect no failure in the disguises. The scene in the Serai proved that they were complete to the native mind. There was just the chance, therefore, that Carnehan and Dravot would be able to wander through Afghanistan without detection. But, beyond, they would find death—certain and awful death.

Ten days later a native correspondent giving me the news of the day from Peshawar, wound up his letter with: "There has been much laughter here on account of a certain mad priest who is going in his estimation to sell petty gauds and insignificant trinkets which he ascribes as great charms to H.H. the Amir of Bokhara. He passed through Peshawar and associated himself to the Second Summer caravan that goes to Kabul. The merchants are pleased because through superstition they imagine that such mad fellows bring good fortune."

The two, then, were beyond the Border. I would have prayed for them, but, that night, a real King died in Europe,[76] and demanded an obituary notice.

———

The wheel of the world swings through the same phases again and again. Summer passed and winter thereafter, and came and passed again. The daily paper continued and I with it, and upon the third summer there fell a hot night, a night-issue, and a strained waiting for something to be telegraphed from the other side of the world, exactly as had happened before. A few great men had died in the past two years, the machines worked with more clatter, and some of the trees in the office garden were a few feet taller. But that was all the difference.

I passed over to the press-room, and went through just such a scene as I have already described. The nervous tension was stronger than it had been two years before, and I felt the heat more acutely. At three o'clock I cried, "Print off," and turned to go, when there crept to my chair what was left of a man. He was bent into a circle, his head was sunk between his shoulders, and he moved his feet one over the other like a bear. I could hardly see whether he walked or crawled—this rag-wrapped, whining cripple who addressed me by name, crying that he was come back. "Can you give me a drink?" he whimpered. "For the Lord's sake, give me a drink!"

I went back to the office, the man following with groans of pain, and I turned up the lamp.

———

[76] Possibly a reference to Czar Alexander II of Russia, assassinated in 1881. [ED.]

"Don't you know me?" he gasped, dropping into a chair, and he turned his drawn face, surmounted by a shock of gray hair, to the light.

I looked at him intently. Once before had I seen eyebrows that met over the nose in an inch-broad black band, but for the life of me I could not tell where.

"I don't know you," I said, handing him the whisky. "What can I do for you?"

He took a gulp of the spirit raw, and shivered in spite of the suffocating heat.

"I've come back," he repeated; "and I was the King of Kafiristan—me and Dravot—crowned Kings we was! In this office we settled it—you setting there and giving us the books. I am Peachey—Peachey Taliaferro Carnehan, and you've been setting here ever since—O Lord!"

I was more than a little astonished, and expressed my feelings accordingly.

"It's true," said Carnehan, with a dry cackle, nursing his feet, which were wrapped in rags. "True as gospel. Kings we were, with crowns upon our heads—me and Dravot—poor Dan—oh, poor, poor Dan, that would never take advice, not though I begged of him!"

"Take the whisky," I said, "and take your own time. Tell me all you can recollect of everything from beginning to end. You got across the Border on your camels, Dravot dressed as a mad priest and you his servant. Do you remember that?"

"I ain't mad—yet, but I shall be that way soon. Of course I remember. Keep looking at me, or maybe my words will go all to pieces. Keep looking at me in my eyes and don't say anything."

I leaned forward and looked into his face as steadily as I could. He dropped one hand upon the table and I grasped it by the wrist. It was twisted like a bird's claw, and upon the back was a ragged red diamond-shaped scar.

"No, don't look there. Look at *me*," said Carnehan. "That comes afterwards, but for the Lord's sake don't distrack me. We left with that caravan, me and Dravot playing all sorts of antics to amuse the people we were with. Dravot used to make us laugh in the evenings when all the people was cooking their dinners—cooking their dinners, and . . . what did they do then? They lit little fires with sparks that went into Dravot's beard, and we all laughed—fit to die. Little red fires they was, going into Dravot's big red beard—so funny." His eyes left mine and he smiled foolishly.

"You went as far as Jagdallak with that caravan," I said at a venture, "after you had lit those fires. To Jagdallak, where you turned off to try to get into Kafiristan."

"No, we didn't neither. What are you talking about? We turned off before Jagdallak, because we heard the roads was good. But they wasn't good enough for our two camels—mine and Dravot's. When we left the caravan, Dravot took off all his clothes and mine too, and said we would be heathen, because the Kafirs didn't allow Mohammedans to talk to them. So we dressed betwixt and between, and such a sight as Daniel Dravot I never saw yet nor expect to see again. He burned half his beard, and slung a sheepskin over his shoulder, and shaved his head into patterns. He shaved mine, too, and made me wear outrageous things to look like a heathen. That was in a most mountaineous country, and our camels couldn't go along any more because of the mountains. They were tall and black, and coming home I saw them fight like wild goats—there are lots of goats in Kafiristan. And these mountains, they never keep still, no more than the goats. Always fighting they are, and don't let you sleep at night."

"Take some more whisky," I said very slowly. "What did you and Daniel Dravot do when the camels could go no farther because of the rough roads that led into Kafiristan?"

"What did which do? There was a party called Peachey Taliaferro Carnehan that was with Dravot. Shall I tell you about him? He died out there in the cold. Slap from the bridge fell old Peachey, turning and twisting in the air like a penny whirligig that you can sell to the Amir. No; they was two for three-ha'pence, those whirligigs, or I am much mistaken and woful sore. . . . And then these camels were no use, and Peachey said to Dravot—'For the Lord's sake let's get out of this before our heads are chopped off,' and with that they killed the camels all among the mountains, not having anything in particular to eat, but first they took off the boxes with the guns and the ammunition, till two men came along driving four mules. Dravot up and dances in front of them, singing—'Sell me four mules.' Says the first man—'If you are rich enough to buy, you are rich enough to rob'; but before ever he could put his hand to his knife, Dravot breaks his neck over his knee, and the other party runs away. So Carnehan loaded the mules with the rifles that was taken off the camels, and together we starts forward into those bitter cold mountaineous parts, and never a road broader than the back of your hand."

He paused for a moment, while I asked him if he could remember the nature of the country through which he had journeyed.

"I am telling you as straight as I can, but my head isn't as good as it might be. They drove nails through it to make me hear better how Dravot died. The country was mountaineous and the mules were most contrary, and the inhabitants was dispersed and solitary. They went up and up, and down and down, and that other party, Carnehan, was imploring of Dravot not to sing and whistle so loud, for fear of bringing down the tremenjus avalanches. But Dravot says that if a King couldn't sing it wasn't worth being King, and whacked the mules over the rump, and never took no heed for ten cold days. We came to a big level valley all among the mountains, and the mules were near dead, so we killed them, not having anything in special for them or us to eat. We sat upon the boxes, and played odd and even[77] with the cartridges that was jolted out.

"Then ten men with bows and arrows ran down that valley, chasing twenty men with bows and arrows, and the row was tremenjus. They was fair men—fairer than you or me—with yellow hair and remarkable well built. Says Dravot, unpacking the guns—'This is the beginning of the business. We'll fight for the ten men,' and with that he fires two rifles at the twenty men, and drops one of them at two hundred yards from the rock where he was sitting. The other men began to run, but Carnehan and Dravot sits on the boxes picking them off at all ranges, up and down the valley. Then we goes up to the ten men that had run across the snow too, and they fires a footy[78] little arrow at us. Dravot he shoots above their heads and they all falls down flat. Then he walks over them and kicks them, and then he lifts them up and shakes hands all round to make them friendly like. He calls them and gives them the boxes to carry, and waves his hand for all the world as though he was King already. They takes the boxes and him across the valley and up the hill into a pine wood on the top, where there was half-a-dozen big stone idols. Dravot he goes to the biggest—a fellow they call Imbra—and lays a rifle and a cartridge at his feet, rubbing his nose respectful with his own nose, patting him on the head, and saluting in front of it. He turns round to the men and nods his head, and says—'That's all right. I'm in the know too, and all these old jim-jams[79] are my friends.' Then he opens his mouth and points down it, and when the first man brings him food, he says—'No'; and when the second man brings him food, he says—'No'; but when one of the old priests and the boss of the village brings him food, he says—'Yes,' very haughty, and eats it slow. That was how he came to our first village, without any trouble, just as though we had tumbled from the skies. But we tumbled from one of those damned rope-bridges, you see and—you couldn't expect a man to laugh much after that?"

"Take some more whisky and go on," I said. "That was the first village you came into. How did you get to be King?"

---

[77] A simple gambling game. [ED.]
[78] Paltry. [ED.]
[79] Knickknacks. [ED.]

"I wasn't King," said Carnehan. "Dravot he was the King, and a handsome man he looked with the gold crown on his head and all. Him and the other party stayed in that village, and every morning Dravot sat by the side of old lmbra, and the people came and worshipped. That was Dravot's order. Then a lot of men came into the valley, and Carnehan and Dravot picks them off with the rifles before they knew where they was, and runs down into the valley and up again the other side and finds another village, same as the first one, and the people all falls down flat on their faces, and Dravot says—'Now what is the trouble between you two villages?' and the people points to a woman, as fair as you or me, that was carried off,[80] and Dravot takes her back to the first village and counts up the dead—eight there was. For each dead man Dravot pours a little milk on the ground and waves his arms like a whirligig and 'That's all right,' says he. Then he and Carnehan takes the big boss of each village by the arm and walks them down into the valley, and shows them how to scratch a line with a spear right down the valley, and gives each a sod of turf from both sides of the line. Then all the people comes down and shouts like the devil and all, and Dravot says—'Go and dig the land, and be fruitful and multiply,'[81] which they did, though they didn't understand. Then we asks the names of things in their lingo—bread and water and fire and idols and such, and Dravot leads the priest of each village up to the idol, and says he must sit there and judge the people, and if anything goes wrong he is to be shot.

"Next week they was all turning up the land in the valley as quiet as bees and much prettier, and the priests heard all the complaints and told Dravot in dumb show what it was about. 'That's just the beginning,' says Dravot. 'They think we're Gods.' He and Carnehan picks out twenty good men and shows them how to click off a rifle, and form fours, and advance in line, and they was very pleased to do so, and clever to see the hang of it. Then he takes out his pipe and his baccy-pouch[82] and leaves one at one village, and one at the other, and off we two goes to see what was to be done in the next valley. That was all rock, and there was a little village there, and Carnehan says—'Send 'em to the old valley to plant,' and takes 'em there and gives 'em some land that wasn't took before. They were a poor lot, and we blooded 'em with a kid[83] before letting 'em into the new Kingdom. That

---

[80] An allusion to Helen of Troy and the Homeric epics. [ED.]

[81] An allusion to Genesis 1. 28. [ED.]

[82] Tobacco pouch. [ED.]

[83] In foxhunting, a newcomer was initiated by being "blooded," but Carnehan may also be referring to the ritual sacrifice of a goat. [ED.]

was to impress the people, and then they settled down quiet, and Carnehan went back to Dravot who had got into another valley, all snow and ice and most mountaineous. There was no people there and the Army got afraid, so Dravot shoots one of them, and goes on till he finds some people in a village, and the Army explains that unless the people wants to be killed they had better not shoot their little matchlocks;[84] for they had matchlocks. We makes friends with the priest and I stays there alone with two of the Army, teaching the men how to drill, and a thundering big Chief comes across the snow with kettle-drums and horns twanging, because he heard there was a new God kicking about. Carnehan sights for the brown of the men[85] half a mile across the snow and wings one of them. Then he sends a message to the Chief that, unless he wished to be killed, he must come and shake hands with me and leave his arms behind. The Chief comes alone first, and Carnehan shakes hands with him and whirls his arms about, same as Dravot used, and very much surprised that Chief was, and strokes my eyebrows. Then Carnehan goes alone to the Chief, and asks him in dumb show if he had an enemy he hated. 'I have,' says the Chief. So Carnehan weeds out the pick of his men, and sets the two of the Army to show them drill and at the end of two weeks the men can manoeuvre about as well as Volunteers.[86] So he marches with the Chief to a great big plain on the top of a mountain, and the Chief's men rushes into a village and takes it; we three Martinis firing into the brown of the enemy. So we took that village too, and I gives the Chief a rag from my coat and says, 'Occupy till I come';[87] which was scriptural. By way of a reminder, when me and the Army was eighteen hundred yards away, I drops a bullet near him standing on the snow, and all the people falls flat on their faces. Then I sends a letter to Dravot wherever he be by land or by sea."

At the risk of throwing the creature out of train I interrupted—"How could you write a letter up yonder?"

"The letter?—Oh!—The letter! Keep looking at me between the eyes, please. It was a string-talk letter, that we'd learned the way of it from a blind beggar in the Punjab."[88]

---

[84] Old-fashioned, inaccurate muskets, which had to be discharged with the use of a slow-burning cord lowered into the breech. [ED.]

[85] A phrase derived from bird hunting meaning shooting at the mass, rather than at a single individual. [ED.]

[86] The name applied to the amateurish predecessors of the regular British Territorial Army. [ED.]

[87] An allusion to Luke 19. 12–27. [ED.]

[88] A former province in the northwestern part of India. [ED.]

I remember that there had once come to the office a blind man with a knotted twig and a piece of string which he wound round the twig according to some cipher of his own. He could, after the lapse of days or hours, repeat the sentence which he had reeled up. He had reduced the alphabet to eleven primitive sounds; and tried to teach me his method, but I could not understand.

"I sent that letter to Dravot," said Carnehan; "and told him to come back because this Kingdom was growing too big for me to handle, and then I struck for the first valley, to see how the priests were working. They called the village we took along with the Chief, Bashkai, and the first village we took, Er-Heb.[89] The priests at Er-Heb was doing all right, but they had a lot of pending cases about land to show me, and some men from another village had been firing arrows at night. I went out and looked for that village, and fired four rounds at it from a thousand yards. That used all the cartridges I cared to spend, and I waited for Dravot, who had been away two or three months, and I kept my people quiet.

"One morning I heard the devil's own noise of drums and horns, and Dan Dravot marches down the hill with his Army and a tail of hundreds of men, and, which was the most amazing, a great gold crown on his head. 'My Gord, Carnehan,' says Daniel, 'this is a tremenjus business, and we've got the whole country as far as it's worth having. I am the son of Alexander by Queen Semiramis,[90] and you're my younger brother and a God too! It's the biggest thing we've ever seen. I've been marching and fighting for six weeks with the Army, and every footy little village for fifty miles has come in rejoiceful; and more than that, I've got the key of the whole show, as you'll see, and I've got a crown for you! I told 'em to make two of 'em at a place called Shu, where the gold lies in the rock like suet in mutton. Gold I've seen, and turquoise I've kicked out of the cliffs, and there's garnets in the sands of the river, and here's a chunk of amber that a man brought me. Call up all the priests and, here, take your crown.'

"One of the men opens a black hair bag, and I slips the crown on. It was too small and too heavy, but I wore it for the glory. Hammered gold it was—five pound weight, like a hoop of a barrel.

"'Peachey,' says Dravot, 'we don't want to fight no more. The Craft's[91] the trick, so help me!' and he brings forward that same Chief that I left at

---

[89] Like all place names used by Carnehan and Dravot in Kafiristan, these are fictional. [ED.]

[90] Alexander the Great, from whom Afghan chiefs claimed descent; Semiramis was queen of Assyria and also the founder of an empire. [ED.]

[91] A name for Freemasonry. [ED.]

Bashkai—Billy Fish we called him afterwards, because he was so like Billy Fish that drove the big tank-engine at Mach on the Bolan[92] in the old days. 'Shake hands with him,' says Dravot, and I shook hands and nearly dropped, for Billy Fish gave me the Grip. I said nothing, but tried him with the Fellow Craft Grip. He answers, all right, and I tried the Master's Grip, but that was a slip.[93] 'A Fellow Craft he is!' I says to Dan. 'Does he know the word?'[94]—'He does,' says Dan, 'and all the priests know. It's a miracle! The Chiefs and the priests can work a Fellow Craft Lodge[95] in a way that's very like ours, and they've cut the marks on the rocks, but they don't know the Third Degree, and they've come to find out. It's Gord's Truth. I've known these long years that the Afghans knew up to the Fellow Craft Degree, but this is a miracle. A God and a Grand-Master of the Craft am I, and a Lodge in the Third Degree I will open, and we'll raise the head priests and the Chiefs of the villages.'[96]

"'It's against all the law,' I says, 'holding a Lodge without warrant from any one; and you know we never held office in any Lodge.'

"'It's a master-stroke o' policy,' says Dravot. 'It means running the country as easy as a four-wheeled bogie[97] on a down grade. We can't stop to inquire now, or they'll turn against us. I've forty Chiefs at my heel, and passed and raised[98] according to their merit they shall be. Billet these men on the villages, and see that we run up a Lodge of some kind. The temple of Imbra will do for the Lodge-room. The women must make aprons[99] as you show them. I'll hold a levee of Chiefs tonight and Lodge tomorrow.'

"I was fair run off my legs, but I wasn't such a fool as not to see what a pull[100] this Craft business gave us. I showed the priests' families how to

---

[92] Mach, a town at the western approach to the Bolan Pass in north-central Baluchistan, was a station on the military railroad line built through the pass in the early 1880s. [ED.]

[93] Secret Masonic handshakes, marking the principal degrees of Masonic rank. Failure to execute a handshake correctly was called a slip. [ED.]

[94] Masons had a secret password. See Knight, "From *The Brotherhood*, 66." [ED.]

[95] They can conduct the rituals of a Masonic Lodge, which were called workings. [ED.]

[96] Dravot proposes to set himself up fraudulently as a Masonic grand master, who had the power to create subsidiary lodges and to raise Masons up the hierarchy of membership, from the second to the third degree, which was the highest degree reached by most in the brotherhood. [ED.]

[97] A railway undercarriage. [ED.]

[98] In Freemasonry, candidates for advancement were given examinations and, if they passed, they were raised to a higher degree. [ED.]

[99] Traditional Masonic costume. The aprons were decorated to indicate one's degree. [ED.]

[100] Advantage or influence. [ED.]

make aprons of the degrees, but for Dravot's apron the blue border and marks was made of turquoise lumps on white hide, not cloth. We took a great square stone in the temple for the Master's chair, and little stones for the officers' chairs, and painted the black pavement with white squares, and did what we could to make things regular.

"At the levee which was held that night on the hillside with big bonfires, Dravot gives out that him and me were Gods and sons of Alexander, and Past Grand-Masters in the Craft, and was come to make Kafiristan a country where every man should eat in peace and drink in quiet, and specially obey us. Then the Chiefs come round to shake hands, and they were so hairy and white and fair it was just shaking hands with old friends. We gave them names according as they was like men we had known in India—Billy Fish, Holly Dilworth, Pikky Kergan, that was Bazar-master[101] when I was at Mhow, and so on, and so on.

"*The* most amazing miracles was at Lodge next night. One of the old priests was watching us continuous, and I felt uneasy, for I knew we'd have to fudge the Ritual, and I didn't know what the men knew. The old priest was a stranger come in from beyond the village of Bashkai. The minute Dravot puts on the Master's apron that the girls had made for him, the priest fetches a whoop and a howl, and tries to overturn the stone that Dravot was sitting on. 'It's all up now,' I says. 'That comes of meddling with the Craft without warrant!' Dravot never winked an eye, not when ten priests took and tilted over the Grand-Master's chair—which was to say the stone of Imbra. The priest begins rubbing the bottom end of it to clear away the black dirt, and presently he shows all the other priests the Master's Mark, same as was on Dravot's apron, cut into the stone. Not even the priests of the temple of Imbra knew it was there. The old chap falls flat on his face at Dravot's feet and kisses 'em. 'Luck again,' says Dravot, across the Lodge to me; 'they say it's the missing Mark that no one could understand the why of. We're more than safe now.' Then he bangs the butt of his gun for a gavel and says: 'By virtue of the authority vested in me by my own right hand and the help of Peachey, I declare myself Grand-Master of all Freemasonry in Kafiristan in this the Mother Lodge o' the country, and King of Kafiristan equally with Peachey!' At that he puts on his crown and I puts on mine—I was doing Senior Warden[102]—and we opens the Lodge in most ample form. It was a amazing miracle! The priests moved in Lodge through the first two degrees almost without telling, as if the memory was

---

[101] A low-ranking, noncommissioned officer in the British Army, who policed the native districts of a town frequented by soldiers and British civilians. [ED.]

[102] A Masonic officer who assisted the master. [ED.]

coming back to them. After that, Peachey and Dravot raised such as was worthy—high priests and Chiefs of far-off villages.[103] Billy Fish was the first, and I can tell you we scared the soul out of him. It was not in any way according to Ritual, but it served our turn. We didn't raise more than ten of the biggest men, because we didn't want to make the Degree common. And they was clamouring to be raised.

"'In another six months,' says Dravot, 'we'll hold another Communication,[104] and see how you are working.' Then he asks them about their villages, and learns that they was fighting one against the other, and were sick and tired of it. And when they wasn't doing that they was fighting with the Mohammedans. 'You can fight those when they come into our country,' says Dravot. 'Tell off every tenth man of your tribes for a Frontier guard, and send two hundred at a time to this valley to be drilled. Nobody is going to be shot or speared any more so long as he does well, and I know that you won't cheat me, because you're white people—sons of Alexander—and not like common, black Mohammedans. You are *my* people, and by God,' says he, running off into English at the end—'I'll make a damned fine Nation of you, or I'll die in the making!'

"I can't tell all we did for the next six months, because Dravot did a lot I couldn't see the hang of, and he learned their lingo in a way I never could. My work was to help the people plough, and now and again go out with some of the Army and see what the other villages were doing, and make 'em throw rope-bridges across the ravines which cut up the country horrid. Dravot was very kind to me, but when he walked up and down in the pine wood pulling that bloody red beard of his with both fists I knew he was thinking plans I could not advise about, and I just waited for orders.

"But Dravot never showed me disrespect before the people. They were afraid of me and the Army, but they loved Dan. He was the best of friends with the priests and the Chiefs; but any one could come across the hills with a complaint, and Dravot would hear him out fair, and call four priests together and say what was to be done. He used to call in Billy Fish from Bashkai, and Pikky Kergan from Shu, and an old Chief we called Kafuzelum[105]—it was like enough to his real name—and hold councils with 'em when there was any fighting to be done in small villages. That was his Council of War, and the four priests of Bashkai, Shu, Khawak, and Madora was his Privy Council. Between the lot of 'em they sent me, with forty men

---

[103] The tribe seems to remember the first two degrees of Masonic ritual but has forgotten the third. Raising was accompanied by the swearing of fearsome, bloodthirsty oaths. [ED.]

[104] A meeting at which a lodge's practices or workings are inspected. [ED.]

[105] A character in a salacious popular song. [ED.]

and twenty rifles, and sixty men carrying turquoises, into the Ghorband [106] country to buy those hand-made Martini rifles, that come out of the Amir's workshops at Kabul, from one of the Amir's Herati [107] regiments that would have sold the very teeth out of their mouths for turquoises.

"I stayed in Ghorband a month, and gave the Governor there the pick of my baskets for hush-money, and bribed the Colonel of the regiment some more, and, between the two and the tribes-people, we got more than a hundred hand-made Martinis, a hundred good Kohat Jezails [108] that'll throw to six hundred yards, and forty man-loads of very bad ammunition for the rifles. I came back with what I had, and distributed 'em among the men that the Chiefs sent in to me to drill. Dravot was too busy to attend to those things, but the old Army that we first made helped me, and we turned out five hundred men that could drill, and two hundred that knew how to hold arms pretty straight. Even those cork-screwed, hand-made guns was a miracle to them. Dravot talked big about powder-shops and factories, walking up and down in the pine wood when the winter was coming on.

"'I won't make a Nation,' says he. 'I'll make an Empire! These men aren't niggers; they're English! Look at their eyes—look at their mouths. Look at the way they stand up. They sit on chairs in their own houses. They're the Lost Tribes, [109] or something like it, and they've grown to be English. I'll take a census in the spring if the priests don't get frightened. There must be a fair two million of 'em in these hills. The villages are full o' little children. Two million people—two hundred and fifty thousand fighting men—and all English! They only want the rifles and a little drilling. Two hundred and fifty thousand men, ready to cut in on Russia's right flank when she tries for India! Peachey, man,' he says, chewing his beard in great hunks, 'we shall be Emperors—Emperors of the Earth! Rajah Brooke will be a suckling to us. I'll treat with the Viceroy [110] on equal terms. I'll ask him to send me twelve picked English—twelve that I know of—to help us govern a bit. There's Mackray, Sergeant-pensioner at Segowli [111]—many's the good dinner he's given me, and his wife a pair of trousers. There's Donkin, the Warder of Tounghoo [112] Jail; there's hundreds that I could lay my hand on if I was in India. The Viceroy shall do it for me. I'll send a man

---

[106] An area north of Kabul. [ED.]

[107] Herat is a city considerably to the west of Kabul, near the border with Iran. [ED.]

[108] Long muskets manufactured in Afghanistan. [ED.]

[109] The Lost Tribes of Israel. [ED.]

[110] The viceroy of India. [ED.]

[111] Segowli (or "Segowlie") is a town in northeastern India. [ED.]

[112] A town in Burma. [ED.]

through in the spring for those men, and I'll write for a dispensation from the Grand Lodge for what I've done as Grand-Master. That—and all the Sniders[113] that'll be thrown out when the native troops in India take up the Martini. They'll be worn smooth, but they'll do for fighting in these hills. Twelve English, a hundred thousand Sniders run through the Amir's country in driblets—I'd be content with twenty thousand in one year—and we'd be an Empire. When everything was shipshape, I'd hand over the crown—this crown I'm wearing now—to Queen Victoria on my knees, and she'd say: "Rise up, Sir Daniel Dravot." Oh, it's big! It's big, I tell you! But there's so much to be done in every place—Bashkai, Khawak, Shu, and everywhere else.'

" 'What is it?' I says. 'There are no more men coming in to be drilled this autumn. Look at those fat, black clouds. They're bringing the snow.'

" 'It isn't that,' says Daniel, putting his hand very hard on my shoulder; 'and I don't wish to say anything that's against you, for no other living man would have followed me and made me what I am as you have done. You're a first-class Commander-in-Chief, and the people know you; but—it's a big country, and somehow you can't help me, Peachey, in the way I want to be helped.'

" 'Go to your blasted priests, then!' I said, and I was sorry when I made that remark, but it did hurt me sore to find Daniel talking so superior when I'd drilled all the men, and done all he told me.

" 'Don't let's quarrel, Peachey,' says Daniel without cursing. 'You're a King too, and the half of this Kingdom is yours; but can't you see, Peachey, we want cleverer men than us now—three or four of 'em, that we can scatter about for our Deputies. It's a hugeous great State, and I can't always tell the right thing to do, and I haven't time for all I want to do, and here's the winter coming on and all.' He put half his beard into his mouth, all red like the gold of his crown.

" 'I'm sorry, Daniel,' says I. 'I've done all I could. I've drilled the men and shown the people how to stack their oats better; and I've brought in those tinware rifles from Ghorband—but I know what you're driving at. I take it Kings always feel oppressed that way.'

" 'There's another thing too,' says Dravot, walking up and down. 'The winter's coming and these people won't be giving much trouble, and if they do we can't move about. I want a wife.'

" 'For God's sake leave the women alone!' I says. 'We've both got all the work we can, though I *am* a fool. Remember the Contrack, and keep clear o' women.'

---

[113] Standard British Army rifle before the Martini-Henry. [ED.]

"'The Contrack only lasted till such time as we was Kings; and Kings we have been these months past,' says Dravot, weighing his crown in his hand. 'You go get a wife too, Peachey—a nice, strappin', plump girl that'll keep you warm in the winter. They're prettier than English girls, and we can take the pick of 'em. Boil 'em once or twice in hot water, and they'll come out like chicken and ham.'[114]

"'Don't tempt me!' I says. 'I will not have any dealings with a woman not till we are a dam' side more settled than we are now. I've been doing the work o' two men, and you've been doing the work o' three. Let's lie off a bit, and see if we can get some better tobacco from Afghan country and run in some good liquor; but no women.'

"'Who's talking o' *women?*' says Dravot. 'I said *wife*—a Queen to breed a King's son for the King. A Queen out of the strongest tribe, that'll make them your blood-brothers, and that'll lie by your side and tell you all the people thinks about you and their own affairs. That's what I want.'

"'Do you remember that Bengali woman I kept at Mogul Serai[115] when I was a plate-layer?' says I. 'A fat lot o' good she was to me. She taught me the lingo and one or two other things; but what happened? She ran away with the Stationmaster's servant and half my month's pay. Then she turned up at Dadur Junction[116] in tow of a half-caste, and had the impidence to say I was her husband—all among the drivers in the running-shed too!'

"'We've done with that,' says Dravot; 'these women are whiter than you or me, and a Queen I will have for the winter months.'

"'For the last time o' asking, Dan, do *not*,' I says. 'It'll only bring us harm. The Bible says that Kings ain't to waste their strength on women,[117] 'specially when they've got a new raw Kingdom to work over.'

"'For the last time of answering[118] I will,' said Dravot, and he went away through the pine-trees looking like a big red devil, the sun being on his crown and beard and all.

"But getting a wife was not as easy as Dan thought. He put it before the Council, and there was no answer till Billy Fish said that he'd better ask the girls. Dravot damned them all round. 'What's wrong with me?' he shouts, standing by the idol Imbra. 'Am I a dog or am I not enough of a man for your wenches? Haven't I put the shadow of my hand over this country? Who stopped the last Afghan raid?' It was me really, but Dravot was too angry to

---

[114]White and pink. [ED.]

[115]A town in northeastern India. [ED.]

[116]A town in Baluchistan, a considerable distance from Mogul Serai. [ED.]

[117]An allusion to Proverbs 31. 3. [ED.]

[118]A phrase from the Anglican marriage ceremony. [ED.]

remember. 'Who bought your guns? Who repaired the bridges? Who's the Grand-Master of the sign cut in the stone?' says he, and he thumped his hand on the block that he used to sit on in Lodge, and at Council, which opened like Lodge always. Billy Fish said nothing and no more did the others. 'Keep your hair on, Dan,' said I; 'and ask the girls. That's how it's done at Home, and these people are quite English.'

"'The marriage of the King is a matter of State,' says Dan, in a white-hot rage, for he could feel, I hope, that he was going against his better mind. He walked out of the Council-room, and the others sat still, looking at the ground.

"'Billy Fish,' says I to the Chief of Bashkai, 'what's the difficulty here? A straight answer to a true friend.'

"'You know,' says Billy Fish. 'How should a man tell you who knows everything? How can daughters of men marry Gods or Devils? It's not proper.'

"I remembered something like that in the Bible;[119] but if, after seeing us as long as they had, they still believed we were Gods, it wasn't for me to undeceive them.

"'A God can do anything,' says I. 'If the King is fond of a girl he'll not let her die.'—'She'll have to,' said Billy Fish. 'There are all sorts of Gods and Devils in these mountains, and now and again a girl marries one of them and isn't seen any more. Besides, you two know the Mark cut in the stone. Only the Gods know that. We thought you were men till you showed the sign of the Master.'

"I wished then that we had explained about the loss of the genuine secrets of a Master-Mason at the first go-off; but I said nothing. All that night there was a blowing of horns in a little dark temple half-way down the hill, and I heard a girl crying fit to die. One of the priests told us that she was being prepared to marry the King.

"'I'll have no nonsense of that kind,' says Dan. 'I don't want to interfere with your customs, but I'll take my own wife.'—'The girl's a little bit afraid,' says the priest. 'She thinks she's going to die, and they are a-heartening of her up down in the temple.'

"'Hearten her very tender, then,' says Dravot, 'or I'll hearten you with the butt of a gun so you'll never want to be heartened again.' He licked his lips, did Dan, and stayed up walking about more than half the night, thinking of the wife that he was going to get in the morning. I wasn't any means comfortable, for I knew that dealings with a woman in foreign parts, though

---

[119]Carnehan may be thinking of the contrary story in Genesis 6. 2. [ED.]

you was a crowned King twenty times over, could not but be risky. I got up very early in the morning while Dravot was asleep, and I saw the priests talking together in whispers, and the Chiefs talking together too, and they looked at me out of the corners of their eyes.

"'What is up, Fish?' I say to the Bashkai man, who was wrapped up in his furs and looking splendid to behold.

"'I can't rightly say,' says he; 'but if you can make the King drop all this nonsense about marriage, you'll be doing him and me and yourself a great service.'

"'That I do believe,' says I. 'But sure, you know, Billy, as well as me, having fought against and for us, that the King and me are nothing more than two of the finest men that God Almighty ever made. Nothing more, I do assure you.'

"'That may be,' says Billy Fish, 'and yet I should be sorry if it was.' He sinks his head upon his great fur cloak for a minute and thinks. 'King,' says he, 'be you man or God or Devil, I'll stick by you today. I have twenty of my men with me, and they will follow me. We'll go to Bashkai until the storm blows over.'

"A little snow had fallen in the night, and everything was white except the greasy fat clouds that blew down and down from the north. Dravot came out with his crown on his head, swinging his arms and stamping his feet, and looking more pleased than Punch.

"'For the last time, drop it, Dan,' says I in a whisper, 'Billy Fish here says that there will be a row.'

"'A row among my people!' says Dravot. 'Not much. Peachey, you're a fool not to get a wife too. Where's the girl?' says he with a voice as loud as the braying of a jackass. 'Call up all the Chiefs and priests, and let the Emperor see if his wife suits him.'

"There was no need to call any one. They were all there leaning on their guns and spears round the clearing in the centre of the pine wood. A lot of priests went down to the little temple to bring up the girl, and the horns blew fit to wake the dead. Billy Fish saunters round and gets as close to Daniel as he could, and behind him stood his twenty men with matchlocks. Not a man of them under six feet. I was next to Dravot, and behind me was twenty men of the regular Army. Up comes the girl, and a strapping wench she was, covered with silver and turquoises, but white as death, and looking back every minute at the priests.

"'She'll do,' said Dan, looking her over. 'What's to be afraid of, lass? Come and kiss me.' He puts his arm round her. She shuts her eyes, gives a bit of a squeak, and down goes her face in the side of Dan's flaming red beard.

"'The slut's bitten me!' says he, clapping his hand to his neck, and, sure enough, his hand was red with blood. Billy Fish and two of his matchlock-men catches hold of Dan by the shoulders and drags him into the Bashkai lot, while the priests howls in their lingo—'Neither God nor Devil but a man!' I was all taken aback, for a priest cut at me in front, and the Army behind began firing into the Bashkai men.

"'God A'mighty!' says Dan. 'What is the meaning o' this?'

"'Come back! Come away!' says Billy Fish. 'Ruin and Mutiny is the matter. We'll break for Bashkai if we can.'

"I tried to give some sort of orders to my men—the men o' the regular Army—but it was no use, so I fired into the brown of 'em with an English Martini and drilled three beggars in a line. The valley was full of shouting, howling creatures, and every soul was shrieking, 'Not a God nor a Devil but only a man!' The Bashkai troops stuck to Billy Fish all they were worth, but their matchlocks wasn't half as good as the Kabul breechload-ers, and four of them dropped. Dan was bellowing like a bull, for he was very wrathy; and Billy Fish had a hard job to prevent him running out at the crowd.

"'We can't stand,' says Billy Fish. 'Make a run for it down the valley! The whole place is against us.' The matchlock-men ran, and we went down the valley in spite of Dravot. He was swearing horrible and crying out he was a King. The priests rolled great stones on us, and the regular Army fired hard, and there wasn't more than six men, not counting Dan, Billy Fish, and me, that came down to the bottom of the valley alive.

"Then they stopped firing and the horns in the temple blew again. 'Come away—for God's sake come away!' says Billy Fish. 'They'll send run-ners out to all the villages before ever we get to Bashkai. I can protect you there, but I can't do anything now.'

"My own notion is that Dan began to go mad in his head from that hour. He stared up and down like a stuck pig. Then he was all for walking back alone and killing the priests with his bare hands; which he could have done. 'An Emperor am I,' says Daniel, 'and next year I shall be a Knight of the Queen.'

"'All right, Dan,' says I; 'but come along now while there's time.'

"'It's your fault,' says he, 'for not looking after your Army better. There was mutiny in the midst, and you didn't know—you damned engine-driving, plate-laying, missionary's-pass-hunting hound!'[120] He sat upon a rock and called me every foul name he could lay tongue to. I was too heart-sick to care, though it was all his foolishness that brought the smash.

---

[120] Someone who begs for a missionary's good-conduct pass. [ED.]

" 'I'm sorry, Dan,' says I, 'but there's no accounting for natives. This business is our Fifty-Seven.[121] Maybe we'll make something out of it yet, when we've got to Bashkai.'

" 'Let's get to Bashkai, then,' says Dan, 'and, by God, when I come back here again I'll sweep the valley so there isn't a bug in a blanket left!'

"We walked all that day, and all that night Dan was stumping up and down on the snow, chewing his beard and muttering to himself.

" 'There's no hope o' getting clear,' said Billy Fish. 'The priests will have sent runners to the villages to say that you are only men. Why didn't you stick on as Gods till things was more settled? I'm a dead man,' says Billy Fish, and he throws himself down on the snow and begins to pray to his Gods.

"Next morning we was in a cruel bad country—all up and down, no level ground at all, and no food either. The six Bashkai men looked at Billy Fish hungry-way as if they wanted to ask something, but they said never a word. At noon we came to the top of a flat mountain all covered with snow, and when we climbed up into it, behold, there was an Army in position waiting in the middle!

" 'The runners have been very quick,' says Billy Fish, with a little bit of a laugh. 'They are waiting for us.'

"Three or four men began to fire from the enemy's side, and a chance shot took Daniel in the calf of the leg. That brought him to his senses. He looks across the snow at the Army, and sees the rifles that we had brought into the country.

" 'We're done for,' says he. 'They are Englishmen, these people, — and it's my blasted nonsense that has brought you to this. Get back, Billy Fish, and take your men away; you've done what you could, and now cut for it. Carnehan,' says he, 'shake hands with me and go along with Billy. Maybe they won't kill you. I'll go and meet 'em alone. It's me that did it. Me, the King!'

" 'Go!' says I. 'Go to Hell, Dan! I'm with you here. Billy Fish, you clear out, and we two will meet those folk.'

" 'I'm a Chief,' says Billy Fish, quite quiet. 'I stay with you. My men can go.'

"The Bashkai fellows didn't wait for a second word but ran off, and Dan and Me and Billy Fish walked across to where the drums were drumming and the horns were horning. It was cold—awful cold. I've got that cold in the back of my head now. There's a lump of it there."

---

[121] 1857 was the year of the Indian Mutiny.

The punkah-coolies[122] had gone to sleep. Two kerosene lamps were blazing in the office, and the perspiration poured down my face and splashed on the blotter as I leaned forward. Carnehan was shivering, and I feared that his mind might go. I wiped my face, took a fresh grip of the piteously mangled hands, and said: "What happened after that?"

The momentary shift of my eyes had broken the clear current.

"What was you pleased to say?" whined Carnehan. "They took them without any sound. Not a little whisper all along the snow, not though the King knocked down the first man that set hand on him—not though old Peachey fired his last cartridge into the brown of 'em. Not a single solitary sound did those swines make. They just closed up tight, and I tell you their furs stunk. There was a man called Billy Fish, a good friend of us all, and they cut his throat, Sir, then and there, like a pig; and the King kicks up the bloody snow and says: 'We've had a dashed fine run for our money. What's coming next?' But Peachey, Peachey Taliaferro, I tell you, Sir, in confidence as betwixt two friends, he lost his head, Sir. No, he didn't neither. The King lost his head, so he did, all along o' one of those cunning rope-bridges. Kindly let me have the paper-cutter, Sir. It tilted this way. They marched him a mile across that snow to a rope-bridge over a ravine with a river at the bottom. You may have seen such. They prodded him behind like an ox. 'Damn your eyes!' says the King. 'D'you suppose I can't die like a gentleman?' He turns to Peachey—Peachey that was crying like a child. 'I've brought you to this, Peachey,' says he. 'Brought you out of your happy life to be killed in Kafiristan, where you was late Commander-in-Chief of the Emperor's forces. Say you forgive me, Peachey.'—'I do,' says Peachey. 'Fully and freely do I forgive you, Dan.'—'Shake hands, Peachey,' says he. 'I'm going now.' Out he goes, looking neither right nor left, and when he was plumb in the middle of those dizzy dancing ropes—'Cut, you beggars,' he shouts; and they cut, and old Dan fell, turning round and round and round, twenty thousand miles, for he took half an hour to fall till he struck the water, and I could see his body caught on a rock with the gold crown close beside.

"But do you know what they did to Peachey between two pine-trees? They crucified him, Sir, as Peachey's hand will show. They used wooden pegs for his hands and his feet; and he didn't die. He hung there and screamed, and they took him down next day, and said it was a miracle that he wasn't dead. They took him down—poor old Peachey that hadn't done them any harm—that hadn't done them any—"

He rocked to and fro and wept bitterly, wiping his eyes with the back of his scarred hands and moaning like a child for some ten minutes.

---

[122]Natives hired to work the large interior fans. [ED.]

"They were cruel enough to feed him up in the temple, because they said he was more of a God than old Daniel that was a man. Then they turned him out on the snow, and told him to go home, and Peachey came home in about a year, begging along the roads quite safe; for Daniel Dravot he walked before and said: 'Come along, Peachey. It's a big thing we're doing.' The mountains they danced at night, and the mountains they tried to fall on Peachey's head, but Dan he held up his hand, and Peachey came along bent double. He never let go of Dan's hand, and he never let go of Dan's head. They gave it to him as a present in the temple, to remind him not to come again, and though the crown was pure gold, and Peachey was starving, never would Peachey sell the same. You knew Dravot, Sir! You knew Right Worshipful Brother Dravot! Look at him now!"

He fumbled in the mass of rags round his bent waist; brought out a black horsehair bag embroidered with silver thread; and shook therefrom on to my table—the dried, withered head of Daniel Dravot! The morning sun that had long been paling the lamps struck the red beard and blind sunken eyes; struck, too, a heavy circlet of gold studded with raw turquoises, that Carnehan placed tenderly on the battered temples.

"You be'old now," said Carnehan, "the Emperor in his 'abit as he lived [123]—the King of Kafiristan with his crown upon his head. Poor old Daniel that was a monarch once!"

I shuddered, for, in spite of defacements manifold, I recognised the head of the man of Marwar Junction. Carnehan rose to go. I attempted to stop him. He was not fit to walk abroad. "Let me take away the whisky, and give me a little money," he gasped. "I was a King once. I'll go to the Deputy Commissioner and ask to set in the Poorhouse till I get my health. No, thank you, I can't wait till you get a carriage for me. I've urgent private affairs—in the south—at Marwar."

He shambled out of the office and departed in the direction of the Deputy Commissioner's house. That day at noon I had occasion to go down the blinding hot Mall, and I saw a crooked man crawling along the white dust of the roadside, his hat in his hand, quavering dolorously after the fashion of street-singers at Home. There was not a soul in sight, and he was out of all possible earshot of the houses. And he sang through his nose, turning his head from right to left:

The Son of Man goes forth to war,
   A golden crown to gain;

---

[123] An allusion to *Hamlet,* echoing Hamlet's words about the appearance of his father's ghost. [ED.]

His blood-red banner streams afar—
Who follows in his train?[124]

I waited to hear no more, but put the poor wretch into my carriage and drove him off to the nearest missionary for eventual transfer to the Asylum. He repeated the hymn twice while he was with me whom he did not in the least recognise, and I left him singing it to the missionary.

Two days later I inquired after his welfare of the Superintendent of the Asylum.

"He was admitted suffering from sunstroke. He died early yesterday morning," said the Superintendent. "Is it true that he was half an hour bare-headed in the sun at mid-day?"

"Yes," said I, "but do you happen to know if he had anything upon him by any chance when he died?"

"Not to my knowledge," said the Superintendent.

And there the matter rests.

---

[124]Verse from a hymn by Reginald Heber, bishop of Calcutta in the 1820s. Carnehan misquotes the second line, which should read "a kingly crown to gain." [ED.]

The Beach of Falesá

Robert Louis Stevenson

CHAPTER I
A South Sea Bridal

I saw that island[1] first when it was neither night nor morning. The moon was to the west, setting, but still broad and bright. To the east, and right amidships of the dawn, which was all pink, the daystar sparkled like a diamond. The land breeze blew in our faces, and smelt strong of wild lime and vanilla: other things besides, but these were the most plain; and the chill of it set me sneezing. I should say I had been for years on a low island near the line,[2] living for the most part solitary among natives. Here was a fresh experience: even the tongue would be quite strange to me; and the look of these woods and mountains, and the rare smell of them, renewed my blood.

The captain blew out the binnacle lamp.[3]

"There!" said he, "there goes a bit of smoke, Mr. Wiltshire, behind the break of the reef. That's Falesá, where your station is, the last village to the east; nobody lives to windward—I don't know why. Take my glass, and you can make the houses out."

I took the glass; and the shores leaped nearer, and I saw the tangle of the woods and the breach of the surf, and the brown roofs and the black insides of houses peeped among the trees.

"Do you catch a bit of white there to the east'ard?" the captain continued. "That's your house. Coral built, stands high, verandah you could walk on three abreast; best station in the South Pacific. When old Adams saw it, he took and shook me by the hand. 'I've dropped into a soft thing here,' says he, 'So you have,' says I, 'and time too!' Poor Johnny! I never saw him again but the once, and then he had changed his tune—couldn't get on with the natives, or the whites, or something; and the next time we came round there he was dead and buried. I took and put up a bit of a stick to him: 'John Adams, *obit* eighteen and sixty-eight. Go thou and do likewise.' I missed that man. I never could see much harm in Johnny."

"What did he die of?" I inquired.

"Some kind of sickness," says the captain. "It appears it took him sudden. Seems he got up in the night, and filled up on Pain-Killer and Kennedy's

---

[1] Falesá is a fictitious island, which Stevenson projected as the site for a cycle of stories set in the South Seas. [ED.]

[2] A coral reef island, as opposed to a "high" or volcanic island, near the equator (or "the line"). [ED.]

[3] A light for reading the ship's compass. [ED.]

Discovery.[4] No go: he was booked beyond Kennedy. Then he had tried to open a case of gin. No go again: not strong enough. Then he must have turned to and run out on the verandah, and capsized over the rail. When they found him, the next day, he was clean crazy—carried on all the time about somebody watering his copra.[5] Poor John!"

"Was it thought to be the island?" I asked.

"Well, it was thought to be the island, or the trouble, or something," he replied. "I never could hear but what it was a healthy place. Our last man, Vigours, never turned a hair. He left because of the beach[6]—said he was afraid of Black Jack and Case and Whistling Jimmie, who was still alive at the time, but got drowned soon afterward when drunk. As for old Captain Randall, he's been here any time since eighteen-forty, forty-five. I never could see much harm in Billy, nor much change. Seems as if he might live to be Old Kafoozleum.[7] No, I guess it's healthy."

"There's a boat coming now," said I. "She's right in the pass; looks to be a sixteen-foot whale; two white men in the stern sheets."[8]

"That's the boat that drowned Whistling Jimmie!" cried the Captain; "let's see the glass. Yes, that's Case, sure enough, and the darkie. They've got a gallows bad reputation, but you know what a place the beach is for talking. My belief, that Whistling Jimmie was the worst of the trouble; and he's gone to glory, you see. What'll you bet they ain't after gin? Lay you five to two they take six cases."

When these two traders came aboard I was pleased with the looks of them at once, or, rather, with the looks of both, and the speech of one. I was sick for white neighbours after my four years at the line, which I always counted years of prison; getting tabooed, and going down to the Speak House to see and get it taken off;[9] buying gin and going on a break, and then repenting; sitting in the house at night with the lamp for company; or walking on the beach and wondering what kind of a fool to call myself for

---

[4] Patent medicines. [ED.]

[5] Dried cocoanut meat, which was pressed out into oil. Copra was the chief commercial resource of the South Seas in the late nineteenth century. It could be diluted with water to cheat the traders. [ED.]

[6] On all South Seas islands, white settlements clustered near the beach in and around the principal harbors. These settlements were referred to simply as the beach, which also served figuratively as a collective term for whites. [ED.]

[7] The captain is thinking of Methuselah, the oldest man mentioned in the Bible, but the name also evokes a character in a bawdy popular song. [ED.]

[8] Open area at the stern of a small boat. [ED.]

[9] Whites who were tabooed, that is, proscribed, usually had to plead their case before native authorities at a public meeting house. [ED.]

being where I was. There were no other whites upon my island, and when I sailed to the next, rough customers made the most of the society. Now to see these two when they came aboard was a pleasure. One was a negro, to be sure; but they were both rigged out smart in striped pyjamas and straw hats, and Case would have passed muster in a city. He was yellow and smallish, had a hawk's nose to his face, pale eyes, and his beard trimmed with scissors. No man knew his country, beyond he was of English speech; and it was clear he came of a good family and was splendidly educated. He was accomplished too; played the accordion first-rate; and give him a piece of string or a cork or a pack of cards, and he could show you tricks equal to any professional. He could speak, when he chose, fit for a drawing-room; and when he chose he could blaspheme worse than a Yankee boatswain, and talk [smut] to sicken a Kanaka.[10] The way he thought would pay best at the moment, that was Case's way, and it always seemed to come natural, and like as if he was born to it. He had the courage of a lion and the cunning of a rat; and if he's not in hell today, there's no such place. I know but one good point to the man: that he was fond of his wife, and kind to her. She was a Samoa woman, and dyed her hair red, Samoa style; and when he came to die (as I have to tell of) they found one strange thing—that he had made a will, like a Christian, and the widow got the lot: all his, they said, and all Black Jack's, and the most of Billy Randall's in the bargain, for it was Case that kept the books. So she went off home in the schooner *Manu'a*, and does the lady to this day in her own place.

But of all this on that first morning I knew no more than a fly. Case used me like a gentleman and like a friend, made me welcome to Falesá, and put his services at my disposal, which was the more helpful from my ignorance of the native. All the [early] part of the day we sat drinking better acquaintance in the cabin, and I never heard a man talk more to the point. There was no smarter trader, and none dodgier,[11] in the islands. [I remember one bit of advice he gave me that morning, and one yarn he told. The bit of advice was this. "Whenever you get hold of any money," says he; "any Christian money, I mean—the first thing to do is to fire it up to Sydney to the bank. It's only a temptation to a copra merchant; some day, he'll be in a row with the other traders, and he'll get his shirt out and buy copra with it. And the name of the man that buys copra with gold is Damfool," says he. That was the advice, and this was the yarn, which might have opened my eyes to

_____

[10] A boatswain is a petty officer on a merchant ship. Smut is obscene matter. *Kanaka* is a Polynesian word meaning either "man" or "mankind," which was used by Europeans to refer derogatively to natives. [ED.]

[11] More cunning. [ED.]

the danger of that man for a neighbour, if I had been anyway suspicious. It seems Case was trading somewhere in the Ellices.[12] There was a man Miller, a Dutchman, there, who had a strong hold with the natives and handled the bulk of what there was. Well, one fine day a schooner got wrecked in the lagoon, and Miller bought her (the way these things are usually managed) for an old song, which was the ruin of him. For having a lot of trade on hand that had cost him practically nothing, what does he do but begin cutting rates? Case went round to the other traders. "Wants to lower prices?" says Case. "All right, then. He has five times the turn-over of any one of us; if buying at a loss is the game, he stands to lose five times more. Let's give him the bed rock; let's bilge the——!" And so they did, and five months after, Miller had to sell out his boat and station, and begin again somewhere in the Carolines.[13]

All this talk suited me, and my new companion suited me, and] I thought Falesá seemed to be the right kind of a place; and the more I drank the lighter my heart. Our last trader had fled the place at half an hour's notice, taking a chance passage in a labour ship[14] from up west. The captain, when he came, had found the station closed, the keys left with the native pastor, and a letter from the runaway, confessing he was fairly frightened of his life. Since then the firm had not been represented, and of course there was no cargo. The wind, besides, was fair, the captain hoped he could make his next island by dawn, with a good tide, and the business of landing my trade was gone about lively. There was no call for me to fool with it, Case said; nobody would touch my things, everyone was honest in Falesá, only about chickens or an odd knife or an odd stick of tobacco; and the best I could do was to sit quiet till the vessel left, then come straight to his house, see old Captain Randall, the father of the beach, take pot-luck, and go home to sleep when it got dark. So it was high noon, and the schooner was under way before I set my foot on shore at Falesá.

I had a glass or two on board; I was just off a long cruise, and the ground heaved under me like a ship's deck. The world was like all new painted; my foot went along to music; Falesá might have been Fiddler's Green,[15] if there is such a place, and more's the pity if there isn't! It was good to foot the grass, to look aloft at the green mountains, to see the men with their green wreaths and the women in their bright dresses, red and blue. On we went,

[12] South Seas islands lying between the Gilbert Islands and Samoa. [ED.]
[13] Islands south of Guam and north of Papua New Guinea, a considerable distance from the Ellices. [ED.]
[14] A ship trading in slave labor. [ED.]
[15] In sailors' folklore, a legendary paradise. [ED.]

in the strong sun and the cool shadow, liking both; and all the children in the town came trotting after with their shaven heads and their brown bodies, and raising a thin kind of a cheer in our wake, like crowing poultry.

"By-the-bye," says Case, "we must get you a wife."

"That's so," said I; "I had forgotten."

There was a crowd of girls about us, and I pulled myself up and looked among them like a Bashaw.[16] They were all dressed out for the sake of the ship being in; and the women of Falesá are a handsome lot to see. If they have a fault, they are a trifle broad in the beam; and I was just thinking so when Case touched me.

"That's pretty," says he.

I saw one coming on the other side alone. She had been fishing; all she wore was a chemise, and it was wetted through, [and a cutty sark[17] at that.] She was young and very slender for an island maid, with a long face, a high forehead, and a [sly], strange, blindish look, between a cat's and a baby's.

"Who's she?" said I. "She'll do."

"That's Uma," said Case, and he called her up and spoke to her in the native. I didn't know what he said; but when he was in the midst she looked up at me quick and timid, like a child dodging a blow, then down again, and presently smiled. She had a wide mouth, the lips and the chin cut like any statue's; and the smile came out for a moment and was gone. Then she stood with her head bent, and heard Case to an end, spoke back in the pretty Polynesian voice, looking him full in the face, heard him again in answer, and then with an obeisance started off. I had just a share of the bow, but never another shot of her eye, and there was no more word of smiling.

"I guess it's all right," said Case. "I guess you can have her. I'll make it square with the old lady. You can have your pick of the lot for a plug of tobacco," he added, sneering.

I suppose it was the smile stuck in my memory, for I spoke back sharp. "She doesn't look that sort," I cried.

"I don't know that she is," said Case. "I believe she's as right as the mail. Keeps to herself, don't go round with the gang, and that. Oh no, don't you misunderstand me—Uma's on the square." He spoke eager, I thought, and that surprised and pleased me. "Indeed," he went on, "I shouldn't make so sure of getting her, only she cottoned to the cut of your jib. All you have to do is to keep dark and let me work the mother my own way; and I'll bring the girl round to the captain's for the marriage."

I didn't care for the word marriage, and I said so.

---

[16] Presumably, a pasha, or high Turkish official. [ED.]

[17] Scotch expression meaning a short shirt. [ED.]

"Oh, there's nothing to hurt in the marriage," says he. "Black Jack's the chaplain."

By this time we had come in view of the house of these three white men; for a negro is counted a white man, and so is a Chinese! a strange idea, but common in the islands. It was a board house with a strip of rickety verandah. The store was to the front, with a counter, scales, and the poorest possible display of trade: a case or two of tinned meats; a barrel of hard bread; a few bolts of cotton stuff, not to be compared with mine; the only thing well represented being the contraband, firearms and liquor. "If these are my only rivals," thinks I, "I should do well in Falesá." Indeed, there was only the one way they could touch me, and that was with the guns and drink.

In the back room was old Captain Randall, squatting on the floor native fashion, fat and pale, naked to the waist, grey as a badger, and his eyes set with drink. His body was covered with grey hair and crawled over by flies; one was in the corner of his eye—he never heeded; and the mosquitoes hummed about the man like bees. Any clean-minded man would have had the creature out at once and buried him; and to see him, and think he was seventy, and remember he had once commanded a ship, and come ashore in his smart togs,[18] and talked big in bars and consulates, and sat in club verandahs, turned me sick and sober.

He tried to get up when I came in, but that was hopeless; so he reached me a hand instead, and stumbled out some salutation.

"Papa's[19] pretty full this morning," observed Case. "We've had an epidemic here; and Captain Randall takes gin for a prophylactic—don't you, Papa?"

"Never took [such thing] my life!" cried the captain indignantly. "Take gin for my health's sake, Mr. Wha's-ever-your-name—'s a precautionary measure."

"That's all right, Papa," said Case. "But you'll have to brace up. There's going to be a marriage—Mr. Wiltshire here is going to get spliced."

The old man asked to whom.

"To Uma," said Case.

"Uma!" cried the captain. "Wha's he want Uma for? 's he come here for his health, anyway? Wha' 'n hell 's he want Uma for?"

"Dry up, Papa," said Case. "'Tain't you that's to marry her. I guess you're not her godfather and godmother. I guess Mr. Wiltshire's going to please himself."

---

[18] Clothes. [ED.]

[19] Please pronounce "pappa" throughout. [Stevenson's note.]

With that he made an excuse to me that he must move about the marriage, and left me alone with the poor wretch that was his partner and (to speak truth) his gull. Trade and station belonged both to Randall; Case and the negro were parasites; they crawled and fed upon him like the flies, he none the wiser. Indeed, I have no harm to say of Billy Randall beyond the fact that my gorge rose at him, and the time I now passed in his company was like a nightmare.

The room was stifling hot and full of flies; for the house was dirty and low and small, and stood in a bad place, behind the village, in the borders of the bush, and sheltered from the trade.[20] The three men's beds were on the floor, and a litter of pans and dishes. There was no standing furniture; Randall, when he was violent, tearing it to laths. There I sat and had a meal which was served us by Case's wife; and there I was entertained all day by that remains of man, his tongue stumbling among low old jokes and long old stories, and his own wheezy laughter always ready, so that he had no sense of my depression. He was nipping gin all the while. Sometimes he fell asleep, and awoke again, whimpering and shivering, and every now and again he would ask me why I wanted to marry Uma. "My friend," I was telling myself all day, "you must not come to be an old gentleman like this."

It might be four in the afternoon, perhaps, when the back door was thrust slowly open, and a strange old native woman crawled into the house almost on her belly. She was swathed in black stuff to her heels; her hair was grey in swatches; her face was tattooed, which was not the practice in that island; her eyes big and bright and crazy. These she fixed upon me with a rapt expression that I saw to be part acting. She said no plain word, but smacked and mumbled with her lips, and hummed aloud, like a child over its Christmas pudding. She came straight across the house, heading for me, and, as soon as she was alongside, caught up my hand and purred and crooned over it like a great cat. From this she slipped into a kind of song.

"Who the devil's this?" cried I, for the thing startled me.

"It's Fa'avao," says Randall; and I saw he had hitched along the floor into the farthest corner.

"You ain't afraid of her?" I cried.

"Me 'fraid!" cried the captain. "My dear friend, I defy her! I don't let her put her foot in here, only I suppose 's [diff'ent] today, for the marriage. 's Uma's mother."

"Well, suppose it is; what's she carrying on about?" I asked, more irritated, perhaps more frightened, than I cared to show; and the captain

---

[20]The trade wind. [Ed.]

told me she was making up a quantity of poetry in my praise because I was to marry Uma. "All right, old lady," says I, with rather a failure of a laugh, "anything to oblige. But when you're done with my hand, you might let me know."

She did as though she understood; the song rose into a cry, and stopped; the woman crouched out of the house the same way that she came in, and must have plunged straight into the bush, for when I followed her to the door she had already vanished.

"These are rum manners," said I.

"'s a rum crowd," said the captain, and, to my surprise, he made the sign of the cross on his bare bosom.

"Hillo!" says I, "are you a Papist?"

He repudiated the idea with contempt. "Hard-shell Baptis'," [21] said he. "But, my dear friend, the Papists got some good ideas too; and tha' 's one of 'em. You take my advice, and whenever you come across Uma or Fa'avao or Vigours, or any of that crowd, you take a leaf out o' the priests, and do what I do. Savvy?" says he, repeated the sign, and winked his dim eye at me. "No, *sir!*" he broke out again, "no Papists here!" and for a long time entertained me with his religious opinions.

I must have been taken with Uma from the first, or I should certainly have fled from that house, and got into the clean air, and the clean sea, or some convenient river—though, it's true, I was committed to Case; and, besides, I could never have held my head up in that island if I had run from a girl upon my wedding-night.

The sun was down, the sky all on fire, and the lamp had been some time lighted, when Case came back with Uma and the negro. She was dressed and scented; her kilt was of fine tapa,[22] looking richer in the folds than any silk; her bust, which was of the colour of dark honey, she wore bare only for some half a dozen necklaces of seeds and flowers; and behind her ears and in her hair she had the scarlet flowers of the hibiscus. She showed the best bearing for a bride conceivable, serious and still; and I thought shame to stand up with her in that mean house and before that grinning negro. I thought shame, I say; for the mountebank was dressed with a big paper collar, the book he made believe to read from was an odd volume of a novel, and the words of his service not fit to be set down. My conscience smote me when we joined hands; and when she got her certificate I was tempted

---

[21] A U.S. Baptist sect known for their extremely strict, Calvinist principles. [ED.]

[22] An unwoven fabric made from the bark of mulberry or breadfruit trees, often elaborately painted. [ED.]

to throw up the bargain and confess. Here is the document. It was Case that wrote it, signatures and all, in a leaf out of the ledger:

[This is to certify that <u>Uma</u> daughter of <u>Fa'avao</u> of Falesá island of——, is illegally married to <u>Mr. John Wiltshire</u> for one night, and Mr. John Wiltshire is at liberty to send her to hell next morning.

John Blackamoor
Chaplain to the Hulks.

Extracted from the register
by William T. Randall
Master Mariner]

A nice paper to put in a girl's hand and see her hide away like gold. A man might easily feel cheap for less. But it was the practice in these parts, and (as I told myself) not the least the fault of us white men, but of the missionaries. If they had let the natives be, I had never needed this deception, but taken all the wives I wished, and left them when I pleased, with a clear conscience.

The more ashamed I was, the more hurry I was in to be gone; and our desires thus jumping together, I made the less remark of a change in the traders. Case had been all eagerness to keep me; now, as though he had attained a purpose, he seemed all eagerness to have me go. Uma, he said, could show me to my house, and the three bade us farewell indoors.

The night was nearly come; the village smelt of trees and flowers and the sea and breadfruit-cooking; there came a fine roll of sea from the reef, and from a distance, among the woods and houses, many pretty sounds of men and children. It did me good to breathe free air; it did me good to be done with the captain and see, instead, the creature at my side. I felt for all the world as though she were some girl at home in the Old Country, and, forgetting myself for the minute, took her hand to walk with. Her fingers nestled into mine, I heard her breathe deep and quick, and all at once she caught my hand to her face and pressed it there. "You good!" she cried, and ran ahead of me, and stopped and looked back and smiled, and ran ahead of me again, thus guiding me through the edge of the bush, and by a quiet way to my own house.

The truth is, Case had done the courting for me in style—told her I was mad to have her, and cared nothing for the consequence; and the poor soul, knowing that which I was still ignorant of, believed it, every word, and had her head nigh turned with vanity and gratitude. Now, of all this I had no guess; I was one of those most opposed to any nonsense about native women, having seen so many whites eaten up by their wives' relatives, and made fools of in the bargain; and I told myself I must make a stand at once, and bring her to her bearings. But she looked so quaint and pretty as she ran away and then awaited me, and the thing was done so like a child or a kind dog, that the best I could do was just to follow her whenever she went on, to listen for the fall of her bare feet, and to watch in the dusk for the shining of her body. And there was another thought came in my head. She played kitten with me now when we were alone; but in the house she had carried it the way a countess might, so proud and humble. And what with her dress—for all there was so little of it, and that native enough—what with her fine tapa and fine scents, and her red flowers and seeds, that were quite as bright as jewels, only larger—it came over me she was a kind of countess really, dressed to hear great singers at a concert, and no even mate for a poor trader like myself.

She was the first in the house; and while I was still without I saw a match flash and the lamplight kindle in the windows. The station was a wonderful fine place, coral built, with quite a wide verandah, and the main room high and wide. My chests and cases had been piled in, and made rather of a mess; and there, in the thick of the confusion, stood Uma by the table, awaiting me. Her shadow went all the way up behind her into the hollow of the iron roof; she stood against it bright, the lamplight shining on her skin. I stopped in the door, and she looked at me, not speaking, with eyes that were eager and yet daunted; then she touched herself on the bosom.

"Me—your wifie," she said. It had never taken me like that before; but the want of her took and shook all through me, like the wind in the luff of a sail.[23]

I could not speak if I had wanted; and if I could, I would not. I was ashamed to be so much moved about a native, ashamed of the marriage too, and the certificate she had treasured in her kilt; and I turned aside and made believe to rummage among my cases. The first thing I lighted on was a case of gin, the only one that I had brought; and, partly for the girl's sake, and partly for horror of the [recollection] of old Randall, took a sudden resolve. I prized the lid off. One by one I drew the bottles with a pocket corkscrew, and sent Uma out to pour the stuff from the verandah.

She came back after the last, and looked at me puzzled like.

["Why you do that?" she asked.]

"No good," said I, for I was now a little better master of my tongue. "Man he drink, he no good."

She agreed with this, but kept considering. "Why you bring him?"[24] she asked presently. "Suppose you no want drink, you no bring him, I think."

---

[23] The forward edge of a sail, which trembled in the breeze. [ED.]

[24] In South Seas pidgin, all pronouns are masculine. [ED.]

"That's all right," said I. "One time I want drink too much; now no want. You see, I no savvy I get one little wifie. Suppose I drink gin, my little wifie he 'fraid."

To speak to her kindly was about more than I was fit for; I had made my vow I would never let on to weakness with a native, and I had nothing for it but to stop.

She stood looking gravely down at me where I sat by the open case. "I think you good man," she said. And suddenly she had fallen before me on the floor. "I belong you all-e-same pig!" she cried.

CHAPTER II
The Ban

I came on the verandah just before the sun rose on the morrow. My house was the last on the east; there was a cape of woods and cliffs behind that hid the sunrise. To the west, a swift cold river ran down, and beyond was the green of the village, dotted with cocoa-palms and breadfruits and houses. The shutters were some of them down and some open; I saw the mosquito bars still stretched, with shadows of people new-awakened sitting up inside; and all over the green others were stalking silent, wrapped in their many-coloured sleeping clothes like Bedouins in Bible pictures. It was mortal still and solemn and chilly, and the light of the dawn on the lagoon was like the shining of a fire.

But the thing that troubled me was nearer hand. Some dozen young men and children made a piece of a half-circle, flanking my house: the river divided them, some were on the near side, some on the far, and one on a boulder in the midst; and they all sat silent, wrapped in their sheets, and stared at me and my house as straight as pointer dogs. I thought it strange as I went out. When I had bathed and come back again, and found them all there, and two or three more along with them, I thought it stranger still. What could they see to gaze at in my house, I wondered, and went in.

But the thought of these starers stuck in my mind, and presently I came out again. The sun was now up, but it was still behind the cape of woods. Say a quarter of an hour had come and gone. The crowd was greatly increased, the far bank of the river was lined for quite a way — perhaps thirty grown folk, and of children twice as many, some standing, some squatted on the ground, and all staring at my house. I have seen a house in a South Sea village thus surrounded, but then a trader was thrashing his wife inside, and she singing out. Here was nothing: the stove was alight, the smoke going up in a Christian manner; all was shipshape and Bristol fashion.[25] To be sure, there was a stranger come, but they had a chance to see that stranger yesterday, and took it quiet enough. What ailed them now? I leaned my arms on the rail and stared back. Devil a wink[26] they had in them! Now and then I could see the children chatter, but they spoke so low not even the hum of their speaking came my length. The rest were like graven images: they stared at me, dumb and sorrowful, with their bright eyes; and it came upon me things would look not much different if I were on the platform of the gallows, and these good folk had come to see me hanged.

I felt I was getting daunted, and began to be afraid I looked it, which would never do. Up I stood, made believe to stretch myself, came down the verandah stair, and strolled towards the river. There went a short buzz from one to the other, like what you hear in theatres when the curtain goes up; and some of the nearest gave back the matter of a pace. I saw a girl lay one hand on a young man and make a gesture upward with the other; at the same time she said something in the native with a gasping voice. Three little boys sat beside my path, where I must pass within three feet of them. Wrapped in their sheets, with their shaved heads and bits of top-knots, and queer faces, they looked like figures on a chimneypiece. Awhile they sat their ground, solemn as judges. I came up hand over fist, doing my five knots, like a man that meant business; and I thought I saw a sort of a wink and gulp in the three faces. Then one jumped up (he was the farthest off) and ran for his mammy. The other two, trying to follow suit, got foul, came to ground together bawling, wriggled right out of [their sheets—and in a moment there were all three of them, two mother naked, scampering for] their lives and singing out like pigs. The natives, who would never let a joke slip, even at a burial, laughed and let up, as short as a dog's bark.

They say it scares a man to be alone. No such thing. What scares him in the dark or the high bush is that he can't make sure, and there might be an army at his elbow. What scares him worst is to be right in the midst of a crowd, and have no guess of what they're driving at. When that laugh stopped, I stopped too. The boys had not yet made their offing, they were still on the full stretch going the one way, when I had already gone about ship and was sheering off the other. Like a fool I had come out, doing my five knots; like a fool I went back again. It must have been the funniest thing to see, and what knocked me silly, this time no one laughed; only one

---

[25] In good business order. [ED.]

[26] "Devil a . . ." is Scotch for "Not a . . .". [ED.]

old woman gave a kind of pious moan, the way you have heard Dissenters[27] in their chapels at the sermon.

"I never saw such [damfool] Kanakas as your people here," I said once to Uma, glancing out of the window at the starers.

"Savvy nothing," says Uma, with a kind of disgusted air that she was good at.

And that was all the talk we had upon the matter, for I was put out, and Uma took the thing so much as a matter of course that I was fairly ashamed.

All day, off and on, now fewer and now more, the fools sat about the west end of my house and across the river, waiting for the show, whatever that was—fire to come down from heaven, I suppose, and consume me, bones and baggage. But by evening, like real islanders, they had wearied of the business, and got away, and had a dance instead in the big house of the village, where I heard them singing and clapping hands till, maybe, ten at night, and the next day it seemed they had forgotten I existed. If fire had come down from heaven or the earth opened and swallowed me, there would have been nobody to see the sport or take the lesson, or whatever you like to call it. But I was to find they hadn't forgot either, and kept an eye lifting for phenomena over my way.

I was hard at it both these days getting my trade in order and taking stock of what Vigours had left. This was a job that made me pretty sick, and kept me from thinking on much else. Ben[28] had taken stock the trip before—I knew I could trust Ben—but it was plain somebody had been making free in the meantime. I found I was out by what might [easy] cover six months' salary and profit, and I could have kicked myself all round the village to have been such a blamed ass, sitting boozing with that Case instead of attending to my own affairs and taking stock.

However, there's no use crying over spilt milk. It was done now, and couldn't be undone. All I could do was to get what was left of it, and my new stuff (my own choice) in order, to go round and get after the rats and cockroaches, and to fix up that store regular Sydney style. A fine show I made of it; and the third morning when I had lit my pipe and stood in the door-way and looked in, and turned and looked far up the mountain and saw the cocoanuts waving and [footed] up the tons of copra, and over the village green and saw the island dandies and reckoned up the yards of print they wanted for their kilts and dresses, I felt as if I was in the right place to

---

[27] Protestant sects, some of them evangelical, that broke away from the established Church of England. [ED.]

[28] Ben Hird is a stock character in *The Island Nights' Entertainments.* [ED.]

make a fortune, and go home again and start a public-house.[29] There was I, sitting in that verandah, in as handsome a piece of scenery as you could find, a splendid sun, and a fine fresh healthy trade that stirred up a man's blood like sea-bathing; and the whole thing was clean gone from me, and I was dreaming England, which is, after all, a nasty, cold, muddy hole, with not enough light to see to read by; and dreaming the looks of my public, by a cant[30] of a broad high-road like an avenue, and with the sign on a green tree.

So much for the morning, but the day passed and the devil anyone looked near me, and from all I knew of natives in other islands I thought this strange. People laughed a little at our firm and their fine stations, and at this station of Falesá in particular; all the copra in the district wouldn't pay for it (I had heard them say) in fifty years, which I supposed was an exaggeration. But when the day went, and no business came at all, I began to get downhearted; and, about three in the afternoon, I went out for a stroll to cheer me up. On the green I saw a white man coming with a cassock on, by which and by the face of him I knew he was a priest. He was a good-natured old soul to look at, gone a little grizzled, and so dirty you could have written with him on a piece of paper.

"Good day, sir," said I.

He answered me eagerly in native.

"Don't you speak any English?" said I.

"[Franch]," says he.

"Well," said I, "I'm sorry, but I can't do anything there."

He tried me awhile in the French, and then again in native, which he seemed to think was the best chance. I made out he was after more than passing the time of day with me, but had something to communicate, and I listened the harder. I heard the names of Adams and Case and of Randall— Randall the oftenest—and the word "poison," or something like it, and a native word that he said very often. I went home, repeating it to myself.

"What does fussy-ocky mean?" I asked of Uma, for that was as near as I could come to it.

"Make dead," said she.

"The devil it does!" says I. "Did ever you hear that Case had poisoned Johnny Adams?"

"Every man he savvy that," says Uma, scornful-like. "Give him white sand—bad sand. He got the bottle still. Suppose he give you gin, you no take him."

---

[29] Now commonly called a pub. [ED.]

[30] A bend or angle. [ED.]

Now I had heard much the same sort of story in other islands, and the same white powder always to the front, which made me think the less of it. For all that, I went over to Randall's place to see what I could pick up, and found Case on the doorstep, cleaning a gun.

"Good shooting here?" says I.

"A 1," says he. "The bush is full of all kinds of birds. I wish copra was as plenty," says he—I thought, slyly—"but there don't seem anything doing."

I could see Black Jack in the store, serving a customer.

"That looks like business, though," said I.

"That's the first sale we've made in three weeks," said he.

"You don't tell me?" says I. "Three weeks? Well, well."

"If you don't believe me," he cries, a little hot, "you can go and look at the copra-house. It's half empty to this blessed hour."

"I shouldn't be much the better for that, you see," says I. "For all I can tell, it might have been whole empty yesterday."

"That's so," says he, with a bit of a laugh.

"By-the-bye," I said, "what sort of a party is that priest? Seems rather a friendly sort."

At this Case laughed right out loud. "Ah!" says he, "I see what ails you now. Galuchet's been at you." *Father Galoshes* was the name he went by most, but Case always gave it the French quirk, which was another reason we had for thinking him above the common.

"Yes, I have seen him," I says. "I made out he didn't think much of [you and] Captain Randall."

"That he don't!" says Case. "It was the trouble about poor Adams. The last day, when he lay dying, there was young Buncombe round. Ever met Buncombe?"

I told him no.

"He's a cure,[31] is Buncombe!" laughs Case. "Well, Buncombe took it in his head that, as there was no other clergyman about, bar Kanaka pastors, we ought to call in Father Galuchet, and have the old man administered and take the sacrament. It was all the same to me, you may suppose; but I said I thought Adams was the fellow to consult. He was jawing away about watered copra and a sight of foolery. 'Look here,' I said, 'you're pretty sick. Would you like to see Galoshes?' He sat right up on his elbow. 'Get the priest,' says he, 'get the priest; don't let me die here like a dog!' He spoke kind of fierce and eager, but sensible enough. There was nothing to say

---

[31] Short for "curious fellow." [ED.]

against that, so we sent and asked Galuchet if he would come. You bet he would. He jumped in his dirty linen at the thought of it. But we had reckoned without Papa. He's a hard-shell Baptist, is Papa; no Papists need apply. And he took and locked the door. Buncombe told him he was bigoted, and I thought he would have had a fit. 'Bigoted!' he says. 'Me bigoted? Have I lived to hear it from a jackanapes like you?' And he made for Buncombe, and I had to hold them apart; and there was Adams in the middle, gone luny again, and carrying on about copra like a born fool. It was good as the play, and I was about knocked out of time with laughing, when all of a sudden Adams sat up, clapped his hands to his chest, and went into the horrors.[32] He died hard, did John Adams," says Case, with a kind of a sudden sternness.

"And what became of the priest?" I asked.

"The priest?" says Case. "Oh! he was hammering on the door outside, and crying on the natives to come and beat it in, and singing out it was a soul he wished to save, and that. He was in a [hell of a] taking, was the priest. But what would you have? Johnny had slipped his cable; no more Johnny in the market; and the administration racket clean played out. Next thing, word came to Randall the priest was praying upon Johnny's grave. Papa was pretty full, and got a club, and lit out straight for the place, and there was Galoshes on his knees, and a lot of natives looking on. You wouldn't think Papa cared that much about anything, unless it was liquor; but he and the priest stuck to it two hours, slanging each other in native, and every time Galoshes tried to kneel down Papa went for him with the club. There never were such larks in Falesá. The end of it was that Captain Randall knocked over with some kind of a fit or stroke, and the priest got in his goods after all. But he was the angriest priest you ever heard of, and complained to the chiefs about the outrage, as he called it. That was no account, for our chiefs are Protestant here; and, anyway, he had been making trouble about the drum for morning school, and they were glad to give him a wipe.[33] Now he swears old Randall gave Adams poison or something, and when the two meet they grin at each other like baboons."

He told this story as natural as could be, and like a man that enjoyed the fun; though, now I come to think of it after so long, it seems rather a sickening yarn. However, Case never set up to be soft, only to be square and hearty, and a man all round; and, to tell the truth, he puzzled me entirely.

---

[32] Delirium tremens. [ED.]

[33] A blow, or a jeer. [ED.]

I went home and asked Uma if she were a Popey, which I had made out to be the native word for Catholics.

"*E le ai!*" says she. She always used the native when she meant "no" more than usually strong, and, indeed, there's more of it. "No good Popey," she added.

Then I asked her about Adams and the priest, and she told me much the same yarn in her own way. So that I was left not much farther on, but inclined, upon the whole, to think the bottom of the matter was the row about the sacrament, and the poisoning only talk.

The next day was a Sunday, when there was no business to be looked for. Uma asked me in the morning if I was going to "pray"; I told her she bet not, and she stopped home herself with no more words. I thought this seemed unlike a native, and a native woman, and a woman that had new clothes to show off; however, it suited me to the ground, and I made the less of it. The queer thing was that I came next door to going to church after all, a thing I'm little likely to forget. I had turned out for a stroll, and heard the hymn tune up. You know how it is. If you hear folk singing, it seems to draw you; and pretty soon I found myself alongside the church. It was a little long low place, coral built, rounded off at both ends like a whale-boat, a big native roof on the top of it, windows without sashes and doorways without doors. I stuck my head into one of the windows, and the sight was so new to me—for things went quite different in the islands I was acquainted with—that I stayed and looked on. The congregation sat on the floor on mats, the women on one side, the men on the other, all rigged out to kill—the women with dresses and trade hats, the men in white jackets and shirts. The hymn was over; the pastor, a big buck Kanaka, was in the pulpit, preaching for his life; and by the way he wagged his hand, and worked his voice, and made his points, and seemed to argue with the folk, I made out he was a gun at the business. Well, he looked up suddenly and caught my eye, and I give you my word he staggered in the pulpit; his eyes bulged out of his head, his hand rose and pointed at me like as if against his will, and the sermon stopped right there.

It isn't a fine thing to say for yourself, but I ran away; and if the same kind of a shock was given me, I should run away again tomorrow. To see that palavering Kanaka struck all of a heap at the mere sight of me gave me a feeling as if the bottom had dropped out of the world. I went right home, and stayed there, and said nothing. You might think I would tell Uma, but that was against my system. You might have thought I would have gone over and consulted Case; but the truth was I was ashamed to speak of such a thing, I thought everyone would blurt out laughing in my face. So I held my tongue, and thought all the more; and the more I thought, the less I liked the business.

By Monday night I got it clearly in my head I must be tabooed. A new store to stand open two days in a village and not a man or woman come to see the trade was past believing.

"Uma," said I, "I think I'm tabooed."

"I think so," said she.

I thought awhile whether I should ask her more, but it's a bad idea to set natives up with any notion of consulting them, so I went to Case. It was dark, and he was sitting alone, as he did mostly, smoking on the stairs.

"Case," said I, "here's a queer thing. I'm tabooed."

"Oh, fudge!" says he; "'tain't the practice in these islands."

"That may be, or it mayn't," said I. "It's the practice where I was before. You can bet I know what it's like; and I tell it you for a fact, I'm tabooed."

"Well," said he, "what have you been doing?"

"That's what I want to find out," said I.

"Oh, you can't be," said he; "it ain't possible. However, I'll tell you what I'll do. Just to put your mind at rest, I'll go round and find out for sure. Just you waltz in and talk to Papa."

"Thank you," I said, "I'd rather stay right out here on the verandah. Your house is so close."

"I'll call Papa out here, then," says he.

"My dear fellow," I says, "I wish you wouldn't. The fact is, I don't take to Mr. Randall."

Case laughed, took a lantern from the store, and set out into the village. He was gone perhaps a quarter of an hour, and he looked mighty serious when he came back.

"Well," said he, clapping down the lantern on the verandah steps, "I would never have believed it. I don't know where the impudence of these Kanakas 'll go next; they seem to have lost all idea of respect for whites. What we want is a man-of-war—a German, if we could—they know how to manage Kanakas."

"I *am* tabooed, then?" I cried.

"Something of the sort," said he. "It's the worst thing of the kind I've heard of yet. But I'll stand by you, Wiltshire, man to man. You come round here tomorrow about nine, and we'll have it out with the chiefs. They're afraid of me, or they used to be; but their heads are so big by now, I don't know what to think. Understand me, Wiltshire; I don't count this your quarrel," he went on, with a great deal of resolution, "I count it all of our quarrel, I count it the White Man's Quarrel, and I'll stand to it through thick and thin, and there's my hand on it."

"Have you found out what's the reason?" I asked.

"Not yet," said Case. "But we'll fix them down tomorrow."

Altogether I was pretty well pleased with his attitude, and almost more the next day, when we met to go before the chiefs, to see him so stern and resolved. The chiefs awaited us in one of their big oval houses, which was marked out to us from a long way off by the crowd about the eaves, a hundred strong if there was one—men, women, and children. Many of the men were on their way to work and wore green wreaths, and it put me in thoughts of the 1st of May at home. This crowd opened and buzzed about the pair of us as we went in, with a sudden angry animation. Five chiefs were there; four mighty stately men, the fifth old and puckered. They sat on mats in their white kilts and jackets; they had fans in their hands, like fine ladies; and two of the younger ones wore Catholic medals, which gave me matter of reflection. Our place was set, and the mats laid for us over against these grandees, on the near side of the house; the midst was empty; the crowd, close at our backs, murmured and craned and jostled to look on, and the shadows of them tossed in front of us on the clean pebbles of the floor. I was just a hair put out by the excitement of the commons, but the quiet civil appearance of the chiefs reassured me, all the more when their spokesman began and made a long speech in a low tone of voice, sometimes waving his hand toward Case, sometimes toward me, and sometimes knocking with his knuckles on the mat. One thing was clear: there was no sign of anger in the chiefs.

"What's he been saying?" I asked, when he had done.

"Oh, just that they're glad to see you, and they understand by me you wish to make some kind of complaint, and you're to fire away, and they'll do the square thing."

"It took a precious long time to say that," said I.

"Oh, the rest was sawder[34] and *bonjour* and that," said Case. "You know what Kanakas are."

"Well, they don't get much *bonjour* out of me," said I. "You tell them who I am. I'm a white man, and a British subject, and no end of a big chief at home; and I've come here to do them good, and bring them civilisation; and no sooner have I got my trade sorted out than they go and taboo me, and no one dare come near my place! Tell them I don't mean to fly in the face of anything legal; and if what they want's a present, I'll do what's fair. I don't blame any man looking out for himself, tell them, for that's human nature; but if they think they're going to come any of their native ideas over me, they'll find themselves mistaken. And tell them plain that I demand the reason of this treatment as a white man and a British subject."

That was my speech. I know how to deal with Kanakas: give them plain sense and fair dealing, and—I'll do them that much justice—they knuckle

---

[34] Flattery. [ED.]

under every time. They haven't any real government or any real law, that's what you've got to knock into their heads; and even if they had, it would be a good joke if it was to apply to a white man. It would be a strange thing if we came all this way and couldn't do what we pleased. The mere idea has always put my monkey up, and I rapped my speech out pretty big. Then Case translated it—or made believe to, rather—and the first chief replied, and then a second, and a third, all in the same style, easy and genteel, but solemn underneath. Once a question was put to Case, and he answered it, and all hands (both chiefs and commons) laughed out aloud, and looked at me. Last of all, the puckered old fellow and the big young chief that spoke first started in to put Case through a kind of catechism. Sometimes I made out that Case was trying to fence, and they stuck to him like hounds, and the sweat ran down his face, which was no very pleasant sight to me, and at some of his answers the crowd moaned and murmured, which was a worse hearing. It's a cruel shame I knew no native, for (as I now believe) they were asking Case about my marriage, and he must have had a tough job of it to clear his feet. But leave Case alone; he had the brains to run a parliament.

"Well, is that all?" I asked, when a pause came.

"Come along," says he, mopping his face; "I'll tell you outside."

"Do you mean they won't take the taboo off?" I cried.

"It's something queer," said he. "I'll tell you outside. Better come away."

"I won't take it at their hands," cried I. "I ain't that kind of a man. You don't find me turn my back on a parcel of Kanakas."

"You'd better," said Case.

He looked at me with a signal in his eye; and the five chiefs looked at me civilly enough, but kind of pointed; and the people looked at me and craned and jostled. I remembered the folks that watched my house, and how the pastor had jumped in his pulpit at the bare sight of me; and the whole business seemed so out of the way that I rose and followed Case. The crowd opened again to let us through, but wider than before, the children on the skirts running and singing out, and as we two white men walked away they all stood and watched us.

"And now," said I, "what is all this about?"

"The truth is I can't rightly make it out myself. They have a down[35] on you," says Case.

"Taboo a man because they have a down on him!" I cried. "I never heard the like."

---

[35] A suspicion. [ED.]

"It's worse than that, you see," said Case. "You ain't tabooed—I told you that couldn't be. The people won't go near you, Wiltshire, and there's where it is."

"They won't go near me? What do you mean by that? Why won't they go near me?" I cried.

Case hesitated. "Seems they're frightened," says he, in a low voice.

I stopped dead short. "Frightened?" I repeated. "Are you gone crazy, Case? What are they frightened of?"

"I wish I could make out," Case answered, shaking his head. "Appears like one of their tomfool superstitions. That's what I don't cotton to," he said. "It's like the business about Vigours."

"I'd like to know what you mean by that, and I'll trouble you to tell me," says I.

"Well, you know, Vigours lit out and left all standing," said he. "It was some superstition business—I never got the hang of it; but it began to look bad before the end."

"I've heard a different story about that," said I, "and I had better tell you so. I heard he ran away because of you."

"Oh! well, I suppose he was ashamed to tell the truth," says Case; "I guess he thought it silly. And it's a fact that I packed him off. 'What would you do old man?' says he. 'Get,' says I, 'and not think twice about it.' I was the gladdest kind of man to see him clear away. It ain't my notion to turn my back on a mate when he's in a tight place, but there was that much trouble in the village that I couldn't see where it might likely end. I was a fool to be so much about with Vigours. They cast it up to me today. Didn't you hear Maea—that's the young chief, the big one—ripping out about 'Vika'? That was him they were after. They don't seem to forget it, somehow."

"This is all very well," said I, "but it don't tell me what's wrong; it don't tell me what they're afraid of—what their idea is."

"Well, I wish I knew," said Case. "I can't say fairer than that."

"You might have asked, I think," says I.

"And so I did," says he. "But you must have seen for yourself, unless you're blind, that the asking got the other way. I'll go as far as I dare for another white man; but when I find I'm in the scrape myself, I think first of my own bacon. The loss of me is I'm too good-natured. And I'll take the freedom of telling you you show a queer kind of gratitude to a man who's got into all this mess along of your affairs."

"There's a thing I am thinking of," said I. "You were a fool to be so much about with Vigours. One comfort, you haven't been much about with me. I notice you've never been inside my house. Own up now; you had word of this before?"

"It's a fact I haven't been," said he. "It was an oversight, and I am sorry for it, Wiltshire. But about coming now, I'll be quite plain."

"You mean you won't?" I asked.

"Awfully sorry, old man, but that's the size of it," says Case.

"In short, you're afraid?" says I.

"In short, I'm afraid," says he.

"And I'm still to be tabooed for nothing?" I asked.

"I tell you you're not tabooed," said he. "The Kanakas won't go near you, that's all. And who's to make 'em? We traders have a lot of gall, I must say; we make these poor Kanakas take back their laws, and take up their taboos, and that, whenever it happens to suit us. But you don't mean to say you expect a law obliging people to deal in your store whether they want to or not? You don't mean to tell me you've got the gall for that? And if you had, it would be a queer thing to propose to me. I would just like to point out to you, Wiltshire, that I'm a trader myself."

"I don't think I would talk of gall if I was you," said I. "Here's about what it comes to, as well as I can make out: None of the people are to trade with me, and they're all to trade with you. You're to have the copra, and I'm to go to the devil and shake myself. And I don't know any native, and you're the only man here worth mention that speaks English, and you have the gall to up and hint to me my life's in danger, and all you've got to tell me is you don't know why!"

"Well, it *is* all I have to tell you," said he. "I don't know—I wish I did."

"And so you turn your back and leave me to myself! Is that the position?" says I.

"If you like to put it nasty," says he. "I don't put it so. I say merely, 'I'm going to keep clear of you; or, if I don't, I'll get in danger for myself.'"

"Well," says I, "you're a nice kind of a white man!"

"Oh, I understand; you're riled," said he. "I would be myself. I can make excuses."

"All right," I said, "go and make excuses somewhere else. Here's my way, there's yours!"

With that we parted, and I went straight home, in a [holy] temper, and found Uma trying on a lot of trade goods like a baby.

"Here," I said, "you quit that foolery! Here's a pretty mess to have made, as if I wasn't bothered enough anyway! And I thought I told you to get dinner!"

And then I believe I gave her a bit of the rough side of my tongue, as she deserved. She stood up at once, like a sentry to his officer; for I must say she was always well brought up, and had a great respect for whites.

"And now," says I, "you belong round here, you're bound to understand this. What am I tabooed for, anyway? Or, if I ain't tabooed, what makes the folks afraid of me?"

She stood and looked at me with eyes like saucers.

"You no savvy?" she gasps at last.

"No," said I. "How would you expect me to? We don't have any such craziness where I come from."

"Ese no tell you?" she asked again.

(*Ese* was the name the natives had for Case; it may mean foreign, or extraordinary; or it might mean a mummy apple; but most like it was only his own name misheard and put in a Kanaka spelling.)

"Not much," said I.

"[Damn] Ese!" she cried.

You might think it funny to hear this Kanaka girl come out with a big swear. No such thing. There was no swearing in her—no, nor anger; she was beyond anger, and meant the word simple and serious. She stood there straight as she said it. I cannot justly say that I ever saw a woman look like that before or after, and it struck me mum. Then she made a kind of an obeisance, but it was the proudest kind, and threw her hands out open.

"I 'shamed," she said. "I think you savvy. Ese he tell me you savvy, he tell me you no mind, tell me you love me too much. Taboo belong me," she said, touching herself on the bosom, as she had done upon our wedding-night. "Now I go 'way, taboo he go 'way too. Then you get too much copra. You like more better, I think. *Tofá, alii,*" says she in the native—"Farewell, chief!"

"Hold on!" I cried. "Don't be in such a [blamed] hurry."

She looked at me sidelong with a smile. "You see, you get copra," she said, the same as you might offer candies to a child.

"Uma," said I, "hear reason. I didn't know, and that's a fact; and Case seems to have played it pretty mean upon the pair of us. But I do know now, and I don't mind; I love you too much. You no go 'way, you no leave me, I too much sorry."

"You no love me," she cried, "you talk me bad words!" And she threw herself in a corner [on] the floor, and began to cry.

Well, I'm no scholar, but I wasn't born yesterday, and I thought the worst of that trouble was over. However, there she lay—her back turned, her face to the wall—and shook with sobbing like a little child, so that her feet jumped with it. It's strange how it hits a man when he's in love; for there's no use mincing things—Kanaka and all, I was in love with her, or just as good. I tried to take her hand, but she would none of that. "Uma," I said, "there's no sense in carrying on like this. I want you stop here, I want my little wifie, I tell you true."

"No tell me true," she sobbed.

"All right," says I, "I'll wait till you're through with this." And I sat right down beside her on the floor, and set to smooth her hair with my hand. At first she wriggled away when I touched her; then she seemed to notice me no more; then her sobs grew gradually less, and presently stopped; and the next thing I knew, she raised her face to mine.

"You tell me true? You like me stop?" she asked.

"Uma," I said, "I would rather have you than all the copra in the South Seas," which was a very big expression, and the strangest thing was that I meant it.

She threw her arms about me, sprang close up, and pressed her face to mine in the island way of kissing, so that I was all wetted with her tears, and my heart went out to her wholly. I never had anything so near me as this little brown bit of a girl. Many things went together, and all helped to turn my head. She was pretty enough to eat; it seemed she was my only friend in that queer place; I was ashamed that I had spoken rough to her: and she was a woman, and my wife, and a kind of a baby besides that I was sorry for; and the salt of her tears was in my mouth. And I forgot Case and the natives; and I forgot that I knew nothing of the story, or only remembered it to banish the remembrance; and I forgot that I was to get no copra, and so could make no livelihood; and I forgot my employers, and the strange kind of service I was doing them, when I preferred my fancy to their business; and I forgot even that Uma was no true wife of mine, but just a maid beguiled, and that in a pretty shabby style. But that is to look too far on. I will come to that part of it next.

It was late before we thought of getting dinner. The stove was out, and gone stone-cold; but we fired up after a while, and cooked each a dish, helping and hindering each other, and making a play of it like children. I was so greedy of her nearness that I sat down to dinner with my lass upon my knee, made sure of her with one hand, and ate with the other. Ay, and more than that. She was the worst cook I suppose God made; the things she set her hand to it would have sickened an honest horse to eat of; yet I made my meal that day on Uma's cookery, and can never call to mind to have been better pleased.

I didn't pretend to myself, and I didn't pretend to her. I saw I was clean gone; and if she was to make a fool of me, she must. And I suppose it was this that set her talking, for now she made sure that we were friends. A lot she told me, sitting in my lap and eating my dish, as I ate hers, from foolery—a lot about herself and her mother and Case, all which would be very tedious, and fill sheets if I set it down in Beach de Mar,[36] but which I must

---

[36] South Seas pidgin, more commonly rendered as "Beach-la-Mar." [ED.]

give a hint of in plain English, and one thing about myself, which had a very big effect on my concerns, as you are soon to hear.

It seems she was born in one of the Line Islands;[37] had been only two or three years in these parts, where she had come with a white man, who was married to her mother and then died; and only the one year in Falesá. Before that they had been a good deal on the move, trekking about after the white man, who was one of those rolling stones that keep going round after a soft job. They talk about looking for gold at the end of a rainbow; but if a man wants an employment that'll last him till he dies, let him start out on the soft-job hunt. There's meat and drink in it too, and beer and skittles,[38] for you never hear of them starving, and rarely see them sober; and as for steady sport, cock-fighting isn't in the same county with it. Anyway, this beachcomber[39] carried the woman and her daughter all over the shop, but mostly to out-of-the-way islands, where there were no police, and he thought, perhaps, the soft job hung out. I've my own view of this old party; but I was just as glad he had kept Uma clear of Apia and Papeete and these flash[40] towns. At last he struck Fale-alii[41] on this island, got some trade—the Lord knows how!—muddled it all away in the usual style, and died worth next to nothing, bar a bit of land at Falesá that he had got for a bad debt, which was what put it in the minds of the mother and daughter to come there and live. It seems Case encouraged them all he could, and helped to get their house built. He was very kind those days, and gave Uma trade, and there is no doubt he had his eye on her from the beginning. However, they had scarce settled, when up turned a young man, a native, and wanted to marry her. He was a small chief, and had some fine mats and old songs in his family, and was "very pretty," Uma said; and, altogether, it was an extraordinary match for a penniless girl and an out-islander.

At the first word of this I got downright sick with jealousy.

"And you mean to say you would have married him?" I cried.

"*Ioe*, yes," said she. "I like too much!"

"Well!" I said. "And suppose I had come round after?"

"I like you more better now," said she. "But, suppose I marry Ioane, I one good wife. I no common Kanaka. Good girl!" says she.

---

[37] A small group of islands at the equator, northeast of Samoa. [ED.]

[38] English ninepins. [ED.]

[39] Derogatory label applied to white roustabouts. [ED.]

[40] *Flash* means cheap, gaudy, trendy. [ED.]

[41] Fictional place name. [ED.]

Well, I had to be pleased with that; but I promise you I didn't care about the business one little bit. And I liked the end of that yarn no better than the beginning. For it seems this proposal of marriage was the start of all the trouble. It seems, before that, Uma and her mother had been looked down upon, of course, for kinless folk and out-islanders, but nothing to hurt; and, even when Ioane came forward, there was less trouble at first than might have been looked for. And then, all of a sudden, about six months before my coming, Ioane backed out and left that part of the island, and from that day to this Uma and her mother had found themselves alone. None called at their house, none spoke to them on the roads. If they went to church, the other women drew their mats away and left them in a clear place by themselves. It was a regular excommunication, like what you read of in the Middle Ages; and the cause or sense of it beyond guessing. It was some *tala pepelo*, Uma said, some lie, some calumny; and all she knew of it was that the girls who had been jealous of her luck with Ioane used to twit her with his desertion, and cry out, when they met her alone in the woods, that she would never be married. "They tell me no man he marry me. He too much 'fraid," she said.

The only soul that came about them after this desertion was Master Case. Even he was chary of showing himself, and turned up mostly by night; and pretty soon he began to table his cards and make up to Uma. I was still sore about Ioane, and when Case turned up in the same line of business I cut up downright rough.

"Well," I said, sneering, "and I suppose you thought Case 'very pretty' and 'liked too much'?"

"Now you talk silly," said she. "White man, he come here, I marry him all-e-same Kanaka; very well then, he marry me all-e-same white woman. Suppose he no marry, he go 'way, woman he stop. All-e-same thief, empty hand, Tonga-heart[42]—no can love! Now you come marry me. You big heart—you no 'shamed island-girl. That thing I love you for too much. I proud."

I don't know that ever I felt sicker all the days of my life. I laid down my fork, and I put away "the island-girl"; I didn't seem somehow to have any use for either, and I went and walked up and down in the house, and Uma followed me with her eyes, for she was troubled, and small wonder! But troubled was no word for it with me. I so wanted, and so feared, to make a clean breast of the sweep[43] that I had been.

---

[42]Black-hearted. [ED.]

[43]Mean-spirited, disreputable person. Derived from *chimney sweep*, the term for one of the lowest, filthiest of jobs. [ED.]

And just then there came a sound of singing out of the sea; it sprang up suddenly clear and near, as the boat turned the headland, and Uma, running to the window, cried out it was "Misi"[44] come upon his rounds.

I thought it was a strange thing I should be glad to have a missionary; but, if it was strange, it was still true.

"Uma," said I, "you stop here in this room, and don't budge a foot out of it till I come back."

CHAPTER III
The Missionary

As I came out on the verandah, the mission boat was shooting for the mouth of the river. She was a long whale-boat painted white; a bit of an awning astern; a native pastor crouched on the wedge of the poop, steering; some four-and-twenty paddles flashing and dipping, true to the boat-song; and the missionary under the awning, in his white clothes, reading in a book, and set him up![45] It was pretty to see and hear; there's no smarter sight in the islands than a missionary boat with a good crew and a good pipe[46] to them; and I considered it for half a minute, with a bit of envy perhaps, and then strolled down towards the river.

From the opposite side there was another man aiming for the same place, but he ran and got there first. It was Case; doubtless his idea was to keep me apart from the missionary, who might serve me as interpreter; but my mind was upon other things. I was thinking how he had jockeyed us about the marriage, and tried his hand on Uma before; and at the sight of him rage flew into my nostrils.

"Get out of that, you low, swindling thief!" I cried.

"What's that you say?" says he.

I gave him the word again, and rammed it down with a good oath. "And if ever I catch you within six fathoms of my house," I cried, "I'll clap a bullet in your measly carcase."

"You must do as you like about your house," said he, "where I told you I have no thought of going; but this is a public place."

---

[44] Pidgin for "Mister"; a term of respect. [ED.]

[45] Scotch expression meaning conceited or vain. [ED.]

[46] Literally, a boatswain's whistle, used for giving orders to the crew; figuratively, an orderly and disciplined ship. [ED.]

"It's a place where I have private business," said I. "I have no idea of a hound like you eavesdropping, and I give you notice to clear out."

"I don't take it, though," says Case.

"I'll show you, then," said I.

"We'll have to see about that," said he.

He was quick with his hands, but he had neither the height nor the weight, being a flimsy creature alongside a man like me, and, besides, I was blazing to that height of wrath that I could have bit into a chisel. I gave him first the one and then the other, so that I could hear his head rattle and crack, and he went down straight.

"Have you had enough?" cried I. But he only looked up white and blank, and the blood spread upon his face like wine upon a napkin. "Have you had enough?" I cried again. "Speak up, and don't lie malingering there, or I'll take my feet to you."

He sat up at that, and held his head — by the look of him you could see it was spinning — and the blood poured on his pyjamas.

"I've had enough for this time," says he, and he got up staggering, and went off by the way that he had come.

The boat was close in; I saw the missionary had laid his book to one side, and I smiled to myself. "He'll know I'm a man, anyway," thinks I.

This was the first time, in all my years in the Pacific, I had ever exchanged two words with any missionary, let alone asked one for a favour. I didn't like the lot, no trader does; they look down upon us, and make no concealment; and, besides, they're partly Kanakaized, and suck up with natives instead of with other white men like themselves. I had on a rig of clean striped pyjamas — for, of course, I had dressed decent to go before the chiefs; but when I saw the missionary step out of this boat in the regular uniform, white duck clothes, pith helmet, white shirt and tie, and yellow boots to his feet, I could have bunged[47] stones at him. As he came nearer, queering[48] me pretty curious (because of the fight, I suppose), I saw he looked mortal sick, for the truth was he had a fever on, and had just had a chill in the boat.

"Mr. Tarleton, I believe?" says I, for I had got his name.

"And you, I suppose, are the new trader?" says he.

"I want to tell you first that I don't hold with missions," I went on, "and that I think you and the likes of you do a sight of harm, filling up the natives with old wives' tales and bumptiousness."

---

[47] Thrown. [ED.]

[48] Studying intently. [ED.]

"You are perfectly entitled to your opinions," says he, looking a bit ugly, "but I have no call to hear them."

"It so happens that you've got to hear them," I said. "I'm no missionary, nor missionary lover; I'm no Kanaka, nor favourer of Kanakas—I'm just a trader; I'm just a common, [low], God-damned white man and British subject, the sort you would like to wipe your boots on. I hope that's plain!"

"Yes, my man," said he. "It's more plain than creditable. When you are sober, you'll be sorry for this."

He tried to pass on, but I stopped him with my hand. The Kanakas were beginning to growl. Guess they didn't like my tone, for I spoke to that man as free as I would to you.

"Now, you can't say I've deceived you," said I, "and I can go on. I want a service—I want two services, in fact; and, if you care to give me them, I'll perhaps take more stock in what you call your Christianity."

He was silent for a moment. Then he smiled. "You are rather a strange sort of man," says he.

"I'm the sort of man God made me," says I. "I don't set up to be a gentleman," I said.

"I am not quite so sure," said he. "And what can I do for you, Mr. ——?"

"Wiltshire," I says, "though I'm mostly called Welsher;[49] but Wiltshire is the way it's spelt, if the people on the beach could only get their tongues about it. And what do I want? Well, I'll tell you the first thing. I'm what you call a sinner—what I call a sweep—and I want you to help me make it up to a person I've deceived."

He turned and spoke to his crew in the native. "And now I am at your service," said he, "but only for the time my crew are dining. I must be much farther down the coast before night. I was delayed at Papa-Malulu[50] till this morning, and I have an engagement in Fale-alii tomorrow night."

I led the way to my house in silence, and rather pleased with myself for the way I had managed the talk, for I like a man to keep his self-respect.

"I was sorry to see you fighting," says he.

"Oh, that's part of [a] yarn I want to tell you," I said. "That's service number two. After you've heard it you'll let me know whether you're sorry or not."

We walked right in through the store, and I was surprised to find Uma had cleared away the dinner things. This was so unlike her ways that I saw she had done it out of gratitude, and liked her the better. She and Mr. Tarleton called each other by name, and he was very civil to her seemingly. But I thought little of that; they can always find civility for a Kanaka, it's us

---

[49] Swindler. [ED.]
[50] Fictional place name. [ED.]

white men they lord it over. Besides, I didn't want much Tarleton just then. I was going to do my pitch.

"Uma," said I, "give us your marriage certificate." She looked put out. "Come," said I, "you can trust me. Hand it up."

She had it about her person, as usual; I believe she thought it was a pass to heaven, and if she died without having it handy she would go to hell. I couldn't see where she put it the first time, I couldn't see now where she took it from; it seemed to jump into her hand like that Blavatsky[51] business in the papers. But it's the same way with all island women, and I guess they're taught it when young.

"Now," said I, with the certificate in my hand, "I was married to this girl by Black Jack the negro. The certificate was wrote by Case, and it's a dandy piece of literature, I promise you. Since then I've found that there's a kind of cry in the place against this wife of mine, and so long as I keep her I cannot trade. Now, what would any man do in my place, if he was a man?" I said. "The first thing he would do is this, I guess." And I took and tore up the certificate and bunged the pieces on the floor.

"*Aué!*"[52] cried Uma, and began to clap her hands; but I caught one of them in mine.

"And the second thing that he would do," said I, "if he was what I would call a man and you would call a man, Mr. Tarleton, is to bring the girl right before you or any other missionary, and to up and say: 'I was wrong married to this wife of mine, but I think a heap of her, and now I want to be married to her right.' Fire away, Mr. Tarleton. And I guess you'd better do it in native; it'll please the old lady," I said, giving her the proper name of a man's wife upon the spot.

So we had in two of the crew for to witness, and were spliced in our own house; and the parson prayed a good bit, I must say—but not so long as some—and shook hands with the pair of us.

"Mr. Wiltshire," he says, when he had made out the lines and packed off the witnesses, "I have to thank you for a very lively pleasure. I have rarely performed the marriage ceremony with more grateful emotions."

That was what you would call talking. He was going on, besides, with more of it, and I was ready for as much taffy[53] as he had in stock, for I felt good. But Uma had been taken up with something half through the marriage, and cut straight in.

---

[51] Madame Blavatsky, a renowned late-century spiritualist, founder of the Theosophical Society. [ED.]

[52] Alas! [Stevenson's note.]

[53] Flattery; literally, a kind of candy. [ED.]

"How your hand he get hurt?" she asked.

"You ask Case's head, old lady," says I.

She jumped with joy, and sang out.

"You haven't made much of a Christian of this one," says I to Mr. Tarleton.

"We didn't think her one of our worst," says he, "when she was at Fale-alii; and if Uma bears malice I shall be tempted to fancy she has good cause."

"Well, there we are at service number two," said I. "I want to tell you our yarn, and see if you can let a little daylight in."

"Is it long?" he asked.

"Yes," I cried; "it's a goodish bit of a yarn!"

"Well, I'll give you all the time I can spare," says he, looking at his watch. "But I must tell you fairly, I haven't eaten since five this morning, and, unless you can let me have something I am not likely to eat again before seven or eight tonight."

"By God, we'll give you dinner!" I cried.

I was a little caught up at my swearing, just when all was going straight; and so was the missionary, I suppose, but he made believe to look out of the window, and thanked us.

So we ran him up a bit of a meal. I was bound to let the old lady have a hand in it, to show off, so I deputised her to brew the tea. I don't think I ever met such tea as she turned out. But that was not the worst, for she got round with the salt-box, which she considered an extra European touch, and turned my stew into sea-water. Altogether, Mr. Tarleton had a devil of a dinner of it; but he had plenty entertainment by the way, for all the while that we were cooking, and afterwards, when he was making believe to eat, I kept posting him up on Master Case and the beach of Falesá, and he putting questions that showed he was following close.

"Well," said he at last, "I am afraid you have a dangerous enemy. This man Case is very clever and seems really wicked. I must tell you I have had my eye on him for nearly a year, and have rather had the worst of our encounters. About the time when the last representative of your firm ran so suddenly away, I had a letter from Namu, the native pastor, begging me to [come] to Falesá at my earliest convenience, as his flock were all 'adopting Catholic practices.' I had great confidence in Namu; I fear it only shows how easily we are deceived. No one could hear him preach and not be persuaded he was a man of extraordinary parts. All our islanders easily acquire a kind of eloquence, and can roll out and illustrate, with a great deal of vigour and fancy, second-hand sermons; but Namu's sermons are his own, and I cannot deny that I have found them means of grace. Moreover, he has a keen curiosity in secular things, does not fear work, is clever at carpentering, and has made himself so much respected among the neighbouring pastors that we call him, in a jest which is half serious, the Bishop of the East. In short, I was proud of the man; all the more puzzled by his letter, and took an occasion to come this way. The morning before my arrival, Vigours had been [set] on board the *Lion,* and Namu was perfectly at his ease, apparently ashamed of his letter, and quite unwilling to explain it. This, of course, I could not allow, and he ended by confessing that he had been much concerned to find his people using the sign of the cross, but since he had learned the explanation his mind was satisfied. For Vigours had the Evil Eye, a common thing in a country of Europe called Italy, where men were often struck dead by that kind of devil, and it appeared the sign of the cross was a charm against its power.

"'And I explain it, Misi,' said Namu, 'in this way: The country in Europe is a Popey country, and the devil of the Evil Eye may be a Catholic devil, or, at least, used to Catholic ways. So then I reasoned thus: if this sign of the cross were used in a Popey manner it would be sinful, but when it is used only to protect men from a devil, which is a thing harmless in itself, the sign too must be [harmless. For the sign is neither good nor bad, even as a bottle is neither good nor bad. But if the bottle be full of gin, the gin is bad; and if the sign be made in idolatry, so is the idolatry bad.'] And, very like a native pastor, he had a text apposite about the casting out of devils.

"'And who has been telling you about the Evil Eye?' I asked.

"He admitted it was Case. Now, I am afraid you will think me very narrow, Mr. Wiltshire, but I must tell you I was displeased, and cannot think a trader at all a good man to advise or have an influence upon my pastors. And, besides, there had been some flying talk in the country of old Adams and his being poisoned, to which I had paid no great heed; but it came back to me at the moment.

"'And is this Case a man of a sanctified life?' I asked.

"He admitted he was not; for, though he did not drink, he was profligate with women, and had no religion.

"'Then,' said I, 'I think the less you have to do with him the better.'

"But it is not easy to have the last word with a man like Namu. He was ready in a moment with an illustration. 'Misi,' said he, 'you have told me there were wise men, not pastors, not even holy, who knew many things useful to be taught—about trees for instance, and beasts, and to print books, and about the stones that are burned to make knives of. Such men teach you in your college, and you learn from them, but take care not to learn to be unholy. Misi, Case is my college.'

"I knew not what to say. Mr. Vigours had evidently been driven out of Falesá by the machinations of Case and with something not very unlike the collusion of my pastor. I called to mind it was Namu who had reassured me about Adams and traced the rumour to the ill-will of the priest. And I saw I must inform myself more thoroughly from an impartial source. There is an old rascal of a chief here, Faiaso, whom I dare say you saw to-day at the council; he has been all his life turbulent and sly, a great fomenter of rebellions, and a thorn in the side of the mission and the island. For all that he is very shrewd, and, except in politics or about his own misdemeanours, a teller of the truth. I went to his house, told him what I had heard, and besought him to be frank. I do not think I had ever a more painful interview. Perhaps you will understand me, Mr. Wiltshire, if I tell you that I am perfectly serious in these old wives' tales with which you reproached me, and as anxious to do well for these islands as you can be to please and to protect your pretty wife. And you are to remember that I thought Namu a paragon, and was proud of the man as one of the first ripe fruits of the mission. And now I was informed that he had fallen in a sort of dependence upon Case. The beginning of it was not corrupt; it began, doubtless, in fear and respect, produced by trickery and pretence; but I was shocked to find that another element had been lately added, that Namu helped himself in the store, and was believed to be deep in Case's debt. Whatever the trader said, that Namu believed with trembling. He was not alone in this; many in the village lived in a similar subjection; but Namu's case was the most influential, it was through Namu Case had wrought most evil; and with a certain following among the chiefs, and the pastor in his pocket, the man was a good as master of the village. You know something of Vigours and Adams, but perhaps you have never heard of old Underhill, Adams' predecessor. He was a quiet, mild old fellow, I remember, and we were told he had died suddenly: white men die very suddenly in Falesá. The truth, as I now heard it, made my blood run cold. It seems he was struck with a general palsy, all of him dead but one eye, which he continually winked. Word was started that the helpless old man was now a devil, and this vile fellow Case worked upon the natives' fears, which he professed to share, and pretended he durst not go into the house alone. At last a grave was dug, and the living body buried at the far end of the village. Namu, my pastor, whom I had helped to educate, offered up a prayer at the hateful scene.

"I felt myself in a very difficult position. Perhaps it was my duty to have denounced Namu and had him deposed. Perhaps I think so now, but at the time it seemed less clear. He had a great influence, it might prove greater than mine. The natives are prone to superstition; perhaps by stirring them up I might but ingrain and spread these dangerous fancies. And Namu besides, apart from this novel and accursed influence, was a good pastor, an able man, and spiritually minded. Where should I look for a better? How was I to find as good? At that moment, with Namu's failure fresh in my view, the work of my life appeared a mockery; hope was dead in me. I would rather repair such tools as I had than go abroad in quest of others that must certainly prove worse; and a scandal is, at the best, a thing to be avoided when humanly possible. Right or wrong, then, I determined on a quiet course. All that night I denounced and reasoned with the erring pastor, twitted him with his ignorance and want of faith, twitted him with his wretched attitude, making clean the outside of the cup and platter,[54] callously helping at a murder, childishly flying in excitement about a few childish, unnecessary, and inconvenient gestures; and long before day I had him on his knees and bathed in the tears of what seemed a genuine repentance. On Sunday I took the pulpit in the morning, and preached from First Kings, nineteenth, on the fire, the earthquake, and the voice, distinguishing the true spiritual power, and referring with such plainness as I dared to recent events in Falesá. The effect produced was great, and it was much increased when Namu rose in his turn and confessed that he had been wanting in faith and conduct, and was convinced of sin. So far, then, all was well; but there was one unfortunate circumstance. It was nearing the time of our 'May' in the island, when the native contributions to the missions are received; it fell in my duty to make a notification on the subject, and this gave my enemy his chance, by which he was not slow to profit.

"News of the whole proceedings must have been carried to Case as soon as church was over, and the same afternoon he made an occasion to meet me in the midst of the village. He came up with so much intentness and animosity that I felt it would be damaging to avoid him.

"'So,' says he, in native, 'here is the holy man. He has been preaching against me, but that was not in his heart. He has been preaching upon the love of God; but that was not in his heart, it was between his teeth. Will you know what was in his heart?' cries he. 'I will show it you!' And, making a snatch at my head, he made believe to pluck out a dollar, and held it in the air.

"There went that rumour through the crowd with which Polynesians receive a prodigy. As for myself, I stood amazed. The thing was a common conjuring trick which I have seen performed at home a score of times; but how was I to convince the villagers of that? I wished I had learned legerdemain instead of Hebrew, that I might have paid the fellow out with his own coin. But there I was; I could not stand there silent, and the best I could find to say was weak.

---

[54] An allusion to Matthew 23. 25–26. [ED.]

"'I will trouble you not to lay hands on me again,' said I.

"'I have no such thought,' said he, 'nor will I deprive you of your dollar. Here it is,' he said, and flung it at my feet. I am told it lay where it fell three days."

"I must say it was well played," said I.

"Oh! he is clever," said Mr. Tarleton, "and you can now see for yourself how dangerous. He was a party to the horrid death of the paralytic; he is accused of poisoning Adams; he drove Vigours out of the place by lies that might have led to murder; and there is no question but he has now made up his mind to rid himself of you. How he means to try we have no guess; only be sure, it's something new. There is no end to his readiness and invention."

"He gives himself a sight of trouble," says I. "And after all, what for?"

"Why, how many tons of copra may they make in this district?" asked the missionary.

"I daresay as much as sixty tons," says I.

"And what is the profit to the local trader?" he asked.

"You may call it three pounds," said I.

"Then you can reckon for yourself how much he does it for," said Mr. Tarleton. "But the more important thing is to defeat him. It is clear he spread some report against Uma, in order to isolate and have his wicked will of her. Failing of that, and seeing a new rival come upon the scene, he used her in a different way. Now, the first point to find out is about Namu. Uma, when people began to leave you and your mother alone, what did Namu do?"

"Stop away all-e-same," says Uma.

"I fear the dog has returned to his vomit," said Mr. Tarleton. "And now what am I to do for you? I will speak to Namu, I will warn him he is observed; it will be strange if he allow anything to go on amiss when he is put upon his guard. At the same time, this precaution may fail, and then you must turn elsewhere. You have two people at hand to whom you might apply. There is, first of all, the priest, who might protect you by the Catholic interest; they are a wretchedly small body, but they count two chiefs. And then there is old Faiaso. Ah! if it had been some years ago you would have needed no one else; but his influence is much reduced, it has gone into Maea's hands, and Maea, I fear, is one of Case's jackals. In fine, if the worst comes to the worst, you must send up or come yourself to Fale-alii, and, though I am not due at this end of the island for a month, I will just see what can be done."

So Mr. Tarleton said farewell; and half an hour later the crew were singing and the paddles flashing in the missionary-boat.

CHAPTER IV

Devil-Work

Near a month went by without much doing. The same night of our marriage Galoshes called round, made himself mighty civil, and got into a habit of dropping in about dark and smoking his pipe with the family. He could talk to Uma, of course, and started to teach me native and French at the same time. He was a kind old buffer, though the dirtiest you would wish to see, and he muddled me up with foreign languages worse than the tower of Babel.

That was one employment we had, and it made me feel less lonesome; but there was no profit in the thing, for though the priest came and sat and yarned, none of his folks could be enticed into my store; and if it hadn't been for the other occupation I struck out, there wouldn't have been a pound of copra in the house. This was the idea: Fa'avao (Uma's mother) had a score of bearing trees. Of course we could get no labour, being all as good as tabooed, and the two women and I turned to and made copra with our own hands. It was copra to make your mouth water when it was done—I never understood how much the natives cheated me till I had made that four hundred pounds of my own hand—and it weighed so light I felt inclined to take and water it myself.

When we were at the job a good many Kanakas used to put in the best of the day looking on, and once that nigger turned up. He stood back with the natives and laughed and did the big don and the funny dog,[55] till I began to get riled.

"Here, you nigger!" says I.

"I don't address myself to you, Sah," says the nigger. "Only speak to gen'le'um."

"I know," says I, "but it happens I was addressing myself to you, Mr. Black Jack. And all I want to know is just this: did you see Case's figure-head about a week ago?"

"No, Sah," says he.

"That's all right, then," says I; "for I'll show you the own brother to it, only black, in the inside of about two minutes."

And I began to walk towards him, quite slow, and my hands down; only there was trouble in my eye, if anybody took the pains to look.

"You're a low, obstropulous[56] fellow, Sah," says he.

---

[55] *Big don* means a pretentious snob; a funny dog is a wise guy. [ED.]

[56] Common corruption of *obstreperous*. [ED.]

"You bet!" says I.

By that time he thought I was about as near as [was] convenient, and lit out so it would have done your heart good to see him travel. And that was all I saw of that precious gang until what I am about to tell you.

It was one of my chief employments these days to go pot-hunting[57] in the woods, which I found (as Case had told me) very rich in game. I have spoken of the cape which shut up the village and my station from the east. A path went about the end of it, and led into the next bay. A strong wind blew here daily, and as the line of the barrier reef stopped at the end of the cape, a heavy surf ran on the shores of the bay. A little cliffy hill cut the valley in two parts, and stood close on the beach; and at high water the sea broke right on the face of it, so that all passage was stopped. Woody mountains hemmed the place all round; the barrier to the east was particularly steep and leafy, the lower parts of it, along the sea, falling in sheer black cliffs streaked with cinnabar;[58] the upper part lumpy with the tops of the great trees. Some of the trees were bright green, and some red, and the sand of the beach as black as your shoes. Many birds hovered round the bay, some of them snow-white; and the flying-fox (or vampire)[59] flew there in broad daylight, gnashing its teeth.

For a long while I came as far as this shooting, and went no farther. There was no sign of any path beyond, and the cocoa-palms in the front of the foot of the valley were the last this way. For the whole "eye" of the island, as natives call the windward end, lay desert. From Falesá round about to Papa-malulu, there was neither house, nor man, nor planted fruit-tree; and the reef being mostly absent, and the shores bluff, the sea beat direct among crags, and there was scarce a landing-place.

I should tell you that after I began to go in the woods, although no one offered to come near my store, I found people willing enough to pass the time of day with me where nobody could see them; and as I had begun to pick up native, and most of them had a word or two of English, I began to hold little odds and ends of conversation, not to much purpose to be sure, but they took off the worst of the feeling, for it's a miserable thing to be made a leper of.

It chanced one day towards the end of the month, that I was sitting in this bay in the edge of the bush, looking east, with a Kanaka. I had given him a fill of tobacco, and we were making out to talk as best we could; indeed, he had more English than most.

---

[57] A pothunter shoots any kind of game that crosses his or her path. [ED.]

[58] A reddish ore found in volcanic rock. [ED.]

[59] In fact, these are two distinct species of bat. [ED.]

I asked him if there was no road going eastward.

"One time one road," said he. "Now he dead."

"Nobody he go there?" I asked.

"No good," said he. "Too much devil he stop there."

"Oho!" says I, "got-um plenty devil, that bush?"

"Man devil, woman devil; too much devil," said my friend. "Stop there all-e-time. Man he go there, no come back."

I thought if this fellow was so well posted on devils and spoke of them so free, which is not common, I had better fish for a little information about myself and Uma.

"You think me one devil?" I asked.

"No think devil," said he soothingly. "Think all-e-same fool."

"Uma, she devil?" I asked again.

"No, no; no devil. Devil stop bush," said the young man.

I was looking in front of me across the bay, and I saw the hanging front of the woods pushed suddenly open, and Case, with a gun in his hand, step forth into the sunshine on the black beach. He was got up in light pyjamas, near white, his gun sparkled, he looked mighty conspicuous; and the land-crabs scuttled from all round him to their holes.

"Hullo, my friend!" says I, "you no talk all-e-same true. Ese he go, he come back."

"Ese no all-e-same; Ese *Tiapolo*," says my friend; and, with a "Good-bye," slunk off among the trees.

I watched Case all round the beach, where the tide was low; and let him pass me on the homeward way to Falesá. He was in deep thought, and the birds seemed to know it, trotting quite near him on the sand, or wheeling and calling in his ears. When he passed me I could see by the working of his lips that he was talking to himself, and what pleased me mightily, he had still my trade mark on his brow. I tell you the plain truth: I had a mind to give him a gunful in his ugly mug, but I thought better of it.

All this time, and all the time I was following home, I kept repeating that native word, which I remembered by "Polly, put the kettle on and make us all some tea," tea-a-pollo.

"Uma," says I, when I got back, "what does *Tiapolo* mean?"

"Devil," says she.

"I thought *aitu* was the word for that," I said.

"*Aitu* 'nother kind of devil," said she; "stop bush, eat Kanaka. Tiapolo big chief devil, stop home; all-e-same Christian devil."

"Well then," said I, "I'm no farther forward. How can Case be Tiapolo?"

"No all-e-same," said she. "Ese belong Tiapolo; Tiapolo too much like; Ese all-e-same his son. Suppose Ese he wish something, Tiapolo he make him."

"That's mighty convenient for Ese," says I. "And what kind of things does he make for him?"

Well, out came a rigmarole of all sorts of stories, many of which (like the dollar he took from Mr. Tarleton's head) were plain enough to me, but others I could make nothing of; and the thing that most surprised the Kanakas was what surprised me least—namely, that he [could] go in the desert among all the *aitus*. Some of the boldest, however, had accompanied him, and had heard him speak with the dead and give them orders, and, safe in his protection, had returned unscathed. Some said he had a church there, where he worshipped Tiapolo, and Tiapolo appeared to him; others swore that there was no sorcery at all, that he performed his miracles by the power of prayer, and the church was no church, but a prison, in which he had confined a dangerous *aitu*. Namu had been in the bush with him once, and returned glorifying God for these wonders. Altogether, I began to have a glimmer of the man's position, and the means by which he had acquired it, and, though I saw he was a tough nut to crack, I was noways cast down.

"Very well," said I, "I'll have a look at Master Case's place of worship myself, and we'll see about the glorifying."

At this Uma fell in a terrible taking; if I went in the high bush I should never return; none could go there but by the protection of Tiapolo.

"I'll chance it on God's," said I. "I'm a good sort of a fellow, Uma, as fellows go, and I guess God'll con me through."

She was silent for a while. "I think," said she, mighty solemn—and then, presently—"Victoreea, he big chief?"

"You bet!" said I.

"He like you too much?" she asked again.

I told her, with a grin, I believed the old lady was rather partial to me.

"All right," said she. "Victoreea he big chief, like you too much. No can help you here in Falesá; no can do—too far off. Maea he small chief—stop here. Suppose he like you—make you all right. All-e-same God and Tiapolo. God he big chief—got too much work. Tiapolo he small chief—he like too much make-see, work very hard."

"I'll have to hand you over to Mr. Tarleton," said I. "Your theology's out of its bearings, Uma."

However, we stuck to this business all the evening, and, with the stories she told me of the desert and its dangers, she came near frightening herself into a fit. I don't remember half a quarter of them, of course, for I paid little heed; but two come back to me kind of clear.

About six miles up the coast there is a sheltered cove they call *Fangaanaana*—"the haven full of caves." I've seen it from the sea myself, as near as I could get my boys to venture in; and it's a little strip of yellow sand. Black cliffs overhang it, full of the black mouths of caves; great trees overhang the cliffs, and dangle-down lianas;[60] and in one place, about the middle, a big brook pours over in a cascade. Well, there was a boat going by here, with six young men of Falesá, "all very pretty," Uma said, which was the loss of them. It blew strong, there was a heavy head sea, and by the time they opened Fanga-anaana, and saw the white cascade and the shady beach, they were all tired and thirsty, and their water had run out. One proposed to land and get a drink, and, being reckless fellows, they were all of the same mind except the youngest. Lotu was his name; he was a very good young gentleman, and very wise; and he held out that they were crazy, telling them the place was given over to spirits and devils and the dead, and there were no living folk nearer than six miles the one way, and maybe twelve the other. But they laughed at his words, and, being five to one, pulled in, beached the boat, and landed. It was a wonderful pleasant place, Lotu said, and the water excellent. They walked round the beach, but could see nowhere any way to mount the cliffs, which made them easier in their mind; and at last they sat down to make a meal on the food they had brought with them. They were scarce set, when there came out of the mouth of one of the black caves six of the most beautiful ladies ever seen: they had flowers in their hair, and the most beautiful breasts, and necklaces of scarlet seeds; and began to jest with these young gentlemen, and the young gentlemen to jest back with them, all but Lotu. As for Lotu, he saw there could be no living woman in such a place, and ran, and flung himself in the bottom of the boat, and covered his face, and prayed. All the time the business lasted Lotu made one clean break of prayer, and that was all he knew of it, until his friends came back, and made him sit up, and they put to sea again out of the bay, which was now quite desert, and no word of the six ladies. But, what frightened Lotu most, not one of the five remembered anything of what had passed, but they were all like drunken men, and sang and laughed in the boat, and skylarked. The wind freshened and came squally, and the sea rose extraordinary high; it was such weather as any man in the islands would have turned his back to and fled home to Falesá; but these five were like crazy folk, and cracked on all sail and drove their boat into the seas. Lotu went to the bailing; none of the others thought to help him, but sang and skylarked and carried on, and spoke singular things beyond a man's comprehension, and laughed out loud when they said them. So the rest of the day Lotu bailed for his life in the bottom of the boat, and was all

---

[60] Vines that tangle themselves into dense thickets. [ED.]

drenched with sweat and cold sea-water; and none heeded him. Against all expectation, they came safe in a dreadful tempest to Papa-malulu, where the palms were singing out, and the cocoanuts flying like cannon-balls about the village green; and the same night the five young gentlemen sickened, and spoke never a reasonable word until they died.

"And do you mean to tell me you can swallow a yarn like that?" I asked.

She told me the thing was well known, and with handsome young men alone it was even common; but this was the only case where five had been slain the same day and in a company by the love of the women-devils; and it had made a great stir in the island, and she would be crazy if she doubted.

"Well, anyway," says I, "you needn't be frightened about me. I've no use for the women-devils. You're all the women I want, and all the devil too, old lady."

To this she answered there were other sorts, and she had seen one with her own eyes. She had gone one day alone to the next bay, and, perhaps, got too near the margin of the bad place. The boughs of the high bush overshadowed her from the cant of the hill, but she herself was outside on a flat place, very stony and growing full of young mummy-apples four and five feet high. It was a dark day in the rainy season, and now there came squalls that tore off the leaves and sent them flying, and now it was all still as in a house. It was in one of these still times that a whole gang of birds and flying foxes came pegging out of the bush like creatures frightened. Presently after she heard a rustle nearer hand, and saw, coming out of the margin of the trees, among the mummy-apples, the appearance of a lean grey old boar. It seemed to think as it came, like a person; and all of a sudden, as she looked at it coming, she was aware it was no boar but a thing that was a man with a man's thoughts. At that she ran, and the pig after her, and as the pig ran it [hollered] aloud, so that the place rang with it.

"I wish I had been there with my gun," said I. "I guess that pig would have [hollered] so as to surprise himself."

But she told me a gun was of no use with the like of these, which were the spirits of the dead.

Well, this kind of talk put in[61] the evening, which was the best of it; but of course it didn't change my notion, and the next day, with my gun and a good knife, I set off upon a voyage of discovery. I made, as near as I could, for the place where I had seen Case come out; for if it was true he had some kind of establishment in the bush I reckoned I should find a path. The beginning of the desert was marked off by a wall, to call it so, for it was more

---

[61] Passed. [ED.]

of a long mound of stones. They say it reaches right across the island, but how they know it is another question, for I doubt if anyone has made the journey in a hundred years, the natives sticking chiefly to the sea and their little colonies along the coast, and that part being mortal high and steep and full of cliffs. Up to the west side of the wall, the ground has been cleared, and there are cocoa palms and mummy-apples and guavas, and lots of sensitive.[62] Just across, the bush begins outright; high bush at that, trees going up like the masts of ships, and ropes of liana hanging down like a ship's rigging, and nasty orchids growing in the forks like funguses. The ground where there was no underwood looked to be a heap of boulders. I saw many green pigeons which I might have shot, only I was there with a different idea. A number of butterflies flopped up and down along the ground like dead leaves; sometimes I would hear a bird calling, sometimes the wind overhead, and always the sea along the coast.

But the queerness of the place it's more difficult to tell of, unless to one who has been alone in the high bush himself. The brightest kind of a day it is always dim down there. A man can see to the end of nothing; whichever way he looks the wood shuts up, one bough folding with another like the fingers of your hand; and whenever he listens he hears always something new—men talking, children laughing, the strokes of an axe a far way ahead of him, and sometimes a sort of a quick, stealthy scurry near at hand that makes him jump and look to his weapons. It's all very well for him to tell himself that he's alone, bar trees and birds; he can't make out to believe it; whichever way he turns the whole place seems to be alive and looking on. Don't think it was Uma's yarns that put me out; I don't value native talk a fourpenny-piece; it's a thing that's natural in the bush, and that's the end of it.

As I got near the top of the hill, for the ground of the wood goes up in this place steep as a ladder, the wind began to sound straight on, and the leaves to toss and switch open and let in the sun. This suited me better; it was the same noise all the time, and nothing to startle. Well, I had got to a place where there was an underwood of what they call wild cocoanut— mighty pretty with its scarlet fruit—when there came a sound of singing in the wind that I thought I had never heard the like of. It was all very fine to tell myself it was the branches; I knew better. It was all very fine to tell myself it was a bird; I knew never a bird that sang like that. It rose and swelled, and died away and swelled again; and now I thought it was like someone weeping, only prettier; and now I thought it was like harps; and there was one thing I made sure of, it was a sight too sweet to be wholesome in a place

---

[62] Mimosa, a plant with leaves that retract when touched. [ED.]

like that. You may laugh if you like; but I declare I called to mind the six young ladies that came, with their scarlet necklaces, out of the cave at Fanga-anaana, and wondered if they sang like that. We laugh at the natives and their superstitions; but see how many traders take them up, splendidly educated white men, that have been bookkeepers (some of them) and clerks in the old country. It's my belief a superstition grows up in a place like the different kind of weeds; and as I stood there and listened to that wailing I twittered in my shoes.

You may call me a coward to be frightened; I thought myself brave enough to go on ahead. But I went mighty carefully, with my gun cocked, spying all about me like a hunter, fully expecting to see a handsome young woman sitting somewhere in the bush, and fully determined (if I did) to try her with a charge of duck-shot. And sure enough, I had not gone far when I met with a queer thing. The wind came on the top of the wood in a strong puff, the leaves in front of me burst open, and I saw for a second something hanging in a tree. It was gone in a wink, the puff blowing by and the leaves closing. I tell you the truth: I had made up my mind to see an *aitu;* and if the thing had looked like a pig or a woman, it wouldn't have given me the same turn. The trouble was that it seemed kind of square, and the idea of a square thing that was alive and sang knocked me sick and silly. I must have stood quite a while; and I made pretty certain it was right out of the same tree that the singing came. Then I began to come to myself a bit.

"Well," says I, "if this is really so, if this is a place where there are square things that sing, I'm gone up anyway. Let's have my fun for my money."

But I thought I might as well take the off chance of a prayer being any good; so I plumped on my knees and prayed out loud; and all the time I was praying the strange sounds came out of the tree, and went up and down, and changed, for all the world like music, only you could see it wasn't human—there was nothing there that you could whistle.

As soon as I had made an end in proper style, I laid down my gun, stuck my knife between my teeth, walked right up to that tree, and began to climb. I tell you my heart was like ice. But presently, as I went up, I caught another glimpse of the thing, and that relieved me, for I thought it seemed like a box; and when I had got right up to it I near fell out of the tree with laughing.

A box it was, sure enough, and a candle-box at that, with the brand upon the side of it; and it had banjo strings stretched so as to sound when the wind blew. I believe they call the thing a Tyrolean[63] harp, whatever that may mean.

---

[63] Æolean. [Stevenson's note.]

"Well, Mr. Case," said I, "you've frightened me once, but I defy you to frighten me again," I says, and slipped down the tree, and set out again to find my enemy's head office, which I guessed would not be far away.

The undergrowth was thick in this part; I couldn't see before my nose, and must burst my way through by main force and ply the knife as I went, slicing the cords of the lianas and slashing down whole trees at a blow. I call them trees for the bigness, but in truth they were just big weeds, and sappy to cut through like carrot. From all this crowd and kind of vegetation, I was just thinking to myself, the place might have once been cleared, when I came on my nose over a pile of stones, and saw in a moment it was some kind of a work of man. The Lord knows when it was made or when deserted, for this part of the island has lain undisturbed since long before the whites came. A few steps beyond I hit into the path I had been always looking for. It was narrow, but well beaten, and I saw that Case had plenty of disciples. It seems, indeed, it was a piece of fashionable boldness to venture up here with the trader, and a young man scarce reckoned himself grown till he had got his breech tattooed, for one thing, and seen Case's devils for another. This is mighty like Kanakas; but, if you look at it another way, it's mighty like white folks too.

A bit along the path I was brought to a clear stand, and had to rub my eyes. There was a wall in front of me, the path passing it by a gap; it was tumbledown and plainly very old, but built of big stones very well laid; and there is no native alive today upon that island that could dream of such a piece of building. Along all the top of it was a line of queer figures, idols or scarecrows, or what not. They had carved and painted faces ugly to view, their eyes and teeth were of shell, their hair and their bright clothes blew in the wind, and some of them worked with the tugging. There are islands up west where they make these kind of figures till today; but if ever they were made in this island, the practice and the very recollection of it are now long forgotten. And the singular thing was that all these bogies were as fresh as toys out of a shop.

Then it came in my mind that Case had let out to me the first day that he was a good forger of island curiosities, a thing by which so many traders turn an honest penny. And with that I saw the whole business, and how this display served the man a double purpose: first of all, to season his curiosities, and then to frighten those that came to visit him.

But I should tell you (what made the thing more curious) that all the time the Tyrolean harps were harping round me in the trees, and even while I looked, a green-and-yellow bird (that, I suppose, was building) began to tear the hair off the head of one of the figures.

A little farther on I found the best curiosity of the museum. The first I saw of it was a longish mound of earth with a twist to it. Digging off the earth with my hands, I found underneath tarpaulin stretched on boards, so that this was plainly the roof of a cellar. It stood right on the top of the hill, and the entrance was on the far side, between two rocks, like the entrance to a cave. I went as far in as the bend, and, looking round the corner, saw a shining face. It was big and ugly, like a pantomime mask, and the brightness of it waxed and dwindled, and at times it smoked.

"Oho!" says I, "luminous paint!"

And I must say I rather admired the man's ingenuity. With a box of tools and a few mighty simple contrivances he had made out to have a devil of a temple. Any poor Kanaka brought up here in the dark, with the harps whining all round him, and shown that smoking face in the bottom of a hole, would make no kind of doubt but he had seen and heard enough devils for a lifetime. It's easy to find out what Kanakas think. Just go back to yourself any way round from ten to fifteen years old, and there's an average Kanaka. There are some pious, just as there are pious boys; and the most of them, like the boys again, are middling honest and yet think it rather larks to steal, and are easy scared and rather like to be so. I remember a boy I was at school with at home who played the Case business. He didn't know anything, that boy; he couldn't do anything; he had no luminous paint and no Tyrolean harps; he just boldly said he was a sorcerer, and frightened us out of our boots, and we loved it. And then it came in my mind how the master had once flogged that boy, and the surprise we were all in to see the sorcerer catch it and bum[64] like anybody else. Thinks I to myself, "I must find some way of fixing it so for Master Case." And the next moment I had my idea.

I went back by the path, which, when once you had found it, was quite plain and easy walking; and when I stepped out on the black sands, who should I see but Master Case himself. I cocked my gun and held it handy, and we marched up and passed without a word, each keeping the tail of his eye on the other; and no sooner had we passed than we each wheeled round like fellows drilling, and stood face to face. We had each taken the same notion in his head, you see, that the other fellow might give him the load of his gun in the stern.

"You've shot nothing," says Case.

"I'm not on the shoot today," said I.

"Well, the devil go with you for me," says he.

"The same to you," says I.

But we stuck just the way we were; no fear of either of us moving.

---

[64] Cry. [ED.]

Case laughed. "We can't stop here all day, though," said he.

"Don't let me detain you," says I.

He laughed again. "Look here, Wiltshire, do you think me a fool?" he asked.

"More of a knave, if you want to know," says I.

"Well, do you think it would better me to shoot you here, on this open beach?" said he. "Because I don't. Folks come fishing every day. There may be a score of them up the valley now, making copra; there might be half a dozen on the hill behind you, after pigeons; they might be watching us this minute, and I shouldn't wonder. I give you my word I don't want to shoot you. Why should I? You don't hinder me any. You haven't got one pound of copra but what you made with your own hands, like a negro slave. You're vegetating—that's what I call it—and I don't care where you vegetate, nor yet how long. Give me your word you don't mean to shoot me, and I'll give you a lead and walk away."

"Well," said I, "you're frank and pleasant, ain't you? And I'll be the same. I don't mean to shoot you today. Why should I? This business is beginning; it ain't done yet, Mr. Case. I've given you one turn already; I can see the marks of my knuckles on your head to this blooming hour, and I've more cooking for you. I'm not a paralee, like Underhill. My name ain't Adams, and it ain't Vigours; and I mean to show you that you've met your match."

"This is a silly way to talk," said he. "This is not the talk to make me move on with."

"All right," said I, "stay where you are. I ain't in any hurry, and you know it. I can put in a day on this beach and never mind. I ain't got any copra to bother with. I ain't got any luminous paint to see to."

I was sorry I said that last, but it whipped out before I knew. I could see it took the wind out of his sails, and he stood and stared at me with his brow drawn up. Then I suppose he made up his mind he must get to the bottom of this.

"I take you at your word," says he, and turned his back, and walked right into the devil's bush.

I let him go, of course, for I had passed my word. But I watched him as long as he was in sight, and after he was gone lit out for cover as lively as you would want to see, and went the rest of the way home under the bush, for I didn't trust him sixpence-worth. One thing I saw, I had been ass enough to give him warning, and that which I meant to do I must do at once.

You would think I had had about enough excitement for one morning, but there was another turn waiting me. As soon as I got far enough round the cape to see my house I made out there were strangers there; a little farther, and no doubt about it. There [were] a couple of armed [sentries] squatting at my door. I could only suppose the trouble about Uma must have come to a head, and the station been seized. For aught I could think, Uma was taken up already, and these armed men were waiting to do the like [by] me.

However, as I came nearer, which I did at top speed, I saw there was a third native sitting on the verandah like a guest, and Uma was talking with him like a hostess. Nearer still I made out it was the big young chief, Maea, and that he was smiling away and smoking. And what was he smoking? None of your European cigarettes fit for a cat, not even the genuine big, knock-me-down native article that a fellow can really put in the time with if his pipe is broke—but a cigar, and one of my Mexicans at that, that I could swear to. At sight of this my heart started beating, and I took a wild hope in my head that the trouble was over, and Maea had come round.

Uma pointed me out to him as I came up, and he met me at the head of my own stairs like a thorough gentleman.

"Vilivili," said he, which was the best they could make of my name, "I pleased."

There is no doubt when an island chief wants to be civil he can do it. I saw the way things were from the word go. There was no call for Uma to say to me: "He no 'fraid Ese now, come bring copra." I tell you I shook hands with that Kanaka like as if he was the best white man in Europe.

The fact was, Case and he had got after the same girl; or Maea suspected it, and concluded to make hay of the trader on the chance. He had dressed himself up, got a couple of his retainers cleaned and armed to kind of make the thing more public, and, just waiting till Case was clear of the village, came round to put the whole of his business my way. He was rich as well as powerful. I suppose that man was worth fifty thousand nuts per annum. I gave him the price of the beach and a quarter cent better, and as for credit, I would have advanced him the inside of the store and the fittings besides, I was so pleased to see him. I must say he bought like a gentleman: rice and tins and biscuits enough for a week's feast, and stuffs by the bolt. He was agreeable besides; he had plenty fun to him; and we cracked jests together, mostly through [Uma for] interpreter, because he had mighty little English, and my native was still off colour. One thing I made out: he could never really have thought much harm of Uma; he could never have been really frightened, and must just have made believe from dodginess, and because he thought Case had a strong pull in the village and could help him on.

This set me thinking that both he and I were in a tightish place. What he had done was to fly in the face of the whole village, and the thing might cost him his authority. More than that, after my talk with Case on the beach, I thought it might very well cost me my life. Case had as good as said he would pot[65] me if ever I got any copra; he would come home to find the best business in the village had changed hands; and the best thing I thought I could do was to get in first with the potting.

"See here, Uma," says I, "tell him I'm sorry I made him wait, but I was up looking at Case's Tiapolo store in the bush."

"He want savvy if you no 'fraid?" translated Uma.

I laughed out. "Not much!" says I. "Tell him the place is a blooming toy-shop! Tell him in England we give these things to the kids to play with."

"He want savvy if you hear devil sing?" she asked next.

"Look here," I said, "I can't do it now because I've got no banjo-strings in stock; but the next time the ship comes round I'll have one of these same contraptions right here in my verandah, and he can see for himself how much devil there is to it. Tell him, as soon as I can get the strings I'll make one for his picaninnies. The name of the concern is a Tyrolean harp; and you can tell him the name means in English that nobody but damfools give a cent for it."

This time he was so pleased he had to try his English again. "You talk true?" says he.

"Rather!" said I. "Talk all-e-same Bible. Bring out a Bible here, Uma, if you've got such a thing, and I'll kiss it. Or, I'll tell you what's better still," says I, taking a header,[66] "ask him if he's afraid to go up there himself by day."

It appeared he wasn't; he could venture as far as that by day and in company.

"That's the ticket, then!" said I. "Tell him the man's a fraud and the place foolishness, and if he'll go up there tomorrow he'll see all that's left of it. But tell him this, Uma, and mind he understands it: If he gets talking, it's bound to come to Case, and I'm a dead man! I'm playing his game, tell him, and if he says one word my blood will be at his door and be the damnation of him here and after."

She told him, and he shook hands with me up to the hilt, and, says he: "No talk. Go up tomollow. You my friend?"

. "No, sir," says I, "no such foolishness. I've come here to trade, tell him, and not to make friends. But, as to Case, I'll send that man to glory!"

So off Maea went, pretty well pleased, as I could see.

-----

[65] Strike, attack. [ED.]

[66] A head-first dive. [ED.]

CHAPTER V
Night in the Bush

Well, I was committed now; Tiapolo had to be smashed up before next day, and my hands were pretty full, not only with preparations, but with argument. My house was like a mechanics' debating society: [67] Uma was so made up that I shouldn't go into the bush by night, or that, if I did, I was never to come back again. You know her style of arguing: you've had a specimen about Queen Victoria and the devil; and I leave you to fancy if I was tired of it before dark.

At last I had a good idea. What was the use of casting my pearls before her? I thought; some of her own chopped hay would be likelier to do the business.

"I'll tell you what, then," said I. "You fish out your Bible, and I'll take that up along with me. That'll make me right."

She swore a Bible was no use.

"That's just your [blamed] Kanaka ignorance," said I. "Bring the Bible out."

She brought it, and I turned to the title-page, where I thought there would likely be some English, and so there was. "There!" said I. "Look at that! *London: Printed for the British and Foreign Bible Society, Blackfriars,*' [68] and the date, which I can't read, owing to its being in these X's. There's no devil in hell can look near the Bible Society, Blackfriars. Why, you silly!" I said, "how do you suppose we get along with our own *aitus* at home? All Bible Society!"

"I think you no got any," said she. "White man, he tell me you no got."

"Sounds likely, don't it?" I asked. "Why would these islands all be chock full of them and none in Europe?"

"Well, you no got breadfruit," said she.

I could have torn my hair. "Now, look here, old lady," said I, "you dry up, for I'm tired of you. I'll take the Bible, which 'll put me as straight as the mail, and that's the last word I've got to say."

The night fell extraordinary dark, clouds coming up with sundown and overspreading all; not a star showed; there was only an end of a moon, and that not due before the small hours. Round the village, what with the lights and the fires in the open houses, and the torches of many fishers moving

---

[67] Mechanics' institutes were widely established in the early and middle decades of the nineteenth century in England to provide adult education for working-class men. [ED.]
[68] The Bible Society sought to make inexpensive Bibles available throughout the world. [ED.]

on the reef, it kept as gay as an illumination; but the sea and the mountains and woods were all clean gone. I suppose it might be eight o'clock when I took the road, laden like a donkey. First there was that Bible, a book as big as your head, which I had let myself in for by my own tomfoolery. Then there was my gun, and knife, and lantern, and patent matches, all necessary. And then there was the real plant of the affair in hand, a mortal weight of gunpowder, a pair of dynamite fishing-bombs, and two or three pieces of slow match that I had hauled out of the tin cases and spliced together the best way I could; for the match was only trade stuff, and a man would be crazy that trusted it. Altogether, you see, I had the materials of a pretty good blow-up! Expense was nothing to me; I wanted that thing done right.

As long as I was in the open, and had the lamp in my house to steer by, I did well. But when I got to the path, it fell so dark I could make no headway, walking into trees and swearing there, like a man looking for the matches in his bed-room. I knew it was risky to light up, for my lantern would be visible all the way to the point of the cape, and as no one went there after dark, it would be talked about, and come to Case's ears. But what was I to do? I had either to give the business over and lose caste with Maea, or light up, take my chance, and get through the thing the smartest I was able.

As long as I was on the path I walked hard, but when I came to the black beach I had to run. For the tide was now nearly flowed;[69] and to get through with my powder dry between the surf and the steep hill, took all the quickness I possessed. As it was, even, the wash caught me to the knees, and I came near falling on a stone. All this time the hurry I was in, and the free air and smell of the sea, kept my spirits lively; but when I was once in the bush and began to climb the path I took it easier. The fearsomeness of the wood had been a good bit rubbed off for me by Master Case's banjo-strings and graven images, yet I thought it was a dreary walk, and guessed, when the disciples went up there, they must be badly scared. The light of the lantern, striking among all these trunks and forked branches and twisted rope-ends of lianas, made the whole place, or all that you could see of it, a kind of a puzzle of turning shadows. They came to meet you, solid and quick like giants, and then span off and vanished; they hove up over your head like clubs, and flew away into the night like birds. The floor of the bush glimmered with dead wood, the way the match-box used to shine after you had struck a lucifer.[70] Big, cold drops fell on me from the branches overhead like sweat. There was no wind to mention; only a little icy breath of a land-breeze that stirred nothing; and the harps were silent.

---

[69] It was nearly high tide. [ED.]

[70] A match. [ED.]

The first landfall I made was when I got through the bush of wild co-coanuts, and came in view of the bogies on the wall. Mighty queer they looked by the shining of the lantern, with their painted faces and shell eyes, and their clothes and their hair hanging. One after another I pulled them all up and piled them in a bundle on the cellar roof, so as they might go to glory with the rest. Then I chose a place behind one of the big stones at the entrance, buried my powder and the two shells, and arranged my match along the passage. And then I had a look at the smoking head, just for good-bye. It was doing fine.

"Cheer up," says I. "You're booked."

It was my first idea to light up and be getting homeward; for the darkness and the glimmer of the dead wood and the shadows of the lantern made me lonely. But I knew where one of the harps hung; it seemed a pity it shouldn't go with the rest; and at the same time I couldn't help letting on to myself that I was mortal tired of my employment, and would like best to be at home and have the door shut. I stepped out of the cellar and argued it fore and back. There was a sound of the sea far down below me on the coast; nearer hand not a leaf stirred; I might have been the only living creature this side of Cape Horn. Well, as I stood there thinking, it seemed the bush woke and became full of little noises. Little noises they were, and nothing to hurt — a bit of a crackle, a bit of a rush — but the breath jumped right out of me and my throat went as dry as a biscuit. It wasn't Case I was afraid of, which would have been common-sense; I never thought of Case; what took me, as sharp as the colic, was the old wives' tales, the devil-women and the man-pigs. It was the toss of a penny whether I should run: but I got a purchase on myself, and stepped out, and held up the lantern (like a fool) and looked all round.

In the direction of the village and the path there was nothing to be seen; but when I turned inland it's a wonder to me I didn't drop. There, coming right up out of the desert and the bad bush — there, sure enough, was a devil-woman, just as the way I had figured she would look. I saw the light shine on her bare arms and her bright eyes, and there went out of me a yell so big that I thought it was my death.

"Ah! No sing out!" says the devil-woman, in a kind of a high whisper. "Why you talk big voice? Put out light! Ese he come."

"My God Almighty, Uma, is that you?" says I.

"*Ioe,*"[71] says she. "I come quick. Ese here soon."

"You come alone?" I asked. "You no 'fraid?"

"Ah, too much 'fraid!" she whispered, clutching me. "I think die."

---

[71] Yes. [Stevenson's note.]

"Well," says I, with a kind of a weak grin, "I'm not the one to laugh at you, Mrs. Wiltshire, for I'm about the worst scared man in the South Pacific myself."

She told me in two words what brought her. I was scarce gone, it seems, when Fa'avao came in, and the old woman had met Black Jack running as hard as he was fit from our house to Case's. Uma neither spoke nor stopped, but lit right out to come and warn me. She was so close at my heels that the lantern was her guide across the beach, and afterwards, by the glimmer of it in the trees, she got her line up hill. It was only when I had got to the top or was in the cellar that she wandered Lord knows where! and lost a sight of precious time, afraid to call out lest Case was at the heels of her, and falling in the bush, so that she was all knocked and bruised. That must have been when she got too far to the southward, and how she came to take me in the flank at last and frighten me beyond what I've got the words to tell of.

Well, anything was better than a devil-woman, but I thought her yarn serious enough. Black Jack had no call to be about my house, unless he was set there to watch; and it looked to me as if my tomfool word about the paint, and perhaps some chatter of Maea's, had got us all in a clove hitch.[72] One thing was clear: Uma and I were here for the night; we daren't try to go home before day, and even then it would be safer to strike round up the mountain and come in by the back of the village, or we might walk into an ambuscade. It was plain, too, that the mine should be sprung immediately, or Case might be in time to stop it.

I marched into the tunnel, Uma keeping tight hold of me, opened my lantern and lit the match. The first length of it burned like a spill of paper, and I stood stupid, watching it burn, and thinking we were going aloft with Tiapolo, which was none of my views. The second took to a better rate, though faster than I cared about; and at that I got my wits again, hauled Uma clear of the passage, blew out and dropped the lantern, and the pair of us groped our way into the bush until I thought it might be safe, and lay down together by a tree.

"Old lady," I said, "I won't forget this night. You're a trump, and that's what's wrong with you."

She humped herself close up to me. She had run out the way she was, with nothing on her but her kilt; and she was all wet with the dews and the sea on the black beach, and shook straight on with cold and the terror of the dark and the devils.

"Too much 'fraid," was all she said.

---

[72] A knot that temporarily binds a rope to a post or spar. [ED.]

The far side of Case's hill goes down near as steep as a precipice into the next valley. We were on the very edge of it, and I could see the dead wood shine[73] and hear the sea sound far below. I didn't care about the position, which left me no retreat, but I was afraid to change. Then I saw I had made a worse mistake about the lantern, which I should have left lighted, so that I could have had a crack at Case when he stepped into the shine of it. And even if I hadn't had the wit to do that, it seemed a senseless thing to leave the good lantern to blow up with the graven images. The thing belonged to me, after all, and was worth money, and might come in handy. If I could have trusted the match, I might have run in still and rescued it. But who was going to trust the match? You know what trade is. The stuff was good enough for Kanakas to go fishing with, where they've got to look lively anyway, and the most they risk is only to have their hand blown off. But for anyone that wanted to fool around a blow-up like mine that match was rubbish.

Altogether the best I could do was to lie still, see my shot-gun handy, and wait for the explosion. But it was a solemn kind of a business. The blackness of the night was like solid; the only thing you could see was the nasty bogy glimmer of the dead wood, and that showed you nothing but it-self; and as for sounds, I stretched my ears till I thought I could have heard the match burn in the tunnel, and that bush was as silent as a coffin. Now and then there was a bit of a crack; but whether it was near or far, whether it was Case stubbing his toes within a few yards of me, or a tree breaking miles away, I knew no more than the babe unborn.

And then, all of a sudden, Vesuvius went off. It was a long time coming; but when it came (though I say it that shouldn't) no man could ask to see a better. At first it was just a son of a gun of a row, and a spout of fire, and the wood lighted up so that you could see to read. And then the trouble began. Uma and I were half buried under a wagonful of earth, and glad it was no worse, for one of the rocks at the entrance of the tunnel was fired clean into the air, fell within a couple of fathoms of where we lay, and bounded over the edge of the hill, and went pounding down into the next valley. I saw I had rather undercalculated our distance, or overdone the dynamite and powder, which you please.

And presently I saw I had made another slip. The noise of the thing began to die off, shaking the island; the dazzle was over; and yet the night didn't come back the way I expected. For the whole wood was scattered with red coals and brands from the explosion; they were all round me on the flat; some had fallen below in the valley, and some stuck and flared in the tree-

[73] Phosphorescent wood glows in the dark. [ED.]

tops. I had no fear of fire, for these forests are too wet to kindle. But the trouble was that the place was all lit up — not very bright, but good enough to get a shot by; and the way the coals were scattered, it was just as likely Case might have the advantage as myself. I looked all round for his white face, you may be sure; but there was not a sign of him. As for Uma, the life seemed to have been knocked right out of her by the bang and blaze of it.

There was one bad point in my game. One of the blessed graven images had come down all afire, hair and clothes and body, not four yards away from me. I cast a mighty noticing glance all round; there was still no Case, and I made up my mind I must get rid of that burning stick before he came, or I should be shot there like a dog.

It was my first idea to have crawled, and then I thought speed was the main thing, and stood half up to make a rush. The same moment from somewhere between me and the sea there came a flash and a report, and a rifle bullet screeched in my ear. I swung straight round and up with my gun, but the brute had a Winchester,[74] and before I could as much as see him his second shot knocked me over like a ninepin. I seemed to fly in the air, then came down by the run and lay half a minute, silly; and then I found my hands empty, and my gun had flown over my head as I fell. It makes a man mighty wide awake to be in the kind of box that I was in. I scarcely knew where I was hurt, or whether I was hurt or not, but turned right over on my face to crawl after my weapon. Unless you have tried to get about with a smashed leg you don't know what pain is, and I let out a howl like a bullock's.

This was the unluckiest noise that ever I made in my life. Up to then Uma had stuck to her tree like a sensible woman, knowing she would be only in the way; but as soon as she heard me sing out, she ran forward. The Winchester cracked again, and down she went.

I had sat up, leg and all, to stop her; but when I saw her tumble I clapped down again where I was, lay still, and felt the handle of my knife. I had been scurried and put out before. No more of that for me. He had knocked over my girl, I had got to fix him for it; and I lay there and gritted my teeth, and footed up the chances. My leg was broke, my gun was gone. Case had still ten shots in his Winchester. It looked a kind of hopeless business. But I never despaired nor thought upon despairing: that man had got to go.

For a goodish bit not one of us let on. Then I heard Case begin to move nearer in the bush, but mighty careful. The image had burned out; there were only a few coals left here and there, and the wood was main dark, but had a kind of a low glow in it like a fire on its last legs. It was by this that I

---

[74] A repeating rifle. [ED.]

made out Case's head looking at me over a big tuft of ferns, and at the same time the brute saw me and shouldered his Winchester. I lay quite still, and as good as looked into the barrel: it was my last chance, but I thought my heart would have come right out of its bearings. Then he fired. Lucky for me it was no shot-gun, for the bullet struck within an inch of me and knocked the dirt in my eyes.

Just you try and see if you can lie quiet, and let a man take a sitting shot at you and miss you by a hair. But I did, and lucky too. A while Case stood with the Winchester at the port-arms;[75] then he gave a little laugh to himself, and stepped round the ferns.

"Laugh!" thought I. "If you had the wit of a louse you would be praying!"

I was all as taut as a ship's hawser[76] or the spring of a watch, and as soon as he came within reach of me I had him by the ankle, plucked the feet right out from under him, laid him out, and was upon the top of him, broken leg and all, before he breathed. His Winchester had gone the same road as my shot-gun; it was nothing to me — I defied him now. I'm a pretty strong man anyway, but I never knew what strength was till I got hold of Case. He was knocked out of time by the rattle he came down with, and threw up his hands together, more like a frightened woman, so that I caught both of them with my left. This wakened him up, and he fastened his teeth in my forearm like a weasel. Much I cared. My leg gave me all the pain I had any use for, and I drew my knife and got it in the place.

"Now," said I, "I've got you; and you're gone up, and a good job too! Do you feel the point of that? That's for Underhill! And there's for Adams! And now here's for Uma, and that's going to knock your blooming soul right out of you!"

With that I gave him the cold steel for all I was worth. His body kicked under me like a spring sofa; he gave a dreadful kind of a long moan, and lay still.

"I wonder if you're dead? I hope so!" I thought, for my head was swimming. But I wasn't going to take chances; I had his own example too close before me for that; and I tried to draw the knife out to give it him again. The blood came over my hands, I remember, hot as tea; and with that I fainted clean away, and fell with my head on the man's mouth.

When I came to myself it was pitch dark; the cinders had burned out; there was nothing to be seen but the shine of the dead wood, and I couldn't remember where I was nor why I was in such pain nor what I was all wetted with. Then it came back, and the first thing I attended to was to

[75] A military stance in which the rifle is held diagonally against the body. [ED.]
[76] A large rope for towing or mooring a ship. [ED.]

give him the knife again a half-a-dozen times up to the handle. I believe he was dead already, but it did him no harm and did me good.

"I bet you're dead now," I said, and then I called to Uma.

Nothing answered, and I made a move to go and grope for her, fouled my broken leg, and fainted again.

When I came to myself the second time the clouds had all cleared away, except a few that sailed there, white as cotton. The moon was up—a tropic moon. The moon at home turns a wood black, but even this old butt-end of a one showed up that forest as green as by day. The night birds—or, rather, they're a kind of early morning bird—sang out with their long, falling notes like nightingales. And I could see the dead man, that I was still half resting on, looking right up into the sky with his open eyes, no paler than when he was alive; and a little way off Uma tumbled on her side. I got over to her the best way I was able, and when I got there she was broad awake, and crying and sobbing to herself with no more noise than an insect. It appears she was afraid to cry out loud, because of the *aitus*. Altogether she was not much hurt, but scared beyond belief; she had come to her senses a long while ago, cried out to me, heard nothing in reply, made out we were both dead and had lain there ever since, afraid to budge a finger. The ball had ploughed up her shoulder and she had lost a main quantity of blood; but I soon had that tied up the way it ought to be with the tail of my shirt and a scarf I had on, got her head on my sound knee and my back against a trunk, and settled down to wait for morning. Uma was for neither use nor ornament, and could only clutch hold of me and shake and cry. I don't suppose there was ever anybody worse scared, and, to do her justice, she had had a lively night of it. As for me, I was in a good bit of pain and fever, but not so bad when I sat still; and every time I looked over to Case I could have sung and whistled. Talk about meat and drink! To see that man lying there dead as a herring filled me full.

The night birds stopped after a while; and then the light began to change, the east came orange, the whole wood began to whirr with singing like a musical box, and there was the broad day.

I didn't expect Maea for a long while yet; and, indeed, I thought there was an off-chance he might go back on the whole idea and not come at all. I was the better pleased when, about an hour after daylight, I heard sticks smashing and a lot of Kanakas laughing and singing out to keep their courage up. Uma sat up quite brisk at the first word of it; and presently we saw a party come stringing out of the path, Maea in front, and behind him a white man in a pith helmet. It was Mr. Tarleton, who had turned up late last night in Falesá, having left his boat and walked the last stage with a lantern.

They buried Case upon the field of glory, right in the hole where he had kept the smoking head. I waited till the thing was done; and Mr. Tarleton prayed, which I thought tomfoolery, but I'm bound to say he gave a pretty sick view of the dear departed's prospects, and seemed to have his own ideas of hell. I had it out with him afterwards, told him he had scamped his duty, and what he had ought to have done was to up like a man and tell the Kanakas plainly Case was damned, and a good riddance; but I never could get him to see it my way. Then they made me a litter of poles and carried me down to the station. Mr. Tarleton set my leg, and made a regular missionary splice of it, so that I limp to this day. That done, he took down my evidence, and Uma's, and Maea's, wrote it all out fine, and had us sign it; and then he got the chiefs and marched over to Papa Randall's to seize Case's papers.

All they found was a bit of a diary, kept for a good many years, and all about the price of copra, and chickens being stolen, and that; and the books of the business and the will I told you of in the beginning, by both of which the whole thing (stock, lock, and barrel) appeared to belong to the Samoa woman. It was I that bought her out at a mighty reasonable figure, for she was in a hurry to get home. As for Randall and the black, they had to tramp; got into some kind of a station on the Papa-malulu side; did very bad business, for the truth is neither of the pair was fit for it, and lived mostly on fish, which was the means of Randall's death. It seems there was a nice shoal in one day, and Papa went after them with the dynamite; either the match burned too fast, or Papa was full, or both, but the shell went off (in the usual way) before he threw it, and where was Papa's hand? Well, there's nothing to hurt in that; the islands up north are all full of one-handed men, like the parties in the "Arabian Nights";[77] but either Randall was too old, or he drank too much, and the short and the long of it was that he died. Pretty soon after, the nigger was turned out of the island for stealing from white men, and went off to the west, where he found men of his own colour, in case he liked that, and the men of his own colour took and ate him at some kind of a corroborree,[78] and I'm sure I hope he was to their fancy!

So there was I, left alone in my glory at Falesá; and when the schooner came round I filled her up, and gave her a deck-cargo half as high as the house. I must say Mr. Tarleton did the right thing by us; but he took a meanish kind of a revenge.

"Now, Mr. Wiltshire," said he, "I've put you all square with everybody here. It wasn't difficult to do, Case being gone; but I have done it, and given my pledge besides that you will deal fairly with the natives. I must ask you to keep my word."

---

[77] Chopping off a hand is the standard punishment for theft in *The Arabian Nights*. [ED.]
[78] A large festive gathering. [ED.]

Well, so I did. I used to be bothered about my balances,[79] but I reasoned it out this way: We all have queerish balances, and the natives all know it, and water their copra in a proportion so that it's fair all round; but the truth is, it did use to bother me, and, though I did well in Falesá, I was half glad when the firm moved me on to another station, where I was under no kind of a pledge and could look my balances in the face.

As for the old lady, you know her as well as I do. She's only the one fault. If you don't keep your eye lifting she would give away the roof off the station. Well, it seems it's natural in Kanakas. She's turned a powerful big woman now, and could throw a London bobby over her shoulder. But that's natural in Kanakas too, and there's no manner of doubt that she's an A 1 wife.

Mr. Tarleton's gone home, his trick[80] being over. He was the best missionary I ever struck, and now, it seems, he's parsonising down Somerset way. Well, that's best for him; he'll have no Kanakas there to get luny over.

My public-house? Not a bit of it, nor ever likely. I'm stuck here, I fancy. I don't like to leave the kids, you see: and — there's no use talking — they're better here than what they would be in a white man's country, though Ben took the eldest up to Auckland, where he's being schooled with the best. But what bothers me is the girls. They're only half-castes, of course; I know that as well as you do, and there's nobody thinks less of half-castes than I do; but they're mine, and about all I've got. I can't reconcile my mind to their taking up with Kanakas, and I'd like to know where I'm to find [them] whites?

---

[79] The adjustable balances of his scales. [ED.]
[80] Sailors' slang for a tour of duty. [ED.]

Heart of Darkness

Joseph Conrad

CHAPTER I

The *Nellie*, a cruising yawl, swung to her anchor without a flutter of the sails, and was at rest. The flood had made,[1] the wind was nearly calm, and being bound down the river, the only thing for it was to come to and wait for the turn of the tide.

The sea-reach[2] of the Thames stretched before us like the beginning of an interminable waterway. In the offing[3] the sea and the sky were welded together without a joint, and in the luminous space the tanned sails of the barges drifting up with the tide seemed to stand still in red clusters of canvas sharply peaked, with gleams of varnished sprits.[4] A haze rested on the low shores that ran out to sea in vanishing flatness. The air was dark above Gravesend,[5] and farther back still seemed condensed into a mournful gloom, brooding motionless over the biggest, and the greatest, town on earth.

The Director of Companies was our captain and our host. We four affectionately watched his back as he stood in the bows looking to seaward. On the whole river there was nothing that looked half so nautical. He resembled a pilot, which to a seaman is trustworthiness personified. It was difficult to realise his work was not out there in the luminous estuary, but behind him, within the brooding gloom.

Between us there was, as I have already said somewhere,[6] the bond of the sea. Besides holding our hearts together through long periods of separation, it had the effect of making us tolerant of each other's yarns — and even convictions. The Lawyer — the best of old fellows — had, because of his many years and many virtues, the only cushion on deck, and was lying on the only rug. The Accountant had brought out already a box of dominoes, and was toying architecturally with the bones.[7] Marlow sat cross-legged right aft, leaning against the mizzenmast.[8] He had sunken cheeks, a yellow complexion, a straight back, an ascetic aspect, and, with his arms dropped,

---

[1] The tide had come in. [ED.]

[2] A reach is a straight portion or a widening of a river. In this case, a sea-reach is the opening out of the Thames at its mouth. [ED.]

[3] That small part of the deep sea seen from the shore. [ED.]

[4] A spar cast diagonally across a fore-and-aft sail. [ED.]

[5] A town east of London, at the mouth of the Thames. [ED.]

[6] A reference to *Youth*, which features these same four men. [ED.]

[7] Dominoes were often made of ivory; hence they were referred to as bones. [ED.]

[8] The mast directly aft of the main mast. [ED.]

the palms of hands outwards, resembled an idol. The Director, satisfied the anchor had good hold, made his way aft and sat down amongst us. We exchanged a few words lazily. Afterwards there was silence on board the yacht. For some reason or other we did not begin that game of dominoes. We felt meditative, and fit for nothing but placid staring. The day was ending in a serenity of still and exquisite brilliance. The water shone pacifically; the sky, without a speck, was a benign immensity of unstained light; the very mist on the Essex marshes was like a gauzy and radiant fabric, hung from the wooded rises inland, and draping the low shores in diaphanous folds. Only the gloom to the west, brooding over the upper reaches, became more sombre every minute, as if angered by the approach of the sun.

And at last, in its curved and imperceptible fall, the sun sank low, and from glowing white changed to a dull red without rays and without heat, as if about to go out suddenly, stricken to death by the touch of that gloom brooding over a crowd of men.

Forthwith a change came over the waters, and the serenity became less brilliant but more profound. The old river in its broad reach rested unruffled at the decline of day, after ages of good service done to the race that peopled its banks, spread out in the tranquil dignity of a waterway leading to the uttermost ends of the earth. We looked at the venerable stream not in the vivid flush of a short day that comes and departs for ever, but in the august light of abiding memories. And indeed nothing is easier for a man who has, as the phrase goes, "followed the sea" with reverence and affection, than to evoke the great spirit of the past upon the lower reaches of the Thames. The tidal current runs to and fro in its unceasing service, crowded with memories of men and ships it has borne to the rest of home or to the battles of the sea. It had known and served all the men of whom the nation is proud, from Sir Francis Drake[9] to Sir John Franklin,[10] knights all, titled and untitled—the great knights-errant of the sea. It had borne all the ships whose names are like jewels flashing in the night of time, from the *Golden Hind*[11] returning with her round flanks full of treasure, to be visited by the Queen's Highness and thus pass out of the gigantic tale, to the *Erebus* and *Terror*,[12] bound on other conquests—and that never returned. It had known the ships and the men. They had sailed from Deptford, from Greenwich,

---

[9] In 1580, Sir Francis Drake became the first man to circumnavigate the globe. [ED.]

[10] The explorer who mapped the coast of Australia, and later died with his entire crew while searching for the Northwest Passage. [ED.]

[11] The ship of Sir Francis Drake. On its return to England, the ship was boarded by Queen Elizabeth, who knighted Drake on the spot. [ED.]

[12] Franklin's two ships on his last, ill-fated expedition. [ED.]

from Erith[13]—the adventurers and the settlers; kings' ships and the ships of men on 'Change;[14] captains, admirals, the dark "interlopers"[15] of the Eastern trade, and the commissioned "generals" of East India fleets.[16] Hunters for gold or pursuers of fame, they all had gone out on that stream, bearing the sword, and often the torch, messengers of the might within the land, bearers of a spark from the sacred fire. What greatness had not floated on the ebb of that river into the mystery of an unknown earth! . . . The dreams of men, the seed of commonwealths, the germs of empires.

The sun set; the dusk fell on the stream, and lights began to appear along the shore. The Chapman lighthouse, a three-legged thing erect on a mud-flat, shone strongly. Lights of ships moved in the fairway—a great stir of lights going up and going down. And farther west on the upper reaches the place of the monstrous town was still marked ominously on the sky, a brooding gloom in sunshine, a lurid glare under the stars.

"And this also," said Marlow suddenly, "has been one of the dark places of the earth."

He was the only man of us who still "followed the sea." The worst that could be said of him was that he did not represent his class. He was a seaman, but he was a wanderer too, while most seamen lead, if one may so express it, a sedentary life. Their minds are of the stay-at-home order, and their home is always with them—the ship; and so is their country—the sea. One ship is very much like another, and the sea is always the same. In the immutability of their surroundings the foreign shores, the foreign faces, the changing immensity of life, glide past, veiled not by a sense of mystery but by a slightly disdainful ignorance; for there is nothing mysterious to a seaman unless it be the sea itself, which is the mistress of his existence and as inscrutable as Destiny. For the rest, after his hours of work, a casual stroll or a casual spree on shore suffices to unfold for him the secret of a whole continent, and generally he finds the secret not worth knowing. The yarns of seamen have a direct simplicity, the whole meaning of which lies within the shell of a cracked nut. But Marlow was not typical (if his propensity to spin yarns be excepted), and to him the meaning of an episode was not inside like a kernel but outside, enveloping the tale which brought it out only

---

[13] Ports on the Thames between London and Gravesend. [ED.]

[14] Short for *Exchange,* where London merchants conducted business, the equivalent of Wall Street in the United States. [ED.]

[15] Unauthorized trading ships. [ED.]

[16] General merchants dealt in miscellaneous goods. The East India Company was granted a monopoly on Indian trade by Queen Elizabeth in 1600 and ceased operations in 1858, in the wake of the Indian Mutiny. [ED.]

as a glow brings out a haze, in the likeness of one of these misty halos that sometimes are made visible by the spectral illumination of moonshine.

His remark did not seem at all surprising. It was just like Marlow. It was accepted in silence. No one took the trouble to grunt even; and presently he said, very slow—

"I was thinking of very old times, when the Romans first came here, nineteen hundred years ago—the other day.... Light came out of this river since—you say Knights? Yes; but it is like a running blaze on a plain, like a flash of lightning in the clouds. We live in the flicker—may it last as long as the old earth keeps rolling! But darkness was here yesterday. Imagine the feelings of a commander of a fine—what d'ye call 'em?—trireme[17] in the Mediterranean, ordered suddenly to the north; run overland across the Gauls in a hurry; put in charge of one of these craft the legionaries—a wonderful lot of handy men they must have been too—used to build, apparently by the hundred, in a month or two, if we may believe what we read. Imagine him here—the very end of the world, a sea the colour of lead, a sky the colour of smoke, a kind of ship about as rigid as a concertina[18]— and going up this river with stores, or orders, or what you like. Sandbanks, marshes, forests, savages—precious little to eat fit for a civilised man, nothing but Thames water to drink. No Falernian wine[19] here, no going ashore. Here and there a military camp lost in a wilderness, like a needle in a bundle of hay—cold, fog, tempests, disease, exile, and death—death skulking in the air, in the water, in the bush. They must have been dying like flies here. Oh yes—he did it. Did it very well, too, no doubt, and without thinking much about it either, except afterwards to brag of what he had gone through in his time, perhaps. They were men enough to face the darkness. And perhaps he was cheered by keeping his eye on a chance of promotion to the fleet at Ravenna[20] by-and-by, if he had good friends in Rome and survived the awful climate. Or think of a decent young citizen in a toga—perhaps too much dice, you know—coming out here in the train of some prefect, or tax-gatherer, or trader even, to mend his fortunes. Land in a swamp, march through the woods, and in some inland post feel the savagery, the utter savagery, had closed round him—all that mysterious life of the wilderness that stirs in the forest, in the jungles, in the hearts of wild men. There's no initiation either into such mysteries. He has to live in the midst of the

---

[17] A large Roman galley. [ED.]
[18] An accordion-like musical instrument favored by sailors. [ED.]
[19] A famous Roman wine. [ED.]
[20] The principal Roman naval base, on the northern Adriatic. [ED.]

incomprehensible, which is also detestable. And it has a fascination, too, that goes to work upon him. The fascination of the abomination—you know. Imagine the growing regrets, the longing to escape, the powerless disgust, the surrender, the hate."

He paused.

"Mind," he began again, lifting one arm from the elbow, the palm of the hand outwards, so that, with his legs folded before him, he had the pose of a Buddha preaching in European clothes and without a lotus-flower— "Mind, none of us would feel exactly like this. What saves us is efficiency— the devotion to efficiency. But these chaps were not much account, really. They were no colonists; their administration was merely a squeeze,[21] and nothing more, I suspect. They were conquerors, and for that you want only brute force—nothing to boast of, when you have it, since your strength is just an accident arising from the weakness of others. They grabbed what they could get for the sake of what was to be got. It was just robbery with violence, aggravated murder on a great scale, and men going at it blind— as is very proper for those who tackle a darkness. The conquest of the earth, which mostly means the taking it away from those who have a different complexion or slightly flatter noses than ourselves, is not a pretty thing when you look into it too much. What redeems it is the idea only. An idea at the back of it; not a sentimental pretence but an idea; and an unselfish belief in the idea—something you can set up, and bow down before, and offer a sacrifice to. . . ."

He broke off. Flames glided in the river, small green flames, red flames, white flames,[22] pursuing, overtaking, joining, crossing each other—then separating slowly or hastily. The traffic of the great city went on in the deepening night upon the sleepless river. We looked on, waiting patiently— there was nothing else to do till the end of the flood; but it was only after a long silence, when he said, in a hesitating voice, "I suppose you fellows remember I did once turn fresh-water sailor for a bit," that we knew we were fated, before the ebb began to run, to hear about one of Marlow's inconclusive experiences.

"I don't want to bother you much with what happened to me personally," he began, showing in this remark the weakness of many tellers of tales who seem so often unaware of what their audience would best like to hear; "yet to understand the effect of it on me you ought to know how I got out there, what I saw, how I went up that river to the place where I first met the

---

[21] Crude expropriation. [ED.]

[22] Marlow is referring to the lights of ships and their reflections. [ED.]

poor chap. It was the farthest point of navigation and the culminating point of my experience. It seemed somehow to throw a kind of light on everything about me—and into my thoughts. It was sombre enough too—and pitiful—not extraordinary in any way—not very clear either. No, not very clear. And yet it seemed to throw a kind of light.

"I had then, as you remember, just returned to London after a lot of Indian Ocean, Pacific, China Seas—a regular dose of the East—six years or so, and I was loafing about, hindering you fellows in your work and invading your homes, just as though I had got a heavenly mission to civilise you. It was very fine for a time, but after a bit I did get tired of resting. Then I began to look for a ship—I should think the hardest work on earth. But the ships wouldn't even look at me. And I got tired of that game too.

"Now when I was a little chap I had a passion for maps. I would look for hours at South America, or Africa, or Australia, and lose myself in all the glories of exploration. At that time there were many blank spaces on the earth, and when I saw one that looked particularly inviting on a map (but they all look that) I would put my finger on it and say, When I grow up I will go there. The North Pole was one of these places, I remember. Well, I haven't been there yet, and shall not try now. The glamour's off. Other places were scattered about the Equator, and in every sort of latitude all over the two hemispheres. I have been in some of them, and . . . well, we won't talk about that. But there was one yet—the biggest, the most blank, so to speak—that I had a hankering after.

"True, by this time it was not a blank space any more. It had got filled since my boyhood with rivers and lakes and names. It had ceased to be a blank space of delightful mystery—a white patch for a boy to dream gloriously over. It had become a place of darkness. But there was in it one river especially, a mighty big river, that you could see on the map, resembling an immense snake uncoiled, with its head in the sea, its body at rest curving afar over a vast country, and its tail lost in the depths of the land. And as I looked at the map of it in a shop-window, is fascinated me as a snake would a bird—a silly little bird. Then I remembered there was a big concern, a Company for trade on that river. Dash it all! I thought to myself, they can't trade without using some kind of craft on that lot of fresh water— steamboats! Why shouldn't I try to get charge of one. I went on along Fleet Street[23] but could not shake off the idea. The snake had charmed me.

"You understand it was a Continental concern, that Trading Society; but I have a lot of relations living on the Continent, because it's cheap and not so nasty as it looks, they say.

---

[23] The central commercial street of London. [ED.]

"I am sorry to own I began to worry them. This was already a fresh departure for me. I was not used to get things that way, you know. I always went my own road and on my own legs where I had a mind to go. I wouldn't have believed it of myself; but, then—you see—I felt somehow I must get there by hook or by crook. So I worried them. The men said 'My dear fellow,' and did nothing. Then—would you believe it?—I tried the women. I, Charlie Marlow, set the women to work—to get a job. Heavens! Well, you see, the notion drove me. I had an aunt, a dear enthusiastic soul. She wrote: 'It will be delightful. I am ready to do anything, anything for you. It is a glorious idea. I know the wife of a very high personage in the Administration, and also a man who has lots of influence with,' &c., &c. She was determined to make no end of fuss to get me appointed skipper of a river steamboat, if such was my fancy.

"I got my appointment—of course; and I got it very quick. It appears the Company had received news that one of their captains had been killed in a scuffle with the natives. This was my chance, and it made me the more anxious to go. It was only months and months afterwards, when I made the attempt to recover what was left of the body, that I heard the original quarrel arose from a misunderstanding about some hens. Yes, two black hens. Fresleven—that was the fellow's name, a Dane—thought himself wronged somehow in the bargain, so he went ashore and started to hammer the chief of the village with a stick. Oh, it didn't surprise me in the least to hear this, and at the same time to be told that Fresleven was the gentlest, quietest creature that ever walked on two legs. No doubt he was; but he had been a couple of years already out there engaged in the noble cause, you know, and he probably felt the need at last of asserting his self-respect in some way. Therefore he whacked the old nigger mercilessly, while a big crowd of his people watched him, thunderstruck, till some man—I was told the chief's son—in desperation at hearing the old chap yell, made a tentative job with a spear at the white man—and of course it went quite easy between the shoulder-blades. Then the whole population cleared into the forest, expecting all kinds of calamities to happen, while, on the other hand, the steamer Fresleven commanded left also in a bad panic, in charge of the engineer, I believe. Afterwards nobody seemed to trouble much about Fresleven's remains, till I got out and stepped into his shoes. I couldn't let it rest, though; but when an opportunity offered at last to meet my predecessor, the grass growing through his ribs was tall enough to hide his bones. They were all there. The supernatural being had not been touched after he fell. And the village was deserted, the huts gaped black, rotting, all askew within the fallen enclosures. A calamity had come to it, sure enough. The people had vanished. Mad terror had scattered them, men, women, and children, through the bush, and they had never returned. What became of the hens I don't know either. I should think the cause of progress got them, anyhow. However, through this glorious affair I got my appointment, before I had fairly begun to hope for it.

"I flew around like mad to get ready, and before forty-eight hours I was crossing the Channel to show myself to my employers, and sign the contract. In a very few hours I arrived in a city that always makes me think of a whited sepulchre.[24] Prejudice no doubt. I had no difficulty in finding the Company's offices. It was the biggest thing in the town, and everybody I met was full of it. They were going to run an over-sea empire, and make no end of coin by trade.

"A narrow and deserted street in deep shadow, high houses, innumerable windows with venetian blinds, a dead silence, grass sprouting between the stones, imposing carriage archways right and left, immense double doors standing ponderously ajar. I slipped through one of these cracks, went up a swept and ungarnished staircase, as arid as a desert, and opened the first door I came to. Two women, one fat and the other slim, sat on straw-bottomed chairs, knitting black wool.[25] The slim one got up and walked straight at me — still knitting with downcast eyes — and only just as I began to think of getting out of her way, as you would for a somnambulist, stood still, and looked up. Her dress was as plain as an umbrella-cover, and she turned round without a word and preceded me into a waiting-room. I gave my name, and looked about. Deal table in the middle, plain chairs all round the walls, on one end a large shining map, marked with all the colours of a rainbow. There was a vast amount of red[26] — good to see at any time, because one knows that some real work is done in there, a deuce of a lot of blue, a little green, smears of orange, and, on the East Coast, a purple patch, to show where the jolly pioneers of progress drink the jolly lager-beer. However, I wasn't going into any of these. I was going into the yellow. Dead in the centre. And the river was there — fascinating — deadly — like a snake. Ough! A door opened, a white-haired secretarial head, but wearing a compassionate expression, appeared, and a skinny forefinger beckoned me into the sanctuary. Its light was dim, and a heavy writing-desk squatted in the middle. From behind that structure came out an impression of pale plumpness in a frock-coat. The great man himself. He was five feet six, I should

<hr>

[24] An allusion to Matthew 23. 27–28. [ED.]

[25] An allusion to the Fates of Greek mythology. [ED.]

[26] On late-nineteenth-century maps of the world, most of which indicated colonial territories through a conventional system of color-coding, red denoted British possessions. Blue signified French colonies, green Italian, orange Portuguese, purple German, and yellow Belgian. [ED.]

judge, and had his grip on the handle-end of ever so many millions. He shook hands, I fancy, murmured vaguely, was satisfied with my French. *Bon voyage.*

"In about forty-five seconds I found myself again in the waiting-room with the compassionate secretary, who, full of desolation and sympathy, made me sign some document. I believe I undertook amongst other things not to disclose any trade secrets. Well, I am not going to.

"I began to feel slightly uneasy. You know I am not used to such cere-monies, and there was something ominous in the atmosphere. It was just as though I had been let into some conspiracy—I don't know—something not quite right; and I was glad to get out. In the outer room the two women knitted black wool feverishly. People were arriving, and the younger one was walking back and forth introducing them. The old one sat on her chair. Her flat cloth slippers were propped up on a foot-warmer, and a cat re-posed on her lap. She wore a starched white affair on her head, had a wart on one cheek, and silver-rimmed spectacles hung on the tip of her nose. She glanced at me above the glasses. The swift and indifferent placidity of that look troubled me. Two youths with foolish and cheery countenances were being piloted over, and she threw at them the same quick glance of unconcerned wisdom. She seemed to know all about them and about me too. An eerie feeling came over me. She seemed uncanny and fateful. Often far away there I thought of these two, guarding the door of Darkness,[27] knitting black wool as for a warm pall, one introducing, introducing con-tinuously to the unknown, the other scrutinising the cheery and foolish faces with unconcerned old eyes. *Ave!* Old knitter of black wool. *Morituri te salutant.*[28] Not many of those she looked at ever saw her again—not half, by a long way.

"There was yet a visit to the doctor. 'A simple formality,' assured me the secretary, with an air of taking an immense part in all my sorrows. Ac-cordingly a young chap wearing his hat over the left eyebrow, some clerk I suppose—there must have been clerks in the business, though the house was as still as a house in a city of the dead—came from somewhere up-stairs, and led me forth. He was shabby and careless, with ink-stains on the sleeves of his jacket, and his cravat was large and billowy, under a chin shaped like the toe of an old boot. It was a little too early for the doctor, so

---

[27] An allusion to Virgil's *Aeneid,* in which the Sybil guards the door to the Underworld (or hell), through which Aeneas must pass. [ED.]

[28] "*Ave!* . . . *Morturi te salutant*" ("Hail! Those about to die salute you") was the greeting Roman gladiators shouted to the emperor of Rome as they entered the arena of combat. [ED.]

I proposed a drink, and thereupon he developed a vein of joviality. As we sat over our vermuths he glorified the Company's business, and by-and-by I expressed casually my surprise at him not going out there. He became very cool and collected all at once. 'I am not such a fool as I look, quoth Plato to his disciples,' he said sententiously, emptied his glass with great resolution, and we rose.

"The old doctor felt my pulse, evidently thinking of something else the while. 'Good, good for there,' he mumbled, and then with a certain eagerness asked me whether I would let him measure my head. Rather surprised, I said Yes, when he produced a thing like calipers and got the dimensions back and front and every way, taking notes carefully. He was an unshaven little man in a threadbare coat like a gaberdine, with his feet in slippers, and I thought him a harmless fool. 'I always ask leave, in the interests of science, to measure the crania of those going out there,' he said. 'And when they come back too?' I asked. 'Oh, I never see them,' he remarked; 'and, moreover, the changes take place inside, you know.' He smiled, as if at some quiet joke. 'So you are going out there. Famous. Interesting too.' He gave me a searching glance, and made another note. 'Ever any madness in your family?' he asked, in a matter-of-fact tone. I felt very annoyed. 'Is that question in the interests of science too?' 'It would be,' he said, without taking notice of my irritation, 'interesting for science to watch the mental changes of individuals, on the spot, but . . .' 'Are you an alienist?'[29] I interrupted. 'Every doctor should be—a little,' answered that original, imperturbably. 'I have a little theory which you Messieurs who go out there must help me to prove. This is my share in the advantages my country shall reap from the possession of such a magnificent dependency. The mere wealth I leave to others. Pardon my questions, but you are the first Englishman coming under my observation . . .' I hastened to assure him I was not in the least typical. 'If I were,' said I, 'I wouldn't be talking like this with you.' 'What you say is rather profound, and probably erroneous,' he said, with a laugh. 'Avoid irritation more than exposure to the sun. Adieu. How do you English say, eh? Good-bye. Ah! Good-bye. Adieu. In the tropics one must before everything keep calm.' . . . He lifted a warning forefinger. . . . 'Du calme, du calme. Adieu.'

"One thing more remained to do—say good-bye to my excellent aunt. I found her triumphant. I had a cup of tea—the last decent cup of tea for many days—and in a room that most soothingly looked just as you would expect a lady's drawingroom to look, we had a long quiet chat by the fireside. In the course of these confidences it became quite plain to me I had

---

[29] In the nineteenth century, a specialist in mental pathologies. [ED.]

been represented to the wife of the high dignitary, and goodness knows to how many more people besides, as an exceptional and gifted creature—a piece of good fortune for the Company—a man you don't get hold of every day. Good heavens! and I was going to take charge of a twopenny-half-penny river-steamboat with a penny whistle attached! It appeared, however, I was also one of the Workers, with a capital—you know. Something like an emissary of light, something like a lower sort of apostle. There had been a lot of such rot let loose in print and talk just about that time, and the excellent woman, living right in the rush of all that humbug, got carried off her feet. She talked about 'weaning those ignorant millions from their horrid ways,' till, upon my word, she made me quite uncomfortable. I ventured to hint that the Company was run for profit.

"'You forget, dear Charlie, that the labourer is worthy of his hire,'[30] she said, brightly. It's queer how out of touch with truth women are. They live in a world of their own, and there had never been anything like it, and never can be. It is too beautiful altogether, and if they were to set it up it would go to pieces before the first sunset. Some confounded fact we men have been living contentedly with ever since the day of creation would start up and knock the whole thing over.

"After this I got embraced, told to wear flannel, be sure to write often, and so on—and I left. In the street—I don't know why—a queer feeling came to me that I was an impostor. Odd thing that I, who used to clear out for any part of the world at twenty-four hours' notice, with less thought than most men give to the crossing of a street, had a moment—I won't say of hesitation, but of startled pause, before this commonplace affair. The best way I can explain it to you is by saying that, for a second or two, I felt as though, instead of going to the centre of a continent, I were about to set off for the centre of the earth.

"I left in a French steamer, and she called in every blamed port they have out there, for, as far as I could see, the sole purpose of landing soldiers and custom-house officers. I watched the coast. Watching a coast as it slips by the ship is like thinking about an enigma. There it is before you—smiling, frowning, inviting, grand, mean, insipid, or savage, and always mute with an air of whispering, Come and find out. This one was almost featureless, as if still in the making, with an aspect of monotonous grimness. The edge of a colossal jungle, so dark-green as to be almost black, fringed with white surf, ran straight, like a ruled line, far, far away along a blue sea whose glitter was blurred by a creeping mist. The sun was fierce, the land seemed to glisten and drip with steam. Here and there greyish-whitish specks showed

[30] An allusion to Luke 10. 7. [ED.]

up, clustered inside the white surf, with a flag flying above them perhaps —
settlements some centuries old, and still no bigger than pin-heads on the untouched expanse of their background. We pounded along, stopped, landed
soldiers; went on, landed custom-house clerks to levy toll in what looked
like a God-forsaken wilderness, with a tin shed and a flag-pole lost in it;
landed more soldiers — to take care of the custom-house clerks, presumably.
Some, I heard, got drowned in the surf; but whether they did or not, nobody seemed particularly to care. They were just flung out there, and on we
went. Every day the coast looked the same, as though we had not moved;
but we passed various places — trading places — with names like Gran' Bassam, Little Popo, names that seemed to belong to some sordid farce acted
in front of a sinister backcloth. The idleness of a passenger, my isolation
amongst all these men with whom I had no point of contact, the oily and
languid sea, the uniform sombreness of the coast, seemed to keep me away
from the truth of things, within the toil of a mournful and senseless delusion. The voice of the surf heard now and then was a positive pleasure, like
the speech of a brother. It was something natural, that had its reason, that
had a meaning. Now and then a boat from the shore gave one a momentary contact with reality. It was paddled by black fellows. You could see
from afar the white of their eyeballs glistening. They shouted, sang; their
bodies streamed with perspiration; they had faces like grotesque masks —
these chaps; but they had bone, muscle, a wild vitality, an intense energy
of movement, that was as natural and true as the surf along their coast.
They wanted no excuse for being there. They were a great comfort to look
at. For a time I would feel I belonged still to a world of straightforward
facts; but the feeling would not last long. Something would turn up to
scare it away. Once, I remember, we came upon a man-of-war anchored off
the coast. There wasn't even a shed there, and she was shelling the bush. It
appears the French had one of their wars going on thereabouts. Her ensign[31] dropped limp like a rag; the muzzles of the long eight-inch guns
stuck out all over the low hull; the greasy, slimy swell swung her up lazily
and let her down, swaying her thin masts. In the empty immensity of earth,
sky, and water, there she was, incomprehensible, firing into a continent.
Pop, would go one of the eight-inch guns; a small flame would dart and
vanish, a little white smoke would disappear, a tiny projectile would give a
feeble screech — and nothing happened. Nothing could happen. There was
a touch of insanity in the proceeding, a sense of lugubrious drollery in the
sight; and it was not dissipated by somebody on board assuring me earnestly

---

[31] Ship's flag. [ED.]

there was a camp of natives—he called them enemies!—hidden out of sight somewhere.

"We gave her her letters (I heard the men in that lonely ship were dying of fever at the rate of three a-day) and went on. We called at some more places with farcical names, where the merry dance of death and trade goes on in a still and earthy atmosphere as of an overheated catacomb; all along the formless coast bordered by dangerous surf, as if Nature herself had tried to ward off intruders; in and out of rivers, streams of death in life, whose banks were rotting into mud, whose waters, thickened into slime, invaded the contorted mangroves, that seemed to writhe at us in the extremity of an impotent despair. Nowhere did we stop long enough to get a particularised impression, but the general sense of vague and oppressive wonder grew upon me. It was like a weary pilgrimage amongst hints for nightmares.

"It was upward of thirty days before I saw the mouth of the big river. We anchored off the seat of the government. But my work would not begin till some two hundred miles farther on. So as soon as I could I made a start for a place thirty miles higher up.

"I had my passage on a little sea-going steamer. Her captain was a Swede, and knowing me for a seaman, invited me on the bridge. He was a young man, lean, fair, and morose, with lanky hair and a shuffling gait. As we left the miserable little wharf, he tossed his head contemptuously at the shore. 'Been living there?' he asked. I said, 'Yes.' 'Fine lot these government chaps — are they not?' he went on, speaking English with great precision and considerable bitterness. 'It is funny what some people will do for a few francs a-month. I wonder what becomes of that kind when it goes up country?' I said to him I expected to see that soon. 'So-o-o!' he exclaimed. He shuffled athwart, keeping one eye ahead vigilantly. 'Don't be too sure,' he continued. 'The other day I took up a man who hanged himself on the road. He was a Swede, too.' 'Hanged himself! Why, in God's name?' I cried. He kept on looking out watchfully. 'Who knows? The sun too much for him, or the country perhaps.'

"At last we opened a reach. A rocky cliff appeared, mounds of turned-up earth by the shore, houses on a hill, others, with iron roofs, amongst a waste of excavations, or hanging to the declivity. A continuous noise of the rapids above hovered over this scene of inhabited devastation. A lot of people, mostly black and naked, moved about like ants. A jetty projected into the river. A blinding sunlight drowned all this at times in a sudden recrudescence of glare. 'There's your Company's station,' said the Swede, pointing to three wooden barrack-like structures on the rocky slope. 'I will send your things up. Four boxes did you say? So. Farewell.'

"I came upon a boiler wallowing in the grass, then found a path leading up the hill. It turned aside for the boulders, and also for an undersized railway-truck lying there on its back with its wheels in the air. One was off. The thing looked as dead as the carcass of some animal. I came upon more pieces of decaying machinery, a stack of rusty rails. To the left a clump of trees made a shady spot, where dark things seemed to stir feebly. I blinked, the path was steep. A horn tooted to the right, and I saw the black people run. A heavy and dull detonation shook the ground, a puff of smoke came out of the cliff, and that was all. No change appeared on the face of the rock. They were building a railway. The cliff was not in the way or anything; but this objectless blasting was all the work going on.

"A slight clinking behind me made me turn my head. Six black men advanced in a file, toiling up the path. They walked erect and slow, balancing small baskets full of earth on their heads, and the clink kept time with their footsteps. Black rags were wound round their loins, and the short ends behind wagged to and fro like tails. I could see every rib, the joints of their limbs were like knots in a rope; each had an iron collar on his neck, and all were connected together with a chain whose bights[32] swung between them, rhythmically clinking. Another report from the cliff made me think suddenly of that ship of war I had seen firing into a continent. It was the same kind of ominous voice; but these men could by no stretch of imagination be called enemies. They were called criminals, and the outraged law, like the bursting shells, had come to them, an insoluble mystery from over the sea. All their meagre breasts panted together, the violently dilated nostrils quivered, the eyes stared stonily uphill. They passed me within six inches, without a glance, with that complete, deathlike indifference of unhappy savages. Behind this raw matter one of the reclaimed, the product of the new forces at work, strolled despondently, carrying a rifle by its middle. He had a uniform jacket with one button off, and seeing a white man on the path, hoisted his weapon to his shoulder with alacrity. This was simple prudence, white men being so much alike at a distance that he could not tell who I might be. He was speedily reassured, and with a large, white, rascally grin, and a glance at his charge, seemed to take me into partnership in his exalted trust. After all, I also was a part of the great cause of these high and just proceedings.

"Instead of going up, I turned and descended to the left. My idea was to let that chain-gang get out of sight before I climbed the hill. You know I am not particularly tender; I've had to strike and to fend off. I've had to resist and to attack sometimes — that's only one way of resisting — without count-

---

[32] Slack parts of a chain or rope. [ED.]

ing the exact cost, according to the demands of such sort of life as I had blundered into. I've seen the devil of violence, and the devil of greed, and the devil of hot desire; but, by all the stars! these were strong, lusty, red-eyed devils, that swayed and drove men — men, I tell you. But as I stood on this hillside, I foresaw that in the blinding sunshine of that land I would become acquainted with a flabby, pretending, weak-eyed devil of a rapacious and pitiless folly. How insidious he could be, too, I was only to find out several months later and a thousand miles farther. For a moment I stood appalled, as though by a warning. Finally I descended the hill, obliquely, towards the trees I had seen.

"I avoided a vast artificial hole somebody had been digging on the slope, the purpose of which I found it impossible to divine. It wasn't a quarry or a sandpit, anyhow. It was just a hole. It might have been connected with the philanthropic desire of giving the criminals something to do. I don't know. Then I nearly fell into a very narrow ravine, almost no more than a scar in the hillside. I discovered that a lot of imported drainage-pipes for the settlement had been tumbled in there. There wasn't one that was not broken. It was a wanton smash-up. At last I got under the trees. My purpose was to stroll into the shade for a moment; but no sooner within than it seemed to me I had stepped into the gloomy circle of some Inferno.[33] The rapids were near, and an uninterrupted, uniform, headlong, rushing noise filled the mournful stillness of the grove, where not a breath stirred, not a leaf moved, with a mysterious sound — as though the tearing pace of the launched earth had suddenly become audible.

"Black shapes crouched, lay, sat between the trees, leaning against the trunks, clinging to the earth, half coming out, half effaced within the dim light, in all the attitudes of pain, abandonment, and despair. Another mine[34] on the cliff went off, followed by a slight shudder of the soil under my feet. The work was going on. The work! And this was the place where some of the helpers had withdrawn to die.

"They were dying slowly — it was very clear. They were not enemies, they were not criminals, they were nothing earthly now — nothing but black shadows of disease and starvation, lying confusedly in the greenish gloom. Brought from all the recesses of the coast in all the legality of time contracts, lost in uncongenial surroundings, fed on unfamiliar food, they sickened, became inefficient, and were then allowed to crawl away and rest. These moribund shapes were free as air — and nearly as thin. I began to distinguish the gleam of eyes under the trees. Then, glancing down, I saw a face near

---

[33] An allusion to Dante's *Inferno*. [ED.]
[34] Charge of dynamite. [ED.]

my hand. The black bones reclined at full length with one shoulder against the tree, and slowly the eyelids rose and the sunken eyes looked up at me, enormous and vacant, a kind of blind, white flicker in the depths of the orbs, which died out slowly. The man seemed young—almost a boy—but you know with them it's hard to tell. I found nothing else to do but to offer him one of my good Swede's ship's biscuits I had in my pocket. The fingers closed slowly on it and held—there was no other movement and no other glance. He had tied a bit of white worsted round his neck—Why? Where did he get it? Was it a badge—an ornament—a charm—a propitiatory act? Was there any idea at all connected with it? It looked startling round his black neck, this bit of white thread from beyond the seas.

"Near the same tree two more bundles of acute angles sat with their legs drawn up. One, with his chin propped on his knees, stared at nothing, in an intolerable and appalling manner: his brother phantom rested its forehead, as if overcome with a great weariness; and all about others were scattered in every pose of contorted collapse, as in some picture of a massacre or a pestilence. While I stood horror-struck, one of these creatures rose to his hands and knees, and went off on all-fours towards the river to drink. He lapped out of his hand, then sat up in the sunlight, crossing his shins in front of him, and after a time let his woolly head fall on his breastbone.

"I didn't want any more loitering in the shade, and I made haste towards the station. When near the buildings I met a white man, in such an unexpected elegance of get-up that in the first moment I took him for a sort of vision. I saw a high starched collar, white cuffs, a light alpaca jacket, snowy trousers, a clean necktie, and varnished boots. No hat. Hair parted, brushed, oiled, under a green-lined parasol held in a big white hand. He was amazing, and had a penholder behind his ear.

"I shook hands with this miracle, and I learned he was the Company's chief accountant, and that all the book-keeping was done at this station. He had come out for a moment, he said, 'to get a breath of fresh air.' The expression sounded wonderfully odd, with its suggestion of sedentary desk-life. I wouldn't have mentioned the fellow to you at all, only it was from his lips that I first heard the name of the man who is so indissolubly connected with the memories of that time. Moreover, I respected the fellow. Yes; I respected his collars, his vast cuffs, his brushed hair. His appearance was certainly that of a hairdresser's dummy; but in the great demoralisation of the land he kept up his appearance. That's backbone. His starched collars and got-up shirt-fronts were achievements of character. He had been out nearly three years; and, later on, I could not help asking him how he managed to sport such linen. He had just the faintest blush, and said modestly, 'I've been teaching one of the native women about the station. It was difficult. She had a distaste for the work.' Thus this man had verily accomplished something. And he was devoted to his books, which were in apple-pie order.

"Everything else in the station was in a muddle—heads, things, buildings. Strings of dusty niggers with splay feet arrived and departed; a stream of manufactured goods, rubbishy cottons, beads, and brass-wire set into the depths of darkness, and in return came a precious trickle of ivory.

"I had to wait in the station for ten days—an eternity. I lived in a hut in the yard, but to be out of the chaos I would sometimes get into the accountant's office. It was built of horizontal planks, and so badly put together that, as he bent over his high desk, he was barred from neck to heels with narrow strips of sunlight. There was no need to open the big shutter to see. It was hot there too; big flies buzzed fiendishly, and did not sting, but stabbed. I sat generally on the floor, while, of faultless appearance (and even slightly scented), perching on a high stool, he wrote, he wrote. Sometimes he stood up for exercise. When a truckle-bed with a sick man (some invalided agent from up-country) was put in there, he exhibited a gentle annoyance. 'The groans of this sick person,' he said, 'distract my attention. And without that it is extremely difficult to guard against clerical errors in this climate.'

"One day he remarked, without lifting his head, 'In the interior you will no doubt meet Mr. Kurtz.' On my asking who Mr. Kurtz was, he said he was a first-class agent; and seeing my disappointment at this information, he added slowly, laying down his pen, 'He is a very remarkable person.' Further questions elicited from him that Mr. Kurtz was at present in charge of a trading-post, a very important one, in the true ivory-country, at 'the very bottom of there. Sends in as much ivory as all the others put together . . .' He began to write again. The sick man was too ill to groan. The flies buzzed in a great peace.

"Suddenly there was a growing murmur of voices and a great tramping of feet. A caravan had come in. A violent babble of uncouth sounds burst out on the other side of the planks. All the carriers were speaking together, and in the midst of the uproar the lamentable voice of the chief agent was heard 'giving it up' tearfully for the twentieth time that day. . . . He rose slowly. 'What a frightful row,' he said. He crossed the room gently to look at the sick man, and returning, said to me, 'He does not hear.' 'What! Dead?' I asked, startled. 'No, not yet,' he answered, with great composure. Then, alluding with a toss of the head to the tumult in the station-yard, 'When one has got to make correct entries, one comes to hate those savages—hate them to the death.' He remained thoughtful for a moment. 'When you see Mr. Kurtz,' he went on, 'tell him from me that everything here'—he glanced at the desk—'is very satisfactory. I don't like to write to him—

with those messengers of ours you never know who may get hold of your letter — at that Central Station.' He stared at me for a moment with his mild, bulging eyes. 'Oh, he will go far, very far,' he began again. 'He will be a somebody in the Administration before long. They, above — the Council in Europe, you know — mean him to be.'

"He turned to his work. The noise outside had ceased, and presently in going out I stopped at the door. In the steady buzz of flies the homeward-bound agent was lying flushed and insensible; the other, bent over his books, was making correct entries of perfectly correct transactions; and fifty feet below the doorstep I could see the still treetops of the grove of death.

"Next day I left that station at last, with a caravan of sixty men, for a two-hundred-mile tramp.

"No use telling you much about that. Paths, paths, everywhere; a stamped-in network of paths spreading over the empty land, through long grass, through burnt grass, through thickets, down and up chilly ravines, up and down stony hills ablaze with heat; and a solitude, a solitude, nobody, not a hut. The population had cleared out a long time ago. Well, if a lot of mysterious niggers armed with all kinds of fearful weapons suddenly took to travelling on the road between Deal and Gravesend, catching the yokels right and left to carry heavy loads for them, I fancy every farm and cottage thereabouts would get empty very soon. Only here the dwellings were gone too. Still, I passed through several abandoned villages. There's something pathetically childish in the ruins of grass walls. Day after day, with the stamp and shuffle of sixty pair of bare feet behind me, each pair under a 60-lb. load. Camp, cook, sleep, strike camp, march. Now and then a carrier dead in harness, at rest in the long grass near the path, with an empty water-gourd and his long staff lying by his side. A great silence around and above. Perhaps on some quiet night the tremor of far-off drums, sinking, swelling, a tremor vast, faint; a sound weird, appealing, suggestive, and wild — and perhaps with as profound a meaning as the sound of bells in a Christian country. Once a white man in an unbuttoned uniform, camping on the path with an armed escort of lank Zanzibaris,[35] very hospitable and festive — not to say drunk. Was looking after the upkeep of the road, he declared. Can't say I saw any road or any upkeep, unless the body of a middle-aged negro, with a bullet-hole in the forehead, upon which I absolutely stumbled three miles farther on, may be considered as a permanent improvement. I had a white companion too, not a bad chap, but

---

[35] Natives of Zanzibar were frequently involved in the slave trade themselves and often served as mercenaries throughout Africa. [ED.]

rather too fleshy and with the exasperating habit of fainting on the hot hillsides, miles away from the least bit of shade and water. Annoying, you know, to hold your own coat like a parasol over a man's head while he is coming-to. I couldn't help asking him once what he meant by coming there at all. 'To make money, of course. What do you think?' he said, scornfully. Then he got fever, and had to be carried in a hammock slung under a pole. As he weighed sixteen stone[36] I had no end of rows with the carriers. They jibbed, ran away, sneaked off with their loads in the night—quite a mutiny. So, one evening, I made a speech in English with gestures, not one of which was lost to the sixty pairs of eyes before me, and the next morning I started the hammock off in front all right. An hour afterwards I came upon the whole concern wrecked in a bush—man, hammock, groans, blankets, horrors. The heavy pole had skinned his poor nose. He was very anxious for me to kill somebody, but there wasn't the shadow of a carrier near. I remembered the old doctor—'It would be interesting for science to watch the mental changes of individuals, on the spot.' I felt I was becoming scientifically interesting. However, all that is to no purpose. On the fifteenth day I came in sight of the big river again, and hobbled into the Central Station. It was on a back water surrounded by scrub and forest, with a pretty border of smelly mud on one side, and on the three others enclosed by a crazy fence of rushes. A neglected gap was all the gate it had, and the first glance at the place was enough to let you see the flabby devil was running that show. White men with long staves in their hands appeared languidly from amongst the buildings, strolling up to take a look at me, and then retired out of sight somewhere. One of them, a stout, excitable chap with black moustaches, informed me with great volubility and many digressions, as soon as I told him who I was, that my steamer was at the bottom of the river. I was thunderstruck. What, how, why? Oh, it was 'all right.' The 'manager himself' was there. All quite correct. 'Everybody had behaved splendidly! splendidly!'—'You must,' he said in agitation, 'go and see the general manager at once. He is waiting!'

"I did not see the real significance of that wreck at once. I fancy I see it now, but I am not sure—not at all. Certainly the affair was too stupid—when I think of it—to be altogether natural. Still. . . . But at the moment it presented itself simply as a confounded nuisance. The steamer was sunk. They had started two days before in a sudden hurry up the river with the manager on board, in charge of some volunteer skipper, and before they had been out three hours they tore the bottom out of her on stones, and she sank near the south bank. I asked myself what I was to do there, now my

---

[36]Two hundred twenty-four pounds. [ED.]

boat was lost. As a matter of fact, I had plenty to do in fishing my command out of the river. I had to set about it the very next day. That, and the repairs when I brought the pieces to the station, took some months.

"My first interview with the manager was curious. He did not ask me to sit down after my twenty-mile walk that morning. He was commonplace in complexion, in feature, in manners, and in voice. He was of middle size and of ordinary build. His eyes, of the usual blue, were perhaps remarkably cold, and he certainly could make his glance fall on one as trenchant and heavy as an axe. But even at these times the rest of his person seemed to disclaim the intention. Otherwise there was only an indefinable, faint expression of his lips, something stealthy—a smile—not a smile—I remember it, but I can't explain. It was unconscious, this smile was, though just after he had said something it got intensified for an instant. It came at the end of his speeches like a seal applied on the words to make the meaning of the commonest phrase appear absolutely inscrutable. He was a common trader, from his youth up employed in these parts—nothing more. He was obeyed, yet he inspired neither love nor fear, nor even respect. He inspired uneasiness. That was it! Uneasiness. Not a definite mistrust—just uneasiness— nothing more. You have no idea how effective such a . . . a . . . faculty can be. He had no genius for organising, for initiative, or for order even. That was evident in such things as the deplorable state of the station. He had no learning, and no intelligence. His position had come to him—why? Perhaps because he was never ill . . . He had served three terms of three years out there . . . Because triumphant health in the general rout of constitutions is a kind of power in itself. When he went home on leave he rioted on a large scale—pompously. Jack ashore—with a difference—in externals only. This one could gather from his casual talk. He originated nothing, he could keep the routine going—that's all. But he was great. He was great by this little thing that it was impossible to tell what could control such a man. He never gave that secret away. Perhaps there was nothing within him. Such a suspicion made one pause—for out there there were no external checks. Once when various tropical diseases had laid low almost every 'agent' in the station, he was heard to say, 'Men who come out here should have no entrails.' He sealed the utterance with that smile of his, as though it had been a door opening into a darkness he had in his keeping. You fancied you had seen things—but the seal was on. When annoyed at meal-times by the constant quarrels of the white men about precedence, he ordered an immense round table[37] to be made, for which a special house had to be built. This was the station's mess-room. Where he sat was the first place—the rest

---

[37] An allusion to the legend of King Arthur and his Knights of the Round Table. [ED.]

were nowhere. One felt this to be his unalterable conviction. He was neither civil nor uncivil. He was quiet. He allowed his 'boy'—an overfed young negro from the coast—to treat the white men, under his very eyes, with provoking insolence.

"He began to speak as soon as he saw me. I had been very long on the road. He could not wait. Had to start without me. The up-river stations had to be relieved. There had been so many delays already that he did not know who was dead and who was alive, and how they got on—and so on, and so on. He paid no attention to my explanations, and, playing with a stick of sealing-wax, repeated several times that the situation was 'very grave, very grave.' There were rumours that a very important station was in jeopardy, and its chief, Mr. Kurtz, was ill. Hoped it was not true. Mr. Kurtz was . . . I felt weary and irritable. Hang Kurtz, I thought. I interrupted him by saying I had heard of Mr. Kurtz on the coast. 'Ah! So they talk of him down there,' he murmured to himself. Then he began again, assuring me Mr. Kurtz was the best agent he had, an exceptional man, of the greatest importance to the Company; therefore I could understand his anxiety. He was, he said, 'very, very uneasy.' Certainly he fidgeted on his chair a good deal, exclaimed, 'Ah, Mr. Kurtz!' broke the stick of sealing-wax and seemed dumfounded by the accident. Next thing he wanted to know 'how long it would take to' . . . I interrupted him again. Being hungry, you know, and kept on my feet too, I was getting savage. 'How can I tell,' I said. 'I haven't even seen the wreck yet—some months, no doubt.' All this talk seemed to me so futile. 'Some months,' he said. 'Well, let us say three months before we can make a start. Yes. That ought to do the affair.' I flung out of his hut (he lived all alone in a clay hut with a sort of verandah) muttering to myself my opinion of him. He was a chattering idiot. Afterwards I took it back when it was borne in upon me startlingly with what extreme nicety he had estimated the time requisite for the 'affair.'

"I went to work the next day, turning, so to speak, my back on that station. In that way only it seemed to me I could keep my hold on the redeeming facts of life. Still, one must look about sometimes; and then I saw this station, these men strolling aimlessly about in the sunshine of the yard. I asked myself sometimes what it all meant. They wandered here and there with their absurd long staves in their hands, like a lot of faithless pilgrims[38] bewitched inside a rotten fence. The word 'ivory' rang in the air, was whispered, was sighed. You would think they were praying to it. A taint of imbecile rapacity blew through it all, like a whiff from some corpse. By Jove! I've never seen anything so unreal in my life. And outside, the silent

---

[38] Possibly, an allusion to John Bunyan's *The Pilgrim's Progress* (1678). [ED.]

wilderness surrounding this cleared speck on the earth struck me as something great and invincible, like evil or truth, waiting patiently for the passing away of this fantastic invasion.

"Oh, those months! Well, never mind. Various things happened. One evening a grass shed full of calico, cotton prints, beads, and I don't know what else, burst into a blaze so suddenly that you would have thought the earth had opened to let an avenging fire consume all that trash. I was smoking my pipe quietly by my dismantled steamer, and saw them all cutting capers in the light, with their arms lifted high, when the stout man with moustaches came tearing down to the river, a tin pail in his hand, assured me that everybody was 'behaving splendidly, splendidly,' dipped about a quart of water and tore back again. I noticed there was a hole in the bottom of his pail.

"I strolled up. There was no hurry. You see the thing had gone off like a box of matches. It had been hopeless from the very first. The flame had leaped high, driven everybody back, lighted up everything—and collapsed. The shed was already a heap of embers glowing fiercely. A nigger was being beaten near by. They said he had caused the fire in some way; be that as it may, he was screeching most horribly. I saw him, later on, for several days, sitting in a bit of shade looking very sick and trying to recover himself: afterwards he arose and went out—and the wilderness without a sound took him into its bosom again. As I approached the glow from the dark I found myself at the back of two men, talking. I heard the name of Kurtz pronounced, then the words, 'take advantage of this unfortunate accident.' One of the men was the manager. I wished him a good evening. 'Did you ever see anything like it—eh? It is incredible,' he said, and walked off. The other man remained. He was a first-class agent, young, gentlemanly, a bit reserved, with a forked little beard and a hooked nose. He was stand-offish with the other agents, and they on their side said he was the manager's spy upon them. As to me, I had hardly ever spoken to him before. We got into talk, and by-and-by we strolled away from the hissing ruins. Then he asked me to his room, which was in the main building of the station. He struck a match, and I perceived that this young aristocrat had not only a silver-mounted dressing-case but also a whole candle all to himself. Just at that time the manager was the only man supposed to have any right to candles. Native mats covered the clay walls; a collection of spears, assegais,[39] shields, knives was hung up in trophies. The business intrusted to this fellow was the making of bricks—so I had been informed; but there wasn't a fragment

---

[39] Small spears, meant for throwing. [ED.]

of a brick anywhere in the station, and he had been there more than a year—waiting. It seems he could not make bricks without something, I don't know what—straw maybe. Anyway, it could not be found there, and as it was not likely to be sent from Europe, it did not appear clear to me what he was waiting for. An act of special creation[40] perhaps. However, they were all waiting—all the sixteen or twenty pilgrims of them—for something; and upon my word it did not seem an uncongenial occupation, from the way they took it, though the only thing that ever came to them was disease—as far as I could see. They beguiled the time by backbiting and intriguing against each other in a foolish kind of way. There was an air of plotting about that station, but nothing came of it, of course. It was as unreal as everything else—as the philanthropic pretence of the whole concern, as their talk, as their government, as their show of work. The only real feeling was a desire to get appointed to a trading-post where ivory was to be had, so that they could earn percentages. They intrigued and slandered and hated each other only on that account, but as to effectually lifting a little finger—oh, no. By heavens! There is something after all in the world allowing one man to steal a horse while another must not look at a halter. Steal a horse straight out. Very well. He has done it. Perhaps he can ride. But there is a way of looking at a halter that would provoke the most charitable of saints into a kick.

"I had no idea why he wanted to be sociable, but as we chatted in there it suddenly occurred to me the fellow was trying to get at something—in fact, pumping me. He alluded constantly to Europe, to the people I was supposed to know there—putting leading questions as to my acquaintances in the sepulchral city, and so on. His little eyes glittered like mica discs—with curiosity—though he tried to keep up a bit of superciliousness. At first I was astonished, but very soon I became awfully curious to see what he would find out from me. I couldn't possibly imagine what I had in me to make it worth his while. It was very pretty to see how he baffled himself, for in truth my body was full of chills, and my head had nothing in it but that wretched steamboat business. It was evident he took me for a perfectly shameless prevaricator. At last he got angry, and, to conceal a movement of furious annoyance, he yawned. I rose. Then I noticed a small sketch in oils, on a panel, representing a woman, draped and blindfolded, carrying a lighted torch. The background was sombre—almost black. The movement of the woman was stately, and the effect of the torchlight on the face was sinister.

---

[40] *Special creation* was the common nineteenth-century term for nonevolutionary theories of divine creation. [ED.]

"It arrested me, and he stood by civilly, holding a half-pint champagne bottle (medical comforts) with the candle stuck in it. To my question he said Mr. Kurtz had painted this—in this very station more than a year ago—while waiting for means to go to his trading-post. 'Tell me, pray,' said I, 'who is this Mr. Kurtz?'

"'The chief of the Inner Station,' he answered in a short tone, looking away. 'Much obliged,' I said, laughing. 'And you are the brickmaker of the Central Station. Every one knows that.' He was silent for a while. 'He is a prodigy,' he said at last. 'He is an emissary of pity, and science, and progress, and devil knows what else. We want,' he began to declaim suddenly, 'for the guidance of the cause intrusted to us by Europe, so to speak, higher intelligence, wide sympathies, a singleness of purpose.' 'Who says that?' I asked. 'Lots of them,' he replied. 'Some even write that; and so *he* comes here, a special being, as you ought to know.' 'Why ought I to know?' I interrupted, really surprised. He paid no attention. 'Yes. Today he is chief of the best station, next year he will be assistant-manager, two years more and . . . but I daresay you know what he will be in two years' time. You are of the new gang—the gang of virtue. The same people who sent him specially also recommended you. Oh, don't say no. I've my own eyes to trust.' Light dawned upon me. My dear aunt's influential acquaintances were producing an unexpected effect upon that young man. I nearly burst into a laugh. 'Do you read the Company's confidential correspondence?' I asked. He hadn't a word to say. It was great fun. 'When Mr. Kurtz,' I continued severely, 'is General Manager, you won't have the opportunity.'

"He blew the candle out suddenly, and we went outside. The moon had risen. Black figures strolled about listlessly, pouring water on the glow, whence proceeded a sound of hissing; steam ascended in the moonlight; the beaten nigger groaned somewhere. 'What a row the brute makes!' said the indefatigable man with the moustaches, appearing near us. 'Serve him right. Transgression—punishment—bang! Pitiless, pitiless. That's the only way. This will prevent all conflagrations for the future. I was just telling the manager . . .' He noticed my companion, and became crestfallen all at once. 'Not in bed yet,' he said, with a kind of servile heartiness; 'it's so natural. Ha! Danger—agitation.' He vanished. I went on to the river-side, and the other followed me. I heard a scathing murmur at my ear, 'Heap of muffs[41]—go to.' The pilgrims could be seen in knots gesticulating, discussing. Several had still their staves in their hands. I verily believe they took these sticks to bed with them. Beyond the fence the forest stood up spec-

---

[41] Bunglers. [ED.]

trally in the moonlight, and through the dim stir, through the faint sounds of that lamentable courtyard, the silence of the land went home to one's very heart—its mystery, its greatness, the amazing reality of its concealed life. The hurt nigger moaned feebly somewhere near by, and then fetched a deep sigh that made me mend my pace away from there. I felt a hand introducing itself under my arm. 'My dear sir,' said the fellow, 'I don't want to be misunderstood, and especially by you, who will see Mr. Kurtz long before I can have that pleasure. I wouldn't like him to get a false idea of my disposition. . . .'

"I let him run on, this papier-mâché Mephistopheles,[42] and it seemed to me that if I tried I could poke my forefinger through him, and would find nothing inside but a little loose dirt, maybe. He, don't you see, had been planning to be assistant-manager by-and-by under the present man, and I could see that the coming of that Kurtz had upset them both not a little. He talked precipitately, and I did not try to stop him. I had my shoulders against the wreck of my steamer, hauled up on the slope like a carcass of some big river animal. The smell of mud, of primeval mud, by Jove! was in my nostrils, the high stillness of primeval forest was before my eyes; there were shiny patches on the black creek. The moon had spread over everything a thin layer of silver—over the rank grass, over the mud, upon the wall of matted vegetation standing higher than the wall of a temple, over the great river I could see through a sombre gap glittering, glittering, as it flowed broadly by without a murmur. All this was great, expectant, mute, while the man jabbered about himself. I wondered whether the stillness on the face of the immensity looking at us two were meant as an appeal or as a menace. What were we who had strayed in here? Could we handle that dumb thing, or would it handle us? I felt how big, how confoundedly big, was that thing that couldn't talk, and perhaps was deaf as well. What was in there? I could see a little ivory coming out from there, and I had heard Mr. Kurtz was in there. I had heard enough about it too—God knows! Yet somehow it didn't bring any image with it—no more than if I had been told an angel or a fiend was in there. I believed it in the same way one of you might believe there are inhabitants in the planet Mars. I knew once a Scotch sailmaker who was certain, dead sure, there were people in Mars. If you asked him for some idea how they looked and behaved, he would get shy and mutter something about 'walking on all-fours.' If you as much as smiled, he would—though a man of sixty—offer to fight you. I would not have gone so far as to fight for Kurtz, but I went for him near enough to a

---

[42] Diabolic agent of Lucifer in Goethe's *Faust* (1808). [ED.]

lie. You know I hate, detest, and can't bear a lie, not because I am straighter than the rest of us, but simply because it appals me. There is a taint of death, a flavour of mortality in lies—which is exactly what I hate and detest in the world—what I want to forget. It makes me miserable and sick, like biting something rotten would do. Temperament, I suppose. Well, I went near enough to it by letting the young fool there believe anything he liked to imagine as to my influence in Europe. I became in an instant as much of a pretence as the rest of the bewitched pilgrims. This simply because I had a notion it somehow would be of help to that Kurtz whom at the time I did not see—you understand. He was just a word for me. I did not see the man in the name any more than you do. Do you see him? Do you see the story? Do you see anything? It seems to me I am trying to tell you a dream—making a vain attempt, because no relation of a dream can convey the dream-sensation, that commingling of absurdity, surprise, and bewilderment in a tremor of struggling revolt, that notion of being captured by the incredible which is of the very essence of dreams. . . ."

He was silent for a while.

" . . . No, it is impossible; it is impossible to convey the life-sensation of any given epoch of one's existence—that which makes its truth, its meaning—its subtle and penetrating essence. It is impossible. We live, as we dream—alone. . . ."

He paused again as if reflecting, then added—

"Of course in this you fellows see more than I could then. You see me, whom you know. . . ."

It had become so pitch dark that we listeners could hardly see one another. For a long time already he, sitting apart, had been no more to us than a voice. There was not a word from anybody. The others might have been asleep, but I was awake. I listened, I listened on the watch for the sentence, for the word, that would give me the clue to the faint uneasiness inspired by this narrative that seemed to shape itself without human lips in the heavy night-air of the river.

" . . . Yes—I let him run on," Marlow began again, "and think what he pleased about the powers that were behind me. I did! And there was nothing behind me! There was nothing but that wretched, old, mangled steamboat I was leaning against, while he talked fluently about 'the necessity for every man to get on.' 'And when one comes out here, you conceive, it is not to gaze at the moon.' Mr. Kurtz was a 'universal genius,' but even a genius would find it easier to work with 'adequate tools—intelligent men.' He did not make bricks—why, there was a physical impossibility in the way—as I was well aware; and if he did secretarial work for the manager, it was because 'no sensible man rejects wantonly the confidence of his superiors.'

Did I see it? I saw it. What more did I want? What I really wanted was rivets, by heaven! Rivets. To get on with the work—to stop the hole. Rivets I wanted. There were cases of them down at the coast—cases—piled up—burst—split! You kicked a loose rivet at every second step in that station yard on the hillside. Rivets had rolled into the grove of death. You could fill your pockets with rivets for the trouble of stooping down—and there wasn't one rivet to be found where it was wanted. We had plates that would do, but nothing to fasten them with. And every week the messenger, a lone negro, letter-bag on shoulder and staff in hand, left our station for the coast. And several times a week a coast caravan came in with trade goods—ghastly glazed calico that made you shudder only to look at it, glass beads value about a penny a quart, confounded spotted cotton handkerchiefs. And no rivets. Three carriers could have brought all that was wanted to set that steamboat afloat.

"He was becoming confidential now, but I fancy my unresponsive attitude must have exasperated him at last, for he judged it necessary to inform me he feared neither God nor devil, let alone any mere man. I said I could see that very well, but what I wanted was a certain quantity of rivets—and rivets were what really Mr. Kurtz wanted, if he had only known it. Now letters went to the coast every week. . . . 'My dear sir,' he cried, 'I write from dictation.' I demanded rivets. There was a way—for an intelligent man. He changed his manner; became very cold, and suddenly began to talk about a hippopotamus; wondered whether sleeping on board the steamer (I stuck to my salvage night and day) I wasn't disturbed. There was an old hippo that had the bad habit of getting out on the bank and roaming at night over the station grounds. The pilgrims used to turn out in a body and empty every rifle they could lay hands on at him. Some even had sat up o' nights for him. All this energy was wasted, though. 'That animal has a charmed life,' he said; 'but you can say this only of brutes in this country. No man—you apprehend me?—no man here bears a charmed life.' He stood there for a moment in the moonlight with his delicate hooked nose set a little askew, and his mica eyes glittering without a wink, then, with a curt Good night, he strode off. I could see he was disturbed and considerably puzzled, which made me feel more hopeful than I had been for days. It was a great comfort to turn from that chap to my influential friend, the battered, twisted, ruined, tin-pot steamboat. I clambered on board. She rang under my feet like an empty Huntley & Palmer biscuit-tin kicked along a gutter; she was nothing so solid in make, and rather less pretty in shape, but I had expended enough hard work on her to make me love her. No influential friend would have served me better. She had given me a chance to come out a bit—to find out what I could do. No, I don't like work. I had rather laze about and think of all the fine things that can be done. I don't like work—no man does—but I like what is in the work—the chance to find yourself. Your own reality—for yourself, not for others—what no other man can ever know. They can only see the mere show, and never can tell what it really means.

"I was not surprised to see somebody sitting aft, on the deck, with his legs dangling over the mud. You see I rather chummed with the few mechanics there were in that station, whom the other pilgrims naturally despised—on account of their imperfect manners, I suppose. This was the foreman—a boiler-maker by trade—a good worker. He was a lank, bony, yellow-faced man, with big intense eyes. His aspect was worried, and his head was as bald as the palm of my hand; but his hair in falling seemed to have stuck to his chin, and had prospered in the new locality, for his beard hung down to his waist. He was a widower with six young children (he had left them in charge of a sister of his to come out there), and the passion of his life was pigeon-flying. He was an enthusiast and a connoisseur. He would rave about pigeons. After work hours he used sometimes to come over from his hut for a talk about his children and his pigeons; at work, when he had to crawl in the mud under the bottom of the steamboat, he would tie up that beard of his in a kind of white serviette[43] he brought for the purpose. It had loops to go over his ears. In the evening he could be seen squatted on the bank rinsing that wrapper in the creek with great care, then spreading it solemnly on a bush to dry.

"I slapped him on the back and shouted 'We shall have rivets!' He scrambled to his feet exclaiming 'No! Rivets!' as though he couldn't believe his ears. Then in a low voice, 'You . . . eh?' I don't know why we behaved like lunatics. I put my finger to the side of my nose and nodded mysteriously. 'Good for you!' he cried, snapped his fingers above his head, lifting one foot. I tried a jig. We capered on the iron deck. A frightful clatter came out of that hulk, and the virgin forest on the other bank of the creek sent it back in a thundering roll upon the sleeping station. It must have made some of the pilgrims sit up in their hovels. A dark figure obscured the lighted doorway of the manager's hut, vanished, then, a second or so after, the doorway itself vanished too. We stopped, and the silence driven away by the stamping of our feet flowed back again from the recesses of the land. The great wall of vegetation, an exuberant and entangled mass of trunks, branches, leaves, boughs, festoons, motionless in the moonlight, was like a rioting invasion of soundless life, a rolling wave of plants, piled up, crested, ready to topple over the creek, to sweep every little man of us out of his

---

[43] French term for a table napkin. [ED.]

little existence. And it moved not. A deadened burst of mighty splashes and snorts reached us from afar, as though an ichthyosaurus had been taking a bath of glitter in the great river. 'After all,' said the boiler-maker in a reasonable tone, 'why shouldn't we get the rivets?' Why not, indeed! I did not know of any reason why we shouldn't. 'They'll come in three weeks,' I said, confidently.

"But they didn't. Instead of rivets there came an invasion, an infliction, a visitation. It came in sections during the next three weeks, each section headed by a donkey carrying a white man in new clothes and tan shoes, bowing from that elevation right and left to the impressed pilgrims. A quarrelsome band of footsore sulky niggers trod on the heels of the donkey; a lot of tents, camp-stools, tin boxes, white cases, brown bales would be shot down in the courtyard, and the air of mystery would deepen a little over the muddle of the station. Five such instalments came, with their absurd air of disorderly flight with the loot of innumerable outfit shops and provision stores, that, one would think, they were lugging, after a raid, into the wilderness for equitable division. It was an inextricable mess of things decent in themselves but that human folly made look like the spoils of thieving.

"This devoted band called itself the Eldorado Exploring Expedition, and I believe they were sworn to secrecy. Their talk, however, was the talk of sordid buccaneers: it was reckless without hardihood, greedy without audacity, and cruel without courage; there was not an atom of foresight or of serious intention in the whole batch of them, and they did not seem aware these things are wanted for the work of the world. To tear treasure out of the bowels of the land was their desire, with no more moral purpose at the back of it than there is in burglars breaking into a safe. Who paid the expenses of the noble enterprise I don't know; but the uncle of our manager was leader of that lot.

"In exterior he resembled a butcher in a poor neighbourhood, and his eyes had a look of sleepy cunning. He carried his fat paunch with ostentation on his short legs, and during the time his gang infested the station spoke to no one but his nephew. You could see these two roaming about all day long with their heads close together in an everlasting confab.

"I had given up worrying myself about the rivets. One's capacity for that kind of folly is more limited than you would suppose. I said Hang!—and let things slide. I had plenty of time for meditation, and now and then I would give some thought to Kurtz. I wasn't very interested in him. No. Still, I was curious to see whether this man, who had come out equipped with moral ideas of some sort, would climb to the top after all, and how he would set about his work when there."

CHAPTER II

"One evening as I was lying flat on the deck of my steamboat, I heard voices approaching—and there were the nephew and the uncle strolling along the bank. I laid my head on my arm again, and had nearly lost myself in a doze, when somebody said in my ear, as it were: 'I am as harmless as a little child, but I don't like to be dictated to. Am I the manager—or am I not? I was ordered to send him there. It's incredible.' . . . I became aware that the two were standing on the shore alongside the forepart of the steamboat, just below my head. I did not move; it did not occur to me to move: I was sleepy. 'It *is* unpleasant,' grunted the uncle. 'He has asked the Administration to be sent there,' said the other, 'with the idea of showing what he could do; and I was instructed accordingly. Look at the influence that man must have. Is it not frightful?' They both agreed it was frightful, then made several bizarre remarks: 'Make rain and fine weather—one man—the Council— by the nose'—bits of absurd sentences that got the better of my drowsiness, so that I had pretty near the whole of my wits about me when the uncle said, 'The climate may do away with this difficulty for you. Is he alone there?' 'Yes,' answered the manager; 'he sent his assistant down the river with a note to me in these terms: "Clear this poor devil out of the country, and don't bother sending more of that sort. I had rather be alone than have the kind of men you can dispose of with me." It was more than a year ago. Can you imagine such impudence!' 'Anything since then?' asked the other, hoarsely. 'Ivory,' jerked the nephew; 'lots of it—prime sort—lots—most annoying, from him.' 'And with that?' questioned the heavy rumble. 'Invoice,' was the reply fired out, so to speak. Then silence. They had been talking about Kurtz.

"I was broad awake by this time, but, lying perfectly at ease, remained still, having no inducement to change my position. 'How did that ivory come all this way?' growled the elder man, who seemed very vexed. The other explained that it had come with a fleet of canoes in charge of an English half-caste clerk Kurtz had with him; that Kurtz had apparently intended to return himself, the station being by that time bare of goods and stores, but after coming three hundred miles, had suddenly decided to go back, which he started to do alone in a small dugout with four paddlers, leaving the half-caste to continue down the river with the ivory. The two fellows there seemed astounded at anybody attempting such a thing. They were at a loss for an adequate motive. As to me, I seemed to see Kurtz for the first time. It was a distinct glimpse: the dugout, four paddling savages, and the lone white man turning his back suddenly on the headquarters, on relief, on thoughts of home—perhaps; setting his face towards the depths of the wilderness, towards his empty and desolate station. I did not know the motive. Perhaps he was just simply a fine fellow who stuck to his work for its own sake. His name, you understand, had not been pronounced once. He was 'that man.' The half-caste, who, as far as I could see, had conducted a difficult trip with great prudence and pluck, was invariably alluded to as 'that scoundrel.' The 'scoundrel' had reported that the 'man' had been very ill—had recovered imperfectly. . . . The two below me moved away then a few paces, and strolled back and forth at some little distance. I heard: 'Military post—doctor—two hundred miles—quite alone now—unavoidable delays—nine months—no news—strange rumours.' They approached again, just as the manager was saying, 'No one, as far as I know, unless a species of wandering trader—a pestilential fellow, snapping ivory from the natives.' Who was it they were talking about now? I gathered in snatches that this was some man supposed to be in Kurtz's district, and of whom the manager did not approve. 'We will not be free from unfair com-petition till one of these fellows is hanged for an example,' he said. 'Cer-tainly,' grunted the other; 'get him hanged! Why not? Anything—anything can be done in this country. That's what I say; nobody here, you under-stand, *here*, can endanger your position. And why? You stand the climate—you outlast them all. The danger is in Europe; but there before I left I took care to—' They moved off and whispered, then their voices rose again. 'The extraordinary series of delays is not my fault. I did my possible.' The fat man sighed, 'Very sad.' 'And the pestiferous absurdity of his talk,' con-tinued the other; 'he bothered me enough when he was here. "Each station should be like a beacon on the road towards better things, a centre for trade of course, but also for humanising, improving, instructing." Conceive you—that ass! And he wants to be manager! No, it's—' Here he got choked by excessive indignation, and I lifted my head the least bit. I was surprised to see how near they were—right under me. I could have spat upon their hats. They were looking on the ground, absorbed in thought. The manager was switching his leg with a slender twig: his sagacious relative lifted his head. 'You have been well since you came out this time?' he asked. The other gave a start. 'Who? I? Oh! Like a charm—like a charm. But the rest—oh, my goodness! All sick. They die so quick, too, that I haven't the time to send them out of the country—it's incredible!' 'H'm. Just so,' grunted the uncle. 'Ah! my boy, trust to this—I say, trust to this.' I saw him extend his short flipper of an arm for a gesture that took in the forest, the creek, the mud, the river—seemed to beckon with a dishonouring flourish before the sunlit face of the land a treacherous appeal to the lurking death, to the hid-den evil, to the profound darkness of its heart. It was so startling that I leaped to my feet and looked back at the edge of the forest, as though I had expected an answer of some sort to that black display of confidence. You know the foolish notions that come to one sometimes. The high stillness confronted these two figures with its ominous patience, waiting for the passing away of a fantastic invasion.

"They swore aloud together—out of sheer fright, I believe—then, pretending not to know anything of my existence, turned back to the station. The sun was low; and leaning forward side by side, they seemed to be tugging painfully uphill their two ridiculous shadows of unequal length, that trailed behind them slowly over the tall grass without bending a single blade.

"In a few days the Eldorado Expedition went into the patient wilderness, that closed upon it as the sea closes over a diver. Long afterwards the news came that all the donkeys were dead. I know nothing as to the fate of the less valuable animals. They, no doubt, like the rest of us, found what they deserved. I did not inquire. I was then rather excited at the prospect of meeting Kurtz very soon. When I say very soon I mean it comparatively. It was just two months from the day we left the creek when we came to the bank below Kurtz's station.

"Going up that river was like travelling back to the earliest beginnings of the world, when vegetation rioted on the earth and the big trees were kings. An empty stream, a great silence, an impenetrable forest. The air was warm, thick, heavy, sluggish. There was no joy in the brilliance of sunshine. The long stretches of the waterway ran on, deserted, into the gloom of over-shadowed distances. On silvery sandbanks hippos and alligators sunned themselves side by side. The broadening waters flowed through a mob of wooded islands; you lost your way on that river as you would in a desert, and butted all day long against shoals, trying to find the channel, till you thought yourself bewitched and cut off for ever from everything you had known once—somewhere—far away—in another existence perhaps. There were moments when one's past came back to one, as it will sometimes when you have not a moment to spare to yourself; but it came in the shape of an unrestful and noisy dream, remembered with wonder amongst the overwhelming realities of this strange world of plants, and water, and silence. And this stillness of life did not in the least resemble a peace. It was the stillness of an implacable force brooding over an inscrutable intention. It looked at you with a vengeful aspect. I got used to it afterwards; I did not see it any more; I had no time. I had to keep guessing at the channel; I had to discern, mostly by inspiration, the signs of hidden banks; I watched for sunken stones; I was learning to clap my teeth smartly before my heart flew out, when I shaved by a fluke some infernal sly old snag that would have ripped the life out of the tin-pot steamboat and drowned all the pilgrims; I had to keep a look-out for the signs of dead wood we could cut up in the night for next day's steaming. When you have to attend to things of that sort, to the mere incidents of the surface, the reality—the reality, I tell you—fades. The inner truth is hidden—luckily, luckily. But I felt it all the same; I felt often its mysterious stillness watching me at my monkey tricks, just as it watches you fellows performing on your respective tight-ropes for—what is it? half-a-crown a tumble—"

"Try to be civil, Marlow," growled a voice, and I knew there was at least one listener awake besides myself.

"I beg your pardon. I forgot the heartache which makes up the rest of the price. And indeed what does the price matter, if the trick be well done? You do your tricks very well. And I didn't do badly either, since I managed not to sink that steamboat on my first trip. It's a wonder to me yet. Imagine a blindfolded man set to drive a van over a bad road. I sweated and shivered over that business considerably, I can tell you. After all, for a seaman, to scrape the bottom of the thing that's supposed to float all the time under his care is the unpardonable sin. No one may know of it, but you never forget the thump—eh? A blow on the very heart. You remember it, you dream of it, you wake up at night and think of it—years after—and go hot and cold all over. I don't pretend to say that steamboat floated all the time. More than once she had to wade for a bit, with twenty cannibals splashing around and pushing. We had enlisted some of these chaps on the way for a crew. Fine fellows—cannibals—in their place. They were men one could work with, and I am grateful to them. And, after all, they did not eat each other before my face: they had brought along a provision of hippo-meat which went rotten, and made the mystery of the wilderness stink in my nostrils. Phoo! I can sniff it now. I had the manager on board and three or four pilgrims with their staves—all complete. Sometimes we came upon a station close by the bank, clinging to the skirts of the unknown, and the white men rushing out of a tumble-down hovel, with great gestures of joy and surprise and welcome, seemed very strange—had the appearance of being held there captive by a spell. The word 'ivory' would ring in the air for a while—and on we went again into the silence, along empty reaches, round the still bends, between the high walls of our winding way, reverberating in hollow claps the ponderous beat of the stern-wheel. Trees, trees, millions of trees, massive, immense, running up high; and at their foot, hugging the bank against the stream, crept the little begrimed steamboat, like a sluggish beetle crawling on the floor of a lofty portico. It made you feel very small, very lost, and yet it was not altogether depressing that feeling. After all, if you were small, the grimy beetle crawled on—which was just what you wanted it to do. Where the pilgrims imagined it crawled to I don't know. To some place where they expected to get something, I bet! For me it crawled towards Kurtz—exclusively; but when the steam-pipes started leaking we crawled very slow. The reaches opened before us and closed behind, as if the forest had stepped leisurely across the water to bar the way for our return. We penetrated deeper and deeper into the heart of darkness. It was very quiet there. At night sometimes the roll of drums behind the curtain of trees would run up the river and remain sustained faintly, as if hovering in the air high over our heads, till the first break of day. Whether it meant war, peace, or prayer we could not tell. The dawns were heralded by the descent of a chill stillness; the woodcutters slept, their fires burned low; the snapping of a twig would make you start. We were wanderers on a prehistoric earth, on an earth that wore the aspect of an unknown planet. We could have fancied ourselves the first of men taking possession of an accursed inheritance, to be subdued at the cost of profound anguish and of excessive toil. But suddenly, as we struggled round a bend, there would be a glimpse of rush walls, of peaked grass-roofs, a burst of yells, a whirl of black limbs, a mass of hands clapping, of feet stamping, of bodies swaying, of eyes rolling, under the droop of heavy and motionless foliage. The steamer toiled along slowly on the edge of a black and incomprehensible frenzy. The prehistoric man was cursing us, praying to us, welcoming us— who could tell? We were cut off from the comprehension of our surroundings; we glided past like phantoms, wondering and secretly appalled, as sane men would be before an enthusiastic outbreak in a madhouse. We could not understand, because we were too far and could not remember, because we were travelling in the night of first ages, of those ages that are gone, leaving hardly a sign—and no memories.

"The earth seemed unearthly. We are accustomed to look upon the shackled form of a conquered monster, but there—there you could look at a thing monstrous and free. It was unearthly, and the men were— No, they were not inhuman. Well, you know, that was the worst of it—this suspicion of their not being inhuman. It would come slowly to one. They howled, and leaped, and spun, and made horrid faces; but what thrilled you was just the thought of their humanity—like yours—the thought of your remote kinship with this wild and passionate uproar. Ugly. Yes, it was ugly enough; but if you were man enough you would admit to yourself that there was in you just the faintest trace of a response to the terrible frankness of that noise, a dim suspicion of there being a meaning in it which you—you so remote from the night of first ages—could comprehend. And why not? The mind of man is capable of anything—because everything is in it, all the past as well as all the future. What was there after all? Joy, fear, sorrow, devotion, valour, rage—who can tell?—but truth—truth stripped of its cloak of time. Let the fool gape and shudder—the man knows, and can look on without a wink. But he must at least be as much of a man as these on the shore. He must meet that truth with his own true stuff—with his own inborn strength. Principles? Principles won't do. Acquisitions, clothes, pretty rags—rags that would fly off at the first good shake. No; you want a deliberate belief. An appeal to me in this fiendish row—is there? Very well; I hear; I admit, but I have a voice too, and for good or evil mine is the speech that cannot be silenced. Of course, a fool, what with sheer fright and fine sentiments, is always safe. Who's that grunting? You wonder I didn't go ashore for a howl and a dance? Well, no—I didn't. Fine sentiments, you say? Fine sentiments be hanged! I had no time. I had to mess about with white-lead and strips of woollen blanket helping to put bandages on those leaky steam-pipes—I tell you. I had to watch the steering, and circumvent those snags, and get the tin-pot along by hook or by crook. There was surface-truth enough in these things to save a wiser man. And between whiles I had to look after the savage who was fireman. He was an improved specimen; he could fire up a vertical boiler.[44] He was there below me, and, upon my word, to look at him was as edifying as seeing a dog in a parody of breeches and a feather hat, walking on his hind-legs. A few months of training had done for that really fine chap. He squinted at the steam-gauge and at the water-gauge with an evident effort of intrepidity—and he had filed teeth too, the poor devil, and the wool of his pate shaved into queer patterns, and three ornamental scars on each of his checks. He ought to have been clapping his hands and stamping his feet on the bank, instead of which he was hard at work, a thrall to strange witchcraft, full of improving knowledge. He was useful because he had been instructed; and what he knew was this—that should the water in that transparent thing disappear, the evil spirit inside the boiler would get angry through the greatness of his thirst, and take a terrible vengeance. So he sweated and fired up and watched the glass fearfully (with an impromptu charm, made of rags, tied to his arm, and a piece of polished bone, as big as a watch, stuck flatways through his lower lip), while the wooded banks slipped past us slowly, the short noise was left behind, the interminable miles of silence— and we crept on, towards Kurtz. But the snags were thick, the water was treacherous and shallow, the boiler seemed indeed to have a sulky devil in it, and thus neither that fireman nor I had any time to peer into our creepy thoughts.

"Some fifty miles below the Inner Station we came upon a hut of reeds, an inclined and melancholy pole, with the unrecognisable tatters of what had been a flag of some sort flying from it, and a neatly stacked woodpile. This was unexpected. We came to the bank, and on the stack of firewood found a flat piece of board with some faded pencil-writing on it. When

---

[44] A relatively simple and compact boiler with a vertical firebox. [ED.]

deciphered it said: 'Wood for you. Hurry up. Approach cautiously.' There was a signature, but it was illegible—not Kurtz—a much longer word. Hurry up. Where? Up the river? 'Approach cautiously.' We had not done so. But the warning could not have been meant for the place where it could be only found after approach. Something was wrong above. But what— and how much? That was the question. We commented adversely upon the imbecility of that telegraphic style. The bush around said nothing, and would not let us look very far, either. A torn curtain of red twill hung in the doorway of the hut, and flapped sadly in our faces. The dwelling was dismantled; but we could see a white man had lived there not very long ago. There remained a rude table—a plank on two posts; a heap of rubbish reposed in a dark corner, and by the door I picked up a book. It had lost its covers, and the pages had been thumbed into a state of extremely dirty softness; but the back had been lovingly stitched afresh with white cotton thread, which looked clean yet. It was an extraordinary find. Its title was, 'An Inquiry into some Points of Seamanship,' by a man Tower, Towson[45]— some such name—Master in his Majesty's Navy. The matter looked dreary reading enough, with illustrative diagrams and repulsive tables of figures, and the copy was sixty years old. I handled this amazing antiquity with the greatest possible tenderness, lest it should dissolve in my hands. Within, Towson or Towser was inquiring earnestly into the breaking strain of ships' chains and tackle, and other such matters. Not a very enthralling book; but at the first glance you could see there a singleness of intention, an honest concern for the right way of going to work, which made these humble pages, thought out so many years ago, luminous with another than a professional light. The simple old sailor, with his talk of chains and purchases, made me forget the jungle and the pilgrims in a delicious sensation of having come upon something unmistakably real. Such a book being there was wonderful enough; but still more astounding were the notes pencilled in the margin, and plainly referring to the text. I couldn't believe my eyes! They were in cipher![46] Yes, it looked like cipher. Fancy a man lugging with him a book of that description into this nowhere and studying it—and making notes—in cipher at that! It was an extravagant mystery.

"I had been dimly aware for some time of a worrying noise, and when I lifted my eyes I saw the wood-pile was gone, and the manager, aided by all the pilgrims, was shouting at me from the river-side. I slipped the book

---

[45] There is no extant book of this title, although J. T. Towson did publish two books of nautical tables. [ED.]

[46] A system for transposing a text so as to conceal its meaning. [ED.]

into my pocket. I assure you to leave off reading was like tearing myself away from the shelter of an old and solid friendship.

"I started the lame engine ahead. 'It must be this miserable trader—this intruder,' exclaimed the manager, looking back malevolently at the place we had left. 'He must be English,' I said. 'It will not save him from getting into trouble if he is not careful,' muttered the manager darkly. I observed with assumed innocence that no man was safe from trouble in this world.

"The current was more rapid now, the steamer seemed at her last gasp, the stern-wheel flopped languidly, and I caught myself listening on tiptoe for the next beat of the float,[47] for in sober truth I expected the wretched thing to give up every moment. It was like watching the last flickers of a life. But still we crawled. Sometimes I would pick out a tree a little way ahead to measure our progress towards Kurtz by, but I lost it invariably before we got abreast. To keep the eyes so long on one thing was too much for human patience. The manager displayed a beautiful resignation. I fretted and fumed and took to arguing with myself whether or no I would talk openly with Kurtz; but before I could come to any conclusion it occurred to me that my speech or my silence, indeed any action of mine, would be a mere futility. What did it matter what any one knew or ignored? What did it matter who was manager? One gets sometimes such a flash of insight. The essentials of this affair lay deep under the surface, beyond my reach, and beyond my power of meddling.

"Towards the evening of the second day we judged ourselves about eight miles from Kurtz's station. I wanted to push on; but the manager looked grave, and told me the navigation up there was so dangerous that it would be advisable, the sun being very low already, to wait where we were till next morning. Moreover, he pointed out that if the warning to approach cautiously were to be followed, we must approach in daylight—not at dusk, or in the dark. This was sensible enough. Eight miles meant nearly three hours' steaming for us, and I could also see suspicious ripples at the upper end of the reach. Nevertheless, I was annoyed beyond expression at the delay, and most unreasonably too, since one night more could not matter much after so many months. As we had plenty of wood, and caution was the word, I brought up in the middle of the stream. The reach was narrow, straight, with high sides like a railway cutting. The dusk came gliding into it long before the sun had set. The current ran smooth and swift, but a dumb immobility sat on the banks. The living trees, lashed together by the creepers and every living bush of the undergrowth, might have been changed into

---

[47]The blade of a paddle wheel. [ED.]

stone, even to the slenderest twig, to the lightest leaf. It was not sleep—it seemed unnatural, like a state of trance. Not the faintest sound of any kind could be heard. You looked on amazed, and began to suspect yourself of being deaf—then the night came suddenly, and struck you blind as well. About three in the morning some large fish leaped, and the loud splash made me jump as though a gun had been fired. When the sun rose there was a white fog, very warm and clammy, and more blinding than the night. It did not shift or drive; it was just there, standing all round you like something solid. At eight or nine, perhaps, it lifted as a shutter lifts. We had a glimpse of the towering multitude of trees, of the immense matted jungle, with the blazing little ball of the sun hanging over it—all perfectly still—and then the white shutter came down again, smoothly, as if sliding in greased grooves. I ordered the chain, which we had begun to heave in, to be paid out again. Before it stopped running with a muffled rattle, a cry, a very loud cry, as of infinite desolation, soared slowly in the opaque air. It ceased. A complaining clamour, modulated in savage discords, filled our ears. The sheer unexpectedness of it made my hair stir under my cap. I don't know how it struck the others: to me it seemed as though the mist itself had screamed, so suddenly, and apparently from all sides at once, did this tumultuous and mournful uproar arise. It culminated in a hurried outbreak of almost intolerably excessive shrieking, which stopped short, leaving us stiffened in a variety of silly attitudes, and obstinately listening to the nearly as appalling and excessive silence. 'Good God! What is the meaning—?' stammered at my elbow one of the pilgrims—a little fat man, with sandy hair and red whiskers, who wore side-spring boots, and pink pyjamas tucked into his socks. Two others remained open-mouthed a whole minute, then dashed into the little cabin, to rush out incontinently and stand darting scared glances, with Winchesters[48] at 'ready' in their hands. What we could see was just the steamer we were on, her outlines blurred as though she had been on the point of dissolving, and a misty strip of water, perhaps two feet broad, around her—and that was all. The rest of the world was nowhere, as far as our eyes and ears were concerned. Just nowhere. Gone, disappeared; swept off without leaving a whisper or a shadow behind.

"I went forward, and ordered the chain to be hauled in short, so as to be ready to trip the anchor and move the steamboat at once if necessary. 'Will they attack?' whispered an awed voice. 'We will all be butchered in this fog,' murmured another. The faces twitched with the strain, the hands trembled slightly, the eyes forgot to wink. It was very curious to see the contrast of expressions of the white men and of the black fellows of our crew, who

---

[48] Repeating rifles. [ED.]

were as much strangers to that part of the river as we, though their homes were only eight hundred miles away. The whites, of course greatly discomposed, had besides a curious look of being painfully shocked by such an outrageous row. The others had an alert, naturally interested expression; but their faces were essentially quiet, even those of the one or two who grinned as they hauled at the chain. Several exchanged short, grunting phrases, which seemed to settle the matter to their satisfaction. Their headman, a young, broad-chested black, severely draped in dark-blue fringed cloths, with fierce nostrils and his hair all done up artfully in oily ringlets, stood near me. 'Aha!' I said, just for good fellowship's sake. 'Catch 'im,' he snapped, with a bloodshot widening of his eyes and a flash of sharp teeth — 'catch 'im. Give 'im to us.' 'To you, eh?' I asked; 'what would you do with them?' 'Eat 'im!' he said, curtly, and, leaning his elbow on the rail, looked out into the fog in a dignified and profoundly pensive attitude. I would no doubt have been properly horrified, had it not occurred to me that he and his chaps must be very hungry: that they must have been growing increasingly hungry for at least this month past. They had been engaged for six months (I don't think a single one of them had any clear idea of time, as we at the end of countless ages have. They still belonged to the beginnings of time — had no inherited experience to teach them, as it were), and of course, as long as there was a piece of paper written over in accordance with some farcical law or other made down the river, it didn't enter anybody's head to trouble how they would live. Certainly they had brought with them some rotten hippo-meat, which couldn't have lasted very long, anyway, even if the pilgrims hadn't, in the midst of a shocking hullabaloo, thrown a considerable quantity of it overboard. It looked like a high-handed proceeding; but it was really a case of legitimate self-defence. You can't breathe dead hippo waking, sleeping, and eating, and at the same time keep your precarious grip on existence. Besides that, they had given them every week three pieces of brass wire, each about nine inches long;[49] and the theory was they were to buy their provisions with that currency in river-side villages. You can see how *that* worked. There were either no villages, or the people were hostile, or the director, who like the rest of us fed out of tins, with an occasional old he-goat thrown in, didn't want to stop the steamer for some more or less recondite reason. So, unless they swallowed the wire itself, or made loops of it to snare the fishes with, I don't see what good their extravagant salary could be to them. I must say it was paid with a regularity worthy of a large and honourable trading company. For the rest, the only thing to eat — though it didn't look eatable in the least — I

---

[49] Brass rods were commonly used as currency in the Congo Free State at this time. [ED.]

saw in their possession was a few lumps of some stuff like half-cooked dough, of a dirty lavender colour, they kept wrapped in leaves, and now and then swallowed a piece of, but so small that it seemed done more for the looks of the thing than for any serious purpose of sustenance. Why in the name of all the gnawing devils of hunger they didn't go for us—they were thirty to five—and have a good tuck-in for once, amazes me now when I think of it. They were big powerful men, with not much capacity to weigh the consequences, with courage, with strength, even yet, though their skins were no longer glossy and their muscles no longer hard. And I saw that something restraining, one of those human secrets that baffle probability, had come into play there. I looked at them with a swift quickening of interest—not because it occurred to me I might be eaten by them before very long, though I own to you that just then I perceived—in a new light, as it were—how unwholesome the pilgrims looked, and I hoped, yes, I positively hoped, that my aspect was not so—what shall I say?—so—unappetising: a touch of fantastic vanity which fitted well with the dream-sensation that pervaded all my days at that time. Perhaps I had a little fever too. One can't live with one's finger everlastingly on one's pulse. I had often 'a little fever,' or a little touch of other things—the playful paw-strokes of the wilderness, the preliminary trifling before the more serious onslaught which came in due course. Yes; I looked at them as you would on any human being, with a curiosity of their impulses, motives, capacities, weaknesses, when brought to the test of an inexorable physical necessity. Restraint! What possible restraint? Was it superstition, disgust, patience, fear—or some kind of primitive honour? No fear can stand up to hunger, no patience can wear it out, disgust simply does not exist where hunger is; and as to superstition, beliefs, and what you may call principles, they are less than chaff in a breeze. Don't you know the devilry of lingering starvation, its exasperating torment, its black thoughts, its sombre and brooding ferocity? Well, I do. It takes a man all his inborn strength to fight hunger properly. It's really easier to face bereavement, dishonour, and the perdition of one's soul—than this kind of prolonged hunger. Sad, but true. And these chaps too had no earthly reason for any kind of scruple. Restraint! I would just as soon have expected restraint from a hyena prowling amongst the corpses of a battlefield. But there was the fact facing me—the fact dazzling, to be seen, like the foam on the depths of the sea, like a ripple on an unfathomable enigma, a mystery greater—when I thought of it—than the curious, inexplicable note of desperate grief in this savage clamour that had swept by us on the river-bank, behind the blind whiteness of the fog.

"Two pilgrims were quarrelling in hurried whispers as to which bank. 'Left.' 'No, no; how can you? Right, right, of course.' 'It is very serious,' said the manager's voice behind me; 'I would be desolated if anything should happen to Mr. Kurtz before we came up.' I looked at him, and had not the slightest doubt he was sincere. He was just the kind of man who would wish to preserve appearances. That was his restraint. But when he muttered something about going on at once, I did not even take the trouble to answer him. I knew, and he knew, that it was impossible. Were we to let go our hold of the bottom, we would be absolutely in the air—in space. We wouldn't be able to tell where we were going to—whether up or down stream, or across—till we fetched against one bank or the other—and then we wouldn't know at first which it was. Of course I made no move. I had no mind for a smash-up. You couldn't imagine a more deadly place for a shipwreck. Whether drowned at once or not, we were sure to perish speedily in one way or another. 'I authorise you to take all the risks,' he said, after a short silence. 'I refuse to take any,' I said shortly; which was just the answer he expected, though its tone might have surprised him. 'Well, I must defer to your judgment. You are captain,' he said, with marked civility. I turned my shoulder to him in sign of my appreciation, and looked into the fog. How long would it last? It was the most hopeless look-out. The approach to this Kurtz grubbing for ivory in the wretched bush was beset by as many dangers as though he had been an enchanted princess sleeping in a fabulous castle. 'Will they attack, do you think?' asked the manager, in a confidential tone.

"I did not think they would attack, for several obvious reasons. The thick fog was one. If they left the bank in their canoes they would get lost in it, as we would be if we attempted to move. Still, I had also judged the jungle of both banks quite impenetrable—and yet eyes were in it, eyes that had seen us. The river-side bushes were certainly very thick; but the undergrowth behind was evidently penetrable. However, during the short lift I had seen no canoes anywhere in the reach—certainly not abreast of the steamer. But what made the idea of attack inconceivable to me was the nature of the noise—of the cries we had heard. They had not the fierce character boding of immediate hostile intention. Unexpected, wild, and violent as they had been, they had given me an irresistible impression of sorrow. The glimpse of the steamboat had for some reason filled those savages with unrestrained grief. The danger, if any, I expounded, was from our proximity to a great human passion let loose. Even extreme grief may ultimately vent itself in violence—but more generally takes the form of apathy. . . .

"You should have seen the pilgrims stare! They had no heart to grin, or even to revile me; but I believe they thought me gone mad—with fright, maybe. I delivered a regular lecture. My dear boys, it was no good bothering. Keep a look-out? Well, you may guess I watched the fog for the signs of lifting as a cat watches a mouse; but for anything else our eyes were of no more use to us than if we had been buried miles deep in a heap of cotton-wool. It felt like it too—choking, warm, stifling. Besides, all I said, though it sounded extravagant, was absolutely true to fact. What we afterwards alluded to as an attack was really an attempt at repulse. The action was very far from being aggressive—it was not even defensive, in the usual sense: it was undertaken under the stress of desperation, and in its essence was purely protective.

"It developed itself, I should say, two hours after the fog lifted, and its commencement was at a spot, roughly speaking, about a mile and a half below Kurtz's station. We had just floundered and flopped round a bend, when I saw an islet, a mere grassy hummock of bright green, in the middle of the stream. It was the only thing of the kind; but as we opened the reach more, I perceived it was the head of a long sandbank, or rather of a chain of shallow patches stretching down the middle of the river. They were discoloured, just awash, and the whole lot was seen just under the water, exactly as a man's backbone is seen running down the middle of his back under the skin. Now, as far as I did see, I could go to the right or to the left of this. I didn't know either channel, of course. The banks looked pretty well alike, the depth appeared the same; but as I had been informed the station was on the west side, I naturally headed for the western passage.

"No sooner had we fairly entered it than I became aware it was much narrower than I had supposed. To the left of us there was the long uninterrupted shoal, and to the right a high, steep bank heavily overgrown with bushes. Above the bush the trees stood in serried [50] ranks. The twigs overhung the current thickly, and from distance to distance a large limb of some tree projected rigidly over the stream. It was then well on in the afternoon, the face of the forest was gloomy, and a broad strip of shadow had already fallen on the water. In this shadow we steamed up—very slowly, as you may imagine. I sheered her well inshore—the water being deepest near the bank, as the sounding-pole informed me.

"One of my hungry and forbearing friends was sounding in the bows just below me. This steamboat was exactly like a decked scow.[51] On the deck there were two little teak-wood houses, with doors and windows. The boiler was in the fore-end, and the machinery right astern. Over the whole there was a light roof, supported on stanchions. The funnel projected through that roof, and in front of the funnel a small cabin built of light

---

[50] Crowded together. [ED.]

[51] A large flat-bottomed boat with square ends, used primarily for carrying sand, gravel, or refuse. [ED.]

planks served for a pilot-house. It contained a couch, two camp-stools, a loaded Martini-Henry[52] leaning in one corner, a tiny table, and the steering-wheel. It had a wide door in front and a broad shutter at each side. All these were always thrown open, of course. I spent my days perched up there on the extreme fore-end of that roof, before the door. At night I slept, or tried to, on the couch. An athletic black belonging to some coast tribe, and educated by my poor predecessor, was the helmsman. He sported a pair of brass earrings, wore a blue cloth wrapper from the waist to the ankles, and thought all the world of himself. He was the most unstable kind of fool I had ever seen. He steered with no end of a swagger while you were by; but if he lost sight of you, he became instantly the prey of an abject funk, and would let that cripple of a steamboat get the upper hand of him in a minute.

"I was looking down at the sounding-pole, and feeling much annoyed to see at each try a little more of it stick out of that river, when I saw my poleman give up the business suddenly, and stretch himself flat on the deck, without even taking the trouble to haul his pole in. He kept hold on it though, and it trailed in the water. At the same time the fireman, whom I could also see below me, sat down abruptly before his furnace and ducked his head. I was amazed. Then I had to look at the river mighty quick, because there was a snag in the fairway. Sticks, little sticks, were flying about—thick: they were whizzing before my nose, dropping below me, striking behind me against my pilot-house. All this time the river, the shore, the woods, were very quiet—perfectly quiet. I could only hear the heavy splashing thump of the stern-wheel and the patter of these things. We cleared the snag clumsily. Arrows, by Jove! We were being shot at! I stepped in quickly to close the shutter on the land-side. That fool-helmsman, his hands on the spokes, was lifting his knees high, stamping his feet, champing his mouth, like a reined-in horse. Confound him! And we were staggering within ten feet of the bank. I had to lean right out to swing the heavy shutter, and I saw a face amongst the leaves on the level with my own, looking at me very fierce and steady; and then suddenly, as though a veil had been removed from my eyes, I made out, deep in the tangled gloom, naked breasts, arms, legs, glaring eyes—the bush was swarming with human limbs in movement, glistening, of bronze colour. The twigs shook, swayed, and rustled, the arrows flew out of them, and then the shutter came to. 'Steer her straight,' I said to the helmsman. He held his head rigid, face forward; but his eyes rolled, he kept on lifting and setting down his feet gently, his mouth foamed a little. 'Keep quiet!' I said in a fury. I might just as well have

---

[52] The Martini-Henry was a standard issue military rifle, with a single-action breech bolt. [ED.]

ordered a tree not to sway in the wind. I darted out. Below me there was
a great scuffle of feet on the iron deck; confused exclamations; a voice
screamed, 'Can you turn back?' I caught sight of a V-shaped ripple on the
water ahead. What? Another snag! A fusillade burst out under my feet. The
pilgrims had opened with their Winchesters, and were simply squirting
lead into that bush. A deuce of a lot of smoke came up and drove slowly
forward. I swore at it. Now I couldn't see the ripple or the snag either. I
stood in the doorway, peering, and the arrows came in swarms. They might
have been poisoned, but they looked as though they wouldn't kill a cat.
The bush began to howl. Our wood-cutters raised a warlike whoop; the
report of a rifle just at my back deafened me. I glanced over my shoulder,
and the pilot-house was yet full of noise and smoke when I made a dash at
the wheel. The fool-nigger had dropped everything, to throw the shutter
open and let off that Martini-Henry. He stood before the wide opening,
glaring, and I yelled at him to come back, while I straightened the sudden
twist out of that steamboat. There was no room to turn even if I had wanted
to, the snag was somewhere very near ahead in that confounded smoke,
there was no time to lose, so I just crowded her into the bank — right into
the bank, where I knew the water was deep.

"We tore slowly along the overhanging bushes in a whirl of broken twigs
and flying leaves. The fusillade below stopped short, as I had foreseen it
would when the squirts[53] got empty. I threw my head back to a glinting
whizz that traversed the pilot-house, in at one shutter-hole and out at the
other. Looking past that mad helmsman, who was shaking the empty rifle
and yelling at the shore, I saw vague forms of men running bent double,
leaping, gliding, distinct, incomplete, evanescent. Something big appeared
in the air before the shutter, the rifle went overboard, and the man stepped
back swiftly, looked at me over his shoulder in an extraordinary, profound,
familiar manner, and fell upon my feet. The side of his head hit the wheel
twice, and the end of what appeared a long cane clattered round and
knocked over a little camp-stool. It looked as though after wrenching that
thing from somebody ashore he had lost his balance in the effort. The thin
smoke had blown away, we were clear of the snag, and looking ahead I
could see that in another hundred yards or so I would be free to sheer off,
away from the bank; but my feet felt so very warm and wet that I had to
look down. The man had rolled on his back and stared straight up at me;
both his hands clutched that cane. It was the shaft of a spear that, either
thrown or lunged through the opening, had caught him in the side just
below the ribs; the blade had gone in out of sight, after making a frightful

---

[53] Rifles. [ED.]

gash; my shoes were full; a pool of blood lay very still, gleaming dark-red under the wheel; his eyes shone with an amazing lustre. The fusillade burst out again. He looked at me anxiously, gripping the spear like something precious, with an air of being afraid I would try to take it away from him. I had to make an effort to free my eyes from his gaze and attend to the steering. With one hand I felt above my head for the line of the steam-whistle, and jerked out screech after screech hurriedly. The tumult of angry and warlike yells was checked instantly, and then from the depths of the woods went out such a tremulous and prolonged wail of mournful fear and utter despair as may be imagined to follow the flight of the last hope from the earth. There was a great commotion in the bush; the shower of arrows stopped, a few dropping shots rang out sharply—then silence, in which the languid beat of the stern-wheel came plainly to my ears. I put the helm hard a-starboard at the moment when the pilgrim in pink pyjamas, very hot and agitated, appeared in the doorway. 'The manager sends me—' he began in an official tone, and stopped short. 'Good God!' he said, glaring at the wounded man.

"We two whites stood over him, and his lustrous and inquiring glance enveloped us both. I declare it looked as though he would presently put to us some question in an understandable language; but he died without uttering a sound, without moving a limb, without twitching a muscle. Only in the very last moment, as though in response to some sign we could not see, to some whisper we could not hear, he frowned heavily, and that frown gave to his black death-mask an inconceivably sombre, brooding, and menacing expression. The lustre of inquiring glance faded swiftly into vacant glassiness. 'Can you steer?' I asked the agent eagerly. He looked very dubious; but I made a grab at his arm, and he understood at once I meant him to steer whether or no. To tell you the truth, I was morbidly anxious to change my shoes and socks. 'He is dead,' murmured the fellow, immensely impressed. 'No doubt about it,' said I, tugging like mad at the shoe-laces. 'And, by the way, I suppose Mr. Kurtz is dead as well by this time.'

"For the moment that was the dominant thought. There was a sense of extreme disappointment, as though I had found out I had been striving after something altogether without a substance. I couldn't have been more disgusted if I had travelled all this way for the sole purpose of talking with Mr. Kurtz. Talking with . . . I flung one shoe overboard, and became aware that that was exactly what I had been looking forward to—a talk with Kurtz. I made the strange discovery that I had never imagined him as doing, you know, but as discoursing. I didn't say to myself, 'Now I will never see him,' or 'Now I will never shake him by the hand,' but, 'Now I will never hear him.' The man presented himself as a voice. Not of course that I did not connect him with some sort of action. Hadn't I been told in all the tones of jealousy and admiration that he had collected, bartered, swindled, or stolen more ivory than all the other agents together. That was not the point. The point was in his being a gifted creature, and that of all his gifts the one that stood out pre-eminently, that carried with it a sense of real presence, was his ability to talk, his words—the gift of expression, the bewildering, the illuminating, the most exalted and the most contemptible, the pulsating stream of light, or the deceitful flow from the heart of an impenetrable darkness.

"The other shoe went flying unto the devil-god of that river. I thought, By Jove! it's all over. We are too late; he has vanished—the gift has vanished, by means of some spear, arrow, or club. I will never hear that chap speak after all—and my sorrow had a startling extravagance of emotion, even such as I had noticed in the howling sorrow of these savages in the bush. I couldn't have felt more of lonely desolation somehow, had I been robbed of a belief or had missed my destiny in life. . . . Why do you sigh in this beastly way, somebody? Absurd? Well, absurd. Good Lord! mustn't a man ever—Here, give me some tobacco." . . .

There was a pause of profound stillness, then a match flared, and Marlow's lean face appeared, worn, hollow, with downward folds and dropped eyelids, with an aspect of concentrated attention; and as he took vigorous draws at his pipe, it seemed to retreat and advance out of the night in the regular flicker of the tiny flame. The match went out.

"Absurd!" he cried. "This is the worst of trying to tell. . . . Here you all are, each moored with two good addresses, like a hulk with two anchors, a butcher round one corner, a policeman round another, excellent appetites, and temperature normal—you hear—normal from year's end to year's end. And you say, Absurd! Absurd be—exploded! Absurd! My dear boys, what can you expect from a man who out of sheer nervousness had just flung overboard a pair of new shoes? Now I think of it, it is amazing I did not shed tears. I am, upon the whole, proud of my fortitude. I was cut to the quick at the idea of having lost the inestimable privilege of listening to the gifted Kurtz. Of course I was wrong. The privilege was waiting for me. Oh yes, I heard more than enough. And I was right, too. A voice. He was very little more than a voice. And I heard—him—it—this voice—other voices—all of them were so little more than voices—and the memory of that time itself lingers around me, impalpable, like a dying vibration of one immense jabber, silly, atrocious, sordid, savage, or simply mean, without any kind of sense. Voices, voices—even the girl herself—now—"

He was silent for a long time.

"I laid the ghost of his gifts at last with a lie," he began suddenly. "Girl! What? Did I mention a girl? Oh, she is out of it—completely. They—the women I mean—are out of it—should be out of it. We must help them to stay in that beautiful world of their own, lest ours gets worse. Oh, she had to be out of it. You should have heard the disinterred body of Mr. Kurtz saying, 'My Intended.' You would have perceived directly then how completely she was out of it. And the lofty frontal bone of Mr. Kurtz! They say the hair goes on growing sometimes, but this — ah — specimen was impressively bald. The wilderness had patted him on the head, and, behold, it was like a ball — an ivory ball; it had caressed him, and — lo! — he had withered; it had taken him, loved him, embraced him, got into his veins, consumed his flesh, and sealed his soul to its own by the inconceivable ceremonies of some devilish initiation. He was its spoiled and pampered favourite. Ivory? I should think so. Heaps of it, stacks of it. The old mud shanty was bursting with it. You would think there was not a single tusk left either above or below the ground in the whole country. 'Mostly fossil,' the manager had remarked disparagingly. It was no more fossil than I am; but they call it fossil when it is dug up. It appears these niggers do bury the tusks sometimes — but evidently they couldn't bury this parcel deep enough to save the gifted Mr. Kurtz from his fate. We filled the steamboat with it, and had to pile a lot on the deck. Thus he could see and enjoy as long as he could see, because the appreciation of this favour had remained with him to the last. You should have heard him say, 'My ivory.' Oh yes, I heard him. 'My Intended, my ivory, my station, my river, my—' everything belonged to him. It made me hold my breath in expectation of hearing the wilderness burst into a prodigious peal of laughter that would shake the fixed stars in their places. Everything belonged to him — but that was a trifle. The thing was to know what he belonged to, how many powers of darkness claimed him for their own. That was the reflection that made you creepy all over. It was impossible — it was not good for one either — trying to imagine. He had taken a high seat amongst the devils of the land — I mean literally. You can't understand. How could you? — with solid pavement under your feet, surrounded by kind neighbours ready to cheer you or to fall on you, stepping delicately between the butcher and the policeman, in the holy terror of scandal and gallows and lunatic asylums — how can you imagine what particular region of the first ages a man's untrammelled feet may take him into by the way of solitude — utter solitude without a policeman — by the way of silence — utter silence, where no warning voice of a kind neighbour can be heard whispering of public opinion? These little things make all the great difference. When they are gone you must fall back upon your own innate strength, upon your own capacity for faithfulness. Of course you may be too much of a fool to go wrong — too dull even to know you are being assaulted by the powers of darkness. I take it, no fool ever made a bargain for his soul with the devil: the fool is too much of a fool, or the devil too much of a devil — I don't know which. Or you may be such a thunderingly exalted creature as to be altogether deaf and blind to anything but heavenly sights and sounds. Then the earth for you is only a standing place—and whether to be like this is your loss or your gain I won't pretend to say. But most of us are neither one nor the other. The earth for us is a place to live in, where we must put up with sights, with sounds, with smells too, by Jove!—breathe dead hippo, so to speak, and not be contaminated. And there, don't you see? your strength comes in, the faith in your ability for the digging of unostentatious holes to bury the stuff in—your power of devotion, not to yourself, but to an obscure, back-breaking business. And that's difficult enough. Mind, I am not trying to excuse or even explain—I am trying to account to myself for—for—Mr. Kurtz—for the shade of Mr. Kurtz. This initiated wraith from the back of Nowhere honoured me with its amazing confidence before it vanished altogether. This was because it could speak English to me. The original Kurtz had been educated partly in England, and—as he was good enough to say himself—his sympathies were in the right place. His mother was half-English, his father was half-French. All Europe contributed to the making of Kurtz; and by-and-by I learned that, most appropriately, the International Society for the Suppression of Savage Customs[54] had intrusted him with the making of a report, for its future guidance. And he had written it too. I've seen it. I've read it. It was eloquent, vibrating with eloquence, but too high-strung, I think. Seventeen pages of close writing he had found time for! But this must have been before his—let us say—nerves went wrong, and caused him to preside at certain midnight dances ending with unspeakable rites, which—as far as I reluctantly gathered from what I heard at various times—were offered up to him—do you understand?—to Mr. Kurtz himself. But it was a beautiful piece of writing. The opening paragraph, however, in the light of later information, strikes me now as ominous. He began with the argument that we whites, from the point of development we had arrived at, 'must necessarily appear to them [savages] in the nature of supernatural beings—we approach them with the might as of a deity,' and so on, and so on. 'By the simple exercise of our will we can exert a power for good practically unbounded,' &c., &c. From that point he soared and took me with him. The peroration was magnificent, though difficult to remember, you know. It gave me the notion of an exotic Immensity ruled by an august Benevolence. It made me tingle with enthusiasm. This was the unbounded power of eloquence—of words—of burning noble words. There were no practical hints to interrupt the magic current of phrases, unless a kind of note at the foot of the last page, scrawled evidently much later, in an unsteady hand, may

---

[54] Perhaps a satirical reference; there is no record of the existence of such a society. [ED.]

be regarded as the exposition of a method. It was very simple, and at the end of that moving appeal to every altruistic sentiment it blazed at you, luminous and terrifying, like a flash of lightning in a serene sky: 'Exterminate all the brutes!' The curious part was that he had apparently forgotten all about that valuable postscriptum, because, later on, when he in a sense came to himself, he repeatedly entreated me to take good care of 'my pamphlet' (he called it), as it was sure to have in the future a good influence upon his career. I had full information about all these things, and, besides, as it turned out, I was to have the care of his memory. I've done enough for it to give me the indisputable right to lay it, if I choose, for an everlasting rest in the dust-bin of progress, amongst all the sweepings and, figuratively speaking, all the dead cats of civilisation. But then, you see, I can't choose. He won't be forgotten. Whatever he was, he was not common. He had the power to charm or frighten rudimentary souls into an aggravated witch-dance in his honour; he could also fill the small souls of the pilgrims with bitter misgivings: he had one devoted friend at least, and he had conquered one soul in the world that was neither rudimentary nor tainted with self-seeking. No; I can't forget him, though I am not prepared to affirm the fellow was exactly worth the life we lost in getting to him. I missed my late helmsman awfully—I missed him even while his body was still lying in the pilot-house. Perhaps you will think it passing strange this regret for a savage who was no more account than a grain of sand in a black Sahara. Well, don't you see, he had done something, he had steered; for months I had him at my back—a help—an instrument. It was a kind of partnership. He steered for me—I had to look after him, I worried about his deficiencies, and thus a subtle bond had been created, of which I only became aware when it was suddenly broken. And the intimate profundity of that look he gave me when he received his hurt remains to this day in my memory—like a claim of distant kinship affirmed in a supreme moment.

"Poor fool! If he had only left that shutter alone. He had no restraint, no restraint—just like Kurtz—a tree swayed by the wind. As soon as I had put on a dry pair of slippers, I dragged him out, after first jerking the spear out of his side, which operation I confess I performed with my eyes shut tight. His heels leaped together over the little door-step; his shoulders were pressed to my breast; I hugged him from behind desperately. Oh! he was heavy, heavy; heavier than any man on earth, I should imagine. Then without more ado I tipped him overboard. The current snatched him as though he had been a wisp of grass, and I saw the body roll over twice before I lost sight of it for ever. All the pilgrims and the manager were then congregated on the awning-deck about the pilot-house, chattering at each other like a flock of excited magpies, and there was a scandalised murmur at my heartless promptitude. What they wanted to keep that body hanging about for I can't guess. Embalm it, maybe. But I had also heard another, and a very ominous, murmur on the deck below. My friends the wood-cutters were likewise scandalised, and with a better show of reason—though I admit that the reason itself was quite inadmissible. Oh, quite! I had made up my mind that if my late helmsman was to be eaten, the fishes alone should have him. He had been a very second-rate helmsman while alive, but now he was dead he might have become a first-class temptation, and possibly cause some startling trouble. Besides, I was anxious to take the wheel, the man in pink pyjamas showing himself a hopeless duffer at the business.

"This I did directly the simple funeral was over. We were going half-speed, keeping right in the middle of the stream, and I listened to the talk about me. They had given up Kurtz, they had given up the station; Kurtz was dead, and the station had been burnt—and so on—and so on. The red-haired pilgrim was beside himself with the thought that at least this poor Kurtz had been properly revenged. 'Say! We must have made a glorious slaughter of them in the bush. Eh? What do you think? Say?' He positively danced, the bloodthirsty little gingery[55] beggar. And he had nearly fainted when he saw the wounded man! I could not help saying, 'You made a glorious lot of smoke, anyhow.' I had seen, from the way the tops of the bushes rustled and flew, that almost all the shots had gone too high. You can't hit anything unless you take aim and fire from the shoulder; but these chaps fired from the hip with their eyes shut. The retreat, I maintained—and I was right—was caused by the screeching of the steam-whistle. Upon this they forgot Kurtz, and began to howl at me with indignant protests.

"The manager stood by the wheel murmuring confidentially about the necessity of getting well away down the river before dark at all events, when I saw in the distance a clearing on the river-side and the outlines of some sort of building. 'What's this?' I asked. He clapped his hands in wonder. 'The station!' he cried. I edged in at once, still going half-speed.

"Through my glasses I saw the slope of a hill interspersed with rare trees and perfectly free from undergrowth. A long decaying building on the summit was half buried in the high grass; the large holes in the peaked roof gaped black from afar; the jungle and the woods made a background. There was no enclosure or fence of any kind; but there had been one apparently, for near the house half-a-dozen slim posts remained in a row, roughly trimmed, and with their upper ends ornamented with round carved balls. The rails, or whatever there had been between, had disappeared. Of course the forest surrounded all that. The river-bank was clear, and on the water-side I saw a white man under a hat like a cart-wheel beckoning per-

---

[55] Red headed. [ED.]

sistently with his whole arm. Examining the edge of the forest above and below, I was almost certain I could see movements—human forms gliding here and there. I steamed past prudently, then stopped the engines and let her drift down. The man on the shore began to shout, urging us to land. 'We have been attacked,' screamed the manager. 'I know—I know. It's all right,' yelled back the other, as cheerful as you please. 'Come along. It's all right. I am glad.'

"His aspect reminded me of something I had seen—something funny I had seen somewhere. As I manœuvred to get alongside, I was asking myself, 'What does this fellow look like?' Suddenly I got it. He looked like a harlequin.⁵⁶ His clothes had been made of some stuff that was brown holland probably, but it was covered with patches all over, with bright patches, blue, red, and yellow—patches on the back, patches on front, patches on elbows, on knees; coloured binding round his jacket, scarlet edging at the bottom of his trousers; and the sunshine made him look extremely gay and wonderfully neat withal, because you could see how beautifully all this patching had been done. A beardless, boyish face, very fair, no features to speak of, nose peeling, little blue eyes, smiles and frowns chasing each other over that open countenance like sunshine and shadow on a wind-swept plain. 'Look out, captain!' he cried; 'there's a snag lodged in here last night.' What! Another snag? I confess I swore shamefully. I had nearly holed my cripple, to finish off that charming trip. The harlequin on the bank turned his little pug nose up to me. 'You English?' he asked, all smiles. 'Are you?' I shouted from the wheel. The smiles vanished, and he shook his head as if sorry for my disappointment. Then he brightened up. 'Never mind!' he cried encouragingly. 'Are we in time?' I asked. 'He is up there,' he replied, with a toss of the head up the hill, and becoming gloomy all of a sudden. His face was like the autumn sky, overcast one moment and bright the next.

"When the manager, escorted by the pilgrims, all of them armed to the teeth, had gone to the house, this chap came on board. 'I say, I don't like this. These natives are in the bush,' I said. He assured me earnestly it was all right. 'They are simple people,' he added; 'well, I am glad you came. It took me all my time to keep them off.' 'But you said it was all right,' I cried. 'Oh, they meant no harm,' he said; and as I stared he corrected himself, 'Not exactly.' Then vivaciously, 'My faith, your pilot-house wants a clean-up!' In the next breath he advised me to keep enough steam on the boiler

---

⁵⁶In traditional French and Italian comedy and pantomime, a character with a shaved head, masked face, and variegated tights, often standing for either comedy or melancholy or both. [ED.]

to blow the whistle in case of any trouble. 'One good screech will do more for you than all your rifles. They are simple people,' he repeated. He rattled away at such a rate he quite overwhelmed me. He seemed to be trying to make up for lots of silence, and actually hinted, laughing, that such was the case. 'Don't you talk with Mr. Kurtz?' I said. 'You don't talk with that man—you listen to him,' he exclaimed with severe exaltation. 'But now—' He waved his arm, and in the twinkling of an eye was in the uttermost depths of despondency. In a moment he came up again with a jump, possessed himself of both my hands, shook them continuously, while he gabbled: 'Brother sailor . . . honour . . . pleasure . . . delight . . . introduce myself . . . Russian . . . son of an archpriest . . . Government of Tambov[57] . . . What? Tobacco! English tobacco; the excellent English tobacco! Now, that's brotherly. Smoke? Where's a sailor that does not smoke?'

"The pipe soothed him, and gradually I made out he had run away from school, had gone to sea in a Russian ship; ran away again; served some time in English ships; was now reconciled with the archpriest. He made a point of that. 'But when one is young one must see things, gather experience, ideas; enlarge the mind.' 'Here!' I interrupted. 'You can never tell! Here I have met Mr. Kurtz,' he said, youthfully solemn and reproachful. I held my tongue after that. It appears he had persuaded a Dutch trading-house on the coast to fit him out with stores and goods, and had started for the interior with a light heart, and no more idea of what would happen to him than a baby. He had been wandering about that river for nearly two years alone, cut off from everybody and everything. 'I am not so young as I look. I am twenty-five,' he said. 'At first old Van Shuyten would tell me to go to the devil,' he narrated with keen enjoyment; 'but I stuck to him, and talked and talked, till at last he got afraid I would talk the hind-leg off his favourite dog, so he gave me some cheap things and a few guns, and told me he hoped he would never see my face again. Good old Dutchman, Van Shuyten. I sent him one small lot of ivory a year ago, so that he can't call me a little thief when I get back. I hope he got it. And for the rest, I don't care. I had some wood stacked for you. That was my old house. Did you see?'

"I gave him Towson's book. He made as though he would kiss me, but restrained himself. 'The only book I had left, and I thought I had lost it,' he said, looking at it ecstatically. 'So many accidents happen to a man going about alone, you know. Canoes get upset sometimes—and sometimes you've got to clear out so quick when the people get angry.' He thumbed the pages. 'You made notes in Russian?' I asked. He nodded. 'I thought they were written in cipher,' I said. He laughed, then became serious. 'I had lots

---

[57] One of the largest federations in central Russia. [ED.]

of trouble to keep these people off,' he said. 'Did they want to kill you?' I asked. 'Oh no!' he cried, and checked himself. 'Why did they attack us?' I pursued. He hesitated, then said shamefacedly, 'They don't want him to go.' 'Don't they?' I said, curiously. He nodded a nod full of mystery and wisdom. 'I tell you,' he cried, 'this man has enlarged my mind.' He opened his arms wide, staring at me with his little blue eyes that were perfectly round."

CHAPTER III

"I looked at him, lost in astonishment. There he was before me, in motley, as though he had absconded from a troupe of mimes, enthusiastic, fabulous. His very existence was improbable, inexplicable, and altogether bewildering. He was an insoluble problem. It was inconceivable how he had existed, how he had succeeded in getting so far, how he had managed to remain—why he did not instantly disappear. 'I went a little farther,' he said, 'then still a little farther—till I had gone so far that I don't know how I'll ever get back. Never mind. Plenty time. I can manage. You take Kurtz away quick—quick—I tell you.' The glamour of youth enveloped his parti-coloured rags, his destitution, his loneliness, the essential desolation of his futile wanderings. For months—for years—his life hadn't been worth a day's purchase; and there he was gallantly, thoughtlessly alive, to all appearance indestructible solely by the virtue of his few years and of his unreflecting audacity. I was seduced into something like admiration—like envy. Glamour urged him on, glamour kept him unscathed. He surely wanted nothing from the wilderness but space to breathe in and to push on through. His need was to exist, and to move onwards at the greatest possible risk, and with a maximum of privation. If the absolutely pure, uncalculating, unpractical spirit of adventure had ever ruled a human being, it ruled this be-patched youth. I almost envied him the possession of this modest and clear flame. It seemed to have consumed all thought of self so completely, that, even while he was talking to you, you forgot that it was he—the man before your eyes—who had gone through these things. I did not envy him his devotion to Kurtz, though. He had not meditated over it. It came to him, and he accepted it with a sort of eager fatalism. I must say that to me it appeared about the most dangerous thing in every way he had come upon so far.

"They had come together unavoidably, like two ships becalmed near each other, and lay rubbing sides at last. I suppose Kurtz wanted an audience, because on a certain occasion, when encamped in the forest, they had

talked all night, or more probably Kurtz had talked. 'We talked of everything,' he said, quite transported at the recollection. 'I forgot there was
such a thing as sleep. The night did not seem to last an hour. Everything!
Everything! . . . Of love too.' 'Ah, he talked to you of love!' I said, much
amused. 'It isn't what you think,' he cried, almost passionately. 'It was in
general. He made me see things — things.'

"He threw his arms up. We were on deck at the time, and the headman
of my wood-cutters, lounging near by, turned upon him his heavy and glittering eyes. I looked around, and I don't know why, but I assure you that
never, never before, did this land, this river, this jungle, the very arch of
this blazing sky, appear to me so hopeless and so dark, so impenetrable to
human thought, so pitiless to human weakness. 'And, ever since, you have
been with him, of course?' I said.

"On the contrary. It appears their intercourse had been very much broken by various causes. He had, as he informed me proudly, managed to
nurse Kurtz through two illnesses (he alluded to it as you would to some
risky feat), but as a rule Kurtz wandered alone, far in the depths of the forest. 'Very often coming to this station, I had to wait days and days before he
would turn up,' he said. 'Ah, it was worth waiting for! — sometimes.' 'What
was he doing? exploring or what?' I asked. 'Oh yes, of course'; he had discovered lots of villages, a lake too — he did not know exactly in what direction; it was dangerous to inquire too much — but mostly his expeditions
had been for ivory. 'But he had no goods to trade with by that time,' I objected. 'There's a good lot of cartridges left even yet,' he answered, looking
away. 'To speak plainly, he raided the country,' I said. He nodded. 'Not
alone, surely!' He muttered something about the villages round that lake.
'Kurtz got the tribe to follow him, did he?' I suggested. He fidgeted a little.
'They adored him,' he said. The tone of these words was so extraordinary
that I looked at him searchingly. It was curious to see his mingled eagerness
and reluctance to speak of Kurtz. The man filled his life, occupied his
thoughts, swayed his emotions. 'What can you expect?' he burst out; 'he
came to them with thunder and lightning, you know — and they had never
seen anything like it — and very terrible. He could be very terrible. You can't
judge Mr. Kurtz as you would an ordinary man. No, no, no! Now — just to
give you an idea — I don't mind telling you, he wanted to shoot me too one
day — but I don't judge him.' 'Shoot you!' I cried. 'What for?' 'Well, I had a
small lot of ivory the chief of that village near my house gave me. You see I
used to shoot game for them. Well, he wanted it, and wouldn't hear reason.
He declared he would shoot me unless I gave him the ivory and then
cleared out of the country, because he could do so, and had a fancy for it,
and there was nothing on earth to prevent him killing whom he jolly well
pleased. And it was true too. I gave him the ivory. What did I care! But I

didn't clear out. No, no. I couldn't leave him. I had to be careful, of course, till we got friendly again for a time. He had his second illness then. Afterwards I had to keep out of the way; but I didn't mind. He was living for the most part in those villages on the lake. When he came down to the river, sometimes he would take to me, and sometimes it was better for me to be careful. This man suffered too much. He hated all this, and somehow he couldn't get away. When I had a chance I begged him to try and leave while there was time; I offered to go back with him. And he would say yes, and then he would remain; go off on another ivory hunt; disappear for weeks; forget himself amongst these people—forget himself—you know.' 'Why! he's mad,' I said. He protested indignantly. Mr. Kurtz couldn't be mad. If I had heard him talk, only two days ago, I wouldn't dare hint at such a thing. . . . I had taken up my binoculars while we talked, and was looking at the shore, sweeping the limit of the forest at each side and at the back of the house. The consciousness of there being people in that bush, so silent, so quiet—as silent and quiet as the ruined house on the hill—made me uneasy. There was no sign on the face of nature of this amazing tale that was not so much told as suggested to me in desolate exclamations, completed by shrugs, in interrupted phrases, in hints ending in deep sighs. The woods were unmoved, like a mask—heavy, like the closed door of a prison—they looked with their air of hidden knowledge, of patient expectation, of unapproachable silence. The Russian was explaining to me that it was only lately that Mr. Kurtz had come down to the river, bringing along with him all the fighting men of that lake tribe. He had been absent for several months—getting himself adored, I suppose—and had come down unexpectedly, with the intention to all appearance of making a raid either across the river or down stream. Evidently the appetite for more ivory had got the better of the—what shall I say?—less material aspirations. However, he had got much worse suddenly. 'I heard he was lying helpless, and so I came up—took my chance,' said the Russian. 'Oh, he is bad, very bad.' I directed my glass to the house. There were no signs of life, but there was the ruined roof, the long mud wall peeping above the grass, with three little square window-holes, no two of the same size; all this brought within reach of my hand, as it were. And then I made a brusque movement, and one of the remaining posts of that vanished fence leaped up in the field of my glass. You remember I told you I had been struck at the distance by certain attempts at ornamentation, rather remarkable in the ruinous aspect of the place. Now I had suddenly a nearer view, and its first result was to make me throw my head back as if before a blow. Then I went carefully from post to post with my glass, and I saw my mistake. These round knobs were not ornamental but symbolic; they were expressive and puzzling, striking and disturbing—food for thought and also for the vultures if there had been any

looking down from the sky; but at all events for such ants as were industri-
ous enough to ascend the pole. They would have been even more impres-
sive, those heads on the stakes, if their faces had not been turned to the
house. Only one, the first I had made out, was facing my way. I was not so
shocked as you may think. The start back I had given was really nothing but
a movement of surprise. I had expected to see a knob of wood there, you
know. I returned deliberately to the first I had seen—and there it was,
black, dried, sunken, with closed eyelids—a head that seemed to sleep at the
top of that pole, and, with the shrunken dry lips showing a narrow white
line of the teeth, was smiling too, smiling continuously at some endless and
jocose dream of that eternal slumber.

"I am not disclosing any trade secrets. In fact the manager said afterwards that Mr. Kurtz's methods had ruined the district. I have no opinion
on that point, but I want you clearly to understand that there was nothing exactly profitable in these heads being there. They only showed that
Mr. Kurtz lacked restraint in the gratification of his various lusts, that
there was something wanting in him—some small matter which, when the
pressing need arose, could not be found under his magnificent eloquence.
Whether he knew of this deficiency himself I can't say. I think the knowledge came to him at last—only at the very last. But the wilderness had
found him out early, and had taken on him a terrible vengeance for the
fantastic invasion. I think it had whispered to him things about himself which he did not know, things of which he had no conception till he
took counsel with this great solitude—and the whisper had proved irresistibly fascinating. It echoed loudly within him because he was hollow at
the core. . . . I put down the glass, and the head that had appeared near
enough to be spoken to seemed at once to have leaped away from me into
inaccessible distance.

"The admirer of Mr. Kurtz was a bit crestfallen. In a hurried, indistinct
voice he began to assure me he had not dared to take these—say, symbols—
down. He was not afraid of the natives; they would not stir till Mr. Kurtz
gave the word. His ascendancy was extraordinary. The camps of these
people surrounded the place, and the chiefs came every day to see him.
They would crawl. . . . 'I don't want to know anything of the ceremonies
used when approaching Mr. Kurtz,' I shouted. Curious, this feeling that
came over me that such details would be more intolerable than those heads
drying on the stakes under Mr. Kurtz's windows. After all, that was only a
savage sight, while I seemed at one bound to have been transported into
some lightless region of subtle horrors, where pure, uncomplicated savagery was a positive relief, being something that had a right to exist—obviously—in the sunshine. The young man looked at me with surprise. I
suppose it did not occur to him Mr. Kurtz was no idol of mine. He forgot

I hadn't heard any of these splendid monologues on, what was it? on love, justice, conduct of life—or what not. If it had come to crawling before Mr. Kurtz, he crawled as much as the veriest savage of them all. I had no idea of the conditions, he said: these heads were the heads of rebels. I shocked him excessively by laughing. Rebels! What would be the next definition I was to hear? There had been enemies, criminals, workers—and these were rebels. Those rebellious heads looked very subdued to me on their sticks. 'You don't know how such a life tries a man like Kurtz,' cried Kurtz's last disciple. 'Well, and you?' I said. 'I! I! I am a simple man. I have no great thoughts. I want nothing from anybody. How can you compare me to . . . ?' His feelings were too much for speech, and suddenly he broke down. 'I don't understand,' he groaned. 'I've been doing my best to keep him alive, and that's enough. I had no hand in all this. I have no abilities. There hasn't been a drop of medicine or a mouthful of invalid food for months here. He was shamefully abandoned. A man like this, with such ideas. Shamefully! Shamefully! I—I—haven't slept for the last ten nights. . . .'

"His voice lost itself in the calm of the evening. The long shadows of the forest had slipped down-hill while we talked, had gone far beyond the ruined hovel, beyond the symbolic row of stakes. All this was in the gloom, while we down there were yet in the sunshine, and the stretch of the river abreast of the clearing glittered in a still and dazzling splendour, with a murky and overshadowed bend above and below. Not a living soul was seen on the shore. The bushes did not rustle.

"Suddenly round the corner of the house a group of men appeared, as though they had come up from the ground. They waded waist-deep in the grass, in a compact body, bearing an improvised stretcher in their midst. Instantly, in the emptiness of the landscape, a cry arose whose shrillness pierced the still air like a sharp arrow flying straight to the very heart of the land; and, as if by enchantment, streams of human beings—of naked human beings—with spears in their hands, with bows, with shields, with wild glances and savage movements, were poured into the clearing by the dark-faced and pensive forest. The bushes shook, the grass swayed for a time, and then everything stood still in attentive immobility.

"'Now, if he does not say the right thing to them we are all done for,' said the Russian at my elbow. The knot of men with the stretcher had stopped too, half-way to the steamer, as if petrified. I saw the man on the stretcher sit up, lank and with an uplifted arm, above the shoulders of the bearers. 'Let us hope that the man who can talk so well of love in general will find some particular reason to spare us this time,' I said. I resented bitterly the absurd danger of our situation, as if to be at the mercy of that atrocious phantom had been a dishonouring necessity. I could not hear a sound, but through my glasses I saw the thin arm extended commandingly, the lower jaw moving, the eyes of that apparition shining darkly far in its bony head that nodded with grotesque jerks. Kurtz—Kurtz—that means "short" in German—don't it? Well, the name was as true as everything else in his life—and death. He looked at least seven feet long. His covering had fallen off, and his body emerged from it pitiful and appalling as from a winding-sheet. I could see the cage of his ribs all astir, the bones of his arm waving. It was as though an animated image of death carved out of old ivory had been shaking its hand with menaces at a motionless crowd of men made of dark and glittering bronze. I saw him open his mouth wide— it gave him a weirdly voracious aspect, as though he had wanted to swallow all the air, all the earth, all the men before him. A deep voice reached me faintly. He must have been shouting. He fell back suddenly. The stretcher shook as the bearers staggered forward again, and almost at the same time I noticed that the crowd of savages was vanishing without any perceptible movement of retreat, as if the forest that had ejected these beings so suddenly had drawn them in again as the breath is drawn in a long aspiration.

"Some of the pilgrims behind the stretcher carried his arms—two shot-guns, a heavy rifle, and a light revolver-carbine—the thunderbolts of that pitiful Jupiter.[58] The manager bent over him murmuring as he walked beside his head. They laid him down in one of the little cabins—just a room for a bed-place and a camp-stool or two, you know. We had brought his belated correspondence, and a lot of torn envelopes and open letters littered his bed. His hand roamed feebly amongst these papers. I was struck by the fire of his eyes and the composed languor of his expression. It was not so much the exhaustion of disease. He did not seem in pain. This shadow looked satiated and calm, as though for the moment it had had its fill of all the emotions.

"He rustled one of the letters, and looking straight in my face said, 'I am glad.' Somebody had been writing to him about me. These special recommendations were turning up again. The volume of tone he emitted without effort, almost without the trouble of moving his lips, amazed me. A voice! a voice! It was grave, profound, vibrating, while the man did not seem capable of a whisper. However, he had enough strength in him— factitious no doubt—to very nearly make an end of us, as you shall hear directly.

"The manager appeared silently in the doorway; I stepped out at once and he drew the curtain after me. The Russian, eyed curiously by the pilgrims, was staring at the shore. I followed the direction of his glance.

---

[58] The chief god in Roman mythology. [ED.]

"Dark human shapes could be made out in the distance, flitting indistinctly against the gloomy border of the forest, and near the river two bronze figures, leaning on tall spears, stood in the sunlight under fantastic head-dresses of spotted skins, warlike and still in statuesque repose. And from right to left along the lighted shore moved a wild and gorgeous apparition of a woman.

"She walked with measured steps, draped in striped and fringed cloths, treading the earth proudly, with a slight jingle and flash of barbarous ornaments. She carried her head high; her hair was done in the shape of a helmet; she had brass leggings to the knee, brass wire gauntlets to the elbow, a crimson spot on her tawny cheek, innumerable necklaces of glass beads on her neck; bizarre things, charms, gifts of witch-men, that hung about her, glittered and trembled at every step. She must have had the value of several elephant tusks upon her. She was savage and superb, wild-eyed and magnificent; there was something ominous and stately in her deliberate progress. And in the hush that had fallen suddenly upon the whole sorrowful land, the immense wilderness, the colossal body of the fecund and mysterious life seemed to look at her, pensive, as though it had been looking at the image of its own tenebrous and passionate soul.

"She came abreast of the steamer, stood still, and faced us. Her long shadow fell to the water's edge. Her face had a tragic and fierce aspect of wild sorrow and of dumb pain mingled with the fear of some struggling, half-shaped resolve. She stood looking at us without a stir, and like the wilderness itself, with an air of brooding over an inscrutable purpose. A whole minute passed, and then she made a step forward. There was a low jingle, a glint of yellow metal, a sway of fringed draperies, and she stopped as if her heart had failed her. The young fellow by my side growled. The pilgrims murmured at my back. She looked at us all as if her life had depended upon the unswerving steadiness of her glance. Suddenly she opened her bared arms and threw them up rigid above her head, as though in an uncontrollable desire to touch the sky, and at the same time the swift shadows darted out on the earth, swept around on the river, gathering the steamer in a shadowy embrace. A formidable silence hung over the scene.

"She turned away slowly, walked on, following the bank, and passed into the bushes to the left. Once only her eyes gleamed back at us in the dusk of the thickets before she disappeared.

"'If she had offered to come aboard I really think I would have tried to shoot her,' said the man of patches, nervously. 'I had been risking my life every day for the last fortnight to keep her out of the house. She got in one day and kicked up a row about those miserable rags I picked up in the storeroom to mend my clothes with. I wasn't decent. At least it must have been that, for she talked like a fury to Kurtz for an hour, pointing at me now and then. I don't understand the dialect of this tribe. Luckily for me, I fancy Kurtz felt too ill that day to care, or there would have been mischief. I don't understand.... No—it's too much for me. Ah, well, it's all over now.'

"At this moment I heard Kurtz's deep voice behind the curtain, 'Save me!—save the ivory, you mean. Don't tell me. Save *me!* Why, I've had to save you. You are interrupting my plans now. Sick! Sick! Not so sick as you would like to believe. Never mind. I'll carry my ideas out yet—I will return. I'll show you what can be done. You with your little peddling notions—you are interfering with me. I will return. I ...'

"The manager came out. He did me the honour to take me under the arm and lead me aside. 'He is very low, very low,' he said. He considered it necessary to sigh, but neglected to be consistently sorrowful. 'We have done all we could for him—haven't we? But there is no disguising the fact, Mr. Kurtz has done more harm than good to the Company. He did not see the time was not ripe for vigorous action. Cautiously, cautiously—that's my principle. We must be cautious yet. The district is closed to us for a time. Deplorable! Upon the whole, the trade will suffer. I don't deny there is a remarkable quantity of ivory—mostly fossil. We must save it, at all events—but look how precarious the position is—and why? Because the method is unsound.' 'Do you,' said I, looking at the shore, 'call it "unsound method"?' 'Without doubt,' he exclaimed, hotly. 'Don't you?' . . . 'No method at all,' I murmured after a while. 'Exactly,' he exulted. 'I anticipated this. Shows a complete want of judgment. It is my duty to point it out in the proper quarter.' 'Oh,' said I, 'that fellow—what's his name?—the brickmaker, will make a readable report for you.' He appeared confounded for a moment. It seemed to me I had never breathed an atmosphere so vile, and I turned mentally to Kurtz for relief—positively for relief. 'Nevertheless, I think Mr. Kurtz is a remarkable man,' I said with emphasis. He started, dropped on me a cold heavy glance, said very quietly, 'He *was*,' and turned his back on me. My hour of favour was over; I found myself lumped along with Kurtz as a partisan of methods for which the time was not ripe: I was unsound! Ah! but it was something to have at least a choice of nightmares.

"I had turned to the wilderness really, not to Mr. Kurtz, who, I was ready to admit, was as good as buried. And for a moment it seemed to me as if I also were buried in a vast grave full of unspeakable secrets. I felt an intolerable weight oppressing my breast, the smell of the damp earth, the unseen presence of victorious corruption, the darkness of an impenetrable night. . . . The Russian tapped me on the shoulder. I heard him mumbling and stammering something about 'brother seaman—couldn't conceal—knowledge of matters that would affect Mr. Kurtz's reputation.' I waited.

For him evidently Mr. Kurtz was not in his grave; I suspect that for him Mr. Kurtz was one of the immortals. 'Well!' said I at last, 'speak out. As it happens, I am Mr. Kurtz's friend—in a way.'

"He stated with a good deal of formality that had we not been 'of the same profession,' he would have kept the matter to himself without regard to consequences. He suspected 'there was an active ill-will towards him on the part of these white men that—' 'You are right,' I said, remembering a certain conversation I had overheard. 'The manager thinks you ought to be hanged.' He showed a concern at this intelligence which amused me at first. 'I had better get out of the way quietly,' he said, earnestly. 'I can do no more for Kurtz now, and they would soon find some excuse. What's to stop them? There's a military post three hundred miles from here.' 'Well, upon my word,' said I, 'perhaps you had better go if you have any friends amongst the savages near by.' 'Plenty,' he said. 'They are simple people—and I want nothing, you know.' He stood biting his lip, then: 'I don't want any harm to happen to these whites here, but of course I was thinking of Mr. Kurtz's reputation—but you are a brother seaman and—' 'All right,' said I, after a time. 'Mr. Kurtz's reputation is safe with me.' I did not know how truly I spoke.

"He informed me, lowering his voice, that it was Kurtz who had ordered the attack to be made on the steamer. 'He hated sometimes the idea of being taken away—and then again. . . . But I don't understand these matters. I am a simple man. He thought it would scare you away—that you would give it up, thinking him dead. I could not stop him. Oh, I had an awful time of it this last month.' 'Very well,' I said. 'He is all right now.' 'Ye-e-es,' he muttered, not very convinced apparently. 'Thanks,' said I; 'I shall keep my eyes open.' 'But quiet—eh?' he urged, anxiously. 'It would be awful for his reputation if anybody here—' I promised a complete discretion with great gravity. 'I have a canoe and three black fellows waiting not very far. I am off. Could you give me a few Martini-Henry cartridges?' I could, and did, with proper secrecy. He helped himself, with a wink at me, to a handful of my tobacco. 'Between sailors—you know—good English tobacco.' At the door of the pilot-house he turned round—'I say, haven't you a pair of shoes you could spare?' He raised one leg. 'Look.' The soles were tied with knotted strings sandal-wise under his bare feet. I rooted out an old pair, at which he looked with admiration before tucking it under his left arm. One of his pockets (bright red) was bulging with cartridges, from the other (dark blue) peeped 'Towson's Inquiry,' &c., &c. He seemed to think himself excellently well equipped for a renewed encounter with the wilderness. 'Ah! I'll never, never meet such a man again. You ought to have heard him recite poetry—his own too it was, he told me. Poetry!' He rolled his eyes at the recollection of these delights. 'Oh, he enlarged my mind!' 'Good-bye,' said I. He shook hands and vanished in the night. Sometimes I ask myself whether I had ever really seen him—whether it was possible to meet such a phenomenon! . . .

"When I woke up shortly after midnight his warning came to my mind with its hint of danger that seemed, in the starred darkness, real enough to make me get up for the purpose of having a look round. On the hill a big fire burned, illuminating fitfully a crooked corner of the station-house. One of the agents with a picket of a few of our blacks, armed for the purpose, was keeping guard over the ivory; but deep within the forest, red gleams that wavered, that seemed to sink and rise from the ground amongst confused columnar shapes of intense blackness, showed the exact position of the camp where Mr. Kurtz's adorers were keeping their uneasy vigil. The monotonous beating of a big drum filled the air with muffled shocks and a lingering vibration. A steady droning sound of many men chanting each to himself some weird incantation came out from the black, flat wall of the woods as the humming of bees comes out of a hive, and had a strange narcotic effect upon my half-awake senses. I believe I dozed off leaning over the rail, till an abrupt burst of yells, an overwhelming outbreak of a pent-up and mysterious frenzy, woke me up in a bewildered wonder. It was cut short all at once, and the low droning went on with an effect of audible and soothing silence. I glanced casually into the little cabin. A light was burning within, but Mr. Kurtz was not there.

"I think I would have raised an outcry if I had believed my eyes. But I didn't believe them at first—the thing seemed so impossible. The fact is, I was completely unnerved by a sheer blank fright, pure abstract terror, unconnected with any distinct shape of physical danger. What made this emotion so overpowering was—how shall I define it?—the moral shock I received, as if something altogether monstrous, intolerable to thought and odious to the soul, had been thrust upon me unexpectedly. This lasted of course the merest fraction of a second, and then the usual sense of commonplace, deadly danger, the possibility of a sudden onslaught and massacre, or something of the kind, which I saw impending, was positively welcome and composing. It pacified me, in fact, so much, that I did not raise an alarm.

"There was an agent buttoned up inside an ulster and sleeping on a chair on deck within three feet of me. The yells had not awakened him; he snored very slightly; I left him to his slumbers and leaped ashore. I did not betray Mr. Kurtz—it was ordered I should never betray him—it was written I should be loyal to the nightmare of my choice. I was anxious to deal with this shadow by myself alone—and to this day I don't know why I was so jealous of sharing with any one the peculiar blackness of that experience.

"As soon as I got on the bank I saw a trail—a broad trail through the grass. I remember the exultation with which I said to myself, 'He can't walk—he is crawling on all-fours—I've got him.' The grass was wet with dew. I strode rapidly with clenched fists. I fancy I had some vague notion of falling upon him and giving him a drubbing. I don't know. I had some imbecile thoughts. The knitting old woman with the cat obtruded herself upon my memory as a most improper person to be sitting at the other end of such an affair. I saw a row of pilgrims squirting lead in the air out of Winchesters held to the hip. I thought I would never get back to the steamer, and imagined myself living alone and unarmed in the woods to an advanced age. Such silly things—you know. And I remember I confounded the beat of the drum with the beating of my heart, and was pleased at its calm regularity.

"I kept to the track though—then stopped to listen. The night was very clear: a dark blue space, sparkling with dew and starlight, in which black things stood very still. I thought I could see a kind of motion ahead of me. I was strangely cocksure of everything that night. I actually left the track and ran in a wide semicircle (I verily believe chuckling to myself) so as to get in front of that stir, of that motion I had seen—if indeed I had seen anything. I was circumventing Kurtz as though it had been a boyish game.

"I came upon him, and, if he had not heard me coming, I would have fallen over him too, but he got up in time. He rose, unsteady, long, pale, indistinct, like a vapour exhaled by the earth, and swayed slightly, misty and silent before me; while at my back the fires loomed between the trees, and the murmur of many voices issued from the forest. I had cut him off cleverly; but when actually confronting him I seemed to come to my senses, I saw the danger in its right proportion. It was by no means over yet. Suppose he began to shout? Though he could hardly stand, there was still plenty of vigour in his voice. 'Go away—hide yourself,' he said, in that profound tone. It was very awful. I glanced back. We were within thirty yards from the nearest fire. A black figure stood up, strode on long black legs, waving long black arms, across the glow. It had horns—antelope horns, I think—on its head. Some sorcerer, some witch-man, no doubt: it looked fiend-like enough. 'Do you know what you are doing?' I whispered. 'Perfectly,' he answered, raising his voice for that single word: it sounded to me far off and yet loud, like a hail through a speaking-trumpet. If he makes a row we are lost, I thought to myself. This clearly was not a case for fisticuffs, even apart from the very natural aversion I had to beat that Shadow—this wandering and tormented thing. 'You will be lost,' I said—'utterly lost.' One gets sometimes such a flash of inspiration, you know. I did say the right thing, though indeed he could not have been more irretrievably lost than he was at this very moment, when the foundations of

our intimacy were being laid—to endure—to endure—even to the end—
even beyond.

"'I had immense plans,' he muttered irresolutely. 'Yes,' said I; 'but if you
try to shout I'll smash your head with—' there was not a stick or a stone
near. 'I will throttle you for good,' I corrected myself. 'I was on the threshold of great things,' he pleaded, in a voice of longing, with a wistfulness of
tone that made my blood run cold. 'And now for this stupid scoundrel—'
'Your success in Europe is assured in any case,' I affirmed, steadily. I did not
want to have the throttling of him, you understand—and indeed it would
have been very little use for any practical purpose. I tried to break the
spell—the heavy, mute spell of the wilderness—that seemed to draw him
to its pitiless breast by the awakening of forgotten and brutal instincts, by
the memory of gratified and monstrous passions. This alone, I was convinced, had driven him out to the edge of the forest, to the bush, towards
the gleam of fires, the throb of drums, the drone of weird incantations; this
alone had beguiled his unlawful soul beyond the bounds of permitted aspirations. And, don't you see, the terror of the position was not in being
knocked on the head—though I had a very lively sense of that danger too—
but in this, that I had to deal with a being to whom I could not appeal in
the name of anything high or low. I had, even like the niggers, to invoke
him—himself—his own exalted and incredible degradation. There was
nothing either above or below him, and I knew it. He had kicked himself loose of the earth. Confound the man! he had kicked the very earth
to pieces. He was alone, and I before him did not know whether I stood
on the ground or floated in the air. I've been telling you what we said—
repeating the phrases we pronounced—but what's the good? They were
common everyday words—the familiar, vague sounds exchanged on every
waking day of life. But what of that? They had behind them, to my mind,
the terrific suggestiveness of words heard in dreams, of phrases spoken in
nightmares. Soul! If anybody had ever struggled with a soul, I am the man.
And I wasn't arguing with a lunatic either. Believe me or not, his intelligence was perfectly clear—concentrated, it is true, upon himself with horrible intensity, yet clear; and therein was my only chance—barring, of
course, the killing him there and then, which wasn't so good, on account
of unavoidable noise. But his soul was mad. Being alone in the wilderness,
it had looked within itself, and, by heavens! I tell you, it had gone mad. I
had—for my sins, I suppose—to go through the ordeal of looking into it
myself. No eloquence could have been so withering to one's belief in mankind as his final burst of sincerity. He struggled with himself, too. I saw it—
I heard it. I saw the inconceivable mystery of a soul that knew no restraint,
no faith, and no fear, yet struggling blindly with itself. I kept my head

pretty well; but when I had him at last stretched on the couch, I wiped my forehead, while my legs shook under me as though I had carried half a ton on my back down that hill. And yet I had only supported him, his bony arm clasped round my neck—and he was not much heavier than a child.

"When next day we left at noon, the crowd, of whose presence behind the curtain of trees I had been acutely conscious all the time, flowed out of the woods again, filled the clearing, covered the slope with a mass of naked, breathing, quivering, bronze bodies. I steamed up a bit, then swung down-stream, and two thousand eyes followed the evolutions of the splashing, thumping, fierce river-demon beating the water with its terrible tail and breathing black smoke into the air. In front of the first rank, along the river, three men, plastered with bright red earth from head to foot, strutted to and fro restlessly. When we came abreast again, they faced the river, stamped their feet, nodded their horned heads, swayed their scarlet bodies; they shook towards the fierce river-demon a bunch of black feathers, a mangy skin with a pendent tail—something that looked like a dried gourd; they shouted periodically together strings of amazing words that resembled no sounds of human language; and the deep murmurs of the crowd, inter-rupted suddenly, were like the responses of some satanic litany.

"We had carried Kurtz into the pilot-house: there was more air there. Lying on the couch, he stared through the open shutter. There was an eddy in the mass of human bodies, and the woman with helmeted head and tawny cheeks rushed out to the very brink of the stream. She put out her hands, shouted something, and all that wild mob took up the shout in a roaring chorus of articulated, rapid, breathless utterance.

"'Do you understand this?' I asked.

"He kept on looking out past me with fiery, longing eyes, with a min-gled expression of wistfulness and hate. He made no answer, but I saw a smile, a smile of indefinable meaning, appear on his colourless lips that a moment after twitched convulsively. 'Do I not?' he said slowly, gasping, as if the words had been torn out of him by a supernatural power.

"I pulled the string of the whistle, and I did this because I saw the pil-grims on deck getting out their rifles with an air of anticipating a jolly lark. At the sudden screech there was a movement of abject terror through that wedged mass of bodies. 'Don't! don't! you frighten them away,' cried some-one on deck disconsolately. I pulled the string time after time. They broke and ran, they leaped, they crouched, they swerved, they dodged the flying terror of the sound. The three red chaps had fallen flat, face down on the shore, as though they had been shot dead. Only the barbarous and superb woman did not so much as flinch, and stretched tragically her bare arms after us over the sombre and glittering river.

"And then that imbecile crowd down on the deck started their little fun, and I could see nothing more for smoke.

"The brown current ran swiftly out of the heart of darkness, bearing us down towards the sea with twice the speed of our upward progress; and Kurtz's life was running swiftly too, ebbing, ebbing out of his heart into the sea of inexorable time. The manager was very placid, he had no vital anxieties now, he took us both in with a comprehensive and satisfied glance: the 'affair' had come off as well as could be wished. I saw the time approaching when I would be left alone of the party of 'unsound method.' The pilgrims looked upon me with disfavour. I was, so to speak, numbered with the dead. It is strange how I accepted this unforeseen partnership, this choice of nightmares forced upon me in the tenebrous land invaded by these mean and greedy phantoms.

"Kurtz discoursed. A voice! a voice! It rang deep to the very last. It survived his strength to hide in the magnificent folds of eloquence the barren darkness of his heart. Oh, he struggled! he struggled! The wastes of his weary brain were haunted by shadowy images now—images of wealth and fame revolving obsequiously round his unextinguishable gift of noble and lofty expression. My Intended, my station, my career, my ideas—these were the subjects for the occasional utterances of elevated sentiments. The shade of the original Kurtz frequented the bedside of the hollow sham, whose fate it was to be buried presently in the mould of primeval earth. But both the diabolic love and the unearthly hate of the mysteries it had penetrated fought for the possession of that soul satiated with primitive emotions, avid of lying fame, of sham distinction, of all the appearances of success and power.

"Sometimes he was contemptibly childish. He desired to have kings meet him at railway-stations[59] on his return from some ghastly Nowhere, where he intended to accomplish great things. 'You show them you have in you something that is really profitable, and then there will be no limits to the recognition of your ability,' he would say. 'Of course you must take care of the motives—right motives—always.' The long reaches that were like one and the same reach, monotonous bends that were exactly alike, slipped past the steamer with their multitude of secular[60] trees looking patiently after this grimy fragment of another world, the forerunner of change, of con-

---

[59] In 1878, when Henry Morton Stanley arrived at the Marseilles Railway Station, he was met by emissaries of King Leopold II of Belgium. [ED.]
[60] In this context, "aged" or "ancient." [ED.]

quest, of trade, of massacres, of blessings. I looked ahead—piloting. 'Close the shutter,' said Kurtz suddenly one day; 'I can't bear to look at this.' I did so. There was a silence. 'Oh, but I will wring your heart yet!' he cried at the invisible wilderness.

"We broke down—as I had expected—and had to lie up for repairs at the head of an island. This delay was the first thing that shook Kurtz's confidence. One morning he gave me a packet of papers and a photograph—the lot tied together with a shoe-string. 'Keep this for me,' he said. 'This noxious fool' (meaning the manager) 'is capable of prying into my boxes when I am not looking.' In the afternoon I saw him. He was lying on his back with closed eyes, and I withdrew quietly, but I heard him mutter, 'Live rightly, die, die . . .' I listened. There was nothing more. Was he rehearsing some speech in his sleep, or was it a fragment of a phrase from some newspaper article? He had been writing for the papers and meant to do so again, 'for the furthering of my ideas. It's a duty.'

"His was an impenetrable darkness. I looked at him as you peer down at a man who is lying at the bottom of a precipice where the sun never shines. But I had not much time to give him, because I was helping the engine-driver to take to pieces the leaky cylinders, to straighten a bent connecting-rod, and in other such matters. I lived in an infernal mess of rust, filings, nuts, bolts, spanners, hammers, ratchet-drills—things I abominate, because I don't get on with them. I tended the little forge we fortunately had aboard; I toiled wearily in a wretched scrap-heap—unless I had the shakes too bad to stand.

"One evening coming in with a candle I was startled to hear him say a little tremulously, 'I am lying here in the dark waiting for death.' The light was within a foot of his eyes. I forced myself to murmur, 'Oh, nonsense!' and stood over him as if transfixed.

"Anything approaching the change that came over his features I have never seen before, and hope never to see again. Oh, I wasn't touched. I was fascinated. It was as though a veil had been rent. I saw on that ivory face the expression of sombre pride, of ruthless power, of craven terror—of an intense and hopeless despair. Did he live his life again in every detail of desire, temptation, and surrender during that supreme moment of complete knowledge? He cried in a whisper at some image, at some vision—he cried out twice, a cry that was no more than a breath—

"'The horror! The horror!'

"I blew the candle out and left the cabin. The pilgrims were dining in the mess-room, and I took my place opposite the manager, who lifted his eyes to give me a questioning glance, which I successfully ignored. He leaned back, serene, with that peculiar smile of his sealing the unexpressed depths of his meanness. A continuous shower of small flies streamed upon the lamp, upon the cloth, upon our hands and faces. Suddenly the manager's boy put his insolent black head in the doorway, and said in a tone of scathing contempt—

"'Mistah Kurtz—he dead.'

"All the pilgrims rushed out to see. I remained, and went on with my dinner. I believe I was considered brutally callous. However, I did not eat much. There was a lamp in there—light, don't you know—and outside it was so beastly, beastly dark. I went no more near the remarkable man who had pronounced a judgment upon the adventures of his soul on this earth. The voice was gone. What else had been there? But I am of course aware that next day the pilgrims buried something in a muddy hole.

"And then they very nearly buried me.

"However, as you see, I did not go to join Kurtz there and then. I did not. I remained to dream the nightmare out to the end, and to show my loyalty to Kurtz once more. Destiny. My destiny! Droll thing life is—that mysterious arrangement of merciless logic for a futile purpose. The most you can hope from it is some knowledge of yourself—that comes too late— a crop of unextinguishable regrets. I have wrestled with death. It is the most unexciting contest you can imagine. It takes place in an impalpable greyness, with nothing underfoot, with nothing around, without spectators, without clamour, without glory, without the great desire of victory, without the great fear of defeat, in a sickly atmosphere of tepid scepticism, without much belief in your own right, and still less in that of your adversary. If such is the form of ultimate wisdom, then life is a greater riddle than some of us think it to be. I was within a hair's-breadth of the last opportunity for pronouncement, and I found with humiliation that probably I would have nothing to say. This is the reason why I affirm that Kurtz was a remarkable man. He had something to say. He said it. Since I had peeped over the edge myself, I understand better the meaning of his stare, that could not see the flame of the candle, but was wide enough to embrace the whole universe, piercing enough to penetrate all the hearts that beat in the darkness. He had summed up—he had judged. 'The horror!' He was a remarkable man. After all, this was the expression of some sort of belief; it had candour, it had conviction, it had a vibrating note of revolt in its whisper, it had the appalling face of a glimpsed truth—the strange commingling of desire and hate. And it is not my own extremity I remember best—a vision of greyness without form filled with physical pain, and a careless contempt for the evanescence of all things—even of this pain itself. No! It is his extremity that I seem to have lived through. True, he had made that last stride, he had stepped over the edge, while I had been permitted to draw back my hesitating foot. And perhaps in this is the whole difference; perhaps all the wisdom, and all truth, and all sincerity, are just compressed into that inappreciable moment of time in which we step over the threshold of the invisible. Perhaps! I like to think my summing-up would not have been a word of careless contempt. Better his cry—much better. It was an affirmation, a moral victory paid for by innumerable defeats, by abominable terrors, by abominable satisfactions. But it was a victory! That is why I have remained loyal to Kurtz to the last, and even beyond, when a long time after I heard once more, not his own voice, but the echo of his magnificent eloquence thrown to me from a soul as translucently pure as a cliff of crystal.

"No, they did not bury me, though there is a period of time which I remember mistily, with a shuddering wonder, like a passage through some inconceivable world that had no hope in it and no desire. I found myself back in the sepulchral city resenting the sight of people hurrying through the streets to filch a little money from each other, to devour their infamous cookery, to gulp their unwholesome beer, to dream their insignificant and silly dreams. They trespassed upon my thoughts. They were intruders whose knowledge of life was to me an irritating pretence, because I felt so sure they could not possibly know the things I knew. Their bearing, which was simply the bearing of commonplace individuals going about their business in the assurance of perfect safety, was offensive to me like the outrageous flauntings of folly in the face of a danger it is unable to comprehend. I had no particular desire to enlighten them, but I had some difficulty in restraining myself from laughing in their faces, so full of stupid importance. I daresay I was not very well at that time. I tottered about the streets—there were various affairs to settle—grinning bitterly at perfectly respectable persons. I admit my behaviour was inexcusable, but then my temperature was seldom normal in these days. My dear aunt's endeavours to 'nurse up my strength' seemed altogether beside the mark. It was not my strength that wanted nursing, it was my imagination that wanted soothing. I kept the bundle of papers given me by Kurtz, not knowing exactly what to do with it. His mother had died lately, watched over, as I was told, by his Intended. A clean-shaved man, with an official manner and wearing gold-rimmed spectacles, called on me one day and made inquiries, at first circuitous, afterwards suavely pressing, about what he was pleased to denominate certain 'documents.' I was not surprised, because I had had two rows with the manager on the subject out there. I had refused to give up the smallest scrap out of that package, and I took the same attitude with the spectacled man. He became darkly menacing at last, and with much beat argued that the Company had the right to every bit of information about its 'territories.' And, said he, 'Mr. Kurtz's knowledge of unexplored regions must have been necessarily extensive and peculiar—owing to his great abilities and to the deplorable circumstances in which he had been placed: there-fore—' I assured him Mr. Kurtz's knowledge, however extensive, did not bear upon the problems of commerce or administration. He invoked then the name of science. 'It would be an incalculable loss if,' &c., &c. I offered him the report on the 'Suppression of Savage Customs,' with the post-scriptum torn off. He took it up eagerly, but ended by sniffing at it with an air of contempt. 'This is not what we had a right to expect,' he remarked. 'Expect nothing else,' I said. 'There are only private letters.' He withdrew upon some threat of legal proceedings, and I saw him no more; but another fellow, calling himself Kurtz's cousin, appeared two days later, and was anxious to hear all the details about his dear relative's last moments. Inci-dentally he gave me to understand that Kurtz had been essentially a great musician. 'There was the making of an immense success,' said the man, who was an organist, I believe, with lank grey hair flowing over a greasy coat-collar. I had no reason to doubt his statement; and to this day I am un-able to say what was Kurtz's profession, whether he ever had any—which was the greatest of his talents. I had taken him for a painter who wrote for the papers, or else for a journalist who could paint—but even the cousin (who took snuff⁶¹ during the interview) could not tell me what he had been—exactly. He was a universal genius—on that point I agreed with the old chap, who thereupon blew his nose noisily into a large cotton hand-kerchief and withdrew in senile agitation, bearing off some family letters and memoranda without importance. Ultimately a journalist anxious to know something of the fate of his 'dear colleague' turned up. This visitor informed me Kurtz's proper sphere ought to have been politics 'on the popular side.' He had furry straight eyebrows, bristly hair cropped short, an eye-glass on a broad ribbon, and, becoming expansive, confessed his opinion that Kurtz really couldn't write a bit—'but heavens! how that man could talk! He electrified large meetings. He had faith—don't you see?—he had the faith. He could get himself to believe anything—anything. He would have been a splendid leader of an extreme party.' 'What party?' I asked. 'Any party,' answered the other. 'He was an—an—extremist.' Did I not think so? I assented. Did I know, he asked, with a sudden flash of cu-riosity, 'what it was that had induced him to go out there?' 'Yes,' said I, and forthwith handed him the famous Report for publication, if he thought fit. He glanced through it hurriedly, mumbling all the time, judged 'it would do,' and took himself off with this plunder.

---

⁶¹Powdered tobacco inhaled through the nostrils; an upper-class affectation long before the late nineteenth century. [ED.]

"Thus I was left at last with a slim packet of letters and the girl's portrait. She struck me as beautiful—I mean she had a beautiful expression. I know that the sunlight can be made to lie too, yet one felt that no manipulation of light and pose could have conveyed the delicate shade of truthfulness upon those features. She seemed ready to listen without mental reservation, without suspicion, without a thought for herself. I concluded I would go and give her back her portrait and those letters myself. Curiosity? Yes; and also some other feeling perhaps. All that had been Kurtz's had passed out of my hands: his soul, his body, his station, his plans, his ivory, his career. There remained only his memory and his Intended—and I wanted to give that up too to the past, in a way—to surrender personally all that remained of him with me to that oblivion which is the last word of our common fate. I don't defend myself. I had no clear perception of what it was I really wanted. Perhaps it was an impulse of unconscious loyalty, or the fulfilment of one of those ironic necessities that lurk in the facts of human existence. I don't know. I can't tell. But I went.

"I thought his memory was like the other memories of the dead that accumulate in every man's life—a vague impress on the brain of shadows that had fallen on it in their swift and final passage; but before the high and ponderous door, between the tall houses of a street as still and decorous as a well-kept alley in a cemetery, I had a vision of him on the stretcher, opening his mouth voraciously, as if to devour all the earth with all its mankind. He lived then before me; he lived as much as he had ever lived—a shadow insatiable of splendid appearances, of frightful realities; a shadow darker than the shadow of the night, and draped nobly in the folds of a gorgeous eloquence. The vision seemed to enter the house with me—the stretcher, the phantom-bearers, the wild crowd of obedient worshippers, the gloom of the forests, the glitter of the reach between the murky bends, the beat of the drum, regular and muffled like the beating of a heart—the heart of a conquering darkness. It was a moment of triumph for the wilderness, an invading and vengeful rush which, it seemed to me, I would have to keep back alone for the salvation of another soul. And the memory of what I had heard him say afar there, with the horned shapes stirring at my back, in the glow of fires, within the patient woods, those broken phrases came back to me, were heard again in their ominous and terrifying simplicity. I remembered his abject pleading, his abject threats, the colossal scale of his vile desires, the meanness, the torment, the tempestuous anguish of his soul. And later on I seemed to see his collected languid manner, when he said one day, 'This lot of ivory now is really mine. The Company did not pay for it. I collected it myself at a very great personal risk. I am afraid they will try to claim it as theirs though. H'm. It is a difficult case. What do you think I ought to do—resist? Eh? I want no more than justice.' . . . He wanted no more than justice—no more than justice. I rang the bell before a mahogany door on the first floor, and while I waited he seemed to stare at me out of the glassy panel—stare with that wide and immense stare embracing, condemning, loathing all the universe. I seemed to hear the whispered cry, 'The horror! The horror!'

"The dusk was falling. I had to wait in a lofty drawing-room with three long windows from floor to ceiling that were like three luminous and bedraped columns. The bent gilt legs and backs of the furniture shone in indistinct curves. The tall marble fireplace had a cold and monumental whiteness. A grand piano stood massively in a corner, with dark gleams on the flat surfaces like a sombre and polished sarcophagus. A high door opened—closed. I rose.

"She came forward, all in black, with a pale head, floating towards me in the dusk. She was in mourning. It was more than a year since his death, more than a year since the news came; she seemed as though she would remember and mourn for ever. She took both my hands in hers and murmured, 'I had heard you were coming.' I noticed she was not very young—I mean not girlish. She had a mature capacity for fidelity, for belief, for suffering. The room seemed to have grown darker, as if all the sad light of the cloudy evening had taken refuge on her forehead. This fair hair, this pale visage, this pure brow, seemed surrounded by an ashy halo from which the dark eyes looked out at me. Their glance was guileless, profound, confident, and trustful. She carried her sorrowful head as though she were proud of that sorrow, as though she would say, I—I alone know how to mourn for him as he deserves. But while we were still shaking hands, such a look of awful desolation came upon her face that I perceived she was one of those creatures that are not the playthings of Time. For her he had died only yesterday. And, by Jove! the impression was so powerful that for me too he seemed to have died only yesterday—nay, this very minute. I saw her and him in the same instant of time—his death and her sorrow—I saw her sorrow in the very moment of his death. Do you understand? I saw them together—I heard them together. She had said, with a deep catch of the breath, 'I have survived'; while my strained ears seemed to hear distinctly, mingled with her tone of despairing regret, the summing-up whisper of his eternal condemnation. I asked myself what I was doing there, with a sensation of panic in my heart as though I had blundered into a place of cruel and absurd mysteries not fit for a human being to behold. She motioned me to a chair. We sat down. I laid the packet gently on the little table, and she put her hand over it. . . . 'You knew him well,' she murmured, after a moment of mourning silence.

"'Intimacy grows quickly out there,' I said. 'I knew him as well as it is possible for one man to know another.'

"'And you admired him,' she said. 'It was impossible to know him and not to admire him. Was it?'

"'He was a remarkable man,' I said, unsteadily. Then before the appealing fixity of her gaze, that seemed to watch for more words on my lips, I went on, 'It was impossible not to—'

"'Love him,' she finished eagerly, silencing me into an appalled dumbness. 'How true! how true! But when you think that no one knew him so well as I! I had all his noble confidence. I knew him best.'

"'You knew him best,' I repeated. And perhaps she did. But with every word spoken the room was growing darker, and only her forehead, smooth and white, remained illumined by the unextinguishable light of belief and love.

"'You were his friend,' she went on. 'His friend,' she repeated, a little louder. 'You must have been, if he had given you this, and sent you to me. I feel I can speak to you—and oh! I must speak. I want you—you who have heard his last words—to know I have been worthy of him. . . . It is not pride. . . . Yes! I am proud to know I understood him better than any one on earth—he told me so himself. And since his mother died I have had no one—no one—to—to—'

"I listened. The darkness deepened. I was not even sure whether he had given me the right bundle. I rather suspect he wanted me to take care of another batch of his papers which, after his death, I saw the manager examining under the lamp. And the girl talked, easing her pain in the certitude of my sympathy; she talked as thirsty men drink. I had heard that her engagement with Kurtz had been disapproved by her people. He wasn't rich enough or something. And indeed I don't know whether he had not been a pauper all his life. He had given me some reason to infer that it was his impatience of comparative poverty that drove him out there.

"'. . . Who was not his friend who had heard him speak once?' she was saying. 'He drew men towards him by what was best in them.' She looked at me with intensity. 'It is the gift of the great,' she went on, and the sound of her low voice seemed to have the accompaniment of all the other sounds, full of mystery, desolation, and sorrow, I had ever heard—the ripple of the river, the soughing of the trees swayed by the wind, the murmurs of wild crowds, the faint ring of incomprehensible words cried from afar, the whisper of a voice speaking from beyond the threshold of an eternal darkness. 'But you have heard him! You know!' she cried.

"'Yes, I know,' I said with something like despair in my heart, but bowing my head before the faith that was in her, before that great and saving illusion that shone with an unearthly glow in the darkness, in the triumphant darkness from which I could not have defended her—from which I could not even defend myself.

"'What a loss to me—to us!'—she corrected herself with beautiful generosity; then added in a murmur, 'To the world.' By the last gleams of twilight I could see the glitter of her eyes, full of tears—of tears that would not fall.

"'I have been very happy—very fortunate—very proud,' she went on. 'Too fortunate. Too happy for a little while. And now I am unhappy for—for life.'

"She stood up. Her fair hair seemed to catch all the remaining light in a glimmer of gold. I rose too.

"'And of all this,' she went on, mournfully, 'of all his promise, and of all his greatness, of his generous mind, of his noble heart, nothing remains—nothing but a memory. You and I—'

"'We shall always remember him,' I said, hastily.

"'No!' she cried. 'It is impossible that all this should be lost—that such a life should be sacrificed to leave nothing—but sorrow. You know what vast plans he had. I knew of them too—I could not perhaps understand—but others knew of them. Something must remain. His words, at least, have not died.'

"'His words will remain,' I said.

"'And his example,' she whispered to herself. 'Men looked up to him—his goodness shone in every act. His example—'

"'True,' I said; 'his example too. Yes, his example. I forgot that.'

"'But I do not. I cannot—I cannot believe—not yet. I cannot believe that I shall never see him again, that nobody will see him again, never, never, never.'

"She put out her arms as if after a retreating figure, stretching them black and with clasped pale hands across the fading and narrow sheen of the window. Never see him! I saw him clearly enough then. I shall see this eloquent phantom as long as I live, and I shall see her too, a tragic and familiar Shade, resembling in this gesture another one, tragic also, and bedecked with powerless charms, stretching bare brown arms over the glitter of the infernal stream, the stream of darkness. She said suddenly very low, 'He died as he lived.'

"'His end,' said I, with dull anger stirring in me, 'was in every way worthy of his life.'

"'And I was not with him,' she murmured. My anger subsided before a feeling of infinite pity.

"'Everything that could be done—' I mumbled.

"'Ah, but I believed in him more than any one on earth—more than his own mother, more than—himself. He needed me! Me! I would have treasured every sigh, every word, every sign, every glance.'

"I felt like a chill grip on my chest. 'Don't,' I said, in a muffled voice.

"'Forgive me. I—I—have mourned so long in silence—in silence. . . . You were with him—to the last? I think of his loneliness. Nobody near to understand him as I would have understood. Perhaps no one to hear . . .'

"'To the very end,' I said, shakily. 'I heard his very last words. . . .' I stopped in a fright.

"'Repeat them,' she said in a heart-broken tone. 'I want—I want—something—something—to—to live with.'

"I was on the point of crying at her, 'Don't you hear them?' The dusk was repeating them in a persistent whisper all around us, in a whisper that seemed to swell menacingly like the first whisper of a rising wind. 'The horror! the horror!'

"'His last word—to live with,' she murmured. 'Don't you understand I loved him—I loved him—I loved him!'

"I pulled myself together and spoke slowly.

"'The last word he pronounced was—your name.'

"I heard a light sigh, and then my heart stood still, stopped dead short by an exulting and terrible cry, by the cry of inconceivable triumph and of unspeakable pain. 'I knew it—I was sure!' . . . She knew. She was sure. I heard her weeping; she had hidden her face in her hands. It seemed to me that the house would collapse before I could escape, that the heavens would fall upon my head. But nothing happened. The heavens do not fall[62] for such a trifle. Would they have fallen, I wonder, if I had rendered Kurtz that justice which was his due? Hadn't he said he wanted only justice? But I couldn't. I could not tell her. It would have been too dark—too dark altogether. . . ."

Marlow ceased, and sat apart, indistinct and silent, in the pose of a meditating Buddha. Nobody moved for a time. "We have lost the first of the ebb," said the Director, suddenly. I raised my head. The offing was barred by a black bank of clouds, and the tranquil waterway leading to the uttermost ends of the earth flowed sombre under an overcast sky—seemed to lead into the heart of an immense darkness.

---

[62]Echoing ironically the Latin proverb, *Fiat justitia, ruat coelum* ("Let justice be done, though the heavens fall"). [ED.]

Part Four

ANCILLARY TEXTS

RECESSIONAL[1]

Rudyard Kipling

God of our fathers, known of old,
  Lord of our far-flung battle-line,
Beneath whose awful Hand we hold
  Dominion over palm and pine—
5 Lord god of Hosts, be with us yet,
Lest we forget—lest we forget!

The tumult and the shouting dies;
  The captains and the kings depart:
Still stands Thine ancient sacrifice,
10   An humble and a contrite heart.
Lord God of Hosts, be with us yet,
Lest we forget—lest we forget!

Far-called, our navies melt away;
  On dune and headland sinks the fire:
15 Lo, all our pomp of yesterday
    Is one with Nineveh and Tyre![2]
Judge of the Nations, spare us yet,
Lest we forget—lest we forget!

If, drunk with sight of power, we loose
20   Wild tongues that have not Thee in awe,
Such boastings as the Gentiles use,

From *The Five Nations.* New York: Doubleday, 1903. 214–15.

[1]"Recessional" was originally published on the front page of the *Times* on 17 July 1897. It appeared opposite Queen Victoria's Jubilee letter to the nation, written in the wake of her Jubilee Day—the celebration of her sixtieth year as Queen—which had been held on 22 June. A recessional hymn is sung while the clergy and choir are withdrawing to the vestry at the conclusion of a service.

[2]Nineveh was the capital city of ancient Assyria; Tyre, a seaport in Lebanon, was the center of Phoenician culture.

Or lesser breeds without the Law—
Lord God of Hosts, be with us yet,
Lest we forget—lest we forget!

25 For heathen heart that puts her trust
In reeking tube and iron shard,
All valiant dust that builds on dust,
And guarding, calls not Thee to guard,
For frantic boast and foolish word—
30 Thy Mercy on thy People, Lord!

                          Amen.

THE WHITE MAN'S BURDEN[1]

Rudyard Kipling

Take up the White Man's burden—
    Send forth the best ye breed—
Go bind your sons to exile
    To serve your captives' need;
5 To wait in heavy harness,
    On fluttered folk and wild—
Your new-caught, sullen peoples,
    Half-devil and half-child.

Take up the White Man's burden—
10   In patience to abide,
To veil the threat of terror
    And check the show of pride;
By open speech and simple,
    An hundred times made plain,
15 To seek another's profit,
    And work another's gain.

Take up the White Man's burden—
    The savage wars of peace—

From *The Five Nations.* New York: Doubleday, 1903. 79–81.

[1] Originally published in the *Times* on 4 February 1899 and in the *New York Sun* on 5 February 1899, "The White Man's Burden" was addressed to the United States at the conclusion of the Spanish-American War, which had resulted in the U.S. acquisition of Cuba and the Philippines as colonies.

Fill full the mouth of Famine
20   And bid the sickness cease;
And when your goal is nearest
The end for others sought,
Watch Sloth and heathen Folly
Bring all your hope to nought.

25 Take up the White Man's burden —
No tawdry rule of kings,
But toil of serf and sweeper —
The tale of common things.
The ports ye shall not enter,
30   The roads ye shall not tread,
Go make them with your living,
And mark them with our dead.

Take up the White Man's burden —
And reap his old reward:
35 The blame of those ye better,
The hate of those ye guard —
The cry of hosts ye humour
(Ah, slowly!) toward the light: —
"Why brought ye us from bondage,
40   Our loved Egyptian night?"

Take up the White Man's burden —
Ye dare not stoop to less —
Nor call too loud on Freedom
To cloak your weariness;
45 By all ye cry or whisper,
By all ye leave or do,
The silent, sullen peoples
Shall weigh your Gods and you.

Take up the White Man's burden —
50   Have done with childish days —
The lightly proffered laurel,
The easy, ungrudged praise.
Comes now, to search your manhood
Through all the thankless years,
55 Cold, edged with dear-bought wisdom,
The judgment of your peers!

From IN THE SOUTH SEAS

Robert Louis Stevenson

For nearly ten years my health had been declining;[1] and for some while before I set forth upon my voyage, I believed I was come to the afterpiece of life, and had only the nurse and undertaker to expect. It was suggested that I should try the South Seas; and I was not unwilling to visit like a ghost, and be carried like a bale, among scenes that had attracted me in youth and health. I chartered accordingly Dr. Merrit's schooner yacht, the *Casco*, seventy-four tons register; sailed from San Francisco towards the end of June 1888, visited the eastern islands,[2] and was left early the next year at Honolulu. Hence, lacking courage to return to my old life of the house and sick-room, I set forth to leeward[3] in a trading schooner, the *Equator*, of a little over seventy tons, spent four months among the atolls (low coral-islands) of the Gilbert group, and reached Samoa towards the close of '89. By that time gratitude and habit were beginning to attach me to the islands; I had gained a competency of strength; I had made friends; I had learned new interests; the time of my voyages had passed like days in fairyland; and I decided to remain. I began to prepare these pages at sea, on a third cruise, in the trading-steamer *Janet Nicoll*. If more days are granted me, they shall be passed where I have found life most pleasant and man most interesting; the axes of my black boys are already clearing the foundations of my future house; and I must learn to address readers from the uttermost parts of the sea.

That I should thus have reversed the verdict of Lord Tennyson's hero[4] is less eccentric than appears. Few men who come to the islands leave them; they grow grey where they alighted; the palm-shades and the trade-wind fans them till they die, perhaps cherishing to the last the fancy of a visit home, which is rarely made, more rarely enjoyed, and yet more rarely re-

Leipzig: Bernhard Tauchnitz, 1901. 9–11, 39–41, 43–45, 46–48, 51–53.

[1] Stevenson suffered all his life from a dangerous and debilitating lung condition, for which he had sought relief in a number of different climates—the Alps, the south of France, the southwest coast of England, and the pine forests of northern New York State. None of these had brought significant improvement, and he had come close to dying numerous times. In the climate of Samoa, however, he discovered immediate relief and enjoyed reasonably good health from his arrival there in December 1889 until his death in December 1894, of a cerebral hemorrhage. [ED.]

[2] The Marquesas, the Paumotus, and the Society Islands. [ED.]

[3] Downwind; in this case, westward. [ED.]

[4] An allusion to Alfred Lord Tennyson's "Ulysses" (1833). [ED.]

peated. No part of the world exerts the same attractive power upon the visitor, and the task before me is to communicate to fireside travellers some sense of its seduction, and to describe the life, at sea and ashore, of many hundred thousand persons, some of our own blood and language, all our contempararies, and yet as remote in thought and habit as Rob Roy or Barbarossa,[5] the Apostles or the Cæsars. [. . .]

At the top of the den there dwelt an old, melancholy, grizzled man of the name of Tari (Charlie) Coffin. He was a native of Oahu, in the Sandwich Islands;[6] and had gone to sea in his youth in the American whalers; a circumstance to which he owed his name, his English, his down-east twang, and the misfortune of his innocent life. For one captain, sailing out of New Bedford, carried him to Nuka-hiva and marooned him there among the cannibals. The motive for this act was inconceivably small; poor Tari's wages, which were thus economised, would scarce have shook the credit of the New Bedford owners. And the act itself was simply murder. Tari's life must have hung in the beginning by a hair. In the grief and terror of that time, it is not unlikely he went mad, an infirmity to which he was still liable; or perhaps a child may have taken a fancy to him and ordained him to be spared. He escaped at least alive, married in the island, and when I knew him was a widower with a married son and a granddaughter. But the thought of Oahu haunted him; its praise was forever on his lips; he beheld it, looking back, as a place of ceaseless feasting, song, and dance; and in his dreams I daresay he revisits it with joy. I wonder what he would think if he could be carried there indeed, and see the modern town of Honolulu brisk with traffic, and the palace with its guards, and the great hotel, and Mr. Berger's band with their uniforms and outlandish instruments; or what he would think to see the brown faces grown so few and the white so many; and his father's land sold for planting sugar, and his father's house quite perished, or perhaps the last of them struck leprous and immured between the surf and the cliffs on Molokai?[7] So simply, even in South Sea Islands, and so sadly, the changes come.

Tari was poor, and poorly lodged. His house was a wooden frame, run up by Europeans; it was indeed his official residence, for Tari was the shepherd of the promontory sheep. I can give a perfect inventory of its

---

[5] In early-eighteenth-century Scotland, Rob Roy Macgregor was a romantic outlaw and an enemy of the British occupying forces. *Barbarossa* ("Red Beard") was the nickname of the twelfth-century emperor Frederick I of Germany. [ED.]

[6] Now the Hawaiian Islands. [ED.]

[7] A famous leper colony was located on the island of Molokai, in the Hawaiian (Sandwich) Islands, on a small promontory that was sealed off from the rest of the island by impassable cliffs. [ED.]

contents: three kegs, a tin biscuit-box, an iron saucepan, several cocoa-shell cups, a lantern, and three bottles, probably containing oil; while the clothes of the family and a few mats were thrown across the open rafters. Upon my first meeting with this exile he had conceived for me one of the baseless island friendships, had given me nuts to drink, and carried me up the den "to see my house"—the only entertainment that he had to offer. He liked the "Amelican," he said, and the "Inglisman," but the "Flessman" was his abhorrence; and he was careful to explain that if he had thought us "Fless," we should have had none of his nuts, and never a sight of his house. His distaste for the French I can partly understand, but not at all his toleration of the Anglo-Saxon. The next day he brought me a pig, and some days later one of our party going ashore found him in act to bring a second. We were still strange to the island; we were pained by the poor man's generosity, which he could ill afford, and, by a natural enough but quite unpardonable blunder, we refused the pig. Had Tari been a Marquesan we should have seen him no more; being what he was, the most mild, long-suffering, melancholy man, he took a revenge a hundred times more painful. Scarce had the canoe with the nine villagers put off from their farewell before the *Casco* was boarded from the other side. It was Tari; coming thus late because he had no canoe of his own, and had found it hard to borrow one; coming thus solitary (as indeed we always saw him), because he was a stranger in the land, and the dreariest of company. The rest of my family basely fled from the encounter. I must receive our injured friend alone; and the interview must have lasted hard upon an hour, for he was loath to tear himself away. "You go 'way. I see you no more—no, sir!" he lamented; and then looking about him with rueful admiration, "This goodee ship—no, sir!—goodee ship!" he would exclaim: the "no, sir," thrown out sharply through the nose upon a rising inflection, an echo from New Bedford and the fallacious whaler. From these expressions of grief and praise, he would return continually to the case of the rejected pig. "I like give plesent all 'e same you," he complained; "only got pig: you no take him!" He was a poor man; he had no choice of gifts; he had only a pig, he repeated; and I had refused it. I have rarely been more wretched than to see him sitting there, so old, so grey, so poor, so hardly fortuned, of so rueful a countenance, and to appreciate, with growing keenness, the affront which I had so innocently dealt him; but it was one of those cases in which speech is vain.

Tari's son was smiling and inert; his daughter-in-law, a girl of sixteen, pretty, gentle, and grave, more intelligent than most Anaho[8] women, and

---

[8] A Marquesan tribe. [ED.]

with a fair share of French; his grandchild, a mite of a creature at the breast. I went up the den one day when Tari was from home, and found the son making a cotton sack, and madame suckling mademoiselle. When I had sat down with them on the floor, the girl began to question me about England; which I tried to describe, piling the pan and the cocoa shells one upon another to represent the houses, and explaining, as best I was able, and by word and gesture, the over-population, the hunger, and the perpetual toil. *"Pas de cocotiers? pas de popoi?"*[9] she asked. I told her it was too cold, and went through an elaborate performance, shutting out draughts, and crouching over an imaginary fire, to make sure she understood. But she understood right well; remarked it must be bad for the health, and sat awhile gravely reflecting on that picture of unwonted sorrows. I am sure it roused her pity, for it struck in her another thought always uppermost in the Marquesan bosom; and she began with a smiling sadness, and looking on me out of melancholy eyes, to lament the decease of her own people. *"Ici pas de Kanaques,"*[10] said she; and taking the baby from her breast, she held it out to me with both her hands. *"Tenez*[11]—a little baby like this; then dead. All the Kanaques die. Then no more." The smile, and this instancing by the girl-mother of her own tiny flesh and blood, affected me strangely; they spoke of so tranquil a despair. Meanwhile the husband smilingly made his sack; and the unconscious babe struggled to reach a pot of raspberry jam, friendship's offering, which I had just brought up the den; and in a perspective of centuries I saw their case as ours, death coming in like a tide, and the day already numbered when there should be no more Beretani,[12] and no more of any race whatever, and (what oddly touched me) no more literary works and no more readers. [. . .]

The thought of death, I have said, is uppermost in the mind of the Marquesan. It would be strange if it were otherwise. The race is perhaps the handsomest extant. Six feet is about the middle height of males; they are strongly muscled, free from fat, swift in action, graceful in repose; and the women, though fatter and duller, are still comely animals. To judge by the eye, there is no race more viable; and yet death reaps them with both hands. When Bishop Dordillon first came to Tai-o-hae, he reckoned the inhabitants at many thousands; he was but newly dead, and in the same bay

---

[9] "No coconut trees? No breadfruit?" [ED.]

[10] Literally: "Here no Kanakas." (*Kanaka* is a Polynesian word meaning either "man" or "mankind," which was used by Europeans to refer derogatively to natives.) [ED.]

[11] "Look" or "see here." [ED.]

[12] Pidgin pronunciation of *Britain.* [ED.]

Stanislao Moanatini counted on his fingers eight residual natives.[13] Or take the valley of Hapaa, known to readers of Herman Melville under the grotesque misspelling of Hapar. There are but two writers who have touched the South Seas with any genius, both Americans: Melville and Charles Warren Stoddard;[14] and at the christening of the first and greatest, some influential fairy must have been neglected: "He shall be able to see," "He shall be able to tell," "He shall be able to charm," said the friendly godmothers; "But he shall not be able to hear," exclaimed the last. The tribe of Hapaa is said to have numbered some four hundred, when the smallpox came and reduced them by one-fourth. Six months later a woman developed tubercular consumption; the disease spread like a fire about the valley, and in less than a year two survivors, a man and a woman, fled from that new-created solitude. A similar Adam and Eve may some day wither among new races, the tragic residue of Britain. When I first heard this story the date staggered me; but I am now inclined to think it possible. Early in the year of my visit,[15] for example, or late the year before, a first case of phthisis appeared in a household of seventeen persons, and by the month of August, when the tale was told me, one soul survived, and that was a boy who had been absent at his schooling. And depopulation works both ways, the doors of death being set wide open, and the door of birth almost closed. Thus, in the half-year ending July 1888 there were twelve deaths and but one birth in the district of the Hatiheu. Seven or eight more deaths were to be looked for in the ordinary course; and M. Aussel, the observant gendarme, knew of but one likely birth. At this rate it is no matter of surprise if the population in that part should have declined in forty years from six thousand to less than four hundred; which are, once more on the authority of M. Aussel, the estimated figures. And the rate of decline must have even accelerated towards the end. [. . .]

The Marquesan beholds with dismay the approaching extinction of his race. The thought of death sits down with him to meat, and rises with him from his bed; he lives and breathes under a shadow of mortality awful to

---

[13] René Ildefonse Dordillon, author of grammars and dictionaries of the Polynesian language, was Bishop of the Marquesas from 1855 until his death in 1888. Tai-o-hae (more commonly spelled "Taiohae") is a large bay on the Marquesan island of Nuka Hiva, and the site of the largest harbor and settlement on the island. Stanislao Moanatini was a European-educated prince of one of the Marquesan tribes and a personal friend of Stevenson's. [ED.]

[14] Author of several books on the South Seas, including *Summer Cruising in the South Seas,* published in 1874. [ED.]

[15] 1888.

support; and he is so inured to the apprehension that he greets the reality with relief. He does not even seek to support a disappointment; at an affront, at a breach of one of his fleeting and communistic love-affairs, he seeks an instant refuge in the grave. Hanging is now the fashion. I heard of three who had hanged themselves in the west end of Hiva-oa during the first half of 1888; but though this be a common form of suicide in other parts of the South Seas, I cannot think it will continue popular in the Marquesas. Far more suitable to Marquesan sentiment is the old form of poisoning with the fruit of the eva, which offers to the native suicide a cruel but deliberate death, and gives time for those decencies of the last hour, to which he attaches such remarkable importance. The coffin can thus be at hand, the pigs killed, the cry of the mourners sounding already through the house; and then it is, and not before, that the Marquesan is conscious of achievement, his life all rounded in, his robes (like Cæsar's) adjusted for the final act. Praise not any man till he is dead, said the ancients; envy not any man till you hear the mourners, might be the Marquesan parody. The coffin, though of late introduction, strangely engages their attention. It is to the mature Marquesan what a watch is to the European schoolboy. For ten years Queen Vaekehu had dunned the fathers; at last, but the other day, they let her have her will, gave her her coffin, and the woman's soul is at rest. I was told a droll instance of the force of this preoccupation. The Polynesians are subject to a disease seemingly rather of the will than of the body. I was told the Tahitians have a word for it, *erimatua,* but cannot find it in my dictionary. A gendarme, M. Nouveau, has seen men beginning to succumb to this insubstantial malady, has routed them from their houses, turned them on to do their trick upon the roads, and in two days has seen them cured. But this other remedy is more original: a Marquesan, dying of this discouragement—perhaps I should rather say this acquiescence—has been known, at the fulfilment of his crowning wish, on the mere sight of that desired hermitage, his coffin—to revive, recover, shake off the hand of death, and be restored for years to his occupations—carving tikis (idols), let us say, or braiding old men's beards. From all this it may be conceived how easily they meet death when it approaches naturally. I heard one example, grim and picturesque. In the time of the smallpox in Hapaa, an old man was seized with the disease; he had no thought of recovery; had his grave dug by a wayside, and lived in it for near a fortnight, eating, drinking, and smoking with the passers-by, talking mostly of his end, and equally unconcerned for himself and careless of the friends whom he infected.

This proneness to suicide, and loose seat in life, is not peculiar to the Marquesan. What is peculiar is the widespread depression and acceptance of the national end. Pleasures are neglected, the dance languishes, the songs are forgotten. It is true that some, and perhaps too many, of them are proscribed; but many remain, if there were spirit to support or to revive them.

From A LETTER TO THE *TIMES*

Robert Louis Stevenson

Sir, I last addressed you on the misconduct of certain officials here, and I was so far happy as to have had my facts confirmed in every particular with but one exception. That exception, the affair of the dynamite,[1] has been secretly smuggled away; you shall look in vain in either Blue Book or White Book[2] for any mention even of the charge; it is gone like the conjuror's orange. I might have been tempted to inquire into the reason of this conspiracy of silence, whether the idea was conceived in the bosoms of the three Powers[3] themselves, or whether in the breasts of the three Consuls because one of their number was directly implicated. And I might have gone on to consider the moral effect of such suppressions, and to show how very idle they were, and how very undignified, in the face of a small and compact population, where everybody sees and hears, where everybody knows, and talks, and laughs. But only a personal question remained, which I judged of no interest to the public. The essential was accomplished. Baron Senft[4] was gone already. Mr. Cedercrantz still lingered among us in the character (I may say) of a private citizen, his Court at last closed, only his pocket open for the receipt of his salary, representing the dignity of the

---

Times 2 June 1894. 17.

[1] Samoan prisoners taken during a political disturbance in 1891 were jailed in Apia, the central town on the main Samoan island of Upolu. A rumor was circulated — most probably by Baron Senfft von Pilsach's government — that the jail had been mined and that it would be blown up if natives attempted to liberate the prisoners. [ED.]

[2] A British Blue Book and a German White Book were published in 1893 on affairs in Samoa. Both substantiated a series of charges Stevenson had made about official misconduct (see Stevenson, *Letters* 1994–95: 8: 31, 87). [ED.]

[3] The three Powers are Britain, Germany, and the United States, which were vying with one another for political control in Samoa. Each nation had a consul, and the three consuls formed a Council of which one was president. [ED.]

[4] The German consul Baron Arnold Senfft von Pilsach (name misspelled in Stevenson's letter) was dismissed, partly as a result of Stevenson's successful agitation against him, in January 1893. Otto Conrad Waldemar Cedercrantz, chief justice of Samoa, was also dismissed by the German government at this time. [ED.]

Berlin Act[5] by sitting in the wind on Mulinuu Point[6] for several consecutive months—a curious phantom or survival of a past age. The new officials were not as yet, because they had not been created. And we fell into our old estate of Government by the three Consuls, as it was in the beginning before the Berlin Act existed; as it seems it will be till the end, after the Berlin Act has been swept away.

It was during the time of this Triumvirate, and wholly at their instigation and under their conduct, that Mataafa[7] was defeated, driven to Manono, and (three warships coming opportunely to hand) forced to surrender. I have been called a partisan of this chief's, and I accept the term. I thought him, on the whole, the most honest man in Samoa, not excepting white officials. I ventured to think he had been hardly used by the Treaty Powers; I venture to think so still. It was my opinion that he should have been conjoined with Malietoa[8] as Vice-King; and I have seen no reason to change that opinion, except that the time for it is past. Mataafa has played and lost; an exile, and stripped of his titles, he walks the exiguous beach of Jaluit,[9] sees the German flag over his head, and yearns for the land wind of Upolu. In the politics of Samoa he is no longer a factor; and it only remains to speak of the manner in which his rebellion was suppressed and punished. Deportation is, to the Samoan mind, the punishment next to death, and thirteen of the chiefs engaged were deported with their leader. Twenty-seven others were cast into the gaol. There they lie still; the Government makes almost no attempt to feed them, and they must depend on the activity of their families and the charity of pitying whites. In the meantime, these very families are overloaded with fines, the exorbitant sum of more than £6600 having been laid on the chiefs and villages that took part with Mataafa.

So far we can only complain that the punishments have been severe and the prison commissariat absent. But we have, besides, to regret the repeated

---

[5] The Berlin Treaty of 1889, signed by the three European powers, had resolved the civil war among native tribes (1887–89) that had been fomented by the Europeans. [ED.]

[6] A spit of land on one side of Apia harbor, occupied by the German government in Samoa. [ED.]

[7] The Samoan chief with the most popular support, who was thus anathema to the three European powers and who led the insurrection of 1893. Native settlements at Manono, an islet where Mataafa had taken shelter, were destroyed by German-backed native forces after Mataafa had surrendered. [ED.]

[8] An older chief who had been forcibly installed as Samoan king by the three powers in 1889. [ED.]

[9] An island in the Marshalls. [ED.]

scandals in connexion with the conduct of the war, and we look in vain for any sign of punishment. The Consuls had to employ barbarous hands; we might expect outrages; we did expect them to be punished, or at least disowned. Thus, certain Mataafa chiefs were landed, and landed from a British man-of-war, to be shamefully abused, beaten, and struck with whips along the main street of Mulinuu. There was no punishment, there was even no inquiry; the three Consuls winked. Only one man was found honest and bold enough to open his mouth, and that was my old enemy, Mr. Cedercrantz. Walking in Mulinuu, in his character of disinterested spectator, gracefully desipient,[10] he came across the throng of these rabblers and their victims. He had forgotten that he was an official, he remembered that he was a man. It was his last public appearance in Samoa to interfere; it was certainly his best. Again, the Government troops in the field took the heads of girls, a detestable felony even in Samoan eyes. They carried them in procession to Mulinuu, and made of them an oblation to that melancholy effigy the King, who (sore against his will) sat on the verandah of the Government building, publicly to receive this affront, publicly to utter the words of compliment and thanks which constitute the highest reward known to Samoan bravery, and crowned as heroes those who should have been hanged like dogs. And again the three Consuls unanimously winked. There was no punishment, there was even no inquiry.

Lastly, there is the story of Manono. Three hours were given to Mataafa to accept the terms of the ultimatum, and the time had almost elapsed when his boats put forth, and more than elapsed before he came alongside the *Katoomba* and surrendered formally to Captain Bickford.[11] In the dusk of the evening, when all the ships had sailed, flames were observed to rise from the island. Mataafa flung himself on his knees before Captain Bickford, and implored protection for his women and children left behind, and the captain put back the ship and despatched one of the Consuls to inquire. The *Katoomba* had been about seventy hours in the islands. Captain Bickford was a stranger; he had to rely on the Consuls implicitly. At the same time, he knew that the Government troops had been suffered to land for the purpose of restoring order, and with the understanding that no reprisals should be committed on the adherents of Mataafa; and he charged the emissary with his emphatic disapproval, threats of punishment on the offenders, and reminders that the war had now passed under the responsibility of the three Powers. I cannot condescend on what this Consul saw during his visit; I can only say what he reported on his return. He reported

---

[10] An archaic word, meaning foolish or idle trifling. [ED.]

[11] Andrew Kennedy Bickford was captain of the British warship HMS *Katoomba*. [ED.]

all well, and the chiefs on the Government side fraternising and making *ava*[12] with those on Mataafa's. It may have been; at least it is strange. The burning of the island proceeded, fruit-trees were cut down, women stripped naked; a scene of brutal disorder reigned all night, and left behind it, over a quarter of the island, ruin. If they fraternised with Mataafa's chieftains they must have been singularly inconsistent, for the next we learn of the two parties, they were beating, spitting upon, and insulting them along the highway. The next morning in Apia I asked the same Consul if there had not been some houses burned. He told me no. I repeated the question, alleging the evidence of officers on board the *Katoomba* who had seen the flames increase and multiply as they steamed away; whereupon he had this remarkable reply—"O! huts, huts, huts! There isn't a house, a frame house, on the island." The case to plain men stands thus:—The people of Manono were insulted, their food-trees cut down, themselves left houseless; not more than ten houses—I beg the Consul's pardon, huts—escaped the rancour of their enemies; and to this day they may be seen to dwell in shanties on the site of their former residences, the pride of the Samoan heart. The ejaculation of the Consul was thus at least prophetic; and the traveller who revisits today the shores of the "Garden Island" may well exclaim in his turn, "Huts, huts, huts!"

The same measure was served out, in the mere wantonness of clan-hatred, to Apolima, a nearly inaccessible islet in the straits of the same name; almost the only property saved there (it is amusing to remember) being a framed portrait of Lady Jersey,[13] which its custodian escaped with into the bush, as it were the palladium and chief treasure of the inhabitants. The solemn promise passed by Consuls and captains in the name of the three Powers was thus broken; the troops employed were allowed their bellyful of barbarous outrage. And again there was no punishment, there was no inquiry; there was no protest, there was not a word said to disown the act or disengage the honour of the three Powers. I do not say the Consuls desired to be disobeyed, though the case looks black against one gentleman, and even he is perhaps only to be accused of levity and divided interest; it was doubtless important for him to be early in Apia, where he combines with his diplomatic functions the management of a thriving business as commission agent and auctioneer. I do say of all of them that they took a very nonchalant view of their duty.

---

[12] Any intoxicating liquor. [ED.]

[13] Margaret Elizabeth, countess of Jersey, had visited Stevenson in Samoa in August 1892, and Stevenson had taken the delighted countess to visit the rebel chief, Mataafa, at his military encampment—an act that scandalized government officials both in Samoa and in London. [ED.]

I told myself that this was the Government of the Consular Triumvirate. When the new officials came it would cease; it would pass away like a dream in the night; and the solid *Pax Romana* of the Berlin General Act would succeed. After all, what was there to complain of? The Consuls had shown themselves no slovens and no sentimentalists. They had shown themselves not very particular, but in one sense very thorough. Rebellion was to be put down swiftly and rigorously, if need were with the hand of Cromwell;[14] at least it was to be put down. And in these unruly islands I was prepared almost to welcome the face of Rhadamanthine[15] severity.

And now it appears it was all a mistake. The Government by the Berlin General Act is no more than a mask, and a very expensive one, for Government by the Consular Triumvirate. Samoa pays (or tries to pay) £2200 a year to a couple of helpers; and they dare not call their souls their own. They take their walks abroad with an anxious eye on the three Consuls, like two well-behaved children with three nurses; and the Consuls, smiling superior, allow them to amuse themselves with the routine of business. But let trouble come, and the farce is suspended. At the whistle of a squall these heaven-born mariners seize the tiller, and the £2200 amateurs are knocked sprawling on the bilge. At the first beat of the drum, the Treaty officials are sent below, gently protesting, like a pair of old ladies, and behold! the indomitable Consuls ready to clear the wreck and make the deadly cutlass shine. And their method, studied under the light of a new example, wears another air. They are not so Rhadamanthine as we thought. Something that we can only call a dignified panic presides over their deliberations. They have one idea to lighten the ship. "Overboard with the ballast, the mainmast, and the chronometer!" is the cry. In the last war they got rid (first) of the honour of their respective countries, and (second) of all idea that Samoa was to be governed in a manner consistent with civilisation, or Government troops punished for any conceivable misconduct. In the present war they have sacrificed (first) the prestige of the new Chief Justice, and (second) the very principle for which they had contended so vigorously and so successfully in the war before—that rebellion was a thing to be punished. [. . .]

The crime of Mataafa is to have read strictly the first article of the Berlin Act, and not to have read at all (as how should he when it has never been

---

[14]Oliver Cromwell, Puritan leader of the English Revolution and head (Lord Protector) of the Commonwealth from 1653 to 1658, used brutal methods to suppress dissent, particularly in Ireland.

[15]Rhadamanthus, son of Zeus and Europa, was judge of the dead in the underworld of Greek mythology.

translated?) the insidious protocol which contains its significance; the crime of his followers is to have practised clan fidelity, and to have in consequence raised an *imperium in imperio*,[16] and fought against the Government. Their punishment is to be sent to a coral atoll and detained there prisoners. It does not sound much; it is a great deal. Taken from a mountain island, they must inhabit a narrow strip of reef sunk to the gunwale in the ocean. Sand, stone, and cocoanuts, stone, sand, and pandanus,[17] make the scenery. There is no grass. Here these men, used to the cool, bright mountain rivers of Samoa, must drink with loathing the brackish water of the coral. The food upon such islands is distressing even to the omnivorous white. To the Samoan, who has that shivering delicacy and ready disgust of the child or the rustic mountaineer, it is intolerable.

From GEOGRAPHY AND SOME EXPLORERS

Joseph Conrad

It is safe to say that for the majority of mankind the superiority of geography over geometry lies in the appeal of its figures. It may be an effect of the incorrigible frivolity inherent in human nature, but most of us will agree that a map is more fascinating to look at than a figure in a treatise on conic sections — at any rate for the simple minds which are all the equipment of the majority of the dwellers on this earth.

No doubt a trigonometrical survey may be a romantic undertaking, striding over deserts and leaping over valleys never before trodden by the foot of civilized man; but its accurate operations can never have for us the fascination of the first hazardous steps of a venturesome, often lonely, explorer jotting down by the light of his camp fire the thoughts, the impressions, and the toil of his day.

For a long time yet a few suggestive words grappling with things seen will have the advantage over a long array of precise, no doubt interesting, and even profitable figures. The earth is a stage, and though it may be an advantage, even to the right comprehension of the play, to know its exact configuration, it is the drama of human endeavour that will be the thing, with a ruling passion expressed by outward action marching perhaps blindly to

---

From *Last Essays*. New York: Doubleday, 1926. 1–4, 10–13, 15–18.

[16] A government within a government. [ED.]

[17] A family of trees and shrubs having daggerlike leaves.

success or failure, which themselves are often undistinguishable from each other at first.

Of all the sciences, geography finds its origin in action, and what is more, in adventurous action of the kind that appeals to sedentary people who like to dream of arduous adventure in the manner of prisoners dreaming behind bars of all the hardships and hazards of liberty dear to the heart of man.

Descriptive geography, like any other kind of science, has been built on the experience of certain phenomena and on experiments prompted by that unappeasable curiosity of men which their intelligence has elevated into a quite respectable passion for acquiring knowledge. Like other sciences it has fought its way to truth through a long series of errors. It has suffered from the love of the marvellous, from our credulity, from rash and unwarrantable assumptions, from the play of unbridled fancy.

Geography had its phase of circumstantially extravagant speculation which had nothing to do with the pursuit of truth, but has given us a curious glimpse of the mediæval mind playing in its ponderous childish way with the problems of our earth's shape, its size, its character, its products, its inhabitants. Cartography was almost as pictorial then as are some modern newspapers. It crowded its maps with pictures of strange pageants, strange trees, strange beasts, drawn with amazing precision in the midst of theoretically conceived continents. It delineated imaginary kingdoms of Monomotapa[1] and of Prester John,[2] the regions infested by lions or haunted by unicorns, inhabited by men with reversed feet, or eyes in the middle of their breasts.

All this might have been amusing if the mediæval gravity in the absurd had not been in itself a wearisome thing. But what of that! Has not the key science of modern chemistry passed through its dishonest phase of Alchemy (a portentous development of the confidence trick), and our knowledge of the starry sky been arrived at through the superstitious idealism of Astrology looking for men's fate in the depths of the infinite? Mere megalomania on a colossal scale. Yet, solemn fooling for solemn fooling of the scientific order, I prefer the kind that does not lay itself out to thrive on the fears and the cupidities of men.

---

[1] Monomotapa was a tribal king in southern Africa, although his name was used by the Portuguese in the sixteenth century to stand for a small kingdom. The kingdom was grossly inflated on European maps, and a legend unaccountably grew up that it was an advanced civilization occupying the whole of southeastern Africa. [ED.]

[2] The imaginary Christian ruler of a mythic, utopian Oriental kingdom, said to have been a descendant of both the Queen of Sheba and the Magi of the Christ story. He was supposedly killed and his state destroyed by Genghis Khan, who was angered that Prester John had refused to give him his daughter in marriage. [ED.]

From that point of view geography is the most blameless of sciences. Its fabulous phase never aimed at cheating simple mortals (who are a multitude) out of their peace of mind or their money. At the most it has enticed some of them away from their homes; to death may be, now and then to a little disputed glory, not seldom to contumely, never to high fortune. The greatest of them all, who has presented modern geography with a new world to work upon, was at one time loaded with chains and thrown into prison. Columbus remains a pathetic figure, not a sufferer in the cause of geography, but a victim of the imperfections of jealous human hearts, accepting his fate with resignation. Among explorers he appears lofty in his troubles and like a man of a kingly nature. His contribution to the knowledge of the earth was certainly royal. And if the discovery of America was the occasion of the greatest outburst of reckless cruelty and greed known to history we may say this at least for it, that the gold of Mexico and Peru, unlike the gold of alchemists, was really there, palpable, yet, as ever, the most elusive of the Fata Morgana[3] that lure men away from their homes, as a moment of reflection will convince any one. For nothing is more certain than that there will never be enough gold to go round, as the Conquistadores found out by experience.

I suppose it is not very charitable of me, but I must say that to this day I feel a malicious pleasure at the many disappointments of those pertinacious searchers for El Dorado who climbed mountains, pushed through forests, swam rivers, floundered in bogs, without giving a single thought to the science of geography. Not for them the serene joys of scientific research, but infinite toil, in hunger, thirst, sickness, battle; with broken heads, unseemly squabbles, and empty pockets in the end. I cannot help thinking it served them right. It is an ugly tale, which has not much to do with the service of geography. The geographical knowledge of our day is of the kind that would have been beyond the conception of the hardy followers of Cortés and Pizarro; and of that most estimable of Conquerors who was called Cabeza de Vaca, who was high-minded and dealt humanely with the heathen nations whose territories he traversed in search of one more El Dorado.[4] It is said they loved him greatly, but now the very memory of those

---

[3] A figure in various chivalric legends (known in the Arthurian cycle as Morgan Le Fay); also the name of a mirage that has appeared in the Straits of Messina, off the coast of Italy, where Morgan's underwater crystal palace is reputed to be. More generally, the term has taken on the meaning of "mirage." [ED.]

[4] Hernando Cortés, the early-sixteenth-century Spanish conqueror of Mexico, defeated Montezuma and brought about the fall of the Aztec Empire in 1521. Francisco Pizarro was a Spanish explorer and the conqueror of Peru, of which he was made governor in 1529. Alvar Nuñez Cabeza de Vaca, Spanish explorer, was a member of the ill-fated expedition

nations is gone from the earth, while their territories, which they could not take with them, are being traversed many times every twenty-four hours by the trains of the Southern Pacific railroad. [. . .]

The voyages of the early explorers were prompted by an acquisitive spirit, the idea of lucre in some form, the desire of trade or the desire of loot, disguised in more or less fine words. But Cook's[5] three voyages are free from any taint of that sort. His aims needed no disguise. They were scientific. His deeds speak for themselves with the masterly simplicity of a hard-won success. In that respect he seems to belong to the single-minded explorers of the nineteenth century, the late fathers of militant geography whose only object was the search for truth. Geography is a science of facts, and they devoted themselves to the discovery of facts in the configuration and features of the main continents.

It was the century of landsmen investigators. In saying this I do not forget the polar explorers, whose aims were certainly as pure as the air of those high latitudes where not a few of them laid down their lives for the advancement of geography. Seamen, men of science, it is difficult to speak of them without admirative emotion. The dominating figure among the seamen explorers of the first half of the nineteenth century is that of another good man, Sir John Franklin,[6] whose fame rests not only on the extent of his discoveries, but on professional prestige and high personal character. This great navigator, who never returned home, served geography even in his death. The persistent efforts extending over ten years to ascertain his fate advanced greatly our knowledge of the polar regions.

As gradually revealed to the world this fate appeared the more tragic in this, that for the first two years the way of the *Erebus* and *Terror* expedition seemed to be the way to the desired and important success, while in truth it was all the time the way of death, the end of the darkest drama perhaps played behind the curtain of Arctic mystery.

The last words unveiling the mystery of the *Erebus* and *Terror* expedition were brought home and disclosed to the world by Sir Leopold McClintock,

---

to Florida in 1527–28, in which only 4 of the 300 men who began the expedition survived. Cabeza de Vaca wandered the coast of the Gulf of Mexico among the Indians for eight years. On his return to Spain, he was rewarded for his discoveries by being appointed governor of a province in Brazil. [ED.]

[5] Captain James Cook, first European explorer of the southern Pacific. Cook was killed by previously quite hospitable islanders in Hawaii in 1779 and was later lionized in British poetry, painting, and nonfiction prose as an innocent martyr of Pacific exploration. [ED.]

[6] The British explorer who died, with the crew of his two ships, the *Erebus* and the *Terror*, while searching for the Northwest Passage in 1847; Franklin had earlier mapped the coast of Australia. [ED.]

in his book, *The Voyage of the* Fox *in the Arctic Seas.* It is a little book, but it records with manly simplicity the tragic ending of a great tale. It so happened that I was born in the year of its publication. Therefore, I may be excused for not getting hold of it till ten years afterwards. I can only account for it falling into my hands by the fact that the fate of Sir John Franklin was a matter of European interest, and that Sir Leopold McClintock's book was translated, I believe, into every language of the white races.

My copy was probably in French. But I have read the work many times since. I have now on my shelves a copy of a popular edition got up exactly as I remember my first one. It contains the touching facsimile of the printed form filled in with a summary record of the two ships' work, the name of "Sir John Franklin commanding the expedition" written in ink, and the pathetic underlined entry "All well." It was found by Sir Leopold McClintock under a cairn and it is dated just a year before the two ships had to be abandoned in their deadly ice-trap, and their crews' long and desperate struggle for life began.

There could hardly have been imagined a better book for letting in the breath of the stern romance of polar exploration into the existence of a boy whose knowledge of the poles of the earth had been till then of an abstract formal kind as mere imaginary ends of the imaginary axis upon which the earth turns. The great spirit of the realities of the story sent me off on the romantic explorations of my inner self; to the discovery of the taste of poring over maps; and revealed to me the existence of a latent devotion to geography which interfered with my devotion (such as it was) to my other schoolwork.

Unfortunately, the marks awarded for that subject were almost as few as the hours apportioned to it in the school curriculum by persons of no romantic sense for the real, ignorant of the great possibilities of active life; with no desire for struggle, no notion of the wide spaces of the world — mere bored professors, in fact, who were not only middle-aged but looked to me as if they had never been young. And their geography was very much like themselves, a bloodless thing with a dry skin covering a repulsive armature of uninteresting bones.

I would be ashamed of my warmth in digging up a hatchet which has been buried now for nearly fifty years if those fellows had not tried so often to take my scalp at the yearly examinations. There are things that one does not forget. And besides, the geography which I had discovered for myself was the geography of open spaces and wide horizons built up on men's devoted work in the open air, the geography still militant but already conscious of its approaching end with the death of the last great explorer. The antagonism was radical.

344 // JOSEPH CONRAD

Thus it happened that I got no marks at all for my first and only paper on Arctic geography, which I wrote at the age of thirteen. I still think that for my tender years it was an erudite performance. I certainly did know something of Arctic geography, but what I was after really, I suppose, was the history of Arctic exploration. My knowledge had considerable gaps, but I managed to compress my enthusiasm into just two pages, which in itself was a sort of merit. Yet I got no marks. For one thing it was not a set subject. I believe the only comment made about it to my private tutor was that I seemed to have been wasting my time in reading books of travel instead of attending to my studies. I tell you, those fellows were always trying to take my scalp. On another occasion I just saved it by proficiency in map-drawing. It must have been good, I suppose; but all I remember about it is that it was done in a loving spirit.

I have no doubt that star-gazing is a fine occupation, for it leads you within the borders of the unattainable. But map-gazing, to which I became addicted so early, brings the problems of the great spaces of the earth into stimulating and directing contact with sane curiosity and gives an honest precision to one's imaginative faculty. And the honest maps of the nineteenth century nourished in me a passionate interest in the truth of geographical facts and a desire for precise knowledge which was extended later to other subjects. [. . .]

Not the least interesting part in the study of geographical discovery lies in the insight it gives one into the characters of that special kind of men who devoted the best part of their lives to the exploration of land and sea. In the world of mentality and imagination which I was entering it was they and not the characters of famous fiction who were my first friends. Of some of them I had soon formed for myself an image indissolubly connected with certain parts of the world. For instance, western Sudan, of which I could draw the rivers and principal features from memory even now, means for me an episode in Mungo Park's[7] life.

It means for me the vision of a young, emaciated, fair-haired man, clad simply in a tattered shirt and worn-out breeches, gasping painfully for breath and lying on the ground in the shade of an enormous African tree (species unknown), while from a neighbouring village of grass huts a charitable black-skinned woman is approaching him with a calabash full of pure cold water, a simple draught which, according to himself, seems to have effected a miraculous cure. The central Sudan, on the other hand, is

---

[7] A Scottish explorer, one of the first Europeans to explore the Niger River, which he mapped in two expeditions. Park published *Travels in the Interior of Africa* in 1779 and was killed by native Africans in 1806. [ED.]

represented to me by a very different picture, that of a self-confident and keen-eyed person in a long cloak and wearing a turban on his head, riding slowly towards a gate in the mud walls of an African city, from which an excited population is streaming out to behold the wonder — Doctor Barth,[8] the protégé of Lord Palmerston, and subsidized by the British Foreign Office, approaching Kano, which no European eye had seen till then, but where forty years later my friend Sir Hugh Clifford, the Governor of Nigeria, travelled in state in order to open a college.

I must confess that I read that bit of news and inspected the many pictures in the illustrated papers without any particular elation. Education is a great thing, but Doctor Barth gets in the way. Neither will the monuments left by all sorts of empire builders suppress for me the memory of David Livingstone.[9] The words "Central Africa" bring before my eyes an old man with a rugged, kind face and a clipped, gray moustache, pacing wearily at the head of a few black followers along the reed-fringed lakes towards the dark native hut on the Congo headwaters in which he died, clinging in his very last hour to his heart's unappeased desire for the sources of the Nile.

That passion had changed him in his last days from a great explorer into a restless wanderer refusing to go home any more. From his exalted place among the blessed of militant geography and with his memory enshrined in Westminster Abbey, he can well afford to smile without bitterness at the fatal delusion of his exploring days, a notable European figure and the most venerated perhaps of all the objects of my early geographical enthusiasm.

Once only did that enthusiasm expose me to the derision of my schoolboy chums. One day, putting my finger on a spot in the very middle of the then white heart of Africa, I declared that some day I would go there. My chums' chaffing was perfectly justifiable. I myself was ashamed of having been betrayed into mere vapouring. Nothing was further from my wildest hopes. Yet it is a fact that, about eighteen years afterwards, a wretched little stern-wheel steamboat I commanded lay moored to the bank of an African river.

---

[8] Heinrich Barth was a German explorer in the service of British expeditions, who traveled through the West Sudan, Chad, and northern Nigeria between 1849 and 1855, during Palmerston's term as prime minister. He published *Travels and Discoveries in North and Central Africa* in 1858. Kano is a city in northern Nigeria on the Jakarta River. In the early nineteenth century, it was the capital of an emirate and the commercial center of a region extending from the Atlantic to the Nile. [ED.]

[9] Dr. David Livingstone, Scottish missionary and explorer, traveled throughout Africa from 1840 onward and died there in 1873, never having found the source of the Nine. He was given a hero's funeral in London in 1874, and his body was buried in Westminster Abbey. [ED.]

Everything was dark under the stars. Every other white man on board was asleep. I was glad to be alone on deck, smoking the pipe of peace after an anxious day. The subdued thundering mutter of the Stanley Falls hung in the heavy night air of the last navigable reach of the Upper Congo, while no more than ten miles away, in Reshid's [10] camp just above the Falls, the yet unbroken power of the Congo Arabs slumbered uneasily. Their day was over. Away in the middle of the stream, on a little island nestling all black in the foam of the broken water, a solitary little light glimmered feebly, and I said to myself with awe, "This is the very spot of my boyish boast."

A great melancholy descended on me. Yes, this was the very spot. But there was no shadowy friend to stand by my side in the night of the enormous wilderness, no great haunting memory, but only the unholy recollection of a prosaic newspaper "stunt" [11] and the distasteful knowledge of the vilest scramble for loot that ever disfigured the history of human conscience and geographical exploration. What an end to the idealized realities of a boy's daydreams! I wondered what I was doing there, for indeed it was only an unforeseen episode, hard to believe in now, in my seaman's life. Still, the fact remains that I have smoked a pipe of peace at midnight in the very heart of the African continent, and felt very lonely there.

But never so at sea. There I never felt lonely, because there I never lacked company. The company of great navigators, the first grown-up friends of my early boyhood. The unchangeable sea preserves for one the sense of its past, the memory of things accomplished by wisdom and daring among its restless waves. It was those things that commanded my profoundest loyalty, and perhaps it is by the professional favour of the great navigators ever present to my memory that, neither explorer nor scientific navigator, I have been permitted to sail through the very heart of the old Pacific mystery, [12] a region which even in my time remained very imperfectly charted and still remote from the knowledge of men.

---

[10] Reshid was the nephew of the Arab slave trader Tippu Tib and his accomplice in the black slave trade. [ED.]

[11] Conrad is referring to the *New York Herald*'s scheme of sending Stanley, then a reporter with the *Herald*, up the Congo to "find" Livingstone (whose whereabouts were no great mystery). Stanley encountered Livingstone on the shores of Lake Tanganyika, which is on the border between present-day Burundi and the Democratic Republic of the Congo. [ED.]

[12] Conrad captained a ship in the South Pacific in 1888 — the very same year in which Stevenson began sailing the South Seas. [ED.]

Part Five

CRITICAL RESPONSES

From The Worst Muckers

Zohreh T. Sullivan

"The Man Who Would Be King" is Kipling's most powerful allegory of empire and kingship, a story of control, desire and subversion, of authority and its discontents, and of the "worst muckers"[1] as world makers and destroyers. A small compendium of his most characteristic concerns, it is enclosed in one of his more elaborate frames that invites the reader to read the lurid embedded tale in its dialectical relationship to the oblique and strange matrix that contains it. The incident chosen for retelling is, as always, a source of displaced personal and political anxiety for the narrator who assumes a stance at once invulnerable, distant, and ironic, but whose rhetoric inadvertently reveals his vulnerability and collusion.

The bare outline suggests a cautionary colonialist allegory about two daring, swashbuckling adventurers who, finding India too confining for their grandiose ambitions, decide to travel to remote, icy, and forbidden Kafiristan in order to become kings. Dravot's and Carnehan's conquest of Kafiristan, accomplished with twenty Martini rifles, a knowledge of British military drill, and a mystique of divine right based on a garbled, half-forgotten version of Masonic ritual, sounds remarkably like a seedy version of the British Raj.[2] That their downfall is provoked by Dravot's hubris encourages us to read the story as a treatment, in schoolboy-thriller form, of Kipling's recurrent "Recessional" theme: England can retain its divinely given right to rule only so long as it retains moral superiority, a "humble and a contrite heart." The partiality of such a reading is demonstrated by the fact that it omits the most important character in the story—the

---

From *Narratives of Empire: The Fictions of Rudyard Kipling.* Cambridge: Cambridge UP, 1993. 99–110.

[1] A mucker is a ne'er-do-well, a backslider. Sullivan is particularly interested in those Kipling figures who express the breakdown of imperial norms for white male behavior—a breakdown that he sees as Kipling's worst fear. [ED.]

[2] *Raj* means rule or sovereignty.

narrator—who compels us to reread its meaning through the complex negotiation between the embedded adventure and the frame. The disturbance in this narrative is created by the collision between its central romantic myth and its distancing realistic, ironic frame whose narrator tempers his dispassionate perceptions of the adventurers with an elegaic and religious sentimentality. The narrator's stance relativizes his relationship to the embedded tale, distances itself from the quest of the adventurers, yet appears incapable of detaching itself from collusion in its implications. That ambivalence, so typical of Kipling, exteriorizes cultural and historical conflicts between the desire to colonize, connect, and possess (country and woman) and the warning against such desire, between the glorification of imperial adventure and the cynical debunking of its origins in greed, self-aggrandizement, and childlike games of power.

Typical of Kipling's narrative strategy, the world of "The Man Who Would Be King" is radically divided. Although the initial and fundamental opposition between "Man" and "King," between the human and his politically symbolic function, is announced in the title, the larger opposition in the story is between the world of the narrator—realistic, seasoned, ironic—and that of the adventurers—romantic, flamboyant, and "mad." The duality makes some parts of the story more dreamlike than others, as if the narrator were the waking self and the embedded tale a dream, a journey into archaic fantasies charged with desire, romance, and unreality. The denied and forbidden aspects of character not accessible but desired by the narrator find expression in the daring of the two bombastic and misguided adventurers whom he glorifies and exoticizes by myth and romance. If this structure, however, would seem to imply a liberating confrontation with the repressed leading to a cathartic resolution of contradiction, the story never realizes that promise. By enveloping the tale in romantic religiosity, Biblical language, and the mythology of Freemasonry, Kipling seems to evade and transcend the social and political. Analogously, he displaces the problem of invasion, lawlessness, and power in the story away from its historical immediacy to the personal; yet he represents that displacement in terms of the overdetermined contradictions of imperial mythology. By displacing the reader's attention from history onto the individual act in order to "manage" and defuse deeply political crises with substitute gratifications, the story becomes a version of what Jameson might call "the modernist project" (266). The theme of the story appears to be an anticolonialist allegory in which the adventurers are an absurd parody of the British in the third world; yet its apparent absurdity is subverted by imagery and language that idealize the imperial mission. And the distance of the frame, which appears at first to counter the inner, individual, and subjective experience, finally supports it through its own neutralizing of irony with compassion.

The conflict between the realistic frame and the romantic story for which it provides a matrix, its two conflicted modes and genres, is partially generated by the historical contradiction of imperial culture: the myth of imperialism is disrupted by the very principle that created it—by colonial man who is neither god nor king, and by the colonized country (Kafiristan) that has already a power, a native presence, and a mother lodge which cannot tolerate the reality of the man beneath the myth.

The doubleness and splitting of the narrator mirror the splitting of the colonial enterprise into agencies of protection and power, of subjugation and powerlessness. The narrator's office and life are invaded by the two adventurers who overpower him with their physical presence and demand his submission to their wishes; but his powerlessness is only temporary because he and his writing will survive into the permanence of recorded fiction. It mirrors too the splitting of Dravot from the ordinary man to the symbolic and divine God-King, a moment that is illuminated by Pierre Bourdieu's reading of political fetishism, "the process in terms of which individuals constitute themselves . . . as a group but through this process lose control of the group in and through which they constitute themselves" (57). Dravot as political fetish consecrates himself with the mystery of leadership through strategies of language and action that ritualize his power. In Bourdieu's scheme, his splitting of the self is necessary to achieve "the oracle effect" through which the individual extinguishes himself in the service of the transcendent and symbolic self. The movement from man to king involves a conversion through which the ordinary person must die so that the symbolic moral person can be born (63).

Whereas the outer story is told by a man about men, the inner story is a temporarily realized dream of heroism and kingship. The man who would be king, Dravot, focuses on the end product—kingship—as the basic unit of his economy around which all else must revolve. But he grows blind to those who grant him that kingship and upon whose labor his status depends. And it is that blindness to his people, to their expectations of him as king, that leads him to his fatal mistake—the marriage that exposes him as a man—a category which his kingship was designed to conceal. The impossible contradiction he is now faced with is quite simple: he cannot be both man and king and must therefore die. Ironically, however, these polarities have been generated by his own desire and are as radically incompatible as those other binary oppositions that the convenient closure of the frame seeks to transcend—native and ruler, the individual and society, nature and culture, the unconscious and the conscious.

The frame narration creates an almost Brechtian estranging effect, at once alienating the reader from the subject matter and compelling her, in spite of the disturbing ambivalence of the narrator, to think about the political dimensions of the enclosed tale. The daring, swashbuckling, romantic adventure into Kafiristan is in part a projection of a narrator who cleaves to the security of margins, of offices, of bureaucracy, and of second-hand reporting of the forbidden adventures of others. But it is also what a Jameson might see as the nostalgic fantasy of an empire in crisis, creating for itself a myth of origins and trying to discover a cause for the still to be dreaded future—the fall of the British Raj. The story of two crazy adventurers will become signs for the tragedy of colonialism: crucified by the men over whom they rule, their end will justify and glorify the means they use to attain it.[3] But it will also be a sign of the Kipling narrator's deepest fear which repeats itself with variations in poems and stories and dreams— the fear of literally and figuratively losing one's head; the story, then, is also an effort to master a recurring fear of self-loss.

The opening paragraph sets up the story's structure of values and voices. The world to which the narrator introduces us is one already structured by unifying tropes of family and social grouping. Although it is a hierarchical world made up of brothers, princes, beggars and kings, the epigraph would seem to suggest a transcendent design available through the Freemason law of equality: "Brother to a Prince and fellow to a beggar if he be found worthy" (153).[4] The narrator's attraction to such a law is based not on his observation of its internal contradiction, but rather on his understanding of the obvious truism, that what lies beneath one's social disguise is impossible to assess: "I have been fellow to a beggar again and again under circumstances which prevented either of us finding out whether the other was worthy" (153). More significantly, he is attracted by transcendent metaphors, by language that extends reality into new dimensions and possibilities (a sort of linguistic colonization), by the analogy between family and class structure, an analogy that can only be sustained by metaphor and not by social or political reality. But the metaphors of Freemasonry, like the metaphors of empire, share the lure of imaginary unity and transcend real political and economic divisions through rituals that deny the absence of "brotherhood" between the colonizer and the colonized, the rich and the

---

[3] For other readings of "The Man Who Would Be King" see Draudt, who argues (unconvincingly) for a Laingian reading of Peachey's madness. See also Shippey and Short, who attempt a linguistic reading of multiple frames as ironic commentary on events and as a method of raising doubt about the reliability of both Carnehan and the "I" narrator; and Meyers or Parry, *Delusions,* who emphasize the moral failures of the adventurers as caricatures of colonialists but ignore the rhetorical complexities of Kipling's discourse. The finest reading of the story, to which all subsequent readings of Kipling's ironic use of the Bible are indebted, is Fussell. [Sullivan's note.]

[4] All parenthetical references to "The Man Who Would Be King" are to this New Riverside Edition. [ED.]

poor, or democracy and dictatorship. The first paragraph, then, introduces a problem of language and metaphor that contains the contradictions between social institutions or law and life ("The Law, as quoted, lays down a fair conduct of life, and one not easy to follow"), but fails to pursue the implications of the dilemma. Rather, the narrator allows himself to be absorbed by the metaphor, to soften his skeptical tone, until the last elegaic sentence of the paragraph which resonates with religiosity and myth: "But today, I greatly fear that my King is dead, and if I want a crown I must go and hunt it for myself" (153).

The rest of the frame is a flashback divided into four scenes recalling the four encounters between the narrator and the adventurers. The shifting stance of the narrator from his initial sense of connection, to detached doubt and distrust, to his eventual reluctant admiration and pity is analogous to the movement of the inner story and also to the change in the initially doubtful stance of Carnehan towards the grandiose dreams of Dravot. The first meeting with Carnehan in the train establishes sufficient kinship to lead the narrator to agree to pass a message on to Dravot at the Marwar Station. The second meeting takes place in the narrator's office late one hot, tense, and anxious night, when Dravot and Carnehan appear with the "contrack" outlining their plan to become kings of Kafiristan. The third meeting occurs the next morning at the town square where the two men, disguised as mad priest and dumb servant, display their facility at deceiving native mobs and at concealing the reality of aggression (rifles and ammunition) under the guise of selling whirligigs to the Amir. Carnehan's story will use the image of the whirligig repeatedly to suggest the unconscious understanding of the deadly implication of the Great Game as it evolves from play to massacre. The last time the narrator meets Carnehan some three years later, the giant who had thought "India isn't big enough for such as us" (161) is now a shrunken, ragged, whining shadow who returns after crucifixion, clutching the decapitated, crowned head of Dravot and survives only long enough to tell his tale to the narrator.

The bonds connecting the narrator as journalist with the adventurers begin with the most obvious, their mutual attraction to India, to travel, to politics and to secret clubs: "He was a wanderer and a vagabond like myself. . . . He told tales of things he had seen and done. . . . We talked politics—the politics of Loaferdom that sees things from the underside where the lath and plaster is not smoothed off—" (154). And the bond of Freemasonry is the hook that connects the narrator with Dravot and their later lives. The deeper connection making the adventurers doubles for the narrator is their gift for story telling and their profession, which is an unlawful version of his restrained double life. The newspaperman's job takes him to "the dark places of the earth, full of unimaginable cruelty, touching the Railway and the Telegraph on one side, and, on the other, the days of Harun-al-Raschid" (157). But whereas the narrator survives such descents into the dark, the adventurers will not. Like them, he too is fascinated with disguise, with power, and with kings: "I did business with divers Kings, and in eight days passed through many changes of life. Sometimes I wore dress-clothes and consorted with Princes and Politicals. . . . Sometimes I lay out upon the ground and devoured what I could get, from a plate made of leaves, and drank the running water, and slept under the same rug as my servant. It was all in the day's work. . . . Then I became respectable, and returned to an Office where there were no Kings" (157, 158). The similarities between the narrator's language and Kipling's letter, between the narrator's meeting with the adventurers and Kipling's meeting with the "brothers" while travelling across India, remind us of the personal sources of fiction and of his investment in the secret societies, clubs, and systems of homosocial bonding that were part of the ideology of empire as family.

The narrator's complaints about the heat, sickness, world politics, and working conditions are repeated in caricature by his storytelling double, Carnehan, who suffers from some of the same distress but reaches different conclusions: "We have been all over India, mostly on foot. We have been boiler-fitters, engine-drivers, petty contractors . . . and we have decided that India isn't big enough for such as us" (161). Flirting on the edge of danger, fantasy, and dream, the narrator's voice is a recurring call to restraint, to stay one's hesitating foot at the edge of the abyss in order to survive self-loss and ascend into the authority of authorship.

The immediate appeal of the vagabonds to the narrator is their ambition, their dream, and their action. In contrast to the narrator, who labors and struggles and sweats thanklessly into the night transforming trauma and distress into palatable newsmatter for the leisure class, Peachey and Dravot are shapers and controllers of destiny, builders of dreams and empires. When they reappear in the narrator's life at three o'clock one hot, tense and anxious morning, clothed all in white, they appear almost as dream figures emerging out of his unconscious. Larger than life, we are told that they were not only too big for India but for the office: "Dravot's beard seemed to fill half the room and Carnehan's shoulders the other half" (161). What they share with the narrator is a sense of defeat by India ruled as it is by a displaced establishment in competition with each other ("they that governs it won't let you touch it" [161]). Because they wish to move from the margins of society into its centers, from being vagabonds to kings (their aim is to "Sar-a-whack" Kafiristan) they decide to pursue their megalomaniacal illusions of power and grandeur into creating an empire: "We shall be Emperors—Emperors of the Earth!" Their announced plan is a familiar one: "We shall go to those parts and say to any king we find—'D'you want to vanquish your foes?' and we will show him how to drill men; for that we know better than anything else. Then we will subvert that King and seize his throne and establish a Dy-nasty" (162). The adventurers, therefore, overcome their sense of defeat by history and class through aggression, cunning and conquest. The narrator trails along their tracks admitting certain connections with them, undercutting others, and finally establishing the authority of his mode over theirs by the fact of his sensibility and survival.

The dynamics between Carnehan and Dravot are a variation on the pattern of opposition set up between the narrator and the adventurers. Dravot the overreacher and visionary is to Carnehan—the cautious worker and the voice of restraint and practicality—what both men are to the narrator. They pay as little heed to his warnings as Dravot pays to those of Carnehan. At first happy to play what appears to be a continuation of their earlier game with whirligigs and concealed rifles, Carnehan later admits, "I knew he was thinking plans I could not advise about, and I just waited for orders" (176). But when Carnehan questions his decisions and his order to arrange a marriage for him with a native woman, it is too late for Dravot, who has by now internalized the illusions and the oracular rhetoric of kingship and power: "You are *my* people, and by God . . . I'll make a damned fine Nation of you, or I'll die in the making! (176) . . . I won't make a Nation . . . I'll make an Empire! These men aren't niggers; they're English!" (177). Dravot's desire to marry is a violation not only of his contract with Carnehan, but of an unspoken code of imperial male bonding that surpasses the love of woman.

Just as the narrator's apparently ethical awareness of problems of lawless imperialism is subverted by his language and his allusions, so too Carnehan's awareness of Dravot's hubris is averted by his elevated language and imagery. These conflicted languages reflect Kipling's ambivalence towards his subject matter which shapes itself into competing voices, frames, and modes. Carnehan's early childlike language describing their methods of subversion ("Dravot he shoots above their heads and they all falls down flat. Then he walks over them and kicks them, and then he lifts them up and shakes hands all round. . . . Then a lot of men came into the valley, and Carnehan and Dravot picks them off with the rifles. . . ." [170, 171]) contrasts with the later more ornate and biblical language of appropriation and kingship. The flatness of the earlier passage, for instance, denies the horror of violence and death and slides into another language of denial—that of the Old and New Testaments. Now wanton killing of "enemies" is followed by an absurd sacramentalizing ritual: "For each dead man Dravot pours a little milk on the ground and waves his arms like a whirligig and 'That's all right,' says he" (171). This ritual is followed by further biblical pronouncements which, increasingly for Carnehan, serve to sanctify their actions: "and Dravot says: 'Go and dig the land, and be fruitful and multiply,' which they did" (171). After acts of colonization described simply as "firing into the brown of the enemy" (172), Carnehan crowns the moment by saying to his Chief, "'Occupy till I come'; which was scriptural" (172).

As Paul Fussell has pointed out, their imperialist enterprise begins in the language of the Old Testament, with allusions to the accounts of creation, the history of early Hebraic kings, and the harmonizing of the tribes of Israel, and ends in the language of the New Testament. Carnehan begins his story by swearing: "It's true. . . . True as gospel. Kings we were, with crowns upon our heads—me and Dravot." During his arbitrations over land wars between villages, Dravot is peacemaker, judge, destroyer, and creator, the first Adam and the second: "And Dravot says, 'Go and dig the land, and be fruitful and multiply,' which they did"; "'That's just the beginning,' says Dravot. 'They think we're Gods. . . . They were a poor lot, and we blooded 'em with a kid before letting 'em into the new Kingdom'" (171). Eventually, their kingdom will be built upon a rock under which is concealed the Masonic mark that makes them also into Gods. Their closest and most loyal friend among the priests and chiefs is Billy Fish; they perceive their people as "The Lost Tribes, or something like it"; Carnehan uses arguments from the Bible to dissuade Dravot from taking a native wife: "The Bible says that Kings ain't to waste their strength on women" (179); and most lurid of all, Carnehan, marked by stigmata, is punished by crucifixion followed by a resurrection ("it was a miracle that he wasn't dead" [184]), after which he returns to civilization to spread the word through our narrator.

But I want to add to Fussell's observations a political dimension that suggests Kipling's perhaps unconscious recognition of the strategy through which kingship separates, isolates, sacramentalizes, and demonizes the man. During the final crisis over desire for a wife, Dravot and his flaming red beard grow to signify ambivalently charged associations: "he went away through the pine-trees looking like a big red devil, the sun being on his crown and beard and all" (179). By this stage in his evolution, Dravot has monopolized and appropriated all meaning and power into himself. He becomes what Nietzsche might call the Antichrist whose hypocrisy consists of living the lie of representing others. But the connection of the demonic with the emblematic color of the British Empire is almost immediately transcended by sentimentality after Dravot's death when the whole narrative is bathed in nostalgia for the man who was once a King—a moment celebrated in the hymn Peachey sings as he shambles out of the narrator's office:

The son of man goes forth to war,
A golden crown to gain;
His blood-red banner streams afar!
Who follows in his train?

Whereas the allusions to the Bible sanctify their venture, and those to Freemasonry transcend the divisions between the colonizers and colonized by presuming archetypal unities,[5] the self-divided Kipling would for other reasons, too, be attracted to an order that encourages the further division between inside and outside. By emphasizing universal brotherhood and a commonality that was nonpolitical and nonreligious, the order attempted what a Kipling was too ready to do—transcend and thereby avoid political and religious division and strife. And so a youthful Kipling would congratulate himself on presuming to have broken barriers in India by associating with natives within a lodge. Just such a division (a point earlier made by Fussell) is celebrated in "The Mother-Lodge":

Outside—"Sergeant! Sir! Salute! Salaam!"
Inside—"Brother," an' it doesn't do no 'arm.

If all plot involves the unfolding of blocked and resisted desire (see Brooks 12), the logical source of narrative desire in Kipling must be found in the narrator who diffuses and represses motive, interest, and intention through his worldweary stance and defensive discourse, and who drives the denied object of unconscious desire into the central embedded story. Yet he suggests the direction of this desire in the nostalgia of his opening paragraph's final hypothetical clause—"I greatly fear that my King is dead, and if I want a crown I must go hunt it for myself" (153)—a clause which also contains the metonymy that moves the narrative and "can never quite speak its name" (Brooks 56). The story that began with acknowledgment of fear and desire ends with a nightmare image of that desire fulfilled— the image of crucified Carnehan carrying the decapitated, shrivelled head of Dravot with a crown: "He fumbled in the mass of rags round his bent waist; brought out a black horsehair bag embroidered with silver thread; and shook therefrom on to my table—the dried withered head of Daniel Dravot! The morning sun that had long been paling the lamps struck the red beard and blind sunken eyes; struck, too, a heavy circlet of gold studded with raw turquoises, that Carnehan placed tenderly on the battered temples."

---

[5] Fussell suggests that in this history of two reprehensible vagabonds Kipling might have intentionally parodied the 1723 book by Anderson that chronicles the almost divine early history of Freemasonry, beginning with Noah, Moses, and Solomon. [Sullivan's note.]

At this point my reading leaves unanswered how the ending resolves the conflict between individual desire and social reality. Social and economic realities are controlled and embodied in the voice of the narrator and later Carnehan when he warns Dravot against giving in to his desire for a native wife. The moment of Dravot's kiss signifies not only his inability to restrain desire, but the racist and political implications of that lawless desire: the Englishman has violated the boundaries proper to his place in the ruling class. But that gesture, accompanied by his proprietary but lower-class responses that provoke and accompany the kiss, complicates the social model and codes that collide against each other here:

> "She'll do," said Dan, looking her over. "What's to be afraid of, lass? Come and kiss me." . . .
> "The slut's bitten me!" says he, clapping his hand to his neck, and, sure enough, his hand was red with blood. (181, 182)

Dravot's desire tests the social code that he has violated with the marriage, and the kiss momentarily allows us to hope for his unifying bond with the natives and for his continued control over them and his bride, but then returns us to the frame with its grotesque image of Carnehan and the surviving narrator/reporter. Although both the narrator and the adventurers work through a desire that can never be fulfilled, the significance of the quest romance is in the effect of again remembering, repeating, and working through the conflict over a desire that must be fulfilled even as it is thwarted and contained. Through his restraint and acquired knowledge, the frame narrator delivers us from the anxieties of illicit desire and conflicted social reality: he suggests a way to live that will allow the colonialist to exert yet contain his desires for power and control—by remaining discreetly in the margins exerting authority through authorship and transforming life into print. The inner story, however, reveals the workings of his repressed desire for "a crown" and for forbidden adventure that necessarily implicates the seeker in power which leads to isolation, self-deception, and tragedy. A frame that contains and controls the inner tragedy is an appropriate form for an ideology that masks the dangers of its own enterprise in comic rhetoric and that transcends its own contradictions with mythology. The anxieties that accompany real kingship and imperialism are confronted on levels that are at once ordinary and symbolic, private and political, with the profound recognition that when power is fetishized into the symbolically sacred, it must destroy its human source. This dream journey to power, kingship, divinity, crucifixion, death, and return, takes the restrained newspaperman not only into forbidden desires and alien territories, but also towards dangerously prophetic insights into the self-destructive mechanisms of imperialism. And Kipling's narrative tests the extent to which the desire unleashed by the mythology of imperialism can violate its sustaining social system and unspoken cultural codes.

Taking Up with Kanakas:
Stevenson's Complex Social Criticism in "The Beach of Falesá"
Katherine Linehan

More than an adventure story, Robert Louis Stevenson's South Sea island tale "The Beach of Falesá," published serially in 1892, is a fascinatingly complex reflection of and commentary on late Victorian attitudes towards race, Empire, and sexuality. It deserves to be better known in the context both of Stevenson's development as a writer and of the literature of imperialism, particularly as an antecedent to Conrad's *Heart of Darkness,* published serially in 1899. Indeed Patrick Brantlinger, in his recent *Rule of Darkness: British Literature and Imperialism, 1830–1914,* suggests that Stevenson's "South Sea stories are as skeptical about the influence of white civilization on primitive societies as anything Conrad wrote" (39). In addition to exploring "The Beach of Falesá" as a reflection of the skepticism about the European presence in Polynesia which Stevenson developed after moving to the South Pacific in 1889, I suggest that Stevenson's critique of colonialism incorporates a remarkable dimension of feminist insight into the parallel workings of racial and sexual domination.

At the same time I want to emphasize how much care is needed in reaching conclusions about the social views transmitted in the story. Both literary and social-psychological complications contribute to the challenge the reader faces. Literary complications inhere partly in a host of aesthetic details which promote interpretive ambiguity, but they derive most of all from the fact that Stevenson hides behind the narrative mask of a heavily racist first-person narrator and subtly contrives to make that protagonist simultaneously the vehicle and object of social criticism. Social-psychological complications are linked to authorial racism and sexism confusingly mingled with intimations of liberal intentions. However, evidence outside the novella allows us perspective on how Stevenson's participation in the cultural ideology of his own day—the heyday of the British Empire and an era

From *English Literature in Transition: 1880–1920* 33 (1990). 407–22.

of painfully conflicted responses to changing sexual mores—carries over at an unconscious level into the tale, producing a story which is at once a critique and an enactment of racism and sexism.[1]

Perhaps the one point on which critics agree is that the story's bluff working-class narrator John Wiltshire, a British trader who comes to the South Sea Island of Falesá prepared to exploit the natives commercially and sexually, is meant to become more appealing to the reader as his loyalties shift from his treacherous fellow-trader, Case, to the loyal, proud island woman Uma whom he learns to love and honor. The tricky question is what to make of the fact that this flashback first-person account of apparent growth into heroism through love for a "kanaka" (native Polynesian) is full of arrogantly bigoted present-tense pronouncements about natives: "I know how to deal with Kanakas. . . . They haven't any real government or any real law, that's what you've got to knock into their heads; and even if they had, it would be a good joke if it was to apply to a white man. It would be a strange thing if we came all this way and couldn't do what we pleased" (206, 207).[2]

With Wiltshire as the teller of the tale, it is not immediately obvious to the reader whether Stevenson portrays such imperialist bravado uncritically, as an amusing embellishment to the character of a heroic man of action, or whether he uses the crudeness of Wiltshire's sentiments to point a moral about the arrogance of imperialism itself, thus giving us a protagonist whose capacity to act upon humanitarian impulses is seriously compromised by his implacably racist mentality. Various aspects of the construction and execution of the tale thicken the smokescreen of indeterminacy surrounding Wiltshire and the story as a whole.

The narration begins with a statement of ambiguity—"I saw that island first when it was neither night nor morning"—and ends with a question—"I'd like to know where I'm to find them whites?" The full content of that closing question, as well as its placement in the final sequence of the narration, compounds difficult judgments for the reader. In the main action, Wiltshire's role has just climaxed in a blaze of glory with the avenging of his own and Uma's honor in a bloody victory over Case. Yet when Wiltshire goes on to bring us up to date on his subsequent life, we resume a prosaic, morally checkered reality. We see him re-engaged in his former shady trading practices and are confronted in his parting words with an expression of

---

[1] Compare the analyses of political complexities in *Heart of Darkness* and *Kim* recently offered (respectively) by Brantlinger in *Rule of Darkness* (255–74) and by Said in *"Kim,"* 27–64. [Linehan's note.]

[2] All parenthetical references to "The Beach of Falesá" are to this New Riverside Edition. [ED.]

perplexity about his mixed-race offspring which jarringly combines parental solicitude with racist denigration: "But what bothers me is the girls. They're only half-castes of course; I know that as well as you do, and there's nobody thinks less of half-castes than I do; but they're mine, and about all I've got. I can't reconcile my mind to their taking up with Kanakas, and I'd like to know where I'm to find [them] whites?" (245). Stevenson indeed contrives to have the very name of his protagonist play upon divergent interpretive possibilities: "Wiltshire" as an evocation of the British county can support patriotic connotations of the working-class British Everyman — cocky, courageous, and fundamentally decent. On the other hand, connotations of the swindler loom large in the version of his name brought to our attention when Wiltshire tells the missionary, Tarleton, " 'I'm mostly called Welsher' " (216).

The difficulty of ascertaining Stevenson's (or more precisely, the implied author's) attitude towards his narrator has led critics to reach dramatically different conclusions about the story's social message. Robert Kiely finds Stevenson essentially uncritical of Wiltshire's racist views.[3] By contrast, Barry Menikoff identifies the tale as "a story rooted in the exposure of white racism," the product of its author's engagement with contemporary social realism. This "profoundly radical social exposé" illustrates "the education of a bigot: how Wiltshire comes to be delivered of prejudices that are so ingrained he cannot consciously rid himself of them" (57, 71, 98). Peter Gilmour takes a middle position, proposing that the story consciously raises issues of racism but ultimately dodges them in favor of the simpler certainties of the adventure story, in the process reducing the natives to the status of "childlike and impressionable" spectators to the all-important "struggle between the decent . . . and the bad white man" (188–201).[4]

The evidence of Stevenson's various writings of the early 1890s suggests that Menikoff is right in claiming that Stevenson translated an angry concern he had come to feel about European commercial exploitation in Polynesia into "The Beach of Falesá." The evidence also suggests that Menikoff glosses over, as Kiely and Gilmour do not, a recidivist strain in Stevenson: a tendency to type Polynesians as children and black-skinned people as savages, reserving attention for white men as figures of high-level moral complexity. Recognizing that Stevenson was subject to the prejudices of

---

[3] "Stevenson deliberately or unconsciously shares in [Wiltshire's] naïveté by failing to introduce even the faintest irony in the tale," Kiely (170–71) asserts, adding in support of that claim: "Wiltshire's insensitive and condescending observations are thoroughly borne out by the behaviour of the characters. Uma and the other natives *do* act and speak like children." [Linehan's note.]

[4] See esp. 192–94. [Linehan's note.]

his time makes us more appreciative, however, of his ability to move towards a critique not just of racism but of the social and sexual politics of imperialism. Indeed, while we end up with a story heavily chauvinistic in the depiction of non-white and female characters, "The Beach of Falesá" is also imaginatively inspired to allegorize relationships among those characters in ways critical of imperialistic and sexual domination.

Amidst the mix of racial attitudes found in Stevenson's late writings, generous humanitarianism forms a central strand, clearly visible even before his first trip to Polynesia. In a travel essay written shortly after his 1879 train journey across America, Stevenson denounces the hostility exhibited by whites towards Chinese: "Of all stupid ill-feelings, the sentiment of my fellow-Caucasians towards our companions was the stupidest and the worse. They . . . hated them *a priori*." He deplores the special injustice attaching to the abuse of native Americans at whose expense European settlement has progressed: "my fellow-passengers danced and jested round them . . . I was ashamed for the thing we call civilisation. We should carry upon our consciences so much, at least, of our forefathers' misconduct as we continue to profit by ourselves" (*Works* 15: 139, 142).

Sympathy for non-whites and indignation over white exploitativeness continue in his South Sea writings. From the beginning of his 1888–89 voyages, Stevenson was fired with interest in and enthusiasm for the native peoples of the eastern South Sea islands. "God's best—at least God's sweetest—works, Polynesians" (*Works* 24: 180) was the phrase he used in a May 1889 letter to his friend Charles Baxter. In the role of self-styled anthropologist and historian, he eagerly began collecting data first for a travelogue reporting on the character and customs of the Polynesian Marquesa and Paumoto Islands and the eastern Micronesian Gilbert Islands (*In the South Seas*) and second for a historical study reporting on the recent politics of Samoa (*A Footnote to History: Eight Years of Trouble in Samoa*). Though showing less animus towards the British or American than the German presence in the Samoas, Stevenson nevertheless repeatedly sounds an alarm over the threat to Polynesian well-being posed by the introduction into the region of European diseases, culture, and commercial adventuring. In *In the South Seas* he also urges the view that supposed racial superiority is in fact relative to historical circumstance: "A polite Englishman . . . is amazed to find [Marquesans] tattooed; polite Italians came not long ago to England and found our fathers stained with woad . . . so insecure, so much a matter of the day and hour, is the pre-eminence of race" (*South Seas* 1971: 12).

Ironically, however, even while Stevenson rejected white supremacy as a wholesale proposition, he did retain a considerable part of its ideology, recognizable in the recapitulation theory which was extremely popular throughout Europe in the late nineteenth century. This theory argues that human development, whether within individuals or social groups, recapitulates earlier evolutionary stages along the path towards maturity.[5] The proposition that ontogeny recapitulates phylogeny (itself now understood as questionable) was thus manipulated to support a view of whites as fully-evolved, brown-skinned people as at a "childhood" level of development, and African blacks as more hedonistically primitive.

Various aspects of the recapitulation theory find echoes in Stevenson's work. Most conspicuous is the conception of the Polynesian as a child, which in Stevenson's case takes on overtones of indulgent paternalism in keeping with his long-standing romantic interest in childhood. Such paternalism emerges, for example, in the characterization (by a presumably reliable narrator) of the Polynesian crew-members in "The Ebb-Tide" (1893) as "kindly, cheery, childish souls" (*Strange Case* 218), or in the representation of the Marquesans studied in *In the South Seas* as being "childishly self-indulgent" (169). A particularly overt equating of Polynesians with children, unself-consciously juxtaposed with criticism of white exploitativeness in Polynesia, occurs in *A Footnote to History:* "The white people . . . are all here after a livelihood. . . . Close at their elbows, in all this contention, stands the native looking on. *Like a child, his true analogue,* he observes, misapprehends, and is usually silent. . . . He looks on at the rude career of the dollar hunt, and wonders. . . . He is strongly conscious of his own position as the common milk cow; and what is he to do?" (*Works* 19: 392–93).

Further evidence suggests that Stevenson's likening of Polynesians to children is part of a larger framework of hierarchical thinking about race probably so unreflectingly absorbed from popular culture that he could not easily see its inconsistency with his own consciously proclaimed egalitarian views. A demeaning stereotype of black-skinned as opposed to brown-skinned people, for example, speaks through Stevenson's description of the Solomon Islanders (a dark-skinned Melanesian people inhabiting the western South Pacific) imported to Samoa as indentured laborers, even allowing for the fact that he is writing in heightened tones to be read by a group of British schoolchildren: "They are not at all like the king and his people, who are brown and very pretty; for these are black as negroes and as ugly as sin, poor souls, and in their own land they live all the time at war, and cook and eat men's flesh" (*Works* 22: 503).[6] A similar hierarchical

---

[5] For an informative discussion of recapitulation theory, see Gould. [Linehan's note.]
[6] Characteristically, however, Stevenson responded with warm sympathy to the needs of a young Solomon Islander who sought shelter at the Stevensons' house from the German plantation where he had been ill-treated. [Linehan's note.]

categorizing around that popular and sensationalized Victorian signifier, cannibalism, occurs in *In the South Seas,* along with language drawn from the recapitulationist model of social evolution as moral maturation: "The higher Polynesian races . . . had one and all outgrown . . . the practice [of cannibalism]. . . . It lingered only in some low islands where life was difficult to maintain, and among inveterate savages" (94). The prominence of whites in comparison to Polynesians in Stevenson's South Seas fiction undoubtedly has mostly to do with his greater familiarity with white culture, but different moral expectations connected to the recapitulationist ideology may be a factor as well. That the white characters in *The Wrecker,* "The Beach of Falesá," and "The Ebb-Tide" show themselves capable of greater extremes of evil than the Polynesians depicted seems to result in part from their being conceived as more adultly complex morally than Polynesians and thus more compellingly enmeshed in dramas of moral choice.

Stevenson's views on race help explain how in "The Beach of Falesá" patronizing authorial stereotypes of non-white characters can and do exist alongside a genuine concern to expose the moral degeneracy of white racism. Authorial values little visible on the surface of Wiltshire's narration find a more direct channel for expression in the creation of plot, character, and dialogue, and Kiely and Gilmour are right in observing that the Polynesians in the story, including Uma, act and speak like children while being relegated to the role of passive onlookers to a struggle which vitally affects them. Recapitulationist thinking may also influence Stevenson's conception of the negro Black Jack as a morally unprincipled partner to Case.

Yet the perpetuation of partly benevolently-inclined stereotypes about non-whites does not preclude a well-founded indignation over the callous exploitation of Polynesians by whites any more inside the story than out. One comment Stevenson made about the story after its completion particularly supports the conjecture that he intended the tale to convey a race-centered critique. In a May 1892 letter to his friend Sidney Colvin, Stevenson defends the roughness of character exhibited by both Wiltshire and Papa Randall (a former British sea captain serving in name as Case's partner but in fact degenerated into a drunken, filthy, fly-ridden wreck of a man): "I think you scarce do justice to the fact that this is a piece of realism *à outrance.* . . . And will you please to observe that almost all that is ugly is in the whites?" (*Works* 17: 147). Manuscript evidence too, as Barry Menikoff demonstrates, testifies to Stevenson's interest in promoting "a realism that depicted the savagery of Polynesian history, a savagery linked to white behavior" (58). Studying changes in language and punctuation introduced by Stevenson's editors, Menikoff points out that the original manuscript reveals a deliberate heightening of racial slurs in Wiltshire's narration, along with other crudities calculated to illustrate "the abuse of men and the exploitation of women" (57). A few additional comments written by Stevenson to Colvin also fit with the reading of critics like Brantlinger and Menikoff who see a critique of white racism implicit in the degeneracy of Papa Randall and see Wiltshire as a morally mixed character, something of a diamond in the rough, whose better side is brought out by his recoil from association with Randall and Case: "Wiltshire . . . had surely, under his beast-ignorant ways, right noble qualities. . . . Papa Randall . . . seemed to me essential as a figure, and essential as a pawn in the game. Wiltshire's disgust for him being one of the small, efficient motives in the story" (*Works* 17: 146–47).

Stevenson's views on sexuality have not commanded as much critical attention as his views on race, nor is extratextual evidence on this point as easily identifiable. My argument for what might be called a proto-feminist insight into the workings of sexual domination is drawn essentially from "The Beach of Falesá" itself. However, it is worth mentioning that the newly-available "The Enchantress" (ca. 1889) lends credibility to speculations about his interest in his late years in the theme of sex-role reversal.[7] In addition, we may note that Stevenson's letters in the 1890s, reflecting as they do his sense of inexperience in fictive treatment of sexuality along with a commitment to deal honestly with the realities of sexual attraction, in some ways anticipate a disjunction in "The Beach of Falesá" between conventional and unconventional thinking about sexuality.

In April of 1891, Stevenson boasts to Colvin that the story he is composing is "(for once in my works) rendered pleasing by the presence of a heroine who is pretty" (*Works* 17: 60). This attention to surfaces is consonant with the actual portrayal of Uma. She gains somewhat in depth as the tale unfolds, but the authorial conception of her remains a simplistic one, relying heavily on the crowd-pleasing appeal of an exotically sensuous yet bravely faithful woman who intuitively recognizes her lover's decency on the very night he prostitutes her, and whose ardent devotion to him is sealed by her literally throwing herself at his feet with the cry, "I belong you all-e same pig!" (198). Racial stereotyping may enter into the portrayal, but as Stevenson's biographer Furnas points out, he had long drawn criticism for creating "stickish" heroines (422) or else for avoiding the depiction of

---

[7]This light piece, composed for shipboard entertainment during the Stevensons' South Sea travels, revolves around an overturning of conventional sex roles which takes the male narrator by surprise. It is interesting for our purposes to note that the narrator associates slavery as well as femininity with his dependent position, declaring to his benefactress: "you are the man in this story, I the woman. . . . You have bought a slave; I hope you like him" (559). [Linehan's note.]

female characters altogether. On the other hand, Furnas also identifies a growing respect for the importance of sexuality in Stevenson's late fiction, stemming, he suggests, from a widening involvement in political and family life and manifesting itself in Stevenson's comment in an 1894 letter to his cousin Bob, "If I had to begin again . . . I believe I should try to honour sex more religiously" (*Works* 24: 433). In this sentiment, as in his willingness to challenge sexual conventions in "The Enchantress" and "The Beach of Falesá," Stevenson was undoubtedly also touched by those late Victorian currents of sexually liberal thinking which can be seen surfacing in the 1890s in controversy over topics like "The New Woman" and novels like Hardy's *Jude the Obscure* [1896]. He certainly does make a point of featuring sexuality as a powerful force first for the worst and then for the best in Wiltshire, and he certainly ran his own obstacle course with publishers in trying to maintain the integrity of that conception.

Several reasons for the complexity and open-endedness of interpretation faced in reading "The Beach of Falesá" are thus more apparent. One presumably falls outside the category of authorial intentionality: the racist element in Stevenson's thinking forms a blind spot which surfaces in the authorial conception of non-white characters and thereby confuses our reading of the ostentatiously bigoted narrator as a vehicle for an anti-racist critique. Another reason presumably falls within the category of authorial intentionality: the consciously anti-racist and anti-puritanical elements in Stevenson's thinking were liable in unvarnished form to prove uncongenial to a Victorian reading audience riding high on late Victorian pride in Empire and little accustomed to unsugared treatments of sexuality, much less interracial sexuality. Not surprisingly, Stevenson's letters to Colvin reveal an anxiety about whether various "novel" elements in the story "may be found unwelcome to that great, hulking, bullering whale, the public" (*Works* 17: 81). It stands to reason then that he would have set up a diversion both in the opacity of Wiltshire's character and, as Menikoff conjectures, in the interweaving of social criticism with swashbuckling romance of the sort he had built his reputation on.[8]

Scrutiny of the text in light of our background investigations reveals a still deeper source of complexity: an unexpected edge of authorial self-awareness about racist ideology. A remarkable feature of "The Beach of Falesá" is that even while Stevenson myopically perpetuates racial and sexual stereotyping in his creation of the Polynesian characters, he far-sightedly

---

[8] Menikoff informs us that the decoy element, if such it was, succeeded only too well among the story's first reviewers, who while enthusiastic about the tale's heroine, love affair, and evocativeness of setting, made virtually no mention of race issues. [Linehan's note.]

and obviously with some degree of authorial control reproduces his own recapitulationist stereotypes in his creation of Wiltshire. Through the filter of educational and class differences, Wiltshire gives forth a brassy echo of Stevenson's own paternalistic and hierarchical thinking, dubbing Uma a "child" (210) and "a kind of a baby" (211), assuring his audience that "to find out what Kanakas think . . . go back to yourself any way round from ten to fifteen years old, and there's an average Kanaka" (232), and engaging at the conclusion of the tale in a sophomorically vindictive account of Black Jack going to the west "where he found men of his own colour, in case he liked that, and the men of his own colour took and ate him at some kind of a corroborree" (244). It is as though through the imaginative freedom conveyed by this narrative mask, Stevenson were able to see himself whole and create a translated, slightly caricatured working-class version of himself to experiment with his own ideas.

This possibility seems more convincing when we consider that Stevenson probably *was* carried outside of himself during this period of his life in ways that he could not easily articulate through letters or essays to friends and readers still living on the other side of the globe. He had moved from the self-confident center of Empire in Victorian England to its battered international fringes in Samoa, and from a footloose bachelor existence as a writer primarily of boys' adventure fiction to the life of sexual engagement and family responsibility that came with his 1880 marriage to the spunky American divorcée and mother of two, Fanny Osbourne. Plunging into a new language, culture, and politics as well as new intimacies of acquaintance, he was "taking up with kanakas" (to use Wiltshire's phrase in his closing line) in ways that must have tested familiar assumptions and values.

My conjecture then is that part of the story's emphasis on uncertainty and ambiguity stems from Stevenson's interest in dramatizing through his tough-talking hero a sense of the unsettling and disorienting shift or even inversion of perspectives that comes with pulling back from the society of white European males and engaging with Polynesia and Polynesians at a level of considerable emotional receptivity. Wiltshire's reluctance to admit to being less than equal to any situation or to feeling emotions not in keeping with his favorite prejudices makes him comically effective as a vehicle for this drama, and allows readers unreceptive to the political significance of the shift in perspectives which occurs over the course of the story to gloss over their full implications.

In any case, whatever the enabling conditions for Stevenson's imagination, it is indeed the case that the text gives evidence of authorial controls working through Wiltshire's limited narrative consciousness, first to set up a politically critical vision of this brashly exploitative trader whose views on race overlap with those expressed elsewhere by Stevenson, and second to deepen that vision by exposing through Wiltshire's unexpected and life-changing involvement with a native woman the interconnectedness of racial and sexual domination.

This interpretation appeals centrally to patterns of language and imagery too carefully orchestrated to be accidental, which comment initially on the arrogant imperiousness linking Wiltshire to Case and then highlight the chastening, humanizing reversal in roles occurring to Wiltshire as his loyalty to Uma subjects him to being cast in the part of the woman, the black, and the slave.

The language of interpersonal relations in particular is fraught with metaphors of political and financial control or subjugation which take on added meaning in light of the historical realities of colonization and empire-building which form a backdrop to the tale. As the story opens, Wiltshire is seen channeling into his relationship with Uma an appetite for power reflected in the images of rulership he employs. When he is about to pick Uma as his mistress, he describes himself surveying the crowd of women around him "like a Bashaw" (192). When he begins to fall in love with her, he tells us that he prefers to speak to her only when he is "master of my tongue" (197). His would-be colonial mastery over her finds its climactic expression in the scene, four days into their relationship, where he takes out on her a frustration for his inability to penetrate the ban mysteriously imposed on him throughout the island:

> . . . I went straight home, in a [holy] temper, and found Uma trying on a lot of trade goods like a baby.
>
> "Here," I said, "you quit that foolery! Here's a pretty mess to have made, as if I wasn't bothered enough anyway! And I thought I told you to get dinner!"
>
> And then I believe I gave her a bit of the rough side of my tongue, as she deserved. She stood up at once, like a sentry to his officer; for I must say she was always well brought up, and had a great respect for whites. (209)

The imposition of a bullying, dehumanizing racial and military master-servant relationship on the emotional intimacy of a budding sexual relationship speaks for the appeal to Wiltshire of claiming in colonial territories racial and sexual prerogatives unavailable to him in England. The point is underscored by the authorial *double entendre* implanted in Wiltshire's earlier imperialist line to the council of island chiefs: "I'm a white man, and a British subject, and no end of a big chief at home; and I've come here to do them good, and bring them civilisation. . . . I demand the reason of this treatment" [206]). The working-class Wiltshire is of course far from being a big chief at home in England (to the genteel Tarleton he will later say "I'm just a common, [low], God-damned white man and British subject, the sort you would like to wipe your boots on" [216]) but he can compensate for that richly in Falesá by obtaining fast money ("I felt as if I was in the right place to make a fortune" [200–201]) and by playing the big chief among the natives, especially at home with his native mistress.

Wiltshire is not alone in his exploitative tendencies. Stevenson's interest in making the story a study of white "ugliness"[9] hinges on a representation of the traders as a group as "parasites" (Wiltshire's word for Case and Black Jack and the pervasive image in his description of Papa Randall) and Case in particular as a supreme manipulator. Case, who makes whites as well as natives pawns in a game played for power, profit, and pleasure, represents a hard-boiled version of Wiltshire's worst tendencies. His role as a trader in souls is epitomized by his sneering assurance to Wiltshire as they look over the native women: "You can have your pick of the lot for a plug of tobacco" (192). Again images of political control strengthen the connection to British colonialism. Wiltshire says of Case at one point, "he had the brains to run a parliament" (207).

However, where Case is a figure of entrenched villainy, Wiltshire's capacity for conscience and self-doubt leaves him contending between affinities to Case and to Uma as between his bad and good angels. Supporting the political dimension of this drama, imagery of social control shifts as love for Uma wins out over solidarity with Case, showing Wiltshire forced to relinquish the superior status and authority he had previously laid claim to.

At first, "ashamed to be so much moved about a native" and yet "ashamed of the marriage too" (197; the reference is to the bogus marriage into which Uma has been conned), Wiltshire shakes off his sense of being "cheap" (196) in his treatment of Uma and strives to repress his vision of her on the night of the pseudo-wedding as "a kind of a countess really . . . and no even mate for a poor trader like myself" (197). The turning point in their relationship occurs when, after Wiltshire's tongue-lashing of Uma in the scene quoted above, she realizes and reveals to him the truth of the trick Case has played on both of them, and offers to leave so that the taboo which attached to her will not interfere with his trade. In what he correctly terms "a very big expression," the normally mercenary Wiltshire fervently responds, "Uma . . . I would rather have you than all the copra in

---

[9]The idea that he finds his subject in a study of white intruders into Polynesia is supported by the fact that "Beach" in the title can refer to the whites of the island collectively as well as to the pidgin English they trade in. See Stevenson's letter of 13 July 1890 to E. L. Burlingame equating "the white population" of Samoa with "The Beach" (Stevenson, *Works* 24: 228). [Linehan's note.]

370 // KATHERINE LINEHAN

the South Seas" (211). Thus begins a portion of the story in which Wiltshire, casting his lot with this native woman, is brought low in a way the story implicitly asks us to recognize as a moral advance. In the remainder of the quarrel scene, the imaging of his reduction of status is physically acted out through his sitting down on the floor with Uma to persuade her not to leave him and then sharing in preparing the dinner he had previously ordered her to have ready.

Subsequently, as Wiltshire endures heightened self-reproach for his deception of Uma and, for a period of some weeks, the social ostracism imposed by the taboo, authorial controls pointedly convey recognition of the connectedness of various forms of social disempowerment and thereby, in this colonial setting, speak for Stevenson's insight into the socially polarizing tendencies of imperialist politics at all levels of social interaction. Imagery and circumstances now associate Wiltshire, in a series of parallel and overlapping role inversions, with blacks or Polynesians rather than whites, laborers rather than masters, and women rather than men. Wiltshire's social contacts are largely restricted to the two women who are his co-sharers in Uma's taboo: Uma and her mother. The three together also become co-workers in the manual labor needed to supply Wiltshire's chief trading commodity: "the two women and I turned to and made copra with our own hands" (223). For this labor, Wiltshire is jeeringly analogized by Case to a black slave: "You don't hinder me any. You haven't got one pound of copra but what you made with your own hands, like a negro slave" (233). In an echo to these socially-imposed taunts, Wiltshire out of guilt towards Uma several times calls himself a "sweep" (216), a slang term taking its negative moral connotation from the association of sooty blackness and degradation with the chimney sweep's dirty job. Possibly the taboo itself, attaching as it does to an ordinary Polynesian woman, carries symbolic weight in the story as a reflection of society's devaluation of the non-male, the non-white, and the non-wealthy. At any rate, within the moral-political scheme of the story, the taboo is unquestionably an effective device for subjecting Wiltshire to ignominies associated with being on the "low" end of a set of social dichotomies which in Polynesia he is accustomed to playing for advantage.

With Wiltshire's immersion in native life and native status comes an opening of new perspectives and new lines of communication. The first step is taken as soon as Wiltshire confesses his love for Uma: "I saw I was clean gone; and if she was to make a fool of me, she must. And I suppose it was this that set her talking, for now she made sure that we were friends. A lot she told me, sitting in my lap and eating my dish, as I ate hers, from foolery—a lot about herself and her mother and Case. . . ." (211). Though sexism will mingle with affectionate respect in their subsequent married relations, this scene marks a crucial transition in Wiltshire's ability to grant Uma the dignity of her selfhood, later to be enhanced by his increasing appreciation of her courage, loyalty, and strength of character. Other self-imposed rules of social exclusion are likewise broken, opening previously closed doors. Despite a continued insistence that "I've come here to trade . . . and not to make friends" (235) and fulminations against missionaries on the grounds—ironically—that "they're partly Kanakaized, and suck up with natives instead of with other white men like themselves" (215), Wiltshire during the period of his taboo reciprocates the friendly overtures of the British missionary Tarleton, the French missionary Galuchet, and various natives who prove willing to converse with him apart from the public eye. As a result, he gains not only companionship but also valuable information about island life and history and rudiments of the native language (which, significantly, he insists upon Tarleton using for the genuine marriage to Uma). Ethnocentrism thus begins to be slightly unsettled, as revealed by occasional cross-cultural insights[10] and symbolically manifested in one scene of Wiltshire alone in the bush in which the spirit of the jungle—in his words, "the queerness of the place" (229)—deeply stirs his imagination. (Here there is unquestionably an echo of Stevenson's experience of emotional engagement with Polynesia, for his inspiration for the story that was to become "The Beach of Falesá" originated, as he reported to Colvin in November of 1890, "in one of my moments of awe, alone in that tragic jungle" [*Works* 17: 14].)

Yet the finest and most solidly realistic touch of all in this carefully engineered narrative lies in Stevenson's refusal to oversimplify the dynamics of individual psychology and social prejudice. We as readers observe Wiltshire in the process of being at least partly "Kanakaized," but he himself is too strongly wed to the ideology of British white male superiority to be able fully to see the lessons we are meant to see. He is converted far more strongly at the emotional than the intellectual level. Comic though this disjunction may sometimes be, it has its disturbing side in the persistence of Wiltshire's racist remarks and colonialist attitudes. Disturbance is amplified through Wiltshire's solicitous closing question about the sexual partnering of mulatto daughters he deems too good for Kanakas and too

---

[10] Male rites of passage, for example, are seen as parallel in European and Polynesian culture: "a young man scarce reckoned himself grown till he had got his breech tattooed, for one thing, and seen Case's devils for another. This is mighty like Kanakas; but if you look at it another way, it's mighty like white folks too" (231). Especially interesting for purposes of this paper is a narratorial observation early in the story which admits insight into the cultural construction of racial categories: "a negro is counted a white man, and so is a Chinese! a strange idea, but common in the islands" (193). [Linehan's note.]

unmarketable for whites (whereas his son can be "schooled with the best"): thus do the racial and sexual inequalities in his loyal, loving marriage to Uma intersect and compound themselves in a society in which Wiltshire's own bigotries are richly replicated.

Perhaps the complexity of judgment invited by Wiltshire's moral character is best summarized, finally, by reference to the Jekyll and Hyde motif Stevenson weaves into Wiltshire's relationship to Case (worth comparing to the Marlow-Kurtz relationship in *Heart of Darkness*). Wiltshire would like to think of himself as the moral superior and total antagonist to Case, but a close reading of the text insists that he be seen as partly complicitous in Case's "devil-work." Various details—Case's marriage to a Samoan woman whom he treats unexpectedly well, Wiltshire's boast to Case of leaving "the marks of my knuckles on your head" (233), and the scene where, with guns on shoulders, the two men "each wheeled round like fellows drilling, and stood face to face" (232)—suggest that the "White Man's Quarrel" (Case's term) they collaborate in is simultaneously a fratricidal (supposing a Cain and Abel allusion) imperialist rivalry for colonial spoils, and the battle of a struggling, normally well-intentioned self divided between impulses of good and evil. The bond between them does not turn Wiltshire into Case in our eyes, but it does serve effectively to dramatize what the story seems to me to be most profoundly about, namely the deep-rooted tenacity of racist, sexist, and selfishly acquisitive habits of mind in the decent sort of fallible common Englishman whom Wiltshire—or Welsher—represents.

Insofar as Stevenson unconsciously imported racist and sexist stereotypes into the creation of the non-white characters in "The Beach of Falesá," he obviously failed to see just how closely he resembled his protagonist in this mix of ingrained prejudice and humanitarian responsiveness to experience. Far more deserving of our attention, however, I would suggest, is the energy and thoughtfulness of imaginative self-transcendence he *did* achieve. Taking up with Kanakas and taking up with marriage late in his life, Stevenson was open-minded enough to develop a new depth of perspective on the cultural assumptions he had grown up with, courageous enough to translate his social criticisms into the fiction-writing on which his livelihood depended, insightful enough to encompass his own failings within a vision of human nature as divided between its narrower and its more generous impulses, and talented enough to fashion his vision and insights into an entertaining, subtly complex, and richly rewarding piece of fiction. Weeks before his death, Stevenson lamented in a letter to his cousin Bob what he saw us certain concessions to conventionality in his work and concluded, "Well, it is so; I cannot be wiser than my generation" (*Works* 24: 433). Though there is some basis for the application of such humility to

"The Beach of Falesá," on balance this story, outstanding even among Stevenson's late works in its forwardness of social vision, argues strongly for a revision of that self-effacing verdict.

An Image of Africa[1]

Chinua Achebe

It was a fine autumn morning at the beginning of this academic year such as encouraged friendliness to passing strangers. Brisk youngsters were hurrying in all directions, many of them obviously freshmen in their first flush of enthusiasm. An older man, going the same way as I, turned and remarked to me how very young they came these days. I agreed. Then he asked me if I was a student too. I said no, I was a teacher. What did I teach? African literature. Now that was funny, he said, because he never had thought of Africa as having that kind of stuff, you know. By this time I was walking much faster. "Oh well," I heard him say finally, behind me, "I guess I have to take your course to find out."

A few weeks later I received two very touching letters from high school children in Yonkers, New York, who—bless their teacher—had just read *Things Fall Apart.*[2] One of them was particularly happy to learn about the customs and superstitions of an African tribe.

I propose to draw from these rather trivial encounters rather heavy conclusions which at first sight might seem somewhat out of proportion to them: But only at first sight.

The young fellow from Yonkers, perhaps partly on account of his age but I believe also for much deeper and more serious reasons, is obviously unaware that the life of his own tribesmen in Yonkers, New York, is full of odd customs and superstitions and, like everybody else in his culture, imagines that he needs a trip to Africa to encounter those things.

The other person being fully my own age could not be excused on the grounds of his years. Ignorance might be a more likely reason; but here again I believe that something more willful than a mere lack of information was at work. For did not that erudite British historian and Regius Professor

---

Massachusetts Review: A Quarterly of Literature, the Arts and Public Affairs 18 (1977): 782–94.

[1] This paper was given as a Chancellor's Lecture at the University of Massachusetts, Amherst, 18 February 1975. [Achebe's note.]

[2] A reference to Achebe's 1958 novel. [ED.]

at Oxford, Hugh Trevor Roper, pronounce a few years ago that African history did not exist?

If there is something in these utterances more than youthful experience, more than a lack of factual knowledge, what is it? Quite simply it is the desire—one might indeed say the need—in Western psychology to set Africa up as a foil in Europe, a place of negations at once remote and vaguely familiar in comparison with which Europe's own state of spiritual grace will be manifest.

This need is not new: which should relieve us of considerable responsibility and perhaps make us even willing to look at this phenomenon dispassionately. I have neither the desire nor, indeed, the competence to do so with the tools of the social and biological sciences. But, I can respond, as a novelist, to one famous book of European fiction, Joseph Conrad's *Heart of Darkness*, which better than any other work I know displays that Western desire and need which I have just spoken about. Of course, there are whole libraries of books devoted to the same purpose, but most of them are so obvious and so crude that few people worry about them today. Conrad, on the other hand, is undoubtedly one of the great stylists of modern fiction and a good storyteller into the bargain. His contribution therefore falls automatically into a different class—permanent literature—read and taught and constantly evaluated by serious academics. *Heart of Darkness* is indeed so secure today that a leading Conrad scholar has numbered it "among the half-dozen greatest short novels in the English language" (Guerard, Introduction 9). I will return to this critical option in due course because it may seriously modify my earlier suppositions about who may or may not be guilty in the things of which I will now speak.

Heart of Darkness projects the image of Africa as "the other world," the antithesis of Europe and therefore of civilization, a place where a man's vaunted intelligence and refinement are finally mocked by triumphant bestiality. The book opens on the River Thames, tranquil, resting peacefully "at the decline of day after ages of good service done to the race that peopled its banks." But the actual story takes place on the River Congo, the very antithesis of the Thames. The River Congo is quite decidedly not a River Emeritus. It has rendered no service and enjoys no old-age pension. We are told that "going up that river was like travelling back to the earliest beginning of the world."

Is Conrad saying then that these two rivers are very different, one good, the other bad? Yes, but that is not the real point. What actually worries Conrad is the lurking hint of kinship, of common ancestry. For the Thames, too, "has been one of the dark places of the earth." It conquered its darkness, of course, and is now at peace. But if it were to visit its primordial relative, the Congo, it would run the terrible risk of hearing grotesque, suggestive echoes of its own forgotten darkness, and of falling victim to an avenging recrudescence of the mindless frenzy of the first beginnings.

I am not going to waste your time with examples of Conrad's famed evocation of the African atmosphere. In the final consideration it amounts to no more than a steady, ponderous, fake-ritualistic repetition of two sentences, one about silence and the other about frenzy. An example of the former is "It was the stillness of an implacable force brooding over an inscrutable intention" and of the latter, "The steamer toiled along slowly on the edge of a black and incomprehensible frenzy." Of course, there is a judicious change of adjective from time to time so that instead of "inscrutable," for example, you might have "unspeakable," etc., etc.

The eagle-eyed English critic, F. R. Leavis, drew attention nearly thirty years ago to Conrad's "adjectival insistence upon inexpressible and incomprehensible mystery." That insistence must not be dismissed lightly, as many Conrad critics have tended to do, as a mere stylistic flaw. For it raises serious questions of artistic good faith. When a writer, while pretending to record scenes, incidents and their impact, is in reality engaged in inducing hypnotic stupor in his readers through a bombardment of emotive words and other forms of trickery much more has to be at stake than stylistic felicity. Generally, normal readers are well armed to detect and resist such underhand activity. But Conrad chose his subject well—one which was guaranteed not to put him in conflict with the psychological predisposition of his readers or raise the need for him to contend with their resistance. He chose the role of purveyor of comforting myths.

The most interesting and revealing passages in *Heart of Darkness* are, however, about people. I must quote a long passage from the middle of the story in which representatives of Europe in a steamer going down the Congo encounter the denizens of Africa:

> We were wanderers on a prehistoric earth, on an earth that wore the aspect of an unknown planet. We could have fancied ourselves the first of men taking possession of an accursed inheritance, to be subdued at the cost of profound anguish and of excessive toil. But suddenly, as we struggled round a bend, there would be a glimpse of rush walls, of peaked grass-roofs, a burst of yells, a whirl of black limbs, a mass of hands clapping, of feet stamping, of bodies swaying, of eyes rolling, under the droop of heavy and motionless foliage. The steamer toiled along slowly on the edge of a black and incomprehensible frenzy. The prehistoric man was cursing us, praying to us, welcoming us—who could tell? We were cut off from the comprehension of our surroundings; we glided past like phantoms, wondering and secretly appalled, as sane men would

be before an enthusiastic outbreak in a madhouse. We could not understand . . . because we were travelling in the night of first ages, of those
ages that are gone, leaving hardly a sign—and no memories.

The earth seemed unearthly. We are accustomed to look upon the
shackled form of a conquered monster, but there—there you could look
at a thing monstrous and free. It was unearthly, and the men were—No,
they were not inhuman. Well, you know, that was the worst of it—this
suspicion of their not being inhuman. It would come slowly to one.
They howled and leaped, and spun, and made horrid faces; but what
thrilled you was just the thought . . . of your remote kinship with this
wild and passionate uproar. Ugly. Yes, it was ugly enough; but if you were
man enough you would admit to yourself that there was in you just the
faintest trace of a response to the terrible frankness of that noise, a dim
suspicion of there being a meaning in it which you—you so remote from
the night of first ages—could comprehend. [280] [3]

Herein lies the meaning of *Heart of Darkness* and the fascination it holds
over the Western mind: "What thrilled you was just the thought of their
humanity—like yours. . . . Ugly."

Having shown us Africa in the mass, Conrad then zeros in on a specific
example, giving us one of his rare descriptions of an African who is not just
limbs or rolling eyes:

And between whiles I had to look after the savage who was fireman. He
was an improved specimen; he could fire up a vertical boiler. He was
there below me, and, upon my word, to look at him was as edifying as
seeing a dog in a parody of breeches and a feather hat, walking on his
hind-legs. A few months of training had done for that really fine chap.
He squinted at the steam-gauge and at the water-gauge with an evident
effort of intrepidity—and he had filed teeth, too, the poor devil, and the
wool of his pate shaved into queer patterns, and three ornamental scars
on each of his cheeks. He ought to have been clapping his hands and
stamping his feet on the bank, instead of which he was hard at work, a
thrall to strange witchcraft, full of improving knowledge. [281]

As everybody knows, Conrad is a romantic on the side. He might not exactly admire savages clapping their hands and stamping their feet but they
have at least the merit of being in their place, unlike this dog in a parody of
breeches. For Conrad, things (and persons) being in their place is of the utmost importance.

Towards the end of the story, Conrad lavishes great attention quite unexpectedly on an African woman who has obviously been some kind of
mistress to Mr. Kurtz and now presides (if I may be permitted a little imi-

---

[3] All parenthetical references to *Heart of Darkness* are to this New Riverside Edition. [ED.]

tation of Conrad) like a formidable mystery over the inexorable immi-
nence of his departure:

> She was savage and superb, wild-eyed and magnificent . . . She stood
> looking at us without a stir, and like the wilderness itself, with an air of
> brooding over an inscrutable purpose. [305]

This Amazon is drawn in considerable detail, albeit of a predictable nature,
for two reasons. First, she is in her place and so can win Conrad's special
brand of approval; and second, she fulfills a structural requirement of the
story; she is a savage counterpart to the refined, European woman with
whom the story will end:

> She came forward, all in black, with a pale head, floating towards me in
> the dusk. She was in mourning. . . . She took both my hands in hers and
> murmured, "I had heard you were coming." . . . She had a mature ca-
> pacity for fidelity, for belief, for suffering. [318]

The difference in the attitude of the novelist to these two women is conveyed in too many direct and subtle ways to need elaboration. But perhaps
the most significant difference is the one implied in the author's bestowal
of human expression to the one and the withholding of it from the other.
It is clearly not part of Conrad's purpose to confer language on the "rudimentary souls" of Africa. They only "exchanged short grunting phrases"
even among themselves but mostly they were too busy with their frenzy.
There are two occasions in the book, however, when Conrad departs somewhat from his practice and confers speech, even English speech, on the savages. The first occurs when cannibalism gets the better of them:

> "Catch 'im," he snapped, with a bloodshot widening of his eyes and a
> flash of sharp teeth — "catch 'im. Give 'im to us." "To you, eh?" I asked;
> "what would you do with them?" "Eat 'im!" he said, curtly. . . . [285]

The other occasion is the famous announcement:

> Mistah Kurtz — he dead. [314]

At first sight, these instances might be mistaken for unexpected acts of generosity from Conrad. In reality, they constitute some of his best assaults. In
the case of the cannibals, the incomprehensible grunts that had thus far
served them for speech suddenly proved inadequate for Conrad's purpose
of letting the European glimpse the unspeakable craving in their hearts.
Weighing the necessity for consistency in the portrayal of the dumb brutes
against the sensational advantages of securing their conviction by clear,
unambiguous evidence issuing out of their own mouth, Conrad chose the
latter. As for the announcement of Mr. Kurtz's death by the "insolent black

head of the doorway," what better or more appropriate *finis* could be written to the horror story of that wayward child of civilization who willfully
had given his soul to the powers of darkness and "taken a high seat amongst
the devils of the land" than the proclamation of his physical death by the
forces he had joined?

It might be contended, of course, that the attitude to the African in
Heart of Darkness is not Conrad's but that of his fictional narrator, Marlow,
and that far from endorsing it Conrad might indeed be holding it up to
irony and criticism. Certainly, Conrad appears to go to considerable pains
to set up layers of insulation between himself and the moral universe of his
story. He has, for example, a narrator behind a narrator. The primary narrator is Marlow but his account is given to us through the filter of a second,
shadowy person. But if Conrad's intention is to draw a *cordon sanitaire* between himself and the moral and psychological malaise of his narrator, his
care seems to me totally wasted because he neglects to hint however subtly
or tentatively at an alternative frame of reference by which we may judge
the actions and opinions of his characters. It would not have been beyond
Conrad's power to make that provision if he had thought it necessary. Marlow seems to me to enjoy Conrad's complete confidence—a feeling rein-
forced by the close similarities between their careers.

Marlow comes through to us not only as a witness of truth, but one
holding those advanced and humane views appropriate to the English
liberal tradition which required all Englishmen of decency to be deeply
shocked by atrocities in Bulgaria or the Congo of King Leopold of the Belgians or wherever. Thus Marlow is able to toss out such bleeding-heart
sentiments as these:

> They were dying slowly—it was very clear. They were not enemies, they
> were not criminals, they were nothing earthly now—nothing but black
> shadows of disease and starvation, lying confusedly in the greenish
> gloom. Brought from all the recesses of the coast in all the legality of
> time contracts, lost in uncongenial surroundings, fed on unfamiliar
> food, they sickened, became inefficient, and were then allowed to crawl
> away and rest. [261]

The kind of liberalism espoused here by Marlow/Conrad touched all the
best minds of the age in England, Europe, and America. It took different
forms in the minds of different people but almost always managed to
sidestep the ultimate question of equality between white people and black
people. That extraordinary missionary, Albert Schweitzer, who sacrificed
brilliant careers in music and theology in Europe for a life of service to
Africans in much the same area as Conrad writes about, epitomizes the
ambivalence. In a comment which I have often quoted but must quote one

last time Schweitzer says: "The African is indeed my brother but my junior brother." And so he proceeded to build a hospital appropriate to the needs of junior brothers with standards of hygiene reminiscent of medical practice in the days before the germ theory of disease came into being. Naturally, he became a sensation in Europe and America. Pilgrims flocked, and I believe still flock even after he has passed on, to witness the prodigious miracle in Lamberene, on the edge of the primeval forest.

Conrad's liberalism would not take him quite as far as Schweitzer's, though. He would not use the word "brother" however qualified; the farthest he would go was "kinship." When Marlow's African helmsman falls down with a spear in his heart he gives his white master one final disquieting look.

> And the intimate profundity of that look he gave me when he received his hurt remains to this day in my memory—like a claim of distant kinship affirmed in a supreme moment. [295]

It is important to note that Conrad, careful as ever with his words, is not talking so much about *distant kinship* as about someone *laying a claim* on it. The black man lays a claim on the white man which is well-nigh intolerable. It is the laying of this claim which frightens and at the same time fascinates Conrad, ". . . the thought of their humanity—like yours. . . . Ugly [280]."

The point of my observations should be quite clear by now, namely, that Conrad was a bloody racist. That this simple truth is glossed over in criticism of his work is due to the fact that white racism against Africa is such a normal way of thinking that its manifestations go completely undetected. Students of *Heart of Darkness* will often tell you that Conrad is concerned not so much with Africa as with the deterioration of one European mind caused by solitude and sickness. They will point out to you that Conrad is, if anything, less charitable to the Europeans in the story than he is to the natives. A Conrad student told me in Scotland last year that Africa is merely a setting for the disintegration of the mind of Mr. Kurtz.

Which is partly the point: Africa as setting and backdrop which eliminates the African as human factor. Africa as a metaphysical battlefield devoid of all recognizable humanity, into which the wandering European enters at his peril. Of course, there is a preposterous and perverse kind of arrogance in thus reducing Africa to the role of props for the breakup of one petty European mind. But that is not even the point. The real question is the dehumanization of Africa and Africans which this age-long attitude has fostered and continues to foster in the world. And the question is whether a novel which celebrates this dehumanization, which depersonalizes a portion of the human race, can be called a great work of art. My answer is: No, it cannot. I would not call that man an artist, for example, who composes an eloquent instigation to one people to fall upon another and destroy them. No matter how striking his imagery or how beautiful his cadences fall such a man is no more a great artist than another may be called a priest who reads the mass backwards or a physician who poisons his patients. All those men in Nazi Germany who lent their talent to the service of virulent racism whether in science, philosophy, or the arts have generally and rightly been condemned for their perversions. The time is long overdue for taking a hard look at the work of creative artists who apply their talents, alas often considerable as in the case of Conrad, to set people against people. This, I take it, is what Yevtushenko is after when he tells us that a poet cannot be a slave trader at the same time, and gives the striking example of Arthur Rimbaud who was fortunately honest enough to give up any pretenses to poetry when he opted for slave trading. For poetry surely can only be on the side of man's deliverance and not his enslavement; for the brotherhood and unity of all mankind and against the doctrines of Hitler's master races or Conrad's "rudimentary souls."

Last year was the 50th anniversary of Conrad's death. He was born in 1857, the very year in which the first Anglican missionaries were arriving among my own people in Nigeria. It was certainly not his fault that he lived his life at a time when the reputation of the black man was at a particularly low level. But even after due allowances have been made for all the influences of contemporary prejudice on his sensibility, there remains still in Conrad's attitude a residue of antipathy to black people which his peculiar psychology alone can explain. His own account of his first encounter with a black man is very revealing:

> A certain enormous buck nigger encountered in Haiti fixed my conception of blind, furious, unreasoning rage, as manifested in the human animal to the end of my days. Of the nigger I used to dream for years afterwards. (Conrad, *Victory* xv)

Certainly, Conrad had a problem with niggers. His inordinate love of that word itself should be of interest to psychoanalysts. Sometimes his fixation on blackness is equally interesting as when he gives us this brief description:

> A black figure stood up, strode on long black legs, waving long black arms. [309]

as though we might expect a black figure striding along on black legs to have *white* arms! But so unrelenting is Conrad's obsession.

As a matter of interest Conrad gives us in a *A Personal Record* what amounts to a companion piece to the buck nigger of Haiti. At the age of sixteen Conrad encountered his first Englishman in Europe. He calls him "my unforgettable Englishman" and describes him in the following manner:

> [his] calves exposed to the public gaze . . . dazzled the beholder by the splendor of their marble-like condition and their rich tone of young ivory . . . The light of a headlong, exalted satisfaction with the world of men . . . illumined his face . . . and triumphant eyes. In passing he cast a glance of kindly curiosity and a friendly gleam of big, sound, shiny teeth . . . his white calves twinkled sturdily. (Meyer 30)

Irrational love and irrational hate jostling together in the heart of that tormented man. But whereas irrational love may at worst engender foolish acts of indiscretion, irrational hate can endanger the life of the community. Naturally, Conrad is a dream for psychoanalytic critics. Perhaps the most detailed study of him in this direction is by Bernard C. Meyer, M.D. In this lengthy book, Dr. Meyer follows every conceivable lead (and sometimes inconceivable ones) to explain Conrad. As an example, he gives us long disquisitions on the significance of hair and hair-cutting in Conrad. And yet not even one word is spared for his attitude to black people. Not even the discussion of Conrad's antisemitism was enough to spark off in Dr. Meyer's mind those other dark and explosive thoughts. Which only leads one to surmise that Western psychoanalysts must regard the kind of racism displayed by Conrad as absolutely normal despite the profoundly important work done by Frantz Fanon in the psychiatric hospitals of French Algeria.

Whatever Conrad's problems were, you might say he is now safely dead. Quite true. Unfortunately, his heart of darkness plagues us still. Which is why an offensive and totally deplorable book can be described by a serious scholar as "among the half dozen greatest short novels in the English language," and why it is today perhaps the most commonly prescribed novel in the twentieth-century literature courses in our own English Department here. Indeed the time is long overdue for a hard look at things.

There are two probable grounds on which what I have said so far may be contested. The first is that it is no concern of fiction to please people about whom it is written. I will go along with that. But I am not talking about pleasing people. I am talking about a book which parades in the most vulgar fashion prejudices and insults from which a section of mankind has suffered untold agonies and atrocities in the past and continues to do so in many ways and many places today. I am talking about a story in which the very humanity of black people is called in question. It seems to me totally inconceivable that great art or even good art could possibly reside in such unwholesome surroundings.

Secondly, I may be challenged on the grounds of actuality. Conrad, after all, sailed down the Congo in 1890 when my own father was still a babe in arms, and recorded what he saw. How could I stand up in 1975, fifty years after his death and purport to contradict him? My answer is that as a sensible man I will not accept just any traveller's tales solely on the grounds that I have not made the journey myself. I will not trust the evidence even of a man's very eyes when I suspect them to be as jaundiced as Conrad's. And we also happen to know that Conrad was, in the words of his biographer, Bernard C. Meyer, "notoriously inaccurate in the rendering of his own history" (30).

But more important by far is the abundant testimony about Conrad's savages which we could gather if we were so inclined from other sources and which might lead us to think that these people must have had other occupations besides merging into the evil forest or materializing out of it simply to plague Marlow and his dispirited band. For as it happened, soon after Conrad had written his book an event of far greater consequence was taking place in the art world of Europe. This is how Frank Willett, a British art historian, describes it:

> Gaugin had gone to Tahiti, the most extravagant individual act of turning to a non-European culture in the decades immediately before and after 1900, when European artists were avid for new artistic experiences, but it was only about 1904–5 that African art began to make its distinctive impact. One piece is still identifiable; it is a mask that had been given to Maurice Vlaminck in 1905. He records that Derain was "speechless" and "stunned" when he saw it, bought it from Vlaminck and in turn showed it to Picasso and Matisse, who were also greatly affected by it. Ambroise Vollard then borrowed it and had it cast in bronze . . . The revolution of twentieth century art was under way! (35–36)

The mask in question was made by other savages living just north of Conrad's River Congo. They have a name, the Fang people, and are without a doubt among the world's greatest masters of the sculptured form. As you might have guessed, the event to which Frank Willett refers marked the beginning of cubism and the infusion of new life into European art that had run completely out of strength.

The point of all this is to suggest that Conrad's picture of the people of the Congo seems grossly inadequate even at the height of their subjection to the ravages of King Leopold's International Association for the Civilization of Central Africa. Travellers with closed minds can tell us little except about themselves. But even those not blinkered, like Conrad, with xenophobia, can be astonishingly blind.

Let me digress a little here. One of the greatest and most intrepid travellers of all time, Marco Polo, journeyed to the Far East from the Mediter-

ranean in the thirteenth century and spent twenty years in the court of
Kublai Khan in China. On his return to Venice he set down in his book entitled *Description of the World* his impressions of the peoples and places
and customs he had seen. There are at least two extraordinary omissions
in his account. He says nothing about the art of printing unknown as yet
in Europe but in full flower in China. He either did not notice it at all or if
he did, failed to see what use Europe could possibly have for it. Whatever
reason, Europe had to wait another hundred years for Gutenberg. But even
more spectacular was Marco Polo's omission of any reference to the Great
Wall of China nearly 4000 miles long and already more than 1000 years
old at the time of his visit. Again, he may not have seen it; but the Great
Wall of China is the only structure built by man which is visible from the
moon![4] Indeed, travellers can be blind.

As I said earlier, Conrad did not originate the image of Africa which we
find in his book. It was and is the dominant image of Africa in the Western
imagination and Conrad merely brought the peculiar gifts of his own mind
to bear on it. For reasons which can certainly use close psychological inquiry, the West seems to suffer deep anxieties about the precariousness of
its civilization and to have a need for constant reassurance by comparing it
with Africa. If Europe, advancing in civilization, could cast a backward
glance periodically at Africa trapped in primordial barbarity, it could say
with faith and feeling: There go I but for the grace of God. Africa is to Europe as the picture is to Dorian Gray—a carrier onto whom the master un-
loads his physical and moral deformities so that he may go forward, erect
and immaculate. Consequently, Africa is something to be avoided just as
the picture has to be hidden away to safeguard the man's jeopardous integrity. Keep away from Africa, or else! Mr. Kurtz of *Heart of Darkness* should
have heeded that warning and the prowling horror in his heart would have
kept its place, chained to its lair. But he foolishly exposed himself to the
wild irresistible allure of the jungle and lo! the darkness found him out.

In my original conception of this talk I had thought to conclude it nicely
on an appropriately positive note in which I would suggest from my priv-
ileged position in African and Western culture some advantages the West
might derive from Africa once it rid its mind of old prejudices and began
to look at Africa not through a haze of distortions and cheap mystifica-
tion but quite simply as a continent of people—not angels, but not rudimentary souls either—just people, often highly gifted people and often

---

[4] About the omission of the Great Wall of China, I am indebted to *The Journey of Marco Polo* as recreated by artist Michael Foreman, published by Pegasus, 1974. [Achebe's note.]

strikingly successful in their enterprise with life and society. But as I thought more about the stereotype image, about its grip and pervasiveness, about the willful tenacity with which the West holds it to its heart; when I thought of your television and the cinema and newspapers, about books read in schools and out of school, of churches preaching to empty pews about the need to send help to the heathen in Africa, I realized that no easy optimism was possible. And there is something totally wrong in offering bribes to the West in return for its good opinion of Africa. Ultimately, the abandonment of unwholesome thoughts must be its own and only reward. Although I have used the word *willful* a few times in this talk to characterize the West's view of Africa it may well be that what is happening at this stage is more akin to reflex action than calculated malice. Which does not make the situation more, but less, hopeful. Let me give you one last and really minor example of what I mean.

Last November the *Christian Science Monitor* carried an interesting article written by its Education Editor on the serious psychological and learning problems faced by little children who speak one language at home and then go to school where something else is spoken. It was a wide-ranging article taking in Spanish-speaking children in this country, the children of migrant Italian workers in Germany, the quadrilingual phenomenon in Malaysia and so on. And all this while the article speaks unequivocally about *language*. But then out of the blue sky comes this:

> In London there is an enormous immigration of children who speak Indian or Nigerian dialects, or some other native language. (Parsons 11)

I believe that the introduction of *dialects,* which is technically erroneous in the context, is almost a reflex action caused by an instinctive desire of the writer to downgrade the discussion to the level of Africa and India. And this is quite comparable to Conrad's withholding of language from his rudimentary souls. Language is too grand for these chaps; let's give them dialects. In all this business a lot of violence is inevitably done to words and their meaning. Look at the phrase "native language" in the above excerpt. Surely the only native language possible in London is Cockney English. But our writer obviously means something else — something Indians and Africans speak.

Perhaps a change will come. Perhaps this is the time when it can begin, when the high optimism engendered by the breathtaking achievements of Western science and industry is giving way to doubt and even confusion. There is just the possibility that Western man may begin to look seriously at the achievements of other people. I read in the papers the other day a suggestion that what America needs at this time is somehow to bring back the extended family. And I saw in my mind's eye future African Peace Corps Volunteers coming to help you set up the system.

Seriously, although the work which needs to be done may appear too daunting, I believe that it is not one day too soon to begin. And where better than at a University?

Heart of Darkness:
Anti-Imperialism, Racism, or Impressionism?

Patrick Brantlinger

In a 1975 lecture at the University of Massachusetts, Nigerian novelist Chinua Achebe attacked *Heart of Darkness* as "racist." Conrad "projects the image of Africa as 'the other world,' the antithesis of Europe and therefore of civilization, a place where man's vaunted intelligence and refinement are finally mocked by triumphant bestiality" ("Image" 374).[1] Supposedly the great demystifier, Conrad is instead a "purveyor of comforting myths" and even "a bloody racist." Achebe adds: "That this simple truth is glossed over in criticisms of his work is due to the fact that white racism against Africa is such a normal way of thinking that its manifestations go completely undetected" ("Image" 379). Achebe would therefore like to strike Conrad's novella from the curriculum, where it has been one of the most frequently taught works of modern fiction in English classes from Chicago to Bombay to Johannesburg.

Achebe's diatribe has provoked a number of vigorous defenses of *Heart of Darkness,* which predictably stress Conrad's critical stance toward imperialism and also the wide acceptance of racist language and categories in the late Victorian period. Cedric Watts, for example, argues that "really Conrad and Achebe are on the same side."[2] Achebe simply gets carried away by his understandable aversion to racial stereotyping. "Far from being a 'purveyor of comforting myths,'" Watts declares, "Conrad most deliberately and incisively debunks such myths." Acknowledging that Conrad

---

Criticism 27 (1985): 363–85.

[1] All parenthetical references to Achebe's essay "An Image of Africa" are to this New Riverside Edition. [ED.] See also Achebe, "Viewpoint" 113. [Brantlinger's note.]

[2] For another defense, see Hawkins, "Racism." Among critics who support Achebe, see Blake, and Redmond. Achebe is, however, in a minority even among nonwestern writers; see Nazareth. [Brantlinger's note.]

employed the stereotypic language common in his day, Watts contends that he nevertheless rose above racism:

> Achebe notes with indignation that Conrad (in the "Author's Note" to *Victory*) speaks of an encounter with a 'buck nigger' in Haiti which gave him an impression of mindless violence. Achebe might as well have noted the reference in *The Nigger of the "Narcissus"* . . . to a "tormented and flattened face—a face pathetic and brutal: the tragic, the mysterious, the repulsive mask of a nigger's soul." He might have noted, also, that Conrad's letters are sprinkled with casual anti-Semitic references. It is the same in the letters of his friend [R. B. Cunninghame] Graham. Both Conrad and Graham were influenced by the climate of prejudice of their times. . . . What is interesting is that the best work of both men seems to transcend such prejudice. (208)

Their work "transcends prejudice," Watts believes, partly because they both attack imperialism. Watts is one of the many critics who interpret *Heart of Darkness* as an exposé of imperialist rapacity and violence. Kurtz's career in deviltry obviously undermines imperialist ideology, and the greed of the "faithless pilgrims"—the white sub-Kurtzes, so to speak—is perhaps worse. "The conquest of the earth," Marlow declares, "which mostly means the taking it away from those who have a different complexion or slightly flatter noses than ourselves, is not a pretty thing when you look into it too much" (251).[3] There is nothing equivocal about that remark; Conrad entertained no illusions about imperialist violence. But Marlow distinguishes between British imperialism and that of the other European powers: the red parts of the map are good to see, he says, "because one knows that some real work is done in there" (254). *Heart of Darkness* is specifically about what Conrad saw in King Leopold's African empire in 1890; the extent to which his critique can be generalized to imperialism beyond the Congo is unclear.

The politics of Conrad's story are complicated by its ambiguous style. I will use "impressionism" as a highly inadequate term to refer to its language and narrative structure, in part because Fredric Jameson uses it in his diagnosis of the "schizophrenic" nature of *Lord Jim* (206–80).[4] Conrad's "impressionism" is for some critics his most praiseworthy quality, while for others it appears instead to be a means of obfuscation, allowing him to mask his "nihilism," or to maintain contradictory values, or both. Interpretations of *Heart of Darkness* which read it as only racist (and therefore

---

[3] All parenthetical references to *Heart of Darkness* are to this New Riverside Edition. [ED.]
[4] See also Watt's discussion of "impressionism" and "symbolism," 168–200. [Brantlinger's note.]

imperialist), or conversely as only anti-imperialist (and therefore anti-racist), inevitably founder on its "impressionism." To point only to the most obvious difficulty, the narrative frame filters everything that is said not just through Marlow, but also through the anonymous primary narrator. At what point is it safe to assume that Conrad/Marlow express a single point of view? And even supposing that Marlow speaks directly for Conrad, does Conrad/Marlow agree with the values expressed by the primary narrator? Whatever the answers, *Heart of Darkness,* I believe, offers a powerful critique of at least certain manifestations of imperialism and racism, at the same time that it presents that critique in ways which can only be characterized as both imperialist and racist. "Impressionism" is the fragile skein of discourse which expresses—or disguises—this "schizophrenic" contradiction as an apparently harmonious whole.

I

In *Conrad and Imperialism,* Benita Parry argues that "by revealing the disjunctions between high-sounding rhetoric and sordid ambitions and indicating the purposes and goals of a civilisation dedicated to global . . . hegemony, Conrad's writings [are] more destructive of imperialism's ideological premises than [are] the polemics of his contemporary opponents of empire" (10). Perhaps. It is at least certain that Conrad was appalled by the "high-sounding rhetoric" which had been used to mask the "sordid ambitions" of King Leopold II of Belgium, Conrad's ultimate employer during his six months in the Congo in 1890. *Heart of Darkness* expresses not only what Conrad saw and partially recorded in his "Congo Diary," but also the revelations of atrocities which began appearing in the British press as early as 1888 and which reached a climax twenty years later, when in 1908 the mounting scandal forced the Belgian government to take control of Leopold's private domain. During that period the population of the Congo was reduced by perhaps one half; as many as 6,000,000 persons may have been uprooted, tortured, and murdered through the forced labor system used to extract ivory and what reformers called "red rubber" from "the heart of darkness."[5] Conrad was sympathetic to the Congo Reform

---

[5] Cookey (35) dates the beginning of British humanitarian protest against Leopold's policies as early as 1888. Morel estimated the decline of the population of the Congo over a twenty-five year period as 8,000,000 (*History* 7). In the appendix, the editors cite the Commission for the Protection of Natives formed by the Belgian government, which in 1919 declared that the population of the Congo may have declined by as much as one half over the same period. Exact figures are, of course, impossible to come by. Roger

Association, established in 1903 partly by his friend Roger Casement whom
he had met in Africa, and Casement got him to write a propaganda letter
in which Conrad says: "It is an extraordinary thing that the conscience of
Europe which seventy years ago . . . put down the slave trade on humanitarian grounds tolerates the Congo state today."[6] There follows some patronizing language contrasting the brutalities visited upon the Congolese
with the legal protections given to horses in Europe, but Conrad's intention is clear enough.

There is little to add to Hunt Hawkins' account of Conrad's relations with the Congo Reform Association. Its leader, Edmund Morel, who
quoted Conrad's letter to Casement in *King Leopold's Rule in Africa* (1904),
called *Heart of Darkness* the "most powerful thing ever written on the
subject" (*History* 205n).[7] But as Hawkins notes, apart from writing the letter to Casement, Conrad backed away from involvement with the Association. Other prominent novelists who'd never been to the Congo contributed as much or more to its work. Mark Twain volunteered "King
Leopold's Soliloquy," and Sir Arthur Conan Doyle wrote a book for the
Association called *The Crime of the Congo*. Hawkins notes that Conrad
"had little faith in agitation for political reform because words were meaningless, human nature unimprovable, and the universe dying" ("Imperialism" 292–93)—hardly views that would encourage engagement in a cause
like that of the Association.

All the same, in at least one other work of fiction Conrad registered his
abhorrence of King Leopold's rape of the Congo. This is the minor but
highly revealing fantasy which Conrad co-authored with Ford Madox
Hueffer, *The Inheritors: An Extravagant Story* (1901).[8] Conrad's role in its
writing may have been slight, but was still substantial enough to make plain
that he shared the views expressed in it. Briefly, the protagonist meets a
beautiful young woman who claims to come from the "fourth dimension"
and to be one of those who "shall inherit the earth."

> The Dimensionists were to come in swarms, to materialise, to devour
> like locusts. . . . They were to come like snow in the night: in the morn-
> ing one would look out and find the world white. . . . As to methods, we
> should be treated as we ourselves treat the inferior races. (16)

Casement offered the perhaps conservative estimate that Leopold's exploitation reduced
the population by 3,000,000. See Legum 35. [Brantlinger's note.]

[6] Conrad's letter is quoted in Morel, *Rule* 351–52. [Brantlinger's note.]

[7] See Hawkins, "Congo Reform"; "Congolese"; and "Imperialism." The Morel quotation
appears in the latter article (293). [Brantlinger's note.]

[8] On the collaboration between Conrad and Hueffer, see Moser 40–47. [Brantlinger's
note.]

Far from being meek, the "inheritors" are obviously modern-day imperialists, satirically depicted as invaders from a "spiritualist" alternative world. But apart from the young woman and one other character, the invasion does not occur during the course of the novel, although the satire upon imperialism is maintained through the portrayal of the Duc de Mersch and his "System for the Regeneration of the Arctic Regions" (46). Like King Leopold, "The foreign financier—they called him the Duc de Mersch—was by way of being a philanthropist on megalomaniac lines." He proves ultimately to be no philanthropist at all, but just the sort of "gigantic and atrocious fraud" that Conrad believed Leopold to be. All one needs to do to read *The Inheritors* as an attack on Leopold's African regime is to substitute "Congo" for "Greenland." The hero, journalist Arthur Granger, helps to expose "the real horrors of the système Groënlandais—flogged, butchered, miserable natives, the famines, the vices, diseases, and the crimes" (280). The authors are not even particular about the color of the eskimo victims: one character says that the Duc "has the blacks murdered" (246–47).

Hueffer and Conrad write some scorching things in *The Inheritors* about "cruelty to the miserable, helpless, and defenceless" (282). But the facts of exploitation in the Congo are perhaps less distressing to them than the lying idealism which disguises it:

> More revolting to see without a mask was that falsehood which had been hiding under the words which for ages had spurred men to noble deeds, to self-sacrifice, to heroism. What was appalling was . . . that all the traditional ideals of honour, glory, conscience, had been committed to the upholding of a gigantic and atrocious fraud. The falsehood had spread stealthily, had eaten into the very heart of creeds and convictions that we learn upon our passage between the past and the future. The old order of things had to live or perish with a lie. (282)

I will come back to the possibility that the worst feature of imperialism for Conrad may not have been its violence toward the "miserable" and "helpless," but the lying propaganda used to cover its bloody tracks.

As Hawkins and others have pointed out, Conrad did not base his critique of imperialist exploitation in *Heart of Darkness* solely on what he had seen in the Congo. What he witnessed was miserable enough, and he was also made personally miserable and resentful by disease and the conviction that his Belgian employers were exploiting him. But, as he assured Casement, while in the Congo he had not even heard of "the alleged custom of cutting off hands among the natives."[9] The conclusion that Casement drew

---

[9] Conrad to Roger Casement, quoted in Morel, *Rule* 117. [Brantlinger's note.]

from this and other evidence was that most of the cruelties practiced in the Congo were not traditional, but were the recent effects of exploitation. The cutting off of hands was a punishment for noncooperation in Leopold's forced labor system, and probably became frequent only after 1890. And just as Conrad had seen little or no evidence of torture, so, Molly Mahood conjectures (12), he probably saw little or no evidence of cannibalism, despite the stress upon it in his story.

It thus seems likely that much of the "horror" either depicted or suggested in *Heart of Darkness* does not represent what Conrad saw, but rather his reading of the literature which exposed Leopold's bloody system between the time of his return to England and the composition of the novella in 1898–99. While Conrad's "Congo Diary" and every facet of his journey to Stanley Falls and back has been scrutinized by Norman Sherry and others, much less attention has been paid to what Conrad learned about the Congo after his sojourn there.[10] The exposé literature undoubtedly confirmed suspicions which Conrad formed in 1890; the bloodiest period in the history of Leopold's regime began about a year later. According to Edmund Morel: "From 1890 onwards the records of the Congo State have been literally blood-soaked. Even at that early date, the real complexion of Congo State philanthropy was beginning to appear, but public opinion in Europe was then in its hoodwinked stage" (*Rule* 103).

The two events which did most to bring Leopold's Congo under public scrutiny after Conrad's time there were the 1891–94 war between Leopold's forces and the Arab slave-traders and the murder of Charles Stokes, English citizen and renegade missionary, by Belgian officials in 1895. The conflict with the Arabs—a "war of extermination," according to Morel—was incredibly cruel and bloody. "The first serious collision with the Arabs occurred in October 27, 1891; the second on May 6, 1892. Battle then succeeded battle; Nyangwe, the Arab stronghold, was captured in January, 1893, and with the surrender of Rumaliza in January, 1894, the campaign came to an end" (*Rule* 23). Conrad undoubtedly read about these events in the press and perhaps also in later accounts, notably Captain Sidney Hinde's *The Fall of the Congo Arabs* (1897). Arthur Hodister, whom Sherry claims as the original of Kurtz, was an early victim of the fighting, having led an expedition to Katanga which was crushed by the Arabs. According to Ian Watt, "*The Times* reported of Hodister and his comrades that 'their heads were stuck on poles and their bodies eaten'" (142). This and many similar episodes during the war are probable sources of Conrad's emphasis upon cannibalism in *Heart of Darkness*.

---

[10]See Sherry, *World;* Jean-Aubry; and Zins. [Brantlinger's note.]

Cannibalism was practiced by both sides in the war, not just the Arabs and their Congolese soldiers. According to Hinde, who must also be counted among the possible models for Kurtz, "The fact that both sides were cannibals, or rather that both sides had cannibals in their train, proved a great element in our success" (124–25).[11] Muslims, Hinde points out, believe that they will go to heaven only if their bodies are intact, as opposed to mutilated, chopped up, eaten. So cannibalism was in part a weapon of fear and reprisal on both sides, and in part also a traditional accompaniment of war among some Congolese societies. Hinde speaks of combatants on both sides as "human wolves" and describes numerous "disgusting banquets" (69). A typical passage in his account reads: "What struck me most in these expeditions was the number of partially cut-up bodies I found in every direction for miles around. Some were minus the hands and feet, and some with steaks cut from the thighs or elsewhere; others had the entrails or the head removed, according to the taste of the individual savage . . ." (131). Hinde's descriptions of such atrocities seem to be those of an impartial, external observer, but in fact he was one of six white officers in charge of some four hundred "regulars" and "about 25,000" "cannibal" troops. His expressions of horror seem only what are expected of an Englishman, but they are also those of a participant and contradict more honest expressions of sadistic fascination with every bloodthirsty detail.

While it seems likely that Conrad read Hinde's lurid account, he must have known about the war from earlier accounts such as those in *The Times*. To cite one other example, in a series of journal extracts published in the *The Century Magazine* in 1896–97, E. J. Glave documented "cruelty in the Congo Free State." According to Glave, "The state has not suppressed slavery, but established a monopoly by driving out the Arab and Wangwana competitors." Instead of a noble war to end the slave trade, which is how Leopold and his agents justified their actions against the Arabs, a new system of slavery was installed in place of the old. Glave continues: "sometimes the natives are so persecuted that they [take revenge] by killing and eating their tormentors. Recently the state post on the Lomami lost two men killed and eaten by the natives. Arabs were sent to punish the natives; many women and children were taken, and twenty-one heads were brought to [Stanley Falls], and have been used by Captain Rom as a decoration round a flower-bed in front of his house" ("Cruelty" 706).[12] Captain Rom, no doubt, must also be counted among the possible models for Kurtz. In

---

[11] Mahood (12) makes the case for Hinde's book as one of Conrad's sources. [Brantlinger's note.]

[12] See also Glave, "New Conditions." [Brantlinger's note.]

any event, the practice of seizing Congolese for laborers and chopping off the hands and heads of resisters continued and probably increased after the defeat of the Arabs, as numerous eyewitnesses testify in the grisly quotations which form the bulk of Edmund Morel's exposés. According to a quite typical account by a Swiss observer: "If the chief does not bring the stipulated number of baskets [of raw rubber], soldiers are sent out, and the people are killed without mercy. As proof, parts of the body are brought to the factory. How often have I watched heads and hands being carried into the factory" (*Red Rubber* 77).

II

When Marlow declares that "the conquest of the earth . . . is not a pretty thing," he goes on to suggest that imperialism may be "redeemed" by the "idea" which lies behind it. But in the real world idealism is fragile, and in *Heart of Darkness,* except for the illusions maintained by a few womenfolk back in Brussels, it has almost died out. In "going native," Kurtz betrays the "civilizing" ideals with which he supposedly set out from Europe. Among the "faithless pilgrims," there are only false ideals and the false religion of self-seeking. "To tear treasure out of the bowels of the land was their desire," says Marlow, "with no more moral purpose at the back of it than there is in burglars breaking into a safe" (275). The true nature of European philanthropy in the Congo is revealed to Marlow by the chain gang and the "black shadows of disease and starvation," left to die in the "greenish gloom," whom he sees at the Outer Station (261). These miserable "phantoms" are probably accurate depictions of what Conrad saw in 1890; they may also be taken to represent what he later learned about Leopold's forced labor system. In any case, from the moment he sets foot in the Congo, Marlow is clear about the meaning of "the merry dance of death and trade" (259). It thus makes perfect sense to interpret *Heart of Darkness* as an attack on imperialism, at least as it was operative in the Congo.

But in the course of this attack, *all* "ideals" threaten to turn into "idols" — "something," in Marlow's words, which "you can set up, and bow down before, and offer a sacrifice to" (251). Conrad universalizes "darkness" partly by universalizing fetishism. Lenin, Rosa Luxemburg, and other Marxist critics of empire described the era of "the scramble for Africa" — roughly 1880 to 1914 — as one when the "commodity fetishism" of "late capitalism" was most intense, a notion which Edward Said touches upon in analyzing *The Nigger of the 'Narcissus'* (*Conrad* 142– 43). If the "natives" in their darkness set Kurtz up as an idol, the Europeans worship ivory, money, power, reputation. Kurtz joins the "natives" in their "unspeakable rites," worshipping his own unrestrained power and lust. Marlow himself assumes the pose of an idol, sitting on shipdeck with folded legs and outward palms like a Buddha. And Kurtz's Intended is perhaps the greatest fetishist of all, idolizing her image of her fiance. Marlow's lie leaves Kurtz's Intended shrouded in the protective darkness of her illusions, her idol-worship.

But the difficulty with this ingenious inversion, through which "ideals" become "idols," is that Conrad portrays the moral bankruptcy of imperialism by showing European motives and actions to be no better than African fetishism and savagery. He paints Kurtz and Africa with the same tarbrush. His version of evil—the form taken by Kurtz's Satanic behavior—is "going native." In short, evil *is* African in Conrad's story; if it is also European, that's because some number of white men in the heart of darkness behave like Africans. Conrad's stress on cannibalism, his identification of African customs with violence, lust, and madness, his metaphors of bestiality, death, and darkness, his suggestion that traveling in Africa is like traveling backward in time to primeval, infantile, but also hellish stages of existence—these features of the story are drawn from the repertoire of Victorian imperialism and racism that painted an entire continent dark.

Achebe is therefore right to call Conrad's portrayal of Africa and Africans "racist." It is possible to argue, as does Parry, that Conrad works with the white-and-black, light-and-darkness dichotomies of racist fantasy in order to subvert them, but she acknowledges that the subversion is incomplete: "Although the resonances of white are rendered discordant . . . black and dark do serve in the text as equivalences for the savage and unredeemed, the corrupt and degraded . . . the cruel and atrocious. Imperialism itself is perceived as the dark within Europe. . . . Yet despite . . . momentous departures from traditional European usage . . . the fiction gravitates back to established practice, registering the view of two incompatible orders within a manichean universe" (*Imperialism* 23). The "imperialist imagination" itself, Parry suggests, works with the "manichean," irreconcilable polarities common to all racist ideology. Achebe states the issue more succinctly: "Conrad had a problem with niggers. . . . Sometimes his fixation on blackness is . . . unrelenting" ("Image" 380).

Identifying specific sources for Conrad's later knowledge of the horrors of Leopold's regime is less important than recognizing that there were numerous sources, swelling in number through the 1890s. Conrad reshaped his firsthand experience of the Congo in the light of these sources in several ways. As I have already suggested, the emphasis on cannibalism in *Heart of Darkness* probably derives in part from Conrad's reading about the war between Leopold's agents and the Arabs. At the same time, the war is not mentioned in the novella—indeed, the Arab rivals of the Belgians for control of the Congo are conspicuous only by their absence. The omission has the important effect of sharpening the light-and-dark dichotomies, the staple of European racism; "evil" and "darkness" are parceled out between only two antithetical sides, European and African, "white" and "black." But while Conrad/Marlow treats the attribution of "evil" to the European invaders as a paradox, its attribution to Africans he treats as a given. Further, the omission of the Arabs means that Conrad does not treat cannibalism as a result of war, but as an everyday custom of the Congolese, even though he probably saw no evidence of it when he was there. Exaggerating the extent and nature of cannibalism is also standard in racist accounts of Africa.

In simplifying his memories and sources, Conrad arrived at the dichotomous or "manichean" pattern of the imperialist adventure romance, a pattern radically at odds with any realist, exposé intention. Perhaps *Heart of Darkness* expresses two irreconcilable intentions. As Parry says, "to proffer an interpretation of *Heart of Darkness* as a militant denunciation and a reluctant affirmation of imperialist civilisation, as a fiction that [both] exposes and colludes in imperialism's mystifications, is to recognise its immanent contradictions" (*Imperialism* 39). Moreover, the argument that Conrad was consciously anti-imperialist, but that he unconsciously or carelessly employed the racist terminology current in his day will not stand up, because he was acutely aware of what he was doing. Every white-black and light-dark contrast in the story, whether it corroborates racist assumptions or subverts them, is precisely calculated for its effects both as a unit in a scheme of imagery and as a focal point in a complex web of contradictory political and moral values.

Conrad knew that his story was ambiguous: he stresses that ambiguity at every opportunity, so that labeling it "anti-imperialist" is as unsatisfactory as condemning it for being "racist." The fault-line for all of the contradictions and ambiguities in the text lies between Marlow and Kurtz. Of course it also lies between Conrad and both of his ambivalent characters, not to mention the anonymous primary narrator. Is Marlow Kurtz's antagonist, critic, and potential redeemer? Or is he Kurtz's pale shadow and admirer, his double, and finally one more idolator in a story full of examples of fetishism and devil worship? Conrad poses these questions with great care, but he just as carefully refuses to answer them.

III

In the world of *Heart of Darkness,* there are no clear answers. Ambiguity, perhaps the main form of "darkness" in the story, prevails. Conrad overlays the political and moral content of his novella with symbolic and mythic patterns which divert attention from Kurtz and the Congo to "misty halos" and "moonshine." The anonymous narrator uses these metaphors to describe the difference between Marlow's stories and those of ordinary sailors:

> The yarns of seamen have a direct simplicity, the whole meaning of which lies within the shell of a cracked nut. But Marlow was not typical . . . and to him the meaning of an episode was not inside like a kernel but outside, enveloping the tale which brought it out only as a glow brings out a haze, in the likeness of one of these misty halos that sometimes are made visible by the spectral illumination of moonshine. (249–50)

The passage announces that locating the "meaning" of the story won't be easy, and in fact may be impossible. It seems almost to be a confession of defeat, or at least of contradiction. Conrad here establishes as one of his themes the problem of rendering any judgment whatsoever—moral, political, metaphysical—about Marlow's narrative. It is precisely this complexity—a theme that might be labeled the dislocation of meaning or the disorientation of values in the story—which many critics have treated as its finest feature.

In *The Political Unconscious,* Fredric Jameson argues that Conrad's stories—*Lord Jim* is his main example—betray a symptomatic split between a modernist "will to style," leading to an elaborate but essentially hollow "impressionism," and the reified, mass culture tendencies of romance conventions. In a fairly obvious way, *Heart of Darkness* betrays the same split, moving in one direction toward the "misty halos" and "moonshine" of a style which seeks to be its own meaning, apart from any "kernel" or center or embarrassingly clear content, but also grounding itself in another direction in the conventions of Gothic romance with their devalued mass culture status—conventions which were readily adapted to the heroic adventure themes of imperialist propaganda. This split almost corresponds to the contradiction of an anti-imperialist novel which is also racist. In the direction of high style, the story acquires several serious purposes, apparently including its critique of empire. In the direction of reified mass culture, it falls into the stereotypic patterns of race-thinking common to the entire tradition of the imperialist adventure story or quest romance. This double, contradictory purpose, characteristic perhaps of all of Conrad's fiction, Jameson calls "schizophrenic" (219).

By "the manichaeanism of the imperialist imagination," Parry means dividing the world between "warring moral forces"—good versus evil, civilization versus savagery, West versus East, light versus darkness, white versus black. Such polarizations are the common property of the racism and authoritarianism which constitute imperialist political theory and also of the Gothic romance conventions which were appropriated by numerous writers of imperialist adventure tales — G. A. Henty, Rider Haggard, Robert Louis Stevenson, Conan Doyle, John Buchan, Rudyard Kipling, and Conrad among them. As Martin Green points out, "Conrad of course offers us an ironic view of that genre. But he affirms its value" (313). Conrad is simultaneously a critic of the imperialist adventure and its romantic fictions, and one of the greatest writers of such fictions, his greatness deriving partly from his critical irony and partly from the complexity of his style — his "impressionism." But the chief difficulty with Jameson's argument, I think, is that the "will to style" in Conrad's text is also a will to appropriate and remake Gothic romance conventions into high art. On some level, the "impressionism" of Conrad's novels and their romance features are identical — Conrad constructs a sophisticated version of the imperialist romance — and in any case both threaten to submerge or "derealize" the critique of empire within their own more strictly esthetic project. As part of that project, providing much of the substance of "impressionism," the romance conventions which Conrad reshapes carry with them the polarizations of racist thought.

In analyzing Conrad's "schizophrenic writing," Jameson notes the proliferation of often contradictory critical opinions which mark the history of his reception: "The discontinuities objectively present in Conrad's narratives have, as with few other modern writers, projected a bewildering variety of competing and incommensurable interpretive options. . . ." Jameson proceeds to list nine different critical approaches, from "the 'romance' or mass-cultural reading of Conrad as a writer of adventure tales [and] the stylistic analysis of Conrad as a practitioner of — [an] 'impressionistic' will to style," to the "myth-critical," the Freudian, the ethical, the "ego-psychological," the existential, the Nietzschean, and the structuralist readings. Jameson leaves off of the list his own Marxist-political reading; what he wishes to suggest is how often criticism ignores or downplays the contradictory politics of Conrad's fiction. Raymond Williams voices a similar complaint:

> It is . . . astonishing that a whole school of criticism has succeeded in emptying *Heart of Darkness* of its social and historical content. . . . The Congo of Leopold follows the sea that Dombey and Son traded across, follows it into an endless substitution in which no object is itself, no social experience direct, but everything is translated into what can be called a metaphysical language — the river is Evil; the sea is Love or Death. Yet only called metaphysical, because there is not even that much guts in it. No profound and ordinary belief, only a perpetual and sophisticated evasion. . . .(145)

There are wonderfully elaborate readings of Marlow's journey as a descent into hell, playing upon Conrad's frequent allusions to Homer, Virgil, Dante, Milton, Goethe, and devil worship. And there are just as many elaborate readings of the story as an "inward voyage" of "self-discovery," in which its geopolitical language is treated as symbolizing psychological states and parts of the mind. Conrad, Albert Guerard reminds us, was Freud's contemporary, and in *Heart of Darkness* he produced the quintessential "night journey into the unconscious" (Guerard, *Conrad* 39).[13] Guerard adds that "it little matters what, in terms of psychological symbolism, we . . . say [Kurtz] represents: whether the Freudian id or the Jungian shadow or more vaguely the outlaw." Perhaps it matters just as little whether we say the story takes place in Leopold's Congo or in some purely imaginary landscape.

The point, however, is not to take issue with Guerard and other critics who concentrate on the "impressionism" of Conrad's story, but rather to restore what their readings neglect. In a great deal of contemporary criticism, words themselves have ceased to have external referents. Williams does not take Jameson's line in accusing Conrad's "will to style" of emptying *Heart of Darkness* of its "social and historical content"; instead, he accuses criticism of so emptying it. The "will to style"—or rather the will to a rarefied critical intelligence—devours us, too, leaving structuralists and deconstructionists, Althusserians and Foucauldians, and so forth. And yet Conrad has anticipated his critics by constructing a story in which the "meaning" does not lie at the center, not even at "the heart of darkness," but elsewhere, in "misty halos" and "moonshine"—forever beyond some vertiginous horizon which recedes as the would-be critic-adventurer sails toward it.

IV

The crowds [in one village] were fired into promiscuously, and fifteen were killed, including four women and a babe on its mother's breast. The heads were cut off and brought to the officer in charge, who then sent men to cut off the hands also, and these were pierced, strung, and dried over the camp fire. The heads, with many others, I saw myself. The town, prosperous once, was burnt, and what they could not carry off was destroyed. Crowds of people were caught, mostly . . . women, and three fresh rope gangs were added. These poor "prisoner" gangs were mere skeletons of skin and bone. . . . Chiyombo's very large town was

---

[13] See also the essays in Conrad, *Heart;* Harkness; and Mudrick. [Brantlinger's note.]

next attacked. A lot of people were killed, and heads and hands cut off and taken back to the officers. . . . Shortly after the State caravans, with flags flying and bugles blowing, entered the mission station at Luanza . . . and I shall not soon forget the sickening sight of deep baskets of human heads. (Morel, *Red Rubber* 49)

While the primary narrator and many critics seem to believe that the meaning of *Heart of Darkness* lies in "the spectral illumination of moonshine," Marlow knows better. "Illumination" proves as false as most white men—as false as white "civilization"; the "truth," or at least the meaning of Conrad's story, lies in "darkness." That is why, once Marlow learns about the shadowy Kurtz, he is so impatient to get to the Central Station. And yet Kurtz seems inadequate as a central character or the goal of Marlow's quest—vacuous, a mere "shade," a "hollow man." That, however, may be part of Conrad's point. Ian Watt has identified at least nine possible models for Kurtz, including Henry Morton Stanley, Arthur Hodister, and Charles Stokes, who left the Church Missionary Society for an African wife and life as a gun-runner and slave-trader (141–45).[14] In 1895 Stokes was executed in the Congo for selling guns to the Arabs, an event which, close on the heels of the war, provided a focus for British public indignation. To Watt's list of models for Kurtz I have already added Captain Hinde, author of *The Fall of the Congo Arabs,* and Captain Rom, who decorated the borders of his flower garden with skulls. The Belgian officer responsible for Stokes's illegal execution, Captain Lothaire, must also be counted.

But just as Conrad probably drew upon many sources in depicting the horrors of the Congo, so he probably had many models for Kurtz in mind. *All* of the white officers in charge of Leopold's empire were in essence Kurtzes, as the eyewitness testimony published by the Congo Reform Association demonstrates. And what about the eyewitnesses? Were they always so objective or so morally appalled as they claimed to be? What about Conrad himself? Although his role in the building of Leopold's "Congo Free State" was minor and also prior to the worst horrors, Conrad must have recognized his own complicity and seen himself as at least potentially a Kurtz-like figure. In the novella, the African wilderness serves as a mirror, in whose "darkness" Conrad/Marlow sees a death-pale self-image.

The massive evidence of wholesale torture and slaughter under the direction of Leopold's white agents suggests not only that there were numerous Kurtzes in the "heart of darkness," but also that, as Hannah Arendt contends in *The Origins of Totalitarianism,* nineteenth-century imperialism prepared the ground in which fascism and Nazism took root after

---

[14] See also Cookey 31–34. [Brantlinger's note.]

World War I. Arendt has Kurtz and other Conrad characters in mind when she describes the appeal of "the phantom world of colonial adventure" to certain types of Europeans:

> Outside all social restraint and hypocrisy, against the backdrop of native life, the gentleman and the criminal felt not only the closeness of men who share the same color of skin, but the impact of a world of infinite possibilities for crimes committed in the spirit of play, for the combination of horror and laughter, that is for the full realization of their own phantom-like existence. Native life lent these ghostlike events a seeming guarantee against all consequences because anyhow it looked to these men like a "mere play of shadows. A play of shadows, the dominant race could walk through unaffected and disregarded in the pursuit of its incomprehensible aims and needs." The world of native savages was a perfect setting for men who had escaped the reality of civilization. (70)

A great many Kurtz-like Europeans "went native" in Africa, often to the extent of practicing genocide as a hobby; some were even rumored to practice cannibalism. According to Sir Harry H. Johnston, first governor of British Central Africa, "I have been increasingly struck with the rapidity with which such members of the white race as are not of the best class, can throw over the restraints of civilization and develop into savages of unbridled lust and abominable cruelty" (68). Kurtz is not a member of the *worst* "class" of the white race, however; Conrad is talking about a quite common pattern of behavior.

One of the most remarkable perversions of the criticism of *Heart of Darkness* has been to see Kurtz not as an abomination—a "hollow man" with a lust for blood and domination—but as a "hero of the spirit." That phrase is Lionel Trilling's. In his well-known essay describing the establishment of the first course in modern literature at Columbia University, Trilling explains why he put Conrad's novella on the reading list:

> Whether or not . . . Conrad read either Blake or Nietzsche I do not know, but his *Heart of Darkness* follows in their line. This very great work has never lacked for the admiration it deserves, and it has been given a . . . canonical place in the legend of modern literature by Eliot's having it so clearly in mind when he wrote *The Waste Land* and his having taken from it the epigraph to "The Hollow Men." ("Modern" 17–18)

Despite the "hollow man" association between Eliot's poem and Conrad's novella, Trilling claims that "no one, to my knowledge, has ever confronted in an explicit way [the latter's] strange and terrible message of ambivalence toward the life of civilization" (17). In *Sincerity and Authenticity*, Trilling adds that Conrad's story is "the paradigmatic literary expression of the modern concern with authenticity," and continues: "This troubling work has no manifest polemical content but it contains in sum the whole of the radical critique of European civilization that has been made by [modern] literature" (106).

Although Trilling mentions the Congolese background of the story, it is less important to him than the larger question of the nature of "European civilization." Marlow's quest for Kurtz becomes a quest for the truth about that civilization. Trilling arrives at his view of Kurtz partly the way Marlow does, because Kurtz at the end of his satanic career seems to confront "the horror, the horror." "For Marlow," says Trilling, "Kurtz is a hero of the spirit whom he cherishes as Theseus at Colonus cherished Oedipus: he sinned for all mankind. By his regression to savagery Kurtz had reached as far down beneath the constructs of civilization as it was possible to go, to the irreducible truth of man, the innermost core of his nature, his heart of darkness. From that Stygian authenticity comes illumination. . . ." (*Sincerity* 108).

Marlow does paradoxically come to admire Kurtz because he has "summed up " or "judged" in his final moments: "He was a remarkable man" (314). Marlow's admiration for Kurtz, however, carries a terrific burden of irony which Trilling seems not to recognize. Kurtz has not merely lost faith in civilization and therefore experimented with "Stygian authenticity" — he is also a murderer, perhaps even a cannibal. He has allowed his idolators to make human sacrifices in his honor and, like Captain Rom, has decorated his corner of hell with the skulls of his victims. I suspect that Trilling arrives at his own evaluation of Kurtz as a "hero of the spirit" in part because he himself does not find "the horror" all that horrible, even though the deaths of 6,000,000 Congolese is a high price to pay for the "illumination" of "Stygian authenticity." But Trilling's interpretation of Kurtz's dying words — "the horror, the horror" — does not take account of what transpired in Leopold's Congo. "For me it is still ambiguous whether Kurtz's famous deathbed cry refers to the approach of death or to his experience of savage life" ("Modern" 18).

According to Trilling's view, either Kurtz thinks death "the horror," or Kurtz thinks African "savagery" "the horror." There is another possibility, of course, which is that Kurtz's dying words are an outcry against himself — against his betrayal of civilization and his Intended, against the smash-up of his early hopes, and also against his bloody domination of the people he has been lording it over. No one would ever mistake Conrad's other traitors to civilization as "heroes of the spirit." I am thinking, for example, of Willems who goes wrong and then "goes native" in *An Outcast of the Islands* [1896], or of the ironically sympathetic murderer Leggatt in "The Secret Sharer" [1910]. Even Lord Jim is no "hero of the spirit," but a moral cripple who manages to regain a semblance of self-respect only after fleeing to Patusan. But how was it possible for Trilling to look past Kurtz's criminal record and identify "the horror" either with the fear of death or with African "savagery"? Achebe gives part of the answer: "white racism against Africa is such a normal way of thinking that its manifestations go completely undetected"—so normal that acts which are condemned as the vilest of crimes when committed in the supposedly civilized West can be linked to a "heroism of the spirit" and to "Stygian authenticity" when committed in Africa against Africans.

But the other part of the answer, it seems to me, is that Trilling is right. Conrad himself identifies with and ironically admires Kurtz. He, too, sees him as a "hero of the spirit," although "the spirit" for Conrad is perhaps not what Trilling thinks it is. For Conrad, Kurtz's heroism consists in staring into an abyss of nihilism so total that the issues of imperialism and racism pale into insignificance. It hardly matters if the abyss is of Kurtz's making. No more than Trilling or perhaps most Western critics, I think, did Conrad concern himself deeply about "unspeakable rites" and skulls on posts. These appear in Marlow's account like so many melodrama props—the evidence of Kurtz's decline and fall, yes—but it is still Kurtz who has center stage, with whom Marlow speaks, who is the goal and farthest point of the journey. Kurtz's black victims and idolators skulking in the bushes are also so many melodrama props.

Kurtz is not only the hero of the melodrama, he is an artist, a "universal genius," and a quite powerful, eloquent "voice" as well. As Achebe points out, the African characters are, in contrast, rendered almost without intelligible language. The headman of Marlow's cannibal crew gets in a few phrases of Pidgin-minstrelese, something about eating some fellow Africans. These are the black Kurtz worshippers, shrieking and groaning incoherently in the foggy shrubbery along the river. Kurtz's "superb and savage" mistress, though described in glowing detail, is given no voice, but in spite of this I like to imagine that she, at least, entertained no illusions about Kurtz or about imperialism, unlike the prim, palefaced knitters of black wool back in Brussels. "It's queer how out of touch with truth women are" (257) says Marlow, but of course he means *white* women. Kurtz's black mistress knows all; it's just unfortunate that Marlow did not ask her for an interview.

The voices which come from the "heart of darkness" are almost exclusively white and male. As a nearly disembodied, pure "voice" emanating from the very center of the story, Kurtz is a figure for the novelist, as is his double Marlow. True, the "voice" which speaks out of the "heart of darkness" is a hollow one, the voice of the abyss; but Marlow still talks of Kurtz's "unextinguishable gift of noble and lofty expression." The "voice" of Kurtz has "electrified large meetings," and through it Kurtz "could get himself to believe anything—anything" (316). Is Conrad questioning or mocking his own "voice," his own talent for fiction-making, for lying? Is he aware that the "will to style," his own tendency to "impressionism," points toward the production of novels which are hollow at the core—which can justify any injustice—which contain, perhaps, only an abyss, a Kurtz, "the horror, the horror"? Yes, I think so. It is just this hollow "voice," so devious and ego-tistical, so capable of self-deception and lying propaganda, which speaks from the center of "the heart of darkness" to "sum up" and to "judge."

Besides a painter, musician, orator, and "universal genius," Kurtz is also, like Conrad, a writer.[15] What he writes can be seen as an analogue for the story and also its dead center, the kernel of meaning or non-meaning within its cracked shell. True, Kurtz has not written much, only seventeen pages, but "it was a beautiful piece of writing." This is his pamphlet for the "International Society for the Suppression of Savage Customs," which Marlow describes as "eloquent, vibrating with eloquence, but too high-strung, I think":

> The opening paragraph . . . in the light of later information, strikes me now as ominous. He began with the argument that we whites, from the point of development we had arrived at, "must necessarily appear to [savages] in the nature of supernatural beings—we approach them with the might as of a deity," and so on, and so on. "By the simple exercise of our will we can exert a power for good practically unbounded," etc., etc. From that point he soared and took me with him. The peroration was magnificent, though difficult to remember, you know. It gave me the no-tion of an exotic Immensity ruled by an august Benevolence. It made me tingle with enthusiasm. This was the unbounded power of eloquence. [And here I will add, "This was the unbounded will to style."] There were no practical hints to interrupt the magic current of phrases, unless a kind of note at the foot of the last page, scrawled evidently much later, in an unsteady hand, may be regarded as the exposition of a method. It was very simple, and at the end of that moving appeal to every altruistic sentiment it blazed at you, luminous and terrifying, like a flash of light-ning in a serene sky: "Exterminate all the brutes!" (294–95)

Viewed one way, Conrad's anti-imperialist story condemns the murderous racism of Kurtz's imperative. Viewed another way, Conrad's racist story voices that very imperative, and Conrad knows it. At the hollow center of *Heart of Darkness,* far from the "misty halos" and "moonshine" where the meaning supposedly resides, Conrad inscribes a text which, like the novel itself, cancels out its own best intentions.

---

[15]Schwartz (72) calls Kurtz a "demonic artist," but does not elaborate on the compari-son between Kurtz and Conrad. [Brantlinger's note.]

But now Kurtz's dying words can be seen as something more than an outcry of guilt, and certainly more than a mere expression of the fear of death or of loathing for African "savagery." They can be seen as referring to the sort of lying idealism which can rationalize any behavior, to a complete separation between words and meaning, theory and practice— perhaps to the "impressionistic" deviousness of art and language themselves. On this metaphysical level, I think, Conrad ceases to worry about the atrocities committed in the Congo and identifies with Kurtz as a fellow-artist, a "hero of the spirit" of that nihilism which Conrad himself found so attractive.

On several occasions, Conrad compared the artist with the empire builder in a way that obviously runs counter to his critique of imperialism in *Heart of Darkness.* In *A Personal Record,* Conrad writes of "that interior world where [the novelist's] thought and . . . emotions go seeking for . . . imagined adventures," and where "there are no policemen, no law, no pressure of circumstance or dread opinion to keep him within bounds." And in the first manuscript of "The Rescuer," which as John McLure points out contains "by far" Conrad's "most sympathetic" treatment of imperialism, empire-builders are "one of those unknown guides of civilization, who on the advancing edge of progress are administrators, warriors, creators. . . . They are like great artists a mystery to the masses, appreciated only by the uninfluential few." [16] Kurtz is empire-builder, artist, universal genius, and voice crying from the wilderness all in one. But he has lost the faith—vision or illusion—which can alone sustain an empire and produce great art. Nihilism is no basis upon which to found or administer a colony, and it is also no basis on which to write a novel, and again Conrad knows it. In suggesting his affinity to Kurtz, he suggests the moral bankruptcy of his own literary project. But once there were empire-builders and great artists who kept the faith. Conrad frequently expresses his admiration for the great explorers and adventurers, from Sir Walter Raleigh and Sir Francis Drake through James Brooke, the white rajah of Sarawak, and David Livingstone, the greatest of the many great explorers of the "Dark Continent."

Conrad's critique of empire is never strictly anti-imperialist. Instead, in terms that can be construed as conservative rather than nihilistic, he mourns the loss of the true faith in modern times, the closing down of frontiers, the narrowing of the possibilities for adventure, the commercialization of the world and of art, the death of chivalry and honor. Here the

---

[16] I owe this point and the quotations which illustrate it to McLure 89–90. [Brantlinger's note.]

meaning of his emphasis on the lying propaganda of modern imperialism becomes evident. What was once a true, grand, noble, albeit violent enterprise is now "a gigantic and atrocious fraud"—except maybe, Marlow thinks, in the red parts of the map, where "some real work is done." Staring into the abyss of his life, or at least of Kurtz's life, Conrad sees in his disillusionment, his nihilism, the type of the whole—the path of disintegration which is modern history. It is not just Africa or even just Kurtz who possesses a "heart of darkness"; Conrad's story bears that title as well.

But I am not going to end by announcing in "a tone of scathing contempt" the death of Conrad's story as a classic, like the insolent manager's boy announcing: "Mista Kurtz—he dead." I agree with Trilling that "authenticity," truth-telling, so far from being a negligible literary effect, is the essence of great literature. The fact that there are almost no other works of British fiction written before World War I which are critical of imperialism, and hundreds of imperialist ones which are racist through and through, is a measure of Conrad's achievement. I do not believe, moreover, that the real strength of Heart of Darkness lies in what it says about atrocities in King Leopold's Congo, though its documentary impulse is an important counter to its "will to style." As social criticism, its anti-imperialist message is undercut both by its racism and by its impressionism. But I know few novels which so insistently invoke an idealism which they don't seem to contain, and in which the modernist "will to style" is subjected to such powerful self-scrutiny—in which it is suggested that the "voice" at the heart of the novel, the voice of literature, the voice of civilization itself may in its purest, freest form yield only "the horror, the horror."

CHRONOLOGY

	Historical Events	Cultural Events
1850		Birth of Robert Louis Stevenson
1853		Elizabeth Gaskell, *Cranford*
1854	Crimean War (1854–56) Conquest of lower Burma	
1855		Charles Kingsley, *Westward Ho!* William Thackeray, *The Newcomes*
1856	Second China War (1856–60)	
1857	Indian Mutiny (1857–58) Attack on Persia	Birth of Joseph Conrad
1858	Founding of the Fenian movement in Ireland	
1859		Charles Darwin, *The Origin of Species*
1861	Acquisition of Lagos, later expanded to all Nigeria	Charles Dickens, *Great Expectations*
1865	Governor Eyre suppresses Jamaican rebellion	Birth of Rudyard Kipling
1868	Acquisition of Basutoland	Wilkie Collins, *The Moonstone*
1871	Stanley "finds" Livingstone at Lake Tanganyika Campaign against Maoris in New Zealand	Charles Darwin, *The Descent of Man*

1872	Acquisition of Dutch posts on the Gold Coast	
1873	Beginning of twenty-year-long economic depression	
1874	Disraeli succeeds Gladstone as prime minister; size of British Empire doubles over next 30 years Acquisition of Fiji Campaign against Ashantis in West Africa	
1876	Queen Victoria crowned Empress of India Creation of *l'Association Internationale du Congo*	George Eliot, *Daniel Deronda*
1878	Second Afghan War (1878–80) Acquisition of Cyprus	
1881	Acquisition of North Borneo	
1882	Conquest of Egypt	
1883		Olive Schreiner, *Story of an African Farm* Robert Louis Stevenson, *Treasure Island*
1884	Creation of *L'Etat Indépendent du Congo* Acquisition of British Somaliland	
1885	Death of General Gordon in the Sudan Acquisition of Bechuanaland Invasion and annexation of upper Burma Congress of Berlin divides Africa among European powers	
1886	First bill for Irish Home Rule defeated in Parliament	
1887	Stanley's expedition up the Congo to relieve the Emin Pasha (1887–90)	H. Rider Haggard, *She*

Acquisition of Kenya, the
New Hebrides, and areas
on the Malay peninsula

1888	Samoan Civil War (1888–89) Acquisition of Brunei	Rudyard Kipling, "The Man Who Would Be King"
1889	Berlin Treaty grants Samoans independent election of king (a promise never kept) Acquisition of Southern Rhodesia	Stevenson arrives in Samoa and settles there
1890	George Washington Williams travels up the Congo Acquisition of Swaziland, Uganda, Zanzibar, and Southern Rhodesia	Conrad travels up the Congo
1891	Acquisition of Nyasaland	
1892	Second bill for Irish Home Rule defeated Acquisition of the Gilbert and Ellice Islands	Robert Louis Stevenson, "The Beach of Falesá"
1893	Samoan insurrection Acquisition of the British Solomons	
1894		Stevenson dies in Samoa
1897		Rudyard Kipling, "Recessional" Bram Stoker, *Dracula*
1898	Acquisition of the Sudan	
1899	Boer War (1899–1902)	Joseph Conrad, *Heart of Darkness*
1900	Samoa divided between Germany and the United States Acquisition of Tonga	Joseph Conrad, *Lord Jim*
1901	Death of Queen Victoria; succeeded by Edward VII	Rudyard Kipling, *Kim*
1902	Creation of Empire Day	J. A. Hobson, *Imperialism*

1904		Joseph Conrad, *Nostromo*
1909	Acquisition of areas on the Malay peninsula	
1912		Arthur Conan Doyle, *The Lost World*
1914	World War I (1914–18)	

WORKS CITED

The "Works Cited" constitutes a thorough bibliography of useful works on the period and of secondary works on Kipling, Stevenson, and Conrad cited in this book.

Achebe, Chinua. "An Image of Africa." *Massachusetts Review: A Quarterly of Literature, the Arts and Public Affairs* 18 (1977): 782–94.

———. "Viewpoint." *Times Literary Supplement* 1 Feb. 1980: 113.

Anderson, James. *The Constitution of the Free-Masons.* London: Senex and Hooke, 1723.

Anonymous. "The Natural History of Morals." Rev. of *History of Civilization in England,* by Henry Thomas Buckley. *North British Review* 8 (1867): 359–403.

Arendt, Hannah. *Imperialism.* New York: Harcourt, Brace and World, 1968.

———. *The Origins of Totalitarianism.* New York: Harcourt, Brace, 1951.

Austen, Jane. *Mansfield Park.* Oxford illustrated ed. Oxford: Oxford UP, 1923.

Bagehot, Walter. "Importance of Obedience and Coherence to Primitive Man." *Fortnightly Review* 8 (1867): 513–20.

———. "Politics and Physics." *Fortnightly Review* 9 (1868): 452–60.

Balfour, Graham. *The Life of Robert Louis Stevenson.* 2 vols. New York: Scribner's, 1901.

Blake, Susan L. "Racism and the Classics: Teaching *Heart of Darkness.*" *College Language Association Journal* 25 (1982): 396–404.

Bonwick, James. "The Australian Natives." *Journal of the Anthropological Institute of Great Britain and Ireland* 16 (1887): 201–10.

Bourdieu, Pierre. "Delegation and Political Fetishism." *Thesis Eleven* 10–11 (1984–85): 56–70.

Brantlinger, Patrick. *Rule of Darkness: British Literature and Imperialism, 1830–1914.* Ithaca: Cornell UP, 1988.

Breeze, David J., and Brian Dobson. *Hadrian's Wall.* London: Lane, 1976.

Brooks, Peter. *Reading for the Plot: Design and Intention in Narrative.* New York: Knopf, 1984.

Carrington, Charles. *Rudyard Kipling: His Life and Work.* Rev. ed. London: Macmillan, 1978.

Charnock, R. S. "Minutes of November 16, 1869." *Anthropological Review* (1870): xiv–xix.

Cole, Sarah. "Conradian Alienation and Imperial Intimacy." *Modern Fiction Studies* 44 (1998): 251–81.

Conrad, Joseph. *The Collected Letters of Joseph Conrad.* Ed. Frederick Karl and Laurence Davies. 5 vols. Cambridge: Cambridge UP, 1986.

———. *Victory.* Garden City: Doubleday, 1921.

Conrad, Joseph, and Ford Madox Hueffer. *The Inheritors: An Extravagant Story.* New York: McLure, Phillips, 1901.

Cookey, S. J. *Britain and the Congo Question, 1885–1913.* London: Longman, 1968.

Darwin, Charles. *The Descent of Man.* Philadelphia: McKay, 1874.

Draudt, Manfred. "Reality or Delusion? Narrative Technique and Meaning in Kipling's *The Man Who Would Be King.*" *English Studies* 69 (1984): 316–26.

Fieldhouse, D. K. *Economics and Empire.* London: Macmillan, 1984.

Final Act of the Conference on the Affairs of Samoa, Signed at Berlin, June 14, 1889. London: HMSO, 1890.

Fleming, Alice Macdonald. "Some Childhood Memories of Rudyard Kipling." *Chambers Journal* 87 (1939): 168–73.

Franklin, John Hope. *George Washington Williams: A Biography.* Chicago: U of Chicago P, 1985.

Furnas, J. C. *Voyage to Windward: The Life of Robert Louis Stevenson.* New York: Sloane, 1951.

Fussell, Paul. "Irony, Freemasonry and Humane Ethics in Kipling's *The Man Who Would Be King.*" *ELH* 25 (1958): 216–33.

Galton, Francis. "Hereditary Talent, and Character." *Macmillan's Magazine* 12 (1865): 157–58.

———. *Inquiries into Human Faculty and Its Development.* 1883. London: Dent, 1911.

Ghose, Indira. *Women Travelers in Colonial India: The Power of the Female Gaze.* New York: Oxford UP, 1998.

Gilmour, Peter. "Robert Louis Stevenson: Forms of Evasion." *Robert Louis Stevenson.* Ed. Andrew Noble. Totowa: Barnes and Noble, 1983.

Glave, E. J. "Cruelty in the Congo Free State." *Century Magazine* 54 (1897): 706.

———. "New Conditions in Central Africa." *Century Magazine* 53 (1896–97): 900–15.

Gould, Steven Jay. *The Mismeasure of Man.* New York: Norton, 1981.

Green, Martin. *Dreams of Adventure, Deeds of Empire.* New York: Basic Books, 1979.

Green, Roger Lancelyn, ed. *Kipling: The Critical Heritage.* London: Routledge and Kegan Paul, 1971.

Grewal, Inderpal. *Home and Harem: Nation, Gender, Empire, and the Cultures of Travel.* Durham: Duke UP, 1996.

Guerard, Albert J. *Conrad the Novelist.* Oxford: Oxford UP, 1958.

———. Introduction. *Heart of Darkness.* New York: New American Library, 1950.

Haggard, H. Rider. *She, King Solomon's Mines, Allan Quatermain: Three Novels.* New York: Dover, 1951.

Harkness, Bruce, ed. *Conrad's* Heart of Darkness *and the Critics.* Belmont: Wadsworth, 1960.

Hawkins, Hunt. "Conrad and Congolese Exploitation." *Conradiana* 13 (1981): 94–100.

———. "Conrad's Critique of Imperialism in *Heart of Darkness*." *PMLA* 94 (1979): 286–99.

———. "Joseph Conrad, Roger Casement, and the Congo Reform Movement." *Journal of Modern Literature* 9 (1981): 65–80.

———. "The Issue of Racism in *Heart of Darkness*." *Conradiana* 14 (1982): 163–71.

Hinde, Captain Sidney L. *The Fall of the Congo Arabs.* London: Methuen, 1897.

Hobsbawm, Eric J. *The Age of Empire: 1875–1914.* London: Weidenfeld and Nicolson, 1987.

Hynes, William. *The Economics of Empire: Britain, Africa, and the New Imperialism, 1870–95.* London: Longman, 1979.

Jameson, Fredric. *The Political Unconscious: Narrative as a Socially Symbolic Act.* Ithaca: Cornell UP, 1981.

Jean-Aubry, Gerard. 1926. *Joseph Conrad in the Congo.* New York: Haskell House, 1973.

Johnston, Sir Harry H. *British Central Africa.* London: Methuen, 1897.

Johnstone, Arthur. *Recollections of Robert Louis Stevenson in the Pacific.* London: Chatto and Windus. 1905.

Jolly, Roslyn. "Robert Louis Stevenson and Samoan History: Crossing the Roman Wall." *Crossing Cultures: Essays on Literature and Culture of the Asia-Pacific.* Ed. Bruce Bennett, Jeff Doyle, and Satendra Nandan. London: Skoob, 1996.

Kiely, Robert. *Robert Louis Stevenson and the Fiction of Adventure.* Cambridge: Harvard UP, 1964.

Kipling, Rudyard. *Something of Myself, For My Friends, Known and Unknown.* New York: Doubleday and Douran, 1937.

Leavis, F. R. *The Great Tradition: George Eliot, Henry James, Joseph Conrad.* New York: Stewart, 1948.

Lecky, William Edward Hartpole. *History of European Morals.* 2 vols. London: Longmans and Green, 1869.

Legum, Colin. *Congo Disaster.* Baltimore: Penguin, 1961.

Long, David. *Towards a New Liberal Internationalism: The International Theory of J. A. Hobson.* Cambridge: Cambridge UP, 1996.

Lubbock, John. *The Origin of Civilization and the Primitive Condition of Man; Mental and Social Condition of Savages.* London: Longmans and Green, 1870.

Mahood, Molly M. *The Colonial Encounter: A Reading of Six Novels.* London: Collins, 1977.

Maine, Henry Sumner. *Ancient Law: Its Connection with the Early History of Society, and Its Relation to Modern Ideas.* London: Murray, 1861.

Marshall, Alfred. *Principles of Economics.* 2 vols. London: Macmillan, 1890.

McClure, John A. *Kipling and Conrad: The Colonial Fiction.* Cambridge: Harvard UP, 1981.

McLennan, John Ferguson. *Primitive Marriage*. Edinburgh: Black, 1865.

Menikoff, Barry. "A Study in Victorian Publishing." Part One in *Robert Louis Stevenson and "The Beach of Falesá": A Study in Victorian Publishing with the Original Text*. Ed. Barry Menikoff. Stanford: Stanford UP, 1984.

Meyer, Bernard, M.D. *Joseph Conrad: A Psychoanalytic Biography*. Princeton: Princeton UP, 1967.

Meyers, Jeffrey. *Fiction and the Colonial Experience*. Ipswich: Boydell, 1973.

Mills, Sara. *Discourses of Difference: An Analysis of Women's Travel Writings and Colonialism*. London: Routledge, 1991.

Morel, Edmund D. *History of the Congo Reform Movement*. Ed. W. R. Louis and Jean Stengers. Oxford: Clarendon, 1968.

———. *King Leopold's Rule in Africa*. 1904. Westport: Negro Universities Press, 1970.

———. *Red Rubber: The Story of the Rubber Slave Trade on the Congo*. London: Unwin, 1906.

Morgan, Susan. *Place Matters: Gendered Geography in Victorian Women's Travel Books about Southeast Asia*. New Brunswick: Rutgers UP, 1996.

Moser, Thomas C. *The Life in the Fiction of Ford Madox Ford*. Princeton: Princeton UP, 1980.

Mudrick, Marvin, ed. *Conrad: A Collection of Critical Essays*. Englewood Cliffs, NJ: Prentice-Hall, 1966.

Nandy, Ashis. *The Intimate Enemy: Loss and Recovery of Self under Colonialism*. Delhi: Oxford UP, 1983.

Nazareth, Peter. "Out of Darkness: Conrad and Other Third World Writers." *Conradiana* 14 (1982): 173–87.

Parry, Benita. *Conrad and Imperialism*. London: Macmillan, 1983.

———. *Delusions and Discoveries: Studies on India in the British Imagination, 1880–1930*. Berkeley: U of California P, 1972.

Parsons, Cynthia. "The 5 Million Children Who Speak a Second Language First." *Christian Science Monitor* 25 Nov. 1974: 11.

Pennefather, F. W. "Natives of New Zealand." *Journal of the Anthropological Institute of Great Britain and Ireland* 16 (1887): 211.

Pratt, Mary Louise. "Arts of the Contact Zone." *Profession* 3 (1991): 33–40.

Rao, K. Bhaskara. *Rudyard Kipling's India*. Norman: U of Oklahoma P, 1967.

Redmond, Eugene B. "Racism, or Realism? Literary Apartheid, or Poetic License? Conrad's Burden in *The Nigger of the 'Narcissus.'*" *The Nigger of the "Narcissus."* Ed. Robert Kimbrough. New York: Norton, 1979.

Ricketts, Harry. *Rudyard Kipling: A Life.* New York: Carroll and Graf, 1999.

Said, Edward W. *Culture and Imperialism.* New York: Random House, 1994.

——. *Joseph Conrad and the Fiction of Autobiography.* Cambridge: Harvard UP, 1966.

——. "*Kim,* The Pleasures of Imperialism." *Raritan* 7. 2 (1987): 27–64.

Schwartz, Daniel R. *Conrad:* Almayer's Folly *to* Under Western Eyes. Ithaca: Cornell UP, 1980.

Sedgwick, Eve Kosofsky. *Between Men: English Literature and Homosocial Desire.* New York: Columbia UP, 1985.

Seeley, J. R. *The Expansion of England: Two Courses of Lectures.* 1884. London: Macmillan, 1909.

Semmel, Bernard. *The Liberal Ideal and the Demons of Empire: Theories of Imperialism from Adam Smith to Lenin.* Baltimore: Johns Hopkins UP, 1993.

Sherry, Norman. *Conrad's Western World.* Cambridge: Cambridge UP, 1971.

——. ed. *Joseph Conrad: A Commemoration.* London: Macmillan, 1976.

Shippey, Thomas, and Michael Short. "Framing and Distancing in Kipling's *The Man Who Would Be King.*" *Journal of Narrative Technique* 2 (1972): 58–87.

Staunton, George. *Embassy to China.* 2 vols. London: Stockdale, 1797.

Stevenson, M. I. *From Saranac to the Marquesas and Beyond.* Ed. Marie Clothilde Balfour. London: Methuen, 1903.

Stevenson, Robert Louis. *Ballads.* New York: Scribner's, 1890.

——. "The Beach of Falesá." Part Two in *Robert Louis Stevenson and "The Beach of Falesá": A Study in Victorian Publishing with the Original Text.* Ed. Barry Menikoff. Stanford: Stanford UP, 1984.

——. "The Enchantress." *Georgia Review* 43 (1989): 550–68.

——. *A Footnote to History: Eight Years of Trouble in Samoa.* London: Cassell, 1892.

——. *In the South Seas.* 1896. London: Chatto and Windus, 1900.

——. *In the South Seas.* 1896. Facsimile reproduction. Honolulu: UP of Hawaii, 1971.

——. *The Letters of Robert Louis Stevenson.* Ed. Sidney Colvin. 5 vols. London: Heinemann, 1924.

——. *The Letters of Robert Louis Stevenson.* Ed. Bradford A. Booth and Ernest Mehew. 8 vols. New Haven: Yale UP, 1994–95.

——. *The Strange Case of Dr. Jekyll and Mr. Hyde and Other Stories.* New York: Scribner's, 1909.

——. *The Works of Robert Louis Stevenson.* 32 vols. New York: Scribner's, 1924.

Stoler, Ann Laura. *Race and the Education of Desire: Foucault's History of Sexuality and the Colonial Order of Things.* Durham: Duke UP, 1995.

Strobel, Margaret. *European Women and the Second British Empire.* Bloomington: Indiana UP, 1991.

Trilling, Lionel: "On the Modern Element in Literature." *Beyond Culture: Essays on Literature and Learning.* New York: Harcourt Brace Jovanovich, 1965.

——. *Sincerity and Authenticity.* Cambridge, MA: Harvard UP, 1972.

Trollope, Anthony. *The Tireless Traveler: Twenty-Five Letters to the Liverpool Mercury; 1875.* Ed. Bradford A. Booth. Berkeley: U of California P, 1978.

Turner, Frederick Jackson. "The Significance of the Frontier in American History." *The Frontier in American History.* New York: Holt, Rinehart and Winston, 1962.

Ware, Vron. *Beyond the Pale: White Women, Racism, and History.* London: Verso, 1992.

Watt, Ian. *Conrad in the Nineteenth Century.* Berkeley: U of California P, 1979.

Watts, Cedric. "'A Bloody Racist': About Achebe's View of Conrad." *Yearbook of English Studies* 13 (1983): 196–209.

Wilde, Oscar. *The Letters of Oscar Wilde.* Ed. Rupert Hart-Davis. New York: Harcourt, Brace and World, 1962.

Willett, Frank. *African Art.* New York: Praeger, 1971.

Williams, Raymond. *The English Novel from Dickens to Lawrence.* New York: Oxford UP, 1970.

Wilson, Angus. *The Strange Ride of Rudyard Kipling.* New York: Viking, 1977.

Wilson, Edmund. "The Kipling That Nobody Read." *Kipling's Mind and Art: Selected Critical Essays.* Ed. Andrew Rutherford. Stanford: Stanford UP, 1964.

Zincke, F. Barham. *Last Winter in the United States; Being Table Talk Collected During a Tour Through the Late Southern Confederation, the Far West, the Rocky Mountains, &c.* London: Murray, 1868.

Zins, Henryk. *Joseph Conrad and Africa.* Nairobi: Kenya Literature, 1982.

FOR FURTHER READING

Below are a few recommended texts not cited in this volume.

BIOGRAPHY AND CRITICISM:
KIPLING, STEVENSON, CONRAD

Bascom, Tim. "Secret Imperialism: The Reader's Response to the Narrator in 'The Man Who Would Be King.'" *English Literature in Transition* 31 (1988): 162–73.

Brown, Tony C. "Cultural Psychosis on the Frontier: The Work of the Darkness in Joseph Conrad's *Heart of Darkness.*" *Studies in the Novel* 32 (2000): 14–28.

Edmond, Ron. *Representing the South Pacific: Colonial Discourse from Cook to Gauguin.* Cambridge: Cambridge UP, 1997.

Karl, Frederick R. *Joseph Conrad: The Three Lives.* New York: Farrar, Straus, and Giroux, 1979.

Levenson, Michael. "The Value of Facts in the *Heart of Darkness.*" *Nineteenth-Century Fiction* 40 (1985): 261–80.

London, Bette. "Reading Race and Gender in Conrad's Dark Continent." *Criticism* 31 (1989): 235–52.

Raval, Suresh. *The Art of Failure: Conrad's Fiction.* Boston: Allen and Unwin, 1986.

Scannell, James. "The Method Is Unsound: The Aesthetic Dissonance of Colonial Justification in Kipling, Conrad, and Green." *Style* 30 (1996): 409–32.

Scheick, William J. "Ethical Romance: Kipling's 'The Man Who Would Be King.'" *Transforming Genres: New Approaches to British Fiction of the*

1890s. Ed. Nikki Lee Manos and Meri-Jane Rochelson. New York: St. Martin's, 1994. 109–29.

Smith, Johanna M. "'Too Beautiful Altogether': Patriarchal Ideology in *Heart of Darkness.*" *Joseph Conrad, Heart of Darkness: A Case Study in Contemporary Criticism.* Ed. Ross C. Murfin. New York: St. Martin's, 1989. 179–95.

Smith, Vanessa. *Literary Culture and the Pacific: Nineteenth-Century Textual Encounters.* Cambridge: Cambridge UP, 1998.

Stewart, David H. "Kipling, Conrad and the Dark Heart." *Conradiana* 19 (1987): 195–205.

Stewart, Garrett. "Lying as Dying in *Heart of Darkness.*" *PMLA* 95 (1980): 319–31.

STUDIES OF IMPERIALISM: HISTORY AND CULTURE

Bhabha, Homi. "Of Mimicry and Man: The Ambivalence of Colonial Discourse." *October* 28 (1984): 125–33.

———. "Signs Taken for Wonders: Questions of Ambivalence and Authority under a Tree Outside Delhi, May 1817." *Critical Inquiry* 12 (1985): 144–65.

Bivona, Daniel. *British Imperial Literature: Writing and the Administration of Empire.* Cambridge: Cambridge UP, 1998.

Bongie, Chris. *Exotic Memories: Literature, Colonialism, and the Fin de Siecle.* Stanford: Stanford UP, 1991.

Boone, Joseph Allen. "Vacation Cruises; or the Homoerotics of Orientalism." *PMLA* 110 (1995): 89–107.

Bristow, Joseph. *Empire Boys: Adventures in a Man's World.* London: Harper, 1991.

Cramb, J. A. *The Origins and Destiny of Imperial Britain and Nineteenth Century Europe.* New York: Dutton, 1915.

Herbert, Christopher. *Culture and Anomie: Ethnographic Imagination in the Nineteenth Century.* Chicago: U of Chicago P, 1991.

Hobson, J. A. *The Psychology of Jingoism.* London: Richards, 1901.

Lane, Christopher. *The Ruling Passion: British Colonial Allegory and the Paradox of Homosexual Desire.* Durham: Duke UP, 1995.

McClintock, Anne. *Imperial Leather: Race, Gender, and Sexuality in the Colonial Conquest.* New York: Routledge, 1995.

Pakenham, Thomas. *The Scramble for Africa.* London: Weidenfeld and Nicolson, 1991.

Pratt, Mary Louise. *Imperial Eyes: Travel Writing and Transculturation.* London: Routledge, 1992.

Rennie, Neil. *Far-Fetched Facts: The Literature of Travel and the Idea of the South Seas.* Oxford: Clarendon, 1995.

Spivak, Gayatri. "Three Women's Texts and a Critique of Imperialism." *Critical Inquiry* 12 (1985): 243–61.

Suleri, Sara. *The Rhetoric of English India.* Chicago: U of Chicago P, 1992.

Torgovnick, Marianna. *Gone Primitive.* Chicago: U of Chicago P, 1990.

Young, Robert J. C. *Colonial Desire: Hybridity in Theory, Culture, and Race.* New York: Routledge, 1995.

RELATED LITERARY, POPULAR, AND OTHER TEXTS

Achebe, Chinua. *Things Fall Apart.* London: Heineman, 1958.

Brontë, Charlotte. *Jane Eyre.* 3 vols. London: Smith, Elder, 1847.

Burton, Richard. *The Lake Regions of Central Africa: A Picture of Exploration.* New York: Harper, 1860.

Collins, Wilkie. *The Moonstone.* London: Tinsley, 1868.

Conrad, Joseph. *Lord Jim.* Edinburgh: Blackwood, 1900.

———. *Nostromo: A Tale of the Seaboard.* London: Harper, 1904.

Darwin, Charles. *The Origin of Species by Means of Natural Selection.* 2nd ed. New York: Burt, 1860.

Defoe, Daniel. *Robinson Crusoe.* 1719. London: Bettesworth, 1724.

Dickens, Charles. *Great Expectations.* 3 vols. London: Chapman and Hall, 1861.

Doyle, Arthur Conan. *The Lost World.* London: Murray, 1912.

Eliot, George. *Daniel Deronda.* Edinburgh: Blackwood, 1876.

Gaskell, Elizabeth. *Cranford.* London: Harper, 1853.

Hugo, Victor. *The Toilers of the Sea.* New York: Harper, 1867.

Kingsley, Charles. *Westward Ho!* 3 vols. Cambridge: Macmillan, 1855.

Kipling, Rudyard. *Kim.* London: Macmillan, 1901.

McClintock, F. Leopold. *The Voyage of the "Fox" in the Arctic Seas.* 1857. London: Murray, 1859.

Rhys, Jean. *Wide Sargasso Sea.* London: Deutsch, 1966.

Schreiner, Olive. *Story of an African Farm.* London: Hutchinson, 1883.

Stanley, Henry Morton. *How I Found Livingstone.* London: Low, 1872.

Stevenson, Robert Louis. *Kidnapped.* London: Cassell, 1886.

———. *The Master of Ballantrae.* London: Cassell, 1889.

———. *South Sea Tales.* Oxford: Oxford UP, 1996.

———. *Treasure Island.* London: Cassell, 1883.

Stoker, Bram. *Dracula.* 1897. New York: St. Martin's, 1999.

Thackeray, William Makepeace. *The Newcomes.* 3 vols. London: Bradbury and Evans, 1855.